GW01003762

LAWYERS AND LAYMEN

LAWYERS AND LAYMEN

Studies in the History of Law
presented to Professor Dafydd Jenkins
on his seventy-fifth birthday
Gŵyl Ddewi 1986

Edited by
T. M. CHARLES-EDWARDS, MORFYDD E. OWEN and D. B. WALTERS

CARDIFF
UNIVERSITY OF WALES PRESS
1986

© University of Wales Press, 1986

British Library Cataloguing in Publication Data

Lawyers and laymen
  1. Law
  I. Charles-Edwards, T. M.
  II. Owen, Morfydd E.
  III. Walters, D. B.
  IV. Jenkins, Dafydd
  340   K230

ISBN 0-7083-0925-9

All rights reserved. No part of this book may be reproduced, stored in a retrieval system, or transmitted, in any form or by any means, electronic, mechanical, photocopying, recording or otherwise, without clearance from the University of Wales Press.

Printed in Wales
by Qualitex Printing Limited
Cardiff

I'R ATHRO EMERITWS DAFYDD JENKINS

Annwyl Dafydd,

   Ni ellir defnyddio ond y Gymraeg i'ch cyfarch, oherwydd o ddyddiau brwd ieuenctid pan ysgrifennwyd *Tân yn Llŷn* hyd at ddyddiau aeddfed *Cyfraith Hywel,* ni bu neb yn fwy taer na chwi dros feithrin yr iaith Gymraeg yn gyfrwng dysg a diwylliant. Yr ydym yn falch fod dau o'ch cydweithwyr wedi dewis ysgrifennu yn y Gymraeg, y naill ohonynt yn ysgolhaig ieuanc a gafodd ei addysg yn Lloegr fel chwithau, y llall yn gyfreithiwr uchel ei barch a'i fri sydd wedi arloesi llwybr i'r Gymraeg yn llysoedd barn ein gwlad.

   Cyfrol ddwyran sydd yma. Y mae'r rhan gyntaf yn deyrnged i chwi fel pen-ynad Cyfraith Hywel—a deall 'ynad' fel term am ddyn a oedd yn ddoeth ddysgedig yn y Gyfraith Gymreig. Ni bydd cynnwys y rhan honno yn ddieithr i chwi—cynnyrch seminar Cyfaith Hywel ydyw llawer ohoni ac fel Athro-ynad y seminar honno, buoch yn gefn ac yn gymorth i'r awduron trwy'r blynyddoedd. Cydnabod eich meistrolaeth ar hanes cyfraith mewn ystyr ehangach a wna ail hanner y gyfrol. Trafodir pynciau sydd yn ymwneud â gweithgarwch cyfreithwyr a llysoedd gan ychydig yn unig o blith yr amryw gyfeillion a oedd yn awyddus i dalu teyrnged i chwi.

   Wrth baratoi'r gyfrol i'r wasg, yr oeddem yn ymwybodol o lawer o bethau: eich cymwynas fel ysgolhaig i astudiaethau cyfreithiol, manylder eich ysgolheictod ond, yn bennaf oll, eich hynawsedd a'ch caredigrwydd. Braint inni fu cael eich cwmni a'ch nawdd ar hyd y blynyddoedd; braint ydyw cael cyflwyno'r llyfr hwn i chwi. Gobeithiwn ei fod yn deilwng ohonoch.

               Ar ran y cyfranwyr a phob un o'ch cyfeillion

Gŵyl Ddewi 1986

TABULA GRATULATORIA

Anders Ahlqvist, Roinn Na Sean-Ghaeilge
Leslie Alcock, University of Glasgow
Rhian M. Andrews, Queen's University, Belfast
Ei Anrhydedd y Barnwr Hywel ap Robert, Penarth
G. M. Ashton, Y Barri
J. H. Baker, St Catharine's College, Cambridge
John Bannerman, Edinburgh University
Gareth A. Bevan, Aberystwyth
Rachel Bromwich, Aberystwyth
A. D. Carr, Bangor
Bosco Costigan, University College, Cork
Brid Máire E. E. Davies, Y Bontfaen
Luned Davies, Y Bontfaen
D. Ellis Evans, Jesus College, Oxford
D. Simon Evans, St David's University College, Lampeter
Edmund Fryde, University College of Wales, Aberystwyth
W. M. Gordon, University of Glasgow
Sir Irvine Goulding, Woking
R. Geraint Gruffydd, Aberystwyth
Geoffrey Hand, University of Birmingham
Alan Harding, University of Liverpool
Marged Haycock, Aberystwyth
John L. Hogg, Reading
Richard W. Ireland, University College of Wales, Aberystwyth
Nansi Jenkins, Harrow Weald
Ben G. Jones, London
E. D. Jones, Aberystwyth
Emyr Wyn Jones, Llansannan, Clwyd
Huw Elwyn Jones, Bangor
Ieuan Gwynedd Jones, Aberystwyth
Marian Henry Jones, Aberystwyth
R. Alwyn Jones, Bangor
Simon Keynes, Trinity College, Cambridge
A. D. E. Lewis, University College, London
Nesta Lloyd, Abertawe

Elfyn Llwyd, Y Bala
Hector L. MacQueen, Edinburgh University
T. J. Morgan, Abertawe
Trevor H. Morgan, Porthaethwy
T. Hywel Moseley, Aberystwyth
Muireann Ni Bhrolcháin, St Patrick's College, Co. Kildare
Donnchadh O Corráin, University College, Cork
Huw a Carys Owen, Caerfyrddin
O. J. Padel, Cornwall
Ei Anrhydedd y Barnwr a Mrs Watkin Powell, Radur, Caerdydd
Brinley Rees, Bangor
John Rhys, Caerdydd
Herbert Protheroe Richards, Caerffili
Brynley F. Roberts, Llyfrgell Genedlaethol Cymru
C. P. Rodgers, University College of Wales, Aberystwyth
Melvyn Rosser, Swansea
Wynne I. Samuel, Caerdydd
W. David H. Sellar, Edinburgh University
Richard Sharpe, Bodleian Library, Oxford
J. G. T. Sheringham, Machynlleth
Beverley a Llinos Smith, Aberystwyth
Ceinwen H. Thomas, Caerdydd
R. L. Thomson, Isle of Man
Count Nikolai Tolstoy, Berkshire
Ian Wyatt Walker, Glasgow
T. Mervyn Ll. Walters, Loughborough
J. E. Caerwyn Williams, Aberystwyth
J. Gwynn Williams, Bangor
D. C. Yale, Christ's College, Cambridge

ABERDEEN	Aberdeen University Library
ABERYSTWYTH	Llyfrgell Genedlaethol Cymru
	Y Llyfrgell, Coleg Prifysgol Cymru, Aberystwyth
CARDIFF	Amgueddfa Werin Cymru
EDINBURGH	Edinburgh University, Old College Libraries
LONDON	Kings College London Library
SURREY	The Library, Public Record Office

ACKNOWLEDGEMENTS

The Editors acknowledge very gratefully the permission to use material given by The Warden and Fellows of Merton College, Oxford for Merton MS Coxe 323; The British Library for MS Cotton Cleopatra A.xiv and MS Cotton Caligula A.iii.

They also wish to express their gratitude to those who have helped in the preparation and production of the book and particularly to Brid Davies, Geraint Gruffydd, Marged Haycock, Kathleen Hughes, Brian Ll. James, Mary Burdett-Jones, Tegwyn Jones, David Johnston, Fergus Kelly, Nesta Lloyd, Eurys Rolant, Siân Rogers, Paul Russell, Ceinwen Thomas, Sabina Thompson, Jenny Walters and Frances White; to Gifford Charles-Edwards for her imaginative handling of illustrations from N.L.W. MS Peniarth 28 and B.L. Add MS 22356 in her design for the dust jacket: to the staff of the University of Wales Press and especially to Anne Howells for her editorial patience.

NOTE ON REFERENCES

In references to periodicals the volume number appears in arabic numerals before the title (full or abbreviated) of the periodical. For the mode of reference to the law texts see the list of *Bibliographical Abbreviations* especially under AL, Bleg, Col, Cyfn, DwCol, Ior, LTWL, VC. Ior and Iorwerth are used indiscriminately to refer to the texts of Llyfr Iorwerth, Cyfn and Cyfnerth for Llyfr Cyfnerth and Bleg and Blegywryd for Llyfr Blegywryd.

CONTENTS

		Page
Dedication		v
Tabula Gratulatoria		vii
Acknowledgements; Notes on References		ix
Table of Contents		xi
Introduction		1
Note on Terminology by T. M. Charles-Edwards		10

PART I: CELTIC SURETYSHIP

The Archaic Core of Llyfr Iorwerth, by Robin Stacey	15
Duw yn Lle Mach: Briduw yng Nghyfraith Hywel, gan Huw Pryce	47
Suretyship in the *Cartulaire de Redon*, by Wendy Davies	72
The General Features of Archaic European Suretyship, by D. B. Walters	92

Texts:

i	Introduction, by T. M. Charles-Edwards	117
ii	The Manuscripts, by Daniel Huws	119
iii	The 'Iorwerth' Text, edited and translated by T. M. Charles-Edwards	137
iv	The 'Cyfnerth' Text, edited and translated by Morfydd E. Owen	179
v	Latin Redaction E, edited and translated by Helen Davies	202
vi	Translation of the Old Irish tract *Berrad Airechta*, by Robin Stacey	210

PART II: LAW-MAKERS AND THE LAW

Legislators, Lawyers and Lawbooks, by Alan Harding	237
The Administration of Law in Medieval Wales: The Role of the Ynad Cwmwd (Judex Patrie), by R. R. Davies	258
The Inns of Court and Legal Doctrine, by J. H. Baker	274
Y Llysoedd, yr Awdurdodau a'r Gymraeg: y Ddeddf Uno a Deddf yr Iaith Gymraeg, gan Ei Anrhydedd y Barnwr Watkin Powell	287
An English Tragedy: the Academic Lawyer as Jurist, by Ian Fletcher	316
Glossary	337
A Bibliography of the Writings of Dafydd Jenkins 1935-83, by Philip Henry Jones	355
Bibliographical Abbreviations	369
Index to Passages cited	375
General Index	381

INTRODUCTION

Maitland remarked that 'law may be taken for every purpose, save that of strictly philosophical inquiry, to be the sum of the rules administered by courts of justice.'[1] Such a view places courts and, sometimes, lawyers at the centre of the picture. Yet there is on this issue of the role of the court and of the lawyer wide variety, as Maitland knew well. In some legal systems, courts are staffed by professional lawyers; in others laymen play a major role as jurymen, suitors or 'doomsmen'; in yet others, there are no professional lawyers at all. Turning from the courts to the rules of law, there is similar variety: on the one hand, there are rules whose operation requires the expertise of the professional; on the other, many legal rules can, indeed must, be operated without the supervision of the lawyer. This is particularly true in a developed economy in which the volume of legal activity and the speed with which legal transactions are made preclude close professional supervision, though of course the lawyer remains ready to be called in if anything goes wrong.

A common view of legal history would claim that there is a gradual change whereby courts come to administer more of the rules by which society is ordered. In this way many rules of morality or custom are transmuted into rules of law. At the same time the growing power of the courts and the increasing complexity of legal business necessitate the emergence of a legal profession. Both the jurisdiction of the court and the professionalism of the lawyer are also fostered by centralized government.

For some legal traditions, notably the English, such a view may work well, yet it is not universally true. A contrary case is provided by Irish and, to a lesser extent, Welsh law. Both Ireland and Wales were politically fragmented and economically rudimentary by the standards of some of their neighbours; yet Ireland and part of Wales had professional lawyers and they concerned themselves with an extraordinarily wide variety of matters ranging from the swarming of bees to questions concerning the inheritance of land. Precisely because the judge normally acted when the aggrieved party approached him and because he often acted as arbitrator, his jurisdiction was as ample as the quarrelsomeness of men. A court might be no more than a judge hearing in his own house a case brought to him by the parties; yet it must be accounted a court rather than some other form of tribunal, for it was the means by which professional lawyers administered the law.

The two parts of the book are directed at some of these contrasts. In the first part, the law discussed is an ordering of society, sanctioned by law but administered by ordinary men with no professional legal competence going about their daily affairs. They make contracts, act as sureties or as witnesses, and so order their world, without the close supervision of the lawyer. In the second part, however, the trained lawyer occupies the centre of the stage, with his lawbooks, his moots and the difficult politics of his profession. The contrast is fundamental in any legal system in which there are professional lawyers. The person who goes shopping in a modern supermarket creates and discharges legal obligations as he passes out past the cash desk. Here the law functions efficiently precisely because the layman can act without the intervention of the professional lawyer. Because of the volume and velocity of exchange, the economy of a developed society requires the professional to remain off-stage in the course of much legal activity. Admittedly, the society which used the law discussed in the first part had a much simpler economy: the assumption is that most transactions are sales of cows, sheep or hens. Since both the volume and the velocity of exchange are so much less, one might be forgiven for supposing that transactions might be made with greater legal ceremony, and that, where there were professional lawyers, they would be more prominent: that exchanges would require more elaborate procedures to make them legally valid and that these procedures would require the supervision of the professional. For Welsh medieval law, however, such a supposition is only very partially true, as the law of suretyship demonstrates.

In the first part, the topic under discussion is, therefore, the medieval Welsh law of suretyship. Suretyship and the giving of gages are essential to the cohesion of any society for they underpin voluntary obligation. (Anyone unfamiliar with the meaning of 'surety' and 'gage' should turn to the Note on Terminology). It is essential to any society that it be possible to make agreements which create obligations where none previously existed and where none would exist if there were no agreement that they should. Such obligations are voluntary in that they are made by a deliberate act: for example, the obligations of a husband or a wife to a spouse are voluntary, but the obligations of a child to its parent are not. Since voluntary obligations are created by agreements, it is essential, first, that it be known what has been agreed, and, secondly, that there be some means by which the agreement should be made effective even if one party defaults on his obligation. It is this underpinning function which is discharged by surety and gage.

The uses of sureties and gages are not confined to the securing of artificial obligations. They may also be used to buttress involuntary obligations, such as those of one neighbour to another or a subject to a ruler. They may be employed to deal with the unintended consequences of voluntary actions, as, for example, where an offender is required to provide surety that he will appear in court or that he will abide by the law in future. In the medieval Welsh law of suretyship, however, much the most prominent function of sureties is to secure agreements. The same is also true of the Irish and Breton material.

The underlying plan of the first part is the same as that of *The Welsh Law of Women*,[2] with certain modifications. One of the standard tractates of the Welsh lawbooks is that on suretyship. Three such tractates have been edited for this volume; as in *The Welsh Law of Women* they have been taken from *Llyfr Iorwerth, Llyfr Cyfnerth* and the Latin tradition. As well as texts there is discussion, partly in the form of separate chapters, partly in the commentary appended to the longest and most systematic tractate, that of *Llyfr Iorwerth* (Ior). By providing text, translation, commentary and discussion, it is hoped that this important but difficult topic may be made accessible to students of Welsh history as well as to those with a comparative interest in the law of suretyship and of contract.

The choice of the law of suretyship as a topic on which a small group of students of Welsh law might work was governed by considerations similar to those which lay behind *The Welsh Law of Women*. In that case, it was intended to provide for Welsh law a volume comparable to *Studies in Early Irish Law*,[3] on this occasion, we knew that we should have as a guide Thurneysen's fundamental work *Die Bürgschaft im irischen Recht* as well as a very important article by Professor D. A. Binchy, 'Celtic Suretyship: a Fossilized Indo-European Institution?'[4] Since Dr Binchy's article, though drawing mainly on the Irish sources, included a brief side-ways glance at Welsh law, his arguments implicitly challenged Welsh legal historians to reconsider their own materials in the light of the work done on Irish law.

This study of suretyship differs from *The Welsh Law of Women* in some important ways. First, it does not concentrate so heavily on Wales. The translation of the main Irish text on suretyship is sufficiently explained by our desire to set Welsh law alongside its Irish counterpart; it makes available some of the results of Thurneysen's researches to those who do not know German. But we have not merely looked across the Irish sea. Brittany offers a most important corrective to the Welsh evidence. The Welsh lawbook is a manual, compiled by one lawyer mainly out of the work of previous lawyers, for the purpose of instructing future lawyers. It is the vehicle of a learned tradition. The Breton evidence examined by Dr Wendy Davies is

earlier and different in kind, consisting almost entirely of a single great
cartulary, that of Redon in south-east Brittany. It is thus focused on
transactions concerning land, whereas the Welsh lawbooks seem mainly to
be thinking of exchanges of movables, in particular livestock. The two
concerns are not unrelated: if in Brittany there was a market in land (as there
was in Ireland, to judge by the laws and by the Book of Armagh), then land
might be exchanged for movable wealth. A contract providing for such an
exchange would normally be guaranteed by sureties on both sides. The one
transaction, therefore, might include debts and sureties in relation to both
land and movables. The focus of the Breton evidence is thus complementary
to that of the Welsh laws and not entirely separate as one might suppose
at first glance. It also has the great virtue for the historian of being precisely
situated in time and place.

Dafydd Walters' chapter goes one step further and looks beyond the Celtic
evidence at some general comparative issues in the law of suretyship. As with
his contribution to *The Welsh Law of Women*, it both serves to introduce
the student of Welsh history to wider issues and also shows how the Celtic
rules may resemble, or differ from, those in other early medieval societies.
In particular he considers Gierke's distinction between mere duty (*Schuld*)
and liability (*Haftung*) and indicates its limited relevance for Celtic law
because of the major role accorded to the enforcing-surety.

Only two chapters directly confront the Welsh law of suretyship. Robin
Stacey's approach is textual. From an analysis of the relationship of the texts
she builds up her case that the tractate on suretyship in *Llyfr Iorwerth* is the
most archaic in doctrine, though it is the least archaic in form. Her argument
reinforces a point long known to legal historians, that late texts may embody
early rules. More generally, her contribution provides a picture of the way
in which the Welsh law of suretyship was evolving. The apparent
timelessness of the lawbooks — a quality properly offensive to the historian
— is again shown to be a superficial characteristic. Admittedly they will not
yield *une histoire événementielle*, for the changes are gradual and long-term; but
they do yield history.

The role of the Church in the development of medieval law is central but
ambiguous. In the twelfth and thirteenth centuries it gave vigorous aid to
the movement towards a more theoretical approach to law and towards modes
of proof relying increasingly on verisimilitude of evidence and cogency of argument. Yet the sacral element in older modes of proof was considerable. By
the eleventh century much medieval law had been impregnated with religious
ideas and ceremonies; this represented, indeed, a major achievement for the
early medieval Church. The post-Hildebrandine papacy, however, desired,
in the sphere of law as elsewhere, to separate *sacerdotium* and *regnum*, and so

encouraged a new secularization of the law of the *regnum*. Though the Welsh lawbooks belong in their present form to the thirteenth century, Huw Pryce shows in his chapter how little they have been affected by this change and thus how important the sacral element remained.

His arguments stand together with one of the main points made in the commentary on the tractate from Ior. The appearance of a commentary is another innovation in the plan of this work as compared with *The Welsh Law of Women*. We were very conscious of the debt that all students of Welsh law have owed over the past twenty years to the commentary provided by Dafydd Jenkins in his edition of *Llyfr Colan*: unless he himself had dealt with a topic in greater detail elsewhere, that commentary has always been the first port of call in any enquiry. The commentary provided here is intended to complement the one in *Llyfr Colan*, concentrating more on the arrangement of the text, less upon a comparison between the chosen text and others.

One of the more interesting aspects of the tract in Ior is the prominence of *cynghawsedd* 'pleading' in the first four paragraphs. Here we have material of the first importance for gauging how the Welsh legal system worked, the importance of the roles of lawyer and layman and of the sacral element in law. We may begin by distinguishing between three ways in which a court may arrive at a decision: the first is that of the ordeal, such as the ordeal by battle beloved of the Anglo-Normans; the second seeks to test the strength of the party's commitment to his position and also that of his friends or relations who act as his oath-helpers; the method by which it tests their resolve is, however, dramatic rather than logical; the third is more direct in that it seeks to elicit the truth by argument in court and by the assessment of the veracity of witnesses; moreover, these witnesses are expected to be independent of either party to the dispute and thus capable of disinterested testimony, whereas the oath-helper is tied to the party on whose behalf he swears. The usual distinction is twofold: between 'irrational' modes including both of the first two, ordeal and compurgation, and the 'rational' mode, namely the third.[5] The Welsh evidence, however, supports a threefold distinction, and suggests that the adjective 'irrational' may not apply to the second.

In cases concerning suretyship, Welsh law adopts the second of these three methods. The tractate in Ior shows clearly how the pressure on the debtor in court is gradually increased.[6] The use of relics and of the religious quality of the oath is essential to the dramatic tension employed to test the resolve of a disputant and of his oath-helpers. In the type of security discussed by Huw Pryce, God is accepted as surety; but if the creditor sometimes accepted God as surety, the judge always accepted him as a witness.[7]

The importance of *cynghawsedd* 'pleading' in the tractate in Ior might lead one to expect that the layman would leave the argument of his case to a professional advocate of some kind. Indeed, in the next tractate in Ior, on land-suits, there is evidence that such a development is under way: the litigant is aided by two assistants who were probably increasingly expected to have had a legal training, the *cyngaws* (the man who shares the *caws*, Latin *causa*) and the *canllaw* (the man who takes him by the hand). On the strength of their arguments and on the wisdom with which they conduct his case, everything stands or falls: into their hands 'he puts loss or gain'. A case concerning land is treated in every way as a serious affair. The plaintiff must obtain the grant of a hearing from the ruler of the territory who, moreover, will preside over the court, accompanied by noblemen, priests and officials. Furthermore, the case is heard by at least two judges and there is thus a minimum of six legally qualified persons present: two judges, and a *cyngaws* and a *canllaw* for each litigant. In the tractate on suretyship, however, neither *cyngaws* nor *canllaw* appear. To initiate proceedings in a case over suretyship, an unsatisfied creditor, having first approached the debtor and the surety, himself goes straight before a single judge. Disputants themselves argue their cases. When a case over suretyship is heard, the only persons involved as principal parties are the creditor, the debtor and the surety. The relative formality of legal proceedings over land may therefore be contrasted with the informality of proceedings over suretyship. The first part of the book illustrates legal self-help.

The contrast between cases concerning suretyship and those concerning land may help towards resolving some of the difficult issues raised by Professor Davies's essay on the Welsh *ynad cwmwd* or *judex patrie*. He draws a number of contrasts, notably between Gwynedd and some parts of Powys, where the professional judge predominates, and the rest of Wales where the verdicts of communities are of greater importance. Even within Gwynedd there is the contrast between the role of the *ynad* as arbitrator and as a professionally trained person accredited by the king's judge, and later by the marcher lord. Before the Edwardian conquest, if we may trust the legal texts, the *ynad* in Gwynedd functioned both as a judge who was sought out by one or both parties to a dispute, as in cases over suretyship, and also as a judge who controlled proceedings and delivered a verdict in cases concerning land; moreover these cases were heard only by the will of the ruler (*brenin* or *arglwydd*) and, moreover, with him presiding over the court. The *ynad* is a judge in both types of hearing; it is we who must accustom ourselves to the notion that his judgeship embraced everything from the most informal arbitration to the solemn hearing of land pleas before the king. Professor Davies is reluctant to term the *ynad* a judge since this might lead us to forget his role as arbitrator; an alternative is to make one's notion of the office of judge more elastic and more true to the evidence.

Professor Davies makes the further point that in the post-conquest period the Welsh *ynad* and his law were exploited by the new lords for their financial advantage. In this way Welsh law became itself an instrument of the late medieval colonialism of which he has written elsewhere.[8] Yet this was preferable to what came later under the Tudors. One way in which lawyer and layman may be divided from each other to the disadvantage of both is if the courts of a country are compelled to use a language which is not that of some or all of the people. This is the problem considered by His Honour Judge Watkin-Powell. He shows that, while great progress has been made in removing the enforced disabilities of Welsh speakers, some serious issues still remain. No volume in honour of Dafydd Jenkins would be complete without mention of the continuing struggle by advocates of the Welsh language for its recognition in public life and, in particular, in the courts.

The two parts of the book also illustrate two legal epochs. In the early middle ages legal activity very rarely made use of writing; the law was predominantly an oral tradition. Professor Harding argues strongly that we should not interpret this tradition as an organic creation of the common people — the theory maintained by nineteenth-century German Romantics. On the contrary, he argues, it was moulded by the co-operation of the king and his *sapientes* as legislators, and perhaps also as judges of difficult cases, who thus established a continuity of law which no single ruler could disregard. In the early middle ages, however, the legal expert in much of western Europe was often no more than a man who happened to be knowledgeable in the law. His expertise was a source of social and political influence but not of his daily livelihood nor was it acquired by a formal education. To the countries discussed by Professor Harding the Celtic legal traditions provide a contrast. Ireland and Wales — the latter only in Gwynedd and parts of Powys as Professor Davies shows — were unusual in having recognisably professional lawyers as soon as there is evidence to show what was going on. Yet both Irish and Welsh law belong to the early middle ages: the administration of justice, as opposed to the instruction of future lawyers, remained almost exclusively an oral business; and in both there is a lack of the intellectual elaboration that came back into law with the renaissance of the eleventh and twelfth centuries. There are very few passages even in the Welsh laws which show the influence of dialectic. All this fits very well Huw Pryce's argument that the sacral element in Welsh law remained crucial, for on this point also Welsh law belonged to the early middle ages.

Even in the English Common Law the replacement of oral by written methods was a very gradual business. The elucidation of the law by the teacher was for long a business of lecture and moot rather than of books. Dr Baker shows how the readings (namely lectures) on the statutes were so important, above all in the fifteenth century, when they played a major part both in legal education and in developing that common learning which lawyers, whether judges, serjeants or apprentices, accepted as authoritative. Such oral exercises were essential to the clarification and systematization of law, especially criminal law; by drawing out the principles upon which decisions had been made they enabled the courts to be more consistent and more confident than they might otherwise have been. Their decline probably owed much to the introduction of printing, even though legal learning continued to be transmitted as much by manuscript as by printed book right into the seventeenth century.

On the other hand Professor Harding argues, among other things, for the crucial role of lawbooks in the development of medieval law in the twelfth and thirteenth centuries. Though one may be surprised to come across the claim of a German scholar that the Carolingian *Lex Saxonum* was the first lawbook in medieval Europe (the claims of the Irish *Senchas Már* are evidently far superior) the golden age of the lawbook was not in the early middle ages but in the twelfth and thirteenth centuries, precisely the period at which Welsh law reached its highest level of development. The circumstances of the time required a legal 'image' of a people, such as the *Sachsenspiegel*, the 'Mirror of the Saxons'. These were to be lawbooks which would bring together recent royal legislation as well as earlier secular law and such church law as had been received as authoritative; but they would reject papal or conciliar decrees considered incompatible with the customs of the realm. The threat of an energetic and expanding canon law, for which custom might be no more than ancient error and the decrees of kings no more than blasphemies promulgated in the face of the people of God, compelled a reconsideration of a people's legal inheritance. Only on the basis of this reconsideration, carried out in lawbooks, was the renewed legislative confidence of the later middle ages possible.

In their lawbooks, their moots and their readings the lawyers of medieval England were part of the revival of learning associated, from the thirteenth century, with the universities. Admittedly the universities included only civil and canon law within their walls while the English common law took root in the inns of court and thus in immediate association with the central courts of the crown; yet it should not be forgotten that the late medieval English university included a surprisingly high proportion of civil as well as canon lawyers.[9] Unlike theologians the students of law did not have to take an arts degree before they could proceed further; whereas theology remained, among the seculars, a study for the able and well patronised few, law was attractive for many. A legal education may thus have had a considerable impact upon the habits of mind of the higher clergy and therefore of many of the leading servants of the crown. One may wonder, after reading Mr Fletcher's essay, whether the challenge posed by the presence of civil and canon lawyers in high places may not have rendered the medieval common lawyers more anxious than their modern heirs to improve legal education.

In the early middle ages the lawyers of the northern Welsh and the Irish were not only unusual in that they formed a distinct profession; the close relationship between poet and lawyer found among the Irish in the seventh century was still flourishing among the Welsh in the thirteenth, as Professor Dafydd Jenkins has demonstrated. Though the learned no doubt stuck together for reasons of self-interest, the consequence may have been a greater receptiveness on the part of lawyers to a common learning which they shared not merely with other lawyers but with poets and theologians. In Ireland, indeed, while the judge was the equal of a carpenter — a high enough status perhaps — the poet was the equal of kings.

[1] PM (reissue of 2nd edn.) i xcv.

[2] WLW.

[3] SEIL.

[4] *Bürgschaft*; D. A. Binchy, 'Celtic Suretyship'.

[5] E.g. J. H. Baker, *An Introduction to English Legal History* (2nd edn., London, 1979), 63.

[6] See the commentary on Ior para. 59.

[7] Cf. the appearance of *Deus* at the head of the witness list in Chad 3 and *Deus omnipotens* in Chad 4, recently discussed by D. Jenkins and M. E. Owen, 'The Welsh Marginalia in the Lichfield Gospels', (1983) 5 *Cambridge Medieval Celtic Studies*, 60.

[8] R. R. Davies, 'Colonial Wales', (1974) 65 *Past & Present*, 3-33.

[9] T. H. Aston, 'Oxford's Medieval Alumni', (1977) 74 *Past & Present*, 10-16; T. H. Aston, G. D. Duncan and T. A. R. Evans, 'The Medieval Alumni of the University of Cambridge', (1980) 86 *Past & Present*, 57-63.

A NOTE ON TERMINOLOGY
T. M. CHARLES-EDWARDS

The first part of this book, on suretyship, is legal history, but it is not written, except for Mr Dafydd Walters' chapter, by legal historians; nor is it written, in the main, for legal historians. The layman, however, may well find the topic of suretyship among the more bewildering mysteries of medieval law. This is often for the trivial reason that the terminology fluctuates: I well remember a whole Trinity term spent working through Stubbs' *Charters* with its plethora of strange entities, *borh, wed, plegius* and the like, with no notion as to whether the modern terms surety and pledge referred to a person or a thing, let alone having a clear idea as to the functions they performed. This note on terminology is intended for those who suffer from the same mystification.

Terminology varies in both texts and modern discussions. To take one example, Pollock and Maitland in their *History of English Law* use pledge for the person appointed to guarantee performance of a contract (as well as some other functions) and gage for the thing given as a guarantee; most recent historians of the early Middle Ages, however, use surety for the person and pledge for the thing. Pollock and Maitland are following their principal sources, which speak of *plegius* and *vadium*; but though 'pledge' undoubtedly originally stood for a person (cf. German *pflegen*), its usual application in modern English is for a thing and thus fluctuation between the old and the new senses of the term causes confusion. To circumvent this difficulty we have on the whole avoided the term 'pledge' entirely.

In our terminology a surety is a person and a gage is a thing. The only exceptions are the chapter by Wendy Davies in Part I in which pledge is used instead of gage and Professor Rees Davies's chapter in Part II in which pledge is used for a surety. Let us take a straightforward example drawn from various bits of our texts. One person (A) agrees to sell a horse to another person (B) for 80 shillings; both the horse and the money are to be handed over at some future date. Both A and B have promised to fulfil their side of the bargain; but both may wish to have some guarantee that the other will discharge his contractual obligation. Suretyship has to do with the guarantee. It is based on the notion that if A cannot entirely trust B, nonetheless there is a better chance of the agreement being carried out if C, a third party, has an obligation to step in if B fails to do what he has promised. Suretyship thus spreads obligation.

The agreement or contract may therefore work as follows. A is a *debtor* to B for the horse, but a *creditor* for the sum of 80 shillings. A will therefore give to B a *surety*, C, to guarantee that the horse will be delivered to B on the appointed day and at the appointed place. Likewise B will give to A a surety, D, to guarantee that the 80 shillings will be forthcoming on the appointed day and at the appointed place. Dafydd Walters explains in his chapter the different ways in which the sureties can guarantee the contract or agreement and the different sorts of obligations, debts and acts they may be required to guarantee. Both the mode of guarantee and the thing guaranteed vary. Here it will be enough to mention the two principal ways in which an Irish or Welsh surety acts to secure a contract. First, he may undertake to compel the debtor (his *principal* in the whole transaction) to perform. C may thus compel A to deliver the horse; D may compel B to pay the 80 shillings. Secondly, a surety may guarantee to discharge the obligation if his principal fails to do so. C might thus promise to deliver a horse of equivalent value, and D might promise to pay 80 shillings from his own pocket. This second form of suretyship (*paying suretyship* as opposed to *enforcing suretyship*) is a form of guarantee by which the surety acts as a substitute for his principal rather than compelling his principal to act. In both cases, therefore, the obligations of the surety are contingent upon the failure of the principal to discharge his obligations by the appointed time and at the appointed place.

A gage is a thing not a person, but the situation in which it is used may be the same as those just mentioned. Indeed, gage and surety may be used side by side. Let us suppose that A has a sword, a much valued heirloom of his family. Everyone knows that he could not bear to lose it and that he would be dishonoured if he did. A may therefore give the sword into the possession (not the ownership) of B as a guarantee that he will deliver the horse in exchange for the 80 shillings. B knows that A is most unlikely to sacrifice the sword for the sake of the horse and is thus assured that the contract will be fulfilled.

There is one important corollary to the function of the surety as a guarantor which has no relevance to the gage. The surety must know what he guarantees. The simplest way in which he may have this knowledge is if he is present at the making of the contract. From this it is a short step to making him participate in a little ceremony by which the agreement is made; one may then even consider his participation to be, in normal circumstances, essential to the making of a legally enforceable agreement. Thus the Welsh *mach* puts one of his hands in the hand of one party to the

contract and the other hand into the hand of the other party. This simple
ceremony (also found, with variations, in other European legal traditions)
ensures that all parties know what is the point at which the agreement is
effectively made and also guarantees that the surety is present. His presence
then allows him to discharge another important function, that of witnessing
to the terms of the agreement. Indeed, his witness is often accepted as
peculiarly authoritative.

Suretyship, then, has to do with agreements (promises, contracts). It can
also be used by rulers and by courts to enforce the performance of non-
contractual obligations; but, on the whole, contractual or debt-suretyship is
more prominent in the Celtic legal texts than any other functions of a surety.
The account given above is therefore limited to contractual suretyship.

PART I: CELTIC SURETYSHIP

THE ARCHAIC CORE OF LLYFR IORWERTH
ROBIN CHAPMAN STACEY

It is hardly possible to discuss early medieval Irish law without using the image of the fossil — an ancient plant once living but long since turned to hard and unchanging stone.[1] Medieval Welsh law, on the other hand, with its curious juxtaposition of the living and the dead, the constantly developing and the eternally static, is more difficult to characterize. The image which is perhaps most appropriate is that of the Egyptian mummy so beloved of early Hollywood moviemakers — an ancient figure, swathed in bandages old and new, who belongs as much to the world which resurrects him as to that of Osiris. For it is the case that the Welsh lawyers, like the Irish, showed a marked propensity to refuse to bury their legal dead. Although Hywel himself was said in the late prologue on the convention at Tŷ Gwyn to have replaced old law with new,[2] his thirteenth-century successors often placed contemporary and archaic practices side by side without noticeable intellectual discomfort. The tremendous reverence and respect accorded Hywel and those provisions which bore his name undoubtedly accounts for much of the desire to preserve the ancient texts.[3] There is but one law according to the Welsh...[and] that is the law of Hywel, says one early fourteenth-century manuscript; alterations made subsequent to Hywel's day are not, in its view, law, but merely good regulations.[4] But it is characteristic of the coexistence of old and new in Welsh law that there was also a practical side to the primitive proverbs and archaic images of the law of Hywel. The most prosperous thirteenth-century litigant was the one who could best adapt this old law to the circumstances of his own case, who could most convincingly show that Hywel was on his side.[5] Medieval Welsh law, like other living things, could thus be geriatric without being dead.

The challenge posed by this bewildering collection of legal material is then to sort out the old from the new, to use the law and attendant legal texts to trace historical developments in Welsh society and institutions. The methods which can be used to do this vary considerably, and not all of them can be used on every body of legal material. One can at least attempt to sniff out the old law by isolating those passages about which there still lingers, in the words of Professor Dafydd Jenkins, 'an ancient and fish-like smell'.[6] But this method has its dangers, since a clever lawyer might well try to give

to a particular case or legal opinion an added sanctity by attaching to it an
ancient clause which may not originally have pertained. A legal passage may
thus aspire to a piscine odour without actually, as it were, having had its
day in the sun.[7] Alternatively, one can attempt to trace legal developments
within the laws themselves. This too has its difficulties, since it is not always
easy to tell an actual change in the law over time from a regional variation
in legal practice.[8] There are, however, two textual yardsticks available to
Welsh historians with which to measure the laws, one of which reflects a
very early, and the other a relatively late, stage in the development of law.
The early Irish legal texts have much to offer to students of Welsh law. In
certain cases, particularly with respect to very old institutions like personal
suretyship, Irish and Welsh law seem literally to fulfil one another; thus it
is that Welsh law preserves the form, and Irish law the formula, of the hand-
in-hand binding of a debt.[9] The second of these 'yardsticks' is difficult to
separate from the lawbooks themselves. These are the Damweiniau,
'Difficult Cases', and the Cynghawsedd, 'Pleading', collections of which are
appended to many legal manuscripts. These short passages reflect, to the
extent that is possible, the teachings and opinions of Welsh lawyers of the
thirteenth century, and they often give more developed versions of
provisions known elsewhere in the lawbooks.[10] Together these early Irish
and relatively late Welsh sources provide a means by which to understand
both where the law has been and where it is heading.

   It is my intention here to engage in some of this 'sorting out' of old and
new by using these sources to isolate the archaic core of the Welsh laws on
personal suretyship. Suretyship, an office through which one man
guaranteed, by virtue of his personal strength or with his liberty or property,
the eventual fulfilment of a legal obligation by another, is a particularly fruitful area for this type of study, as it is one of the oldest institutions visible
in the lawbooks. It is also a topic on which the comparative approach with
Irish law is especially possible and relevant — possible, as there is extant an
Old Irish tract on the subject,[11] and relevant, as there is good evidence to
suggest a close relationship between the Irish *naidm* and the Welsh *mach*
sureties. There is certainly a linguistic correlation; the Irish term *naidm*, the
verbal noun of *naiscid*, 'binds', was not the original name of this surety. In
the archaic stratum of the Irish texts appears the original name of this surety,
macc, cognate with Welsh *mach*, both from a Common Celtic *makkos*.[12]
By the time of the compilation of the Irish tract, circa AD 700, the original
term *macc* had been replaced by *naidm* in order to avoid confusion with the
Irish word for 'boy,' *macc*, Welsh *mab*, from Celtic *mak^wk^wos*.[13] The
structural similarity between the offices of the *naidm* and the *mach* is as
conclusive as the linguistic relationship, and this close correspondence not

only justifies, but renders necessary, the comparative approach taken here.

Information on the Welsh *mach* is to be found in suretyship tractates contained in all of the important books of the Welsh laws except Latin C, which is incomplete, and in all of the early manuscripts of these books except Cyfnerth *U*, the one on which Owen based his Gwentian Code. Since Sir Goronwy Edwards first introduced the term 'tractate' to describe the various constituent sections of the Welsh lawbooks,[14] many interesting conclusions on the nature of these tractates and on their relationships to one another have emerged. Because many of these tractates must have been composed from a number of different sources, it is clear that the stemma for any given tractate must be established independently. Even within a single lawbook, the stemma of one tractate may or may not correspond to that of another. Dr Charles-Edwards has shown that with respect to the tractate on the law of women the common ancestor of Latin Redactions A and B drew material from an early Cyfnerth version, from a Iorwerth text, and from other unknown sources.[15] In the suretyship tractate, however, the contribution of a Cyfnerth text to the original Latin version was not nearly as extensive.[16] This discovery has more than just a textual significance for historians, since it is only logical that if the stemmas of these tractates must be established independently, the relationship between the law contained in them must be judged separately as well.

In terms of both language and content, the lawbooks tend to divide first into Northern and Southern texts, and then into the three traditions so familiar to Welsh legal historians: Cyfnerth, Iorwerth, and Blegywryd. Scholars have often observed that although all three of the main legal traditions harbour within themselves the most blatant and unrepentant archaisms, Cyfnerth· is the most primitive of the three with respect to the stage of law that it reflects, despite the fact that its earliest manuscripts are no older than the fourteenth century. The Latin tradition is thought to represent the next stage in legal development, and Iorwerth to be the most developed and the most sophisticated of the three. This observation has been verified with respect to many different subjects, most notably the officers of the court,[17] *galanas* 'feud',[18] and commutation.[19] T. Jones Pierce concluded that

> from the point of view of content the books of *Cyfnerth, Blegywryd,* and *Iorwerth* stand in related chronological sequence — and in the order named...the silence of *Cyfnerth* on those manifestations of a changing order of society, known to have had their beginnings no earlier than the middle of the twelfth century, and which are featured prominently in the work of Iorwerth...suggests that...this deals with a phase in Welsh legal history which antedates the phase revealed in Iorwerth...[20]

Iorwerth had quite lost the 'primitive flavour' which he felt to characterize Cyfnerth and the Latin tradition because there 'the older matter seem[ed] to have changed so much under the pressure of the new political and social atmosphere of the times...'[21]

There can be little doubt but that these observations are, in general, correct. In matters like *galanas*, Iorwerth does seem to record the most, and Cyfnerth and the Latin tradition the least, developed law, although as Jones Pierce himself noted, the Southern texts were not immune to progress.[22] But more is known now about the importance of tractates than it was in 1952 when Jones Pierce's article first appeared, and it seems appropriate to suggest here that the relative sophistication of the three traditions, like the stemmatic relationships between them, must be evaluated separately for each individual tractate. The three suretyship texts might seem on a superficial examination to conform to the general pattern. The short 'primitive' clauses of Cyfnerth certainly invoke the style and tone of an ancient legal tract in a way that Ior's rambling and sometimes argumentative style does not.[23] Iorwerth's tractate is by the far the longest and most elaborate of the three — fully twice as long as the longest Cyfnerth text — a fact which itself suggests that Ior's compiler made many additions to whatever old material he may have had before him. And in fact Ior does contain a large amount of what is obviously recent law, as its compiler evidently made liberal use of *Damweiniau* and *Cynghawsedd*. These passages dominate Ior's tractate, and the presence of these relatively late legal genres suggests that the tractate as we have it today was probably compiled not long before the earliest manuscript that contains it.[24] It must be remembered, however, that even a tractate which appears, in terms of its length and degree of detail, to be highly advanced, may yet conceal within it an older core which reflects an early stage in the development of legal institutions. This is, I would argue, the case with the Iorwerth tractate on personal suretyship. Despite its present elaborate appearance, the Iorwerth text is more closely tied to early law than is that of the Latin tradition or even Cyfnerth, and its archaisms deserve some attention.

The best introduction to the *mach*'s suretyship and to the old rules and concepts that lie concealed in the Iorwerth tractate is the Old Irish material on the *naidm*.[25] The *naidm* filled many roles in a contractual obligation, but his most important tasks were to bind the obligation itself on the two parties involved, to witness the various stages of the contract, and to enforce those payments or promises to which his contracting party had committed himself. As the person that bound creditor and debtor to one another and to their respective obligations, the *naidm* was essential to the actual existence of the agreement. His appointment was not done before or after the binding of the obligation as was the appointment of the other sureties of Irish law; the *naidm*'s appointment *was* the 'binding' of the debt, and therein lay the true significance of his name, which means, literally, 'binding'. He was, in a very real sense, the claim, the living 'bond' of the obligation.[26]

As the witness of the obligation, the *naidm* was required to remember the details of the promises made, and his testimony as to the specifics of the obligations incurred could not be challenged by ordinary witnesses.[27]. His witnessing duties did not end with the binding of the debt, for he was required to witness also other stages of the debt and repayment process. Although the *naidm*'s primary duty after the binding of the obligation was to enforce the claim against a recalcitrant defendant, he was not allowed to begin enforcing until he had himself seen the defendant refuse the plaintiff's claim.[28] Only after seeing the debtor's default could the *naidm* force the guilty party to come to law, and he was entitled to use physical compulsion and distraint to enforce the claim.[29] What the *naidm* specifically did not do in a contractual obligation was to pay the debt upon the defendant's default. For this purpose Irish law recognized another surety, the *ráth*, who operated alongside the *naidm* in order to provide payments for obligations that the *naidm* had bound but was unable to enforce successfully.

Although the *mach* of the thirteenth century had clearly come a long way from the private law officer envisaged in the eighth-century Irish texts, the medieval Welsh sources, and particularly the Iorwerth tractate, show clearly that the *mach*'s primary obligations in his suretyship were exactly those required of the *naidm*. Like the *naidm*, the *mach* was present at the binding of the contract itself, and joined hands with the principals to confirm the transaction.[30] The extant descriptions of the binding procedure do not allow us to say with certainty that the *mach* acted in this ritual as the literal bond which united creditor and debtor, but it is quite likely that he did, and that the hand-to-hand binding was a symbolic expression of this aspect of the *mach*'s office. Certainly the *mach* was, like the *naidm*, identified in the oldest texts with the claim itself; a defendant, for example, who wished to deny his obligation did so by denying not the creditor or his claim, but rather the *mach* himself.[31] But a passage found only in the Ior tractate directly expresses this archaic concept: a claimant who refused law before the two knees of the judge lost his *mach* and thereby his claim, *cane phara e haul namen hyt tra parhao e mach*, 'since the claim lasts only while the *mach* lasts'.[32]

The *mach* also, again like the *naidm*, acted as the chief witness for the transaction, and the testimony of both prevailed over that of ordinary witnesses. In the period reflected in the oldest stratum of all of the tractates, the *mach*'s testimony on the details of the debt could not be challenged if he confirmed his testimony on oath.[33] The *naidm* was a witness not only

for the conditions of the original agreement, but for the defendant's refusal
as well; once again, this very important aspect of the surety's function can
be paralleled in the Welsh texts only in the Iorwerth tractate, where a *mach*
was forbidden to begin enforcing the claim against the debtor *ony bey ryuot
negydyaeth en e vyd*, 'unless there had been a denial in his presence', or unless
he had previously seen such a denial.[34] Texts of the Latin and Cyfnerth
traditions require the plaintiff to obtain the *mach*'s permission before he
could grant the defendant additional time in which to pay the debt.[35]

The third, and in many ways most important aspect of the *naidm*'s role
as surety was his enforcement of the claim, and there can be no doubt but
that enforcement was the primary duty of the *mach* as well. All of the
tractates regulate the manner in which a *mach* could distrain on a debtor's
property,[36] and Colan even defines the *mach*'s office in terms of
enforcement:

> *Ny dyly vn dyn bot yn uach kynnogyn canys deu dyn e delan uot; canys pan holo
> er haulur, reyt eu urth y mach y kymell, a pan gemello y mach nyt oes kynnogyn
> y kymeller arnau; ac urth henny ny eyll er un dyn bot yn uach ac yn kynnogyn.*[37]

> A single man is not entitled to be a surety-debtor because they should be two
> men; since when the creditor makes his claim, it is necessary to have the surety
> to enforce it, and when the surety enforces, there is no debtor against whom
> to enforce; and because of that the same man cannot be [both] surety and
> debtor.

Only Ior of the three legal traditions sets the amount of the gage to be taken
— the other texts speak of distraint in this context — and it is interesting
that the amount that a Welsh debtor would lose by defaulting on his debt
is exactly equivalent to the amount of the penalty charged to a defaulting
debtor in early Irish law.[38] And as the *naidm* was allowed to use physical
force in getting the debtor to comply with law, so too apparently was the
mach, since if a defendant resisted a *mach*'s attempt to deliver the defendant's
gage to the creditor, the *mach* was obliged *kemryt e fonnaut gentaf o byd emlad*,
'to take the first blow if there is fighting'.[39] This provision, which reflects
a stage in the development of law when legal enforcement was entirely
private, is to be found in the Ior tractate, in Latin A, B, and E, and in a
slightly less graphic form — less fishlike perhaps — in Cyfnerth: *a godef
arna6 y gofut a del*, 'let him suffer the affliction that may come'.[40] It is
obviously an old regulation, but the fact that the wording in the Latin texts
is closer to that of Iorwerth than to that of Cyfnerth suggests either that
Ior's is the original version or that the original Latin text borrowed this
provision from Ior or Ior sources. In either case, Iorwerth preserves what
appears to be the most primitive version of this ancient passage.

One can, therefore, still see in the thirteenth-century lawbooks a *mach* the nature of whose suretyship corresponded extremely closely to those of the Old Irish *naidm*, despite the centuries which separate the manuscripts that describe them. This correspondence is particularly remarkable in light of the fact that at least some of these practices — the "first blow" suffered by the distraining surety, and the close identification of the surety with the claim — must certainly have been obsolescent by the thirteenth century. Much of the evidence for these older practices is to be found only in the Ior tractate. Iorwerth's compiler has clearly had access to some old legal provisions that are no longer extant elsewhere.[41] There is, however, more to Ior's preservation of such archaisms than mere chance. Even on those points where changes in the law over time allow one to compare directly the various suretyship tractates, Iorwerth's alone reflects the earlier rules.

One of the clearest examples of this is to be found in the passages which discuss the participation of legally incompetent people in contractual relationships. Early Irish law was very definite on this subject; none of the standard legal incompetents — slaves, pilgrims, fools, monks, sons of living fathers, women — were allowed either to *act* as a surety for someone else or to *give* a surety to guarantee an agreement that they themselves had made.[42] Of these two restrictions, the inability to give surety had the more serious implications for the individual's standing in law. A person who could not be a surety might still have been able to make binding legal contracts, but a person who could not give a surety could not enter into such arrangements and had, therefore, no effective legal competence at all.[43] Eventually, in Ireland as elsewhere, changes in the social and economic position of some of these individuals, particularly of women, loosened these restrictive rules, and some late commentaries on Irish law allow women to make valid contracts and even to act as sureties for restricted amounts with their husband's permission.[44]

Welsh law also prohibits legal incompetents from acting in contractual arrangements, and the passage on this matter must be one of the oldest passages in the lawbooks, as it occurs in all of the redactions which contain the suretyship tractate.[45] There are two distinct textual traditions on this issue, the Northern tradition represented by the Iorwerth version of the passage, and the Southern by the version found in Cyfnerth and in the texts of the Latin tradition.[46] It is clear that the Cyfnerth and Latin tradition texts both derive ultimately from a canon in the early eighth century *Collectio Canonum Hibernensis* which forbids legal incompetents to act as sureties.[47] At least one text must have intervened between the original Irish canon and the passages as they appear in the Welsh tractates, since the texts of the Cyfnerth and the Latin traditions are more similar to one another than they are to the Irish original. The Welsh texts omit completely the *brutus* 'fool', and the *virgo sancta*, 'holy virgin', mentioned in the canon, and both add to the list the *scholaris nisi consentiente magistro*, 'the student unless with the permission of his teacher'. The intervening text would, therefore, have included an exile (rendered *alltut* in Welsh), a monk without his abbot's permission, a son without the consent of his father, a student without the consent of his teacher, the slave (*caeth*) and a *femina nisi domina*, 'a woman unless she is a lady'. This last, which must originally have reflected women's changing economic status in Ireland,[48] has been radically transformed by the texts of the Latin tradition, all of which have *nisi domina principalis debitoris*, 'unless she is the lady of the principal debtor'. Cyfnerth's reading here, *na gwreic onyt ar yr hyn ymedho arna6*, 'nor a woman except for that over which she has control', appears at first to have departed from the original, but is actually likely to be a direct translation of the Latin *nisi domina*, a fact which shows both that *principalis debitoris* was an addition unique to the Latin tradition, and that the text intervening between the canon and the Welsh texts must have been in Latin. Both the Cyfnerth and the Latin traditions add further material to their passages, and it is probable that at least the Latin additions were made relatively late in the transmission process, since their use of the term *principalis debitor* is redolent of the twelfth-century revival of Roman law.[49] Interestingly, Cyfnerth's translation of the *nisi domina* phrase seems to envisage a woman acting as debtor-surety for herself, a practice not permitted in early law. The redactor of Colan, whom we know to have been working with both a Latin text and a version of Iorwerth,[50] chose to base his passage on the Latin source, adding clauses to his list that can only have come from a text of the Latin tradition.[51]

The odd man out in this happy group is Iorwerth's passage, and its reading is sufficiently unusual to make one suspect that Colan's choice to rely on the Latin text was deliberate, and was made because its redactor considered the Iorwerth version to be archaic and no longer in accord with contemporary law. Although the ultimate source for the Iorwerth passage was probably neither the Irish canon nor the Latin text which intervened between the canon and the various Southern redactions of it,[52] the Iorwerth passage fits easily into the general tradition of Old Irish law on legal incompetents.[53] Women are noticeably absent from the list, but they may well have been deleted from it at some point in the transmission of the text because they were to be considered elsewhere in the Iorwerth suretyship tractate.[54] In any case, Ior's passage is not as odd in the people that it excludes from suretyship as in the manner in which it seeks to exclude them. Two unusual aspects of the Iorwerth version suggest that it reflects an early stage in the development of the law on incompetents in legal affairs.

Iorwerth is the only redaction which does not mention that these legal incompetents could act as sureties if they obtained the permission of those under whose authority they fell. This omission is, in itself, not conclusive, since one could well construe the clause added by Ior to the list — *p(h)ob den ny allo hep kanhyat arall guassanaethu keureyth*, 'each person who cannot serve law without the permission of another' — to mean that Ior's incompetents, like those of the other texts, could act as sureties with the consent of their superiors. The fact still remains, however, that Ior's failure to mention this option indicates that the original from which Ior's compiler was working dated from a period when legal incompetents were not allowed to act as sureties in any circumstances.

This is particularly suggestive when considered alongside the most striking aspect of Ior's incompetence passage. All of the texts discussed to this point have referred strictly to the ability to *be* a surety, but Iorwerth goes beyond this to prevent its incompetents from even *giving* sureties:

> *Llawer o denyon ne dele menet en uach na rody mach: sef achaus yu, cane deleant hue guadu mach my deleant huenteu rody mach...* [55]

> Many [types of] people are entitled to act as *machs* nor to give a *mach*. This is the reason [for that] — since they are not entitled to deny a *mach*, they are not entitled to give a *mach*...'

We have already remarked that the prohibition against giving sureties is one that takes us back to a very early period of total legal incompetence; it is Iorwerth, and Iorwerth alone, that preserves this archaic rule. The reasoning by which Ior's compiler defends this rule is worth some attention as a revealing bit of lawyer's logic, although one must suspect that the lawyer in question is here working from a minor to a major premise: since they are not entitled to deny a *mach* they are not entitled to give a *mach*. The logic appears to be as follows: a debtor who wished to deny a surety and thereby his debt, had to confirm his denial by an oath on relics. If the supposed *mach* did not counter-swear against him on the same relics, the single oath of the debtor sufficed to free him from the claim, and the *mach* thereby became responsible for the debt. If the surety did counter-swear in the appropriate manner, the debtor had then to present a compurgation of six of his relatives in order to free himself from the claim made against him. [56] An incompetent, who would presumably not be capable of presenting such a compurgation, would be unable to protect himself from a false claim, and it was, therefore, for his own protection that he was not allowed to give a surety at all.

The logic of this rationale is important for the next issue to be examined, the legal competence of women, which is discussed in Ior and Colan in the

context of the three useless suretyships. There is another text to consider here as well. Ior manuscript G, Peniarth 35, contains a provision on women which is obviously old, and which has led Dr Charles-Edwards to suggest that the quire in which it is found may have formed part of an earlier, now lost lawbook — perhaps the Llyfr Cynog mentioned in Cyfnerth and the Latin tradition as an early source.[57] The G passage is a clear and unambiguous statement of early law: *Nyt mach a rodo g6reic 6rya6c, ac ny diga6n hitheu bot un uach*, 'the *mach* that a married woman[58] gives is not a [valid] *mach*, and she cannot be a *mach*'.[59] Iorwerth's own testimony, however, appears on first sight to agree with that of Cyfnerth and the Latin tradition, and to reflect the growing competence of women in contractual affairs:

> ...*nyt mach mach gureyc. Sef yu henne, ny dele gureyc bot en uach, urth na eyll guraged guadu mach, ac na dele hythey reythwyr y'u guadu hy. E kyureyth a dyweyt hagen bot en uach e mach a rodho gureyc, canys puebennac a allo anylessu da, keureyth a deweyt bot en ryd ydau e dylessu; a chanys gureyc a eyll anylessu da, e kyureyth a deweyt bot en reyt mach e genthy hytheu a bot en uach e mach a rodho. A chanys gur a watta hy, guyr a dele hytheu egyt a hy e wadu mach.*[60]

...the *mach* of a woman is not a [valid] *mach*. This is [the meaning of] that — a woman is not entitled to be a *mach*, since women are not entitled to deny a *mach*, and [a female surety] is not entitled to a compurgation of men to deny her. The law says that the *mach* that a woman gives is a [valid] *mach*, since the law says that is lawful for whoever is able to invalidate [an exchange of] goods to [be able to] render them immune from claim. Since a woman can invalidate [an exchange of] goods, the law says that is necessary [to take] a *mach* from her [to guarantee] the immunity [of the exchange], and that the *mach* that she gives is a [valid] *mach*. Since it is a man that she denies, she is entitled to have men together with her to deny a *mach*.

It is clear that by the time the Ior compiler was at work, women, though still not allowed to act as sureties, could now give sureties to guarantee the agreements into which they entered.

The Iorwerth passage is not, however, as simple as it appears. The wording of the first part of this passage suggests strongly that the original with which the Ior compiler was working contained a rule which, though phrased differently from that in G, reflected the same early stage in the legal competence of women. The proverb with which the text opens — *nyt mach mach gureyc*, 'the surety of a woman is not a [valid] surety' — offers both syntactical and content-related reasons for one to suspect that it is old. The sentence order — copula, predicate, subject — would seem to date it no later than the early Middle Welsh period,[61] and although the meaning of the phrase 'the *mach* of a woman' is ambiguous, there are good reasons to believe, against Ior's own interpretation, that it referred originally to the surety given by a woman, and not to that 'consisting of' a woman. The same proverb occurs in the Damweiniau attached to several of the Ior manuscripts, where it is interpreted as the surety 'given by' a woman.[62] Indeed, that is the meaning that one would expect from the possessive genitive — the surety belonging to, i.e. given by, a woman — since the usual way to express the meaning favoured by Ior's compiler would be with the preposition o, as in Colan 52's *reyth o wyr*, a compurgation consisting of men.[63] Colan's redactor, who seems in general to have little interest in preserving practices that he felt to be irrelevant to contemporary law, adds the preposition o, abandons the archaic syntax of the Ior passage, and adds to his sentence a stipulation that can only have come from the Latin text with which he was working: *nyt mach o wureyc ony byt argluydes*, 'a female surety is not a [valid] surety unless she is a lady'.[64]

It seems likely, therefore, that Ior's compiler has either intentionally or unintentionally misunderstood the proverb he had before him. This becomes even more likely upon examination of the reasoning by which the Ior compiler defends his interpretation. He would have one believe that women could not act as sureties, because women could not deny a surety, and because a female surety was not entitled to male compurgators to deny her. The argument appears to be as follows. If a woman claimed to be a surety, and the accused debtor wished to deny that she was a surety, the debtor would have to present a compurgation of women to make this denial, since a woman was not entitled to be denied by male compurgators. However, since women were not permitted to participate in such compurgations of suretyship, a female surety could thus not be denied at all. Women were therefore prohibited from being sureties in order to protect innocent people from the sinister accusations of dishonest claimants and their unscrupulous female accomplices. This reasoning is highly suspect, but it may not have been entirely the product of the compiler's own fertile brain. There is good reason to suspect that at least part of the rationale offered here was original to the material with which the compiler was working, and that it, like the proverb with which this provision opens, originally explained a woman's inability to *give* a surety.

It is certainly true that women were not allowed to participate in the important compurgations of suretyship, *galanas*, 'feud', and *lledrat*, 'theft', for such participation is prohibited elsewhere in the Laws of Women.[65] Much less certain is Ior's assertion that women who are to be denied cannot be denied by men but must be denied by other women. Colan 52 states specifically that women can, and in these special cases, *must*, be denied by men, and in all of the other sex-segregated compurgations described in the

laws the sex of the oath-helpers matches that of the person making the
denial, and not the person against whom they are swearing. Thus a woman
accused of sexual intercourse would clear herself with the oaths of fifty
women even though her accuser was a man.[66] Ior's compiler has adduced
a principle unknown in Welsh law to support his own interpretation of the
older passage. Confronted with a text, the original of which would have said
something like *nyt mach mach gureyc, canys ny eyll gureyc wadu mach*, 'the
surety [given by], a woman is not a [valid] surety, since a woman cannot
deny a surety,' and which would have been very close to the rationale offered
in Ior's incompetence passage, *cane deleant hue guadu mach ny deleant huenteu
rody mach*, 'since they are not entitled to deny a surety they are not entitled
to give a surety',[67] the compiler made two important changes in order to
make sense of his own presumed link between being and denying a surety.
He first pluralized the subject of the last clause so that it would appear to
refer to 'women in general', and not to the single 'woman' of the proverb,
and he then added to the text the provisions that women could not be denied
by male oath-helpers, and that men also could only be denied by men.

There is in fact extant another version of the three useless suretyships that
provides some support for this hypothesis. This short Latin passage is to be
found only in Latin E, well outside the suretyship tractate; it is impossible
to say with certainty from where Latin E obtained it, but it is suggestive
that the passage which follows it also treats of suretyship, is unattested
otherwise in the Southern texts, and corresponds directly to Ior 71/1.[68] The
sentence, which has none of the intricate reasoning that characterizes the Ior
version, reads like a Latin translation of the old original with which Ior's
editor may have been working: *Tercia est fideiussio mulieris, quia ipsa non potest
fideiussorem negare, et ideo non potest fideiubere*, 'the third [useless suretyship]
is the suretyship of a woman, because she herself cannot deny a surety, and
therefore she cannot be (?)/give (?) a surety'.[69] This appears at first every
bit as ambiguous as Ior's Welsh version, since the meaning of *fideiussio
mulieris* is as obscure as the meaning of *mach gureyc*, and since the verb
fideiubere can mean either to give or to be a surety. It does, however, imply
that Ior's mention of the male compurgators was an addition to a sentence
which originally did not mention them, and its use of *ipsa*, the feminine
singular intensive pronoun, referring of necessity in this context to the
mulier of the first clause, renders the sentence less ambiguous than it appears.
The person unable to deny a surety is not here 'women in general', as it is
in Ior's 'revised' version, but rather 'she herself', a fact which renders the
original meaning of the passage pellucidly clear, since a woman who acts as
a surety in a given transaction would herself have no need to deny one. Only
if one understands the passage to say that a woman cannot give a surety

because she cannot deny one is the difficulty resolved. It was, I suspect, from the Welsh original of this text that Ior's compiler wrote his own version.

One can, therefore, recognize three stages in the texts on women G represents the very earliest stage, where women could neither give nor act as sureties.[70] Colan and the texts of the Cyfnerth and the Latin traditions represent the latest stage visible in the lawbooks, since women and other incompetents could certainly give sureties, and could, under certain circumstances, even act as sureties. Ior's tractate reflects, in a very confused fashion, both of these stages at once. Both the proverb and the rationale which accompanied it referred originally to a woman's ability to give a surety, but Ior's compiler, anxious that his lawbook reflect what he knew to be contemporary practice, chose nevertheless to reinterpret rather than to abandon the old material with which he was working.

We turn now to another aspect of suretyship in which Ior's tractate again appears closer to earlier law than does that of Cyfnerth or the Latin tradition. It has long been understood that, like the Irish *naidm*, the *mach* was not originally liable for the debt upon the default of the debtor.[71] By the time of the major legal compilations, however, two varieties of financially liable *mach* had emerged — a *mach* whose liability stemmed from his own failure to perform the characteristic duties (*teithi*) of his office, and a surety liable only because his principal had defaulted. A *mach* who did not fulfil the *teithi* of his suretyship, whether by refusing to give a counter-oath against a denying debtor,[72] or by taking distraint in an improper manner or amount,[73] was thought to have brought his loss upon himself, and was not, therefore, eligible for compensation. It is difficult to know whether this was an old concept; the practice of making a surety liable in this manner for errors he had himself committed was unknown in early Ireland,[74] but the word *teithi* is cognate with the Irish *téchtae*, a technical legal term which seems in some contexts to have much the same meaning of 'characteristics, proper attributes'.[75] Certainly the fact that this practice is associated in all three legal traditions with the requirement that a distraining surety accept the 'first blow' must at least suggest that it was a tradition of long standing.[76]

The second kind of financially liable *mach*, the true paying-surety, was a figure unknown in early Welsh law. Certain stages of his development are, however, still visible in passages like the following from the Ior tractate:[77]

> O deruyd e den kemryt mach ar da a guedy henne dyhol e kennogen... sef a wyl e keureyth ena, bot en yaun rannu e gollet eregthunt en deu hanner: talu o'r mach e neyll hanner e'r haulur, canys hager yu talu o'r mach kubel ac ef en wyreon, ac nat tegach colly kubel o'r haulur yr credu ohonau ew y mach...O deruyd deuot e kennogen eylweyth e'r wlat tra'e keuen, venteu a deleant kemell eu da arnau ef, ac ena e mae yaun caffael o'r mach hanner o'r da hunnu.[78]

> If it happens that a man takes a *mach* [to guarantee] goods, and after that the
> debtor is banished...this is what the law 'sees' to be proper — the loss is to
> be divided in two halves between [the creditor and the surety]: the *mach* pays
> the one-half to the claimant since it is unfair that the *mach* should pay all and
> he innocent [of the default], and it is not more fair for the claimant to lose
> all on account of having trusted in the *mach*...If it happens that the debtor
> comes back to the land after that, they are entitled to enforce [payment of]
> their goods from him, and then it is proper for the *mach* to get half of those
> goods.

Although the surety of this passage no longer enjoyed the complete financial
immunity that characterized the suretyship of the *naidm*, he was not yet a
true *Zahlbürge*. The general presumption of the provision is clearly that in
normal circumstances an innocent *mach* would not be required to pay any
part of the debt at all, and this surety was, therefore entitled to claim and
to enforce his compensation when circumstances permitted.

The evolution of the true paying-surety may well have been a long
process, but it was a natural one. The thirteenth century witnessed many
significant changes in the economic and commercial spheres, as the use of the
currency became more common, and the exploitation of trade and commerce
more organized.[79] Increasingly complex and increasingly professional
transactions required more security than that which could be offered by the
simple enforcing surety, and the existence of two potential debtors against
whom a creditor or a lord could urge a claim must considerably have
streamlined the debt and repayment process. Moreover, paying sureties had
existed elsewhere in Europe — including Ireland — for many centuries, and
Welsh rulers were certainly aware of this. Such rulers must also have been
aware of the role played by such sureties in English courts, where they served
to insure that the king received payments due to him, and they would
certainly have realized the potential benefits of such a system. Thus as the
mach's other functions were gradually usurped by the growing power of
rulers and their courts,[80] payment of the obligation replaced enforcement as
the surety's most important responsibility.[81]

Those who have written on the subject have generally assumed that by
the thirteenth century, the *mach*'s evolution from an enforcing to a true
paying surety had been completed in all parts of Wales.[82] This assumption,
while probably correct, has caused certain facts about the actual evidence for
the paying surety to be ignored. It is clear that the original Latin text to
which the books of the Latin tradition trace their ancestry was familiar with
a paying surety. Each of the texts of the Latin tradition joins Latin A in
stipulating that:

Fideiussor existens solvendo, fideiussor vero minime non solvat antequam debitor deficiet. Debitor vero non deficiet dum legi paruerit. Lex autem eius est et ius, si ita habuerit tria indumenta, id est, try tudedyn, ut duo solvat et tercium retineat.[83]

Where a surety exists for the payment [of a debt], the surety nonetheless does not pay before the debtor defaults. A debtor however does not default while he holds to law. His[84] law and the custom it is, however, if in those circumstances [the debtor] has three garments, i.e. three garments, that he pay two and retain the third.

All of the Latin texts use the term *principalis debitor*, which while admittedly ambiguous, as it is used in thirteenth-century English law for both the debtor and his principal paying surety,[85] nevertheless envisages a financially liable *mach*.[86] While early law required the son or kinsmen of a dead debtor to pay the debt that they had inherited, Latin A's tractate and Latin B's and E's lawbook place that burden squarely on the surety, an obvious example of how the advent of a paying *mach* had changed the law on the inheritance of a debt.[87] One might even see in the Latin tradition's addition of a 'man more powerful than he' to its list of legal incompetents a reference to a paying surety. This addition would make little sense in the context of a purely enforcing surety, since a powerful man would seem the ideal enforcer; the difficulties involved in forcing a powerful individual to pay a debt incurred as a result of a debtor's default make the provision immediately intelligible.[88] Thus while one cannot say with certainty that at the time of the compilation of the tractate of the Latin tradition the *mach* was always, or even primarily, a paying surety, it is clear that the practice was sufficiently common as to influence both vocabulary and law on other topics.

Evaluating Cyfnerth's tractate on this point is slightly more difficult, since while there is clear evidence there for a paying surety, the ultimate source for this evidence casts doubt upon the conclusions which can be drawn from it. Cyfnerth manuscripts *V*, *W*, and *X* and Latin A, B, and E contain a payment schedule which sets out in detail a number of fixed payment dates on which a *mach* could expect a defaulting debtor to repay the debt; after these payment dates had come and gone without payment by the debtor, the *mach* had then himself to reimburse the creditor.[89] Cyfnerth adds to its version of the payment schedule its provision on the surety's compensation.[90] The ultimate source for this payment schedule is another Irish canon from the *Collectio Canonum Hibernensis* relating to the Irish paying surety, the *ráth*,[91] as is clear from the chart below:

Sinodus Hibernensis: 15 (days)..20..30..40..payment.
         Item, *pro vivo:* 10...........5........payment.
         Item, *pro mortuo:* 30...................payment.

Latin A: 12.......20..30..40..payment.

Latin B:	12 . . . . 20 . . 30 . . . . . payment.
Item, *re viva:*	10 . . . . 5 . . . . payment.
Item, *re mortua*	30 . . . . payment.

Latin E:	12 . . . . 20 . . 30 . . . . . payment.
Item, *re viva:*	9 . . . . 5 . . . . payment.
Item, *re mortua:*	30 . . . . payment.

Cyfnerth:

| *da bywawl:* | 15 . . . . 10 . . . 5 . . . . . payment. |
| *da marwawl:* | 15 . . . . 30 . . 50 . . . . . payment. |

Again it is apparent that at least one text must have intervened between the Irish canon and the Cyfnerth and the Latin tradition versions of it, since the phrasing of the Welsh passages is very different from that of the Irish original. But whereas the details of the payment schedule in the Latin tradition match almost exactly those in the Irish text, with one small and easily explicable error (xii for xv), the schedule laid out in Cyfnerth is irreconcilable with that of the canon. Cyfnerth must have drawn here on another, perhaps more local tradition. [92] The only other evidence in Cyfnerth for a paying surety is a provision which allows nine days for a surety to prepare payment *os ef ehunan ae tal gyssefin*, 'if it is he himself who pays first'. [93] This clause occurs also in Latin B, D, and E, but with a significant difference; the Latin texts, which allow only eight days, all omit the word *first*, and without this qualification the sentence could apply to a normally non-paying surety who is forced to pay because of his own failure to perform the duties expected of him. [94] These difficulties must cast some doubt on Cyfnerth's evidence for a paying surety, but one can nevertheless say that it, like the texts of the Latin tradition, is familiar with the institution. And if the icthyoid aroma arising from the passages associated in both traditions with the paying surety is a genuine one, the transition from enforcing to paying surety may well have occurred relatively early in south Wales.

It is easy to summarize the evidence in the Iorwerth tractate for the true paying surety because it quite simply does not exist. The only paying sureties with which Ior's tractate is familiar are those who pay as a result of their own errors, or those who pay half for an exiled debtor. [95] The difficulty posed by Ior's silence is to determine the extent to which it can be said to be a significant one. Here it seems appropriate to draw a distinction between an argument made on the basis of the absence of certain evidence or types of evidence and one made on the basis of the silence of a given text on a particular subject. An argument based on absence may be suggestive, but it is difficult to put much weight on it; it may well be significant that only

Ior makes the archaic identification of claim and surety directly, but as the subject is not one that the very short texts of the Latin tradition could be expected to address, the absence of evidence on this point proves little. The argument based on silence is more persuasive. If a text is tremendously full and detailed, as is Ior's tractate, and if it makes some attempt to cover a topic in a full and organized fashion, as does Ior, then its silence on an issue of central importance, like the financial liability of the *mach*, is a significant one, and needs to be explained. [96]

The obvious explanation for this silence would be that paying sureties were unknown in north Wales at the time that the tractate as we have it was compiled. It is certainly possible that paying sureties developed earlier in the more anglicized South than they did in the North, as the practice of allowing a man to stand surety for his own debt seems to have done. [97] There is, however, fairly good evidence to suggest that paying sureties were known in northern Wales by the thirteenth century. It is certainly the case that the *mach gorfodog*, a special *mach* for criminal affairs described in Ior outside the suretyship tractate, was liable for the sum owed by his principal. [98] One of the pleas now extant only in the fifteenth-century Ior manuscript *F*, but which was probably once attached to the early fourteenth-century manuscript *G* as well, [99] defines payment as one of the primary duties of suretyship:

> *c(h)an adefeist dy vot yn vach, ti a dyly talu neu gymhell; kanys kyfreith mach yv pan adefho y vechniaeth talu neu gymell.* [100]
>
> since you acknowledged yourself to be a *mach*, you are obliged either to pay or to compel; since the law [concerning], a *mach* is that when he acknowledges his suretyship [he is] to pay or to compel.

If it is true, as has already been suggested, that the date of the compilation of the Ior tractate as we have it was not far removed from that of the first Ior manuscripts, it would seem likely that paying sureties would indeed have been known to the compiler of the Ior tractate.

If the solution to this problem is not the historical one, then it must be a textual one, and it must lie in the manner in which the Ior tractate was compiled. The archaic provisions that we have discussed here suggest that Ior's compiler must, at the very least, have had access to a variety of old materials which were not available to the editors of the tractates of the Cyfnerth and the Latin traditions. But this may be only half of the truth. The range of subjects covered in the older stratum of the tractate would in itself suggest that Ior's compiler was working from an early suretyship tractate, and not simply from scattered old materials of heterogeneous origins. And if one imagines such an early tractate as the core of the one which we now have, determining the organization of the later work and controlling the subjects which the later compiler did and did not address, Ior's silence on the paying surety is entirely comprehensible. As a sculptor uses separate bits of clay to flesh out a wire figure erected earlier, so Ior's compiler may have added his separate bits, his *Damweiniau* and *Cynghawsedd*, to the already formed tractate which was before him. Those subjects treated in the earlier work for which he had relevant *Cynghawsedd* were enlarged and fleshed out with the more recent material, but those topics not mentioned in the early tractate, and for which he had no relevant later texts, were ignored. Thus it is that the late provision on the surety seeking the lord's permission to take an outsize gage is placed with the early description of the procedure to be followed in taking a gage,[101] but paying sureties, which would not have existed at the time the original tractate was composed and on which the compiler must not have had any late material, are not mentioned at all. Indeed the occasional repetition of a given provision, like that which requires a surety who does not counter-swear against a denying debtor to pay the debt, might well be evidence of this technique if it could be shown that one of the provisions comes from the later, and the other from the earlier, stratum of the tractate.[102]

The idea that an archaic text may lie at the core of the extant Ior tractate is not an inherently unlikely one, given what we know about the transmission of the Welsh legal texts and the age of suretyship itself as an institution, and it would account plausibly for the various peculiarities of that tractate. The existence of such a tractate is, however, less interesting than the nature and extent of it. The problems involved in isolating this core are those posed by Welsh law as a whole, for we do not yet have the sort of understanding of Welsh law that would allow us to classify as old or new law every sentence in the present tractate. One can, however, obtain a broad outline of the contents of the early text by isolating from the rest subjects or sections which a comparison with Irish law would suggest to be close to early law, or which seem to have been of particular importance to the compiler and around which a number of later texts have clustered. The resulting outline, with those subjects on which Ior's tractate seems to place special importance underlined looks like this:

<u>Denying a surety</u>

<u>Denying suretyship</u>

<u>Taking a gage</u>

One day surety forbidden

<u>Dead surety</u>

Dead debtor

Women (three useless suretyships)

Legal incompetents

Debtor and surety meet on the bridge of one tree
Identification of surety and claim

Though it is at present impossible to demonstrate with certainty that any one of these subjects appeared in an earlier tractate, one can nevertheless say that this outline reflects at least the basic structure of the *extant* Ior tractate, and that its relationship to an earlier source remains to be proved.

We find this 'proof' in the suretyship tractate in Cyfnerth, commonly thought to be the most primitive of the lawbooks. The tractate is in fact missing from Cyfnerth manuscript *U*, but since it is to be found in five Cyfnerth manuscripts, *V*, *W*, *Mk*, *X* and *Z* we must assume that this is a lacuna in *U*. *X* and *Z*'s tractate are the shortest and most primitive, and it is clear that manuscripts *V*, *Mk* and *W* have borrowed heavily from a Iorwerth text; everything printed in WML after 88.8 (Cyfnerth 36) was, for example, taken directly from Ior, and cannot be considered part of the original Cyfnerth tractate.[103] In order, therefore, to obtain the same sort of rough outline for the Cyfnerth that we have made for the Iorwerth tractate, one must ignore all the material found only in *Mk*, *V* and *W* and not found in *X* and *Z*, on the suspicion that it represents an addition to the original. This I have done in making the following outline, which I here place beside that made above of the Iorwerth tractate:

IORWERTH	CYFNERTH
Denying a surety	Denying a surety
Denying suretyship	Denying suretyship
Taking a gage	Taking distraint
One day surety forbidden	
	Payment schedule
Dead surety	Dead surety
Dead debtor	Dead debtor
Women	
Legal incompetents	Women and legal incompetents

Bridge of one tree

Identification of surety and claim

My point is, I hope, made for me by this chart. The subjects covered in both of the tractates are the same. What we are looking at now, I propose, is an

outline of a tractate which was the ultimate, though not the immediate,
source for both Ior and Cyfnerth's suretyship tractate — an *Urtext* indeed.

To say that the present Cyfnerth and Ior stem ultimately from the same
source is not, of course, to say that either or both necessarily reproduce the
actual law contained in that source. Changes in the substance and the
wording of the original legal material could have been introduced at any
point in the transmission of either tractate; the similarities noted above speak
only to the contents and the organisation of the hypothetical *Urtext*. It is
however, at least suggestive that the procedures outlined by the two
lawbooks on the taking of distraint, the denial of sureties and suretyship, and
the death of a debtor, are substantially the same.[104] Although one must
always admit the possibility of later redactors making similar changes to two
different texts, it is more likely that the texts in these cases do actually
preserve the practices originally detailed in the core tractate. Indeed in at least
one passage even the wording of the Cyfnerth and Ior versions is strikingly
similar:

O deruyd lludyas rody guestel, e mach byeu hebrug e guestel ygyt ar haw-lwr[105] hyt en dyogel, ac a dele kemryt e fonnaut gentaf o byd emlad. Ac ony wna henne, talet ehun e delyet. (Ior 62/3-4)	Mach adyly d6yn gauel gyt ar ha6l6r hyt yn diogel, agodef arna6 y gofut adel. Ac ony wna hynny, talet ehunan. (Cyfnerth 8)
If it happens that there is hindrance to [the *mach*] giving the gage, it pertains to the *mach* to accompany the gage together with the creditor to a safe place, and he is obliged to take the first blow if there is fighting. And if he does not do that, let he himself pay the debt.	The *mach* is obliged to distrain together with the creditor to a safe place, and to suffer the affliction that may come. And if he does not do that, let he himself pay.

There are in fact only two subjects discussed in the core tractate on which
Ior and Cyfnerth differ significantly from one another, and in both instances
it is possible to determine with some degree of certainty which reflects the
earlier stage in law. I have already argued that Ior's provisions on legal
incompetents return us to a very early period in Welsh history; Cyfnerth
would here seem to have 'modernised' its lawbook by substituting for the
original passage an Irish canon more in accord with the actual legal practices
of the day.[106] With respect to the procedure to be followed after the death
of a surety, however, it is Cyfnerth which seems to retain more of the
substance of the old law. Ior requires the surety's son to assume his father's

responsibilities, while Cyfnerth urges the creditor to confirm the suretyship of the dead man by a compurgation over his grave.[107] These provisions are not, as they stand, irreconcilable; Cyfnerth does not, after all, stipulate by whom the debtor's heirs would be compelled to meet their obligations. But since the practice of swearing an oath over a dead man's grave is one that might be most reasonably associated with an early period in law,[108] and since the suretyship of the *naidm* was not heritable in early Irish law,[109] Cyfnerth's reading would appear to be the older of the two. It is in any case remarkable that despite the numerous changes that must have been made in this ancient tractate over the years, its framework and perhaps something of its contents are still dimly visible in the Iorwerth and Cyfnerth lawbooks of the thirteenth and fourteenth centuries.

The obvious question raised by these observations is the extent to which the texts of the Latin tradition reflect this hypothetical *Urtext*, but this they do not do at all. Indeed the individual tractates do not seem to follow any particular organizing principle, and they certainly do not follow the outline that has been suggested for the Ior and Cyfnerth texts. This seems at first somewhat surprising, since the redactions of the Latin tradition are thought to come ultimately from an original Latin text which itself stems at least in part from an early Cyfnerth book; thus it is that one can speak of a 'Southern' as opposed to a 'Northern' tradition. The suretyship tractate seems, however, to adhere only half-heartedly to this general pattern, in that the original Latin tractate would seem to have borrowed only relatively little from a Cyfnerth source. Only one short sequence is likely to have come from an early Cyfnerth tractate, and even within this sequence one of the provisions of the Latin tradition is much closer to the Ior version of the sentence than it is to the Cyfnerth version.[110] The stemma given below and the charts in Table 1 show the relationship of the Latin tradition as a whole to Cyfnerth texts and sources, and of the individual Latin texts to one another. It is always very difficult to tell whether a given text has used another, or whether the two are descended instead from the same source. Dr Emanuel suggested that the compiler of Latin B used Latin A directly,[111] but the significant differences in phrasing and the occurence in Latin A's tractate of provisions that appear in Latin B only outside the main tractate suggest to me that they descend from a common source. Emanuel's conclusion that Latin E used Latin B is, however, accurate, in my opinion.[112] Latin E looks very like a corrected and improved version of the particularly poorly arranged Latin B; not only does it correct the most blatant of the errors of Redaction B, it also draws into its tractate sections relating to suretyship that are found in Latin B only outside the main tractate.[113]

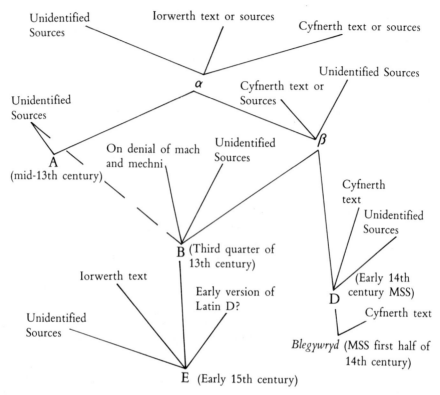

(Dates given are of the earliest extant manuscript)

The most striking aspect of the texts of the Latin tradition is the very advanced stage of law that they all reflect. All of the extant versions derive from a single and now missing Latin text (designated α in the stemma). But even this earliest text, which can, to a certain extent, be reconstructed through a comparison of the extant books, contains a significant amount of relatively late law. We have already determined that its laws on incompetents are the most developed of all of the lawbooks, and it, like the Latin tradition in general, is clearly familiar with the paying surety.[114] α even allows men to stand as sureties for their own debts, an undoubtedly late practice which is not permitted by the other two legal traditions.[115] The recent date of many of the Latin provisions, coupled with the disorganized character of certain of the Latin lawbooks, strongly suggest that the suretyship tractate of the Latin tradition was not so much a thoughtful compilation of old and new law as a careless collection of miscellaneous provisions which does not much predate the earliest extant manuscript.

Not every tractate in the lawbooks will prove to possess such an archaic core, although it is certainly suggestive that the Iorwerth tractate on women seems to have been patterned on a list of unions of declining status similar to the undoubtedly archaic *Nau Kynywedi Teithiauc.*[116] Suretyship was an ancient and vitally important institution, and we are lucky to have had in the Iorwerth and Cyfnerth compilers men conscious of their dual role as both purveyors of contemporary law and historians of an impressive legal tradition. It would obviously be of great interest to know the date at which the tractate from the Iorwerth and Cyfnerth texts ultimately derive took shape, but here our sources fail us. We can remark only that it would seem to have preceded the division of the laws into Northern and Southern traditions, and that many of the practices that would seem on Iorwerth's testimony to have been described in it were consistent with what is known of the eighth-century Irish *naidm.*[117] By the thirteenth century a plethora of materials, old and new, had collected around this central core, and suretyship then became, in the despairing words of a late jurist, 'one of the three complexities of law', because the regulations and procedures associated with it were 'difficult to remember and reduce to rule'.[118] The mummy was thus alive and prospering in the last century of Welsh independence, but the many wrappings wound around him by time could not entirely obscure the ancient figure that lay within.

[1] This paper was presented in something very like its present form to the Sixth International Colloquium on Welsh Law, held at Gregynog Hall in September of 1983. I would like to thank all of those at the conference for their helpful and encouraging remarks and suggestions especially Dr T. M. Charles-Edwards.

[2] Bleg 2.5-8. On this prologue, see J. Goronwy Edwards, 'Hywel Dda and the Welsh Lawbooks', CLP, 137-160.

[3] T. Jones Pierce, 'Social and Historical Aspects of the Welsh Laws', reprinted in J. Beverly Smith, ed., *Medieval Welsh Society* (Cardiff, 1972), 353-368, 357-358.

[4] '*Kyfreith*', as opposed to '*Llunnyeith da*'. This is found in manuscript G (Peniarth 35) only: AL VIII.xi.3.

[5] Note, for example, how the principle of 'one tongue urging and another denying' could be applied to different types of cases. AL VIII.v.2, AL VII.i.43, Ior 59/1. A defendant who could successfully claim that there was but 'one tongue accusing and another denying' in his case obtained thereby the right to make a denial of the charge to which there could be no response.

[6] Dafydd Jenkins, 'Legal and Comparative Aspects of the Welsh Laws', (1963) WHR 51-59, p. 56.

[7] This has almost certainly happened in the suretyship tractate itself, where what appears to be the same passage in origin is attached to different provisions in Cyfnerth and the Latin tradition: Lat A 5, Lat B 1/12, Lat D 22, Lat E 1/11, Bleg 41.7-8, Cyfn 17,18.

All Latin text references are to tractates as defined in the **Key** which follows this article, and to the sentences numbered 1- final in each of those individual tractates.

[8] Latin D's requirement that the lord enforce a debt on behalf of a dead *mach* (Lat D 30-31, Bleg 42.1-7) rather than the son mentioned in Ior 64/5 (Col 104) may or may not reflect the increasing role of lordship in legal enforcement.

[9] Bleg 40.6-22, Lat D 8-13, Ior 68/8, DwCol 462-468, CIH 595.2, 5, 13.

[10] This is of course a generalization, and it must be recognized that there are exceptions to this characterization. The *Damwein* itself is an ancient legal form, and some of the *Damweiniau* found in these later collections are recognizably 'old law': AL IV.iv.4. Even *Cynghawsedd*, a legal genre whose roots lie in a curial, and therefore relatively late, legal procedure, make frequent use of old images and provisions; note for example the provision which requires a distraining surety to take the 'first three blows' — a familiar and fishlike rule put here into triadic form for greater effect — and then encourages him to bring a plaint for *sarhad* to his lord! (AL XIV.xxii.10)

[11] CIH 591.8-599.38.

[12] CIH 595.21-22, 595.37-596.1, 598.16, 19, 22, 26, 31, etc.

[14] Daniel Binchy, 'Celtic Suretyship', 355-367, 360-361.

[14] According to Dafydd Jenkins in WLW 2-3.

[15] T. M. Charles-Edwards, 'The Relationship of the Tractates in Latin Redactions A and B to those in *Llyfr Iorwerth* and *Llyfr Cyfnerth*', WLW 180-185.

[16] Above, p. 36.

[17] Stephen J. Williams, in the Bleg introduction, xix-xxv.

[18] T. Jones Pierce, 'The Kindred and the Bloodfeud', reprinted in Smith, *Medieval Welsh Society*, 289-308.

[19] T. Jones Pierce, 'The Growth of Commutation in Gwynedd during the Thirteenth Century', reprinted in *Medieval Welsh Society*, 103-125. Aled Rhys Wiliam repeats this evaluation of the three legal traditions in his introduction to *Llyfr Iorwerth*, xxi.

[20] T. Jones Pierce, 'Bloodfeud', 295.

[21] T. Jones Pierce, 'Bloodfeud', 296.

[22] T. Jones Pierce, 'The Laws of Wales — the Last Phase', reprinted in *Medieval Welsh Society*, 369-389, 383, note 51.

[23] See, for example, the long theological argument with which Ior bolsters its ruling on the issue of the denial of an inherited suretyship: Ior 64/6-7.

[24] That is, in the thirteenth century. Also indicative of a fairly late date is the price of the horse mentioned in Ior 62/12 and Col 98; see Professor Jenkins's note on this on §60 of *Lyfr Colan*.

[25] On the duties and privileges of the *naidm* the standard work is still Rudolf Thurneysen, *Die Bürgschaft im irischen recht: Abhandlungen der Preussischen Akademie der Wissenschaften* (1928) nr. 2, 56-61.

[26] Cf. 'Die *naidms*...sind eine Art Oberaufseher über den Vertrag, man mochte sagen: der Vertrag in Person'. *Bürgschaft* 57.

[27] CIH 593.18.

[28] CIH 594.23-25.

[29] CIH 7.9, 9.5, 239.37, 397.35-36.

[30] CIH 593.2-5, 595.1-15, Ior 68/8, Bleg 40.6-22, Lat D 8-13, DwCol 462-468, and AL X.vii.40-43. Lat D has erred in twice substituting debitor for creditor, a mistake which almost certainly stems from a mistranslation of the Welsh word *dylyawdyr*, 'creditor,' as 'debtor' (from the more common word *dyledwr*). Lat A makes this same error in sentence 13. Note that while an Irish debt had to be 'counter-bound', in that both contracting parties appointed sureties to one another to guarantee proper comportment in respect of the debt, there is no hint of such an arrangement in the Welsh laws.

[31] Cyfn 11, Ior 58/8, 59/1-2, 4, Col 78-79.

[32] Ior 67/2 and see also 63/1.

[33] Ior 56/5, Col 88, Lat A 124.18, Lat B 216.8, Lat D 367.4-5, Lat E 458.3, Bleg 38.18-20, DwCol 390, 397. Cyfn 82.

[34] Ior 62/5-6, Col 93. These passages bristle with textual difficulties which the helpful note in *Llyfr Colan* largely resolves: 59-60.

[35] Cyfn 4, Bleg 40.2, Lat B 11/1, Lat D 6, Lat E 1/20.

[36] Ior 62/1-4, Col 92-99, Lat A 10-11, Lat B 11/13-14, Lat D 18-19, Bleg 41.1-4, Lat E 1/30-31, Cyfn 8.

[37] Col 101.

[38] That is, one third of the amount of the debt. This is an issue on which there is some disagreement, since the phrasing of the relevant passages (Ior 62/2 and Col 92) is ambiguous. Professor Dafydd Jenkins, in his note to Col 92 (p. 59), suggests that the 'third' in question is a third of the gage itself, and not a third of the debt; the gage is therefore equal to 1½ times the original debt, and the amount that a debtor would lose through his default one-half of the debt. As Professor Jenkins notes, in Ior 62/7 a creditor who has lost his debtor's gage must return a halfpenny to the debtor 'since a halfpenny is a third of a legal penny'. There are, however, other passages in the laws which would suggest that the 'third' mentioned in Ior 62/2 and Col 92 is in fact a third of the debt itself, and that a defaulting Welsh debtor, like a defaulting Irish debtor, would lose as a penalty an amount equal to a third of his debt: Ior 62/10 in the Peniarth 35 (f. 21v) version, and AL VIII.xi.6. Most conclusive is Lat E in LTWL 508.12-13: *Vadium legale est quarta pars quae* (from E4) *cadat sub ipso*, 'A legal gage is a quarter part which belongs to that same [gage].' According to this passage, if the amount of the debt was a penny, the amount of the gage would be 1⅓ pence, and the penalty charged a defaulting debtor a third of the debt itself. This interpretation still leaves unexplained how 'a halfpenny is a third of a legal penny', as it is in Ior 62/7, but this problem too can be resolved. A halfpenny is the smallest monetary unit mentioned in the thirteenth-century English sources; it was not a minted coin, but was rather made by clipping in half a coin that had been minted as a full penny. It is unlikely that a coin smaller than a halfpenny (in this case a third of a penny) could exist, since the coin could not bear additional clipping. Ior 62/7 might well have been intended only to specify that whenever a fraction smaller than a halfpenny was due, the amount should be rounded to the nearest halfpenny. If this interpretation is correct, it is interesting that it is once again Ior and Lat E, both of which have been traditionally regarded as sophisticated and late legal compilations, that preserve the old tradition.

[39] Ior 62/3.

[40] Cyfn 8, Lat A 10-11, Lat B II/13-14, Lat E I/30-31, Ior 62/3-4, Col 92. Lat D 18 and Bleg 41.1-3 would seem to have deliberately omitted the provision on the first blow.

[41] See Professor Jenkins's notes to Col 92.59.

[42] CIH 593.35-40.

[43] Thus T. M. Charles-Edwards in an unpublished article, 'NLW Peniarth MS. 35 (G)'. I would like to thank Dr Charles-Edwards for allowing me to see this paper.

[44] Cf. Cyfn 25, 26 and Ior 66/7.

[45] D. A. Binchy, 'The Legal Capacity of Women in Regard to Contracts', SEIL, 207-234.

[46] Ior 66/7, Col 116, Cyfn 25, 26, Lat A 7, Lat B 1/15, Lat D 35-36, Lat E 1/15, Bleg 42.16-21.

[47] H. Wasserschleben, ed., *Die irische Kanonensammlung* (Leipzig, 1885) XXXIV, 3, 144. On the relationship between the Irish and the Welsh texts, see Rudolf Thurneysen, 'Aus dem irischen Recht V. Zu der Etymologie von irischen *ráth*, 'Bürgschaft', und zu der irischen

Kanonensammlung und der Triaden', (1929-1930) 18 ZcP 364-375, 368-369.

[48] Binchy, in 'Legal Capacity', 224-234, connects the growing competency of women in contract with changes in the amounts of property women brought into marriage. See also the Col note 113, 63. MS *X* has interesting variants (see below p. 200 n.3).

[49] LTWL 39.

[50] See Professor Jenkins's introduction to *Llyfr Colan* pp. xxvi-xxx on Ior as a source for Col, and pp. xxx-xxxii on the Latin text used by the Col redactor.

[51] Examples of clauses taken by Col from a Latin text would include *heb ganyat y abat, heb gannyat y athro*, and *dyn a uo cadarnach no ef* (Col 116).

[52] This is likely to be a controversial conclusion, but in order to believe that the Ior version also stemmed originally from the Irish canon one would have to accept that the Ior compiler added the very early provision against incompetents giving sureties, and dropped the relatively late consent clauses that are found throughout the Latin tradition. Both of these seem extremely unlikely changes for a compiler to make — the restrictions on the giving of sureties are too obviously 'old law', and the consent clauses equally obviously relevant to the period in which the compiler was working.

[53] See, for example, CIH 592.26-31, 536.23-24, 459.16-17.

[54] In Ior 65/7-11, the three useless suretyships.

[55] Ior 66/7.

[56] The fullest account of the denial procedure is found in Ior 58-60.

[57] Charles-Edwards, 'NLW Peniarth MS. 35 (G)'. G does not, however, contain the prohibition against legal incompetents giving sureties. This omission might suggest that *na rody mach* was an addition by the Ior compiler, but *na rody mach* is found in all of the Ior manuscripts except G, and it seems unlikely that a thirteenth century compiler would add something so obviously outdated to one of his provisions.

[58] This qualification does not significantly affect the meaning of the provision. *Gwreic* itself is used in the lawbooks to mean a woman who has had sexual relations; *gwreic wryawc* means only that the woman in question has a husband at the time (i.e. she is not a widow). It is the position of such a woman that is most at issue here: Charles-Edwards, 'NLW Peniarth MS. 35 (G)'.

[59] Peniarth 35, f. 23r.

[60] Ior 65/7-10.

[61] GMW 145, n.3.

[62] AL IV.iv.4 (Ior manuscripts *A,E,F,G,* and *U*).

[63] GMW 231. See Charles-Edwards, NLW Peniarth MS. 35 (G) for this argument.

[64] Col 113.

[65] Ior 55/2, Col 52.

[66] Ior 46/9, 10, Cyfnerth 73/24a (in WLW 138-139), Lat A 52/49-51 (WLW 156-157).

[67] Ior 66/7.

[68] LTWL 504.14-15 = Ior §71/1.

[69] LTWL 504.11-13.

[70] Charles-Edwards, 'NLW Peniarth MS. 35 (G)' reaches this conclusion with respect to G, Ior and Col.

[71] Dafydd Jenkins, 'Legal and Comparative Aspects,' 54-55 and 58, and see D. A. Binchy, 'Celtic Suretyship', 360-362 on the *naidm*.

[72] Ior 59/5, 60/5-6.

[73] Ior 62/3-4, 62/10-11, AL X.vii.39.

[74] Except insofar as a surety who refused to act would forfeit his honour, which he could redeem only by payment of his honour-price: *Bürgschaft*, 60.

[75] See examples cited under column 101 in DIL *T- tnuthaigid.*

[76] Lat A 10-11, Lat B 11/13-14, Lat E 1/30-31, Cyfn 8, Ior 62/3-4.

[77] From manuscript *E*; found in all for manuscripts except *B* and *K*.

[78] Ior 64/1-3.

[79] T. Jones Pierce, 'The Growth of Commutation', especially pp. 114-124, and 'Social and Historical Aspects', especially 355-356.

[80] The later law envisages significant changes in the *mach*'s role as chief witness of the transaction (Lat E 1/50, DwCol 402, AL VI.i.65, V.ii.63, V.ii.68, VIII.xi.29, Cyfn 83, Bleg 126.5-13), and as enforcer of the obligation (AL VIII.iii.6, V.ii.66, XIV.xli.12, X.v.9, XIV.xxv.4).

[81] The compensation of such a paying surety is mentioned only once in the Welsh lawbooks, and that only in a passage that could scarcely have been of any particular comfort to sureties concerned about their own financial well-being (Cyfn 17, 18). One must assume that a paying surety would indeed have been entitled to compensation for his loss; it is only natural that details relating to a relatively recent aspect of the *mach*'s office might not have been sufficiently integrated into a tractate on the subject.

[82] See, for example, note 81, 58, in Col and WTL 11, 15-19.

[83] Lat A 3-5, Lat B 1/10-12, Lat D 20-22, Lat E 1/9-11, Bleg 41.4-8.

[84] That is, Hywel's law? Or should this be translated 'its', as referring to the law of suretyship?

[85] See, for example, Memoranda Roll 23 Henry III, King's Remembrancer (E.159/17 m.) and Fine Roll 23 Henry II (C.60/36 m.6).

[86] Lat A 6, 7, 8, 21, 23, Lat B 1/1, 4, 15, Lat D 1, 14, 35, Lat E 1/1, 15, 35, etc.

[87] Ior 64/10, Col 107, Cyfn 19, Lat A 21-23, Lat B IV/1-2, Lat D 32-33, Lat E 11/1-2, Bleg 42.7-12.

[88] For a similar provision in early Irish law, see CIH 1122.4-5.

[89] Lat A 8-9, Lat B VII/1-4, Lat E 35-38, Cyfn 10-18.

[90] Cyfn 17, 18, Compare with this Lat A 5, Lat B 1/12, Lat D 22, Lat E 1/11, Bleg 41.7-8.

[91] *Kanonensammlung*, XXXIV, 4. Thurneysen, 'Zu der irischen Kanonensammlung', 369-370.

[92] Manuscript Q has evidently used either Cyfn or the source from which Cyfn drew this table, since its schedule is exactly the same as that in Cyfn. AL X.vii.44.

[93] Cyfn 6.

[94] Lat B 11/15, Lat D 15, Lat E 1/32.

[95] On the former, see above, pp. 27f. On the latter: there are two passages in Ior which could be taken as evidence for a true paying surety and one of these (Ior 62/12) is obviously of a late date. Both Ior 62/12 and Ior 63/3 mention a creditor who takes the gage of a *mach*, and they seem to imply that a creditor could take a gage from the surety for the payment of the debt upon the debtor's default. A close examination of the relevant passages shows, however that the *guestel e mach*, the 'gage of the surety', is not a separate gage given by the surety to guarantee that he will pay the debt, but is rather the gage taken by the *mach* from the debtor. What is from the surety's point of view the gage of the debtor is from the creditor's point of view the gage of the surety, since it is from the surety that he receives it. This is made clear by the wording of the passages in question. The Welsh lawbooks usually use the preposition *ar* to indicate the person from whom the gage is taken; compare then Ior 63/3 *ny dele mach duen guestel y ar e kennogen*, 'the surety is not entitled to take a gage *from* the debtor', with this clause from the same passage: *ne dele er haulur duen guestel e mach*, 'the creditor is not entitled to take the gage of the mach'. Note also how in Ior 62 the surety is sometimes spoken of as the taker, and sometimes as the giver, of a gage. In this passage,

as above, the difference between the giver and the taker lies in the point of view adopted.
[96] Mr. James Campbell made this point with reference to the government of Offa's Mercia in a lecture given at the University of Oxford in the spring of 1982.
[97] Lat A 13-14, Lat B 1/16-7, Lat D 26-27, Lat E 1/18-19, Bleg 41.16-25.
[98] Ior 70/1.
[99] The first ten paragraphs of the plea are missing in G (Peniarth 35), but G then resumes its narrative in the middle of a sentence in paragraph ten, and follows F closely from that point to the end of the plea. It is, therefore, most likely that the rest of the paragraphs now missing in G were once included in it: AL VIII.i.1-11.
[100] AL VIII.i.8. Note also that Colan's incompetence passage takes the *dyn a uo cadarnach no ef*, 'man more powerful than he', from the Latin text, and that this is a provision which may have reference to a paying surety: Col 116, and above, p. 29.
[101] Ior 62/1-4, 62/12.
[102] Ior 59/5, 60/6.
[103] Cyfn 36 = Ior 64/5, Cyfn 27-30 = Ior 63/2, Cyfn 73 = Ior 64/8,11 (by implication), Cyfn 48 = Ior 62/7, Cyfn 49, 50 = Ior 62/10-11, Cyfn 51 = Ior 62/8. Likewise the W additions: Cyfn 31-35 = Ior 64/1-4, Cyfn 37-47 = Ior 58-59, Cyfn 74-76 = Ior 64/13.
[104] Cyfn 31 = Ior 58-60 (a lengthy section of *Cynghawsedd* with which Ior's redactor has replaced the original clause); Cyfn 2 = Ior 61/2-4; Cyfn 8 = Ior 62/3-4; Cyfn 19 = Ior 64/10. Note that in this last passage Cyfn preserves the older practice of placing the responsibility for an inherited debt on the shoulders of the 'three nearest degrees' (of kindred), while Ior makes only the son responsible.
[105] I have supplied a reading from manuscript C (B.L. Cotton MS Caligula A iii) (see below). The text of Wiliam's edition which is based on manuscript B (B.L. Cotton MS Titus Dii) reads *ygyt ac ef*, 'together with him', but as B and K (Peniarth 40) are the only Ior manuscripts to differ from the reading in manuscript C, *ygyt ar hawlwr* is likely to be the closest to the original.
[106] I think this solution more likely than the alternative, i.e. that Ior's *na rody mach* 'nor to give a *mach*', represents an addition to the original core text made early in the transmission of the Iorwerth version of it. I would further suggest that Ior's proverb on women was also a part of the original tractate, although it might well have been presented originally in a context other than that of the three useless suretyships; a Cyfnerth redactor would then presumably have dropped this passage when it became irrelevant to the practices of his own day, or, perhaps, when he incorporated the Irish canon into his text.
[107] Cyfn 21, 22, Ior 64/5.
[108] Similar provisions are found in Anglo-Saxon law (Ine c. 53), and also in late Manx law: *Old Historians of the Isle of Man* (1871), 24. And although I still think it likely that this is an archaic practice, it should be noted that a record of such a custom exists in a London municipal legal collection of the early thirteenth century: Mary Bateson, 'A London Municipal Collection of the Reign of John', (July 1902) 17 EHR 480-511, p. 493 = f. 98b of B.L. Add MS 14252.
[109] Although the *naidm's* office was not hereditary, that of the Irish paying surety, the *ráth*, clearly was. Since the *mach* of the thirteenth-century texts is almost certainly a paying surety, heritability of the office may well have begun when the *mach* changed from a primarily enforcing to a primarily paying surety.
[110] Cf. Lat A 10-11, Lat B 11/13-14, Lat E 1/30-31 Cyfn 8, Ior 62/3-4.
[111] LTWL 14-16.
[112] LTWL 74-75.
[113] For example, Lat B VII/1-4 = Lat E 1/35-38; Lat B III/1-2 = Lat E 1/41; Lat B

V/1-3 = Lat E 1/42-43. Lat E moves the paragraph on *dirwy* which Lat B would appear to have interpolated into the middle of its main suretyship tractate to the end of its tractate, and rephrases Lat B 1/8-9 to make it more intelligible (Lat E 1/5).

[114] Lat A 3-5, Lat B 1/10-12, Lat E 1/9-11, Lat D 20-22, Bleg 41.4-8, and Lat A 6, Lat B 1/6, Lat E 1/8, Lat D 19.

[115] Lat A 13-14, Lat B 1/16-17, Lat D 26-27, Bleg 41.16-25, Lat E 1/18-19. Note that Ior is clearly aware of the practice, since it goes to the trouble to prohibit it: Ior 63/2, Col 101.

[116] T. M. Charles-Edwards, 'Nau Kynywedi Teithiauc', WLW, 23-39, 27.

[117] If it could be determined at what point women began to enjoy some limited capacity with regard to contract, one would at least have a *terminus ad quem* for some of the Ior material. Unfortunately this is a subject of particular obscurity, as Dr Wendy Davies notes in her *Wales in the Early Middle Ages* (Leicester, 1982), 78-79. Her own research into the Llandaff charters has revealed a very few examples of women involved in land grants (140 ca. 655, 190b ca. 705, and 207 ca. 760), but these were all royal women, and most of the grants were made in association with or by permission of their husbands. Dr Davies concludes that 'There is nothing to suggest that non-royal women had any role in the disposal of property'. (Wendy Davies, *An Early Welsh Microcosm* (London, 1978), 56) For what it is worth the Irish texts which reflect this sort of limited capacity in contract are linguistically datable to the period ca. 700-750: Binchy, 'Legal Capacity', 215-217. For the date of *Cáin Lánamna* see Dr Charles-Edwards's review of CIH (1980) 20 *Studia Hibernica* 141-62.

[118] AL X.vii.27 (manuscript Q, with P and S variants).

KEY TO TABLE

LATIN A: LTWL pp. 124-125
LATIN B I: LTWL pp. 216-217
LATIN B II: LTWL pp. 217-218
LATIN B III: LTWL p. 250
LATIN B IV: LTWL p. 254
LATIN B V: LTWL p. 254
LATIN B VI: LTWL p. 255
LATIN B VII: LTWL p. 256
LATIN B VIII: LTWL p. 258
LATIN D: LTWL pp. 367-369
LATIN E I: LTWL pp. 458-461
LATIN E II: LTWL p. 501
LATIN E III: LTWL p. 501
LATIN E IV: LTWL p. 504
LATIN E V: LTWL p. 505
BLEG: *Llyfr Blegywryd* p. 39 = *Dyledion*, pp. 40-42 = *Meichiau*

TABLE 1: THE LATIN TRADITION AND BLEGYWRYD
TABLE OF EQUIVALENT SENTENCES

Lat E	Lat B	Lat A	Lat D/Bleg	Cyfn	Ior	Other
I/1	I/1	—	1/39.24-25	—	—	—
I/2	I/2	—	2/39.25-27	—	—	—
↓I/3	↓I/3	—	↓3/39.27-29	—	—	—
I/4	I/4+	—	+14/40.23-24	—	—	—
I/5	I/8–9					
	VI/1-2	—	—/—	—	64/1-4	—
I/6	I/5	—	8/40.6-9	—	(cf. 68/8)	—
—	—	—	9-13/40.9-22+	—	—	—
I/7	I/7	2	−4/39.29-30	—	—	—
—	—	—	5/—	—	—	—
I/8	I/6	6	19/41.3-4	—	—	—
I/9	I/10	3	20/41.4-5	—	—	VIII.iii.
I/10	I/11	4	21/41.5-6	—	—	—
I/11	I/12	↓5	22/41.7-8	(cf. 17,18)	—	(cf. VIII.iii.2)
I/12	I/13–	19-	23/41.9-12	2,3	(cf. 61)	—
↓I/13	↓I/14	↓20	↓24/41.14-15	82	(cf. 61/5)	—
I/14	—	—	—/—	—	—	—
I/15	I/15	7	35/42.16-20 | 25		66/7	Ir. canon
—	—	—	↓36/42.20-21 ↓26		—	—
↓I/16	|II/10+	—	—/—	—	—	—
↓I/17	↓II/11					
	243.41-2	15-18	17/40.29-41.1	—	—	—
I/18-19	I/16-17	13-14X	26-27/41.16-25	—	—	—
I/20	|II/1	—	6/40.1-4	4	(cf. 58/3)	—
I/21	II/2	—	—/—	—	—	—
I/22-23	II/3-4	—	—/—	—	58-60	—
I/24	II/5	—	—/—	—	—	—
I/25	II/6	—	(cf. 23/41. 9-12)	3	68/4 (cf. 68/2-3, 5-6)	—
I/26	II/7	—	—/—	—	—	—
I/27	II/8	—	—/—	—	—	—
I/28	II/9	—	—/—	—	—	—
I/29	II/12	↑12	16/40.26-28 |7+		—	—
I/30-31	II/13-14	|10-11X	−18/41.1-3X ↓8		62/3-4	—
I/32	II/15	—	15/40.24-25 ↑6		—	—
I/33	II/16	—	7/40.5-6 |5–		—	G f.24r
↓I/34	↓II/17	—	|28/41.26-27 ↑80		—	—
—	—	—	↓29/41.27-31 |81		—	—

————————————————————————— END OF LATIN B I AND II

TABLE CONTINUED

Lat E	Lat B	Lat A	Lat D/Bleg	Cyfn	Ior	Other
I/35-36	VII/1-2	8-9-	—/—	10-18	—	Ir. canon
I/37-38	VII/3-4	—	—/—		—	Ir. canon
I/39-40	243.36-9	128.35-37	374.33-5	Welsh/ 77 – +		
			117.7-10			
I/41	III/1-2	—	—/—		—	—
I/42	V/1 –	1 –	—/—	—	—	—
I/43	V/3	—	—/—	—	—	—
I/44	—	—	—/—	—	—	—
I/45	—	—	—/—	—	64/4	—
I/46	—	—	—/—	—	58/1-3	—
I/47	—	—	—/—	(cf. 23,24)	(cf.66/ 8-11)	—
I/48	—	—	—/—	—	—	DwCol 117
I/49	—	—	—/—	—	—	(cf. DwCol 5)
I/50	—	—	—/—	—	—	(cf. DwCol 402-3)
I/51	—	—	—/—	—	—	—

——————————————————————————————END OF LATIN E

II/I	IV/I	21	—/—	—	—	—
—	—	22	—/—	—	—	—
II/2	IV/2	23	—/—	—	—	—
II/3	IV/3	24	—/—	—	—	—

——————————————————————————————END OF LATIN E II

| III/I | V/2 | — | —/— | — | — | — |

——————————————————————————————END OF LATIN E III

| IV/1-4 | — | — | —/— | — | 65 | — |
| IV/5 | — | — | —/— | — | 71/1 | — |

——————————————————————————————END OF LATIN E IV

—	—		—/—	63	—	—
	VIII/2	—	—/—	—	—	—
	VIII/1	—	—/—	—	—	—

——————————————————————————————END OF LATIN E V

TABLE CONTINUED

Lat E	Lat B	Lat A	Lat D/Bleg	Cyfn	Ior	Other
—	—	—	25/41.12-14	11	—	—
—	—	—	—/126.5-13	83	—	—
—	—	—	30/42.1-5	↓ 21,22	—	—
—	—	—	31/42.6-7	—	—	—
—	—	—	32-33/42.7-12		—	—
—	—	—	↓ 34/42.13-15	↓	—	—
—	—	—	373.38-40/42.2 2-26	—	—	—
—	—	—	373.41/42.27-28	—	—	—

NOTE: Arrows indicate sentence sequences within an individual lawbook.

DUW YN LLE MACH: BRIDUW YNG NGHYFRAITH HYWEL
HUW PRYCE

Y mae'r rheolau ar fechni yng Nghyfraith Hywel yn ddrych sy'n nodweddiadol o ddyfeisgarwch dynol y rhai a'u lluniodd ond ni ddylem anghofio eu bod hefyd yn dyst i ddibyniaeth y gyfraith ar ragdybion crefyddol a chydweithrediad eglwysig.[1] Yn debyg i gyfreithiau seciwlar eraill yr Oesoedd Canol, at Dduw, yn y pen draw, y trôi'r gyfraith Gymreig pan fyddai angen arni brawf diymwad o wirionedd gosodiad neu gyhuddiad a lefarwyd mewn achos, er enghraifft, geiriau cynnogn yn gwadu mach neu eiriau mach yn gwadu ei fod yn fach, a hynny drwy drefnu llw.[2] Yn ogystal gellid galw ar ymyrraeth Duw wrth ffurfio contract yn y lle cyntaf. Yr enw ar y ffurf honno ar gontract oedd *briduw*, ac mae'n bleser mawr gennyf gyflwyno'r sylwadau canlynol arni i'r Athro Dafydd Jenkins, nid yn unig fel ymgais i godi cwr arall o'r llen ar fechnïaeth Geltaidd ond hefyd fel ymateb, digon cyfyngedig ei sylw mae'n wir, i'r argyhoeddiad a fynegodd ef dros ugain mlynedd yn ôl fod 'angen astudio perthynas y gyfraith Gymreig â'r Eglwys yn fanylach'.[3]

Cafwyd sawl cynnig ar ddehongli ystyr ac etymoleg *briduw* gan ysgolheigion. Bu'r rhan fwyaf ohonynt o'r farn mai math o lw ydoedd a gyfatebai i'r arfer o 'wystlo ffydd'.[4] Yn wir, aeth Gwilym Prys Davies mor bell ag awgrymu fod briduw wedi ei chreu gan ganonwyr yn y ddeuddegfed ganrif ar lun y 'gwystl ffydd' (Saes. *pledge of faith*) fel ffordd o gael gwŷr y gyfraith i gydnabod yr addewid noeth yn egwyddor gyfreithiol, a bod gwŷr cyfraith Gwynedd wedi ateb yr her eglwysig yn y drydedd ganrif ar ddeg drwy seciwlareiddio briduw a'i phatrymu ar fechni.[5] Yn fwy diweddar, fodd bynnag, dadleuodd D. A. Binchy fod gwreiddiau hynafol, cyn-Gristnogol o bosibl, i friduw, a'i bod wedi ei christnogeiddio cyn iddi lanio fel crair o'r gorffennol pell ar ddalennau llyfrau Cyfraith Hywel.[6] O ran ei hetymoleg, mynnai Timothy Lewis a T. P. Ellis fod briduw i'w hesbonio drwy lygriad o'r Lladin *Pro Deo*,[7] ond ni dderbyniwyd hyn gan ysgolheigion diweddarach a gynigiai'n fwy argyhoeddiadol ei tharddu o'r ddau air Cymraeg *bri* a *Duw*, gyda *bri* yn golygu 'anrhydedd'.[8]

Yn y papur hwn, byddaf yn bwrw golwg fanwl dros y prif adrannau sy'n ymwneud â briduw yn y llyfrau cyfraith er mwyn ceisio egluro eu cynnwys, sefydlu'r berthynas destunol rhyngddynt, ac yn olaf, mentro rhai casgliadau cyffredinol ynghylch arwyddocâd briduw yng Nghyfraith Hywel. Gellir rhannu'r adrannau yn ddau brif ddosbarth. Cynrychiolir Dosbarth I gan Lyfr Cyfnerth, Testun Lladin D a Llyfr Blegywryd, a Dosbarth II gan (i) Testun Lladin B a (ii) Llyfrau Iorwerth a Cholan. At yr adrannau hyn gellir ychwanegu amryw o reolau eraill yn Llyfr y Damweiniau ac mewn llyfrau diweddarach. Y mae dwy nodwedd sydd yn gyffredin i'r ddau Ddosbarth, sef eu bod yn ymwneud yn bennaf â sut i *wadu* briduw, a bod y dull o wadu wedi ei batrymu ar un dull o wadu mach.

I

Yn Llyfr Cyfnerth y ceir fersiwn gwreiddiol Dosbarth I:

E neb a watto mach: rodet y l6 ar y seithuet o'r dynyon nessaf y werth, petwar o parth y tat a deu o parth y vam ac ynteu ehunan seithuet. Y neb a watto mechniaeth: rodet y l6 ar y seithuet yn y kyffelyp vod, ac ony byd y genedyl yn vn wlat ac ef, rodet y l6 ehunan uch pen seith alla6r kyssegyr yn vn gantref ac ef, kanys uelly y g6edir bri du6. [9]

Pwybynnag a wado fach, rhodded ei lw gyda'r chwe dyn sydd agosaf eu gwerth [10] iddo, sef pedwar o ochr ei dad a dau o ochr ei fam ac yntau ei hun yn seithfed. Pwybynnag a wado fechnïaeth, rhodded ei lw yn un o saith yn yr un modd; ac oni bydd ei dylwyth [11] yn yr un wlad ag ef, rhodded ei lw ei hunan uwchben saith allor gysegredig yn yr un cantref ag ef, canys dyna sut y gwedir briduw.

Sylwer nad â briduw yn uniongyrchol y mae a wnelo'r ail reol yma; yn hytrach, cymhwysir rheol ar sut i wadu briduw at sut y dylai mach wadu mechnïaeth pan na fydd ganddo 'y genedyl yn vn wlat ac ef'.[12] A bwrw bod *gwlad* a *chantref* yn dermau cyfystyr yma gellid dadlau fod y saith allor yn cymryd lle'r saith person a fyddai fel arfer yn ffurfio'r rhaith. [13] Ymddengys fod pwy bynnag a luniodd yr adran ar fach yn gwadu ei fod yn fach yn Nhestun Lladin D yn benthyca o'r adran yn Llyfr Cyfnerth:

Fideiussor negans fideiussionem suam de septimo proximorum sibi in redemptione negabit, vel solus iurans super vii altaria dedicata, os briduw a diwad. *Si partim negat et partim profitetur, solus semel iurabit. Et sic* kynnogyn, *si fideiussionem negaverit, scilicet, de septimo.* [14]

Bydd mach sydd yn gwadu ei fechnïaeth, yn ei gwadu drwy raith y saith aelod o'i dylwyth sydd agosaf ato fel y dylent dalu [ei alanas], neu [bydd] yntau ei hunan yn gwadu ar saith allor gysegredig, os briduw a wada. Os gwada ran a chyfaddef rhan, bydd ef ei hunan yn tyngu [llw] unwaith. Ac felly y dyledwr, yn sicr, os bydd ef wedi gwadu mechnïaeth, sef drwy lw saith aelod o'i dylwyth.

Seilir yr adran hon ar adran yn Nhestun Lladin A,[15] ond daw'r deunydd ychwanegol am saith allor a briduw o'r rheol yn Llyfr Cyfnerth a ddyfynnwyd uchod. Yn ôl Testun Lladin D, fodd bynnag, mae'r mach ei hunan yn gwadu briduw, hynny yw, yn lle cymryd cymal Llyfr Cyfnerth am fach yn gwadu ar saith allor fel *cyffelybiaeth* â briduw, fe'i deëllir fel *disgrifiad* ohoni, er nad oes unrhyw reswm pam y dylai gwadu briduw berthyn i fach rhagor neb arall. Mae'n fwy na thebyg na ddeallai lluniwr Testun Lladin D, nac awdur Llyfr Blegywryd ar ei ôl, beth yn hollol oedd briduw, a bod y rheol wedi ei gwthio i mewn i'w llyfrau er mwyn cryfhau eu naws eglwysig.[16] Dylid nodi yn ogystal na cheir unrhyw gyfeiriadau pellach at friduw yn Nhestun Lladin D a Llyfr Blegywryd, a bod llyfrau diweddarach y Deheubarth heb ddatblygu unrhyw reolau newydd amdani.[17] Teg casglu felly nad creadigaeth newydd cyfraith y Deheubarth, dan ddylanwad y canonwyr, mo friduw; gellir olrhain ei phresenoldeb yn y llyfrau deheuol at un rheol yn Llyfr Cyfnerth.[18]

II

Bid a fo am ei gwreidddiau yr oedd a wnelai datblygiad briduw â thraddodiad cyfreithiol Gwynedd, fel y dengys y rheolau amdani yn Nosbarth II. Mae'n debyg fod Testun Lladin B wedi ei ysgrifennu yn y Gogledd,[19] ac er iddo gasglu ei ddeunydd amrywiol o sawl man, gellir mentro fod y rheol dan sylw yma o darddiad gogleddol oherwydd y tebygrwydd rhyngddi a'r rheolau mwy datblygedig yn Llyfr Iorwerth a Llyfr Colan, llyfrau sy'n gynnyrch diamheuol dysg gyfreithiol Gwynedd. Yn ôl pob un o'r tri llyfr hyn, gwedir briduw drwy raith yn hytrach na thrwy lw yr unigolyn ar allorau, hynny yw, cymhwysir y dull arferol o wadu mach neu fechni at friduw hithau.

(i) Digwydd yr adran o Destun Lladin B yn ail gasgliad y llyfr hwnnw o reolau ar fechnïaeth, ac nis ceir mewn unrhyw lyfr arall ac eithrio Testun Lladin E. Gan nad yw'n tarddu o Destun Lladin A, rhaid bod i'r adran ffynhonnell arall, efallai'r un a oedd hefyd y tu ôl i'r adran o Lyfr Iorwerth. Anodd credu bod yr adran o Destun Lladin B yn dibynnu ar eiddo Llyfr Iorwerth o gofio bod yr ail yn fanylach a llawnach, nac ychwaith fod yr adran o Lyfr Iorwerth yn ddyledus yn uniongyrchol i'r un o Destun Lladin B oherwydd y nifer o wahaniaethau pwysig sydd rhyngddynt o ran eu cynnwys. Eto, y mae digon yn gyffredin rhyngddynt i awgrymu fod y ddau lyfr yn dystion annibynnol yn y fan hon i'r un ddysgeidiaeth gyfreithiol (sef bod angen rhaith i wadu briduw)—dysgeidiaeth sydd yn wahanol i eiddo Llyfr Cyfnerth—a bod y ddysgeidiaeth honno ar glawr rywbryd cyn cofnodi rheolau Testun Lladin B a Llyfr Iorwerth erbyn canol y drydedd ganrif ar ddeg.[20]

Dyma'r adran o Destun Lladin B sy'n trafod briduw:

Si fideiussor fatetur esse in commercio, super illum primo veniet iuramentum ut fateatur super quod fuit fideiussor. Si totum negat quod non sit fideiussor, super kennogyn *primo veniet iuramentum. Et si fideiussor contra iuret,* kennogyn *denegat illum cum vii hominibus. Si manu, id est, fide, confirmatur commercium, redditur, si negatur, non. Negatio est eius* bridwy *iuramentum vii hominum. Similiter est negatio fideiussoris si contra iuretur, vel fideiussori. Et si non, non debet nisi iuramentum ipsius solius super quod ponatur fideiussor. Nullum commercium est commercium sine fide vel fideiussore.* [21]

Os cydnebydd mach ei fod yn [ymwneud â] masnach, daw'r llw arno ef yn gyntaf, er mwyn iddo gydnabod yr hyn y bu'n fach arno. Os gwada'r [dyledwr] yn gyfan gwbl ei fod yn fach, ar y dyledwr y daw'r llw yn gyntaf. Ac os tynga'r mach yn ei erbyn, bydd y dyledwr yn gwadu hynny gyda saith o ddynion. Os cadarnheir masnach trwy law, hynny yw, trwy ffydd, telir [y ddyled]. Trwy lw saith o ddynion y gwedir y friduw honno. Yn yr un modd y gwedir mach, os tyngir yn ei erbyn, neu, yn hytrach, [wadu] 'r mach [gan y dyledwr].[22] Ac oni [wneir] ni ddylai ond ei lw ei hunan fod ar yr hyn y mae'n fach arno. Nid masnach mo fasnach heb na ffydd na mach.

Noder pwyslais y rheolau ar swyddogaeth fasnachol mechnïaeth a briduw yma: defnyddir y gair *commercium* ('masnach', 'cyfnewid masnachol')—gair nas ceir yn unrhyw ran arall o'r Testunau Lladin sy'n ymdrin â mechni—droeon, gan ddiweddu â dihareb fod rhaid wrth naill ai ffydd neu fach ar gyfer cyfnewid dilys.[23] Trawiadol hefyd yw'r gyffelybiaeth a wneir rhwng briduw a *fides* ('ffydd'); yn wir, unwaith yn unig y defnyddir y gair briduw ei hunan, a hynny yn yr un cyd-destun â Llyfr Cyfnerth, sef lle y sonnir am wadu briduw.

Yn ôl Testun Lladin B, felly, golygai briduw ddull o ymrwymo mewn contract ar sail ffydd yn hytrach na thrwy fach. Ceir enghreifftiau eraill yn y llyfrau cyfraith o addewidion a rhwymedigaethau drwy *fides*, *ffydd*, neu *gred*, er mai un yn unig ohonynt sy'n adleisio adran Testun Lladin B a chyplysu ffydd â briduw.[24] Sonnir am roi a chymryd ffydd neu gred mewn testunau rhyddiaith Cymraeg Canol eraill megis *Culhwch ac Olwen* a *Pheredur*.[25] Ymddengys mai addewid neu rwymedigaeth difrifol a wneid, mwy na thebyg trwy i'r person a roddai ei ffydd gydio yn llaw y person a'i cymerai ganddo wrth roi'r addewid.[26] Yng ngoleuni'r cyfeiriadau llenyddol gellir awgrymu bod rhoi ffydd wedi datblygu erbyn c.1100 fan bellaf[27] fel ffurf o rwymedigaeth ar gyfer gwneud rhywbeth yn y dyfodol. Yr oedd yn wahanol i ymrwymo drwy lw, ac yn annibynnol ar gyfraith mechnïaeth.[28]

Erbyn ysgrifennu Testun Lladin B yn ystod hanner cyntaf y drydedd ganrif ar ddeg mae'n fwy na thebyg nad oedd gwahaniaeth sylfaenol rhwng briduw a'r arfer frodorol o 'roi ffydd', er bod *gwreiddiau* briduw yn wahanol, fel y gwelwn yn y man. Yn y ddeuddegfed ganrif hawliai'r eglwys yn Lloegr a rhannau eraill o Ewrop fod pob rhwymedigaeth *fide interposita* yn ddarostyngedig i'w llysoedd hi,[29] ac erbyn diwedd y ganrif ystyriai'r gyfraith ganon fod ffydd yn gyfartal â llw addewid fel dull o ffurfio rhwymedigaeth.[30] Er y gwyddys fod ffydd fel y deëllid hi gan y canonwyr wedi ei defnyddio i ffurfio cytundebau mewn rhai mannau ac mewn rhai cylchoedd yng Nghymru yn ystod y ddeuddegfed ganrif a'r drydedd ar ddeg, gan osod y cytundebau hynny dan awdurdodaeth eglwysig,[31] y mae'n anodd dal fod y rheolau cyfraith ar ffydd a chred yn ddyledus i'r syniadau canonaidd hyn, oherwydd nid oes sôn o gwbl ynddynt am lysoedd yr eglwys.[32]

(ii) Am yr ymdriniaeth fwyaf llawn a manwl â briduw yn llyfrau Cyfraith Hywel rhaid troi at Lyfr Iorwerth, at adran fer y ceir fersiwn mwy cryno ohoni yn Llyfr Colan.[33] Yn y rhan gyntaf o'r adran eglurir canlyniadau cyfreithiol 'rhoddi briduw ar beth', ac yn arbennig y drefn briodol ar gyfer gwadu hynny (68/1-6), ac yna, yn yr ail ran, ychwanegir nifer o reolau craill ar y pwnc (68/7-10). Fel yr adrannau byr ar amod (69) a gorfodogaeth (70), daw'r adran ar ddiwedd y traethawd ar fechni. Yn wir, patrymir y rhan gyntaf o'r adran ar reolau a geir yn y traethawd hwnnw (58-60) ar sut y dylai cynnogn wadu mach, ac fel gyda'r rheolau am fach yn gwadu ei fechni (61/1-4) y mae'n debyg fod manylion y rheolau hynny wedi eu cymryd yn ganiataol a'u haddasu at y rhai am wadu briduw. Felly wrth ddadansoddi'r adran ar friduw rhaid ystyried y rheolau am fechni yr un pryd, a thrwy ehangu'r drafodaeth yn y modd hwn bydd yn bosibl i ni oleuo ryw ychydig ar gyd-destun crefyddol y traethawd ar fechni.[34]

(a) [1] O dervyd y dyn rody bry Dyw ar peth, talet new gwadet mal y dywetto kyvreyth. [2] Sef a dyweyt e kyvreyth, ony gwrthtyghir arnaw, bot en dygawn y lw ehwn. [3] Os gwr(th)twng a vyd arnaw, galwet enteu am vrawt.

Os digwydd i ddyn roi briduw ar beth, taled neu waded fel y dywedo'r gyfraith. Dyna a ddywed y gyfraith fod ei lw ei hunan yn ddigonol, oni thyngir yn ei erbyn. Os tyngir yn ei erbyn, galwed yntau am ddyfarniad.

Gellir cymharu 68/1 â'r frawddeg ganlynol yn adran Testun Lladin B: Si manu, id est, fide, confirmatur commercium, redditur; si negatur, non.[35] Mae 68/2-3 yn gyson â'r rheolau yn 59 sy'n esbonio sut y dylai cynnogn wadu mach a sut y caiff y mach wrthdyngu. Yn ôl y rheolau hynny rhaid i'r cynnogn dyngu llw ar ei ben ei hun ar grair sydd yn llaw yr ynad, a dyna ddiwedd ar y mater o safbwynt y cynnogn oni ddewisa'r mach wrthdyngu a chyhuddo'r cynnogn — tra bo ei enau yn dal ar y crair — o fod wedi tyngu anudon a mynnu brawd (sef dyfarniad) gan yr ynad.[36]

Mae'r holl amgylchiadau y tyngid llwon o danynt yng Nghyfraith Hywel yn bwnc rhy fawr i'w drafod yma, ond y mae un agwedd arno y carwn oedi gyda hi am ychydig cyn symud ymlaen, sef y defnydd o greiriau. Cyfeirir yn fynych at dyngu ar greiriau yn y llyfrau cyfraith; yn wir, nid oedd llw

yn ddilys fel arfer heb ei dyngu 'i Dduw ac i'r crair'.[37] Weithiau dywedir
mai mewn eglwys, ger yr allor neu arni, y tyngir ar grair neu greiriau,[38]
ond droeon eraill sonnir am fynd â chreiriau allan o eglwys er mwyn eu
defnyddio mewn achos a gynhelid mewn rhyw fan arall.[39] Tanlinellir
pwysigrwydd cyfreithiol creiriau gan dair rheol yn Llyfr y Damweiniau:

> *Puybennac a decco kreyreu y datleu, ac eu keyssyau o'r llall en erbyn e kreyryeu a
> doeth ganthau ef, nyny a dewedun na dyly hunnu e kreyryeu ef yny daruo y datleu
> eff; o hynny allan kyffredyn uyd e kreyreu y paub en y maes. Nyt reyt kreyreu en
> datleu a kymeller emenwuent egluys canys plas keureythyaul ev. O deruyd bot
> keureyth en datleu ac na bo kreyreu yn y maes, nyny a dewedun na deleyr oet y
> keyssyau kreyryeu namyn tra gatwo er egnat y urautle, a hynny en ewyllys er egnat.*[40]

Pwybynnag a ddygo greiriau i achos cyfreithiol, ac y bydd rhywun arall yn
gofyn am eu cael yn ymyl y creiriau a ddygodd ef, ni a ddywedwn nad oes
gan hwnnw yr hawl i'w greiriau ef hyd oni therfyno ei achos ef; o hynny
ymlaen, bydd y creiriau yn gyffredin i bawb yn y maes. Nid oes rhaid wrth
greiriau mewn achos a gynhelir mewn mynwent eglwys, canys mangre
gyfreithiol ydyw. Os digwydd fod achos cyfreithiol ymlaen ac nad oes creiriau
yn y maes, ni a ddywedwn na ddylid oedi i geisio creiriau ond tra arhoso yr
ynad yn ei frawdle a hynny yn ôl ewyllys yr ynad.

Awgryma'r rheol gyntaf fod gan unigolion eu hoff greiriau, a hwyrach y bu
peth cystadleuaeth am gael defnyddio creiriau neilltuol.[41] Edrydd Gerallt
Gymro hanes am yr Arglwydd Rhys yn mynd mor bell â dwyn torch Cynog
Sant a'i chadw yng nghastell Dinefwr, nes iddo ennyn dialedd Duw arno am
ei haerllugrwydd, a gwyddys fod gan y tywysog Dafydd ap Llywelyn
(1240-46) groes sanctaidd y byddai'n tyngu llwon arni.[42] Dengys rheolau
Llyfr y Damweiniau hefyd fod achosion yn cael eu cynnal y tu allan, 'yn y
maes', neu mewn mynwentydd. Condemniwyd beilïaid Llywelyn ap
Gruffudd am 'weinyddu barn a chynnal achosion ar ddyddiau Sul a gŵyl
mewn mynwentydd a mannau eraill a gysegrwyd i Dduw, a hyd yn oed
mewn eglwysi' gan esgob a chabidwl Llanćwy yn 1276,[43] ac o ddarllen
canonau cynghorau eglwysig gwelwn fod yr un arferion ar gael yn Lloegr
yn y drydedd ganrif ar ddeg.[44] Yr oedd mynwentydd ac eglwysi yn lleoedd
cyhoeddus ac mae'r amlygrwydd a roddid iddynt wrth weinyddu'r gyfraith,
yn ogystal â'r defnydd helaeth o greiriau, yn dyst huawdl i'r cyfuniad o
elfennau sanctaidd a seciwlar yng ngweinyddiad cyfraith frodorol Cymru.

   Beth yn hollol oedd y creiriau? Dosberthid creiriau yn ddau brif fath yn
yr Oesoedd Canol, sef rhai corfforol a rhai anghorfforol. Cyrff neu ran o
gyrff y saint oedd y cyntaf, tra cynhwysai'r ail unrhyw beth a gysylltid â
sant.[45] Ychydig iawn o gyfeiriadau sydd gennym at greiriau corfforol yng
Nghymru;[46] ac awgryma'r dystiolaeth yn gryf mai'r math anghorfforol a
fu fwyaf niferus a phoblogaidd, ac mai ar y rhain y tyngid llwon fel arfer.

Mewn darn enwog, sylwodd Gerallt Gymro ar hoffter y Cymry, fel y
Gwyddyl a'r Albanwyr, o glychau llaw, baglau a chreiriau eraill, gan honni
ei bod yn llawer gwell gan y pobloedd hyn dyngu llwon ar greiriau o'r fath
nag ar yr Efengylau.[47] Cawn gadarnhad o'i sylwadau ym mucheddau'r
saint[48] ac mewn barddoniaeth o'r unfed ganrif ar ddeg a'r ddeuddegfed,[49]
a hefyd gan ambell reol yn y llyfrau cyfraith eu hunain. Yn ôl Llyfr Cyfnerth
yr oedd yn ofynnol i ŵr a wadai iddo gael cyfathrach rywiol â gwraig yn
'llwyn a pherth' roi ei lw 'y gloch heb taua6t yndi',[50] ac y mae nifer o'r
llyfrau'n datgan bod yn rhaid tyngu llw ar fagl a llyfr Efengyl pan fyddai
ar eglwys eisiau profi terfynau ei thiroedd.[51] Dylem ddeall *crair* yn y
cyfreithiau fel 'gwrthrych sanctaidd' (cf. Saes. *halidom*), yn debyg i'r *mind*
a ddefnyddid mewn cyfraith Wyddelig gynnar,[52] a chan fod creiriau o'r fath
yn niferus ac uchel eu parch nid yw'r cyfeiriadau lu atynt yn y llyfrau cyfraith
yn syndod.

(b)   [4]*Esef a varn e kyureyth, y lw ar y seythvet o'y gwadu: pedwar o kenedyl y tat a
    dev o kenedyl y vam ac ehvn en seythvet.*

    Dyma a farn y gyfraith, ei lw yn un o saith er mwyn gwadu ['r briduw]:
    pedwar o ochr ei dad a dau o ochr ei fam ac ef ei hun yn seithfed.

Yr un yw byrdwn Llyfr Colan: 'keureyth a uarn e lu ar y viiuet o'y wadu,
a hynny yn unwet a reyth mach'.[53] Yn ôl Llyfr Iorwerth dyma gyfansoddiad
rhaith cynnogn sy'n gwadu mach ar ôl i hwnnw ei wrthdyngu, a cheir yr
un rheol yn Llyfr Cyfnerth;[54] dywed y Testunau Lladin, ar y llaw arall, fod
y mach yn tyngu *gyda* saith aelod arall o'i genedl, ac nid fel y seithfed, ond
efallai iddynt gamddeall ffynhonnell Gymraeg yn y fan hon.[55] Dywed rheol
arall yn Llyfr Iorwerth fod i wraig sy'n gwadu briduw wragedd eraill yn
ffurfio'r rhaith gyda hi.[56]

(c)   [5]*Oet e reyth honno wythnos o'r Svl rac wynep.*[57]
    Amser cynnal y rhaith honno yw wythnos i'r dydd Sul canlynol.

Cyfetyb y rheol hon i 60/3 o Lyfr Iorwerth eithr yno ychwanegir: 'ac
esef lle er rodyr er reyth honno en llann e bo y dwfyr swyn a'y vara efferen;[58]
ac esef amser e kymeryr e rwng e Benedycamvs a rody e bara efferen'. Mae'r
manylion hyn ynglŷn ag amseriad a lleoliad y rhaith yn arbennig o werthfawr
i ddeall agweddau crefyddol a litwrgaidd cyfraith mechnïaeth yn Llyfr
Iorwerth. Gadewch inni ystyried *dwfr swyn* a *bara offeren* yn gyntaf. Fel y
nododd T. P. Ellis, nid sagrafennau mo'r rhain, eithr elfennau a ddosberthid
ymhlith y gynulleidfa ar ddiwedd gwasanaeth yr offeren y priodolid iddynt
rinweddau iachaol ac amddiffynnol.[59] Y term technegol am fara offeren yw
eulogia(e) a gellir olrhain yr arfer o'i rannu ymysg y bobl i'r chweched ganrif
yng Ngâl, er na ddaeth yn arferol i'w ddosbarthu *ar ôl* yr offeren tan ganol

y nawfed ganrif. Yn ei *Capitula presbyteris data* (852) gorchmynnodd Hincmar o Reims y dylai pob offeiriad ar ddydd Sul neu ŵyl fendithio'r bara nas cysegrwyd ar gyfer y Cymun a'i rannu ymysg pawb yn yr eglwys a oedd heb gymuno. Eglurodd hefyd fod yn rhaid i'r offeiriad gysegru dŵr cyn yr offeren a'i daenellu dros y gynulleidfa wrth iddynt ddod i mewn i'r eglwys (sef defod yr *asperges*) ac yna, ar ddiwedd y gwasanaeth, câi'r gynulleidfa fynd â pheth o'r dŵr adref gyda hwy mewn dysglau a'i daenellu dros eu tai, eu caeau, eu gwinllannoedd, eu gwartheg a hyd yn oed eu bwyd a'u diod eu hunain er mwyn eu diogelu rhag drwg. Diolch i ddosbarthiad eang y canonau hyn lledaenwyd yr arfer o rannu bara a dŵr ar ôl yr offeren at eglwysi eraill Ewrop yn ail hanner y nawfed ganrif ac wedyn. Erbyn y ddeuddegfed ganrif, o leiaf yn Ffrainc, yr oedd yr arfer o rannu'r bara wedi gafael gymaint nes i'w gymryd gael ei ystyried yn weithred *a gymerai le*'r Cymun, a bu raid i synodau yn y drydedd ganrif ar ddeg wahardd rhoi'r bara yn lle'r Cymun mewn gwasanaethau offeren.[60]

Mae'r datblygiad olaf hwn yn hawdd i'w ddeall o gofio mai pur anaml y cymunai pobl yn y cyfnod hwnnw. Dyfarnodd Pedwaredd Synod y Lateran (1215) nad *rhaid* i leygwyr gymuno'n amlach nag unwaith y flwyddyn, sef adeg y Pasg.[61] I'r gynulleidfa bob dydd Sul, dosbarthu'r bara a'r dŵr ar ddiwedd yr offeren oedd y weithred a arhosai yn y cof, yn hytrach na'r Cymun, a dyna ragdyb rheol Llyfr Iorwerth. Oherwydd prinder tystiolaeth, mae'n amhosibl dweud pryd y cychwynnodd yr arfer yng Nghymru: y *terminus a quo* yw ail hanner y nawfed ganrif, ond dengys deddfwriaeth eglwysig o Loegr yn y drydedd ganrif ar ddeg fod yr arfer yn fyw yng nghyfnod ysgrifennu'r llawysgrifau cynharaf sydd gennym o Lyfr Iorwerth, ac felly beth bynnag yw ei dyddiad gwreiddiol, byddai'r rheol hon yn ystyrlon i bobl yn oes Llywelyn Fawr, yn ôl pob tebyg.[62]

Dywed 60/3 hefyd fod y rhaith i'w chymryd 'rhwng y *Benedicamus* a rhoddi y bara offeren'. Fformwla oedd *Benedicamus Domino* a ddefnyddid ar ddiwedd yr offeren, naill ai i ddynodi bod y gwasanaeth ar ben ac felly i ollwng y gynulleidfa ymaith neu ynteu i gyhoeddi bod gwasanaeth arall i'w ddilyn. Fel arfer cwblheid yr offeren â'r fformwla *Ite missa est*, a cheir peth ansicrwydd pryd y dechreuwyd dweud *Benedicamus Domino* yn ei lle ac o dan ba amgylchiadau. Awgryma rhywfaint o dystiolaeth mai *Benedicamus Domino* a glôi'r offeren yn rheolaidd yn yr eglwys Ffrancaidd erbyn y nawfed ganrif, ac yr oedd Jungmann o'r farn mai hi o bosibl oedd fformwla ddiweddu arferol y litwrgi Galicanaidd. Nis gwelir yn litwrgi Eglwys Rufain, fodd bynnag, tan tua chanol y ddeuddegfed ganrif, ac nid oes unrhyw arlliw ohoni yno cyn *c.*1000. Yn yr unfed ganrif ar ddeg ceisiodd Bernold o Konstanz (†1100) esbonio'r gwahaniaeth rhwng *Ite missa est* a *Benedicamus Domino* drwy ddweud mai'r fformwla gyntaf a fyddai'n arferol ar ddiwedd offeren gyda *Gloria* a'r ail mewn gwasanaethau offeren eraill. Esboniodd hefyd, fel awduron eraill ar ei ôl, y gellid defnyddio *Benedicamus Domino* pan fyddai'r gwasanaeth yn parhau, er enghraifft ar ddiwedd offeren ganol nos y Nadolig a ddilynid gan Foliannau.[63]

Ymddengys mai fel fformwla ollwng ymaith y deëllir *Benedicamus* yn Llyfr Iorwerth: nid oedd rhannu'r bara offeren yn rhan gynhenid o'r offeren, ac y mae llyfr cyfraith arall yn cyfeirio at gynnal rhaith mewn achos anghyfarch 'kyn gwaret o'r yfeiriat y wisc amdano na rannv bara'.[64] Os felly, rhaid mai dyma'r fformwla arferol, ac anodd derbyn awgrym T. P. Ellis fod y rheol yn rhagweld peidio â chymryd y rhaith ond ar adegau arbennig o'r flwyddyn, megis y Grawys ac ar rai gwyliau eglwysig eraill.[65] Nid yw'n amhosibl, fodd bynnag, mai er mwyn cyhoeddi defod led-litwrgaidd, sef y rhaith, y defnyddiwyd y *Benedicamus* yn y cyswllt hwn, a hwyrach na fu'r fformwla'n arferol fel arall.[66] Yn anffodus, oherwydd ei mynegiant cryno a'r diffyg tystiolaeth arall am *Benedicamus Domino* yng Nghymru erys union arwyddocâd y rheol yn dywyll, ac felly hefyd ei dyddiad. Os cymerwn *Benedicamus* fel fformwla ar gyfer gollwng y bobl ymaith o'r eglwys ar ddiwedd yr offeren yna, ar gorn y dystiolaeth Ffrancaidd, gall fod wedi ei harfer gan eglwysi yng Nghymru ers y nawfed ganrif o leiaf, eithr, pe bwriedid hi ar gyfer cyhoeddi'r rhaith, ac atal y bobl rhag ymadael â'r eglwys, byddai'r unfed ganrif ar ddeg yn fwy tebygol fel *terminus a quo*.

Rhaid gwahaniaethu, wrth gwrs, rhwng pryd y gallasai'r defodau litwrgaidd o rannu bara a dŵr, a dweud y *Benedicamus*, fod wedi dechrau yng Nghymru, a phryd y cyfansoddwyd y rheol gyfreithiol sy'n eu cymryd yn ganiataol. Gellid dadlau bod y defodau litwrgaidd wedi dechrau yn gynnar, o bosibl tua diwedd y nawfed ganrif;[67] eithr yn ôl pob tebyg cyfansoddwyd y rheol gyfreithiol yn ddiweddarach, yn y ddeuddegfed ganrif neu'r drydedd ganrif ar ddeg. Buasai'r sôn am fara offeren a dwfr swyn bron yn sicr yn ystyrlon yr adeg honno, a dylid nodi fod y rhan fwyaf o'r dystiolaeth o'r cyfandir am y fformwla *Benedicamus Domino* yn perthyn i ddiwedd yr unfed ganrif ar ddeg ac i'r ddeuddegfed ganrif. Yn destunol, mae'n awgrymog na cheir yr un manylion yn Llyfr Cyfnerth nac yn y Testunau Lladin, a bod yr holl enghreifftiau o'r termau *bara offeren* a *dwfr swyn* ar gadw naill ai mewn llyfrau cyfraith o Wynedd y tybir iddynt gael eu cyfansoddi yn eu crynswth yn y drydedd ganrif ar ddeg neu mewn llyfrau sy'n seiliedig arnynt. A bwrw bod traethawd Llyfr Iorwerth ar fechnïaeth yn rhoi cig ar esgyrn traethawd cynharach,[68] dichon mai i'r cig y perthyn yr elfennau litwrgaidd, gyda'r amcan o egluro'r gyfraith yn fanylach ac mewn modd a fuasai'n ddealladwy yn hanner cyntaf y drydedd ganrif ar ddeg.

(ch) [6] *O cheffyr e reyth, dogyn ew; o dygwyd e reyth y'r dyn, kamlwrw y'r brenyn a'r eglwys byt en y ol, a thalet e delyet en kvbyl.*

Os ceir y rhaith o'i blaid, dyna ddigon. Ond os syrthia'r rhaith yn erbyn y dyn, [telir] *camlwrw* i'r brenin a bydd yr eglwys ar ei ôl, a thaled yntau y ddyled i gyd.

Drwy gymharu'r rheol hon â 60/4 o Lyfr Iorwerth daw'n amlwg fod a wnelo ei hail hanner â chanlyniadau tyngu anudon: 'Ac o cheyff e reyth, dogen yu ydau; ony keyff enteu e reyth, talet er haul, ac o men er argluyd erlyt keureyth anudon arnau, erlynhet.' Diffinir *cyfraith anudon* yn Llyfr Cyfnerth fel cosb ddeublyg, sef camlwrw (tair buwch neu 15 swllt) i'r brenin a phenyd, a diau mai dyna ystyr 60/4 a 68/6 o Lyfr Iorwerth.[69] Erbyn y ddeuddegfed ganrif hawliai'r eglwys mai hi yn unig oedd biau'r awdurdod dros achosion o dor ffydd ac anudon, ac y mae dysgeidiaeth Cyfraith Hywel ar y pwnc yn ymdebygu yn fwy i'r sefyllfa a fodolai'n gynharach yn yr Oesoedd Canol yn Ewrop.[70] Ychydig iawn y gellir ei ddysgu am anudon yn y llyfrau cyfraith: canolbwyntia'r rhelyw o'r rheolau ar y cyfyngiadau cyfreithiol a ddeuai i ran rhywun a gafwyd yn euog o anudon, er enghraifft ei wahardd rhag bod yn dyst, ac ni fanylir ar amgylchiadau tyngu anudon yn y lle cyntaf nac ar y camlwrw a'r penyd.[71]

Yr oedd y rhan gyntaf o adran Llyfr Iorwerth ar friduw wedi ei phatrymu'n agos felly ar reolau manylach y llyfr hwnnw ynghylch cynnogn yn gwadu mach, a thrwy ddadansoddi'r rheolau hynny daw'n eglur fod y broses o wadu rhwymedigaeth — boed drwy fechni, neu drwy friduw — yn golygu cryn fesur o gydweithrediad eglwysig. Os yw'r dull o wadu briduw wedi ei seciwlareiddio ar un olwg yn Llyfr Iorwerth o'i gymharu â Llyfr Cyfnerth, gyda rhaith o saith person yn disodli llw ar saith allor, nis seciwlareiddiwyd yn llwyr, a chawn brawf pellach o natur grefyddol briduw yn yr ail ran o'r ymdriniaeth â hi yn Llyfr Iorwerth.

(d) [7]*O dervyd y dyn kymryt bry Dyw y gan arall a dywedwyt pan yw ar pedeyr ar vgeynt e mae, a'r llall en adef bot bry Dyw ar chwech keynnyawc, esef a dyweyt e kyvreyth delyw ohonaw ef bot en atverwr pahar e mae y vry Dyw, ay ar pedeyr ar vgeynt ay ar chwech keynnyawc, kanyt edyw en gwadv bry Dyw, a henny wrth y lw.*[72]

Os digwydd i berson gymryd briduw gan rywun arall a dweud ei bod ar [rywbeth sy'n werth] 24 ceiniog, a bod y llall yn cydnabod bod y friduw ar 6 cheiniog, dywed y gyfraith y dylai'r ail berson ddatgan ar beth y mae ei friduw — ai ar 24 ceiniog, ai ar 6 cheiniog — gan nad ydyw ef yn gwadu briduw, a hynny ar ei lw.

Yn wahanol i ran gyntaf yr adran, lle trôi'r ymdrafodaeth gyfreithiol ar fodolaeth rhwymedigaeth a ffurfiwyd drwy friduw, nid oes ddadl yma ynghylch bodolaeth y rhwymedigaeth ond yn hytrach ddadl ynghylch ei maint. Mewn rheol gynharach datganwyd mai'r mach a gâi dyngu llw i ddatgan y swm pan fyddai anghytundeb rhwng y cynnogn a'r hawlwr

ynghylch ei maint,[73] ond gan nad oes mach dynol mewn rhwymedigaeth
drwy friduw ni ellir addasu'r rheol honno'n uniongyrchol at y dyledwr sy'n
cael tyngu ar faint ei friduw.[74]

(dd)   [8]*Ket dyweter y bot en vry Dyw, e kyvreyth a dyweyt nat bry Dyw eny kyvarfo e
       llaw a'y gylyd, ac nat mach ac nat gorvodawc eny kyvarfo e teyr llaw y gyt.*[75]

       Er y dyweder ei bod yn friduw, y gyfraith a ddywed nad briduw oni chyfarfo
       y ddwy law â'i gilydd, ac nad oes mach na gorfodog oni chyfarfo y tair llaw
       ynghyd.

Dyma un o'r ychydig reolau ar sut y gwnaed briduw. Fe'n hatgoffir o
adran Testun Lladin B a'i sôn am gytundeb 'drwy law, hynny yw, ffydd',
er y tebyg yw fod y ddefod am ffurfio rhwymedigaeth drwy fach ym meddwl
lluniwr y rheol yma.[76]

(e)   [9]*Er eglwys a'r brennyn a delyant kymhell bry Dyw, kanys Dyw a kymerwyt en lle
       mach, a'r eglwys pyew y wahard am bry Dyw, a'r brennyn y kymhell.*[77]

       Yr eglwys a'r brenin a ddylai orfodi briduw oherwydd Duw a gymerwyd yn
       lle mach, a'r eglwys biaul['r hawl] i'w wahardd am friduw a'r brenin i'w
       orfodi.

Mewn rhwymedigaeth drwy fechnïaeth y mach a fyddai'n gyfrifol am
'gymell' y cynnogn i dalu ei ddyled, ond yma, gan na fedr Duw gymell yn
uniongyrchol, rhaid i'r eglwys a'r brenin (sef y tywysog) weithredu ar ei
ran. Codai'r angen am gymell briduw yn ôl pob tebyg pan fyddai person
yn gwrthod talu naill ai ar ôl cyfaddef iddo roi briduw (68/1) neu ar ôl iddo
golli'r rhaith wrth geisio ei wadu (68/6). Rhagwelir ymyrraeth gan y brenin
neu'r arglwydd mewn rhan arall o'r traethawd ar fechnïaeth: pan fydd farw
mach heb etifedd i gyflawni ei ddyletswydd ar ei ôl, yna daw'r arglwydd i
wasanaethu yn ei le fel mach.[78] Nid yw ystyr *gwahardd* yn gwbl glir. Mae'n
fwy na thebyg mai gwaharddiad ar dderbyn bara offeren a dwfr swyn, neu
hyd yn oed esgymundod, a olygir.[79] Yn sicr, fel gyda thyngu anudon,
rhagwelai'r gyfraith gydweithrediad rhwng yr awdurdodau lleyg ac
eglwysig er mwyn gwarantu rhwymedigaeth drwy friduw.

(f)   [10]*Kanys y gan pob dyn a vedydyer e delyr kymryt bry Dyw, ac y gan gwr ac y gan
       gwreyc; wrth henny e dely a gwr a gwreyc y rody hythev hyt en oet map seyth mlwyd
       a el adan law y peryglawr.*

       Oherwydd oddi wrth bob person a fedyddier, boed yn ŵr ynteu yn wraig, y
       dylid cymryd briduw; gan hynny fe ddylid ei rhoi gan wryw yn ogystal â chan
       fenyw, hyd yn oed gan blentyn saith mlwydd a êl o dan law ei gyffeswr.

Datgan y rheol hon fod hawl gan unrhyw aelod o'r eglwys dros saith
mlwydd oed i roi briduw, ac fel y rheol flaenorol, pwysleisia natur ddwyfol

y dull hwn o ymrwymo mewn contract. Y cymal olaf sydd fwyaf anodd ei ddehongli. Awgrymodd Aled Rhys Wiliam fod yr ymadrodd 'mynd o dan law' yn cyfateb i ymadrodd mewn Gwyddeleg Modern sy'n golygu 'bedydd esgob' (*dul fo láim*).[80] Yn y testun *Ríagail Pátraic* y cawn yr unig enghraifft o hyn mewn Hen Wyddeleg, wrth drafod cwblhau a pherffeithio bedydd drwy 'fynd o dan law yr esgob'.[81] Yn y rheol Gymraeg, fodd bynnag, cyfeirir at blentyn saith mlwydd oed 'a el adan law y *peryglawr*': nid oes sôn yma am *esgob*, er mai esgobion yn unig a gâi gonffirmio fel arfer yn Eglwys y Gorllewin ers y bedwaredd ganrif.[82] Nid esgob mo'r periglor, eithr math o offeiriad. Yn wir, defynyddir *periglor* ac *offeiriad* yn y llyfrau cyfraith weithiau fel petaent yn ddau derm cyfystyr: er enghraifft, yn ei fersiwn o Ior 68/10 sonia Llyfr Colan am fod 'dan llau effeyryat'.[83] Er bod tarddiad y gair *periglor* yn ansicr,[84] y mae'n bur ddiogel y golygai offeiriad, ac offeiriad a wrandawai ar gyffes yn fwyaf arbennig, erbyn y ddeuddegfed ganrif fan bellaf.[85] A derbyn hynny, go brin fod y periglor yn gweinyddu bedydd esgob yn y cyfnod y cyfansoddwyd Llyfr Iorwerth,[86] ac felly rhaid chwilio am ddehongliad arall o'r ymadrodd 'mynd o dan law' yn Ior 68/10.

Dylid nodi na chyfyngid y weithred o osod llaw ar ben rhywun i fedydd esgob yn unig: gweithred a arwyddai fendith ydoedd yn y bôn, ac felly, gellid ei chymhwyso at unrhyw ddefod eglwysig lle y byddai'n rhaid i'r gweinidog roi ei fendith, er enghraifft ar ddiwedd gwasanaeth yr offeren neu ar ôl gwrando ar gyffes.[87] A chofio'r dystiolaeth sy'n awgrymu mai offeiriad a wrandawai ar gyffes oedd y periglor, y mae'n bur debyg fod yr ymadrodd 'adan law y peryglawr' yn Llyfr Iorwerth yn cyfeirio at gyffes a chymun cyntaf y plentyn. Yn ôl Pedwaredd Synod y Lateran (1215), yr oedd yn rhaid i bawb gyffesu ar ôl iddynt gyrraedd oedran rheswm, yn ogystal â derbyn y cymun o leiaf unwaith y flwyddyn,[88] a dichon fod y rheol gyfreithiol Gymreig yn cymryd yn ganiatol y byddai plentyn saith mlwydd oed wedi ei gynysgaeddu â rheswm ac o ganlyniad yn gallu dirnad ystyr pechod ac arwyddocâd y cymun. Dywed rheol arall yn Llyfr Iorwerth mai dyna'r oedran y cymerai plant 'wedd Duw' arnynt drwy fynd o dan law yr offeiriad neu'r periglor, ac o hynny allan caent dyngu llw ar eu pen eu hunain yn lle cael eu tadau i dyngu drostynt.[89] Y syniad, mae'n debyg, ydoedd na ddylai plentyn dyngu llw i Dduw, na rhoi briduw, nes iddo allu deall hanfodion y ffydd Gristnogol fel yr amlygid hwy yn sagrafennau'r cyffes a'r cymun. Y mae hyn hefyd yn gyson â hoffter gwŷr y gyfraith o rannu bywyd dynion a merched yn gyfnodau o saith mlynedd, gyda hawliau a rhwymedigaethau cyfreithiol priodol ynghlwm wrth bob cyfnod.[90]

III

Carwn gloi drwy grynhoi canlyniadau'r arolwg hwn o'r rheolau sy'n ymdrin â briduw ac yna mentro rhai casgliadau mwy cyffredinol am ddatblygiad ac arwyddocâd briduw yng Nghyfraith Hywel. Yn gyntaf, yn llyfrau cyfraith Gwynedd y ceir yr wybodaeth fanylaf am y pwnc ac nid oes unrhyw sail destunol dros gredu fod briduw yn greadigaeth newydd canonwyr y Deheubarth; yn wir, y mae lle cryf i amau nad oedd gan awduron Testun Lladin D a Llyfr Blegywryd unrhyw amcan am ystyr y term, a'u bod wedi codi briduw o Lyfr Cyfnerth gyda'r bwriad o gryfhau naws eglwysig eu llyfrau. Os felly, rhwng rheolau Llyfr Cyfnerth ac eiddo Testun Lladin B, Llyfr Iorwerth a Llyfr Colan y cyfyd y gwahaniaeth sylfaenol ar y pwnc. Cyfeiriad anuniongyrchol yn unig sydd gan Lyfr Cyfnerth at friduw, ond dengys fod modd ei wadu drwy dyngu llw ar saith allor mewn un cantref. Gan nad yw'r rheol yn fenthyciad diweddar gan destunau Llyfr Blegywryd, teg casglu ei bod yn rhan gysefin o Lyfr Cyfnerth ac felly y byddid yn disgwyl, ar dir testunol cyffredinol, iddi fod yn gynharach nag ymdriniaeth Llyfr Iorwerth â'r pwnc. Gellid mentro ymhellach fod y rheol am wadu briduw ar saith allor o leiaf mor hen â'r ddeuddegfed ganrif, canys y mae'n dra thebyg fod rheol newydd am ei gwadu drwy raith eisoes yn bod cyn i Destun Lladin B a Llyfr Iorwerth lunio eu rheolau ar friduw erbyn canol y drydedd ganrif ar ddeg.

Erbyn y drydedd ganrif ar ddeg ni welai llunwyr Testun Lladin B a Llyfr y Damweiniau unrhyw wahaniaeth rhwng briduw a rhwymedigaeth drwy ffydd neu gred. Gwelsom fod nifer o reolau eraill yn cydnabod cytundebau neu addewidion drwy ffydd, ac yng ngoleuni ffynonellau llenyddol eraill ymddengys fod hon yn ffordd frodorol, gyn-Normanaidd o ffurfio rhwymedigaeth a ragflaenai'r ddysgeidiaeth ganonaidd ar *fides* yn y ddeuddegfed ganrif. Ymhellach, y mae rheolau sawl llyfr cyfraith, gan gynnwys Testun Lladin B a Llyfr Iorwerth, yn awgrymu bod ffurf briduw yn debyg i eiddo rhwymedigaeth drwy ffydd, sef fod person yn gwneud datganiad a fyddai'n ei rwymo tra'n cydio yn llaw y person y ffurfiai gontract ag ef. Efallai y daethpwyd i synio am friduw fel rhwymedigaeth drwy ffydd mewn contractau lle y byddid fel arall yn defnyddio mach neu amodwyr. Ac er nad oes dystiolaeth i awgrymu mai fersiwn o'r llw addewid ydoedd, unwaith y datblygid y cysyniad o friduw fel math o 'ffydd' ni fuasai fawr o wahaniaeth yn ymarferol rhyngddi a llw, o gofio bod y gyfraith ganon yn trin ffydd a llw yn gyfartal erbyn diwedd y ddeuddegfed ganrif.

Ond y mae'r ymgais i esbonio briduw fel ffydd, ynghyd ag ymdriniaeth llyfrau'r Deheubarth â'r gair, yn awgrymu ei bod mewn gwirionedd yn hynafol erbyn y drydedd ganrif ar ddeg, a dichon fod Llyfr Iorwerth yn

llygad ei le pan ddywed fod Duw wedi ei gymryd yn lle mach. Daw bron
pob cyfeiriad at friduw yn y llyfrau cyfraith yng nghyd-destun mechnïaeth
ac yn Llyfr Iorwerth cyplysir briduw â'r un berfau â mach, sef *rhoi, cymryd*
a *gwadu*. Hyd yn oed petasai'r geiriau 'kanys Dyw a kymerwyt en lle mach'
yn los diweddar gan ŵr cyfraith o'r drydedd ganrif ar ddeg, y mae'r cysyniad
ei hunan yn hen. Fe'i gwelir eisoes yn Nhrydedd Gainc y Mabinogi a gellir
tybio ei fod o darddiad canoloesol cynnar.[91] Fel y dengys D. A. Binchy
mae'r arfer o warantu rhwymedigaethau drwy feichiau goruwchnaturiol yn
gyntefig iawn: ceir enghreifftiau yng nghyfraith gynnar Rhufain a'r Hen
Destament yn ogystal â llên gynnar Iwerddon,[92] er mai ychydig o le sydd
i fechnïaeth oruwchnaturiol neu sanctaidd yn y traethodau cyfraith
Gwyddelig cynnar. Cyfeiria'r traethawd *Coibnes uisci thairidne* (a
gyfansoddwyd tua chanol y seithfed ganrif) at gontract lle y gelwir ar 'wŷr
y nef ac Efengyl Crist' fel meichiau, a dywed fod yn rhaid i bob *déorad Dé*
'alltud Duw' (math o bererin) orfodi (sef, yn ieithwedd Cyfraith Hywel,
gymell) eu mechni. Dyna'r rheol sydd agosaf i'r rheolau Cymreig ar friduw
a geir yng nghyfraith gynnar Iwerddon.[93]

Y rheol gyfraith gynnar debycaf i friduw, fodd bynnag, yw cymal 33 o
Gyfreithiau Alfred sy'n egluro'r broses ar gyfer hawlio a gwadu addewid
drwy *godborh* (llyth. 'mach Duw'): rhaid i'r hawlwr dyngu mewn pedair
eglwys, a'r amddiffynnwr, os dymuna ei ryddhau ei hunan, mewn
deuddeg.[94] Mae'r tebygrwydd rhyngddi a'r rheol am wadu ar saith allor yn
Llyfr Cyfnerth yn drawiadol, er nad yw'n ddigon agos i awgrymu dylanwad
uniongyrchol gan y naill reol ar y llall. Serch hynny y mae, efallai, yn
arwyddocaol nad oes sôn am *godborh* mewn unrhyw gasgliad arall o gyfraith
Eingl-Seisnig, ac o gofio cysylltiadau Alfred â Chymru ni ddylid diystyru'r
posibilrwydd ei fod wedi mabwysiadu arfer Gymreig yn y fan hon.[95] O leiaf
awgryma'r rheol Eingl-Seisnig y geill fod gwreiddiau cynnar i'r cysyniad o
gymryd Duw yn fach yng Nghyfraith Hywel hithau, a bod briduw fel y
crybwyllir hi yn Llyfr Cyfnerth o darddiad cyn-Normanaidd.

Nid oes fodd i ni wybod ai creadigaeth gwŷr y gyfraith oedd y gair briduw
yn wreiddiol ynteu term a fabwysiadwyd ganddynt ac iddo ystyr ehangach
na ffurf ddwyfol ar fechni. A derbyn ei fod yn enw cyfansawdd (*bri + Duw*)[96]
golygai naill ai 'anrhydedd' neu 'nerth' Duw. Nid yw'n amhosibl, mewn
cymdeithas a ddibynnai ar syniadau am anrhydedd a gwarth, fod llw a
warentid gan anrhydedd Duw wedi ei ystyried yn un arbennig o ddwys na
ellid mo'i dorri heb ennyn digofaint Duw am Ei sarhau.[97] Erbyn cyfnod
cyfansoddi'r rheolau cyfraith sydd gennym, fodd bynnag, nid ymddengys fod
llw ynghlwm wrth friduw,[98] a hwyrach fod i'r elfen *bri* ystyr arferol ei
chytras Gwyddeleg *bríg*, sef 'nerth, gallu', ac felly galw ar allu Duw i
warantu contract a wneid pan roddai rhywun friduw.[99]

Gwelsom fod a wnelo'r rhelyw o'r rheolau cyfraith Cymreig â chanlyniadau ffurfio rhwymedigaeth drwy friduw, ac yn arbennig â sut y dylid ei gwadu. Cymharol ychydig, gan hynny, a ddywedir am swyddogaeth briduw yn gyffredinol. Gellir tybio mai ffurf o ymrwymo ydoedd yn wreiddiol ar gyfer y sawl a fethai â chael mach a heb berthnasau'n byw yn ddigon agos i ffurfio rhaith; pwysleisir yr ail bwynt yn Llyfr Cyfnerth. Buasai briduw felly yn ffurf addas ar gyfer alltudion (yn ystyr dechnegol y cyfreithiau), gan gynnwys masnachwyr: y mae'n ddiddorol nodi bod ffurf debyg yn rhan o gyfraith fasnach Llundain cyn Statud Masnachwyr Edward I (1285).[100] Ond cyfyngwyd yn arw ar y swyddogaeth hon pan ofynnwyd am raith er mwyn gwadu briduw. Yn ôl Llyfr Iorwerth, pe dymunai rhywun ffurfio contract heb fach gallai ddewis rhwng briduw ac amod, er y byddai angen amodwyr ar gyfer yr ail; ac wrth gwrs, gallai'r hawlwr mewn contract drwy friduw ddisgwyl derbyn cymorth pwerus yr eglwys a'r fraich seciwlar pan wawriai'r dydd o dalu'r ddyled yn ôl iddo.[101]

Yn anffodus, ni fedrwn ddweud pa mor weithredol oedd briduw erbyn cyfnod ysgrifennu'r llawysgrifau cynharaf o Lyfr Iorwerth. Rhaid cofio fod y traethawd ar fechni yn rhagdybio gweithrediadau llafar yn unig ac o'r herwydd prin fydd yr olion ysgrifenedig ohonynt mewn ffynonellau eraill. Dichon fod awdur y traethawd yn ailwampio ffynhonnell gynharach ac er iddo ychwanegu elfennau diweddarach ati ni raid i hynny olygu fod y rheolau yn weithredol o hyd. Gallasai cofnodi'r rheolau am friduw fod yn rhan o gynhyrchu *lex scripta* heb fod iddi unrhyw arwyddocâd yn y gyfraith fel y'i gweinyddid yng Ngwynedd Llywelyn Fawr.[102] Ar y llaw arall mae'n bosibl fod y rheolau hynny, er yn hynafol, yn dal i gyfateb i syniadau byw am fechni dwyfol, yn yr un modd ag y parhâi sefydliad tebyg i *godborh* cyfreithiau Alfred yng nghyfraith fasnachol Llundain tan y drydedd ganrif ar ddeg.[103] Efallai y dylem osgoi ceisio creu darlun unffurf o hanes cyfraith rhwymedigaethau yng Nghymru: gallasai hen ffurfiau fel briduw fod wedi goroesi, mewn rhai cylchoedd ac ar gyfer rhai mathau o gontract o leiaf, ochr yn ochr â ffurfiau mwy diweddar fel ffydd a'r llw addewid, hyd at y drydedd ganrif ar ddeg. Mae'n amlwg nad adlewyrcha rheolau Llyfr Iorwerth yr holl ffyrdd neu hyd yn oed y prif ffyrdd o ffurfio contract neu gytundeb yng Nghymru'r ddau Lywelyn. Ceir digon o dystiolaeth i gytundebau *gwleidyddol* y drydedd ganrif ar ddeg i brofi bod pob math o sancsiynau, yn sanctaidd ac yn seciwlar, wedi eu hychwanegu atynt (gan gynnwys ymostwng i awdurdod preladau ac ymwadu â'r hawl i apelio at y gyfraith sifil a chanon) fel y'u ceir hwy mewn cymalau-sancsiwn cytundebau Seisnig y cyfnod.[104] Nid ar gorn gosodiadau Cyfraith Hywel y ffurfiwyd rhwymedigaethau gwleidyddol pwysig megis Cytundeb Trefaldwyn; y mae'r rheini'n perthyn i fyd gwahanol diplomyddiaeth ryngwladol. Ond i'r rhelyw o boblogaeth Cymru hwyrach fod hen ddulliau llafar mechnïaeth a briduw yn fwy addas wrth iddynt brynu defaid neu werthu ieir, ac ar y lefel ddi-nod honno o gontract a chymdeithas a ffynnai'r rhan hon o'r gyfraith frodorol o hyd. Ysywaeth, fel gyda chynifer o agweddau ar y cyfreithiau, nid yw'r dystiolaeth angenrheidiol gennym i brofi a oedd hyn yn wir neu beidio.[105]

Eto, os oes rhaid cyfaddef fod yna lawer na allwn ei wybod am friduw, y mae un casgliad cyffredinol y gellir ei wneud ar gorn y drafodaeth hon cyn tewi. Gwelsom fod rheolau manwl Llyfr Iorwerth yn enwedig yn dyst i gydymdreiddiad yr agweddau sanctaidd a seciwlar ar gymdeithas y tueddir i ystyried eu bod yn gyffredin yn Ewrop nes i'r cyfnewidiadau mawr a achoswyd gan lwyddiant y diwygiad pabaidd, datblygiad y gyfraith ganon a'r twf yn awdurdod y llysoedd eglwysig weddnewid y sefyllfa a phennu ffin fwy pendant nag o'r blaen rhwng y *regnum* a'r *sacerdotium*, y tymhorol a'r ysbrydol, yn ystod y ddeuddegfed ganrif.[106] Er bod olion o'r ffin honno i'w canfod ar ddalennau'r llyfrau cyfraith Cymreig,[107] bu eu hawduron ar y cyfan yn gyndyn i addasu'r gyfraith frodorol at y safonau a'r disgwyliadau newydd ac yn fwyaf arbennig i gydnabod mai'r eglwys yn unig a gâi farnu, yn ôl rheolau o'i dewis a'i hawduraeth hi, bynciau megis priodas, cymynnu, anudon, a thor ffydd. Ar y naill law, dyma greu cyfraith fwy seciwlar yn ôl safonau'r ddeuddegfed ganrif a'r drydedd ganrif ar ddeg, er enghraifft drwy gadw'r rheolau ar ysgar, ond ar y llaw arall, fel y dengys y rheolau ar friduw, dyma ddiogelu safle'r eglwys yng ngweinyddiad y gyfraith seciwlar i raddau pellach na'r cyffredin yn y cyfnod hwnnw. Hwyrach fod y cydweithredu rhwng y gyfraith a'r eglwys a welir mor amlwg yn y rheolau ar fechni a briduw yn nodweddiadol o berthynas y gyfraith Gymreig â'r eglwys yn gyffredinol; yn sicr, ni ellir gobeithio deall y berthynas honno yn llawnach heb gofio bod y gyfraith y mynnodd Peckham ei thadogi ar y Diafol hefyd wedi cymryd Duw yn lle mach.[108]

[1] Carwn gydnabod yn ddiolchgar y cymorth caredig a gefais gan y diweddar Athro Idris Foster, yr Athro Fergus Kelly a Mr Peter Llewellyn wrth imi baratoi'r papur hwn. Yr wyf hefyd yn ddyledus iawn i Ms Morfydd Owen a'r Dr Nesta Lloyd am wella mynegiant y papur, a diolchaf i Ms Owen a'r Dr Thomas Charles-Edwards am nifer o awgrymiadau gwerthfawr ynglŷn â'i gynnwys.
[2] Cf. E. V. Colman, 'Reason and Unreason in Early Medieval Law', (1974) 4 *Journal of Interdisciplinary History* 587; D. Jenkins; 'The Medieval Welsh Idea of Law', (1981) 49 *T.v.R.* 332-33. Ni ddefnyddir y diheurbrawf fel dull prawf yng Nghyfraith Hywel, er y ceir adlais cynnar o bosibl o ddiheurbrawf drwy frwydr yng Nghainc Gyntaf y Mabinogi: T. M. Charles-Edwards, 'The Date of the Four Branches of the Mabinogi', (1970) THSC 284-86. Esbonia llyfr cyfraith diweddar fod Hywel Dda wedi dileu'r 'hayarn twymyn', 'y dwfyr brwt' a 'gornest' a ddefnyddid fel profion yng Nghyfraith Dyfnwal Moelmud: AL XIV.xiii.4.

[3] Col xxxiii n. 34.

[4] E.e., John Davies yn ei *Dictionarium Duplex* (1632): GPC, *s.v. briduw;* LW 558; D. Jenkins, *Cyfraith Hywel,* ail arg. (Llandysul, 1976), 85.

[5] G. P. Davies, 'Rhwymedigaethau Cytundebol yn y Gyfraith Gymreig' (Traethawd Ll.M. Prifysgol Cymru, 1952), 44-49.

[6] D. A. Binchy, 'Celtic Suretyship', 357; y mae'r ddadl o blaid gwreiddiau hynafol briduw hefyd wedi ei derbyn gan Morfydd Owen (1964-65) 8 *Llên Cymru* 247 a chan Dafydd Jenkins, *Cyfraith Hywel,* 85.

[7] T. Lewis, *A Glossary of Medieval Welsh Law* (Manceinion, 1913), 45; T. P. Ellis, *Welsh Tribal Law and Custom in the Middle Ages* (Rhydychen, 1926), ii.3.

[8] Cynigiwyd hyn eisoes gan A. W. Wade-Evans: WML, 328. Gw. hefyd Bleg 184; Col 64; D. Jenkins, *Cyfraith Hywel,* 85.

[9] WML 85.4-11 (llsgr. *V*). Digwydd y darn yn llsgrau, *W, X* a *Mk* yn ogystal, ond nis yn *U.*

[10] Sef y gwerth a delid i'w *genedl* pe lleddid ef, ac felly yn fesur o'i statws.

[11] Sef ei genedl (Saes. *kindred*): cf. M. E. Owen yn WLW 54-55.

[12] Y mae'r gymhariaeth, a wneir yn y rheol, rhwng briduw a mechnïaeth yn chwithig. Ni ellir cael sefyllfa debyg i'r eiddo'r mach sy'n gwadu ei fechnïaeth mewn rhwymedigaeth drwy friduw, oherwydd Duw yn unig sydd yn cyfateb i'r mach yno. Byddai cyffelybiaeth rhwng gwadu briduw a sefyllfa'r dyledwr sydd yn gwadu mach yn taro'n well.

[13] Am enghraifft arall lle yr ymddengys fod llyfr cyfraith yn cymryd *gwlad* a *chantref* fel termau cyfystyr, gw. LTWL 385.35-41 (D). Defnyddiwyd y gair *patria,* y term Lladin arferol am *wlad,* am gantref Arwystli mewn siarter gan Madog ap Maredudd o Bowys (†1160): Llyfrgell Gyhoeddus Amwythig, Llsgr. 1 (Cartwlari Haughmond), ff.215r. Cf. 'Wynnstay MSS. — Charters of Trefeglwys', gol. R. Williams, (1860) 6 *Arch. Camb.* 331. Ni raid meddwl bod *gwlad* bob amser yn gyfystyr â *chantref* (gallai gyfeirio hefyd at ardal o faint mwy): fy mhwynt yma yw y gellid cyffelybu'r ddau derm weithiau.

[14] LTWL 369.1-5. Cf. Bleg 41.9-15: 'Mach a watto y vechni, gwadet ar y seithuet o'r dynyon nessaf y werth. Ac os briduw a watta, ehunan a twg vch seith allawr kyssegredic, neu seith weith ar yr un allawr. Os y talawdyr a watta y mach, gwadet ar y seithuet o'r dynnyon nessaf y werth. Os mach a watta ran o'e vechni ac adef ran arall, ef ehunan vn weith a'e twg.' Er nad cyfieithiad slafaidd o adran Llad. D mo hwn mae'n amlwg ei fod wedi ei seilio arni, neu ar fersiwn ohoni. Y prif wahaniaethau rhyngddynt yw bod Bleg yn newid trefn y ddwy frawddeg olaf, yn ychwanegu cymal am dyngu saith waith ar un allor ac yn newid geiriau Cymraeg Llad. D.

[15] LTWL 125.33-36.

[16] Diddorol nodi bod Llad. E yn nes at ystyr Cyfn a heb ychwanegu cyfeiriad at friduw: 'Fideiussor negans fideiussionem cum septem manibus proximorum negabit, vel ipse solus in septem altaribus consecratis.' (LTWL 459.1-2) Mae'r darn yn seiliedig ar un yn Llad. B (LTWL 217.2-3) ond deillia'r cymal olaf naill ai o Cyfn neu o Llad. D neu Bleg; mae'r ychwanegiad pellach 'et septies super eodem altari' mewn fersiwn arall o Llad. E yn awgrymu bod arno ef, o leiaf, ddyled destunol i Bleg (LTWL 459 n. 1).

[17] Deillia pob enghraifft yn llsgrau. *S, J* a *Q* o Cyfn, Bleg neu Ior, ac eithrio un rheol yn *S*: AL XI.v.43. Ceir cryn sôn am friduw yn llsgr. *H* (o'r 14eg g.), llawysgrif na wyddys ei tharddiad: AL XIV.i.10; iii.12, 24; xxi.16; xxii.1,2,4; xxxvi.4; xl.31. Cf. hefyd AL VIII.i.7 (llsgr. *F*).

[18] Y mae tarddiad daearyddol Cyfn yn ansicr. Dichon i'r Llyfr Cyfnerth gwreiddiol gael ei lunio yng Ngwynedd, nes iddo gael ei ddisodli yno gan Lyfr Iorwerth: Col xxiv-v. A barnu oddi wrth eu rhaglithiau a'u rheolau ar werthoedd coed, y mae'r fersiynau o Cyfn sydd ar

glawr, fodd bynnag, yn dwyn cysylltiadau â'r canolbarth a'r de: WML 334-37; W. Linnard, 'Beech and the Lawbooks', (1978-80) 28 BBCS 605-07.

[19] LTWL 40-44.

[20] Ar oed llsgr. gynharaf Llad. B, gw. LTWL 172. Ysgrifennwyd y llsgrau. cynharaf sydd gennym o Ior tua chanol y 13eg g., a thybir i'r architeip gael ei lunio yn ystod hanner cyntaf y ganrif honno, yn oes Llywelyn Fawr: D. Jenkins, 'The Medieval Welsh Idea of Law', 324.

[21] LTWL 217.33-218.4. Cf. LTWL 459.26-35 (E).

[22] Dylid nodi i'r enw *fideiussor* 'mach' ymddangos ddwywaith yn y frawddeg hon, y tro cyntaf yn y cyflwr genidol a'r ail dro yn y cyflwr derbyniol. Mae'n fwy na thebyg fod copïydd y frawddeg wedi sylwi bod yr ymadrodd *negatio fideiussoris* yn amwys: gellid ei gymryd fel 'gwadu o'r mach [ei fod yn fach]', h.y. drwy gymryd y mach yn oddrych y gwadu. Trwy ychwanegu'r cymal *vel fideiussori*, dangosir yn glir mai gwrthrych y gwadu ydyw (dilynir y berf *negare* a'r enw *negatio* gan y cyflwr derbyniol). Cadarnheir hyn gan y frawddeg nesaf: ni fyddai diben i'r mach dyngu ynghylch maint ei rwymedigaeth oni bai iddo dderbyn eisoes ei fod yn fach.

[23] *Dictionary of Medieval Latin from British Sources. Fascicule II C*, paratowyd gan R. E. Latham (Llundain, 1981), s.v. *commericum*.

[24] G.C.II.xvii.18: 'Y neb a gynheuo tan yn odyn arall, kymeret fyd y neb a crasso arna6 g6edy ef y uot yn diogel yg guyd tyston neu yna diffodo y tan; ony wna hynny talent y collet ell deu yn deuhanner.' Digwydd y rheol hefyd ym mhob un o'r llyfrau Lladin ac eithrio C (LTWL 123.23-26, 212.1-5, 378.10-14, 452.9-13), Bleg 50.16-22 a chyda *cred* yn lle *ffydd* yn Ior 117/4 a Col 426. Rheolau Llad. A a Cyfn yn unig sy'n datgan bod angen cymryd y ffydd yng ngŵydd tystion neu yn gyhoeddus. Yn ôl Llad. A a llyfrau eraill pe cipiai dyn ferch 'yn llathrudd' ac addo rhywbeth iddi 'drwy ffydd neu ar y creiriau', ac yna gwadu hynny, derbynnid llw'r ferch fel tystiolaeth am yr addewid: LTWL 143.37-41, 343.14-18, 473.21-5; Bleg 63.15-22; Ior 47/1. Mae'n drawiadol fod y rheol yng nghanol Cyfraith y Gwragedd ac yn wir, yn Llsgr. Peniarth 28 o Lad. A, daw rhwng dwy reol a ysgogodd feirniadaeth weladwy y darllenydd a ychwanegodd farciau – *nota* wrth ymyl y dalennau ar ysgar a phriodas! Gw. D. Huws, 'Leges Howelda at Canterbury', (1975-76) 19 NLWJ 344 n.14. Medd Llyfr y Damweiniau 'nat oes kret namyn bri du6': AL VI.i.40 (llsgr. *D*).

[25] RM 117.14-17, 118.4-6, 120.13-17; *Historia Peredur vab Efrawc*, gol. G. W. Goetinck (Caerdydd, 1976), 38.11,14; *Ystorya de Carolo Magno*, gol. S. J. Williams (Caerdydd, 1930), 50.20-28, 76.6-7, 87.22-24 a chymharer 90.25-6.

[26] Cf. 'Si manu, id est, fide' Llad. B: LTWL 217.37. Yn ôl Llad. D a Bleg rhoddid ffydd wrth i fach, dyledwr a hawlwr roi eu dwylo ynghyd mewn contract drwy fechni; LTWL 368.17-23; Bleg 40.14-22. Ar gydiad llaw fel dull o ffurfio contract mewn cyfraith Germanaidd gynnar, gw. PM ii.188-89.

[27] Sef y dyddiad y tybir ddarfod cyfansoddi *Culhwch* yn ei ffurf bresennol: I. Foster, 'Culhwch ac Olwen', *Y Traddodiad Rhyddiaith yn yr Oesau Canol*, gol. G. Bowen (Llandysul, 1974), 65.

[28] Gwahaniaethir rhwng mechni, ffydd a llw mewn rheol arall yn Llad. B: LTWL 218.5-7; ac y mae'r gwahaniaeth rhwng ffydd a llw ymhlyg yng ngeiriau rheol Llad. A ar ferch 'lathrudd' sef 'firmans illud fide sua vel super reliquias', ond nid erys yn fersiwn Bleg o'r rheol: Bleg 63.18. Ar ddiflaniad y gwahaniaeth rhwng ffydd a llw, gw. isod, t.000 a n.30 a chymharer y dyfyniad o'r '*Vita Dauidis II*' yn n. 31.

[29] PM ii. 195-203; Councils and Synods... relating to the English Church I. *AD 871-1204*, gol. D. Whitelock, M. Brett a C. N. L. Brooke (Rhydychen, 1981), 869-70.

[30] Decretalau Gregori IX, *Lib.* I, *tit*.40, *c*.3; *Lib*.III, *tit*. 21, *c*.2: Liber Extra 1.40.3;3.21.2., ii Friedberg 219, 530. Ar y llw addewid (Saes. *promissory oath*) gw. A. Esmein, 'Le serment

promissoire dans le droit canonique', (1888) 12 *Nouvelle revue historique de droit* 248-77, a R. Naz, 'Serment promissoire', yn *Dictionnaire de droit canonique* (Paris, 1935-65), vii.993-1001. Ni ellir sicrwydd ar wreiddiau'r llw addewid ond erbyn y 13eg g. fe'i hesbonnir gan y canonwyr fel llw sy'n rhwymo'r dyledwr i dalu Duw fel y prif hawlwr, gyda'r hawlwr dynol yn eilradd iddo (a bu angen cryn ddyfeisgarwch ar y canonwyr er mwyn egluro sut y câi'r hawlwr eilradd hwnnw ryddhau'r dyledwr o'i ddyled yn enw Duw fel petai!); ac er bod peth anghydweld a fyddai'n briodol neu beidio i'r hawlwr eilradd ddwyn achos gerbron llys eglwysig yn erbyn dyledwr a wadai ei ddyled, cytunai'r canonwyr fod angen rhyw fath o sancsiynau eglwysig er mwyn gorfodi'r dyledwr ⸗'w dalu. Derbynnid y byddid yn tyngu'r llw 'yn gorfforol', h.y. ar yr Efengyl. Nid llw fel y cyfryw oedd rhoi neu 'wystlo' ffydd, ond o ddeall ffydd fel ffydd Gristnogol bu'n hawdd i'r eglwys hawlio awdurdod dros achosion a drôi arni a barnu *fideilaesio* 'tor ffydd' yn ogystal â *periurium* 'anudon' yn ei llysoedd. Am gymalau ynglŷn â thorri a gwystlo ffydd mewn siarteri Seisnig c.1180-c.1240, gw. D. Postles, 'Pledge of Faith in Transaction of Land'. (1984) 7 *Journal of the Society of Archivists* 295-98.

[31] B. G. Charles, 'The Records of Slebech', (1947-48) 5 NLWJ 190 (cytundeb drwy gymod David FitzGerald, esgob Tyddewi, 1148-76); M. Richter, 'A New Edition of the So-Called Vita Dauidis Secundi', (1966-68) 22 BBCS 249 ('tactis sacrosanctis reliquiis et fide confirmauit); 'Cartularium Prioratus S. Johannis Evang. de Brecon', gol. R. W. Banks, (1883) 14 *Arch. Camb.* 167 (1216-30), 278 (1218); Llyfrgell Genedlaethol Cymru, Llsgr. Peniarth 231B, 79-80 (1270), 82. Am gytundebau *'bona fide'* o'r 13eg g., gw. *Littere Wallie*, gol. J. G. Edwards (Caerdydd, 1940), 13, 45-46, 53, 64, 49, 85-86.

[32] Profir a wnaed addewid drwy ffydd i ferch a gipiwyd 'yn llathrudd' neu beidio drwy lw'r ferch ar greiriau, tra yn ôl adran Llad.B gwedir ffydd/briduw drwy raith: gw. uchod, t.50 a n.28. Ychydig o sôn sydd am lysoedd eglwysig o gwbl yn llyfrau Cyfraith Hywel. Digwydd y term *cabidwl* (Llad. *capitulum*) yn Ior, Llyfr y Damweiniau a Llsgrau. cyfraith o'r 15fed g., lle y golyga lys ar gyfer naill ai tenantiaid yr eglwys (Ior 83/10) neu fynaich a chlerigwyr (DwCol 472, AL.X1.ii.1-2). Gan nad oes gennym chwaith gofnodion llysoedd eglwysig, anodd barnu pa mor aml y deuai achosion o anudon a thor ffydd ger eu bron, er y ceir mewn dryll o gofnodion llys consistori Tyddewi enghreifftiau o ganol y 14eg g.: H. D. Emanuel, 'Early St. Davids Records', (1953) 8 NLWJ 259, 261-62.

[33] Ior 68, Col 126-31.

[34] Nodir darlleniadau amrywiol Ior 58-70 yn y gwahanol Isgrau. isod, tt.140-62. Yma gelwir sylw at yr amrywiadau mwyaf perthnasol i'r drafodaeth bresennol yn unig. Dyfynnaf o lsgr. *C.*

[35] LTWL 217.37-38.

[36] Mae llsgr. G yn hepgor 'nawdd Pab Rhufain' yn 59/3, ac nid oes sôn am anudon yn fersiwn llsgrau. *A* ac *E* o 59/7.

[37] Ar y gwahaniaeth rhwng 'dweud ar air' a 'thyngu i'r crair', gw. Col 355, 496. Derbynnid tystiolaeth lleidr ar fin cael ei grogi yn erbyn ei gyd-leidr 'heb grair': WML 41.17.

[38] E.e. mewn achos o wadu neu dadogi mab (WML 129. 17-22, Ior 100/2) neu ddogn fanag (Col 367), neu wrth sefydlu ynad llys (LTWL 235.33-36, Bleg 17.2-7).

[39] Ior 59/3, 106/9; DwCol 191, AL VIII.xi.25, IX.ii.9. Yn ôl Cyfn 'dy6 Llun dydd y lauurya6 y keissa6 creireu a defneu y tygu y tir': G.C.II.xxxvii.1; cf. AL XIV.xx.12.

[40] DwCol 131-33. Yn ôl llsgrau. *S, K* a *Tim* 'plas y creiriau' ac nid 'plas cyfreithiol' yw'r fynwent yn 132: gw., e.e., *The Laws of Howel Dda*, gol. T. Lewis (Llundain, 1912), 87.

[41] Rhaid i lofrudd 'kemryt kreyr a creto ydaw' (myfi biau'r italeiddio) os dymuna gael person y tybia ei fod yn aelod o'i genedl i dyngu a ydyw'n aelod ai peidio, ac felly penderfynu a oes raid i hwnnw gyfrannu 'ceiniog paladr' yn lle galanas: Ior 106/9.

[42] *Giraldi Cambrensis Opera*, gol. J. S. Brewer, J. R. Dimock a G. F. Warner (Rolls Series, Llundain, 1861-91), vi.112 (*Itinerarium Kambriae*, II.2); *Littere Wallie*, gol. J. G. Edwards,

10, 11 (1241). Ni wyddys ai'r un yw'r groes â'r 'Groes Naid' a fu ym meddiant olynydd Dafydd, sef Llywelyn ap Gruffudd, ac a drosglwyddwyd i Edward I yn sgil y Goncwest: cf . E. Owen, 'The Croes Nawdd', (1932) 43 *Y Cymmrodor* 1-18, yn arbennig, 10; W. C. Tennant, 'Croes Naid', (1951-52) 7 BLWJ 103.

[43] *Councils and Ecclesiastical Documents relating to Great Britain and Ireland*, gol. A. W. Haddan a W. Stubbs (Rhydychen, 1869-71), i.513 (*c*. 18).

[44] *Councils and Synods with Other Documents relating to the English Church. II. A.D. 1205-1313*, gol. F. M. Powicke a C. R. Cheney (Rhydychen, 1964), 35-6, 93, 135, 174, 195, 274, 321, 351, 410, 461, 519. Pwysleisiodd un o Statudau Wells (?1258), mewn gwrthgyferbyniad llwyr i DwCol 132, na ddylid cynnal achosion mewn mynwentydd *oherwydd* bod ynddynt gyrff saint a haeddai barch: ibid., 601 (*c*. 19). Dengys esboniadau o'r 12fed g.-14eg g. ar y traethodau cyfraith Hen Wyddeleg fod tyngu llwon mewn mynwentydd yn rhan arferol o weithrediadau cyfreithiol yn y cyfnod hwnnw: gw., e.e., CIH 820.42 (dyledus wyf i'r Athro Kelly am y cyfeiriad hwn), a *Dictionary of the Irish Language* (Royal Irish Academy, Dulyn, 1913-76), s.v. *reilic.*

[45] C. Thomas, *The Early Christian Archaeology of North Britain* (Rhydychen, 1971), 135. Cf. W. Davies, *Wales in the Early Middle Ages* (Caer Lŷr, 1982), 179-83. Yr wyf yn ddiolchgar i'm gwraig, y Dr Nancy Edwards, am drafodaeth fuddiol ar greiriau yn gyffredinol.

[46] Ni ddarganfuwyd corff Dewi Sant tan yn hwyr yn y 13eg g., ac yn ôl eu Bucheddau claddwyd Padarn ac Illtud yn Llydaw, Carannog yn Iwerddon a Chadog (yn ôl un traddodiad yn ei Fuchedd) yn ne'r Eidal: F. G. Cowley, 'A Note on the Discovery of St. David's Body', (1962) 19 BBCS 47-8; VSB 264 (*c*. 27), 228 (*c*. 24), 146 (*c*. 6), 110 (*c*. 40). Bu raid i'r esgob Urban o Landaf deithio mor bell ag Ynys Enlli er mwyn darganfod corff un o nawddsaint ei eglwys, Dyfrig, ynghyd â dannedd y meudwy Elgar, yn 1120: LL, 5, 84-6. Cawn un cyfeiriad at dyngu llwon drwy estyn llaw drwy dwll mewn sarcoffagws ym Muchedd Cadog (c.36): VSB 100, Cf. C. Thomas, *The Early Christian Archaeology of North Britain*, 138, 140-44. Nid oes sôn o gwbl, hyd y gwn i, am ysgriniau'n cynnwys *brandeae* yn y ffynonellau Cymreig: cf. ibid., 136-7.

[47] *Giraldi Cambrensis Opera*, vi.26-7 (*Itin. Kamb.*, I.2); cf. ibid., 17-18 (*Itin. Kamb.*, I.1).

[48] VSB 86, 94-6 (Buchedd Cadog, *cc*. 27, 33, 34: hanesion am gloch a llyfr Efengyl Gildas a chyllell Cadog); LL, 106 (cloch Teilo). Cf. *Vitae Sanctorum Hiberniae*, gol. C. Plummer (Rhydychen, 1910), i.cv n. 9. Y mae gennym chwe chloch law yn weddill o Gymru'r oesoedd canol: (J.) Fisher, 'The Welsh Celtic Bells', (1926) 81 *Arch. Camb.* 324-34.

[49] I. Williams 'An Old Welsh Verse', *The Beginnings of Welsh Poetry*, ail arg. (Caerdydd, 1980), 182 a chymharer y nodyn ar *creiriou*, t. 185 (englyn i fagl St Padarn, Cyrwen); *Hen Gerddi Crefyddol*, gol. H. Lewis (Caerdydd, 1931), xxxv.81 (clychau Tywyn yng nghân Llywelyn Fardd i Gadfan).

[50] WML 97.9 (llsgr.*W*).

[51] WML 47.23-48.7; LTWL 131.19-21 (A), 226.33-6 (B), 288.18 (C), 383.12-18 (D); Bleg 71.1-3; Col 455.

[52] *Dictionary of the Irish Language*, s.v. *mind.* Cysylltid *mind* mor agos â'r weithred o dyngu llw nes i'r gair fagu'r ystyr ychwanegol o 'lw'.

[53] Col 128.

[54] Ior 60/2; Cyfn 1-3.

[55] LTWL 125.34-5, 217.36-7, 369.1-2.

[56] Ior 65/11. Ceir y darlleniad 'gwŷr' yn lle 'gwragedd' mewn dwy lsgr. ddiweddar yn unig, sef *D* a Pheniarth 39.

[57] Ni chynnwys Col 128 fanylion Ior 68/5-6, mwy na thebyg am eu bod wedi eu cymryd yn ganiataol yn yr ymadrodd 'yn unwet a reyth mach'.

⁵⁸ Darlleniad llsgrau. *A* ac *E* yma yw 'e guarrandaho ef eferen'.

⁵⁹ T. P. Ellis, 'The Catholic Church in the Welsh Laws', (1931) 42 *Y Cymmrodor* 42-3, 46-8, 68.

⁶⁰ J. A. Jungmann, *The Mass of the Roman Rite: Its Origins and Development (Missarum Sollemnia)*, cyfieith. F. A. Brunner (Efrog Newydd, 1951-55), ii.452-54; A. Franz, *Die kirchlichen Benediktionen im Mittelalter* (Freiburg, 1909), i.86-109, 247-58; A. A. King, *Holy Water* (Llundain, 1926), 97-103. Am enghreifftiau cynnar o'r *eulogiae* a'r gred yn rhinweddau iachaol bara a dŵr cysegredig, er nid yng nghyd-destun defod ar gyfer y bobl ar'ôl gwasanaeth yr offeren fel a ddisgrifir yn Hincmar a ffynonellau eraill, gw. *Adomnan's Life of Columba*, gol. A. O. a M. O. Anderson (Llundain, 1961), 332, 340, 352 (II.4, 6, 13), a *La Vie de Saint Samson*, gol. R. Fawtier (Paris, 1912), 140 (*c.* 45). (Dyledus wyf i'r diweddar Athro Foster am y ddau gyfeiriad olaf.)

⁶¹ *Sacrorum Conciliorum nova et amplissima Collectio*, gol. J. D. Mansi (Fflorens, Fenis, Paris, 1759-1927), xxii.1010 (*c.* 21). Dyna hefyd farn Gerallt yn ei *Gemma Ecclesiastica* (1197) er iddo ddyfynnu canonau a fynnai fod lleygwyr yn derbyn y cymun o leiaf dair gwaith y flwyddyn: *Giraldi Cambrensis Opera*, ii.117 (I.41).

⁶² *Councils and Synods...relating to the English Church. II. A.D. 1205-1313*, 166, 175, 180, 303, 312. Am gyfeiriadau at y *panis benedictus* yn unig, gw. ibid., 63, 80, 154, 513. Rhaid i'r caplan roi'r *aqua benedicta* i'r esgob ar ôl yr offeren a'r Efengyl yn ôl Statudau Esgobol Llywelyn de Bromfield, esgob Llanelwy 1293-1314: Llyfrgell Genedlaethol Cymru, Llsgr. Peniarth 231B, 13. Am ymgais aflwyddiannus i waredu tai ym Mhenfro o rithiau stwrllyd drwy daenellu dwfr swyn, gw. *Giraldi Cambrensis Opera*, vi.94 (*Itin. Kamb.* I.12).

⁶³ J. A. Jungmann, *The Mass of the Roman Rite*, ii.433-36. Gw. hefyd *Tractatus de Sacramentis Altaris* Steffan o Autun (12fed g.): *Patrologiae...Latina*, gol. J. P. Migne (Paris, 1844-64), clxxii.1303. ('Diaconus missae finem imponit, decantans *Benedicamus Domino*, vel *Ite missa est*, in diebus festivis, vel *Requiescant in pace*, ut in mortuorum exsequiis.') (Diolchaf i Mr Peter Llewellyn am y cyfeiriad hwn.)

⁶⁴ AL IX.vi.4.

⁶⁵ T. P. Ellis, 'The Catholic Church in the Welsh Laws', 46.

⁶⁶ Cf. natur led-litwrgaidd y diheurbrawf.

⁶⁷ Y mae'r posibilrwydd o ddylanwad Carolingaidd ar Gymru, drwy Asser o bosibl, yn berthnasol yma: cf. D. P. Kirby, 'Asser and his Life of King Alfred', (1971) 6 SC 35 n. 1.

⁶⁸ Gw. papur Robin Stacey uchod tt.18, 31-2.

⁶⁹ WML 108.20-109.5. Cf. DwCol 128.

⁷⁰ PM ii.541-43; R. Naz, 'Parjure', *Dictionnaire de droit canonique*, vi.1232-33. Digwydd y gyfatebiaeth agosaf y gwn amdani mewn cyfreithiau eraill i'r rheol Gymreig ar 'gyfraith anudon' yn un o Aseisiau honedig David I, brenin yr Alban (1124-53), sy'n gorchymyn penyd yn ogystal â dirwy o wyth fuwch i'r brenin am anudon: *The Acts of the Parliaments of Scotland*, gol. T. Thomson a C. Innes (Caeredin, 1814-75), i.324 (*Assise Regis David, c.* 12). Yn anffodus ni ellir sicrwydd ar na dilysrwydd na dyddiad y rheol gan nad oes gennym dystiolaeth ddiogel fod a wnelo Aseisiau David â'r brenin hwnnw mewn gwirionedd: A. A. M. Duncan, 'Regiam Maiestatem. A Reconsideration', *Juridical review* (1961) 206-08; *idem, Scotland. The Making of the Kingdom* (Caeredin, 1975), 108 n.12. (Diolchaf i Mr David Sellar am gadarnhau'r pwynt olaf ynghylch dilysrwydd a dyddiad yr Aseisiau.)

⁷¹ Gw., e.e., WML 119.18-120.6, LTWL 132.11-12, 254.1-3, 366.21-6, Bleg 37.17-25, Col 529.

⁷² Yr un yw sylwedd Col 129.

⁷³ Ior 61/5. Gw. hefyd Cyfn. 82, LTWL 125.23-6, 217.1-4, 369.3-4, Bleg 41.14-15.

⁷⁴ Am reol debyg i Ior 68/7 mewn llyfr cyfraith diweddarach, gw. AL XIV.xxii.2 (llsgr. *H*).

[75] Mae Col 130 yn llawer mwy cryno: 'Nyt brydyw yn y gyuaruo y llau a'y gylyt.' Cf. AL VI.i.40 (llsgr. *D*); VIII.i.7 (llsgr. *F*).

[76] Gw. papur Robin Stacey, t.19 uchod.

[77] Hepgorir yr eglurhad yng nghymal cyntaf Col 131.

[78] Ior 64/8-10. Yn 1276 cyhuddwyd Llywelyn ap Gruffudd gan esgob a chabidwl Llanelwy o orfodi pobl i dalu dirwyon a warantid gan feichiaid mewn achosion o ddyweddiad, a benthyciad, a hynny yn rhinwedd y meichiaid: *Councils and Ecclesiastical Documents*, gol. A. W. Haddan a W. Stubbs, i.515 (*c.* 24). Ai ymgais ar ran y tywysog i ehangu ei awdurdod dros gontractau a sicrheid drwy feichiaid a welir yma?

[79] Gorchmynnai rhai statudau esgobol yn Lloegr yn y 13eg g. wahardd pobl rhag derbyn bara offeren (a weithiau dwfr swyn hefyd) er mwyn eu disgyblu: *Councils and Synods... relating to the English Church. II. A.D. 1205-1313*, 154, 166, 175, 180, 303, 312; ac ymddengys i'r gwaharddiad gael ei ystyried fel y cam disgyblu olaf cyn cyhoeddi esgymundod llawn: ibid., 63. Fel gydag anudon â chanlyniadau cyfreithiol esgymundod y mae a wnelo rhelyw rheolau Cyfraith Hywel ar y pwnc, er y ceir yn Ior 45/8 ddatganiad y bydd pwy bynnag a dorro gymyn (sef ewyllys) gyfreithiol yn esgymunedig fel *publican*. Gellir cymharu'r cydweithrediad rhwng yr eglwys a'r awdurdod seciwlar a ragwelir yn Ior 68/9 â'r arfer o 'anrheithio' eiddo person a esgymunwyd ers mis a diwrnod: DwCol 371. Yn Lloegr yr oedd y cyfnod yn hwy, sef deugain niwrnod: PM i.478-80. Diau y croesawai eglwyswyr yng Nghymru gymorth y braich seciwlar gymaint â'i gymrodyr mewn rhannau eraill o Ewrop, ac ni raid ddehongli y sancsiwn 'ddwbl' yn Ior 68/9 fel mynegiant o ymyrraeth seciwlar ormesol â hawliau eglwysig. Yn 1261 dyfarnodd y cymodwyr rhwng Llywelyn ap Gruffudd a Rhisiart, esgob Bangor, y dylai'r tywysog ddal unrhyw un a esgymunwyd pe derbyniai gais am hynny gan yr esgob: *Councils and Ecclesiastical Documents*, gol. A. W. Haddan a W. Stubbs, i.490.

[80] Ior 115; diolchaf i Mr Eurys Rolant am ei awgrymiadau gwerthfawr, ac yn arbennig, am ei sylwadau ar fy ymdriniaeth â Ior 63/10.

[81] 'The Rule of Patrick', gol. J. G. O'Keeffe, (1904) 1 *Ériu* 218.

[82] Yn wreiddiol gweinyddid bedydd a bedydd esgob yr un pryd yn y Gorllewin, ac fe'u cyfunid mewn un offis o hyd yn y Llyfrau Sagrafen Galicanaidd a Gelasiaidd. Parhâi'r arfer hon yn Eglwys y Dwyrain lle y câi'r offeiriad weinyddu'r ddwy ddefod. Ond yn y Gorllewin bu tuedd i wahanu'r ddwy o'r bedwaredd ganrif ymlaen, a'r offeiriad yn gweinyddu bedydd yn unig a'r esgob yn conffirmio wedyn, er y gwyddys am rai enghreifftiau o offeiriaid yn conffirmio ar ôl hyn, gan ddefnyddio crism a oedd wedi ei gysegru'n barod gan yr esgob. Gw. A. J. Maclean, 'The Theory and Practice of Confirmation in the Church up to the Reformation', yn *Confirmation or the Laying on of Hands* (Llundain, 1926), i.25-59.

[83] Col 131. Cf. Ior 97/6, lle y ceir *periglor* yn llsgrau. *D* ac *E*, ac *offeiriad* yn llsgrau. *B* ac *C*.

[84] Cynigiodd Whitley Stokes (a Timothy Lewis a Ludwig Bieler ar ei ôl) darddu'r gair o'r Traethawd Hen Wyddeleg ar Lyfr Offeren Stowe, lle y ceir glos sydd yn disgrifio'r weddi *Miserere mei Deus* – a offrymai'r offeiriad wrth iddo gynnig y caregl i Dduw – fel *oratio periculosa*. Enw ar yr offeiriad hwnnw oedd *periglor*: T. Lewis, *A Glossary of Medieval Welsh Law*, 45; *The Irish Penitentials*, gol. L. Bieler (Dulyn, 1963), 62, 126, 241-42. Am destun o'r Traethawd, gw. *Thesaurus Palaeohibernicus*, gol. W. Stokes a J. Strachan (Caergrawnt, 1901-03), ii.253. Fel yr awgrymodd yr Athro Foster imi, fodd bynnag, y mae'n anodd credu y buasai glos un unigolyn mewn Hen Wyddeleg yn esgor ar derm gweddol gyffredin am eglwyswr yn y Gymraeg, ac er gwaethaf amheuon Ifor Williams, efallai y dylem edrych yn hytrach i gyfeiriad yr enw Lladin *parochia* am darddiad periglor. (Cynigiodd L. Mühlhausen darddu *periglor* o'r Lladin *paroch(1)iarius*: cf. adolygiad J. Vendryes, (1917-19) 37 RC 371. Ym marn Ifor Williams, ar y llaw arall, o hwnnw y disgwylid datblygu *pereigliawr*: CA 301. Eto,

hwyrach i ffurf Ladin fel *parochialarius* droi yn *periglawr*, fel y tybir i'r Llad. *librarius* droi yn *llyfrawr* yn Gymraeg: cf. *Armes Prydein*, gol. I. Williams (Caerdydd, 1955), llin. 193 a nodyn, t. 67.) O'r 12fed g. ymlaen daeth *parochia* i olygu 'plwyf' yng Nghymru, ond cyn hynny yr oedd i'r gair ystyr letach, sef 'cylch awdurdod' eglwys neu fynachlog, neu 'esgobaeth': T. M. Charles-Edwards, 'The Seven Bishop-Houses of Dyfed', (1970-72) 24 BBCS 258; J. Conway Davies, *Episcopal Acts and Cognate Documents relating to Welsh Dioceses, 1066-1272* (Caerdydd, 1946-48), ii.589-94. Efallai i *periglor* ddynodi offeiriad a chanddo awdurdod eang dros *parochia* yn yr hen ystyr yn wreiddiol, ond wrth i *parochia* ddod i olygu 'plwyf', ac felly i gyfeirio at gylch llai o faint, nid oedd rheswm mwyach am wahaniaethu yn ymarferol rhwng *periglor* ac *offeiriad*. Fodd bynnag, nid yw'r rhelyw o'r enghreifftiau o *periglor* mewn Cymraeg Canol yn cynnig sail dros gadarnhau'r ddamcaniaeth mai o enw Lladin a gynhwysai'r elfen *parochia(l)* y tarddodd y gair, er y dylid crybwyll *Canu i Dyssilio* Cynddelw, lle y sonnir am beriglor pobl Gwynedd ac am beriglor pobl Powys: *Hen Gerddi Crefyddol*, gol. H. Lewis (Caerdydd, 1931), xvi.173, 232. Ond dichon mai gormodiaith arferol bardd sy'n canu clodydd ei wrthrych (eglwys Meifod yma) a welir yn y llau. hyn, ac ni ddylid rhoi gormod o bwysau arnynt wrth geisio olrhain ystyr wreiddiol *periglor*.

[85] Cyplysir *periglor* â chyffes a phenyd yn yr enghreifftiau canlynol o'r Hen Ganu: *The Book of Taliesin*, gol. J. G. Evans (Llanbedrog, 1910), 9.10 ('At (6yn) bryt 6rth penyt perigla6r'); *Hen Gerddi Crefyddol*, xxxvi.1-6, yn arb. llin. 2, a chymharer ibid., xiv.63-66, yn arb. llin.65 ('...pan beriglwyf'), a xv.9-10. Gw hefyd LLA 136,145; I. Williams, 'Rhinweddau Croen Neidr', (1927-29) 4 BBCS 35.19-20. Yn yr enghreifftiau nesaf defnyddir periglor i olygu offeiriad yn gyffredinol, heb briodoli iddo swyddogaeth cyffeswr: *Hen Gerddi Crefyddol*, xix.28; *The Poetry in the Red Book of Hergest*, gol. J. G. Evans (Llanbedrog, 1911), 582.33-4, 1054.12, 1238.31; *LL A* 96; H. Lewis 'Englynion i'r Offeren', (1929-31) 5 BBCS 16-37. J. E. Caerwyn Williams, 'Gvyrthyeu Saint Edmund Archescop Keint', (1947-48) 5 NLWJ 60.5, 55; E. G. B. Phillimore, 'A Fragment from Hengwrt MS. No. 202', (1886) 7 *Y Cymmrodor* 137.1-3 ('Teir bendith ny adant dyn y newyn nac y noethi os keif. Bendith y ber(i)-glawr. A bendith y argl6yd priodawr. A bendith kerda6r o lin gerd.') Yr enghraifft gynharaf, o bosibl, yw llin. 961 o'r *Gododdin*: 'peleidyr pwys preiglyn benn periglawr'. Ceir cryn betruster, fodd bynnag, ai dyma'r un gair â'r gair am eglwyswr a geir yn yr enghreifftiau eraill uchod: CA, 300-1; K. Jackson, *The Gododdin* (Caeredin, 1969), 147. (Diolchaf i Mr P. J. Donovan am ddanfon imi ffotocopïau o'r slipiau ar *periglor* sydd yn archif GPC.)

[86] Mae'n dra thebyg fod y syniad mai priod waith yr esgob yn unig oedd conffirmio wedi gafael yng Nghymru erbyn cyfnod y Normaniaid, fan bellaf: cf. VSB, 266 (Buchedd Padarn, c. 30): T. Morris, 'The Liber Pontificalis Aniani of Bangor', (1962) *Trafodion Cymdeithas Hynafiaethwyr a Naturiaethwyr Môn* 81 (*Ordo* 'ad consignandum pueros': dyddia'r *Liber Pontificalis* o ddiwedd y 13eg g. neu o'r 14eg g. gynnar.)

[87] A. J. Maclean (fel n. 82), 46. Cf. *Giraldi Cambrensis Opera*, ii. 25 (*Gemma Ecclesiastica*, 1.7).

[88] *Sacrorum Conciliorum...Collectio*, gol. J. D. Mansi, xxii.1007, 1010 (c. 21): 'Omnis utriusque sexus fidelis, postquam ad annos discretionis pervenerit, omnia sua solus peccata confiteatur...propria sacerdoti...' Ymddengys fod plant bach iawn wedi derbyn y cymun yn Eglwys y Gorllewin o'r 3edd g. hyd c.800, ond o hynny ymlaen daeth yn arferol i gyfyngu'r cymun i blant a oedd wedi cyrraedd oedran rheswm: H. Leclercq, 'Communion des enfants', *Dictionnaire d'archéologie chrétienne et de liturgie*, Cyfrol III, Rhan 2 (Paris, 1914), 2440-45.

[89] Ior 97/5-6, 99/1.

[90] Cf. C. McAll, 'The Normal Paradigms of a Woman's Life in the Irish and Welsh Texts', WLW. 7-8, 16, 20. Yn ôl Isidor o Seville (†636), yn *Etymologiae* xi.2, gellid rhannu

blynyddoedd cynnar dyn yn *infantia* 'babandod' (hyd at saith mlwydd oed) ac yna yn *pueritia* 'bachgendod' (hyd at bedair ar ddeg oed): *Patrologiae Latina*, gol. J. P. Migne, lxxxii. 415. Mae'n bosibl fod y dosbarthiad hwn wedi dylanwadu ar wŷr y gyfraith yng Nghymru er nad adlewyrchir y cyfnod nesaf yn Isidor — sef *adolescentia* (hyd at wyth ar hugain oed) — yn y llyfrau cyfraith Cymreig.

[91] PKM 57. 18-20: 'Mi a rodaf Duw y uach it, na weleisti gedymdeith gywirach noc y keffy di ui, tra uynho Duw it uot uelly.' (Manawydan wrth Gigfa ferch Gwyn Gloyw.)

[92] Gw. uchod, n. 6. Cf. A. Esmein, 'Le serment promissoire dans le droit canonique', 250-51; Genesis xxxi.44-55.

[93] D. A. Binchy, 'Irish Law Tracts Re-edited. I' (1955) 17 *Ériu* 56, 66-7 (7); ceir rhagor o dystiolaeth gyfreithiol am statws uchel y *deorad Dé* erbyn canol y 7fed g. yn T. M. Charles-Edwards, 'The Social Background to Irish *Peregrinatio*', (1976) 11 *Celtica* 53. Mewn llythyr ataf y mae'r Athro Fergus Kelly yn nodi ei fod yn drawiadol gyn lleied o sôn sydd am fechnïaeth oruwchnaturiol yn y ffynonellau cyfraith Gwyddelig cynnar, er bod cryn lawer o ddeunydd ar fechnïaeth wedi goroesi ynddynt.

[94] Liebermann i.66; am drafodaeth, gw. ibid., ii.332, 345-46. Sylwyd ar y tebygrwydd rhwng briduw a *godborh* gan T. P. Ellis (*Welsh Tribal Law and Custom*, ii.4, 379-80) a D. A. Binchy (uchod, n.6). Nid adlewyrchir y gwahaniaeth terminolegol sydd ymhlyg rhwng *godborh* a *menniscborh* yng Nghyfreithiau Alfred yn llyfrau Cyfraith Hywel: Liebermann i.48 (Af 1.8).

[95] Gwyntyllir y posibilrwydd y gallasai cyfraith Cymru fod wedi dylanwadu weithiau ar gyfraith Eingl-Seisnig yn D. Jenkins, 'The Medieval Welsh Idea of Law', 338.

[96] Digwydd y ddau air ar wahân mewn rhai llsgrau. o Gyfraith Hywel: Cyfn 3 (llsgr. *V*); uchod, tt.51, 56-7 (llsgr. *C*); AL V.ii.96 (llsgr. *D*).

[97] Am enghraifft o lw i anrhydedd *person* mewn llenyddiaeth Wyddeleg gynnar, gw. T. M. Charles-Edwards, 'Honour and Status in Some Irish and Welsh Prose Tales', (1978) 29 *Ériu*, 140. Cf. hefyd yr ymadrodd Hen Wyddeleg 'tyngaf i'r duw y twng fy *túath* iddo': *idem*, 'Native Political Organization in Roman Britain and the Origin of MW *brenhin*', yn *Antiquitates Indogermanicae*, gol. M. Mayhofer *et al.* (Innsbruck, 1974), 37.

[98] Gw. uchod, tt.57, 59.

[99] *Dictionary of the Irish Language*, s.v. *bríg*. Nid oes i'r ymadrodd 'gwir Duw' (sy'n cyfateb i'r Hen Wyddeleg *fír nDé*) yr un ystyr â briduw canys dull o *brofi* achos, yn hytrach na gwarantu ymrwymiad, ydyw: T. M. Charles-Edwards, 'The Date of the Four Branches of the Mabinogi', 284-85.

[100] PM ii.215.

[101] Ior 68/9. Y mae Dafydd Jenkins o'r farn fod amod wedi disodli briduw er mwyn ateb yr angen am ffurf ar gontract a fyddai'n symlach na mechni: *Cyfraith Hywel*, 85. Yn anffodus heb ragor o dystiolaeth mae'n amhosibl barnu pa mor boblogaidd fu briduw ar *unrhyw* adeg na beth yn hollol oedd ei phwrpas o'i chymharu â mechni ac amod.

[102] Cf. C. P. Wormald, '*Lex Scripta* and *Verbum Regis*...', yn *Early Medieval Kingship*, gol. P. H. Sawyer ac I. N. Wood (Leeds, 1977), 105-38, yn arb. t. 115.

[103] Gw. n.100. Yn ôl Ioan o Gaersallog cynigiodd Harri II Dduw yn wystl wrth iddo addo maddau i Becket yn 1170: *The Letters of John of Salisbury*, gol. W. J. Millor *et al.* (Llundain, 1955-79), ii.694. Hefyd yn berthnasol i'r drafodaeth ar hirhoedledd y cysyniad o fechnïaeth oruwchnaturiol yw hanesion Gerallt Gymro am groeslun mawr a ddefny ddid fel mach yn Eglwys Grist, Dulyn, ar ôl Goresgyniad 1169: *Giraldi Cambrensis Opera*, v.128-29 (*Topographia Hibernica*); a chymharer *Expugnatio Hibernica, The Conquest of Ireland, by Giraldus Cambrensis*, gol. A. B. Scott a F. X. Martin (Dulyn, 1978), 68, 166 (I.17, II.14).

[104] *Littere Wallie*, passim. Cf. J. E. Sayers, *Papal Judges Delegate in the Province of Canterbury*

1198-1254 (Rhydychen, 1971) 251-53.

[105] Ymddengys fod rhyw ffurf ar y gyfraith Gymreig ar fechnïaeth yn weithredol o hyd yng Ngogledd Cymru tua diwedd y 13eg ganrif oherwydd y mae Statud Rhuddlan (1284) yn cynnwys achosion a drôi ar gontractau, dyledion a meichiau ymhlith yr achosion y gellid eu barnu o dan y gyfraith frodorol yn y Dywysogaeth: *Statutes of the Realm* (Record Commission, Llundain, 1810-28), i.68.

[106] Cf. P. Brown, 'Society and the Supernatural: A Medieval Change', (1975) 104 *Daedalus* 133-51.

[107] e.e. Ior 81/13, 87/5-6.

[108] *Registrum Epistolarum Fratris Johannis Peckham,* gol. C. T. Martin (Rolls Series, Llundain, 1882-85), ii.475-6.

SURETYSHIP IN THE *CARTULAIRE DE REDON*
WENDY DAVIES

In the village communities surrounding Redon, in eastern Brittany, the mechanisms of suretyship were used for a range of normal social processes during the ninth century, and there is much practical detail in the earliest Cartulary from Redon about the people who served as sureties and the contexts in which they did so. Since our knowledge of such process in the early middle ages is so often derived from legal tracts, codes and formularies, rather than from cases, this evidence of practice is particularly important, although it has attracted rather less attention from scholars than has the vernacular terminology associated with it.[1] It is therefore my intention to indicate the range of information provided by the Cartulary about the occurrence and behaviour of ninth-century sureties in this region and to investigate the social role and status of the persons chosen to act as such.

The monastery of Redon was founded in AD 832, and had the patronage of the Carolingian emperor Louis and of his representative in Brittany, Nominoe. It was endowed with many small grants of property in its neighbourhood in the decades following its foundation, and it purchased and leased others; records of the grants and sales, together with documents arising from previous transactions, were copied in the eleventh century into the *Cartulaire de Redon*.[2] This collection includes 283 charters of the ninth and early tenth century, and a further sixty-two, which may not have been included in the medieval cartulary, are known from early modern transcripts.[3] Three quarters of the total relate to the forty years following the foundation and constitute — for the ninth century — a remarkable number of documents concerning a limited area. Further, since many properties came to Redon together with extant documentation about them, the collection includes material from at least one generation previous to 832 and material about transactions to which Redon was not party. The importance of the corpus for European history in the early middle ages cannot be overemphasized, quite apart from its long-recognized importance for Celtic studies: since most documents record small-scale, private transactions, it provides a very considerable body of detailed, localisable information about individuals and personal relationships in a peasant society, some two centuries before the record-making revolution of the central middle ages.

Eastern Brittany (the counties of Vannes, Rennes and Nantes, that is modern Morbihan, Ille-et-Vilaine and Loire-Atlantique), together with Anjou and Maine to the east of it (modern Maine-et-Loire and Mayenne), is a zone of fluctuating cultural and political status, and this was never more so than in the early middle ages. Often claimed as an integral part of the vast Frankish state, it was sometimes clearly ruled by the Franks; equally clearly sometimes it was not, as was nearly always the case with the lands to the west; at other times it was politically dominated by the aristocratic families of north-west France. The ninth century was a period in which there were some obvious changes in political status: early in the century the Franks, under the Carolingian dynasty, took control of the whole peninsula of Brittany and between 820 and 832 appointed a Breton (Nominoe) as their representative in the area; this meant some level of political unification for the peninsula, for the first time; by 842 Nominoe had revolted, and he and his successors (the *principes*) ruled Brittany (and sometimes the lands to the east of it) as a single unit, more or less independently, for much of the ninth century. The area that is covered by the Redon material (the whole of south-eastern Brittany) includes much of the intermittently Frankish counties of Rennes and Nantes, and also much of the rarely Frankish county of Vannes, which lay west of the River Vilaine (sometimes cited as a boundary) (see fig. 1). The entire area, then, might be expected to show some traces of institutions introduced by the Carolingians in the ninth century, and/or institutions associated with the *principes*, and the eastern part of it might have had traces of Frankish institutions of longer standing. These possibilities have to be borne in mind when considering the suretyship material and its parallels.

Redon itself actually lies on the River Vilaine. The area surrounding it, the subject of the charters, was an area of mixed farming practices and was — for the ninth century — intensively exploited. At the beginning of the century many of the farmers were independent peasant proprietors, with plots of up to sixty hectares, and they often had associated dependent serfs; there were few large-scale landowners until the extension of Redon's interests. Although much settlement was dispersed, agrarian society was composed of village-based units, known as *plebes*, and each *plebs* had its focal nucleated settlement and church. The peasant community regulated its own business and relationships within the *plebs*, often under the chairmanship of a distinctive 'officer', the machtiern. He was a man who might, for example, initiate dispute settlement proceedings (although he did not himself serve as judge) and might preside over the performance of transactions in which sureties were used (but only rarely served as such himself). Machtiernships were often hereditarily transmitted, through families whose property

interests spanned two or three *plebes* — a wider area, that is, than the peasant
norm; machtierns do not appear to have been appointees of government,
neither Frankish nor Breton; and, though some aspects of the exercise of
their office was clearly proprietary, their responsibility seems essentially to
have been to the village community.[4]

*   *   *   *   *

Breton suretyship has traditionally been viewed in Irish terms. The model
of early Irish suretyship devised by Thurneysen, and more recently discussed
by Professor Binchy, depends on the identification of three distinctive
functions for sureties, with distinctive persons to perform them: the *naidm*,
the binding surety who witnessed a contract, enforced what had been
contracted and distrained on the property of a guilty party — by physical
compulsion if necessary; the *ráth*, the paying surety who made good any
deficit — from his own property; and the *aitire*, the hostage surety who
guaranteed the enforcement of an obligation with his own person. The
relative importance of each function (and person) is supposed to have
changed over time (with a trend away from physical compulsion towards
payment) but *ráth* and *naidm* could each still play a part in one transaction
at the time that the classical Irish law tracts were compiled.[5] Breton terms
have been supposed to indicate equivalents to the first and second Irish
functions, and possibly the third. It has therefore been argued that the
dilisidus of the Redon Cartulary was the equivalent of Irish *ráth*, and that
'machtierns' in the same text performed the binding and enforcing role of
the Irish *naidm* (earlier *macc*); hence, two distinctive types of surety are
supposed to have existed in the ninth century, exercising two different
functions.[6] I shall begin consideration of the problems of Breton suretyship
with an outline of the material that occurs in the Cartulary, paying particular
attention to evidence that the texts themselves provide about function and
refraining from arguing by analogy, Irish or otherwise. Thereafter I shall
proceed to the social and political questions with which this paper is
primarily concerned.

Two terms for surety are constantly used in the Redon charters: the Latin
fideiussor and — less frequently — a Latinised vernacular word, *dilisid(us)*
(occasionally *dilisit*). *Fideiussor* is the classical Roman legal term for one of the
accessories undertaking to pay if a principal debtor did not, guaranteeing any
kind of obligation.[7] It was also used in a variety of early medieval contexts
for those who put down pledges (gages), who guaranteed other people's
debts to creditors, who guaranteed other people's pledges in default
(appearing for them in court) or who acted as oath-helpers.[8] *Dilisidus*

presumably stands for a vernacular equivalent to *fideiussor*, since *dilis* means 'sure' and its Irish and Welsh cognates (*díles* and *dilys*) were used with reference to property that was 'outside legal process' (because ownership was total) and therefore secure.[9] The two Redon terms are sometimes used together in the charter texts and sometimes separately. Hence, 'et obligamus (sic) vobis fideiussores vel dilisidos in securitate ipsius terrae, his nominibus...' (CR 91); or 'et dederunt fideiussores iiii in securitate...' (CR 73); or 'et dederunt dilisidos in securitate...' (CR 132). I see no substantive significance in the recorder's preference for one or other or both terms, and the differences are probably to be explained by differences in record-making habits rather than by intrinsic differences in the transactions.[10] Very occasionally, a third term, *securator*, was employed but no distinction is implied in the nature of the sureties so designated (CR 63, 118, 271). No common Latin words are used for any pledge although the *pignus* of classical Roman terminology is reflected in *pignoratio* and *terra pignorantiae* (CR 86, 193). The Latinised Frankish *uuadio* and *uuadiatio* and the vernacular Breton *aruuistl* each occur once; the contexts clearly indicate 'pledge' or 'gage' put down, the former case in Guérande (near the mouth of the Loire) in 870, the next in Bains in 833 and the last in Molac (west of the Vilaine) in 849 (CR 234, 182, 251).

There are eighty-seven charters that mention sureties in the Redon collection; since two are doublets of the same transaction, one pertains to the eleventh century and another to the twelfth, there remain eighty-four records of ninth-century business using sureties, and my subsequent comments will be confined to these. 292 sureties are cited in the course of these transactions.[11] Of the eighty-four occasions, nine fell before 832 (the foundation date of Redon); 73 per cent fell in the thirty years between 840 and 870, and 31 per cent in the decade 860-870. These proportions reflect the survival of charters in the ninth century and make no particular point about suretyship. The second proportion also reflects the fact that many tenancy disputes were resolved and new tenancies created in the 860s.

The surviving corpus of Redon charters records transactions that took place throughout south-east Brittany — a distance of 100km east-west — but by far the greater proportion of properties lay within 40km of Redon itself, most of these lying to the north of Redon and west of the River Vilaine (see fig. 1). Sureties were named for transactions performed in all parts covered by the charters as also for properties distributed throughout the area. (Although transactions concerning any named property were sometimes performed on the land in question, more frequently they were transacted in some appropriate village meeting-place; sometimes they occurred at a distance from the relevant *plebs*, in Redon or some other monastery or

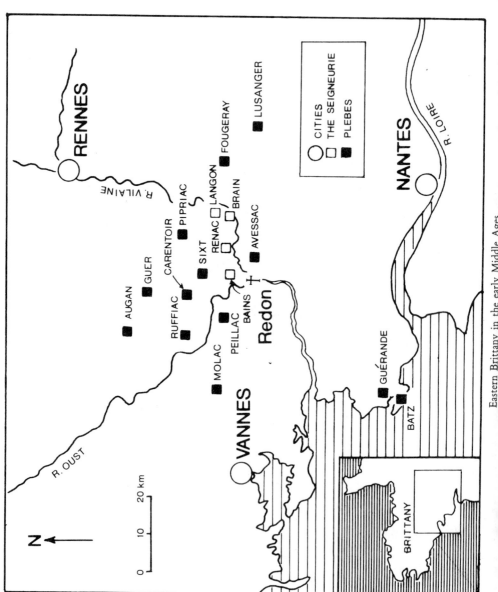

Eastern Brittany in the early Middle Ages

aristocratic residence. For analytical purposes, place of performance needs to be distinguished from the location of the property in question.) Remarkably, 37 per cent of the transactions naming sureties relate to the *plebes* of Ruffiac and Carentoir and, less remarkably, 21 per cent relate to the four *plebes* surrounding Redon (Bains, Brain, Langon and Renac).[12] Admittedly, a quite disproportionate number of charters refers to Ruffiac and Carentoir (22 per cent), but it is an unusually high proportion of these charters that records the use of sureties. It is also notable that nearly all transactions involving saltpans had sureties named (eight of eleven). The apparent preponderance of sureties in some parts is curious and it is also curious that only one of the Langon transactions names sureties (this *plebs* was not far from Redon and the scene of much judicial business) and none of the early Lusanger sales does so. Although these oddities in the distribution pattern cannot at the moment be explained, it is important to observe that the use of sureties was almost as characteristic of the eastern parts of the area as of the western. Although there are considerably fewer surety transactions recorded east of the Vilaine, the proportion is only slightly less than the proportion of eastern records.

Different occasions and transactions provoked the use of sureties in ninth-century Brittany, although it is notable that all concern land transactions and not exchanges of movables: there are thirty-seven cases of sale, twenty of 'pledge' or 'landgage',[13] sixteen of dispute settlement (especially when sureties were given for the future payment of render by the loser), four of agreement to future payment of render with no dispute noted (though possibly implied), and seven miscellaneous occasions. 67 per cent of transactions naming sureties, then, occurred in straightforward cases of the exchange of landed property rights, either fully or partially, for money. Sureties were only rarely used for ordinary *grants* of property; although they were not invariably named in sales they were nearly always characteristic of pledges.

Here is a typical example of the use of sureties in a sale; for ease of comprehension, here and subsequently, I summarise the charter text rather than give a literal translation: Couuetic sold one of his properties, Ranscaman Baih [in Ruffiac], together with its serf, to the smith Carantcar and his wife Uuentamau for 17 *solidi* 4 *denarii*, totally, with full powers of alienation; he assigned Catuuotal, Haeldifoes and Omnis as sureties for the security of the land; if he or his coheirs or relations should contravene the sale, he should pay 34 *solidi*. [There follows a list of twenty-one witnesses, including the vendor, but neither the purchaser nor the sureties.] It was performed on the land in question, on Tuesday, the kalends of March, in the reign of King Charles, with Nominoe holding Brittany and Susannus as bishop [1 March, 847]; Abbot Haeldetuuid made the record (CR 64).

The money sanction is not an invariable aspect of these records, although it is common; when it does occur it is nearly always twice the value of the price paid, or thereabouts.[14] The role of the sureties is never explicitly stated but CR 259 specifies that five sureties were assigned to ensure that land purchased by the abbot for 8 *solidi* would never revert to the vendors nor their descendants (871-77, unlocated). In another case, in Ruffiac in 866, the four sureties of a sale that took place in 857 were produced in court to testify to the validity and totality of the sale when the vendor disputed it. Here the testimony of the sureties was distinguished from that of the witnesses to the original transaction and must be presumed to have had a special status (CR 139).

Transactions of pledge (or 'landgage') are those in which property rights were handed over, for a limited term, for payment; at the end of the term the period could be extended but ultimately both property and payment were due to return to their original owners.[15] When the payment was *not* repaid then the property did not revert either and the transaction effectively constituted a sale on rather light terms. This is a typical example: Iuduuallon gave 20 *solidi* to Iarncon for one and a half parcels of land, *pars* Roetanau and *pars* Eusirgid [probably in Carentoir], and the three men on them, Tiarnoc and his sons Couualin and Uuorethemel; Iarncon gave Iuduuallon three sureties, Iarnbud, Mertinhoiarn and Tanetuuallon. This was for seven years and a week, and thereafter another seven years and a week, and thereafter a third seven years and a week. It was performed on Saturday after Christmas Day in the year that the Emperor Charles died, before [eleven named] witnesses [30 December 813]. If Iarncon and/or his children had not redeemed the land after three times seven years and a week, then Iuduuallon and his wife Ibiau and son Uuallon should own it fully, with powers of alienation and without obligation to pay render to anyone. Lathoiarn recorded this (CR 135).

The way in which these transactions are recorded suggests that usually land was handed over as security for the loan of money; the land was the pledge (gage) and the reason for the transaction seems to have been the pledgor's need for cash.[16] Indeed, the vernacular term *aruuistl*, 'pledge, gage', was explicitly used in this sense.[17] The Latin word *venditio* was also sometimes employed to describe pledge transactions although they are clearly to be distinguished from real sales: the sums of money that changed hands were lower, often no more than the value of rent expected during the term of the pledge; pledged land was sometimes subsequently sold to the pledgee for a further payment (cf. CR 182 and 181); and pledged land might well be redeemed at the end of the specified term. There can have been little long-term benefit to the lessor/pledgor for at the end of the term he may have received his land back but he had lost the income from it during the period of the pledge.[18] It is extremely difficult to see why landowners should have entered into such arrangements except under local political pressure or a short-term need for cash, as once explicitly occurred (CR 234).

The precise actions that sureties were to take in pledge transactions is nowhere specified. However, since the sureties in these transactions were named by the man who provided the land and not by the man who provided the cash there is some suggestion that their role was an enforcing one: it was not their job to pay up if the deal failed but rather to make sure that use of the land was secured to the man who had paid for it, the pledgee.[19] This is, in fact, virtually explicit in the example cited above.

A fifth of the eighty-four cases using sureties are cited in the context of procedures following the settlement of disputes, often to ensure the enforcement of the terms of the settlement. In seven of these, sureties were named for the regular payment of render from tenants; the disputes that these settlements followed were either of the type in which owner A maintained that tenant B's payments had lapsed or of the type in which ownership had been disputed between two proprietors, C and D. In the former type, B agreed to pay regularly in future; in the latter type, it was agreed that C should own the disputed property but D should hold it from him and pay rent. So, for example, between 836 and 842 the abbot and monks of Redon accused Anauhocar and his family of wrongly farming a virgate called Puz, and appealed to the ruler of Brittany, Nominoe, to intervene; Nominoe ordered that the case be heard locally and six men testified against the laymen; thereafter three sureties were given by Anauhocar to Redon both for the land (*in securitate supradictae terrae*) *and* for subsequent annual payment (CR 61). Here the sureties performed two potentially separable functions: they both secured the land to Redon and they also guaranteed the payments. The few records that detail the provision of sureties for payment of future rent, without reference to previous disputes, may in fact have followed comparable settlements: for example, in 868 Maenhoiarn and his brother provided Redon with two sureties for the payment of 2 *solidi*, every Martinmas, for a parcel in Carentoir (CR 134).

In one of the records about rent it is specified that sureties were assigned by the tenant against future claims by his family: in Carentoir, in 863, two sureties were named for payment of the rent and a further four for the security of the property. (*Et dedit Uuruueten duos fideiussores ad supradictum abbatem...ut omnibus annis redderet censum ad kalendas octobris, id est, duos solidos, sine repugnatione; et dederunt supradictus Uuruueten et Pivetat iiii fideiussores in securitate ut nec ipsi nec parentes eorum nec filii eorum post eos dicant accepisse se in hereditate illam supradicta[m] partem.* CR 63) On another four occasions sureties were explicitly assigned after dispute settlement in order to guarantee that the loser and his progeny would not bring another case.[20] In Renac in the late 850s the abbot of Redon and Torithgen, son of Houuen, settled that some disputed properties should be split between the two; Torithgen gave six sureties that neither he nor his progeny would bring another case against the abbot over these lands, and also that — in that event — his share would be forfeited to the abbot (CR 29).[21] All of these cases suggest that one role of the sureties was to enforce: their function was to persuade the man who had named them to keep the terms of the settlement (and, at least once, it was to oversee, and presumably effect, forfeiture). Sometimes, by contrast, it is suggested that they guaranteed payments; when this happened sureties for the payment are often distinguished from others in the same transaction. In cases where no rent was due, however, an enforcing role must be implied: in Pipriac in the very late ninth century the line of the abbot's boundaries was questioned; when the bounds were agreed, sureties were given to the abbot by the peasants that they would stick to the agreed line (CR 47). In a different type of case, c.863, Cunatam handed over a serf to Redon, in recompense for raiding, stealing and causing havoc in Redon property; he assigned two sureties for the serf (CR 32, cf. 163). In practical terms, this presumably meant that they guaranteed that the serf's produce went to Redon and not to Cunatam.

The most detailed comments on the functions of sureties occur in a record of 858 about the consequences of assault. A cleric, Anau, tried to kill the priest Anauhoiarn (a priest attached to Redon); Anau gave his vineyard in Ruffiac to Redon in compensation for the assault, and named three sureties for the security of the grant. Thereafter, he named those three and a further three men as sureties that he would do no wrong to Redon's men in the future; if the sureties came to hear of any bad intention of his, they were to warn the abbot; and if Anau actually committed any further offence they were to give his worth (*precium*) to the abbot and pursue him to death. These men had more than a paying and distraining function: in effect they were to adopt a policing role and administer punishment (CR 202). In this case the social function of the sureties is quite explicit: they were the means by which stability and security in this society was maintained, for they constituted the machinery to check and balance the interests of individuals and particular families. It is a nice indication of the fact that the surety system could be fundamental to social order in a world in which the notion of order was not the monopoly (nor even the preserve) of the state.

There is no further detail on the functions of sureties in this material. In most cases the sureties in these Breton villages were personal guarantors that the legal obligations of others would be fulfilled, as sureties were everywhere. There is really very little detail of how this was done, although payment from the sureties' own property and physical compulsion are both implied. Clearly both did occur — and both might occur with reference to the same transaction, either with one set of sureties or with more. It therefore looks as if a surety might perform his guaranteeing role in a number of ways: he presumably used the method that fitted the particular circumstances and did not follow a rigid system. As a comment on practice this makes sense and is what we might expect from records of practice; it is therefore particularly inappropriate to force the material to fit the formulations of lawyers.

*   *   *   *   *

The charters themselves include some information about the social and economic status of the people who served as sureties in these transactions. The number of sureties used on each occasion varied: usually two, three or four, it was exceptionally one, five or six and very exceptionally eight, nine or twelve. Where property was sold or pledged, there is only one type of correlation between the number of sureties and the size or value of the property, or the length of the pledge (landgage) transaction: if the property was *very* small, valued at less than 10 *solidi*, there were usually two sureties. Otherwise, valuable properties might have few sureties, like two for a sale worth 29*s*.3*d*., in 856 (CR 172), and less valuable ones might have many, like twelve for a sale worth 16*s*. 6*d*., in 849 (CR 58). Nor is there any obvious distinction between numbers used in different decades of the ninth century. As one might expect, then, the reasons for the variation in numbers presumably lay in the status and economic resources of the sureties and in the particular social circumstances that attended each case; possibly, since it was a peasant community, they had to cover the obligation between them — in a society of small proprietors this may sometimes have involved several people of moderate means.[22]

Direct information about the status of the sureties is infrequently recorded, but occurs sufficiently often to be interesting. Of 292 citations of sureties, and about 200 different individuals, a small number were local office holders, either lay or clerical.[23] At least nine of the people used as sureties also served as *scabini* in their localities, that is they served on the panels of judgement-finders used in court cases — free, local, respectable, propertied men, such as Arthbiu of Bains or Uuolethec of Augan.[24] At least eight were people called upon to give evidence, as impartial witnesses, in court cases — again, these were local, respectable men, usually referred to as *seniores* of their respective *plebes*.[25] A couple also served as *mair*.[26] On three occasions the sureties were machtierns. This very limited occurrence is particularly interesting in view of the probable meaning of the element *mach* in the word 'machtiern' — 'surety', like Welsh *mach*: if machtierns had originally been *distinguished* by functioning as sureties, they had clearly lost the distinction by the ninth century. Use of machtierns for these purposes was clearly exceptional and only seems to have occurred for special types of case, as in the settlement following the assault by Anau on a Redon priest (CR 202).[27] Clerics also sometimes functioned as sureties, but not very often: there were certainly two priests and a deacon, and maybe twice that number, but not more.[28] In fact, overall, it is the low proportion of lay and clerical office holders that is striking; 20 per cent at most. Clearly persons of special standing in the village community were sometimes used as sureties but much more often less distinctive members were chosen.

Indeed, although some people stood as sureties for several transactions in their local communities, it was much more characteristic to do so once only: of the 200 individuals used as sureties, less than 20 per cent stood more than once. Now it was characteristic, with a few notable exceptions, for surety transactions (like most others) to be performed in the *plebs* in which the property lay: Guérande transactions took place in Guérande, Augan transactions in Augan, Fougeray transactions in Fougeray, and so on.[29] The norm, then, was that surety transactions were narrowly local affairs that were particular to a particular local group of people.[30] Moreover, the people who served as sureties were men of very limited geographical range. Where people served on more than one occasion, they normally did so in the same *plebs* (or within the block of *plebes* near Redon that constituted the *seigneurie*); the only possible exception to this concerns Iudlin, who served in Batz and neighbouring Guérande in the 850s and 860s (CR 60, 95).[31] So, Catbud served four times in Carentoir between 833 and 866 and Maenuili served a most unusual six times in Ruffiac between 821 and 848; Loieshoiarn served twice in Carentoir, Nominoe and Noli twice in Ruffiac, Breselan twice in Guérande, Iunetmonoc twice in Renac, and so on. The same type of observation may be made of those who only served once as surety: we do not often find them doing business outside their own *plebs* (unless within the *seigneurie*), and if we do, then usually that business did not take them beyond the neighbouring *plebs*. Hence, Christian was surety and sometimes witness in Peillac, *c*.867; Finitan in Molac, *c*.820-27; Greduuocon in Sixt, and (called *senior* of Sixt) gave evidence as impartial witness in Bains, all between 834 and 851; Rethuualart was surety and witness at least ten times in Ruffiac, and witness possibly in Augan and Guer, between 832 and 866 — he was also called as witness for one party in dispute in Ruffiac in 846. Iudrith (of the *seigneurie*) served three times as surety in Renac, Bains and

Brain between 832 and 870, and witnessed at least eight times in those *plebes* with reference to properties in the *seigneurie*.[32]

As for the economic status of the sureties, it is sometimes made clear that they were propertied men. They appeared as donors, vendors, purchasers and pledgors of land in their own right. Uuordoital was a donor of property in Ruffiac, as well as a surety and frequent witness there.[33] Kinetuuant was a pledgor of property in Guérande as well as surety and witness there, 859-66. Cathoiarn was vendor of property in Carentoir as well as witness there, and three times surety and frequent witness in Ruffiac.[34] Tiarnan was donor of property in Bains, a judgement-finder in Langon, surety in Renac and Brain and witness throughout the *seigneurie*.[35] Nothing, however, suggests that these were the properties of great aristocrats: they consisted of small units, a few 10 or 20 hectare parcels at most, and they were not widely scattered. Usually they lay in the *plebs* in which the owner served as surety. The only consistent exceptions to this pattern relate to the *seigneurie*, as in the case of Tiarnan above: here men might well have property in one *plebs* of the group and serve in another. All these people, then, were well-off peasants; they were neither great lords nor country gentlemen and nothing suggests that they had either military capacity or interests. Quite often, by the 860s, they were the men who had made grants to Redon and then taken tenancies on the lands they formerly owned.

There is another characteristic of those who served as sureties that may incidentally throw some light on the way they performed their role. Sometimes the close family (brothers or sons) of one party to a transaction was named as surety; and in one case local elders stated, in a judgement, that it would be most suitable if an accused man's brother stood as surety for his agreed settlement (CR 264). On other occasions people who were themselves liable to make future payments (in a joint transaction) stood as surety for each other: for example, four men from Peillac (A, B, C, D) defaulted on dues owed to Redon; the agreement was renewed in 867, with the new abbot, and they all gave sureties for payment of the render in the future; A gave B and D, while B gave A, D and another (X); C gave X and two others (Y and Z), and the last, D, gave Z (CR 96). This may well suggest that one function of many of the sureties was to resign their own personal interests in the property transferred, whether they had family or other involvements. If a man named his brother, or another potentially interested person, as surety for a sale then the surety was directly committed to the totality of that sale and — in agreeing to stand — publicly resigned his own interest.

*   *   *   *   *

The Redon material nicely demonstrates the use of sureties in eastern Brittany in different types of land transaction during the ninth century. Nothing suggests that the practice was exclusive either to Frankish or to Breton parts. When property rights were transferred for money, sureties are recorded often enough to suggest that their use was a norm. They were provided by the vendors or pledgors of land, to guarantee that the property rights really would change hands and that the original owners would neither work nor take profits nor renders from the lands they had alienated. Sureties were also sometimes used to guarantee payment of regular rent from tenants to landlords, particularly when the rents had been disputed between the parties but possibly in other circumstances too. Further, as might be expected, they were used to guarantee that the terms of a settlement arrived at after dispute would be respected by all parties, especially by any loser, whether or not the settlement involved subsequent regular payments. On occasion great care was taken over the selection of sureties, and decisions over appropriate people to carry out the task were sometimes a part of settlement proceedings. On others, small payments might be made to them (CR 111, 136) and they were invariably distinguished from ordinary witnesses to business, who themselves had to be of suitable standing. They did, then, have a special, and valued, role to play. Practical detail of what this role involved is rare, although both enforcing and paying activities are sometimes indisputable and the sureties named after Anau's assault also had a punishing function. We should not forget, however, that several aspects of the operation of suretyship remain uncertain: as well as the lack of precise description of action taken, or envisaged, by the parties to an agreement, we lack evidence of the machinery for implementing the *stipulatio* (sanction); and, apart from the pledge transactions themselves, we do not know if pledges were sometimes put down in the course of action by sureties, as part of the enforcing process, for example.[36] Usually the people chosen to act as sureties were free, male, respected members of the local village community, although we lack evidence on the manner of their selection and on the qualifications for eligibility;[37] they seem to have been reasonably well propertied peasants, with limited interests; they sometimes held some local lay or clerical office but they were not rich or powerful men and they were not the representatives of any higher level of government. Suretyship was essentially a village-based business and the sanctions which the institution imposed operated within communities in which reputation was of importance to individual and to family and essential to the viability of working relationships.[38]

In many ways these Breton practices were not at all distinctive: the use of sureties was widespread in early medieval Europe, in continental as well as insular regions, as it also had been in the ancient world, and the contexts in which sureties were principally used involved debt and court procedure. Payment of fines and compensations by a guilty man — especially composition for homicide — was often treated like contract and sureties were therefore used to guarantee the contractual obligation; a similar approach influenced the use of sureties for appearance in court by an accused man and for future good behaviour of a guilty one. The use of pledges (landed and movable) was also widespread on the continent, both to guarantee obligations in dispute settlement procedure and — as in the Redon cases — to establish security for raising a loan.[39] Pledging (*rewadiare*) and the use of *fideiussores* were established Frankish practices, both Merovingian and Carolingian, but were also common in Byzantine and Lombard Italy and in Visigothic Spain as well as in Anglo-Saxon England.[40] None of this is very surprising, especially when we recall the Roman law of contract — particularly with respect to debt and loan — and the emphases it received in the late Empire: the *Digest*, quoting late commentators, is explicit on the appropriate use of pledge *and* surety in raising loans; the *Theodosian Code* often notes the particular significance of pledging for those who took leases on imperial property; and at least once, in language reminiscent of the Redon material, the *Code* specifies the need for tenants of imperial property to provide sureties for the payment of their rent.[41]

There are two aspects of Breton suretyship in the ninth century which are relatively uncommon: the use of sureties in transactions of sale (of land) and the use of sureties for 'policing'. With reference to sale, three contexts provide apparently close parallels. The legal text known as *Excerpta de libris Romanorum et Francorum*, of pre-ninth-century Breton or near Breton origin, includes a provision that unless something acquired by purchase has *fideiussores*, or the *auctor* (former owner) to answer for it, it could be regarded as stolen; in other words, it requires sales to have guarantors.[42] Secondly, the early eighth-century Irish canonical collection known as *Collectio Canonum Hibernensis* includes a chapter on *fideiussores* and *stipulationes*, mostly with reference to debt. Section 6, *de eo, quod aliquis non debet emere aut vendere sine ratis et stipulationibus*, appears to have precisely the same requirement in mind: sales should not take place without guarantors as well as sanctions, and the section goes on to cite the authority of Jerome, Augustine and an (?) Irish synod.[43] Thirdly, Anglo-Saxon legal codes, especially of the tenth century, constantly repeat the requirement that every man needs a guarantor for his transactions; no-one could buy or exchange without surety *and* witness.[44] The *Excerpta*, the *Collectio* and the Anglo-Saxon codes seem to be articulating principles that were actually implemented in the transactions recorded in the Redon corpus, although they sometimes explicitly refer to exchanges of movables.[45] The *requirement* that sureties be available for goods sold looks like a northern European application of trends visible in Roman Vulgar Law: the legal evidence suggests increasing emphasis on the need for witnesses when titles were transferred by sale, and the need for sureties in some circumstances was also occasionally specified.[46]

It is extremely difficult to parallel — precisely — the policing function of the sureties of CR 202 although late tenth-century English legislators seem to have envisaged a very similar financial role for sureties for a guilty man.[47] The detail of the 'policing' of 202 is unusual, however, for the sureties' capacity to punish seems to have been viewed as an entirely private matter between the contracting parties and the guarantors of their contracts. In the several early medieval contexts in which citizens formed bands for the pursuit of bad men — sixth- and ninth-century Francia, tenth-century England — the bands were mobilised because of state direction and interest, and they were sometimes accompanied by an appropriate officer such as a *comes* or *grafio*.[48] The Breton material suggests unusually private machinery for mobilising the band that was to ride out in pursuit.

*　　*　　*　　*　　*

The Breton practice evidenced in the ninth century does not look entirely distinctive, and it certainly does not look distinctively Celtic, although there are points of contact with both Welsh and Irish practice. The contexts in which sureties were used, especially since they refer to landed property, are often as reminiscent of late Roman, Visigothic, Lombard, Frankish and even Anglo-Saxon practice, if not more so; it is therefore strained to force the Breton evidence exclusively into a native Irish model. It is also strained to suppose the Breton terms refer to persons of distinctive function: enforcing and paying both clearly occurred and both methods could be employed by a single *fideiussor*.[49] However, what is most interesting in all of this is not so much the parallels here and there, since suretyship was common in European societies, but the differences of emphasis and the possible social and political explanations for those differences. Use of sureties in the sale of landed property seems to have been a local intensification of a general trend in post-Roman Europe rather than a totally distinctive practice. It presumably reflects a society in which the number of transactions was limited and their security potentially fragile. It might well be pointing to the limited occurrence of sale and to the limited mobility of property, rather than — as might at first appear — to the contrary; it might therefore be effectively pointing to the strength of family interests, operating as a restraint on freedom of alienation.

Use of sureties for policing, to constrain and punish bad men, is an interesting extension of the machinery of suretyship, personal guarantors of contract between individuals operating as a means of guaranteeing order in the community. The absence of state interest is very marked, by contrast with the use of comparable machinery elsewhere in Europe in the early middle ages, and suggests an absence of state institutions. It serves to reinforce the impression, also conveyed by other aspects of the Redon material, that the affairs of local village communities were regulated by the peasant cultivators themselves, men who had little contact with an outside wider world. By the twelfth century, partly because of the increased power of Redon itself, that was to change; in the mid-ninth century the change was still some time away.

---

[1] L. Fleuriot, 'Un fragment en Latin de très anciennes lois bretonnes armoricaines du vi siècle', (1971) 78 *Annales de Bretagne* 622-24, 648-54; M. Planiol, *Histoire des Institutions de la Bretagne* (5 vols., 2nd. ed. Mayenne, 1981-4), ii. 72f, 159, 166f.
I am extremely grateful for the comments made on this paper by Julia Smith, Chris Wickham and, of course, the editors. I am also indebted to the staff of the Computer Centre at University College London for their tolerance during my preparation of a Redon database and, in particular, to Chris Horsbrugh for writing the programs which allowed me to interrogate it. The section of this paper which deals with the characteristics and occurrence of different individuals depends upon a computer-assisted analysis of the incidence of the 6600 personal names and 1100 place-names that occur in the ninth-century charters of the *Cartulaire de Redon*. I shall discuss the technical aspects of this in my forthcoming book *Villages, Villagers and the Structure of Rural Society in Early Medieval Brittany* (Duckworth, 1986). Considerable assistance with clerical support has been provided by the British Academy, to which I owe especial thanks.
[2] *Cartulaire de Redon*, ed. A. de Courson (Paris, 1863), hereafter CR. The manuscript is in the care of the archbishop of Rennes.
[3] Nearly all of these were printed by de Courson in an Appendix to CR and the rest were printed by H. Morice, *Mémoires pour servir de preuves à l'histoire écclésiastique et civile de Bretagne* (3 vols., Paris, 1742-46), i. col. 265, 271f, 295, 297, 308; most of the transcripts from which they were printed are difficult to locate.
[4] For machtierns see my 'On the distribution of political power in Brittany in the mid-ninth century' in *Charles the Bald: Court and Kingdom*, ed. M. Gibson and J. Nelson with D. Ganz, British Archaeological Reports, International Series 101 (1981), 87-107, and J. G. T. Sheringham, 'Les machtierns' (1981) 58 *Mémoires de la Société d'Histoire et d'Archéologie de Bretagne* 61-72. Despite many attempts I have been unable to consult F. Burdeau, 'Les Machtierns', Mémoire, Agregation de Droit Romain, Rennes, 1967. For other aspects of social structure and economy see my forthcoming *Villages, Villagers*. For detailed discussion of dispute settlement procedure see my 'Disputes, their conduct and their settlement in the village communities of eastern Brittany in the ninth century' (1985) 1 *History and Anthropology* 289-312 and my 'People and places in dispute in ninth-century Brittany' in *Settlement of Disputes in Early Medieval Europe*, ed. W. Davies and P. Fouracre (Cambridge, 1986).
[5] D. A. Binchy 'Celtic Suretyship', 355-67; see also *ante*, Stacey.
[6] Cf. L. Fleuriot, 'Fragment' (1971) 78 *Annales de Bretagne* 651.
[7] J. A. C. Thomas, *Textbook of Roman Law* (Amsterdam, 1976) 335.

[8] See above, p.85 and nn.39 and 40.

[9] Cf. Ior 65/3-6; CG 83f.

[10] There are two tendencies: 1) both words tend to be used in first person records and one or other in third person records; 2) both are used up to and including the 840s, while one or other might be used at any time in the ninth century, early or late. This reflects changes in diplomatic practice characteristic of the 840s. There are no apparent regional distinctions in the choice of terms nor do they vary consistently in accordance with the type of transaction to which they refer. (I shall discuss the diplomatic of these charters in *Villages, Villagers.*)

[11] See above pp.81-3.

[12] These four adjacent *plebes* were controlled by Redon by the 850s, and a fifth — Massérac — was added by 890, forming a compact block of territory (*seigneurie*) over which the abbot and monks had a type of proprietary right (without affecting individual ownership of property within the *plebes*); in practice this meant that the abbot had rights to certain dues and rights of jurisdiction in the area, and that it was immune from state intervention. See further *Villages, Villagers.*

[13] See above, p.78.

[14] This was common late and post-Roman practice in continental Europe; see E. Levy, *Weströmisches Vulgarrecht. Das Obligationenrecht* (Weimar, 1956) 213-20.

[15] The verb of action in these records is usually Latin *pignorare* (sic), 'to pledge, pawn, mortgage', or Latinised Germanic *uuadiare*, 'to give surety'; again, I see no significance in the choice of term except with respect to recording practice.

[16] Transactions of this type were not uncommon in late and post-Roman Europe, particularly in order to raise cash; see J. A. C. Thomas, *Textbook of Roman Law*, 330-2; *Digest*, 18.1.81, *Digesta*, ed. T. Mommsen, i (Berlin, 1868; see further below, n. 41); *Les diplômes originaux des merovingiens*, ed. P. Lauer and C. Samaran (Paris, 1908), no. 25, 18 (in which land was pledged to the abbot of St Denis in order raise money to pay a fine in seventh-century Francia). Rather later, the 'beneficial lease' of twelfth- and thirteenth-century England represented a comparable development, and so — occasionally — did the landgage of late medieval Wales, although the latter was more usually associated with a shortage of land rather than a shortage of cash; see H. D. Hazeltine, 'The gage of land in medieval England' (1903-4) 17 *Harvard Law Review* 552f and Ll. B. Smith, 'The gage and the land market in late medieval Wales' (1976) 29 *Economic History Review* 537-50.

[17] The word was used in a different sense in Ior 57/3, 65/3; see Glossary.

[18] It would be possible to read CR 68 as suggesting that the pledgor received an annual income for twenty-one years of 18*d.*; the text, however, is corrupt and it is by no means certain that this *is* the meaning.

[19] The one pledge that has a money sanction attached may imply that if the terms were not met an appeal should be made to the machtiern, who would take action; however, this charter has lacunae and no argument can depend on it (CR 265).

[20] CR 29, 118, 127, 180: *pro se et suos semine et omnibus suis ingeniis* (sic) (CR 29).

[21] In fact, it is not clear if the half-parcel that he handed over was the subject of the dispute or another parcel, in lieu; neither possibility alters the fact that he was liable to forfeit a share of the disputed parcel.

[22] One clause in a Visigothic law tract, however, made the point that *each fideiussor* should have the means to meet the cost, even if there were several of them; E. Levy, *Weströmisches Vulgarrecht*, 201. Such rules might also have been applicable in Brittany.

[23] 'About 200' since identifications cannot always be certain.

[24] Arthbiu (CR 124, 192; 29, 58, 96, 155); Catlouuen (124, 192; 58); Framuual (180); ? Hitin (180); Houuori (147; 146); Iarndeduuid (147; 148, 220); Notolic (192; 29, 132);

Tiarnan (124; 53, 58); Uuatin (124, 192; 58); Uuolethec (147, ?180; 196).
[25] Cumiau (CR 106; A17); Greduuocon (106; A17); ?Haeluuocon (106; 96); Hincant (61); ?Houuori (205; 146, cf. 147); Iarnhatoeu (106; 181); Iarnhebet (106; 121, 182); Maenuuoron (106; 181, 199); ? Uuallon (106; 58). Whether or not these men really were impartial is impossible to deduce; functionally, however, they were distinct from partial witnesses; see further my 'Disputes' (1985) 1 *History and Anthropology* 298-300.
[26] Cumiau (A17); Uuolethec (111; 196). The precise function of the *mair* is unclear; he may have been a ruler's agent or steward of an estate (cf. Carolingian *maiores*). See further my 'Disputes' (1985) 1 *History and Anthropology* n. 12.
[27] Welsh *mach* and Old Breton *meich* would certainly support this meaning, although Sir Ifor Williams suggested that *mach* in 'machtiern' was a cognate of Irish *mass*, 'great, fine'; see further the discussions of Fleuriot and Planiol (above, n.1), Sheringham and myself (above, n.4). The machtierns are Ratfred (105; 202); Ratuili (111, 113, 143; 202); Uuorgost (116; 136); and possibly Catusloiant (198; 172). If *mach* in 'machtiern' means 'surety' it makes such more sense to suppose that machtierns had some responsibility for overseeing suretyship rather than for being sureties themselves, somewhat as sergeants of the peace in late medieval Britain saw that suspects produced sureties for their appearance in court. In the ninth century machtierns may have been involved in transactions that had gone wrong, as one pledge charter clearly implies (CR 265). Hence, although it is imperfect, the material in the Redon Cartulary suggests that machtierns were only rarely sureties themselves, although they might sometimes have had an enforcing role in investigating problem transactions; in the latter, however, they were external to the original contract and not part of the contractual relationship.
[28] Priests: Arblant (249); Rihouuen (156; 202); ? Haeluuocon (76; 96); ?Maenuuethen (248; 256); ?Unum (93, 248; 249). Deacons: Loiesuuotal (271); ?Haelhouuen (38; 39, 82).
[29] This is true of at least 69 per cent of the surety cases; only 12 per cent *certainly* took place elsewhere; the remainder are unlocated. See above, p.75, for the overall distribution of surety transactions.
[30] The chief exception to the predominant geographical pattern concerns Carentoir, for which apparently ordinary property transactions took place in Bains and Renac. Additionally, two Carentoir, one Ruffiac and one Pleucadeuc transaction took place at Lisnouuid, which is unlocated but lay within Ruffiac or Carentoir. At the least, then, in two cases and possibly three this place functioned as a regional centre for Ruffiac, Carentoir and neighbouring *plebes*. Surety transactions performed in Bains and Renac, as might be expected, usually related to the *plebes* of the *seigneurie* (see above, n. 12). Surety transactions only took place at Redon itself in the exceptional case of the settlement following Anau's assault.
[31] These were not necessarily, however, separate *plebes*. Roenuuallon might possibly be another exception (CR 34, 88, 133, 181, 256).
[32] CR 53, 58; 29, 32, 74, 163, 185, 207, 216, 233.
[33] CR 153; 144; 112, 144, 172, 173, etc.
[34] Morice, *Preuves*, i. col. 295; CR 151, 160, 171; 8, 9, 155, etc.
[35] CR 71; 124; 53, 58; 181.
[36] CR 274 states that, after some havoc caused by his tenants in the early tenth century, Bishop Bili and his brother gave security for their good behaviour in the future (*securitatem dare*). The manner of reference certainly leaves open the possibility that some pledge may have been put down, but it might equally indicate that the two men merely gave assurances.
[37] Lombard law, for example, specified that sureties needed sufficient property to meet the obligation if necessary to do so and that they should come from the debtor's own district (Liutprand 128, 38); MGH Leges, iv, *Leges Langobardorum*, ed. F. Bluhme (Hanover, 1868), 161, 125.

[38] Suretyship in early medieval Brittany may have been more complex than the processes
evidenced in the Redon Cartulary, for there exists in Old Breton a range of words that may
relate to suretyship that are not evidenced in this text: *guuistl* (glossing *obses*), *rad* (glossing
stipulationes) and *meich* (glossing *ratas*). They occur in contexts that do not elucidate precise
meaning and do not distinguish between the import of the different words. It is therefore
conceivable that some ninth-century people perceived distinctive types of surety, although
there are considerable problems with this terminology and although this clearly was not so
with the people who drew up the Redon texts. For the problems, see L. Fleuriot, 'Fragment'
(1971) 78 *Annales de Bretagne* 648-54 and DGVB 75, 141, 193, 204, 253, 293. *Guuistl* may
merely mean 'hostage' and may not imply 'hostage surety', although *aruuistl* clearly does refer
to the gage put down and the tenth- or eleventh-century *Vita Gildae*, c.21, seems to refer
to hostage sureties: *Nisi enim beatum virum Gildam mihi fideiussorem dederis...*; *Gildae. De
Excidio Britanniae*, ed. and trans. H. Williams, Cymmrodorion Record Series 3 (2 vols.,
London, 1901), ii.356. CR 105 could be taken to indicate hostage sureties but not certainly
so.

[39] See above n. 16; J.-O. Tjäder, *Die nichtliterarischen lateinischen papyri Italiens aus der Zeit
445-700* (Lund, 1955) i.232, where *fideiussores* were appointed in a tutelage case; *MGH Legum*,
Sectio v, *Formulae Merowingici et Karolini Aevi*, ed. K. Zeumer (Hanover, 1886) 88 (Marculf
II), although pledges were not used, be it noted, in formulas of sales or exchange; cf. the
use of *fideiussores* in a variety of contexts in the taking of evidence in court and presenting
of cases, ibid. 60, 67 (Marculf I); they were often cited in standard formulas in charter texts,
particularly when freedoms were granted in the eighth and ninth centuries, for example MGH
Diplomata Karolinorum, ed. E. Muhlbacher (Hanover, 1906) i.199 and MGH *Diplomata Regum
Germaniae ex stirpe Karolinorum*, ed P. Kehr (Berlin, 1934) i.67; MGH *Leges*, iv, *Leges
Langobardorum*, ed. F. Bluhme (Rothari 192, 346, Liutprand 36-41, 108) 46f, 79, 125f, 151.
The Lombard laws have much detail (and modifications to it over the years) about surety and
pledge procedure, especially in cases of debt.

[40] See further Davies and Fouracre, *Settlement of Disputes*, for discussion of the use of *fideiussor*
in a great variety of early medieval contexts. See further below, nn. 44 and 48.

[41] *Digest*, 18.1.81, on whether or not land pledged as security for a loan would become the
surety's by purchase if the surety himself paid the loan after the appointed term; *Codex
Theodosianus*, 1.11.1, 2.30, 2.31.1, 10.3.4, *The Theodosian Code*, trans. C. Pharr (Princeton,
1952) 23, 60f, 270; J. A. C. Thomas, *Textbook of Roman Law*, 330-35.

[42] *The Irish Penitentials*, ed. L. Bieler (Dublin, 1963) 136-59, clauses A19/P28; cf. A30, on
the requirement to pledge for future payment in cases of failure to pay tribute (*pignus det*);
cf. A44/P48 on the sacrilege of invoking God as *fideiussor* (although the meaning here is
presumably 'oath-helper'). Professor Fleuriot argued that this text was Breton and of sixth-
century date, 'Fragment' (1971) 78 *Annales de Bretagne* 612-18; though the argument for the
provenance is a strong one and it is very difficult to locate it other than in the east
Breton/Anjou/Maine zone the argument for the date is less convincing and I cannot date it
more precisely than fifth- to eighth-century inclusive (the manuscript is a ninth-century one
and the content would be difficult to explain in a pre-fifth-century context). Although the
formulation and terminology is quite different, the Frankish ruling that movables might be
regarded as stolen property if witnesses to their transfer could not be provided seems to
indicate a comparable pre-occupation and — interestingly — the area north of the Loire is
specified in this context; *Pactus Legis Salicae*, ed. K. A. Eckhardt (Göttingen, 1955) clause
47, 292-6.

[43] *Die Irische Kanonensammlung*, ed. F. W. H. Wasserschleben (2nd. ed., Leipzig, 1885), lib.
34, 123. I am here understanding *ratus* as a Latinisation of Irish *ráth* although it may merely

have its common Latin meaning of 'sure'. Although the word *fideiussor* is not used in this clause *ratus* must stand for 'surety'; hence, the requirement that there be sureties and sanction (*stipulatio*) appears to be just the practice used in sale in ninth-century Brittany. Breton manuscripts are the source of much Irish canonical material; cf. Paris Bib. Nat., Lat. MSS 3182 and 12021. The comparability of the material in the *Collectio* is best explained in the context of the establishment of the early Irish church and the accompanying transmission of late Roman ideas; cf. D. Ó Corráin, L. Breatnach, A. Breen, 'The Laws of the Irish' (1984) 3 *Peritia* 382-438 for evidence of the absorption of biblical ideas in native secular material.

[44] I Atr. 3, III Atr. 5 (*The Laws of the Kings of England from Edmund to Henry I*, ed. A. J. Robertson (Cambridge, 1925) 54, 66); I Edw. 1, cf. Hl. and E. 16 (*The laws of the earliest English kings*, ed. F. L. Attenborough (Cambridge, 1922) 114, 22).

[45] Cf., especially, CR 124 where failure to produce sureties in a dispute about ownership provoked a judgement that the property be awarded to the other party. The prominence of the notion of sale in the Breton practice is emphasized by the fact that pledges are sometimes referred to as *venditiones* (although they are to be distinguished from real sales in perpetuity, as indicated above, p.78).

[46] E. Levy, *West Roman Vulgar law. The Law of Property* (Philadelphia, 1951) 129, 160. Cf. E. Levy, *Weströmisches Vulgarrecht*, 222: *Si venditor non fuerit idoneus, fideiussorem dare debet emptori* (Codex Euricianus); and ibid. 233, where Levy cites both Jerome and Augustine on the giving of an *arra* as an earnest in a pledge for sale; even classical Roman lawyers occasionally conceived the possibility of personal sureties being used in sale, *Digest*, 18.1.83; *Codes Theodosianus*, 8.18.1.

[47] I Atr 1.5 and 1.7 (Robertson, *Laws*, 52), in which sureties were to pay the wergeld of the accused to the lord entitled to fines incurred by him.

[48] MGH *Legum*, Sectio ii.1, *Capitularia Regum Francorum*, ed. A. Boretius (Hanover, 1883) 9; MGH *Legum*, Sectio ii.2, *Capitularia Regum Francorum*, ed. A. Boretius and V. Krause (Hanover, 1897) 277f; I Edg. 2, II Cnut 20 (Robertson, *Laws*, 16, 184); cf. I Edm. 7.1, I Atr 1 (Robertson, *Laws*, 10, 52) for sureties for the good behaviour of accused men; perhaps the *gorfodog* of late medieval Wales should be viewed in the same light, Ior 68/17, 70. In fact two of the sureties named in the Anau case (CR 202) were machtierns; however, the case is not comparable to the European examples cited here — even if it were argued that machtierns were representatives of state — since there are two of them, they are not called machtierns in the record and are not cited as leaders; they appear to have been involved by one of the parties to the agreement and not to have acted in any official capacity.

[49] Even where legal tracts from other parts of Europe suggest that payment was the norm, practice often involved more distraint than payment; this is well-evidenced in Lombard Italy. Despite the legislation of Rothari and Liutprand (see above nn. 37 and 39), *fideiussores* in one case of 761 gave a house (from the property of the accused) to the accuser because the pledge could not be found; *Il Regesto di Farfa*, ed. I. Georgi and U. Balzani (5 vols., Rome, 1879-1914) ii. docs.44, 45, pp.51f. (I am grateful to Chris Wickham for making this point to me with some force.)

THE GENERAL FEATURES OF ARCHAIC EUROPEAN SURETYSHIP

D. B. WALTERS

I. INTRODUCTION

Put simply, and therefore somewhat imprecisely, a surety is a person whose participation in an agreement or transaction between others (who for the present may be called the principals) is intended to make sure what would otherwise be unsure. The idea is found widely in the law both of 'archaic' and 'developed' societies, that is, in societies where the observance of law is for the most part voluntary and its enforcement dependant on individual or collective self-help, and in those where the observance of law and the regulation of the means for its enforcement lie in impartial hands which any aggrieved person can invoke.[1] Of course the contrast is incomplete; there is evidence of external law enforcement in early European law,[2] and some developed legal systems leave the business of enforcing civil (though not criminal) judgments very much to the interested party.

This essay will be largely concerned with matters of analysis and classification, and with the answers which have been suggested to the following questions raised by the surviving references to suretyship in archaic law: How did the need for suretyship and other forms of security arise? What were its forms? How did the existence of a surety help a creditor to get satisfaction, and its corollary, what happened to the surety if satisfaction was not forthcoming? These questions have provoked an extensive literature[3] and little more than a summary can be offered here. Professor Binchy's paper 'Celtic Suretyship, a fossilized Indo-European institution?' first published in 1970[4] provides a useful starting-point for those for whom this is uncharted territory.

Although it is anachronistic to describe the archaic law of suretyship in the language of developed law, it is well-nigh inescapable if endless circumlocution is to be avoided. There are in any case respectable precedents for doing so.[5] We may call the apparent principals, as we would the parties to any contract[6] *debtor* and *creditor*, *promisor* and *promisee* or *obligor* and *obligee*, and it is convenient to keep to the first pair. But the legal significance of these words, like the debt which is their subject,[7] is wider than is generally given them in everyday life. *Debt* is not restricted to notions of money or its equivalent, but includes the sense of 'anything that can be owed' including services, behaviour of a stated kind, the production of a person, immunity and so on, as well as the more obvious sense of the duty to transfer something with a money value, or the units in which that value is calculated, money itself. The fulfilment of the debtor's promise, irrespective for the moment of who fulfils it, may also be called *payment* or *performance* whatever the subject-matter.

In developed law a surety is a species of the genus *security*, a legal institution which employs things and rights as well as persons to secure the performance of an obligation on which a principal (the debtor) defaults. Modern security is thus essentially collateral or ancillary to some other principal obligation.[8] In archaic law it is not so; the 'absence of any public enforcement of private engagements',[9] like the general absence of 'credit'[10] in the sense of a promise of future performance in return for a present benefit conferred on the debtor (the executory contract of modern law), made the participation of sureties essential to the formation of agreements which gave rise to 'debt' (a term which is discussed below[11]) as well as to the performance of other acts.[12] The archaic surety was for long central to the agreements in which he appeared, whereas his modern counterpart is peripheral. In both legal orders, however, archaic or developed, the function of suretyship or indeed of any species of security may be stated in general terms to be to ensure or secure the fulfilment or performance of expectations arising out of someone's undertaking to transfer something, to do some act, or to refrain from some action (*dare*, *facere*, *non facere*)[13] for the benefit of some other or others. How, when, by whom and with what this performance is to be achieved, whether distinctly from performance by the debtor or alternatively to his default, and whether with his co-operation or against his will are among the matters which vary considerably and which call for discussion. Three simplified illustrations from developed law may make the possible forms of security clearer:

(1) I wish to borrow from you. You are willing to lend, on terms favourable to yourself, if, in addition to proof of my solvency and my promise to repay, I furnish you with security. Then if I default, you have a choice. You may sue me on my promise, or resort to the security and directly or indirectly satisfy your claim out of that, either specifically or equivalently.[14]

(2) I wish to sue or appeal against a judgment. In certain cases the court will only grant me leave to bring the action or appeal if I provide security for the costs I will incur if I lose.

(3) I am charged with having committed a serious crime by a peace officer with power to have me promptly detained. I wish to remain at liberty until my trial or until the prosecution is abandoned. In certain

circumstances I can obtain temporary freedom if I can find bail, that is, sureties to answer for my appearance in court at the start of the trial and who forfeit the sums they offer as security if they fail to produce me.[15] In the first and second cases the security may be *personal* in the shape of sureties or *real* in the shape of property (or rights to property), convertible into money if necessary. In the third case *bail* is strictly a synonym for sureties, although it also is used of, firstly, the sum to be forfeited if the accused fails to 'surrender to his bail', i.e. to the sureties who have bound themselves to produce him in court if he does not appear voluntarily, and secondly, the fact of thus being at liberty, 'on bail'; the accused is 'admitted to bail' i.e. delivered into the custody not of the State but of his bail, his sureties. Despite the survival in some common-law jurisdictions of the phrase in the bail-bond that the bail are bound 'body for body' with the accused,[16] in fact neither in this nor any other case of suretyship in developed law is any surety at risk as to liberty or life, but only as to fortune[17], unlike the hostage and self-surety of archaic law.[18] To that extent all modern security is resolvable, directly or indirectly, into money.

It is possible that the emergence of suretyship marks an important addition to the forms of archaic social solidarity. If we take the chief of these to have been the reciprocal relationships created by kinship, alliance by marriage and clientship, the possibility of entering into binding legal relations with a person who was not a kinsman, ally by marriage, lord or fellow-client must have been enhanced by the 'security' which suretyship afforded. An example of the second is given by the late Anglo-Saxon tract on marriage *Be wifmannes beweddunge*,[19] where sureties and gages were required from the groom firstly for his suitable maintenance of his wife, secondly for the repayment of her rearing-fee and thirdly for three marriage prestations — something akin to morning-gift, dower, and to ensure the division of their common property: 'he is to strengthen all that he promises with gage and his friends (or: kinsmen) are to stand surety for it'.[20]

II.1 DEBT AND LIABILITY (SCHULD UND HAFTUNG)

A century and less ago, studies in the texts of early Germanic law led some writers[21] to draw conclusions about the nature and location of debt and liability arising from those legal relationships we call obligations.

In any obligation there are a number of ingredients, the chief of which these writers identified as follows:

(i) a *legal duty*, i.e. something which ought to be done, defined by law and laid on the person (the debtor): it may arise from a wrong done to another (the creditor), e.g. by harming his body, or from a promise. Until the duty has been discharged, the creditor is left with an unsatisfied claim for redress against the debtor;

(ii) *liability* for that wrong or failure to keep a promise, so that it can only be put right by recourse on the creditor's part to something or someone burdened with that liability;

(iii) the expectation of *performance*, specifically or equivalently according to its nature, of the legal duty in favour of the creditor. This expectation may be satisfied either (a) voluntarily, by the debtor or on his behalf, or (b) involuntarily, by appropriation or realisation of the thing or person bearing liability;[22] and

(iv) a duty on the creditor's part to *accept performance* when made in accordance with the agreement (a duty which is reciprocal to the debtor's), including the duty to refrain from doing anything which might frustrate performance.[23]

The German technical terms are *Schuld* (wrong, debt, duty) for the duty owed in (i) and (iv), both debtor and creditor being called *Schuldner;*[24] *Haftung* (being bound, obliged, liable) for the liability in (ii); *Leistung* for performance in (iii) and (iv) and *Forderung* for the creditor's demand for performance as in (iii).

Gierke and his predecessors argued that in early society generally, *Schuld* and *Haftung* were so distinct that the *Schuldner* owed the debt but was not liable for it and the *Hafter* bore the liability but did not owe the debt. The *Haftung* might be borne by some *thing* given by or for the debtor to the creditor (or seized or detained by him, according to the circumstances) and held by or for him. This thing might be a forfeitable real security, *Pfand,*[25] consisting of an item of property equal to or exceeding the value of the debt, or it might be a human gage,[26] the body of a person taken by or given as hostage to the creditor. Alternatively, again as dictated by the circumstances, the *Haftung* might be borne by a person, not in the creditor's hands, whose status *vis-à-vis* both creditor and debtor was such that the creditor trusted him[27] to secure performance specifically or equivalently. *Haftung* is then seen to be nothing other than security; and personal security is suretyship, *Bürgschaft:*[28] the *Hafter* is a *Bürge*. Leaving aside *Pfand* for the moment, the person whose detention is intended to compel performance of the debt is called in Germanic law *Geisel*, hostage, and his liability-suretyship, *Geiselschaft* or *Geiselbürgschaft.*[29] The person whose status convinces the creditor of his ability to compel performance by or for the debtor may be regarded as the debtor's supervisor, *Auf-* or *Vor-steher*, i.e. someone to enforce (*durchsetzen, erzwingen*) performance by using his status to influence (*einwirken, beeinflussen*) the debtor. He is thus a surety for performance (*Leistung*) by or for the debtor and his suretyship is *Leistungsbürgschaft;*[30] if that performance consists of the debtor's appearance (*Gestellung*) in some legal act or process, it is called *Gestellungsbürgschaft*. The *Geisel* would normally be a dependant and inferior of the debtor,[31] but the *Leistungsbürge* would be his superior or, among the higher social classes, possibly his peer.[32] These two forms might be found at the same epoch; the surety who pays if the debtor defaults (*Zahlbürge* or *Zahlungsbürge*, the ordinary collateral surety of modern law[33]) appears to be a later development, also found with the other forms, but eventually replacing both.

An early illustration of suretyship for performance and for payment being offered in the alternative is provided by an episode, a story within a story, in the eighth book of the *Odyssey*. To entertain Odysseus, the bard Demodocus sang of Ares' adultery with Aphrodite, the wife of Hephaestus. Suspicious of their affair, Hephaestus made a metal net in his smithy and, having suspended it over his bed like a tester, trapped the lovers in *flagrante delicto*. Calling in his fellow-gods to witness his cuckoldom, he demanded the return of Aphrodite's bride-price which he had paid to her father Zeus. The gods' mirth at the spectacle was brought to an end by Poseidon, who urged Hephaestus to free Ares:

'Unloose him, and I promise you that he himself shall compensate you, as you require, in the presence of the immortal gods.'

Hephaestus demurred at Poseidon's offer, saying that to have in hand[34] a surety for an untrustworthy debtor was of little value, adding, how in any case could the penalty of being publicly bound be imposed on a god like Poseidon, if it turned out that Ares escaped the debt as well as the net? (The net that had enmeshed Ares would, as it were, be used to bind Poseidon.) Poseidon then offered an alternative suretyship:

'Hephaestus, if Ares indeed fails to pay and makes off, I will pay you myself'.

To this Hephaestus consented, and sprang the trap.[35] In this illustration, the surety for another's performance vowed more than his honour, since in theory he was liable to be bound, physically not metaphysically, if the debtor defaulted. (We shall consider Poseidon's second offer, payment, in section IV.)

The dichotomy between *Schuld* and *Haftung* is exposed most clearly when real as well as personal security is considered. Only a person can be said to owe a duty, but a thing, real security, (including the person of any *Geisel*, hostage-surety) can be given or taken into the creditor's hands[36] and *bound*, subjected to the power of the creditor in a way that the debtor, not in the creditor's hands, is not (save in the special form of self-suretyship, *Selbstverknechtung*, discussed in the next section.)[37] Words commonly used in archaic law for liability have the primary meaning of being literally bound, e.g. *obligare* (and its resolution *solvere*), *nestigan*,[38] *haften*, just as in English the modern use of *bind*, *be bound* (and their resolution in *release*, *be released*) of duties legal and moral reminds us of the original form of the liability, since the literal sense will precede the metaphorical. One is led to assume that *Geiselschaft*, hostage-suretyship and *Pfand*, moveable real security, were once not only imperfectly differentiated, since the hostage was 'an animated gage' but, perhaps along with debtor-bondage, *Selbstverknechtung*, were the earliest forms of security and if so, the argument in favour of the separate identification of *Schuld* and *Haftung*, at least at this early stage, is a strong one. Certainly the two ideas can be usefully distinguished for purposes of legal analysis, at any epoch.[39]

The distinction between *Schuld* and *Haftung* may be illustrated by reference (1) to a wrong which ought to be put right by a payment in money or kind and (2) to a duty owed as the result of an undertaking or agreement — in the language of developed law, by reference to delict or tort and to contract.

(1) It has been suggested[40] that perhaps the earliest example of a duty (*Schuld*) being owed according to law was payment of compensation to compose the blood-feud, following murder or other outrage. The debtor (which includes the murderer or other wrongdoer and those of his kin who ought, according to law, to share in making the payment) owes this sum to the creditor, i.e. to those of the murdered person's kin entitled to receive it, including the victim in outrages short of murder.[41] But in the nature of things the creditor may not be able to enforce his claim against the debtor specifically, although the law says that the debtor should pay and that the creditor should not resort to the feud.[42] Any performance by the debtor will be voluntary and if he does not pay he cannot be made to pay. Perhaps he simply cannot. In societies where only certain members enjoy legal capacity (heads of kindred, *patresfamiliarum*) liability might only attach to them, not to those in their power, their *munt* or *manus*. If so, although the wrongdoer incurs the debt, its discharge lies with or through another. Perhaps he is a head of kindred but refuses to pay; it may be that nothing happens because he is too powerful. His refusal may lead to outlawry, which affects his property as well as his person. In that case the creditor might have recourse to the property, just as he might seize the debtor's person if he dare, or slay him. Much depends on the relative strength of the parties, and it is easy to see how a bold creditor might tire of waiting for compensation and, short of raising the feud, seize the debtor's property or dependants instead of having him outlawed, in the hope of coercing him to perform. The fragility of legal institutions where law enforcement is a matter of self-help is obvious

in such cases, as the Icelandic Saga literature shows.[43] If the debtor absconds or is outlawed, leaving nothing and no-one against which the creditor can proceed, then no-one has *Haftung* and the creditor is unsatisfied,[44] just like a modern judgment-creditor whose insolvent debtor 'disappears'. What is sought by the creditor is immediate and enforceable liability, not moral liability: having established an 'ought', *das Sollen*, he seeks the corresponding 'is', *das Sein*.[45]

(2) In the previous example the force of *Schuld* was 'duty arising from wrong, breach of the law'.[46] Let us now consider cases which are, in modern terms, contractual, i.e. based on an undertaking given by the debtor to the creditor or on an agreement between them. Even in those archaic societies which may not have admitted the possibility of credit, i.e. which may not have recognised enforceable promises of future payments in return for present benefits, voluntary indebtedness might still have arisen. Thus in the previous example the debtor might have been willing to compose the feud but he and his kindred might have needed time to raise the sum due.[47] Or, because of some disaster, a man might have lost his livelihood, and sought food in time of famine or because he had been driven from his home by invaders, and found someone willing to relieve his need.[48] In these cases, for the victim's kin to agree to a postponement of the payment, or for the wealthy man to relieve the other's need against the expectation of future payment, would give rise to *Schuld* without *Haftung*, for the same reasons as before: there would be no way to enforce the debt specifically against the non-solvent or recalcitrant debtor. Now although traditions of hospitality or of religious or moral precept may work powerfully to constrain those with the means to relieve the urgent needs of others, permanent and unreciprocated generosity tends to depress the status of the recipient.[49] These considerations apart, the victim's kin or the wealthy man would only be likely to agree to postpone performance of the debt in return for some present security which would thus bear liability for that performance. The debtor must therefore furnish the creditor with security, some thing either of such value in the eyes of the creditor that he can recoup the debt by appropriating or realising it, or of such value to the debtor that he will do all in his power to discharge the debt and redeem it rather than forfeit it. The respective estimates of the security's value in the eyes of creditor and debtor may well coincide.

Using the categories of developed law we may be tempted to say that the security in question is either *real* (a *res* or thing): a gage (*Pfand, pignus, fiducia cum creditore contracta, vadium*, etc.)[50] or *personal* (consisting of belief, 'credit', in the promise of someone other than the principal debtor). But where security takes the form of a hostage (*Geisel, obses, obstagium,* etc.)[51] this distinction is not valid, as the terminology employed shows.[52] In true hostageship, where the person was bound or confined (as opposed to being a debtor-bondsman working off his own debt: see section II.3 below), the hostage was a *res* and the security he represented to the creditor was real, not personal.[53]

According to the German theory which we have been considering, the giving and accepting of security is a distinct transaction entered into at the time the debt is incurred. Such a real or personal security passes in to the power of the creditor and bears the liability created by the debt. It does so in two stages: up to the time for performance its retention by the creditor is intended to coerce the debtor to perform, and when that time expires, the debt being unpaid, the security is forfeited to the creditor, who appropriates or otherwise realises it, in order to satisfy what is due if he can. His risk of loss is thus minimised.[54] He cannot compel the debtor to perform his undertaking specifically, but as he already holds a security, he can obtain an equivalence.[55] We cannot say, as in modern law, that the creditor has a choice of remedies, to sue the debtor or enforce the security: he is limited to the latter if the debtor does not voluntarily perform. The proposition is that a secured transaction gives rise to parallel legal relationships, one between the debtor and the creditor creating the unenforceable *Schuld* and the other between the creditor and the security (person or thing) which bears the liability, the *Haftung*, but which only does so because of the existence of the *Schuld.*[56]

At a later stage of legal development, the giving of real security may become formalised and symbolic[57] and personal security takes additional forms besides (and later instead of) hostageship. In more developed law, the supporters of this theory agree, *Schuld* and *Haftung* are normally united in the person of the debtor.[58]

The theory that *Haftung* was originally distinct from *Schuld* and vested in someone other than the debtor can be tested by examining voluntary suretyship in Celtic law,[59] which Gierke and his predecessors ignored. To find where liability lay, we may ask what befell the surety who evaded or neglected his office, what befell him if despite his efforts the debtor defaulted, and whether a defaulting debtor had to compensate a surety called on to act on his account.

In Irish law there are three principal types of surety (leaving aside for the moment the hostage-surety used to secure obligations between kingdoms, the *giall*). The *macc* or *naidm* was an enforcing surety. He is said to have three functions: he witnesses[60] the terms of the transaction and its progress towards performance or evasion; he swears that the debtor will perform;

and, as *naidm* 'binding' signifies,[61] he binds the debtor to performance, using all necessary force, once he is aware of defaults (BA 30, 43, 44).[62] Professor Binchy argues that his status is noble, enabling him to coerce a debtor, and that his office derives from a society still in 'the infancy of political organisation'.[63] But he does not assume personal liability: what he puts at risk is his 'face' or honour.[64]

Aitire (literally 'betweenship') is sometimes a generic term for surety, but it is also used for a hostage-surety who has to surrender to the creditor if the debtor defaults (BA 65f). That his liability to fall into the creditor's hands is postponed until default marks him off from the *gíall* 'hostage', and shows that credit is involved.[65] The creditor requires the *aitire* to swear that, if the debtor defaults, he will surrender himself to the creditor: 'you will be ready [and] willing to put your foot in a fetter [and] your neck in a chain [and] to remain in the stocks or in prison until you are released from it by debt-payments [by the debtor], or until you can give a gage for yourself after the forfeiture [period]' (BA 65f). Once he has remained in detention for ten days, he may ransom himself by payment of the sum by which an ordinary captive may be ransomed. He may then enforce on the debtor his own, now very heavy, compensation as well as compelling him to discharge the original debt.[66]

The paying-surety, the *ráth*, acts in conjunction with one or more *naidm*-sureties.[67] He also exchanges *naidm*-sureties with the debtor, guaranteeing to discharge his office and receiving security that the debtor would indemnify him for any loss (BA 74).[68] His liability can arise in two stages: (1) if the debtor can not pay as stipulated, the *ráth* can pay immediately, but he may also give a gage to guarantee later payment (BA 63). If the debtor still does not pay, the *ráth* has to pay himself, on pain of forfeiting his gage. The debtor then owes heavy compensation to the *ráth* (BA 71).

According to Professor Binchy, however, this complex system had only recently evolved by the date of BA (i.e. *c.* 700).[69] According to him, there were two earlier stages:

(1) there are two forms of security, the *naidm* and the *gíall*, enforcing-surety and hostage;

(2) the *gíall* splits into two, the *gíall* for public obligations and the *aitire* for private ones;

(3) the *aitire* in turn splits into two, the *aitire* himself taking on the specialized role of guarantor of inter-tribal treaties and leaving the securing of private contracts to the *ráth*, a paying-surety.

Whatever the truth of this theory, it is clear that the strategy underlying Irish suretyship at the time of BA is to separate the function of discharging the debt from that of enforcing it. The security of the creditor consists in the probability that either (1) the primary *naidm* will compel the debtor to pay or (2) the *naidm* who secures the *ráth*'s obligation will compel the latter to pay. Both the debtor and the *ráth* have a *naidm* standing behind them. The ultimate liability, however, is that of the debtor, since the *ráth* can, again with the help of a *naidm*, compel the debtor to compensate him for any loss he has incurred on the other's behalf. If all goes according to plan, the debtor will pay in the end, either to the creditor or to the *ráth*. Of the theory that where there is a surety, the debtor owes but is not liable, there is no sign. The early Irish evidence, therefore, tells against Gierke's theory.[70]

II.2 ENFORCEMENT OF OBLIGATIONS

The distinction between the ideas of debt and liability is useful even if their primitive location in separate persons is unproved.[71] If no security was given when the debt arose (as in the illustration of the bloodfeud) the person or the property of the debtor might, as in Irish law, be saddled with liability against his will. Frankish law illustrates this in *Pactus Legis Salicae, c.*50,[72] where the unsatisfied creditor denounces the defaulting debtor to a public officer, to have him 'bound'[73] and ordered not to pay any other debt until the one in issue is discharged. The procedure for renewing the demands for the debt and the imposition of additional penalties for its refusal, is then set out. For present purposes the central element is revealed when the creditor, having been refused payment at the local assembly, takes his claim before the *Grafio*, relates the proceedings to date and says:

> ego super me et \<super\> furtunam meam pono quod \<tu\> securus mitte in furtunam suam manum

Assisted by seven *rachinburgi*, elders familiar with the law,[74] the *Grafio* makes a final appeal to the debtor at his house to pay or have an appraisal made by two of the *rachinburgi*; but if he refuses or is absent, then

> rachineburgii adpretiatum pretium quantum valuerit debitus, quod debet, hoc de furtuna illius tollant

i.e. they appraise and distrain to the value of the debt. Not only is this an example of involuntary security; it owes its authorisation in part to the creditor's promise, his *fides facta*,[75] that he gages his own fortune as security for the legitimacy of his claim. Maitland noted the popularity of the *fides facta* with the Church, since it seemed innocent of obvious pagan associations.[76]

II.3 SELF-SURETYSHIP AND DEBT-BONDAGE[77]

The conjunction of debt and liability in the person of the unsecured debtor is not only the norm in developed law. In archaic law too, in addition to any right the creditor might have to distrain against the debtor's movable property, it is found in those cases where a man has nothing to offer a prospective creditor by way of security, not even a dependant. In such a case he offered himself. If the theory of von Amira and Gierke is right, self-suretyship must be later than hostage-suretyship and real security, since it represents an enhanced risk to the creditor, justifiable perhaps only in the context of the economic advantage its successful achievement would give the creditor. Obviously it represents a last resort for both parties. The debtor passes into the power of the creditor, usually, it must be assumed, to work off the debt by labour as a bondsman, whereas the hostage-surety might be passive and the subject fettered in those cases where his detention was designed to coerce the debtor into prompt performance. A passive self-surety in the creditor's hands is worth little — indeed, he is a charge on the creditor: *Geiselmahl, köstliches Mahl*,[78] 'A hostage's meal is a banquet'. If he cannot or may not work off his debt, the debtor's only hope is that some magnanimous person will ransom him, a duty proclaimed in Jewish law and a cornerstone of the Christian doctrine of the Redemption.[79]

M. I. Finley introduced his paper 'Debt-bondage and the problem of slavery'[80] with the story of how Herakles, suffering from a disease, consulted the Delphic oracle and learned that his sickness was a punishment for a treacherous murder. He was told that he would only be cured if he had himself sold into labour-bondage for a period in return for a price which he was to give to his victim's kin. He was then sold to Omphale, the Lydian queen, and purged his guilt in her service.[81] The story raises many questions, but it depicts an institution by which a man's labour could be given or demanded, not only under a contract of employment but by total, if temporary, surrender of the labourer. If the price could be paid by the creditor at the outset, as in the story, so too could bondage be entered into to satisfy a debt previously incurred, as Finley demonstrates elsewhere.[82] The earliest allusion to the story of Herakles is in the *Agamemnon* of Aeschylus (mid 5th cent. BC),[83] but some time in the first quarter of the sixth century BC,[84] Solon had introduced drastic reforms in the face of crushing indebtedness and consequential political unrest. Those needing credit who had property had gaged it, those without had pledged their bodies; and the latter were sold into slavery if they defaulted. Solon ordered the cancellation of all debts, the removal of the stones, ὅροι[85] which were placed on lands subject to debt, the ransom of debt-bondsmen and the prohibition of such loans on the body for the future, in an ordinance called the σεισάχθεια, 'the shaking-off of burdens'.[86] Whatever its long-term effects, which are disputed, it shows how widespread the problem of secured but irredeemable debt had become in sixth century BC Athens.[87]

The possible transition from the debt-bondage of a man who is his own surety to 'true obligation by way of self-guarantee' was discussed by de Zulueta in his commentary on the *Institutes* of Gaius[88] in a speculative note:

> The starting-point is that a man needing credit — it may be a loan, or time in which to find the ransom from some vengeance threatened on account of his wrongdoing — and not being able to obtain it on his mere promise, which would be unenforceable, gets a friend or kinsman to give himself as a bondsman to the creditor. The bondsman (*nexus*) will owe no debt; he will simply be a hostage. The debtor will not be *nexus*, but to release the hostage by duly meeting the debt will be both his right against the creditor and his duty to the hostage. In describing this situation it is convenient to use the Germanistic terms *Schuld* for the debtor's unenforceable duty to the creditor and *Haftung* for the engagement of the hostage, but it must be borne in mind that while *obligatio* in its basic sense fairly corresponds to *Haftung*, there is no Latin equivalent for *Schuld*, and if no Latin term, no clear Roman concept.[89]

The *nexus* was not, in historical times, a passive hostage for a debtor. He was a freeman who became indebted[90] and surrendered himself to his creditor to work off the debt by his labour, regaining his liberty when the debt was paid: *liber qui suas operas in servitutem pro pecunia quam debebat, dum solveret, nexus vocatur.*[91] There were however other early Roman debtors who became their creditors' fettered captives, *addicti* and *iudicati*,[92] whose fate was death or sale into slavery *trans Tiberim* if their debts were not paid within sixty days' imprisonment; thus active debt-bondage and passive bondage were both encountered. The *Lex Poetilia*, *c.* 313 BC,[93] by restricting fetters to offenders and prohibiting any debtor for a loan to be *nexus* in future, ordering the release of all existing *nexi*, is very close in spirit to Solon's reforms nearly three centuries earlier. The varieties of debt-bondsmen in the world of antiquity[94] form a subject apart, however, which cannot be pursued further here.

II.4 OTHER DEVELOPMENTS

We have already seen that suretyship might be potential, as with the Irish *aitire*. In the Genesis story, Judah offered to stand surety to Jacob for the safe return of Benjamin from Egypt, under pain of perpetual dishonour should he fail.[95] Archaic society recognised such promises given by the honourable, together with a form of what we might fairly call political hostageship: confinement to quarters of a person or his household as surety for the payment of a debt or the appearance of persons (*Einlager*[96]). The rules concerning the exchange of foster-children or ambassadors are not without this ingredient, so that each family, each State, might be surety for the good treatment of the other. Another adaptation of potential hostageship is Frankpledge and its antecedents, where inferior members of society stood in mutual suretyship, not always voluntary, for the good conduct of their fellows.[97]

III. SURETIES FOR PERFORMANCE, INCLUDING APPEARANCE: LEISTUNGSBÜRGEN AND GESTELLUNGSBÜRGEN

The suretyship where liberty or property is not immediately exposed to the risk of forfeiture, but where instead the surety's honour is the creditor's security that the debtor will perform, was commonly employed for *Leistungsbürgschaft*, suretyship for performance, and its variant designed to secure the appearance of a person, *Gestellungsbürgschaft*.[98] In its aboriginal form *Leistungsbürgschaft* seems to have supposed the intervention between the principals of a person whose honour was so exalted that the creditor was willing to accept his promise, perhaps made by oath,[99] that the debtor would perform, the debtor being so overawed as to obey him.[100]

However, creditors must have found the sanction of the surety's dishonour no adequate substitute for equivalent performance if the debtor defaulted, and thus sought the power to obtain redress from the surety, as the Homeric extract above illustrates. In time the surety came, in Binchy's phrase, 'to enforce, by all means available to him...including the use of violence' performance by the debtor and those means included taking hostages or gages for it or distraining upon default. The papyrus document cited below illustrates such double security. Obviously by this stage the debtor is *liable* for the debt he *owes: Haftung* and *Schuld* are united in his person because the surety is now an enforcer of the debtor's liability towards the original creditor.[101]

A number of names have been suggested for him: he is the 'influencing surety' (*le garant influent*,[102]) the 'reprisal-taking surety' (*Repressalienbürge*[103]) the 'enforcing surety' illustrated by Irish law,[104] the 'supervising surety' and, by reference to the object he promised to achieve, the 'surety for performance', *Leistungsbürge*, the term adopted here.[105]

Germanic law provides evidence of additions to the *Leistungsbürge's* honour as the force constraining the debtor to perform. He acquired the right to proceed against the debtor's person or property in order to coerce him,[106] but he also put his own person or property at risk to the claims of the creditor, either because he knew the creditor might proceed against him or it after the debtor's default or, at the time his suretyship was accepted by the creditor, by gaging his property or offering to surrender his person into the creditor's power or service.[107]

The developed form of *Geiselbürgschaft* called *Einlager* or *Leibbürgschaft*,[108] together with real security in the form of a gage given or distraint taken, seem to have been used in combination from an early stage of the development of *Leistungsbürgschaft*. Perhaps they were always combined with it save in those cases where the status of the *Leistungsbürge* was such that no additional security taken by him or for him was thinkable.

The *mach* of Welsh law in Ior, who is an enforcing surety, is fully discussed elswhere.[109] In the other Welsh traditions, Cyfn, Bleg etc. he has become a paying surety, though with some signs of the earlier role of enforcement. However, a surety for appearance in court (*Gestellungsbürge*) is referred to in Ior 67/4; and it is recognised that the *gorfodog* or bail, who is said to be truly liable 'body for body' ('for every *cerydd*, charge, to which the wrongdoer is exposed': a wrongdoer whom the text takes to have committed homicide), may himself take sureties from the wrongdoer *ar ei amrygoll*, for the risk he runs of total ruin (Ior 70/2,3).

Medieval Welsh literature provides clear examples of various kinds of suretyship. In the First Branch of the *Mabinogi*, where Pwyll and Gwawl are rivals for the hand of Rhiannon, Gwawl (despite his trickery) is worsted and trapped in a bag. He secures his release by agreeing to a series of stipulations. Rhiannon advises Pwyll:

'Thou are now in a position in which it is proper for thee to content suitors and minstrels. Leave Gwawl there to give to all in thy stead' said she, 'and take security from him (*a chymer gedernit* [mod. W. *cadernid*] *y ganthaw*) that he will never lay claim (*na bo ammouyn*) nor seek vengeance (*na dial*) for this. And that is punishment a-plenty for him. 'He shall have that gladly' answered the man out of the bag. 'And gladly will I accept it' said Pwyll 'by the counsel of Hefeydd and Rhiannon'. 'That is our counsel' said they. 'I accept it' said Pwyll; 'do thou [Gwawl] seek sureties for thyself' (*Keis ueicheu drossot*). 'We will answer for him' said Hefeydd 'until his men are free to answer for him'. And with that he was let out of the bag and his chief men were freed. 'Demand now sureties of Gwawl' (*Gouyn ueithon y Wawl weichau*) said Hefeydd, 'We know who should be taken from him.' Hefeydd listed the sureties (*Riuaw y meicheu a wnaeth Heueyd*). 'Do thou thyself draw up thy terms' (*dy ammot*) said Gwawl. 'I am content' (*Digawn yw gennyf i*) said Pwyll, 'even as Rhiannon drew them up'. The sureties went on those terms (*meicheu a aeth ar yr ammot hwnnw*). 'Aye, lord' said Gwawl, 'I am wounded and have received great bruises, and have need of a bath; and with thy permission (*gan dy gannyat ti*) I will go my way. And I will leave noblemen here in my stead to answer to all who shall make request of thee.' 'Gladly' said Pwyll. . .'[110]

Cadernid is used in the Welsh Laws of 'confirm by sureties' or 'by oath'.[111] In this episode sureties are provided for Gwawl's good conduct upon release including his renunciation of any claim to Rhiannon or to vengeance for the insult he has (no doubt justifiably) sustained, and for the performance of his promise to make the gifts on the occasion of the marriage of Pwyll and Rhiannon which Pwyll would otherwise have made to the wedding-guests.

IV. THE PAYING OR PERFORMING SURETY

If the *Leistungsbürge* came to put at risk not so much his honour as his person if the debtor defaulted, by active involvement in enforcing the debt, or by refusing to act unless first given rights against the debtor's property, by gage or distraint, it is a short step to make the substance of his promise the direct acceptance of liability, to be met out of his own property subject to indemnity by the debtor. So we come to the paying surety of developed law, the *Zahlungsbürge* in German terminology,[112] the collateral surety who is equally liable for the debt with the debtor but to whom the creditor looks only in the event of the debtor's default, like the Irish *ráth* and the *mach* of the non-Iorwerth texts in Welsh law.[113]

The acceptable suretyship which Poseidon offered Hephaestus is a paying suretyship, and it is significant that the two forms, enforcing and paying, were regarded as co-existing and alternative at that period. Before the complete emergence of negotiated credit as a commercial possibility, however, the creditor-lender will take additional security along with the surety's promise to pay in the event of the debtor's default. A good illustration is provided by a papyrus document, a bond of suretyship, dated AD 94 at Oxyrhynchus. It has three parties: Lucia, the borrower; Heraklides, the lender; and Serapion, who looks like a professional surety. In order to raise the loan Lucia had to give Heraklides a gage (ὑποθήκη) of her lands, substantially more valuable than the amount of the loan, as well as providing a paying surety in the person of Serapion. The document sets out the terms for the repayment of the loan with interest about two years later and identifies the land gaged. It also states that although Serapion stands surety for repayment by Lucia, she indemnifies him against any liability he might incur thereby. There then follow two conditions (very like a modern bond): (1) If Lucia defaults and Serapion is called on to honour his suretyship, paying off her debt, the lands Lucia gaged to Heraklides shall pass in perpetuity to Serapion (they would be released by Heraklides when Serapion paid off Lucia's debt) as if he had purchased them, and Lucia has to complete his title to them. (2) Any infringement of her promises by Lucia shall not only be invalid but shall render her immediately liable to a penalty of 1000 silver drachmae payable to Serapion and a like sum to the fisc, her original undertaking remaining in force and Serapion having a right of execution against Lucia personally, her gaged lands and other property —

large security for a two-year loan of 3500 drachmae at 1 per cent per month.[114]

It is common to find gage[115] combined with paying suretyship, as it is with *ráth* (BA 51a), though in Ior it is associated with an enforcing surety (Ior 62). Such combinations are understandable; the anxiety of creditors is not easily allayed and, in Plucknett's phrase, they like to assemble 'every contractual engine known to the law'[116] to reinforce their expectation of payment.

In some cases the supposed enforcing surety is really nothing more than a stakeholder, who holds the debtor's gage in the following transaction: the debtor, on assuming or acknowledging his debt, hands a gage to the creditor who passes it to a surety named by the debtor and acceptable to the creditor. If the debtor pays or performs, the surety returns the gage to him; if he defaults, the surety gives the gage to the creditor (or realises it for the creditor's benefit). Here the surety's role is reduced to a minimum.

In another transaction with both *wed* or gage and suretyship, the gage is symbolic: a staff or wand, a little stick or stalk of straw, the ring with a coin in a wedding (i.e. betrothal). Two main theories have been proposed about the staff or stick, one that it is an application to a suretyship contract of the formalities associated with the conveyance of land, in which the stick is the *festuca*;[117] the other, that it is the badge carried by a messenger as his authority for the debtor's and creditor's request that the person presented with the staff (*Stab, wadia*) should assume the function of surety between them.[118]

The proposition that the paying surety developed from the surety for performance or enforcement can be tested by reference to Welsh law. In Ior 62, if the debtor refuses payment, his *mach*, surety, takes an adequate gage from him (62/1,2). If necessary the creditor and surety take the gage together, but if the debtor resists, the surety is to 'receive the first blow' in any fight (62/3, cp.BA 44) or pay the debt himself. If this gage is not redeemed, it becomes forfeit to the creditor, the surety having thus taken it as part of his duty but on the creditor's behalf. This suggests an evolution from enforcing to paying suretyship in which the seizure of a gage or distress from the debtor for the creditor by the surety is an important element, with payment out of his own property by the surety only as a penalty for failure to enforce.[119] Paying suretyship presumably also replaced the security affected by symbolic *wed* or gage as such symbols were discarded under rationalist influences. The *fideiussio* of Roman law[120] and its Frankish imitations[121] represent an advanced state of this evolution. What distinguishes archaic from developed law in this respect is the widespread reliance of the former on suretyship to fence in obligations of all kinds, substantive and procedural,[122] in a society which did not command adequate impersonal means to hold men to their obligations.

V. CONCLUSION

Recent studies published by the *Société Jean Bodin pour l'histoire comparative des Institutions* illustrate the universality of the concepts and techniques discussed in this paper. In particular the analysis proposed by the Society's President, M. John Gilissen, in the essay prefaced to the last of the three volumes of the Society's *Recueils* devoted to this subject between 1969 and 1974[123] gives us a valuable means by which to classify any given type of suretyship. A summary of M. Gilissen's analysis is printed in the appendix below.

Despite its varied forms in time and place, and leaving aside divergent conceptual developments like the warranty of quality or title, all suretyship takes the general form of a third party's promise that the debtor will perform his promise, on pain of the surety forfeiting reputation, property or liberty, though subject to compensation from the debtor in the last two cases. If that looks like too energetic a wielding of Ockham's razor, we may say that two types of personal security have survived into the private law of the modern world from the legal orders of classical antiquity and medieval society. One is the procedural surety for appearance, who undertakes to produce his principal before a person exercising lawful authority, judicial or otherwise, on pain of forfeiting a sum of money or other property should he fail to produce him. The other is the substitute debtor surety. Having exacted a price from the debtor (an insurance premium), he either pays or performs what the defaulting debtor owes the creditor, in the majority of cases where personal performance by the debtor is not essential to the discharge of the obligation incurred; or he indemnifies the creditor in the event of the debtor's default by compensating him in those rarer cases where no-one but the debtor could have performed precisely what was promised.

APPENDIX

Summary of the analysis of personal security proposed by M. John Gilissen in his 'Esquisse d'une histoire comparée des sûretés personnelles', (1974) XXVIII *Recueils de la Société Jean Bodin*, 5-127 with some Celtic and other examples added.
Leaving aside his references to purely modern phenomena (certain forms of commercial corporation, State institutions with economic functions, and the like), the author distinguishes three variable and three invariable elements in suretyship. The proposed invariables are:
(1) There must be three parties (*garanti* or debtor, *bénéficiaire* or creditor and *garant* or surety).

(2) The surety must guarantee something for the creditor's benefit.
(3) What is guaranteed must be the usual subject-matter of contract (*dare, facere, non facere*).

The three variables are:

(1) Who guarantees, i.e. the identity of the surety and his position *vis-à-vis* creditor and debtor.
(2) How he guarantees.
(3) What he guarantees.

These variables may be elaborated:

(1) Who guarantees? It may be a single individual, or groups (kindred, villagers, all the clients or villeins or tenants of a given lord, etc.)
(2) How? The types of surety defined by role are suggested to be:
   (i)   The hostage, including detainee under house-arrest etc, (*le garant ôtage*),
   (ii) The influencing surety (*le garant influent*)
   (iii) The enforcing surety (*le garant exécuteur*), including the surety for appearance (*le garant de présence*).
   (iv) The indemnifying surety (*le garant de dédommageant*).
   (v)   The paying or performing surety (*le garant payant ou exécutant*).
(3) What? The surety guarantees on behalf of the debtor one or more of five things:
   (i)   The debtor's appearance (*présence*) (see 2 (iii) above).
   (ii) His integrity (i.e. the surety gives a 'character' or 'solvency reference').
   (iii) The quality or characteristics (cf. W. *teithi*) of some thing which is the subject of a contract (e.g. the covenant against eviction and for quiet enjoyment by seller to buyer).
   (iv) That the debtor will keep the peace (*obses pacis*, cf. Irish *gíall*).
   (v)   That a debt will be paid or a loan repaid, or returned specifically or equivalently.

The author then lists three ways in which suretyship and any associated real security may arise:

(1) *ex voluntate*, by agreement between the parties;
(2) *ex lege*, involuntarily i.e. by operation of law, as in the case of distress or other legally authorised execution against the person or property of a defaulter; or
(3) 'naturally' i.e. as a concomitant of the surety's membership of a group whose members stand surety for one another (e.g. a kinship group, a subject people, Frankpledge etc.).

The analysis is related to specific examples, either suggested by the contributors or provided by M. Gilissen.

---

[1] The distinction is therefore not dependent on universal chronology but on development within a given legal tradition: cf. PM i, 6. For anthropological comment see e.g. M. Gluckman, *Politics Law & Ritual in Tribal Society* (Oxford, 1965), 113 et sqq.; S. Roberts, *Order & Dispute: An Introduction to Legal Anthropology* (Harmondsworth, 1979), 26, 41 & cf. 39; E. A. Hoebel, *Law of Primitive Man* (Cambridge, Mass., 1961), passim.

[2] See e.g. the procedure given to recover a debt in PLS *c*. 50 (see below. p.95-6).

[3] See e.g. Appendix, 108-9, Bibliography and refs. at n. 21, etc.

[4] Binchy, 'Celtic Suretyship'; page references are given to the original version published in 1970 and (in brackets) to the reprint of 1972; and cf. Binchy, 'Distraint', 1973 esp. 32-3.

[5] 'There were *obligati* before there were *obligations*' Cuq, 1904, cited de Zulueta, *Gaius*, ii, 144 and n. 3; cf. Binchy, 'Celtic Suretyship', n. 4.

[6] In some contracts, e.g. loan, one party is debtor and the other creditor, at least as to the chief element (the thing lent). In an executory contract, i.e. as yet unperformed on at least one side, each party is creditor of the other's promise and each debtor to the other. See further Section II, esp. pp.95-6; Hübner, 68, 466-7.

[7] See Section II, below.

[8] For *obligation* as a legal bond (*vinculum iuris*) see below n. 38. In imitation of classical Roman Law (e.g. Gaius, *Institutes*, 3.88) the plural is the usual name for all acts, omissions and undertakings which give rise to some species of legally enforceable liability, and the Law of Obligations thus came to be one of the major divisions of private law.

[9] Binchy, 'Celtic Suretyship', 357 (362).

[10] See p.103.

[11] See pp.94-96.

[12] See D. Jenkins, 'Legal & Comparative Aspects of the Welsh Laws' (1963) *WHR* Special Welsh Laws Number, at 54-5; Binchy 'Celtic Suretyship', 355-60 (360-5).

[13] See Kaser, *RRP* §34.I (tr. 144); note the form *praestare* (<*praes stare*, stand surety for). RPR gives cross-references to the fuller treatment of topics in Kaser's *Das Römische Privatrecht* (RPR) 2nd edn. Munich, 2 vols, vol. i, 1971 (early, pre-classical & classical law), vol. ii, 1975 (post-classical developments).

[14] Specifically, i.e. by appropriating the security as it stands so that it becomes the property of the creditor, or equivalently, i.e. by realising the security (e.g. by way of exchange, or by sale including agreeing to its ransom), the creditor appropriating the thing exchanged or the price obtained.

[15] For other forms of bail in AN law (mainprise), see *replevina* etc. in Niermeyer, *Lexicon Minus*; for *replegiatio* etc. as in *Revised Medieval Latin Wordlist*, see PM ii, 584, 589-590 & Bracton ii, 391, 6th to 2nd line from foot, (fol. 139).

[16] See e.g. *Jacob's Law Dictionary*, s.v. bail, cited by Holmes, 197 n. 11 & cf. Binchy, 'Celtic Suretyship', n. 10.

[17] Binchy, 'Celtic Suretyship', 358 (364).

[18] See pp.96-99, 101, 104-105. For literary examples in Welsh custom see nn. 29, 115 and Section III, pp.105-106.

[19] Liebermann i, 442; transl. *English Historical Documents,* i 2nd edn. no. 130; text and trans., *Councils and Synods,* 1:1 (Oxford 1981), ed. D. Whitelock, M. Brett & C. N. L. Brooke, no. 58, 427-431.

[20] Trans. as in *Councils and Synods,* 1:1 (previous note), 430. For a parallel in the collective liability of the debtor's kin to suffer distraint in Irish law, see Binchy, 'Distraint', 1973, 33.

[21] See notably K. von Amira, *Obligationsrecht,* i and ii; Gierke esp. §2 (*Schuld*) 7ff; §3 (*Haftung*) 11 ff; Brunner, ii, §121, 684 ff, *das Betreibungsverfahren,* 'the pursuit of claims'. Among Romanists, see de Zulueta, *Gaius* ii, 142-6; Buckland, §CXLII at 406-7 and Kaser, RPR §39.I.1, (trans. 167).

[22] This leaves open the question of what happened if there were failure on the part of the supposed earliest form of *Leistungsbürge,* whose security was his divinity, honour, etc; cf. Section III, pp.104-106.

[23] See Hübner, 68. In contracts like those of employment (in civilian terminology *locatio conductio operarum* or *l.c operis faciendi* and later analogies) there will inevitably be a delay

between incurring a debt (to pay the price of goods made, etc. or wages for services rendered) and the time at which liability to pay arrives; see the discussion in Holmes, Lect. IX at 263.

[24] Similarly Old Irish *féchem* is both creditor and debtor in the modern sense: see BA 49. Modern German *Glaübiger* (creditor, i.e. the one who 'believes' or 'trusts' in the eventual performance of or for the debtor) is rarely used before 16th cent., Hübner 466-7. *Schuldner* is a late derivative of *Schuld*, which in turn is formed from the OHG verb *sculan*; cp. English 'shall' <OE *sceal*; *sollen*, earlier *solan*, *solen*, is in origin a by-form of *sculan*: see F. Kluge, *Etymologisches Wörterbuch der deutschen Sprache*, (20th edn., ed. W. Mitzka, Berlin, 1967), s.vv. *Schuld* and *sollen*.

[25] For *Pfand* (gage) see Gierke 4, and standard German authors cited in this paper, indices s.v., (the verb is *verpfänden*); *Pfändung*, (vb. *pfänden*) is distress, distraint (to distrain).

[26] See also section II.3.p.101 ff.

[27] For *Treue* and its compounds in the sense of 'trusted', 'relied upon' see Gierke c. 2 (§§11-15).

[28] The *Hafter* or *Bürge* do not owe the debt personally at this stage of legal development, according to the theory; Gierke, 58 & n. 33; Hübner, 470.

[29] *Geisel* is a possible borrowing from the Common Celtic word **gheistlos*> Irish *gíall* (for which see Binchy, CG, legal glossary s.v.), W. *gwystl*. A triad in Bleg (111.5-11) lists three women whose sons take their mothers' *tref*, the first being a woman given as a *gwystl* by her father and whose son is born during her *gwystloriaeth* (hostageship). For Welsh literary examples see PKM 72. 18-21 (*Math*: hostages secure a truce) and *Owein*, ed. R. L. Thomson (Dublin, 1975), 24, lines 652-7 (hostage-sureties, *gwystlyon*, offered by the earl to secure his own ransom). In Ior *gwystl* is used for gage: see e.g. Ior 62/1 etc., and T. M. Charles-Edwards' note, p.169 and cf. Ior 77/37. For *Pfand* etc. see n. 25 and the next para. in the text.

[30] See Kaser *RPR* 57.II. 1-2 (trans. 232-6) relating it in Roman law to the archaic *sponsio*; and cf. his *Das altrömische Ius* (Göttingen, 1949), §28 *Die sponsio*, esp. 262-7; Binchy, 'Celtic Suretyship', (361-62); Gierke 5; Planitz/Eckhardt, 220 (*Leistung am Dritte*); and s.v. *Bürgschaftsleistung* in other German authors. For *Geisel-* and *Gestellungsbürgschaft* see Conrad, i, 163 et sqq. & 422; Planitz/Eckhardt, 60.

[31] i.e. if given, not taken; in the latter case, the creditor seizes whom he can, whatever his rank.

[32] For the lord's obligations to his vassal sued by a stranger, see PM i, 306-7, and n. 1 at 307 for an illustration.

[33] *Zahl* — or *Zahlungsbürgschaft*; cf. mod. German *Schadloshaftung*, liability to indemnify, to 'make free from damage, harm' & *Zahlungsverbindlichkeit*, 'liability to pay'.

[34] Greek ἐγγύη means something put into the palm, ἐυ + γύαλον 'in the hollow' i.e. hand; cf. Irish *Gaib fort laim*, *Gait it laim*, 'Take on' or 'in [to] your hand', BA para. 51 a, b, c,; cf. Latin *manus*, Germ. *munt*. The double use of the net, to bind Ares or Poseidon, is suggested rather than expressed. The antithesis of l. 351 is difficult to reproduce in translation; speaking of the worthlessness of any (enforcing) surety for an untrustworthy debtor, Hephaestus says δειλαί τοι δειλῶν γε καὶ ἐγγύαι ἐγγυάασθαι. Homer attributed personal experience of going unpaid to Poseidon. In Iliad 21.435-60 Poseidon complained of Apollo's Trojan partisanship, although the pair of them had once been compelled by Zeus to work for the Trojan King Laomedon disguised as θῆτες, journeymen labourers with neither property nor kin and *adscripti glebae*, building Troy's walls and herding Laomedon's cattle. Laomedon defaulted and packed them off unpaid: cf. M. I. Finley, *The World of Odysseus* (2nd edn., London, 1978), 57.

[35] Odyssey 8.266-359; the passage quoted is 347-358. See generally A. Ehler, 'Die Bürgschaft Poseidons im 8 Gesange der Odysee' (1947) 65 *ZRG/RA* 312-9.

[36] See refs to *hand* in n. 34.

[37] And see e.g. Hübner, 470.

[38] In PLS c. 50, discussed below, p.95/96. For 'bind', *ligare* in *obligatio* as *iuris vinculum* see e.g. Buckland, cxl.III, 405-9; Kaser RPR 32 (trans. 135 ff).

[39] Gierke did not claim finality for the theory; op. cit., conclusion, 387-8.

[40] Hübner, 68, 459-460, 469-470: F. Pringsheim, *The Greek Law of Sale* (Weimar, 1950), 20; cf. PM ii, 450-1, Brunner, ii, 692 ff. (§123 *die Fehde*) and index s.v. *Busse* (composition).

[41] See e.g. J. M. Wallace-Hadrill, 'The Bloodfeud of the Franks' in *The Long-Haired Kings* (coll. essays, London, 1962, repr. 1982), 121 et sqq.

[42] E.g. the Lombard *Edictus Rothari*, cc. 45, 74; and cf. cc. 143, 162, 188, 190, 214.

[43] See P. Hallberg, *The Icelandic Saga*, trans. P. Schach (Lincoln, Nebraska, 1962), c. 8, esp. 104-08. Good examples are *Eyrbyggja Saga*, transl. H. Palsson and P. Edwards (Edinburgh, 1973), cc. 9-10 and 18-19. *Beowulf*, e.g. 1. 1384-85, emphasises vengeance for wrongs but only rarely mentions composition, e.g. 1. 2282.

[44] For *Schuld ohne Haftung* see Gierke, 98-99.

[45] For the connection between *sollen* and *Schuld* see n. 24.

[46] Hübner, 472; PM ii, 451; Wallace-Hadrill, 'The Bloodfeud of the Franks', 122-26.

[47] 'Credit' is agreed time to pay; cf. de Zulueta, *Gaius*, ii, 144, and Plucknett, 629.

[48] Consider the various suretyships arising in the story of Jacob and his children in Genesis 28-46:7: for debtor-bondage see Genesis 29:15-30, and below, section II. 3.

[49] M. Mauss, *The Gift* (trans. I. Cunningham, London, 1954), *passim*. It was Laban's offer of wages which prevented Jacob's subsequent labour for him amounting to a gift: Genesis 29:15.

[50] For med. Lat. words for a gage see Niermeyer, *Lexicon Minus*, esp. s.vv. *cautela*, *impignorare*, *inwadiamentum*, *pignorare*, *plevium*, *wadiare* etc.; for distraint see also s.vv. *districtus*, *distringere*, *diswadiare*, *namiare* ff. For Roman *fiducia cum creditore* see Buckland, §CLXVI, 473-76; Kaser, RPR §31.III (trans. 129-134). A good example of gage and surety where a gage is held until a surety be forthcoming is Charlemagne's *Capitulatio de Partibus Saxoniae* (MGH *Leges, Fontes iuris... in usum scholarum*, 4, *Leges Saxonum*, ed. C. von Schwerin, Hanover, 1918), c. 27.

[51] For med. Latin words for hostage-surety see Niermeyer, *Lexicon Minus*, s.vv. *obstaticare* etc., *reprensalia* and some of the terms listed in n. 50, esp. *plevius*. Charlemagne's *Capitulatio de Partibus Saxoniae*, c. 25, forbade Saxons to use human gages (hostage-sureties); cf. the *Divisio Regnorum* or *Imperii* of 806, c. 13 (trans. H. R. Loyn and J. Percival *The Reign of Charlemagne*, London, 1975, 94), on hostage-sureties transferred from one kingdom to another.

[52] Cf. reff. to Niermeyer in two previous nn. A good example is *vadii loco* for a person 'as gage', as in *Leges Henrici Primi*, c. 89.3, ed. L. J. Downer (Oxford, 1972), 278, who translates it as 'by way of pledge'. On the ambiguity of 'pledge' and 'gage' in English see above. p.10.

[53] *Real* and *personal* are used in two distinct ways in legal English: (1) they qualify the two species into which the law of property is divided, *real* meaning freehold land and certain associated rights, and *personal* meaning all other property (anomalously including leases of land). The distinction reflects the separate systems of succession on death which formerly prevailed, and exists (or existed) in many legal systems. (2) *Real* security, however, means some *res* furnished as security for debt, and *personal* security refers to the liability assumed by a *person* who promises to pay or perform if the debtor defaults. Since the hostage is delivered to the creditor and does not make any promise, his role is analogous to that of the gage and he can therefore be termed a real security. Similar distinctions and terminology are employed in other legal systems.

54 Minimised, not eliminated, because of the risk that the security might perish.

55 Cf. Hübner, 468, penultimate line.

56 See n. 21 and Hübner, 463, reff. at his n. 2.

57 See Niermeyer, *Lexicon Minus*, s.v. *wadiatio*, and p.353 below.

58 Gierke, §3.1 (p. 12), *Selb- & Unselbständig Haftung*; and see n. 39.

59 Some Irish suretyships were involuntary: BA 23, 24 (not discussed here); cf. Binchy, 'Distraint', 1973 for distraint in Irish Law, esp. 27-34, discussing Irish *athgabál*, Welsh *gafael*, *adafael (cynnogn)* and Breton *adgabael*. For Welsh Law see n. 70.

60 In technical terms, his witness was constitutive,*not just evidentiary, i.e. without him the transaction was invalid. See BA 43 and 58-63, esp. 58.3; cf. Ior 65/1-2.

61 Binchy, 'Celtic Suretyship', 360 (366); cf. BA 25, 84.

62 Binchy, 'Celtic Suretyship', 361 (367) and his n. 19.

63 Binchy, 'Celtic Suretyship', 361-62 (367-68).

64 cf. BA 35, 36, 66 (where *aitire* = surety in general); Binchy, 'Celtic Suretyship', 362 (368) and his n. 20.

65 See pp.94-96, 337.

66 See generally Binchy, 'Celtic Suretyship', 363-64 (369-71).

67 BA 74-77.

68 cf. the later Roman law rules (Glossary, s.v. *fideiussio*); and cf. Ior 62/12-13.

69 Binchy, 'Celtic Suretyship', 357-59 (362-64), 362-66 (368-72).

70 For the corresponding Welsh material see Robin Stacey's chapter and the commentary on Ior.

71 As it is, for example, by J. Yver, 'Les sûretés personelles en Normandie', (1971) 29 *Rec. Soc. Jean Bodin* 221-262 at 233, commenting on Gierke's *Schuld und Haftung*; cf. PM ii, 470 et sqq.

72 See *de fide(s) facta(s) PLS* cc. 50.1; 52.5; 56.1, 2, 6a; 57.2; 58.6; 112; 113; for *sub fidem habere* see Beyerle, 'Der Ursprung der Bürgschaft', 607; *Lex Ribuaria*, c. 58.21; *Edictus Rothari*, 360-63, where, following class. Latin, *sacramentum* is used for oath.

73 *Nestigan*, transl. *verstricken* by Eckhardt, i.e. 'entangle, ensnare, enmesh', and so 'bind' (literally or figuratively); cf. *obligare* (n. 38) and *haften* (section II. 1).

74 Cf. PLS c. 57.

75 Germ. *Treugelübde, Treugelöbnis*, 'vow of faith, by or on one's faith or trustworthiness'; cf. Hübner, 493 et sqq.

76 PM ii, 189, 197. The earliest recorded form of this *fides* was, however, a flamboyant and irrational oath: Tacitus, *Germania*, 24.4. For extra-judicial distress and distress following judgement, as in *PLS* c. 50, see Brunner, §§111 and 112 (584 et sqq.), and for the form *Strud* or *Raub*, ibid., 595, and Hübner, §69B (477 et sqq.). For *namium, namiare* see n. 50.

77 Debt-bondage includes the use of hostages who are not debtors, already discussed. See Gierke, 5.IV (65), Brunner, i, 141-42, 353-54, ii, §111(584 et sqq.) and §116, esp. 624-26.

78 Cited Hübner, 483, Gilissen, 57.

79 Debtor-redemption was recognised in Frankish law: *PLS* c. 58 (*de chrenecruda*), para. 6; if a killer or his kin cannot raise the sum to compose the feud and *si eum in compositione nullus ad fidem tulerit, hoc est ut eum redemat de <hoc> quod non persolsit, <tunc> de sua vita componat*: if no one vouches for him (by *fides facta*) to redeem him, since he has not paid, he pays with his life. Compare this with the provision to protect foreign merchant creditors in England under the statutes of Acton Burnell (1282) and of Merchants (1285): see T. F. T. Plucknett, *Legislation of Edward I* (Oxford, 1949), 138-43. Jewish law made the ransoming of native bondsmen etc. a duty (e.g. Leviticus, 25:35-55) and the prophets spoke constantly of Israel's redemption from captivity and, by analogy, from sin (e.g. Isaiah, cc. 36-48): see R. Yaron,

114   LAWYERS AND LAYMEN

'Redemption of Persons in the Ancient Near East', (1959) 6 *RIDA* 155-76, and E. Neufeld, *'Ius Redemptionis* in Ancient Hebrew Law', (1961) 8 *RIDA* 28-40. The New Testament employs this language (e.g. Galatians, 3:19-4:7.) applying it to the combined effect of the central mysteries of the Christian faith.

[80] c. 9 in the collection, *Economy and Society in Ancient Greece*, ed. B. D. Shaw and R. P. Saller (London, 1981).
[81] *Ibid.*, previous note; and cf. c. 7 in the same collection.
[82] Op. cit., c. 4.
[83] Op. cit., c. 7.
[84] About 594/3 BC, or possibly two decades later.
[85] For ὅροι see Finley, op. cit., c. 4 and his detailed treatment with texts in *Studies in Land and Credit in Ancient Athens, 500-200 BC* (New Brunswick, 1951, repr. 1973), *passim*.
[86] *Athenian Constitution*, cc. 2, 5-8, esp. c. 6.
[87] For the significance of Greek social habits and law for subsequent European legal history see e.g. K. R. Popper, *The Open Society and its Enemies* (4th edn., London, 1962), i, 171-75.
[88] De Zulueta, *Gaius*, ii, 143-45; the quotation is from 144.
[89] De Zulueta, *Gaius*, ii, 144. For the *fideiussor*, the paying surety of classical and later Roman law, see Glossary.
[90] Whether personally or by way of succession (see Livy's account of the circumstances in which L. *Poetilia, c.* 313 BC was introduced, discussed by G. MacCormack in (1973) 19 *Labeo*, 306 et sqq.). For *nexus* or *nexum* see Buckland §CL and Kaser RPR §39.I.1 (trans. 167 et sqq.).
[91] Varro (116-27 BC), *De Lingua Latina*, 7.105, cited by e.g. A. Watson, *Rome of the XII Tables — Persons and Property* (Princeton, 1975), c. 9 at 112-13.
[92] *Addicti* and *iudicati* were roughly speaking insolvent civil debtors and condemned criminals respectively. For *addicti* see M. I. Finley, *Ancient Slavery and Modern Ideology* (London, 1980), 143 and his n. 63 at 183; it later came to imply compulsory public labour by defaulting debtors, even though debt-bondage to the creditor had been abolished by L. *Poetilia*: see Buckland §§CCXI and CCXII (*manus iniectio*, the seizure of the defendant debtor etc.), 618-23; Kaser, RPR §81.III.
[93] See nn. 90-91 above.
[94] For which see Finley, op. cit. (as n. 80), c. 9, §III, for Greece, and Watson, op. cit. (as n. 91), 111, n. 1 and reff. for Rome. 'Sell' and 'buy' can mean 'transfer', 'acquire' in many archaic laws (Finley, op. cit.: Pringsheim, op. cit., as n. 40).
[95] Genesis 43:3-11.
[96] For *Einlager (Einquartierungspflicht)* see Brunner, ii, 307, Hübner, 482-83 and Planitz/Eckhardt, 223 (s.v. *Leibbürgschaft*, 'body suretyship').
[97] For Frankpledge and its forerunners see II Cnut c. 20 (Liebermann, i, 322), discussed e.g. in PM ii 529; W. A. Morris, *The Frankpledge System* (New York, 1910), 14-15; Plucknett 97; P. H. Sawyer, *From Roman Britain to Norman England* (London, 1978), 198-99; H. R. Loyn, *The Governance of Anglo-Saxon England, 500-1087* (London, 1984), 147; see also PM i, 564-65, 568-71 (the tithing), 580-81 (view of Frankpledge); for mainpast see PM i, 419, ii, 530-2.
[98] See Binchy, 'Celtic Suretyship', 356-57 (361-62); Brunner, i, 286 and n. 25. For the kinsman as the usual *Gestellungsbürge* see Planitz/Eckhardt, 60.
[99] An oath might be 'by the gods' or the natural elements (Binchy, 'Celtic Suretyship', 357 [362]) and later bind the oath-taker's honour, as does the *fides facta* (above 96, 101).
[100] There is a hint of hypocrisy in Hephaestus' deference in accepting Poseidon as paying-surety for Ares (above, 96): "It is neither allowable nor fitting to deny *your* request [that

I free Ares on such favourable terms]''; Od. 8. 358.

[101] As they are in debtor-bondage, above, 102.

[102] Gilissen, 61.

[103] W. Ogris, 'Die persönlichen Sicherheiten im Spätmittelalter', (1965) 82 ZRG/GA 140-89, part II, 4, 160-65; Repressalienbürgschaft is one of Ogris's eight categories; id., (1971) Rec. Soc. Jean Bodin, 19-20. The surety takes reprisals against the defaulting debtor before the creditor takes them against him.

[104] Binchy, 'Celtic Suretyship', 356-57 (361-62), 361-63 (367-69).

[105] See above, 95 and n. 30.

[106] Cf. PLS c. 50 (and above, 101).

[107] There are many variants: see Hübner, 479-85 and n. 96 above for Einlager, since in some of its forms the 'hostage' took service under the 'host'.

[108] See n. 96.

[109] See Robin Stacey, above, pp.19-21, and notes to Ior, esp. to para. 62.

[110] PKM 17.15-18.15; R. L. Thomson, Pwyll Pendeuic Dyuet (Dublin, 1957), 11. 391-422; the transl. is adapted from G. Jones and T. Jones, The Mabinogion (London, 1949, revised 1974), 16. Such peace-sureties are not discussed in the legal tractates on suretyship. On the general context of the passage see J. K. Bollard, 'The Structure of the Four Branches of the Mabinogi', (1974/75) THSC, 250-76, esp. 253-63, 271-74.

[111] Cadernid, 'confirmation, security', cf. the verb cadarnhau as in Bleg 125.4, in a triad saying that a summons is 'confirmed' inter alia by suretyship (mechniaeth); and cf. DwCol 244 and AL V.ii.20. In Ior 77/36 (cf. Col 502), which describes landsuit procedure, the judges are to 'take security', kemryt kedernyt, of the parties to abide by their judgement, yet to be delivered, and sureties (mach) from both sides for their fee. Ior 77/37 (cf. Col 502, second half) further says that after judgement in such cases, the king ('lord' Col) is to release the parties' gwystlon from their prison, a clear example of gwystl as hostage-surety; cf. n. 29.

[112] Zahl- or Zahlenbürge, 'paying-surety'; Schadlosbürge, 'indemnifying surety' (the first pays the debt specifically, the second makes good the debt in some other way): Binchy, 'Celtic Suretyship', 356 (361); Conrad, i, 422 and nn. at 426; Planitz/Eckhardt, 223-24; Gilissen, 67, 84.

[113] Above, pp.100-1 and nn. 67-70.

[114] A. S. Hunt and C. C. Edgar (eds.), Select Papyri (Loeb Class. Lib., London and Cambridge, Mass., 1932), no. 57, and cp. beneficium cedendarum actionum in Glossary s.v. fideiussio. Pringsheim (op. cit. as n. 40), 7-8, points out that these papyri record essentially Greek, not Roman law and Rhodian rather than Attic law, since Ptolemaic Egypt followed the law of Rhodes.

[115] For gage see e.g. Brunner, ii, 493-97, esp. 496; J. H. Wigmore, 'The Pledge-Idea: a Study in Comparative Legal Ideas', (1896/97) 10 Harvard Law Review, 321-50, 389-417, and (1897/98) 11 Harvard Law Review, 18-39; H. D. Hazeltine, 'The Gage of Land in Med. England', (1903/04) 17 Harvard Law Review, 549-57 and (1904/05) 18 Harvard Law Review, 36-50.

[116] Plucknett, 629.

[117] For festuca see PM ii, 85-86 and 186.

[118] For stab and wadia see Hübner, 497-503; F. Beyerle, 'Der Ursprung der Bürgschaft', Appendix II, 'Der Stab als Wettsymbol', 635. The clearest Germanic legal text is the Lombardic, Leges Langobardorum, 643-866, ed. F. Beyerle (Germanenrechte, Neue Folge, Westgermanisches Recht, 2nd ed., Witzenhausen, 1962), glossary s.v. uuadium. The theory is von Amira's: see his Der Stab in der germanischer Rechtssymbolik (Munich, 1909).

[119] In those Welsh legal texts which treat the mach as a paying surety, e.g. Cyfn 6, the mach

must give permission before the creditor distrains to compel the debtor to pay: Cyfn 4. Creditor and surety co-operate in levying the distress (Cyfn 8), a sign that this *mach* had developed from an enforcer of the Ior kind. (I am indebted to Dr Thomas Charles-Edwards for these references).

[120] For *fideiussio* etc. see the Glossary. It belongs to developed law so that its inclusion in this paper would be inappropriate. For gage-taking (distraint) in Irish law see Binchy, 'Distraint', 33.

[121] Cf. its use in the Marculfian Formulary (MGH *Leges, Formulae Merowingici et Karolini Aevi*, ed. K. Zeumer, Hanover, 1886), I.3, 43ff. in a clause forbidding a grantee to take or to seize (*tollere*) houses, foodrents, *vel fideiussores. . . nec. . . de quaslibet causas distringendum nec nulla redibutione reuirendum. . . Fideiussores* may mean peace-pledges or hostage-sureties.

[122] See e.g. the extensive references to procedural sureties in E. de Haas and G. D. G. Hall, *Early Registers of Writs* (SS 87, 1970), e.g. Analytical Index, 350, 372; and cp. R. C. van Caenegem, *Royal Writs. . . from the Conquest to Glanvill* (SS 77, 1958-59), index s.vv. distraint, pledge; M. M. Bigelow, *History of Procedure in England from the Norman Conquest, 1066-1204* (London, 1880, c.s. (distraint) and index s.vv. security, sureties; *Dialogus de Scaccario*, ed. C. Johnson (Nelson Med. Classics, London, 1950), lxii-lxiii.

[123] See Bibliographical Abbreviations.

THE TEXTS
i INTRODUCTION
T. M. CHARLES-EDWARDS

The choice of texts to illustrate the Welsh law of suretyship has been governed by different considerations in each case. Here, and in the commentary on Ior, a distinction has been made between northern and southern texts, so that Ior and Col are regarded as northern and Cyfn and Bleg as southern. The Latin texts vary in that they have both northern and southern connections. It should be said, however, that this distinction does not imply, necessarily, that the ultimate origin of a lawbook is northern or southern as the case may be, only that in its existing form it appears to have northern or southern connections. In the case of Ior at least it is clear that the origin is indeed northern, but for Cyfn this is more questionable.

The edition of Ior is an experiment. First, it uses a different principal MS from that preferred by Dr A. R. Wiliam in his edition of *Llyfr Iorwerth*. The reason for this change is the important observations on the MSS made by Mr Daniel Huws. Secondly, it tries to reconstruct the original text on the basis of a new stemma.

The choice of *W* among the MSS of Cyfn was dictated by its inclusion of more material derived from Ior than any other of the Cyfn MSS. It thus contains the basic stock of material common to the Cyfn MSS as a whole but also demonstrates the influence of Ior in the south no later than the beginning of the fourteenth century, about the time that the first MS. of Ior with a southern provenance (G) was written. The Latin lawbook Redaction A also betrays the influence of a northern text, very probably that of Ior itself, in the thirteenth century (WLW 180-85), so that it is likely that copies of Ior began to penetrate Deheubarth very soon after the date of its compilation in the early thirteenth century. On the other hand, the Latin tradition as a whole shows traffic in the opposite direction, from the south into Gwynedd. The main stock of the Latin texts is southern, but Latin C especially, and also Latin B and E, show signs of having been compiled in the north. The thirteenth century was evidently a period of active interchange of legal texts between different parts of Wales.

For a Latin text, Merton College MS 323 was chosen because it is the archetype of one of the branches of the textual tradition of Latin Redaction E. Since the text printed in Emanuel's *Latin Texts of the Welsh Laws* was based on the archetype of the other branch, it was decided that this would be the most helpful text to print. Redaction E was chosen because it presents a relatively full version of the tractate.

ii THE MANUSCRIPTS
DANIEL HUWS

B.L. COTTON CALIGULA A. iii (ff. 149-198)

Folios 149-198 of B. L. Cotton Caligula A. iii, a composite Cottonian volume, comprise an imperfect text of Llyfr Iorwerth known since the publication of Aneurin Owen's *Ancient Laws and Institutes of Wales* by the siglum C, which will be used in this description. Until now the fullest description has been that of Gwenogvryn Evans, RMWL ii 945-6.

Because of its very defective state (38 of an original 88 leaves are missing) C has received less attention than some of the other thirteenth-century lawbooks. It is an early one, perhaps the earliest. And it is one whose place of origin seems close to identification, if ultimately elusive. For these reasons, what is formally a description has been allowed here and there to burst its seams.

Preparation of the manuscript

The parchment is thick, with many original holes, some large, e.g. f. 184. The leaves measure 220 × 165 mm but have been heavily cropped on all three sides, in s. xvi or later; originally the book must have measured about 260 × 180 mm, much larger than any of the other surviving thirteenth-century Welsh lawbooks. Written space is 175 × 125 mm (the height is 180 mm in quire 7, 185 mm in quire 6). In two columns, apart from the list of values on ff. 191ᵛ-192ᵛ which is in three. Ruled in plummet; written below the top line; 26 lines to the page in quires 1-5, 31 in quires 6 and 28 in quires 7-8. For a vernacular MS the ruling is unusually complicated: the top two, middle three and bottom two lines go right across the page; marginal bounding lines are double; columns are separated by a triple line; the outer edges of margins are defined by bounding lines, as though in preparation for a surrounding gloss. In the inner margins, near the gutter, are sets of four stab holes, common to each quire.

Foliation

There are four foliations. The earliest, of s. xvi/xvii, is in ink in the centre of the upper margins of rectos, 1-50. The second, made after incorporation in the Cottonian binding, s. xvii, also in ink, is in the top right hand corners of rectos, running 153-210 (jumping from 180-191). The third is a B.M. foliation, in pencil of s. xix, 152-201. The fourth, the current B.L. foliation, in pencil, dates from 1896 (see end flyleaf) and runs 149-198. These foliations show that the many missing leaves indicated by the collation and by the lucanae in the text were all gone before c. 1600. They also show that between each foliation there was rearrangement of the manuscript. The arrangement reflected by the pre-Cottonian foliation is: f. 180 (the folio number cannot be read but that this leaf came first is evident from its position in the second and third foliations), quires 1-4, quire 6 (apart from f. 180), quires 7-8, quire 5. This arrangement is wrong and cannot be the original. The text shows that the most recent rebinding and foliation at last restored the original order. The removal of f. 180 to the beginning of the manuscript was obviously prompted by a perceived need for a preface; the proper one was missing and someone replaced it by the preface to *Llyfr Prawf*.

Collation

The quiring was originally regular, in eights. The losses are many:

Folios	Quire	
149-154	1⁸	wants 4 and 5, 1 and 8 are singletons
155-162	2⁸	
163-169	3⁸	wants 5
170-172	4⁸	wants 1, 2, 4, 5 and 8
173-179	5⁸	wants 8
180-186	6⁸	wants 2
187-192	7⁸	wants 4 and 5
193-198	8⁸	wants 1 and 8, the latter probably blank

There is a large roman II at the end of quire 1 but no other original quire signatures survive (they have all doubtless been cut away by binders). The losses indicated by the collation are confirmed by the text (see below). The text also confirms that one quire has been lost before quire 1 (as indicated by the signature) and suggests that two complete quires are wanting between quire 1 and quire 2.

Script

Gwenogvryn Evans, mistakenly it seems, suggested that the manuscript was written by two scribes.[1] He was led to his opinion by the compressed text of ff. 180-182; his reference to an 'intermediate stage' suggests that he may have had his doubts. From the beginning of quire 1 up to f. 177 the spacing of the text is generous, remarkably so in quires 2 and 3 (see for example f. 159ᵛ in plate 1). On f. 177ᵛ the scribe begins to cram his text; the amount of text to the page increases by about a third, without departing from the original ruling. His aim evidently was to complete his text of *Cyfreithiau gwlad* within the quire. We must suppose either that he had no more parchment ready to hand or, more likely, that he preferred cramming his text to having a single (and easily lost) leaf at the end of his quire. This bears on a point which will be made later: that when the scribe completed quire 5 the following three quires containing *Llyfr Prawf* either had already been written or else had not been conceived of by the scribe as a mere continuation of the text he was engaged on.

Llyfr Prawf, *Liber probationis*, is in quires 6-8. It begins on f. 180 in a browner ink than has appeared in the preceding quires. Perhaps in order to match the compressed text of the end of quire 5 (supposing that quires 1-5 had been written first), the script at the beginning of quire 6 is similarly compact (see f. 180 in plate 1) and the number of lines is greater. But gradually the scribe relaxes again. By quire 8 the script is once more wide-spaced as in the early part of the manuscript. Before beginning quire 8 the scribe paused. He now had some new black ink. The pause may have given time for calculation; the scribe realized perhaps that he had more than enough space in his last quire of eight to complete his text comfortably.

The scribe I take to have been writing about the middle of the 13th century, perhaps not a young man, old-fashioned in his ways. He also wrote, in smaller script, Peniarth 44, containing a version of *Brut y Brenhinedd* not known from any other independent source,[2] and Llanstephan 1, the earliest manuscript of a fairly widespread version of *Brut y Brenhinedd*.[3] None of these manuscripts is dated or datable; we may note however that in Peniarth 44 but not the other two the writing is above the top line. English scribes began to write below the top ruled line about 1230.[4] It looks as though, conservative though he may have been, the scribe of these manuscripts fell victim to a change of fashion. He was evidently writing after 1230. How quickly such a fashion might have penetrated Wales is matter for speculation. With regard to the date of C we also need to note Dafydd Jenkins's demonstration that *Llyfr Iorwerth* can hardly have been compiled long before 1240;[5] and also on the other hand the suggestion below that C may preserve *Llyfr Iorwerth* in the earliest form that has come down to us.

The first striking feature of the script of our manuscript at its most relaxed is the wide spacing not only of the lines but also of letters within words (see plates), giving it an almost tentative air. Except when the text becomes compressed the 'biting' of *de* and *do* is no more than one would expect in a late twelfth-century manuscript.

The *a* is always open; *d* always round; *g* has a conspicuous tag to its tail; round *r* only occurs after *o*; majuscule *R* is occasionally used at the end of words; final *s* is always round (in this at least the scribe is not old-fashioned); the shaft of *t* does not go above the cross stroke; *v* used for *w* has not begun to develop a distinct form; *w* is four-stroked, still clearly two *v*s; *y*, formed of two parallel curves, is always dotted.

Ascenders and descenders are generally short. Ascenders have a conspicuous spur. Cursive forms of a few majuscule initials occur sporadically, notably *A* and *S*.

An unusual practice of the scribe is his placing of accents on double vowels e.g. *áá* (ff. 155, 156, 183, 194ᵛ), *éé* (f. 180), *óó* (f. 164ᵛ) perhaps *w̃* (treated as a double *u*, e.g. ff. 149ᵛ, 162ᵛ, it is hard to be sure whether the strokes are accents or mere flourishes). He does the same in Peniarth 44 and Llanstephan 1. This practice of accenting double vowels occurs also in Strata Marcella charters of s. xii/xiii and an Abbey Dore MS of 1244.[6] Characteristic of the scribe's Welsh orthography is his avoidance of *i* (he writes *y*) and his general use of *u* only in conjunction with *v* or *w*.[7]

Punctuation is normally by point and *punctus elevatus*(⁏). A few times however the scribe introduces an eccentric archaism. On ff. 157ᵛ, 170, 171 and 183 he uses the mark., and on f. 163ᵛ the mark.., at the end of a paragraph. This is a remarkable survival of Insular punctuation marks.[8] Hyphens are regularly used in words broken at the end of lines. Deletion is by erasure or expunction.

For the explicit, *Explicit libellus probationis legum curialium Wallie. Amen*, on f. 198ᵛ, the scribe (I assume it was the same one) adopted a formal chancery hand, which one might confidently have dated to s. xiii¹, with high ascenders (about four times the height of minims) with four notches on their shafts, *a* and *s* almost as tall as other ascenders.

Rubrication

The hand of the headings written in red appears indistinguishable from that of the scribe of the text apart from one feature: in the headings the final shaft of *m* and *n* is sometimes given a double curve (e.g. ff. 176ᵛ, 177, 187 and the *explicit*). That the scribe and rubricator were one and the same person who used this decorative feature only in his headings seems probable. Of his other two manuscripts the scribe appears to have rubricated Llanstephan 1 himself while the rubrication of Peniarth 44 (which has penwork in a corrosive green) is probably by another hand.

The spaces for initials in C are in quires 1-5 marked by the scribe with a low point and in quires 6-8 with a diagonal stroke; there are no guide letters. The red appears to be red lead; it has in many letters darkened by oxidation, mostly so where the letters are near the outside edge of the page,

ÿar e dayar. E sef ath
aws ew ket boet kÿv
reÿth er rwng dÿn
aÿ gÿlÿd ar e dayar
hon. nÿt oes kÿvre
ÿth er rwng dÿawul
aÿ gÿlÿd. Ac nÿt oes
kÿvreÿth er rwng

e mach peÿ bÿw.
dervÿd ÿ dÿn kÿmrÿt
mach ÿ kan arall ar
peth a chÿn dÿvot oet
e dÿlÿet marw e kÿn
nogÿn. e mach a delÿ
kÿmhell map e kÿn
nogÿn megÿs e kÿnno
gÿn.

(a)

amser glÿndÿt bÿnÿv. c
ena ededrÿchassant ekÿvreÿ
thÿev. arhon aveÿ re trom o
nadvnt ÿ helcavÿnhav. arhon
aveÿ re eskavÿn onadvnt ÿ
hachwanegv. eth oz kÿvre
ÿthÿev a adassant val edoeÿdÿ
nt. peth arall avÿnnassant ÿ
enendav. ereÿll adÿleassant

enitev pÿev ÿ ellvng ef ar er ar
glÿpÿd. ar arglwÿd pÿev eskÿn
nv ÿdav entev egneÿdÿaeth. ac
en varnedÿc e vravt a varnibo
entev o hennÿ allan. Ac entev
pÿev rodÿ pedeÿr arvgeÿnt ÿr
egnat llÿs enÿ obÿr. O dervÿd
ÿdav entev barnv kam vravt
o hennÿ allan. nÿ delÿ entev ÿ
tavavt

(b)

1. B.L. Cotton Caligula A.iii, (a) f.159ᵛ (b) f.180

tra vo vyw.
loſevrn llo e vlwydyn
kyntaf keynnyavc. k.
ew y werth. er eyl vlwy
dyn dwy. k. en etryded
vlwydyn teyr. keynnyavc.
ar pedwared vlwydyn pe
deyr keynnyavc ac evelly
e byd.

Wy bynnac a wrth o
dynawet. yavn ew ydav
y orvot rac try heynt
e gwarthec ac en ragor
tac e clafry hyt wyl
padryc. E nep ay pryno
a del y y kady entey en
lle yach. ac en ty ny ryffo
olafry ſeyth mlyned gynt
endav. O werth e moch
ac ev teythy e traetha hyn.

werth porchell or nos
e ganher eny el y ton
voy keynnyavc. k. ew
y werth. hyt ra vo
en dynv dwy keynny
avc. k. E ſef ew henny
try mys. Ac o henny eny
el e moch yr koet ba
nv vyd.

a phedeyr keynnyavc
k. ew y gwerth. Ac o
wyl yevan hyt e ka
lan pymthec vyd y
gwerth. O r kalan hyt
wyl yevan eyl werth.
chwech cheynnyavc k.
ew y gwerth. ac ena
a dan e koet val y mae
a dec arvgeynt ew y
gwerth.

Teythy hwch ew na
vo baed redavc. ac
uat yſſo y pherchyll.
ay gorvot teyr nos a
thry dyew rac e veny
glavc. ſleu ot yſt y pher
chyll nev o byd baed
redavc atverer y thru
yan gwerth. Kymeynt
ew gwerth y hael ay
gwerth ehvn. kyme
ynt ew gwerth e baed
a gwerth teyr or moch.
O werth e deveyt ac ev
teythy e traetha hyn.

oen or nos e gan
her hyt kalan gay
af

2. B.L. Cotton Caligula A.iii, f.189

sometimes giving the illusion that two reds, one dark and one pale, have been used. The text is indented only for the large initials. Others are squeezed awkwardly into the narrow column formed by the bounding lines (see plates). The large initials vary from 9-line (f. 180, at the beginning of *Llyfr Prawf*) through all sizes down to 5-line, without suggesting a deliberate hierarchy of corresponding complexity. Some of the large initials are split, i.e. a narrow unpainted seam divides the limbs of letters down the middle. In form the initials could be twelfth-century.

Line-filling at the end of paragraphs only occurs in quires 6-8. There is foliage (e.g. f. 186ᵛ), interlace (e.g. f. 189, see plate 2) and chain (e.g. f. 190ᵛ).

Drawings

In the lower margins of several pages, always provoked by a run-on of the text, there are drawings, probably the work of the scribe although they can hardly be seen as an integral part of the decoration of the manuscript; they are in a brown ink and red indistinguishable from those used by the scribe. All the drawings have suffered from the heavy cropping of the book. The subjects are: f. 159ᵛ, a bird, ? St. John's eagle; f. 180, a winged monster, ? St. Mark's lion; ff. 189 and 194ᵛ, similar versions of a winged monster; ff. 189 ʳ⁻ᵛ, 194, a man's head both full-face and in profile with a square cap (see plates). The bird and winged monster resemble in their style the evangelist symbols in early Insular gospel books.[9] It is interesting that a Welsh scribe in the 13th century should resort to such models; indeed, that he should have been able to.

Text

This is not the place for a detailed discussion of the text of C. But the codicological implications ought to be spelt out.

Aled Rhys Wiliam chose Cotton Titus B ii ('B') as the basis of his text of *Llyfr Iorwerth*. He sums up its quality: 'The text of B (excluding the *Cynghawsedd* at the end) is the shortest coherent version of the Book of Iorwerth, and the only one of the thirteenth-century which is arranged in correct order'.[10] He suggests that B probably represents the 'original Book of Iorwerth'; more faithfully than any other manuscript.

When, with an eye on the collation of the manuscript (see above), the text of C is collated with Aled Rhys Wiliam's *Llyfr Iorwerth*, calculating from the surviving leaves how much text has been lost on the wanting ones, it will be seen that except at one point (to which we return) the text of C and

B go hand in hand. It would be perverse to contend that C, before it suffered mutilation did not include the complete text of *Llyfr Iorwerth*, in the same order as B. Of C it can reasonably be said that it was as coherent as B, was shorter and was not followed by the *Cynghawsedd*. The one indisputable virtue of B is that its text is complete.

The major divergence between the texts of B and C comes at the beginning of *Llyfr Prawf*. C, alone among the thirteenth-century manuscripts, has a preface to *Llyfr Prawf*, followed by a section on judgeship. There follows the tractate on *galanas*; this, in C, as in the other manuscripts of *Llyfr Iorwerth*, is substantially different and shorter than that in B.

A number of questions have in the past been raised about these textual differences and their bearing on the 'original' *Llyfr Iorwerth*. They bear looking at again in the light of two observations. Firstly, that C, to judge by its script, and other features, might be a generation earlier than B. Secondly, and more significantly, that whereas in B *Llyfr Prawf* is an integral part of the lawbook, with merely a brief incipit in mid-page to announce its beginning, in C *Llyfr Prawf* is physically separate, in three quires which in the number of lines and other respects differ from the earlier quires. There is on these limited grounds a *prima facie* case for considering that C may offer the more primitive form of *Llyfr Iorwerth*.

The questions, then, are these. Given a long and short of form of a preface, is the short the embryo of a later one or the rump of an earlier one? In the case of the long preface to *Llyfr Prawf* in C the answer hitherto has been that it is probably a later expansion.[11] What also perhaps now needs to be considered is the possibility that *Llyfr Prawf* may originally have had independent existence, circulating on its own, a possibility suggested by the make-up of C, and that the need for a status-giving preface might then be greater than when the text of *Llyfr Prawf* had been subsumed in what we now know as *Llyfr Iorwerth*.

The most primitive form of *Naw affaith galanas* seems to be that represented in a late manuscript, Peniarth 34 ('F').[12] The version in C, with which several other manuscripts are in fairly close agreement, contains additional matter; B, which in this section has no close affiliations with other early manuscripts, contains much more additional matter, mostly different.[13] Which of the two sets of additional matter represents the earliest development is a question not yet answered.

A third question is: what originally consituted *Llyfr Prawf*? In B an explicit comes at the end of the tractate on *Gwerth gwyllt a dof*. There follows what Aled Rhys Wiliam refers to as the 'appendix', while conceding that it is an integral part of *Llyfr Iorwerth*, even of *Llyfr Prawf*. In C, as we have seen, the explicit of *Liber probationis* comes at the very end of the whole text;

the 'appendix' is embraced in *Llyfr Prawf*. This is consistent with the statement in the preface: *Ar llyvyr hvn a elwyr e llyvyr prav sef ev henny teyr kolovyn kyvreyth a gwerth gvyllt a dof ac a berthyn ar hynny*. But this again is evidence which can be used to argue in either of two directions.

The sentence which introduces the 'appendix' in B and C offers an important and equally ambivalent difference. In B, where other manuscripts attribute the following text to Iorwerth ap Madog the credit is simply given to *y doethyon*. Aled Rhys Wiliam, following one obvious line of reasoning, makes this impersonality a main plank in his case for the text of B being our closest to that which left the hands of the compiler, Iorwerth.[15] Another line of argument might be that B's text simply reflects some lawyer's pragmatic dislike of fuss and that the excision of any preamble to *Llyfr Prawf* exemplifies the same tendency. In introducing the 'appendix', C, alone among the manuscripts, gives the compiler the fuller form of his name by which Dafydd Jenkins was able to identify him, *Yorverth vap Madavc vap Rahavt*. That C knows and records Iorwerth's grandfather's name is again a fact that one can interpret as one will.

C makes much greater use of headings than B. In this respect B may be considered more primitive. Headings are a sophistication and mark an advance. In C, like the lay-out, they may well represent the influence on the scribe of well-organised Latin codices, in particular perhaps books of canon law.

History of the manuscript: the evidence

Conjecture about the place of origin of the manuscript is largely dependent on the evidence that can be assembled about its later history. For this reason, before indulging in speculation, the evidence, mostly a matter of marginalia, is presented straight, in roughly chronological order.

I   In the top left hand corner of f. 196ᵛ is a cropped note of s. xiii/xiv

ap mad ap hyuel

orane   super toredulam
        terra monacorum
llwyt de
filius eius
*iu*ssores in
au' et ph'
pro feodo
llanvawr
proxima post

sancti johannis
e. anno. d.
iiii

All lines are acephalous. The relationship of the words in the top four lines (roughly reproduced above) is unclear. More text is probably cut away above the top surviving line.

II   At the foot of f. 166ʳ is a baffling line of writing, its lower part somewhat cropped, s. xiii/xiv:

mab keillʋleuki gilamv.ac klein inrodion

III   Written across the lower margins of ff. 197ᵛ-198 in a hand of s. xiv, legible only in part, is a note beginning:

Nota quod genus humanum duobus regitur naturali videlicet iure et moribus. Naturale est quod in lege [   ] continetur [   ] quisque iubetur alii facere quod sibi wlt fieri et modo unde in ewangelio 'omnia quecunque [   ] ut faciant vobis homines et vos eadem facite illis'.

This is an echo of the opening of the *Decretum* of Gratian.

IV   In yellowish ink a hand of s. xiv² wrote tags in shaky Latin and Welsh on ff. 152ᵛ,169 ('universis sante matris ecclesie fulis [sic]'), 170ᵛ ('bendycedic vo llaw a yscriuenot hyn') and 181ᵛ. On f. 184 he wrote something more interesting:

bit crama can iar
bit drydar can lew
bit oual ar kar
bit kywir baclawc

For texts of the *Bidiau* to which these lines belong, see K. Jackson, *Early Welsh Gnomic Poems* (Cardiff, 1935), 35.

V   A poor hand of s. xiv/xv wrote in the margin of f. 163ᵛ, again cropped, followed by an erasure:

fen
horf
wyw   mad' ap ff ai kanawt

No poet of the name Madog ap Ffylip is known.

VI   Across the lower margin of f. 151ᵛ, partly cropped and partly erased, in a hand of s. xv/xvi, are some twenty lines of a cywydd to a patron, possibly called Tomos, of which the most substantial surviving portion appears to read

meistyr irroddlyn rryd
wr dwr dinid
omos noswaith
rth yved med maith
h amyl gellwerriaw
wnn avr oth law

VII Marginal notes in the hand of Gruffudd Hiraethog showing an interest in the text and unusual words, e.g., f. 149 *bardd tevlv*, f. 150ᵛ *kweranav*, f. 158ᵛ *kynogyn*.

VIII A cropped note in the margin of f. 150v in a hand of s. xvi, conceivably a note meant for the attention of Gruffudd Hiraethog:

n dda
ydiw
deg
hynny
ruffuth

IX On f. 177ᵛ and again on f. 178 are the initials 'H T', probably s. xvi.

X On f. 160ᵛ, written in the same italic hand, s. xvi², the names 'Robart Edwards' and 'Roger Eytton'.

XI In 1605 the manuscript was seen and collated with another text by John Jones, Gellilyfdy, see *RMWL* i 1046-8 and Ior xxvii. According to John Jones the manuscript had belonged to Richard Langford of Trefalun.

XII Running the length of the outer margin of f. 186ᵛ, partly cut away, pre-dating the Cottonian binding and probably medieval is a fluent drawing of two intertwined dragons.

XIII When and how the manuscript came into Cotton's hands is not clear. Of his friends, Richard Broughton, a justice of Great Sessions on the Chester circuit, and Hugh Holland, a native of Denbigh, had connections with north east Wales; while Francis Tate, justice on the Brecon circuit of Great Sessions, is known to have been interested in Welsh law.[16]

History of the manuscript: conclusions

The evidence helps us greatly to narrow the field, but does not allow us to locate conclusively either the place of origin or the medieval home of the manuscript. What follows shows that the manuscript was written in an ecclesiastical milieu, not to say a monastic one, Welsh, probably Cistercian; that it remained in such a milieu at least into the 14th century; that its geographical associations are all with north east Wales; that the case for Valle Crucis is strong, while Strata Marcella and Basingwerk remain possibilities.

Ecclesiastical, probably monastic, production is suggested by the page layout, reminiscent of canon law books; by the very size of the manuscript, so much bigger than the other contemporary Welsh lawbooks, a library book rather than a pocket book; by the language (Latin) and script of the explicit; by the derivation of the drawings (if that suggestion is accepted) from the evangelist symbols. The nature of the text of the two other manuscripts written by our scribe speaks for a house sympathetic to Welsh vernacular literature; one cannot but think of the Cistercians. The *correctus* written at the end of quires in Llanstephan 1 is evidence of a well-organised scriptorium which in mid-thirteenth-century Wales could hardly have been other than monastic.[17] The accenting of double vowels is a contemporary usage in two Welsh Cistercian houses.

That during the fourteenth century the manuscript remained in a similar milieu is indicated by marginal item I with its reference to *terra monacorum* and its use of the year AD for dating rather than the regnal year; by marginal item III with its echo of Gratian's *Decretum*; by marginal item IV with its Latin tags.

The presence of a Welsh lawbook in a monastery need cause no surprise. It would have been needed for legal purposes if for no other. Although no surviving lawbook is of proven association with a Welsh religious house, we do have several references to *llyfr y Ty Gwyn*.[18]

Marginal item I refers to a fee which is evidently in Llanfor. Strata Marcella owned land there and so too did Basingwerk.[19] The same marginal note refers to *super toredulam*. *Toredula* is a rare word, meaning kiln, perhaps limekiln.[20] Valle Crucis and Basingwerk lie close by the limestone belt of north east Wales; neither Strata Marcella nor Llanfor are close to limestone.

Of the manuscripts which contain the *Bidiau* stanzas to which the lines in marginal item IV belong, one which reads close to our lines is Peniarth 27ii, written by Gutyn Owain. Although Gutyn Owain has one cywydd to Thomas Pennant, abbot of Basingwerk, and wrote one manuscript which came to rest there,[21] both his poetry and scribal activity link him far more closely with Valle Crucis than with anywhere else.

The fragments of a cywydd in marginal item VI do not come from any surviving cywydd to an abbot of Basingwerk, Valle Crucis or Strata Marcella. If it is *Tomos* which provides the cynghanedd with *noswaith*, the date would allow identification of the subject with Thomas Pennant.

We now need to look at the 16th-century evidence of provenance. The

'HT' of marginal item IX is not readily identifiable. The presence of Gruffudd Hiraethog's notes, on the other hand, and the names of Robart Edwards and Roger Eytton, direct us firmly towards north east Wales, the home ground of Gruffudd and of the Eytons.

It is time to introduce a stranger, Edward ap Rhys ap Dafydd of Eglwyseg. Edward ap Rhys (*fl.* 1503-45), held many offices during a long life, among them auditor and recorder of Powis, steward or deputy steward of several lordships including Bromfield' and Yale, and Chirk, and deputy steward of Valle Crucis. [22] There is a cywydd to him by Gruffudd Hiraethog and another, an elegy, by Morus ap Hywel ap Tudur. [23] Both pay tribute to his learning, first Gruffudd:

A pherffaith ei deiriaith deg
Ac â'i lys yn Eglwyseg

Athro pen ysgrifenwyr
I ddysgu oedd, ddwy oes gwyr

Then Morus ap Hywel:

Tai Eglwyseg, teg lysoedd
Ar lun a sut Orliawns oedd,
Llawn ddamwain, lluniodd yma,
Llafur a dysg llyfrau da.
Ni wyr heb fai ond rhai'u trin
Gwedi Edwart gwaed Edwin.

Edward ap Rhys looks like one who might have had both the opportunity and the inclination to rescue books at the time of the Dissolution. He was a patron of Gruffudd Hiraethog, the most scholarly bard of his generation; Morus ap Hywel implies that he was known for his collection of books. Next to nothing is known of the first post-Dissolution generation of owners of monastic books in north Wales. Was Edward ap Rhys one of them?

Edward's eldest son was John ap Rhys, otherwise John Price, holder of many public offices who died in 1593. [24] Gruffudd Hiraethog in Peniarth MS 134 refers to a book written by Thomas ab Ieuan ap Deicws for John abbot of Valle Crucis (1503-?27) which was then, in 1550, in the possession of John ap Rhys of Rhisgog. [25] Rhisgog is about a mile from Valle Crucis. Is this possibly the son of Edward ap Rhys before he established himself at Eglwyseg? [26] Here, at any rate, is one of the Valle Crucis books barely ten years after the Dissolution.

Edward ap Rhys had a daughter Margaret who married Edward ap Roger Eyton. Edward ap Roger of Ruabon is best known for his great compilation

of Welsh pedigrees, Peniarth MS 128. Edward ap Roger's father was a
Roger Eyton; a brother of Edward's was also called Roger Eyton; so too
was one of his sons.[27] Allowing that Edward ap Rhys may have been owner
of C, it is easy to conceive how it might have passed on to his bookish son-
in-law. The Roger Eyton named in the book is most likely to be the son
of Edward ap Roger; the writing looks like that of his generation. Both
Edward ap Rhys and his son John were patrons of Gruffudd Hiraethog; and
Gruffudd used Edward ap Roger's collection of pedigrees. C might therefore
have been in the possession of any one of these three when Gruffudd
annotated it. The Robart Edwards whose name is paired with that of Roger
Eytton may well have been Robert Edwards of Stansty.[28]

Lastly, we need to look at the evidence for localizing the two other
manuscripts written by the scribe of C. Most striking, in that it is based
solely on the textual affiliations of Peniarth 44 and Llanstephan 1, is Professor
B. F. Robert's conclusion that they were most likely written at Basingwerk,
Strata Marcella or Valle Crucis, the latter being much the most favoured
candidate.[29]

The internal evidence of provenance in the two manuscripts confirms their
north east Wales associations. Peniarth 44 has on f. 48 (once a flyleaf), in
a hand of s. xv/xvi, brief annals about the rising of Owain Glyndŵr
referring to events in Aberconwy, Ruthin, Fyrnwy and Denbigh; on f. 19ᵛ
in a hand of s. xv is the name 'Bellyn ap D'd Ieuann', Belyn being very much
a north east Wales name; the first certainly identifiable owner is Jasper
Gryffyth. The first known owner of Llanstephan 1 is John Lloyd of Blaen-y-
ddol, a schoolmaster at Ruthin.[30]

[1] RWML ii, 945.
[2] See B. F. Roberts, *Astudiaeth destunol o'r tri chyfieithiad Cymraeg cynharaf o Historia regum Britanniae* (unpublished University of Wales Ph.D. dissertation, 1969) cxiv-clxxxiv; more briefly B. F. Roberts, *Brut y Brenhinedd, Llanstephan MS 1 Version* (Dublin, 1971), xxviii-xxix, and E. Reiss, 'The Welsh versions of Geoffrey of Monmouth's *Historia*' (1968) 4 WHR 109.
[3] See B. F. Roberts, *Brut y Brenhinedd, Llanstephan MS. 1 Version* (Dublin, 1971).
[4] N. R. Ker, 'From 'above top line' to 'below top line'' (1960) 5 *Celtica* 13-16.
[5] Dafydd Jenkins, 'Iorwerth ap Madog' (1953) 8 NLWJ 164-170, and 'A family of medieval Welsh lawyers' in Dafydd Jenkins (ed.), *Celtic Law Papers* (Bruxelles, 1973), 123-133.
[6] N.L.W., Wynnstay Deposit (1945), Strata Marcella charters 4 and 23 (the numbers follow those of J. Conway Davies in 51 *Montgomeryshire Collections*, 164-187); Egerton MS 3088, see A. G. Watson, *Catalogue of dated and datable Manuscripts c.700-1600 in the Department of Manuscripts, the British Library* (London, 1979), 117 and plate 139.
[7] On his orthography see B. F. Roberts, *Brut y Brenhinedd* (as above) xxxix-xliii.
[8] Cf. D. Huws, *The Medieval Codex: with reference to the Welsh Law Books* (Aberystwyth, 1980), 7.
[9] There are, for instance, some similarities to the symbols in BL Harley 1023 and its possible model, the Book of Armagh, see J. J. G. Alexander, *Insular Manuscripts, 6th to the 9th century*

(London, 1978), nos. 76 and 53, plates 341, 344, 229 and 230. All four evangelist symbols are used similarly in another Welsh lawbook N.L.W. MS 20143A ('Y'), in the lower margins of ff. 29, 38^v, 39 and 79^v.

[10] Ior xxxvi.

[11] Ior xxv, Col 86.

[12] (1914) BBCS, 95, Ior xxvi, Col 87-8.

[13] Ibid.

[15] Ior xxxv-xxxvi.

[16] H. I. Bell (1936) THSC, 25-27; Nesta Jones (1968) THSC, 99-109.

[17] This is the only instance of which I know, where the correction of quires in a Welsh manuscript is thus marked.

[18] Dafydd Jenkins has collected the references in Col 136-7.

[19] K. Williams-Jones, *The Merioneth Lay Subsidy Roll 1292-3* (Cardiff, 1976), 7, D. H. Williams, 'Strata Marcella Abbey' (1976) 11 *Cistercian Studies* 187 and 'Basingwerk Abbey' (1981) 2 *Citeaux* 96, 108.

[20] R. E. Latham, *Revised Medieval Latin Word-List from British and Irish Sources* (London, 1965).

[21] N.L.W. MS 7006, *Llyfr Du Basing*. The evidence for a Basingwerk provenance seems sound. Valle Crucis is a likelier place of origin.

[22] The cywyddau of Gruffudd Hiraethog and Morus ap Hywel ap Tudur (see note 23) both mention several of his offices. Much about him can be gathered from Peniarth MS 354, a precedent book which belonged to him and is largely in his hand; it contains a wide range of documents relating both to English Common Law and canon law. To a number of documents Edward ap Rhys is himself a party; there seems no reason to doubt that in this they reflect original documents. Unfortunately, the documents are seldom dated. A chronology of Edward ap Rhys's life would have to be constructed from other sources. In the precedent book, he is described as 'of Stradmarchell' and 'of Wrexham' as well as 'of Eglwyseg'. The earliest dated document in which he is named (f. 50) is his commission as deputy steward of Euas in 1503. The latest reference I have found to him is in N.L.W. Chirk Castle D80 in which as deputy steward of Bromfield and Yale and Chirk he held court at Llangollen in 1545. A discreditable anecdote in Cardiff MS 5.51, p. 868, tells how Edward ap Rhys acquired his Llanfyllin estate, later the inheritance of the recusant Prices of Llanfyllin. In the lay subsidy roll of 1543-4 (I rely on the transcript in N.L.W. MS 1816OD) Edward ap Rhys of Eglwyseg is the third most highly rated person in the hundred of Bromfield. For the pedigree of Edward ap Rhys, and his children, see (1889) *Arch. Camb.* 245-7, Peniarth MS 128, p. 142, Peniarth MS 177, p. 152.

[23] Gruffudd Hiraethog's cywydd I take from Brogyntyn MS 2, p. 512 (there are two other MSS); Morus ap Hywel's from BL Add MS 14967, p. 230, the only copy, in the hand of Edward ap Roger, Edward ap Rhys's son-in-law, see below. I have standardised the spelling and punctuated the quotations.

[24] See, for example, the indexes to J. R. S. Phillips, *The Justices of the Peace in Wales and Monmouthshire 1541 to 1689* (Cardiff, 1975), R. Flenley, *A Calendar of the Register of the Council...of Wales and the Marches...1569-1591* (London, 1916), *Calendar of Patent Rolls*. There are cywyddau to him by Gruffudd Hiraethog and William Llŷn and a cywydd marwnad by Edward ap Raff; see also cywyddau in Mostyn MS 147, pp. 258-73.

[25] See RMWL i 842.

[26] I have failed to find any John ap Rhys of Rhisgog in the pedigree books. He is named in the lay subsidy roll of 1543-4.

[27] Pedigree in Peniarth MS 128, p. 896.

[28] Pedigree in Peniarth MS 287, p. 214. BL Add 21253, a Valle Crucis MS of sermons, belonged in 1633 to 'John Edwards of Stanstie' (f. 185).
[29] B. F. Roberts, *Brut Tysilio* (Swansea, 1980), 18-20.
[30] On John Lloyd see B. F. Roberts, 'Llythyrau John Lloyd at Edward Lhuyd' (1971) 17 NLWJ 88-96.

B.L., COTTON CLEOPATRA A.xiv (ff. 34-107)

Earlier descriptions are in RMWL ii 950-1 and WML xiv-xv. Aneurin Owen's W. for text see WML.

Preparation of the manuscript

The parchment is stiff, with some original holes. 74ff. Measures 165 × *c*. 120 mm, cropped at the time of the Cottonian binding. Written space 130 × 85 mm. Ruled in brown lead with double outer margins and a single inner. 21 long lines, written below the top line. Stab marks common to the leaves of each quire occur in two pairs in the top and bottom of inner margins.

Foliation

Paginated 1-144 in s. xvi[2] by the Welsh annotator (see below) omitting ff. 94[v], 95[r-v] and 107[v], evidently on the grounds that they bore no text. Cottonian foliation 33-106. Current B.L. foliation 34-107 in the lower right hand corners.

Collation

1-2[8], 3[6], 4-9[8], 10[6]. No signatures survive in quire 1. Quire 2 is signed [*a* i] — *a iiii* in plummet in the centre of the lower margin of leading leaves; similarly through to *g i* — *g iiii* in quire 8. No signatures survive in quires 5, 9 and 10. Catchwords are in plain rectangular frames. The text ends on the penultimate leaf of quire 3, on the fourth from the end of quire 8 and on the penultimate of quire 10. In other words, the manuscript comprised three free-standing parts, quires 1-3, 4-8 and 9-10; these contain respectively *Cyfreithiau llys*, *Cyfreithiau gwlad* and the Triads. One interpretation of this is that the manuscript represents a reordering of the text. The second of the three parts may have been written first: the ink in quires 4-5 is blackish, turning to brown on f. 69[v]; a scribal addition on f. 57 is in brown ink; the remainder of the manuscript, including quires 1-3, is in brown ink. A later series of quire signatures G-Q goes with the Cottonian binding.

Script

The text is all by one hand, that of the scribe of the Book of Taliesin (Peniarth 2) who also wrote Mostyn 117 (*Brut y Brenhinedd*), Harleian 4353 (*Cyfraith Hywel*, 'V', closely related to our MS) and Peniarth 6iv (a fragment of *Gereint*). On this identification see Marged Haycock, *Llyfr Taliesin: Astudiaethau ar rai Agweddau* (University of Wales Ph. D. dissertation, 1983) 5-7. The character of the hand is described by N. Denholm-Young, *Handwriting in England and Wales* (Cardiff, 1954) 44. Haycock notes that in Cleopatra as in Mostyn 117 the scribe usually writes *gu-* where in the other manuscripts he writes *g6-*, and dots his *y* which in the others he leaves undotted; she suggests, plausibly, that these two manuscripts were written earlier than the others, that the scribe in these respects simply moved with fashion. Haycock dates him s. xiv[1], which seems right.

Punctuation is by point and *punctus elevatus*. Deletion is by expunction and insertion by caret and interlining or a *signe-de-renvoi* and marginal note. The scribe is fond of placing a dot inside majuscule letters and of stretching a final *n* as a line-filler at the end of a paragraph.

Rubrication

On ff. 34, 56 and 95, i.e. at the beginning of each of the three free-standing parts, are three-line initials in red and blue, with penwork in red, and red and blue extensions into the margins; elsewhere, two-line initials with red penwork. Alternate red and blue initials in the text. By Welsh standards the initials are skilful. Probably they are not the work of the scribe, others of his manuscripts having only plain initials. On ff. 42, 71[v] and 88 as line-fillers there are monsters drawn in red.

Binding

The covers of the Cottonian binding, of calf with Cotton's arms in gilt, are laid down on the modern covers. Sewing holes show that the pre-Cottonian binding of our manuscript was on three bands.

History of the manuscript

The pages left blank in the manuscript were host to a variety of additions in s. xiv[2] and s. xv, many of them later erased with greater or lesser success. On f. 107 in a hand of s. xiv[2] are what may be part of a prayer, a scriptural tag (*Fuit homo missus a deo...*) and four Latin verses beginning *O dives dives*

134 LAWYERS AND LAYMEN

non in omni tempore vives (For other texts see H. Walther, *Initia carmina ac versuum medii aevi posterioris latinorum* (Göttingen, 1959) 12601). Below, these verses are repeated in reverse order by a hand of s. xv[1] which continues for five further lines, scantly legible.

On ff. 94[r-v] and 95[v], in one hand of s. xiv[2], evidently all mere pentrials, are opening formulae of deeds, including a conveyance of a burgage in Cardiff, a gift from [ ] vabe *Rimy* to Robert Grandior, and mention of Ieuan ap Dd' ap [ ], [ ] ap Blethyn and Ior' ap *Rimy* ap Ro [ ]; formulae from court roles, with mention of *hondrod de Kerfill'*; and openings of letters, in French (*Cher et bien amie...*). On f. 55 are similar pentrials in a hand of s. xiv/xv naming Johannes Vechan, Ieuan ap Phelippe Hir, Dd' ap Fillippe Hir and Johannes ap Gwyll'.[1] On ff. 43[v]-44 are yet more such pentrials of the same date naming Johannes filli and Johannes vabe Ll'. On f. 94 in a hand of s. xv are words hard to read, seemingly in cipher: y boforus ahoxtro*de* *subult* *i*hsxur.

On f. 95, written in large textura between two vertically ruled lines and filling most of the page, is *Semper occederat*[ ], perhaps s. xiv[2]. The motto remains unidentified.

On many pages there is annotation of the text in black ink, in Welsh, by a secretary hand of s. xvi[2]. The writer shows a general interest in Welsh law. The same hand appears to have been responsible for the pagination and also, to judge by the ink, for a series of marginal marks made up of various combinations of dots and dashes.[2] On several pages, e.g. ff. 78[r-v] and 101[r-v] are scribbled words in Welsh and crude drawings, in yellowish ink, s. xv or xvi.

On f. 34 is the signature 'Robert Cotton Bruceus' and also in Cotton's hand *Liber Cardiff de consuetudinibus Walliae*. This does not sound like Cotton's invention; perhaps he took it from the original cover of the MS where it may have been written in the period when the law of Hywel Dda survived as customary law for the Welshry in the lordship of Glamorgan and Morgannwg. Following Cotton's contents list on f. 1 is written *Cyfraith Hywel Dda. i. Leges Hoeli Boni Walliae*; the hand is that of Moses Williams, who also wrote the word *breyr* on f. 89.

Origin of the manuscript

Cotton's title, taken with the evidence of the marginalia, suggests that the manuscript was in Cardiff or thereabouts by the end of s. xiv and may have remained there until his own time. Beyond its presence in Cardiff one needs to consider all the manuscripts of the Taliesin scribe together. Haycock (op.

cit. 11-17), noting that on linguistic grounds he is south Welsh and that the milieu in which he was working (albeit maybe as a professional scribe) was most likely to be a Cistercian monastery of Welsh sympathies, arrives at a short list of Strata Florida, Whitland and Cwmhir. The case for Strata Florida is perhaps weakened by the absence of the Taliesin hand from *Llawysgrif Hendregadredd* where so many contemporary hands appear (see (1981) 22 NLWJ 1-26). The case for Cwmhir is strengthened by the early Radnorshire associations of the Book of Taliesin (Haycock 17-22).

[1] The pedigree of Phylip Hir of Meisgyn and his descendants is in P. C. Bartrum, *Welsh Genealogies AD 300-1400* (Cardiff, 1974), iv, 816; Dafydd ap Phylip Hir was an ancestor of Rice Merrick of Cotrell.
[2] B. Ll. James (ed.), *Rice Merrick, Morganiae Archaiographia* (Cardiff, 1983), xxxi, suggests on genealogical grounds, that Rice Merrick may have owned our MS. That Rice Merrick may be the Welsh annotator is a possibility I have not been able to test.

OXFORD, MERTON COLLEGE MS 323

The manuscript is described by H. D. Emanuel (with references to earlier descriptions) in LTWL 410-2.

Material, preparation of manuscript, foliation

On paper, of two watermarks, the one hard to make out, the other a pot, close to Briquet 12725 (1581). The page measures 310×210 mm, written space 245×155 mm. 29 long lines. Foliated i-iv, 1-53, 54-59. Folios iii-iv and 54-57 are contemporary flyleaves, ff. i-ii and 58-59 are later ones.

Collation

This is deduced from the watermarks and confirmed by the sewings, visible in all but quire 2: 1^{18}, 2^8, 3^{14}, 4^{18} (wants 18).

Script

The text is written by John Dee in a calligraphic secretary hand, with words in Welsh, proper names and glosses in italic. I am grateful to have my suspicion that the hand is Dee's confirmed by Professor Andrew Watson; the manuscript will be listed DM 160 in the forthcoming catalogue of Dee's library by R. J. Roberts and A. G. Watson.

Binding

Speckled calf, blind-tooled with double fillet and rectangular panel formed by a roll, s. xvii/xviii.

Text

There is little to add to Emanuel's comment on the text beyond the fact that the glosses (both interlined and embodied in the text) in Greek, Latin, Italian and English may now reasonably be attributed to Dee, and so too probably the liberties taken with the text (see Emanuel's comment, LTWL 410-1). Only a selection of glosses is printed in Emanuel's apparatus. One substantial gloss omitted by Emanuel occurs on f. 6, beside the break of paragraph corresponding to LTWL 441...*penkenid/Distein*...The gloss reads *Haec omissa sunt per interpretem quae tamen in Brytanico textu habentur. Os is kynted...Rann deuvarch idau or ebrann.* The Welsh text corresponds to Bleg 10 line 26 to 11 line 9; more particularly it reads with Cotton Titus D ix ('L'), a MS in which Dee's hand appears, e.g. on f. 59.

History of the manuscript

Dee probably wrote the manuscript in 1585 × 1588. It is not, as Emanuel noticed, in Dee's 1583 catalogue of his MSS. On f. 1 Dee added his own pedigree in the margin, including his children and their birthdates; the births of the four elder children, up to Michael Pragensis born in 1585, belong to the first writing while those of the younger four born 1588-95 are later additions. The presence of the pedigree on this page is clearly due to the descent from Hywel Dda.

On f. iii are calculations by Dee, made in 1600. Their evident import is a prognosticated reform of the laws of Wales 666 years after their making and therefore reckoned to come in the year 1610.

The manuscript was acquired by Thomas Allen (his signature on f. iii and a reference to our MS by Richard James in Bodleian James MS 6, p. 84, see LTWL 411), probably after 1625 (see A. G. Watson, 'Thomas Allen of Oxford and his Manuscripts', in M. B. Parkes & A. G. Watson (ed.), *Medieval Scribes, Manuscripts and Libraries: Essays presented to N. R. Ker* (London, 1978), 279-314, esp. 290). Given to Merton by Thomas Clayton, warden of the college, in 1680 (f. iii). Merton pressmarks F.2.4 and F.2.4 Arch. on f. iii.

iii THE 'IORWERTH' TEXT
EDITED AND ᵢTRANSLATED BY T. M. CHARLES-EDWARDS

The text of the tractate from Ior is an attempt to reconstruct, as far as possible, the archetype. It is based upon a stemma which, while it owes much to that proposed by Dr A. Rh. Wiliam, also differs from it in important respects, I hope to present the evidence for this revised stemma in a forthcoming article. The sigla are those of Aneurin Owen with the addition of Lew (William Maurice's siglum for Peniarth MS 39) and Tim (after Timothy Lewis who edited it). The present locations of the MSS are given as B.L. (British Library) or N.L.W. (National Library of Wales, Aberystwyth) for MSS in those collections.

A: N.L.W., Peniarth MS 29, "The Black Book of Chirk', *c.* 1250, ff 17r-21r (pp. 43-51 of *Facsimile of the Chirk Codex of the Welsh Laws*, ed. J. Gwenogvryn Evans (Llanbedrog, 1909).

B: B.L., Cotton MS Titus D ii, s. XIII², ff. 20r-25v (the base of *Llyfr Iorwerth*, 34-45).

C: B.L., Cotton MS Caligula A iii, *c.* 1250, ff. 155v-164r.

D: N.L.W., Peniarth MS 32, *c.* 1400, pp. 52-67; in the hand of the main collaborator of Hywel Fychan in the Red Book of Hergest.

E: B.L., Additional MS 14931, s. XIII², pp. 34-42 (ff. 17v-21v); a paragraph almost at the end of the MS was added by the scribe of *B*.

G: N.L.W., Peniarth MS 35, s. XIV¹, ff. 26r-30r (65/1-71/1 only; in the same hand as the Cynf. MS *U* (N.L.W., Peniarth MS 37).

J: Jesus College, Oxford, MS 57, *c.* 1400, pp. 269-77 (breaks off at 65/2); written by Hywel Fychan; ed. M. Richards, *Cyfreithiau Hywel Dda o Lawysgrif Coleg yr Iesu Rhydychen LVII* (Cardiff, 1957), 131-34.

K: N.L.W., Peniarth MS 40, s. XV, ff. 24v-33v.

Lew: N.L.W., Peniarth MS 39, s. XV, contains 61/5-71/1, but the MS is disarranged so that its material from the tractate is to be found as follows:

61/5-64/13 = ff. 48v15-54v9
65/1-66/5 = ff. 19v7 – 21v16
66/5-67/4 = ff. 47r1-48v14
68/1-4 = f. 54v10-16
68/4-71/1 = ff. 23r1-26r4

Tim: N.L.W., Llanstephan MS 116, *s.*XV, pp. 67-71, containing 62/5-67/4 with several omissions and dislocations; Miss Morfydd Owen has identified the hand as that of the Bleg. MS *S*, which also derives from the Teifi Valley; ed. T. Lewis, *The Laws of Howel Dda* (London, 1912), with the same pagination as the MS.

Stemma of Ior's tractate on suretyship

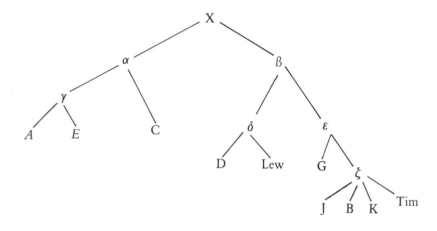

Since some details of the phrasing as well as the orthography of the archetype cannot be recovered, it is necessary to take one early MS as a basis. The choice of British library, Cotton MS Caligular A. iii (Aneurin Owen's *C*) is sufficiently explained by Mr Daniel Huws's observations on the manuscript in his contribution to this volume. The stemma given above is only certainly applicable to the tractate on suretyship and the succeeding tractate on land-suits. For earlier parts of Ior there are fewer MSS; but the main elements of the stemma may be valid for the whole text of Ior as far as the beginning of the Test Book (*Llyfr Prawf*). From that point onwards *B* and *C* occupy different positions in the tradition of the text. In particular, *C* ceases to be closely related to *A* and *E* and joins a group consisting of *D*, *K*, *Lew*, the lost MS of Llanforda and probably also *G*. This may explain an important aspect of the physical make-up of *C* noticed by Mr. Huws.

The Tractate

Ior §58

[1]AM HAWL VACH A CHYNNOGYN E TRAETHA HYNN. [2]O dervyd y dyn rody mach y arall ar peth, yavn ew ydav rydhaw e mach. [3]O vn o try achavs e byd ryd mach: ay o talw trostaw ay o wystlaw ay o gwadw mach. [4]Os y gwadw a vynn, val hynn e gwedyr: dyvot ar er egnat, a'r egnat pyew keyssyaw y gan e dwy pleyt adef ay mach e gwr ay nyt mach. [5]"Mach," hep er havlvr; "Na vac," hep e kynnogyn. Ena e mae yavn y'r egnat govyn y'r mach, "A wyt vach ty?". [6]"Wyf," hep e mach; "Kvbyl gwat," hep e kynnogyn, "nat wyt vac ty y kenhyfy nac ar henny nac ar dym." [7]"Dyoer," hep e mach, "val e mae gorev e dely mach heprwng y vot en vach, er hebrynghafy ve mot en vach." [8]"Dyoer," hep e kynnogyn, "val e mae gorev e dylyaf ynhev gwadv mach, mynhew a'th gwadaf ty."

[1] — AEJD; Kyfreith am uach K   E TRAETHA HYNN] — B.
[3] o try] or try C;   o talw] C omits o.
[4] e gwedyr] C adds mach;   dyvot] B adds e due pleyt ar mach;   e dwy pleyt]
C omits e;   adef] — EK;   e gwr] CJ add raccw.
[5] Mach] — A; C adds dyoer.
Na] — A;   vac] C adds dyoer.
y'r mach] — AE.
[7] e dely mach] e delyafy mach with yafy cancelled C.
[8] e dylyaf ynhev] deleuah hi A; dyly mach y E; e dele kynnogen ß;
mynhew a'th gwadaf ty] mynheu ay gwadaw EAJ.

Ior §59

[1]Ena e mae yavn y'r egnat edryc pa delw e dely ef y wadw: sef a wyl e kvyreyth ena, kanyt oes namyn y vn tavavt ef ehvn en gyrrw arnaw, na dely namyn y vn tavavt entev o'y gwadv. [2]"Ye," hep e kynnogyn, "mynhev a'y gwadaf ef." [3]Ena e mae yavn y'r egnat kymryt e kreyr en y law a dywedwyt vrth e kynnogyn, "Navd Dyw ragot, a navd Pap Rwveyn, a navd de arglwyd, na dos en llw kam. [4]Od aa entew y'r llw, tyghet y Dyw en e blaen ac y'r kreyr essyd en llaw er egnat hyt nat mach ef y kanthaw ef nac ar a dyweyt nac ar dym. [5]Ony vrthtwng e mach arnaw byt ryd e kynnogyn o'r havl a thalet e mach kvbyl o'r dylyet y'r havlvr. [6]Os ef a gwna e mach gvrthtvng ar e kynnogyn, gwrthtyghet tra vo e kynnogyn en rody y enew y'r kreyr gwedy e thygho. [7]Ac esef val y gwrthtwng: "Myn e kreyr essyd ena, mach wyfy y kenhyty ar er hynn re dywedeysy ac anvdon re tyngheysty; ac vrth e gwrthtwng re gwneythvmy arnaty, myvy a vynnaf barnw brawt ymy o'r egnat."

Ior §58

[1]THIS TREATS OF A CLAIM OF SURETY AND DEBTOR. [2]If it happens that a man gives a surety to another for something, it is right that he should free the surety. [3]A surety is free for one of three reasons: either payment on his behalf or giving a gage or denial of a surety. [4]If he (the debtor) should wish to deny, denial is made thus: [they] come before the judge, and it is proper for the judge to ask the two parties to recognise either that the man is surety or that he·is not. [5]"Surety," says the claimant; "He is not surety," says the debtor. Then it is right that the judge should ask the surety, "Are you surety?" [6]"I am," says the surety; "a complete denial," says the debtor, "[namely] that you are not a surety given by me neither for that nor for anything." [7]"God knows," says the surety, "as a surety should best assert that he is a surety, so do I assert that I am surety." [8]"God knows," says the debtor, "as I should best make a denial, I deny you."

Ior §59

[1]Then it is right that the judge should see how he (the debtor) should deny him (the surety): this is the view the law takes in that case, since there is only the one tongue of the latter making the charge against him, he, for his part, is only entitled to his one tongue to deny him. [2]"Yes," says the debtor, "I deny him." [3]Then it is right that the judge should take the relics in his hand and say to the debtor, "The protection of God before you and the protection of the Pope of Rome and the protection of your lord, do not proceed to a false oath." [4]If he should proceed to the oath, let him first swear to God and to the relics that are in the hand of the judge that the other is not surety for him neither for what he says nor for anything. [5]If the surety does not counter-swear against him, let the debtor be free from the claim and let the surety pay the whole debt to the claimant. [6]If the surety should counter-swear against the debtor, let him counter-swear while the debtor is putting his mouth to the relics after he has sworn. [7]And this is how he

[1] e dely ef y wadw] e deleyr guadu mach *BK*; y mae ia6n g6adu mach *D*; y dyly gwadu y mach J;   y vn tavavt ef ehvn en] un tauaut e mach e *BD*; un tauaut y kynnogyn y *E*.
[2] Ye] dyoer *C*;   a'y gwadaf ef] a'th wadaf ty ß.
[3] vrth e kynnogyn] —*B*;   na dos] nat elych *D*.
[4] dyweyt] dywaut *EA*.
[5] vrthtwng] *here and elsewhere C writes this as two words* (g)vrth twng;   o'r havl] *BK add* am e guat redygones;   o'r dylyet] — *AE*.
[7] re dywedeysy] a dywedassam ny *EA*;   ac anvdon...y arnaty] — *AE*; barnw] — ß; ymy o'r] yr J; e gan er ß.

Ior §60

[1] Ac ena e mae yavn y'r egnat menet allan y barnw brawt. [2] Ac esef a wyl e kyvreyth ena, llw e kynnogyn ar y sseythvet o'y wadv, chwegwyr ac ef ehvn en seythvet, pedwar onadvnt o parth y tat, a'r dev o parth y vam, ac ef ehvn en sseythvet; ac esef en nesset e delyant e gwyr henny bot ydaw ac e delywynt talw galanas y gyt ac ef a'y chymryt. [3/1] Ac esef ew oet er reyth honno, wythnos o'r Swl nessaf rac wynep; [3/2] ac esef lle er rodyr er reyth honno, en llann e bo y dwfyr swyn a'y vara efferen; [3/3] ac esef amser e kymeryr e rwng e Benedycamws a rody e bara efferen. [4] Ac o cheyff entew e reyth honno, dogyn ew ydaw; ony cheyff entev er reyth, talet er hawl, ac o mynn er arglwyd erlyt kyvreyth anvdon arnaw, erlynet. [5] Pa vach bynnac a vrthtygho ar e kynnogyn, ryd vyd o'r havl ac o'r vechny, kanys gwnaeth teythy mach a'r hynn a dyley. [6] Pa vach bynnac entew ny vrthtygho, talet ehvn er havl, kany gwnaeth teythy mach a'r hynn a dyley. [7] Pan adefho mach vrth er egnat y vot en vach, yavn ew y'r havlvr ena tystv re adef ohonaw, rac kylyaw ohonaw eylweyth.

[1] — *C*.
[2] o'y wadv] y wadu y uechny *EA*;   en nesset] *BC omit* en; yn gynesset *D*;   bot ydaw] *CK add* en kyn nesset;   talw galanas y gyt ac ef a'y chymryt] kymryt...ay thalw *C*;...ay chymryt ygyt ac ew *EA*.
[3/1] nessaf rac wynep] *EA omit* rac wynep; ß *omits* nessaf.
[3/2] er reyth honno] *EA add* ydau ew;   e bo y dwfyr swyn a'e vara] y gwarandawho ew *EA*.
[3/3] kymeryr] ß *adds* e reyth honno;   rody] — *A*.
[5] ryd vyd] byt ryd *B*.
[6] ny vrthtygho] ß *adds* ar e kennogen;   er havl] e delyet ar havl *C*; y dylyet *J*.

counter-swears: ''By the relic which is there I am a surety given by you upon that which I have said, and you have sworn a perjury; and because of the counter-oath that I have sworn against you, I wish to have the judge give judgment for me.''

Ior §60

[1] And then it is right for the judge to go out to judge a judgment. [2] And this is the view that the law takes in that case: the oath of the debtor as one of seven [is required] to deny it, six men and himself as seventh, four of them from the father's side, and two from the mother's, and himself as seventh; and these men ought to be sufficiently near to him that they ought to pay and receive wergeld together with him. [3/1] And this is the appointed time for that compurgation, a week from the next Sunday following; [3/2] and the place in which that compurgation is given is the church in which are his holy water and his Mass-bread; [3/3] and the time at which it is taken is between the Benedicamus and the distribution of Mass-bread. [4] And if he obtain that compurgation, that is sufficient for him; and if he does not obtain the compurgation, let him pay what is claimed, and if the lord wishes to prosecute the law of perjury against him, let him prosecute. [5] Any surety who counter-swears against the debtor is free of the claim and of the suretyship, since he has done what pertains to a surety. [6] Let any surety, however, who does not counter-swear, himself pay what is claimed, since he has not done what pertains to a surety and what he is obliged to do. [7] When a surety acknowledges before a judge that he is a surety, it is right that the claimant should then testify that he has acknowledged him, lest he should subsequently withdraw.

Ior §61

¹O dervyd y dyn kymryt mach ar peth y gan arall, yavn ew y'r dyn dody oet ar e peth a delyo, a phan del er oet yavn ew ydaw ehwn govyn e kynnogyn kessevyn, ac os negyf vyd e kynnogyn ydaw, devet ar y vach a holet y vach, a dywedet vot e kynnogyn en negyf ydaw. ²Os ef a dyweyt e mach gwadv hyt nat mach, devent hyt ar er egnat, a holet er havlvr e mach rac dev glyn er egnat. ³Ac os ef a vynn e mach gwadw ac na gwrthyngho er havlvr arnaw, byt ryd e mach o'r havl am e gwat redygones. ⁴Os ef a wna er havlvr gwrthtwng ar e mach a galw am vrawt ar er egnat vrth e gwrthtwng redygones, yavn ew y'r egnat barnw ar e mach y lw ar y sseythvet en vn ffvnvt ac y dywedassam ny wuchot. ⁵O dervyd y dyn kymryt mach y gan arall ar peth a dyvot y dwy pleyt y gyt, er havlwr a'r kynnogyn a'r mach, a holy o'r havlvr e mach a dywedwyt y vot en vach ar peth mawr, ac atteb o'r kynnogyn a dywedwyt y vot en vach ar peth bychan, a hep gwadw e vechny, yawn ew y'r egnat ena barnw bot en edvryt e mach pahar e mae mach, ay ar peth mawr ay ar peth bychan; a henny wrth lw e mach, kanys mach adevedyc ew. ⁶O dervyd y dyn kymryt llawer o veychyew ar peth, a mynnv ew gwadw o'r kynnogyn, kymeynt ac y dywedassam ny wuchot y gwadw mach a daw y wadw pob vn onadvnt wyntew herwyd val y dywedassam wuchot. ⁷Rey a vynn ac vn seyth wyr gwadw ket ed vo pedwar mach ar vgeynt; e kyvreyth eyssyoes a dyweyt hyt nat yavn ac nat adwuyn. ⁸O dervyd y dyn tebygv bot en ryd mach o'y vechny o talv peth o'r dylyet a hep talw kvbyl, e kyvreyth a dyweyt hyt na byd ryd a dylyw ohonaw bot en vach ar e keynnyavc dywethaf mal ar e kyntaf.

---

¹ ar peth] — *BKJ*;　　　　　a holet y vach] — *JK*.
² gwadv] — *E*　　　devent] *CD:* deuet *other MSS;*　　　er havlvr e mach] y haul *EA;* er haulur ef *B;* y vach *J;*　　　a holet...er egnat] — *D*.
³ gwadw] *C adds* hyt nat mach; *J adds* nat mach; er havlvr] ß; e kynnogyn α.
⁴ er havlvr] ß; e kynnogyn α;　　　　gwrthtwng redygones] *C omits* twng;　　　barnw ar e mach] ar ya mach barnu *EA;* barnu arnau *B:* barnu llw y mach ar y seithuet *J;*　　　y lw ar y sseythvet]; e llv ar guat β; i l6 *K; C adds* ac esef nesset e dely e gwyr henny vot ydaw val e dylewynt kymryt galanas y gyt ac ef ay chymryt a henny; *for J see previous note;* en vn ffvnvt ac] *ACD;* yn vn furv ac *E;* mal *BJK*.
⁵ ar peth mawr] — *B;*　　　　ar peth mawr...y vot en vach] — *K;*　　　barnw] — *C;*　　　　edvryt] deturyt *AEBLew.*
⁶ kymryt] rodi *K;*　　　herwyd val e dywedassam ny wuchot] — *B;* ual i dywetp6yt uchot *K;*　　　dywedassam] dreckassam *A;* trythassam *E;*　　　herwyd] — *Lew.*
⁷ Rey] *C adds* or egneyt;　　　e kyvreyth] nyny a dywedvn *EA and similarly throughout the tractate;*　　　hyt nat yavn ac nat adwuyn] hyt nat yaun *EA,* hyt nat adwuyn *CDJLew;* — hyt *K.*
⁸ na byd ryd] *C omits* ryd;　　　dywethaf] dyweth *C.*

Ior §61

[1] If it happens that a man accepts a surety for something from someone else, it is right that the man set a fixed time-limit on the thing to which he is entitled, and when the time comes, it is right that he should first ask the debtor, and if the debtor refuses him, let him come to the surety and let him put his claim to his surety, and let him say that the debtor is refusing him. [2] If the surety says that he denies that he is a surety, let them come to the judge, and let the claimant plead his claim against the surety before the judge. [3] And if the surety wishes to deny [that he is a surety] and the claimant does not counter-swear against him, the surety is free of the claim on account of the denial that he has made. [4] If the claimant counter-swears against the surety and calls for a judgment from the judge on account of the counter-oath that he has made, it is right that the judge judge that the surety should swear his oath as one of seven in the same way as we said above. [5] If it happens that a man accepts a surety from someone else for something and the two parties come together, the claimant and the debtor and the surety, and the claimant makes his claim against the surety and says that he is surety for a large debt, and the debtor replies and says that he is surety for a small debt, and without denying his suretyship, it is right that the judge should then judge that the surety is to declare for what he is surety, whether for a large debt or for a small debt; and that is to be decided according to the oath of the surety, since he is an acknowledged surety. [6] If it happens that a man accepts many sureties for something, and the debtor wish to deny them, as many as we said above were to deny a surety are to come forward to deny each one of them in the way we said above. [7] Some propose that the denial should be made with the one set of seven men though there be twenty-four sureties; but the law says that that is not right and is not appropriate. [8] If it happens that a man suppose that a surety is free of his suretyship by the payment of part of the debt and not the whole, the law says that he is not free and he is obliged to be surety for the last penny just as for the first.

Ior §62

[1] O dervyd bot mach adevedyc ar peth a bot negydyaeth kan e kynnogyn am talw, yawn ew y'r mach rody gwystyl kyvreythyavl. [2] Ac esef ew gwystyl kyvreythyawl e trayan en gwell no'r tal. [3] O dervyd llvdyas rody gwystyl, e mach pyew heprwng e gwystyl y gyt a'r hawlwr hyt en dyogel, ac a dely kymryt e ffonnawt kyntaf o byd emlad. [4] Ac ony gwna henny talet ehvn e dylyet. [5] O dervyd y vach keyssyaw dwyn gwystyl hep e kynnogyn en y kyffroy, ny dely y dwyn: ny dely mach dwyn gwystyl hep e kynnogyn ony byd negydyaeth kyndrychavl en y wyd. [6] O gweles ef negydyaeth en erbyn er hawlwr kynt no henny, entev a eyll rody gwystyl e kynnogyn y'r havlwr en y absen.

[7] O chanhyatta e kynnogyn y'r mach rody gwystyl pvnt en lle vn keynnyavc, a chynn oet e gwystyl kolly e gwystyl, ny dyweyt e kyvreyth delyw ohonaw trachevyn namyn dymey, kanys henny ew trayan e keynnyavc kyvreyth. [8] O dervyd y dyn rody kywerthyd pvnt en lle vn keynnyawc eg gwystyl, a dygwydaw e gwystyl, ny wrthveryr y'r kynnogyn kymeynt ac vn fyrdlyng, kanys ef ehvn a lygrws breynt e gwystyl.

[9] Pwy bynnac a gwystlo gwystyl adevedyc a thebygw ohonaw ef vrth nat oes vach arnaw bot en anylys e gwystyl hvnnw, e kyvreyth a dyweyt dygwydaw e gwystyl hvnnv a'y vot en dylys.

[10] O dervyd y'r mach rody peth mawr eg gwystyl peth bychan, kyvreythyavl ew y'r havlwr kymryt er hynn a roder ydaw eg gwystyl; a chen kollo hwnnw kynt no'r oet, ny dywc ef namyn e trayan trachevyn. [11] E mach hagen a'y dywc en kvbyl y'r kynnogyn, kanys agkyvreythyawl y dwc.

[12] O dervyd bot mach ar devdec keynnyavc, a dyvot oet e devdec keynnyavc, ac nat oes ar helw e kynnogyn namyn march a talho dec pvnt, a dyvot er havlwr a'r mach y kymhell ew devdec keynnavc, a dywedwyt o'r kynnogyn, "Nyt oes kenhyfy a talwyf ychwy namyn ve march, a hvnnv nys talafy ychwy ac nys gwystlaf," ny dely e mach eyssyoes dwyn gwystyl arnaw ef, ac ny dely er havlwr dwyn gwystyl e mach, namyn kyrchw er arglwyd elldev, a mynegy y'r arglwyd nat oes kanthav namyn peth mawr, ac na deleyr dwyn e peth mawr hvnnv eg gwystyl peth bychan. [13] Ac ena e mae yavn y'r arglwyd rody kannyat y'r mach y rody gwystyl mawr en lle e peth bychan rac bot en kolledyc er havlwr.

[14] O dervyd y dyn rody mach y arall ar peth, a gwedy rody e mach mynet y nawd rac e delyet, e kyvreyth a dyweyt na dely nawd rac henny, ac e dely e mach rody y wystyl y'r havlwr, nev entew a gwatto y vechny.

---

[1] ar peth] — AEJ; add yr havlwr. kan e kynnogyn] — AE; rody gwystyl kyvreythyavl] CJ

Ior §62

¹ If it happens that there is an acknowledged surety for something and that the debtor refuses to pay, it is right that the surety should give a lawful gage. ² And the lawful pledge is a third more than the payment. ³ If it happens that the giving of a gage is hindered, it is the job of the surety to bring the gage, together with the claimant, to a safe place, and he ought to take the first blow if there is fighting. ⁴ And if he does not do that, let him pay the debt himself. ⁵ If it happens that the surety seek to take a gage without the debtor urging it, he is not entitled to take it: a surety is not entitled to take a gage in the absence of the debtor unless there is a face to face refusal in his presence. ⁶ If he has previously seen a refusal against the claimant, he is entitled to give the debtor's gage to the claimant in his (the debtor's) absence.

⁷ If the debtor permits the surety to give a gage worth a pound in the place of one worth a penny, and before the time limit for the gage he loses the gage, the law says that he is only entitled to a halfpenny back, because that is a third of a lawful penny. ⁸ If it happens that a man give the value of a pound instead of a penny as a gage, and the gage is forfeit, not even as much as a farthing is returned to the debtor, since he himself debased the status of the gage. ⁹ Whoever should give an acknowledged gage and suppose that because there is no surety for it that gage is not immune from claim, the law says that that gage is forfeit and that it is immune from claim. ¹⁰ If it happens that a surety give something valuable as a gage for something cheap, it is lawful for the claimant to take what is given to him as a gage; and though he should lose it before the time-limit, he only gives a third back in compensation. ¹¹ The surety, however, pays compensation in full to the debtor, since he took it unlawfully. ¹² If it happens that there is a surety for twelve pence, and the time-limit for the twelve pence is up, and there is nothing in the possession of the debtor except a horse worth ten pounds, and the claimant and the surety come to enforce [payment of] their ten pence, and the debtor says, "I have nothing that I can pay you except my horse, and as for that, I shall not give it to you in payment and I shall not give it as a gage," the surety is nevertheless not entitled to take a gage from him, and the claimant is not entitled to take the surety's gage, but they are both to seek out the lord, and they are to explain to the lord that he only has a valuable thing in his possession, and that that valuable thing ought not to be taken as a gage for something cheap. ¹³ And then it is right that the lord should give the surety permission to give a valuable gage instead of the cheap thing lest the claimant should suffer loss. ¹⁴ If it happens that a man give a surety to another for something, and after the surety has been given

² Ac esef ew gwystyl kyvreythyawl] — *EJK; the main scribe of E adds* ar uod *in the left margin;* e] e e *C.*

³ y gyt a'r hawlwr] ygyt ac ef *BK.*

⁵ (a) O dervyd...en y kyffroy]

y vach keyssyaw] keyssyau or mach β; dwyn gwystyl] d6yn gauael *JK;* d6yn gafel neu 6ystyl *Tim;* hep e kynnogyn en y kyffroy] *CKLew;* hep ekanogon hep kefroi or kanogon er haul *A;* heb y kynnogyn ep gyfroy ar y kynnogyn yr haul *E; B omits* en y kyffroy; heb yr ha6l6r yn y gyffroi *D;* heb y kynogyn y kyffroi *Tim;* y tala6dyr yn y absen *J;*

(b) ny dely y dwyn] *B;* nys dyly *DJ;* — *KLew; EA add* gvystyl; ny dely ef dwyn gwystyl hep e kynnogyn *C;* nys dyly y d6yn *Tim;*

(c) ny dely mach...hep e kynnogyn] — *BDJTim; EA omit* hep;

(d) ony byd...en y wyd] *EA;* ony bey ryuot negydyaeth en y vyd *B;* kyndrychavl] eny kyndrychavl *C;* k*yfreith*a6l *DJLew;* — *Tim;* en y wyd] yny ofyn *Tim;* gantha6 gysseuin *J.*

⁶ gwystyl] *B adds* keureythyaul. 7-8. — *J.*

⁷ y'r mach] — *B;* a chynn oet e gwystyl] a chyn yr oet gvystyl *EA;* henny] dymey *B.*

⁸ kywerthyd] gwystyl *C;* eg gwystyl] — α; wrthveryr] *CLew;* vruernyr *A;* uernyr *ETim (cf. Col);* arueryr *B;* atuerir *D;* di6ygir *K;* ac vn fyrdlyng] a dim *AE.*

⁹ — *Tim;* adefedyc] α *J;* — ß; dygwydaw e gwystyl hvnnv] e dyguyd e guestel hunnu *B; AE omit* e gwystyl.

¹⁰ kymryt er hynn] kymryt y peth *EA;* kymryt y rym *Lew;* i gymryt *K;* a roder ydaw] *B adds* er e ueynt; ny dywc ef] *C adds* yr mach ay rodassey attaw ef; ni dicuit ef *with* hu *written above the* cu *of* dicuit *A;* ny dygvyd ew *with* dygwyd *deleted and replaced by* dyvc *in the left margin, all by the main scribe, E;* ny d6c *Tim;* nyt atuer er haulur *B;* trachevyn] *EA add* yr mach ay rodes atav.

¹¹ hagen] — *EA.*

¹² a dyvot oet e devdec keynnyavc] — *BDTim;* a talho dec pvnt] *EA omit* a talho; a dalei...*DKTim; KJTim omit* dec; ny dely e mach eyssyoes dwyn gwystyl] — *EA;* eyssyoes] yna *DJ;* — *Tim;* dwyn] rodi *J;* gwystyl] gafel *Tim;* kanthav] racv *EA.*

¹³ ac yna i mae ir argl6yd rodi peth ma6r yng6ystyl peth bychan *etc. K;* en lle e] am e *B; Lew omits* en lle; peth] — *C.*

¹⁴ rody mach] *B adds* ar delyet; ar peth] — *AB.*

Ior §63

¹ Ny dely nep kymryt mach en vn dydyavc, kanys onys havl en e dyd hvnnv nevt edyw en amser nat oes vach ydaw. ² Ny dely dyn kymryt mach kynnogyn, kanys dev ardelw ynt ac na cheyff entew namyn dewys y ardelw: os o vechny e dewys y ardelw nyt oes kynnogyn; os o kynnogyn e dewys nyt oes vach; ac wrth henny ny eyll vn dyn sevyll en vach kynnogyn. ³ Ny dely mach dwyn gwystyl ar e kynnogyn ac ef en negessev y arglwyd new en y negessev ehvn nev en wan; ac ny dely er hawlwr dwyn gwystyl e mach eg kehyt a henny o espeyt.

he seeks protection from the debt, the law says that he is not entitled to protection from that, and that the surety ought to give a gage to the claimant, or else he should deny his suretyship.

Ior §63

[1] No one should accept a surety for one day, for unless he claims it on that day, it is then a period in which he has no surety. [2] No one should accept someone who is both surety and debtor, for they are two legal roles and that person must choose his role: if he chooses to put himself forward as a surety there is no debtor; if he chooses to put himself forward as a debtor there is no surety; and because of that no man may act as both surety and debtor. [3] No one is entitled to take a gage from the debtor while the latter is engaged in the pressing affairs of his lord or in his own pressing affairs or is sick; and the claimant is not entitled to take the surety's gage in the same period of time.

[1] neut edyw en amser]...ar amser *EA*; neut aeth dros amser *D*.
[2] os o vechny e dewys y] *AE omit* dewys y;   os o kynnogyn e dewys] *AETim omit* e dewys; *Lew has* e dewys *deleted after* vach;   en vach kynnogyn] en vach ac en kynnogyn *CDLewTim*.
[3] gwystyl] gafel na g6ystyl *K*;   en negessev y arglwyd new en y negessev ehvn] *DLew reverse order;*   espeyt] *J adds* Teirg6eith y mae yr mach keissya6 y tala6dyr yny atlam kynn d6yn y auael ac onys keiff yn hynny ryd y6 ida6 rodi y auael yr ha6l6r.

Ior §64

[1] O dervyd y dyn kymryt mach ar da ac gwedy henny dyhol e kynnogyn, ay o achavs galanas ay o achavs lledrat ay o agkyvreyth arall ny del y o ef e gwlat, a mynnv o'r havlvr e da y gan e mach, esef a wyl e kyvreyth bot en yavn rannv er regthvnt en dev hanner e kollet: talw o'r mach e neyll hanner y'r havlwr kanys hagyr ew talw o'r mach kvbyl ac ef en wyryon, ac nat tegach kolly o'r havlwr kvbyl a recredw ohonaw entew e mach. [2] A llena e tredyd lle e ran e kyvreyth herwyd kyvreyth Hewel. [3] O dervyd dyvot e kynnogyn y'r wlat tra'y kevyn gwedy henny, wyntew a delyant kymhell ew da arnaw ef, ac ena e mae yavn kaffael o'r mach hanner o'r da hvnnv. [4] A llyna e lle e byd kymhellwr e mach ar da ydaw ehwn. [5] O dervyd bot mach ar delyet a chyn no dyvot oet e delyet marw e mach ac adaw map ohonaw, e map a dely sevyll en dylyedyon y tat. [6] Rey a dyweyt o mynn e map hvnnv gwadv e vechny e mae wuch pen bed y tat e gwat ar kyvreyth; e kyvreyth eyssyoes a dyweyt na deleyr kanys e doethyon a dyweyt nat erlyt kyvreyth e byt dyn na nef ed el nac wffern namyn hyt eny el ef y ar e dayar. [7] Esef achaws ew, ket boet kyvreyth er rwng dyn a'y gylyd ar e dayar hon, nyt oes kyvreyth er rwng dyawul a'y gylyd ac nyt oes kyvreyth er rwng eghyl a'y gylyd namyn ewyllys Dyw; ac wrth henny dyn a el y ar e dayar honn nyt oes ydaw entew kyvreyth namyn kytvot e neyll rey onadvnt. [8/1] Ac wrth henny e mae yawn y vap e mach marw gwassanaethw kyvreyth tros y tat mal y gwassanaeythey y tat pey byw. [8/2] Ony byd map ydaw er arglwyd a dely bot en vap ydaw. [9] Ac o byd reyt kymhell ef a dely kymhell mal y deley y mach pey byw. [10] O dervyd y dyn kymryt mach y kan arall ar peth a chyn dyvot oet e dylyet marw e kynnogyn, e mach a dely kymhell map e kynnogyn megys e kynnogyn. [11] O dervyd na bo map ydav, savet er arglwyd en lle map ydaw a thalet trostaw; ac os gwadw a vynn, gwadet ehwn mal e gwattey e gwr ed aeth en vap ydaw yr y da. [12] Kan bw gwell kanthaw ef mynet en vap y'r gwr raccw yr y da no bot en arglwyd, byt entew em breynt e gwr ed aeth en vap ydaw, a gwadet ar y seythvet e vechny; a'r gwyr henny ny delyant hanvot o kenedyl e kynnogyn namyn o kenedyl e brennyn, kany deyryt kenedyl e kynnogyn y'r brennyn ket gwatto e brennyn e mach. [13] Eny dygwydo gwat ar vap am vechny y tat, ny dely nep o kenedyl y vam gwadw dym tros y tat ef.

Ior §64

[1] If it happens that a man accepts a surety for goods, and subsequently the debtor is banished, whether because of feud or because of theft or for some other unlawful act so that he is not entitled [to remain in] the land, and the claimant wishes to have the goods from the surety, this is the view that the law takes, that it is right that they divide the loss equally between them: the surety is to pay one half to the claimant because it is unseemly that the surety should pay the whole though he is innocent, and it is no fairer that the claimant should lose the whole because he, for his part, trusted the surety. [2] And that is one of the three places in which the law makes a division according to the law of Hywel. [3] If it happens that the debtor subsequently returns to the land they are entitled to compel him to pay their goods, and then it is right that the surety should receive half of those goods. [4] And that is the place in which the surety is an enforcer for his own goods. [5] If it happens that there is a surety for a debt and before the time-limit for the debt is up the surety dies and leaves a son, the son should act in respect of the obligations of the father. [6] Some say that if that son wishes to deny his suretyship he makes a denial in law over the grave of the father; the law, however, says that he ought not, since the wise say that the law of this world does not pursue a man whether he go to heaven or to hell but only until he departs from this earth. [7] And this is the reason: though there be law between one man and another on this earth, there is no law between one devil and another nor between one angel and another except for the will of God; and therefore for a man who departs from this earth there is no law except that each of them should be at peace with the other. [8/1] And because of that it is right that the son of the dead surety should do what is lawful on behalf of his father just as the father would have done had he been alive. [8/2] If he has no son the lord should act as his son. [9] And if it be necessary to enforce he should enforce just as the surety should have done if he had been alive. [10] If it happens that a man takes a surety from someone for something and before the time-limit for the debt is up the debtor dies, the surety should compel the debtor's son [to pay] just as he would the debtor. [11] If it happens that he has no son, let the lord stand in the place of his son and let him pay on his behalf; and if he wishes to deny, let him deny as

¹ ay o achavs lledrat ay o agkyvreyth arall] *EAJ substitute* achavs *for* agkyvreyth arall; *B substitutes* agkyureythyeu, *and KLew* aghyfreithieu ereill; *D omits* achavs; agheneu ereill *Tim*;   na delyo ef] *EAJ* add bot yn;   y'r havlwr] yr kynnogyn *C*; ar kynnogyn e llall *EA*;   nat tegach] hagyr *E*; hegar *A*;   a recredw ohonaw entew e mach] — *BKTim*, ar recredw . . . *C*; yr . . . *E*.
² kyvreyth herwyd] — *Tim*;   herwyd kyvreyth Hewel] *CLew*; her6yd kyfreith 6yned *K*; heruit kereihaul *A*; yn gyureithyaul *E*; en deu hanner *BDJ*.
⁶ o mynn e map hvnnv gwadv] ony mynn y mab seuyll yn *Tim*; o men e mab hunnu seuyll en *BDKLew*.
8/²bot en] seuyll en lle ß.   9. deley] kemhelley ß.
¹¹en lle map ydaw] yny le *EA*;   a thalet trostaw] *BKTim add* neu wadet.
¹²o kenedyl e kynnogyn] o genedyl y mach *EA*;   kany deyryt kenedyl e kynnogyn] kanys ny. . . ; *for* kynnogyn *EA substitute* mach.
¹³Ene] ony *B*;   *dygwydo*] diguatho *A*; dywato *E*;   ar vap] — *A*.

Ior §65

¹TEYR OVER VECHNY ESSYD: kyntaf ew onadvnt pan prynno dyn peth y gan arall yr aryant, a chymryt mach arnaw ac na chymerer mach ar er aryant, a bot en edyvar kan perchynnavc er aryant e kyvnewyt. ²Kany mynn mwynhaw e mach essyd ydaw ar e peth y kymyrth, ac nat oes vach y'r llall a kymhello ydaw e kyvnewyt, wrth henny e mae over e mach o'r neyll tv kany mynn e perchennawc ef. ³Er eyl ew, o dervyd y dyn rody mach y arall ar anylys en ryth dylys, a dyvot perchennawc e da o'e anylyssw, yavn ew y kaffael o'r perchennawc er eydaw; ket roder mach ar peth, ny deleyt y rody ac nyt yawn y kechwyn o'r llaw e mae endy eny del arwystyl kystal ac ef y kan er arwayssaf. ⁴O dervyd y'r arwayssaf dywedwyt na dely talw namyn kymeynt ac a kavas ef yr e march, e kyvreyth eyssyoes a dyweyt delyw ohonaw ef talw gwerth kyvreyth e march pa ryw varch bynnac vo. ⁵Ac wrth na eyll e mach kynnal e kyvechny ed aeth en vach arney, am henny e gelwyr en over vach. ⁶E da anylys redywedassam ny wuchot, pwybynnac a dygwydho eg kam am y kychwynnyat byt er arglwyd en y ol. ⁷Tredyd ew nyt mach mach gwreyc. ⁸Esef ew henny, ny dely gwreyc bot en vach, kany dely gwraged gwadw mach, ac na dely hythew reyth o wyr o'y gwadw. 9/¹E kyvreyth a dyweyt bot en vach mach a rodo gwreyc, kanys pwybynnac a allo anylyssw da e kyvreyth a dyweyt bot en kyvreyth ydav y dylyssw. 9/²Kanys gwreyc a eyll anylyssw da, e kyvreyth a dyweyt bot en reyt mach ar dylysrwyd y kenthy, a bot en vach e mach a rodo hythew. ¹⁰Kanys gwr a gwatta hy, gwyr a dely hythew y gyt a hy y gwadw mach. ¹¹O dervyd y gwreyc rody bry Dyw ar peth a'y gwadw ohoney en kyvreythyawl, e kyvreyth a dyweyt e mae gwraged a'y gwatta y gyt a hy.

¹ OVER] OVEN *C*;   kyntaf ew onadvnt] — *AE*; un etc. ß; *DJ omit* onadvnt; arnaw] ar y peth ß;   arnaw ac na chymerer mach] — *B*.

would the man whose son he has become for the sake of the goods. [12]Since he prefers to become a son to that man for the sake of the goods rather than be lord, let him have the status of the man whose son he has become, and let him deny his suretyship as one of seven; and those men should not belong to the debtor's kindred but to the king's kindred, since the debtor's kindred does not pertain to the king though the king deny the surety. [13]When it falls to the son to make a denial concerning the suretyship of the father, no one from his mother's kindred is entitled to deny anything on behalf of his father.

Ior §65

[1]There are three useless suretyships: the first of them is when someone buys something from another for money, and a surety is accepted for the thing and a surety is not accepted for the money, and the owner of the money changes his mind about the exchange. [2]Since he does not wish to make use of the surety that he has for the thing that he received, and the other party has no surety who can enforce the exchange for him, as a consequence the surety from the one side is useless since the owner does not desire [to use] him. [3]The second is if it happens that a man gives a surety to another for something which does not belong to him in the belief that it is his, and the owner of the goods comes to reclaim them, it is right that the owner should get what is his; though a surety be given for something, there was no entitlement to give him, and it is not right that it should leave the hand in which it is until there comes a substitute of equal value to it from the warrantor. [4]If it happens that the warrantor says that he should only pay as much as he got for the horse, nevertheless the law says that he should pay the legal value of the horse whatever sort of horse it may be. [5]And because the surety cannot sustain his suretyship for which he became a surety, for that reason he is called a useless surety. [6]The goods that he did not own which we mentioned above, let the lord pursue whoever should be found to be at fault concerning their change of possession. [7]The third is that a woman's surety is no surety. [8]That is, a woman is not entitled to be a surety, since women are not entitled to deny a surety, and she is not entitled to have men as compurgators to deny it. [9/1]The law says that the surety that a woman gives is a surety, because whoever can reclaim ownership of goods, the law says that it is lawful for him to transfer ownership which is immune from claim. [9/2]Since a woman can reclaim goods, the law says that it is necessary to have from her a surety as to immunity from claim,

² nat oes vach] *B omits* vach;   y'r llall] *BKTim add* ar er aryant.
³ Er eyl ew] — *AE*;   ar anylys] ar peth anylys ß;   kaffael o'r perchennawc]
BGKTim add e da;   ar peth, ny] arnau cane *BGKTim*;   nyt yawn] ny deleyr ß.
⁴ yr e march] er e peth ß; *BGK add* pa ryu beth bennac vo;   ef talw] —
BGK;   march] peth *β*;   varch] beth *β*.
⁵ kyvechny] keuechny *A*; gynegny *E*; kyvnewyt *C*; vechny ß; uechniaeth *G*;
am henny] — ß.
⁶ anylys] — *B*;   wuchot] yma *EA*;   am y kychwynnyat] kychwynnyat amdanau
B; am gychwynnedigaeth y da hvnnv *E*.
⁸ Esef] sef *C with space left for large E*;   kany dely] urth na eyll *B*;   reyth o wyr]
reythwyr *BGTim*.
^{9/1-2} E kyvreyth...a eyll anylyssv da] — *AE*;
^{9/1} bot en kyvreyth] *Clew*, bot en kyfreytha6l *D*; bot yn kyfreithia6n *K*; bot yn ia6n *GTim*;
bot en ryd *B*.
^{9/2} kyvreyth] kyvreyt *C*;   reyt] ryd reyd *E*;   mach ar dylysrwyd] *Tim omits*
mach ar; *B omits* ar dylysrwyd.
¹¹ gwraged] g6yr *DLew*.

Ior §66

¹Rey a dyweyt na dygwyd gwystyl o law vach hyt em pen vn dyd a
blwydyn; e kyvreyth a dyweyt e dygwyd gwystyl o law try dyn en y oet.
²Esef ew e try dyn henny, mach ac arglwyd a pherchennavc da. ³Sef achaws
ew, kanys er arglwyd a vyd mach ar pob da adevedyc; vrth henny e dygwyd
o'y law entew e gwystyl new o law y wassanaethwyr. ⁴O law arglwyd nev
o lav vach nyt reyt mach ar dylyssrwyd gwystyl, kany gwadant wy y rody,
ac wyntew en delyw bot en veychyew ar dylysrwyd e gwystyl hvnnv vyth.
^{4a}Er arglwyd essyd vach ar pob da adevedyc o'r ny vo mach arnaw. ⁵Y gan
perchen e da e deleyr kymryt mach ar dylysrwyd e gwystyl, rac y gwadv
ohonaw ef ay yr chwant e da ay yr peth arall nas rodassey.

⁶Ny dely nep dywedwyt nat el en vach tros y gylyd or byd kyvryw gwr
ac e delyo mynet en vach. ⁷Llawer o kyvryw dynyon ny delyant mynet en
vach na rody mach; sef achaws ew henny, kany delyant wy gwadw mach,
ny delyant rody mach: nyt amgen, a manach ac ermydwr a dyn agkyfyeyth
ac escolheyc escol a phop dyn ny allo hep kanhyat arall dyvot y wassanaethw
kyvreyth. ⁸O dervyd y dyn rody mach ar dylyet ar oet a dygwydaw er oet
en vn o'r teyr gwyl arpennyc, e Nodolyc a'r Pasch a'r Swl Gwynn, yr holy
ohonaw ny chyll onyt y annot. ⁹Os dyw Nodolyc e kyffry y hawl, ny cheyff
attep hyt trannoeth gwedy dyw Kalan. ¹⁰Os dyw Pasch vyd, dyw Mavrth
gwedy dyw Pasch bychan. ¹¹Os dyw Swl Gwyn vyd, dyw Mavrth gwedy
y'r swl nessaf y'r Swl Gwynn. ¹²A'r teyr wythnos henny a elwyr oc ew
breynt en vn dyd dydon. ¹³Nyt reyt kymryt mach ar aryant nac ar tlyssew
treygledyc, kae a chyllell a gwregys, nac arvew hevyt. ¹⁴O dervyd y vach
a chynnogyn kyvarvot ar pont vn pren, ny dely bot en negyf ydaw hep

and that the surety that she gives is a surety. [10] Since a man denies her, she
is entitled to have men along with her to deny a surety. [11] If it happens that
a woman gives the Honour of God for something and she makes a lawful
denial, the law says that it is women who deny it together with her.

Ior §66

[1] Some say that a gage is not forfeit from the hand of a surety for a period
of a day and a year; the law says that a gage is forfeit from the hand of three
persons at its appointed time. [2] Those three persons are as follows: a surety
and a lord and an owner of goods. [3] The reason is because the lord is surety
for all acknowledged goods; as a consequence the gage is forfeit from his
hand or from that of his servants. [4] There is no need for a lord or a surety
to give a surety for a gage's immunity from claim, since they do not deny
having given it, and they themselves should always be sureties for that gage's
immunity from claim. [4/a] The lord is surety for all acknowledged goods
which have no surety for them. [5] From the owner of the goods a surety for
immunity from claim should be accepted, lest he should deny [the
transaction] either because he desires the goods or for some other reason [and
says] that he did not give them. [6] No one ought to say that he will not act
as surety for another if he be the sort of man that ought to act as surety.
[7] Many sorts of person are not entitled to act as surety nor to give surety;
and this is the reason, because they are not entitled to deny a surety they
are not entitled to give a surety; namely, a monk and a hermit and a person
who does not speak Welsh and a pupil in a school and every person who
cannot, without the permisson of another, come to act at law. [8] If it happens
that a man gives a surety for a debt with a fixed time-limit and the time-limit
expires on one of the three special feasts, Christmas and Easter and Whitsun,
even though he should make his claim he does not lose anything except for
the delay. [9] If he makes his claim at Christmas, he does not obtain an answer
until the day after the 1st of January. [10] If it is Easter, the Tuesday after Low

gwnevthvr vn o try pheth: ay talw ay gwystlaw ay kyrchw kyvreyth; ac ny dely ef kychwyn y vawt hyt y savdyl hep gwnevthvr vn o'r try henny. [15]O byd negyf ef o gwnevthvr vn o'r try henny, rodet e mach y wystyl entew y'r havlwr. [16]O byd gwell kanthav entew, kyrchet kyvreyth dyannot.

[2] mach ac arglwyd] argluyd a mach ß.
[3] kanys] — D; adefedyc] ß adds ny bo mach arnau; o'y law entew e gwystyl] e guestel o'e lau enteu ß.
[4] nev o law vach] — D. [4a] — ß; C omits vach.
[5] ohonaw ef] ß adds eylweyth; peth] da B.
[7] nyt] yt C with space left for a large N; ermydwr] meud6y Tim; ny allo hep kannyat arall dyvot y wassanaethw kyvreyth] CG; ny allho dyuot heb ganhyat arall y wassanaythu kyureyth EA; B omits dyvot y; ny allo dyuot y wassanaethu kyfreith heb gannyat arall DKLew; ny allo dyfod heb genad arall dyfod y 6ssanaethu kyfreith with second dyfod deleted Tim.
[9] e kyffry y hawl, ny cheyff] A adds hi haul ny keif; E adds y haul nac.
[10-11] dyw Mavrth] trannoeth EA; nessaf y'r Swl Gwynn] y drinda6t DKLewTim.
[14] hep gwnevthvr] o wneythur ß; gwystlaw] g6adu D.
[15] gwnevthvr] — AE.

Ior §67

[1]Ny deleyr rody oet wrth porth am hawl vach a kynnogyn kanys dyannot e dely vot. [2]O dervyd y havlwr gwrthot kyvreyth rac dev glyn egnat, byt ryd e mach a byt kolledyc entew o'y hawl, kany phara y hawl namyn tra parhao y mach. [3]Os e kynnogyn a wrthyt kyvreyth, byt e mach en vach adevedyc a'r hawl en yr, a chymhell o'r mach y'r hawlwr y delyet.

[4]O damweynhya y dew dyn bot kyvreyth er regthvnt, a'r neyll onadvnt en galw ar vach ar kyvreyth, a'r llall en dewedwyt na dely ef rody mach namyn delew ohonaw ef oet wrth y porth, a dywedwyt o'r hawlvr, "Dyoer," hep ef, "mach a delyaf y; dely mach ny dely dym" — "Dyoer," hep e llall, "nyt mach ar ny bo mach ar dym, ac y my ny deleyr dym kanys adevedyc kennyt ty na deley ty dym" — e kyvreyth a dyweyt na dely mach ar kyvreyth kan ardelws e llall o oet wrth porth ac nat oes oet en hawl vach a chynnogyn.

[2] kany phara] kanys ny para α.
[3]byt] C; a bot D; bot other MSS; a'r hawl...mach] ar yr ha6l; y mach a dyly D; y delyet] kubel oe delyet ß.
[4]damweynhya] dervyd DTim; ar vach] am vach ß; rody mach] BK add ar keureyth; Lew omits rody; ac y my ny deleyr dym] — D; na deley ty dym] AE add ymi C adds ac nat delyet dym; e llall] — AE; ynteu D; oet wrth porth] ß adds a phey rodey e mach keureyth dynannot a uedey.

Sunday. [11]If it is Whitsun, the Tuesday after the first Sunday after Whitsun. [12]And those three weeks are called in virtue of their privilege the sole free day. [13]It is not necessary to take a surety for money nor for easily movable valuables, brooch and knife and girdle, nor for arms. [14]If it happens that a surety and a debtor meet on a bridge consisting of a single log, he (the debtor) is not entitled to refuse him or to avoid doing one of three things: either pay or give a gage or go to law; and he is not entitled to move his finger to his heel without doing one of those three things. [15]And if he refuse to do one of those three things, let the surety give that person's gage to the claimant. [16]If he, the debtor, should prefer, let him go to law without delay.

Ior §67

[1]A fixed period of delay for seeking assistance should not be granted in a plea of surety and debtor since it ought to be without delay. [2]If it happens that a claimant refuses to go to law before a judge, let the surety be free and let the claimant be deprived of his claim, since the claim continues only as long as the surety continues. [3]If the debtor refuses to go to law, let the surety be an acknowledged surety and the claim be undecayed, and let the surety enforce the debt for the claimant. [4]If it happens that two men be at law and one of them calls for a surety for law, and the other says that he ought not to give a surety but he is entitled to a fixed delay for assistance, and the claimant says, "God knows," he says, "I am entitled to a surety; he who is entitled to a surety is not entitled to anything" — "God knows," says the other, "he who is not a surety for anything is not a surety, and from me there is no debt owing since you have admitted that you are not entitled to anything" — the law says that he is not entitled to a surety for law since the other based his position on a fixed delay for assistance and there is no fixed delay in a plea of surety and debtor.

Ior §68
AM VRY DYW E TRAETHA HYN.

[1]O dervyd y dyn rody bry Dyw ar peth, talet new gwadet mal y dywetto kyvreyth. [2][S]ef a dyweyt e kyvreyth, ony gwrthtyghyr arnaw, bot en dygawn y lw ehwn. [3]Os gwr[th]twng a vyd arnaw, galwet entew am vrawt. [4]Esef a varn e kyvreyth, y lw ar y seythvet o'y gwadw: pedwar o kenedyl y tat a dev o kenedyl y vam ac ehvn en seythvet. [5]Oet e reyth honno wythnos o'r Svl rac wynep. [6]O cheffyr e reyth, dogyn ew; o dygwyd e reyth y'r dyn, kamlwrw y'r brenyn a'r eglwys byt en y ol, a thalet e delyet en kvbyl. [7]O dervyd y dyn kymryt bry Dyw y gan arall a dywedwyt pan yw ar pedeyr ar vgeynt e mae, a'r llall en dywedwyt ac en adef bot bry Dyw ar chwech keynnyawc, esef a dyweyt e kyvreyth delyw ohonaw ef bot en atverwr pahar e mae y vry Dyw, ay ar pedeyr ar vegeynt ay ar chwech keynnyavc, kanyt edyw en gwadv bry Dyw, a henny wrth y lw. [8]Ket dyweter y bot en vry Dyw, e kyvreyth a dyweyt nat bry Dyw eny kyvarfo e llaw a'y gylyd, ac nat mach ac nat gorvodawc eny kyvarfo e teyr llaw y gyt. [9]Er eglwys a'r brennyn a delyant kymhell bry Dyw, kanys Dyw a kymerwyt en lle mach, a'r eglwys pyew y wahard am bry Dyw, a'r brennyn y kymhell. [12]Kanys y gan pob dyn a vedydyer e deleyr kymryt bry Dyw, ac y gan gwr ac y gan gwreyc; wrth henny e dely a gwr a gwreyc y rody hythev hyt en oet map seyth mlwyd a el adan law y peryglawr.

[1] bry Dyw] bridui *A*.
[2] gwrthtyghyr] gurthdug *EAB*.
[4] a varn] a wyl *B*;   kyvreyth] ß *adds* ydau;   kenedyl y tat] parth y tat *EA*; kenedyl y vam] parth y uam *EA*.
[5] wythnos] pytheunos *EA*.
[6] dogyn] k6byl *D*; digon *K*;   ew] *B adds* ydy;   e reyth y'r dyn] yny reith *EA*;   a'r eglwys byt en y ol] *KG omit* byt; ac yr egluis bit *A*; a byt er egluys en e ol *B*.
[7] *Here C prefixes the heading* Am vry dyw ew hyn;   bry Dyw] bridui *A*;   pan yw] e mae *B*;   en dywedwyt ac en adef] en dywedwyt ac — *AE*; ac en adef — ß;   bry Dyw] bridu *A*;   chwech] *CBKGLew*; deudec *D*; — *AE*;   chwech] *CBKGLew*; deudec *D*; — *AE*;   a henny wrth y lw] — *AE*; *D adds* yr creir.
[8] Ket dyweter y bot en vry Dyw] — *AE*;   e llaw a'y gylyd] *BKG*; y lla6 yny gilyd *DLew*;   y teyr llau y gyt *α*;   eny kyvarfo] — *C*.
[9] Dyw] dyn *C*;   a'r eglwys] yr egluys *E*; ac urth henne er eglues *B*.
[10] y rody hythev] rody (roy *A*) bruduv *EAD*; peryglawr] perigleu *G*; offeiryat *D*.

Ior §69
O VRY DYW E TRAETHWYT WUCHOT AC O AMVOT EW HYNN.

[1]Pwy bynnac a gwnel amvot dedvavl a'y gylyd, doent e dew amvotwr y gyt, a dywedent ew hamvot val e mynnoent y gwnevthwr, a rodent wyntev en

Ior §68
THIS TREATS OF THE 'HONOUR OF GOD'

[1] If it happens that a man gives the Honour of God [as a guarantee] for something. Let him pay or let him deny as the law may prescribe. [2] And this is what the law prescribes: unless a counter-oath be sworn against him, his own oath is sufficient. [3] If there is a counter-oath against him, let him call for judgement. [4] And this is what the law judges: his oath as one of seven [is required] to deny it, four from his paternal kindred and two from his maternal kindred and himself as the seventh. [5] The fixed time for that compurgation is a week from the Sunday following. [6] If the compurgation is obtained, it is sufficient; if the man's compurgation fails, the king takes a *camlwrw* and let the church pursue him, and let him pay the debt in full. [7] If it happens that a man takes the Honour of God from someone else and says that it is for 24d., and the other acknowledges that the Honour of God guarantees 6d., this is what the law says, that he is to recall what his Honour of God guarantees, whether 24d. or 6d., since he is not denying the Honour of God; and that [declaration] is to be upon his oath. [8] Though it should be said to be the Honour of God, the law says that it is not the Honour of God until the one hand should meet with the other, and that there is no surety and there is no gorfodog until the three hands meet together. [9] The church and the king should enforce the Honour of God, since God is taken in place of a surety, and the church should excommunicate him for the sake of the Honour of God and the king should enforce it. [10] For the Honour of God should be accepted from every person who has been baptised, both from man and from woman; because of this both man and woman are entitled to give it, even a child of seven years who goes under the authority of a priest.

Ior §69
ABOVE THE HONOUR OF GOD WAS DISCUSSED, AND THIS IS ABOUT *AMOD*

[1] Whoever should make a lawful *amod* with another, let the two *amod*-men come together, and let them declare their *amod* as they may wish to make

llaw er amvotwyr kadw er amvot ar e llvn y hadavssant. ²O dervyd y dyn gwnevthvr amvot ac na mynho y kadw ac na gwatto entew er amvot, er arglwyd pyew kymhell y kadw val y hatvero er amvotwyr. ³O dervyd y dyn mynnv gwadv y amvot ac arall en y errw arnaw er amvot ac entew en gwadv ehwn, e kyvreyth a dyweyt na daw arnaw ef namyn y lw ehwn o'y wadw ony byd gwrthtwng arnaw. ⁴Os gwrthtwng a vyd arnaw galwet er havlvr am vravt; ac esef a vernyr ydaw, y lw ar y seythvet o'y gwadv, a henny val e gwatter mach, a'r oet a vo ar reyth mach y vot ar hvnnv. ⁵O dervyd ena mynnv llyssw vn o'r reythwyr henny, nyt oes lys arnaw namyn na hanvo o'y kenedyl val na delyo vot en reythwr ydaw. ⁶Sef val e dely bot en reythwr ydaw; en kynnesset ac e talo galanas y gyt ac ef ac e kymero trostaw; ac wrth lw e reythwr bot en wyr y kerennyd. ⁷O dervyd y dyn gwnevthwr amvot a'y gylyd hep amvotwyr a'r llaw yn y gylyd, a'r neyll en mynnv gwadv, ny daw arnaw namyn y lw ehvn o'e gwadw. ⁸O dervyd y dyn emadav ac arall am peth eg gwyd tystyon a mynnv ohonaw y gwadw, e kyvreyth a dyweyt na dely ef y gwadw eny pallo e tystyon. ⁹O dervyd y dyn emadaw ac arall am peth hep tystyon en e lle, nyt amvot hvnnw, a chanyt amvot gwadet o'e lw ehwn. ¹⁰Ny dely nep gwnevthvr amvot tros y gylyd kany phara amvot namyn en oes a dyn a'y gwnel. ¹¹Ny eyll e tat adav amvot ar e map namyn kan y kanhyat e map mwy noc a eyll e map gwnevthvr amvot ar torr e tat a'r tat en vyw. ¹²Amvot a tyrr dedyf. ¹³Ket gwneler amvot en erbyn e kyvreyth, dyr ew y kadw.

¹ doent] *CDKW*; doet *AEBGLew*; dew] du *A*; duyn *E*; a rodent... amotwyr] — *D*; kadw] k6d6 *D*; hadavssant] dywedassant *EA*.
³ gwadv y amvot] guad y amod *A*; guadu amot ß; en y errw] yn gyrru *EAB*; en gwadv ehwn] yn gwadu hunnu *EA*; en e wadu ehun *BKG*; ehun yn g6adu *D*; ac ynteu yn g6adu ehun *Lew*; na daw] *C adds* dyweyt (*deleted*) *after* na; na da *A*; nat a *E*; gwrthtwng arnaw] byd arnau gurthtug *B*.
⁴ er havlvr] — *B*; gwatter] gwedyr *EA*; ar reyth] *C omits* ar; y vot] — *B*.
⁵ ydaw] — *AE*; arno *K*.
⁶ talo] talhoent *E*; deleho talu *BK*; ac e kymero] ac y cymeront *E*; ay chymryt *CB*; trostaw] — *AE*; wyr] *C adds* a dyweyt a.
⁷ gwneythwr amvot a'y gylyd] ay gylyd gwneuthur amuot *EA*; hep amvotwyr] *C adds* en e lle; *DLew add* namyn; a'r neyll] *EA add* onadunt; namyn] namy *C*.
⁸ ac] ac ac ac *C*; am peth eg gwyd tystyon] eg guyd testyon am peth *BKG*; a mynnv ohonaw y gwadw] *AE omit* ohonaw; a mennu eylweyth e wadu ohonau *BGK*; a mynnu y wadu ohona6 eilweith *DLew*.
⁹ emadaw ac arall am peth] *AEB omit* am peth.
¹⁰ kany phara] kanys ny phara α; a'y gwnel] *A omits* y.
¹¹ eill] dele *BGK*; mwy noc a eill] m6y noc y geill *GK*; *BCLew omit* mwy; ac ny eyll *EAD*; *C adds* nev na dely.
¹³ dyr ew y kadw] dyr yu y wadu *EA*; dir6y y g6adu *D*.

it, and let them put it into the hand of the *amod*-men that they should preserve the *amod* in the manner that they promised to do. [2] If it happens that a man make an *amod* and not want to keep it, and he does not deny the *amod*, it belongs to the lord to compel him to keep it as the *amod*-men may remember it. [3] If it happens that a man wishes to deny his *amod* and another man charges him with the *amod* and he denies [it] alone, the law says that he is only required to swear an oath by himself to deny it unless there is a counter-oath against him. [4] If there is a counter-oath against him, let the claimant call for judgement; and this is what is adjudged to him, his (the defendant's) oath as one of seven to deny it, and that is to be in the manner in which a surety is denied, and the fixed time that is [required] for a surety's compurgation is to be [required] for this. [5] If it then happens that [the claimant] wants to object to one of these compurgators, there is no objection to them except that he does not stem from his kindred, so that he is not entitled to be his compurgator. [6] This is how he is entitled to be his compurgator, [namely that he is] sufficiently close to him that he may pay wergeld together with him and may receive it for him; and [the declaration that] the kinship is true [is to be] on the oath of the compurgator. [7] If it happens that a man makes an *amod* with another without *amod*-men and the one hand in the other, and one party wishes to deny [it], he is only required to swear by himself in order to deny it. [8] If it happens that a man makes a promissory agreement with another concerning something in the presence of witnesses and he wishes to deny it, the law says that he is not entitled to deny it until the witnesses should fail. [9] If it happens that a man makes a promissory agreement with another without witnesses present, that is no *amod*, and since it is not an *amod*, let him deny it by swearing an oath by himself. [10] No one is entitled to make an *amod* on behalf of another for an *amod* endures only in the lifetime of the person who makes it. [11] The father cannot leave an *amod* to the son unless with the son's permission, any more than the son can make an *amod* against the will of the father while the father is alive. [12] *Amod* prevails over law. [13] Though an *amod* be made contrary to the law, it is right to maintain it.

Ior §70
AM ORVODOGAETH E TRAYTHA HYNN

[1] Pwy bynnac a kymero arall ar y orvodogaeth, dygwydet em pob keryd o'r a oed ar e dyn a kymyrth attav. [2] O myn entew y dyeyssywaw o'r dyn a kymmyrth ef ar y orvodogaeth, kymeret entew meychyew y gan e dyn hwnnw ar y amrykoll; ac onys kymer, ket delyo ef gwnevthwr yawn tros y orvodogaeth am e dyn, ny dely e dyn gwnevthvr ydaw ef vn yavn, kanyt emedewys ac ef. [3] Os e gorvodavc a kymer meychyew y kan e llofrvd ar y dyeyssywaw, ny byd nawd ydaw entew rac e meychyew henny. [4] O dervyd y dyn kymryt arall ar y orvodogaeth ac oet arnaw, a chyn no'r oet dylyssw o'r llofrvd e gorvodawc, talet e gorvodawc trostaw kwbyl. [5] O dervyd y dyn adaw gorvot peth y arall y kanthaw, en y pen ehwn ed a pa peth a orwu arnaw, ay bychan ay llawer, kanys ef ehwn a credwyt.

[1] orvodogaeth] orvodgaeth C;   o'a oed] or a uo E; or a pot A.
[2] ar y orvodogaeth] CD; ata6 ary orvodogaeth Lew; uot trostau BKG; drostau EA;   am e dyn] — A;   gwnevthvr ydaw ef vn yavn] A omits gwnevthvr; gwneythur yaun ydau ew EG; wneythur vnia6n ida6 ef Lew.
[5] a orwu arnaw] oruo EA; oruc G; orw Lew.

Ior §71

[1] Try pheth ny deleyr nawd racdwnt kan ew bot en kyvadevedyc: gorvodogaeth a mechnyaeth a gorescynn.

[1] mechnyaeth] meychnyaeth C.

Ior §70
THIS TREATS OF GORFODOGAETH

[1] Whoever should accept another on his *gorfodogaeth*, let him be liable concerning every accusation that there was against the man whom he has accepted. [2] If he wishes to be indemnified by the man whom he accepted on his *gorfodogaeth*, let him take sureties from that man for his indemnity; and if he does not take them, though he ought to do justice to the man in respect of his *gorfodogaeth*, the man is not obliged to do him justice, since he did not promise him [to do so]. [3] If the *gorfodog* takes sureties from the offender in respect of his indemnity, there is no protection for that man against those sureties. [4] If it happens that a man accepts another on his *gorfodogaeth* with a time-limit upon it, and before the time-limit the offender causes him to be liable, let the *gorfodog* pay everything on his behalf. [5] If it happens that a man promises to take responsibility (*gorfod*) for something on behalf of another, it is on his head whatever he is responsible for, whether little or much, for he, and no other, has been trusted.

Ior §71

There are three things against which there should be no protection since they are acknowledged: *gorfodogaeth* and suretyship and possession-taking.

COMMENTARY

§58

The tractate beings with *cynghawsedd*, namely model pleading to serve as a guide as to how a case should be argued in court. 58-60 constitute one set of such model pleadings. First, however, we have a triad, the three ways in which a debtor may free his surety from his suretyship. Different forms of the triad occur elsewhere, though not always with the same constituent items (see Col 74n). It is quite likely therefore that the lawyer who composed the *cynghawsedd* used an existing triad as a starting-off point.

The pleading starts on the basis that the debtor has taken the third way of freeing his surety, that of denying that the man was his surety at all (the other two, paying and giving a gage, would not normally issue in court proceedings). It may seem odd that a lawbook should provide a detailed account of how a debtor may free his surety by denying that he ever was a surety (cf. *Llyfr Iorwerth*, note ad loc.), but there is really no difficulty. The court itself is to decide whether the man who purports to be his surety is indeed his surety. The proceedings are not designed as a way by which a debtor may dishonestly free the surety from his suretyship, but rather, as we shall see, as a carefully calculated method of testing the debtor's denial of the surety. Moreover, there was no other way in which a purported debtor could deny a debt (which perhaps he did not owe) than to deny the purported surety (who might, perhaps, be in league with a man who falsely claimed to be the man's creditor); for while the surety retained his status as a surety, the debt endured (cf. 67/2), and the onus of proof remained upon the purported debtor.

58 contains the opening cut and thrust of denial and assertion. We are to assume that the creditor, the debtor and the surety are already before the judge. 58/4-5 cover the first round which is between the creditor and the debtor, the creditor acknowledging the surety and the debtor denying him. The judge then turns to the purported surety and asks him if he is indeed surety for the debt (58/5). He acknowledges that he is and is promptly denied by the debtor (58/6). 58/7-8 contain the next round, dictated by the judge's question: the surety has been confronted with the debtor's denial and now makes a second assertion of his suretyship, couched this time in a much more formal style. In 58/8, however, he is again denied in equally formal style by the debtor. The second round, therefore, is between surety and debtor: the creditor retires into the background once the surety has acknowledged his office: he must sit tight and hope that the surety will press home his assertion of his suretyship.

58/1. MS *C* is rich in rubricated titles for tractates. This one has no claim to be part of the original text of Ior, but it has been retained because of the convenience of having an early title for the tractate.

58/3. Cf. Cyfn 4 (WML 85.12-17).

58/5/1 & 2. *C*'s addition of *dyoer* confuses the gradual rise in solemnity from bare assertion to solemn declaration.

58/8. *E*'s error suggests that, even though it was not copied from *A*, its exemplar had an orthography similar to that of *A* at this point since something like *deleuah* must lie behind *E*'s *dyly mach*.

§59

The judge has had his answer to the questions put in 58/4-5, and the surety and the debtor have crossed swords over the surety's reply. The judge now continues to dictate how the pleading of the case shall develop (for the control exercised by the judges see AL VII.i. 9: *byt e kyfreyth e medyant er egneyt, ac nyt kanyat namyn a ganhyatoent*, 'And from this point let the legal proceedings be under the control of the judges, and there is no permission except what they may permit'). The exchange in 59/1-4 is thus between the judge and the debtor, not between the debtor and the surety. The creditor, for his part, continues to be silent. The judge's role in 59/1-4 is to push the debtor on to the next level of solemnity: the oath on relics. He begins by obtaining a plain denial by the debtor (given in 59/2), repeating the denial of 58/5, but now made directly to the judge rather than in response to the surety.

59/1 shows that the judge cannot proceed straight from assertion to compurgation by-passing the oath on relics. The reason given, however, is odd, for it is not the surety's success in obtaining compurgators (more than the 'one tongue' of 59/1) which will, in 60/2, push the debtor on from the oath on relics to compurgation. The reason given in 59/1 suggests a clash between groups of compurgators similar to the clash of witnesses envisaged for land-suits by 77/1-32. Our tractate, like the treatment of land-suits in *Llyfr Cynghawsedd*, 'The Book of Pleading', avoids such clashes. In *Llyfr Cynghawsedd* this is done by the principle that the argument between the two parties continues until one side makes a straight denial of the last position that the other party has taken up. If the denial is only partial (like the distinctions made in formal disputation in the schools, when a proposition so distinguished is denied in one form, but accepted in the other), the argument will continue, for a new position has been taken up. A flat denial, however, destroys the mobility of the argument, and thus compels recourse to the sworn evidence appropriate to the case (in *Llyfr Cynghawsedd* generally the oaths of *gwybyddiaid*, 'eye-witnesses'). The person whose assertion has been flatly denied claims the right to bring forward his witnesses (e.g. AL VII.i.21-22). In our tractate, there are two differences: it is not a group of eye-witnesses that will support the debtor's denial, but a group of compurgators, men who must swear an oath supporting that of their principal rather than offering their own independent testimony (Ior 80/4-8; AL VII.i.13-19); and, secondly, it is not the person who has been denied (the surety in this case), but the person who has made the denial, who must bring forward a group of other men to swear on his behalf. The second point is important, for, whereas it seems to be assumed in *Llyfr Cynghawsedd* that it is an advantage to be flatly denied and thus to have the right to bring forward one's eye-witnesses, here it is the debtor who is on the defensive, so that it is evidently not thought to be an advantage to be driven to the point at which one must have recourse to compurgation to support one's case.

166   LAWYERS AND LAYMEN

The apparent assumption behind 59/1, however, is at variance with this scheme by which only one side brings forward its witnesses or compurgators as the case may be, and thus there is no question of any clash between opposing groups of compurgators. It may be a relic of an earlier version which adopted a similar strategy to that followed in Ior's tractate on land-suits, in which case there would be just such a clash between two groups of compurgators like the clash between two groups of witnesses in the tractate on land-suits. In our tractate in its present form, however, the rationale of the strategy appears to be that the judge should test the denial by the debtor and, in doing so, should proceed from one level of solemnity to the next. He should not try to leap over the middle level, that of the oath on relics, so as to get straight to the final level, that of compurgation. In other words there are three main levels:

(1) assertion: (a) plain assertion (58/5-6; repeated, by the debtor only, and directly to the judge, 59/2);
(b) solemn assertion (58/7-8);
(2) oath on relics and counter-oath (59/3-7)
(3) compurgation (only on the debtor's side) (60/2-4).

The testing of the debtor must proceed gradually, building up the pressure from one level to the next.

59/2. The ß reading *a'th wadaf ty* would suggest, wrongly, that the exchange is still between surety and debtor.

59/3. The mention of the pope is not found elsewhere in Ior; cf., however, WML 52.11-13; LTWL 388.29-33. It is not immediately obvious why the judge should preface his injunction to the debtor "do not proceed to a false oath" with the mention of the protection of God, pope or lord. The text does not say whether the judge is promising protection to the debtor or declaring that the procedure as such is under protection. At all events it can hardly be thinking of the primary meaning of *nawdd* which is 'safe-conduct' (cf. CG, Legal Glossary, under *snádud*). One may, however, compare the action of the priest in the procedure known as *dogn-fanag* 'full indication', where he is said to *croessy Duu racdau na tygo anudon* 'invoke God by making the sign of the cross before him so that he may not swear a false oath' (Ior 113/3). This suggests that the judge must be declaring that the legal procedure of swearing an oath on relics is under the protection of God, pope and lord, a protection which would be violated by perjury. Perjury, of course, was an offence against canon law, and this may account, in a church by now more or less post-Gregorian even in Wales, for the mention of the pope in Ior. It is worth noting that there is no invocation of the saint by whose relics the oath is taken: this is not so surprising in the thirteenth century as it would have been in an early medieval text.

59/5. Failure to counter-swear is the first circumstance in which a surety in Ior finds himself compelled to pay the whole debt to the creditor. In 62/4 he must pay if he fails to enforce the debt to the point at which he runs the risk of physical injury. In 64/1 he may have to pay half, possibly only temporarily. In the southern lawbooks, however, the surety may pay if his principal defaults: see Cyfn 10-16, Lat E 9, 35-38.

59/6. The timing achieves the maximum tension between the authority of the relics coupled with the counter-oath of the surety, on the one hand, and the oath of the debtor, on the other. It is notable that the surety does not kiss the relics: this indicates that the procedure is designed to test the debtor not the surety.

59/7. The surety's counter-oath requires the judge to proceed to the next level of solemnity, compurgation.

§60

This paragraph deals with the third stage in the testing of the debtor, compurgation.

60/1. Cf. 76/3 where it is said that the judges in land-suits go out to consult, away from the parties to the dispute, and 77/35 where the judges come to their 'judgement-place' to make the final judgement. Here, the *brawd* is not a final judgement, but a determination of the next step in the procedure. The sentence is not, however, clear and is omitted by C.

60/2. The composition of the group of compurgators is common when it is made up of kinsmen: cf. 47/4, 68/4, 69/4, but contrast 111/17-20.

60/3. For the meaning of *dwfyr swyn*, *bara efferen* and *Benedycamws* (i.e. Benedicamus) see above pp. 53-55.

60/4. For *kyfreyth anvdon* see Col 81n.

60/5-6. Cf. 59/5.

60/7. If a surety acknowledged by the creditor fails, the creditor loses his case. It might thus be in his interest to disavow his surety if he had not already (cf.58/5) acknowledged him.

§61

Paragraphs 58-60 have dealt with a single situation: the denial by the debtor of the surety. In this paragraph we have much briefer indications of the appropriate pleadings in other situations: (1) when the debtor refuses to pay and the surety denies his suretyship (61/1-4); 61/4 shows that the procedure in this situation closely follows that set out in paragraphs 58-60; (2) creditor, surety and debtor all acknowledge the suretyship, but the creditor and the debtor disagree as to the amount of the debt (61/5). 61/6-7 is a supplementary note on compurgation when there is a plurality of sureties, and 61/8 is another supplementary note on the necessity for the whole debt to be paid before the surety is free from his suretyship.

61/1. The *oed*, appointed date at which the debt should be paid, is an essential part of the procedure (cf. BA 51-54). The creditor does not yet know if either surety or debtor will refuse him what he asks from them.

Negyf is a variant form of *negydd*; cf. *tyfyn* for *tyddyn*, and, in the reverse direction, Caerdydd for Caerdyf, Eiddionydd for Eifionydd. In 62/1-6 it (or *negydyaeth*) signifies refusal to pay rather than the denial of the surety and thus of the debt. Here also it may be refusal rather than denial.

61/3-4. The agreement of *A*, *E* and *C* in reading *e kynnogyn* in place of *er havlvr* is important evidence for the existence of the *α* branch of the MS tradition (see above pp. 137-38). They have confused the situation here (a dispute between creditor and surety) with that of 59-60 (a dispute between surety and debtor).

61/5. This situation is also described in 56/5: the surety is one of the *naw tafodiog* 'nine tongued-ones'.

61/6-7. On the difference between Ior and Col here see Col p. xxvii. It appears that Col agrees with the opinion stated and rejected in 61/7. There may be two contrary principles involved in the problem. (a) The creditor's hope that the surety will confirm his suretyship against the debtor's denial depends upon the debtor being tested by assertion, oath upon relics and finally compurgation. If, therefore, the debtor can employ the one set of compurgators to deny more than the one surety, the creditor has, in this respect, no more security from twenty-four sureties than he would have had from one, for they can all be denied by the one group of seven compurgators. There is, however, the other principle that a man is not prevented from swearing one oath by having previously sworn another (see Col. p. xxvii). If this principle were to prevail, it might be expected that one group of compurgators might deny more than one surety. For a similar issue in Irish law see BA para. 26.

61/7. The different readings for *hyt nat yavn ac nat adwuyn* are interesting. The archetype must have had both *yavn* and *adwuyn*; *AE* (i.e. *γ*) simplified one way; *CJ* and *DLew* independently simplified the other way leaving only *B* and *K* with the original.

61/8. The payment in question may either be by the debtor, as in 58/3, or by the surety, as in 59/5.

§62

There is a sharp break at this point. The *cynghawsedd* of 58-61 is at an end, and with it the proccupation with proceedings in court. We now have what is likely to be an earlier stratum of the text, one which is concerned with the *mach* as an enforcing agent. The difference is shown by 62/3-4 when compared with 59/5-6. In 62/3-4 the *mach* will have to pay if he does not "take the first blow" in any fighting (cf. Cyfn 8, Lat E 30); in 59/5-6 he had to pay if he did not counter-swear at the proper time. In 62, therefore, the moment of crisis is extra-curial; in 59 it is curial. On the other hand, the difference between 58-61 and 62 is not simply one of strata. In the first place, the comparison made by Robin Stacey (above pp. 32-34) between the order of Cyfn and that of Ior suggests that 58-61 have quite a long textual history behind them, and that it was probably only recently that the text had been recast as *cynghawsedd*. Secondly, in 58-61/4 the surety is not acknowledged, whereas here he is a *mach adevedyc*, 'acknowledged surety' (62/1). The *negydyaeth* of 62/1, 5-6 must, therefore, be refusal to pay rather than denial of the surety.

The fact remains, however, that one of the most striking differences between Ior and the Irish tract BA lies precisely here, in the absence of any concern in the Irish text with the possibility that the debtor will deny the surety. Partly, no doubt, the reason lies in the great formality with which an Irish contract was made, with a plurality of sureties (including sureties from both parties to the contract) as well as witnesses. In such circumstances the likelihood that a debtor could deny a surety or that a man who claimed falsely to be a creditor could bring all the sureties and the witnesses to support his claim, was very slight. Ior mentiones witnesses in 69/8, but this is in the context of *amod*, a form of contract without a *mach*. The prominence of a debtor's denial of a surety in Ior suggests that many contracts were made with only one surety on either side; whereas an Irish contract would not only have (1) the primary *naidm*-sureties to bind the contract, but also (2) *ráth*-sureties, and then (3) further *naidm*-sureties to guarantee that the principal parties to the contract would indemnify their *ráth*-sureties for any loss the latter might incur on their behalf, while (4) the *ráth*-sureties themselves gave *naidm*-sureties to guarantee that they would discharge their obligations if called on to do so (BA, paras. 63, 74-78). If the witnesses are then added, it is easy to see that the Irish contract was far too public and formal an affair for denial to be much of a risk. The very formality of the full-dress Irish contract had its corollary in the important class of contracts which did not require sureties before they were valid (BA, paras. 1ff.). Since the Welsh contract appears to have been a much simpler and less formal affair, it is not surprising that the Welsh laws do not bother to define such a class of every-day contracts not requiring a surety.

There may also be other reasons why Ior should be so concerned with the debtor's denial of the surety. The difference between the Irish and the Welsh laws may turn partly on the relationship between the debtor and the surety. If the surety was someone such as a senior kinsman or a lord, the debtor could hardly deny him without the surety's dishonourable collusion; but if he were not closely associated with the debtor, it would be easier to deny him. At an early period, therefore, when the *mach* was primarily an extra-curial enforcing agent for contractual debt, it would be normal for him to be closely associated with the debtor and the issue covered by 58-61/4 would be of peripheral importance (cf. *Bürgschaft*, 59; Binchy, 'Celtic Suretyship', 361-62 [367-68]). The central position assigned in Ior to the denial of the surety by the debtor is thus a mark of change away from a law which works almost exclusively through the ordinary institutions of social control, such as lordship and kinship, towards a legal system more closely controlled by the courts.

62/1-4. In Ior, as in Col, the surety enforces the debt upon the debtor by taking from him a gage, *gwyst(y)l*. Since the gage is of greater value than the debt, the debtor is constrained to pay. If he fails to do so by the appointed time (the *oet* of 62/7 etc.), the gage is forfeit to the creditor. The procedure is different in the southern texts: they envisage the surety distraining the movables of the debtor. This conception of distraint as the means by which the *mach* enforces payment of the debt has affected some of the MSS. containing the Ior tractate on suretyship which were written in South Wales (e.g. *JKTim* in 62/5; *Tim* in 62/12; *JK* in 63/3). In part, the difference between taking a gage and distraining is one of conception rather than of substance, for in both traditions the *mach* removes the debtor's property in order to compel him to pay. There is, however, one highly significant difference: the debtor might encourage the surety to take a gage (62/5, 7) whereas he would not encourage him to distrain. By thus permitting a gage to be taken, the debtor won extra time for himself (the *oet* was now that of the gage, not that of the original debt) at the rist of losing more than the value of the original debt.

Both Welsh traditions differ from early Irish law. The latter envisages the *naidm* (*mac*) taking whatever means lie to hand so as to compel the debtor to pay (BA paras. 42, 44, 46; and see *Bürgschaft*, 56-57). These may include distraint, but also force applied to the person of the debtor. Giving a gage is, in Irish law, characteristic of the *ráth* rather than of the *naidm* (BA paras. 63, 76b, c, d, 77, 79, 80; for discussion, *Bürgschaft* (pp. 36-37), whereas in general the *mach* of Ior corresponds to the Irish *naidm* or *mac*. It might be objected that the gage given by the *ráth* guarantees payment by the *ráth* of the debt should the debtor have defaulted, whereas the *mach* in Ior takes the debtor's gage, by force if necessary, and gives it to the creditor. This is true, but not quite the whole truth. In 62/12 the debtor can neither pay nor give a gage because his disposable assets consist of objects of much higher value than the debt. In this situation, "the surety is nevertheless not entitled to take a gage from him (the debtor), and the claimant is not entitled to take the surety's gage." There are two distinct takings of a gage in this passage, though there are probably not two distinct gages. The idea is perhaps that the one article of value might be given by, or taken from, the debtor to guarantee his payment of the debt, and then given by the surety to the creditor so that the latter had security that the debt would be paid. The one gage would thus guarantee that both the debtor's and the surety's obligations would be discharged. When the debtor willingly gave the gage to the surety, he would thus give him a guarantee, and the surety would then use the same gage to give the creditor his guarantee. While, therefore, the *mach* of Ior preserves much of the character of the Irish *naidm/mach* as an enforcing surety, the importance of the gage in his role is reminiscent of the Irish *ráth*. As a whole, therefore, the way the *mach* functions in Ior appears to be a novel and ingenious combination of the two types of security, the gage and the surety. It was presumably based on the general principle that a defendant in any case could give a gage to guarantee that he would pay the debt or abide by the decision of a court. The crucial change introduced in the legal tradition represented by Ior is thus the notion that if the debtor refuses in the presence of the surety either to pay the debt or to give a gage, the surety can then take a gage by force. The one legal instrument, the gage, thus does duty both for the situation in which the debtor is compliant and the situation in which he refuses to pay.

62/5-6. Cf. Col 93n. The MS. readings suggest that this sentence caused considerable difficulty. The confusion is clear in *AE*'s *hep e kanogon hep kefroi or/ar kanogon er haul* and *D*'s *hep yr ha6l6r yn y gyffroi*. The difficulty was to distinguish between (a) the creditor's role in starting the process of enforcing the debt (cf. 61/1) and (b) the possible role of the debtor in offering to hand over a gage or encouraging the surety to take one. The *negydyaeth* 'refusal' of 62/1 was made in the first place to the creditor. The surety, for his part, should not act unless the creditor has first asked the debtor and has been refused (61/1). D and E appear to think that this is what is involved in 62/5. The agreement of *CKLew* (i.e. one α and two ß MSS.) shows that D and E are wrong and that the situation is not (a) but (b). The rule stated in 62/5-6 is therefore this: the surety cannot accept a refusal made only to the creditor as a sufficient ground for him to take the gage by force. The refusal must be made in his presence. The context for the rule is perhaps that the creditor should normally go first to the surety as soon as the debtor has failed to pay on the appointed day, and they should then go together to the debtor (contrary, admittedly, to the way it is put in 61/1; but cf. BA 44). If the debtor then refuses to pay, the refusal will be in the presence of the surety. The rule given in 62/5-6 is also in accord with the surety's role as a privileged witness to the contract (56/5, 61/5) and as the binding force within the contract (67/2).

62/7. On the *keynnyavc kyvreyth* see WML 330 and also the different interpretation proposed above, p.39, n.38.

62/7-13. One of the main reasons why a debtor might offer a gage rather than paying the debt immediately, even though the gage was of higher value than the debt (62/2), was that the debtor might have assets sufficient to pay the debt, but not the precise article or sum owed. A corollary of this difficulty is that he may also not have an article of a value one third in excess of the debt and thus suitable as a lawful gage. His appropriate action is then to seek the permission of the territorial ruler (62/12-13).

62/14. Cf. 70/5, 71/1-2. Contrast BA, 45-46.

§63

With the end of 62, the relatively systematic part of the tractate is at an end. 63 has a unity, but it is one of form (*Ny dely...*), not of substance.

63/2. On the difference of view on this point between the northern lawbooks and Bleg see Col 101n. On the term *ardelw* see Col 381n. *Mach kynnogyn* is a dvandva compound, 'one who is both surety and debtor'.

63/3. The additional sentence in *J* is clearly of southern origin since it envisages the use of distraint not a gage.

§64

Unlike 63, 64 has a unity of substance rather than of form: the consequences of the removal from the jurisdiction, by death or by exile, of a party to the contract, either debtor or surety, with the consequence that he is unable to discharge or to enforce the debt. 64/1-4 deal with the exile of the debtor; 64/5-9 deal with the death of a surety; 64/10-13 with the death of the debtor.

64/1-4. The phrases *a llena e tredyd lle* and *a llyna e lle* in 64/2 and 4 suggest that these sentences embody rules perceived by the compiler as traditional; cf. Lat E 45, and, for another of the three, the last sentence of AL VII.i.9.

64/5-9. The argument given in 64/6-7 appears to be of ecclesiastical origin, but I do not know the source. The effect of the argument is that although the son inherits the suretyship of the father, he does not inherit the ability to deny the suretyship, a power his father possessed.

§65

The triad also occurs in Col 111-113. Cf. also the triad *teir balauc uechny* 'three buckle suretyships', DwCol 462-65, and a similar triad VC II.vi.46-48, from *K*.

65/1-2. Both parties to a contract must give and receive at least one surety, though one side may give more than the other (61/6). A similar issue is covered in BA 27, but with the difference that it requires both parties to a contract to appoint a *naidm*-surety given by one of them; thus the creditor, as well as the debtor, should appoint a *naidm*-surety given by the debtor. This is the point made by the first two items in the triad *teir balauc uechny*. It was essential that the *mach* should take the hand both of the debtor and of the creditor. If he only took the hand of one party to the contract, he would then have been appointed only by the one side and the suretyship was *balawc*, properly attached only at the one end (see Bleg 40.10n. for the metaphor underlying the term *balawc*).

65/3-6. Cf. BA 51a where the formula includes a guarantee of *dílse* and *dílmaine*, namely that the thing exchanged is the property of the man who proposes to give it in exchange and that it cannot be claimed by a third party. With land the issue might arise as to whether it was inherited land, and thus whether the donor had the right to alienate it, even though the land was certainly his (cf. the Breton *dilisidus*, above pp. 74-75; *dilis* = Irish *díles*, Welsh *dilys*).

en ryth dylys. Cf. the cognate Irish phrase *i rricht*, e.g. *Bethu Phátraic*, 130: *Iar sin dochóid Foilgi co tarat fúasma tría Odrán hi richt Patraic*, 'Then Foilge went and gave a spear-thrust through Ordrán mistaking him for Patrick.' In 62/3-6, the recipient of the goods bought them in good faith and therefore has a right as against the seller to an *arwystyl* 'substitute'. On the other hand, the true owner has a right to recover his property. It does not matter whether the seller was in good faith (the phrasing of 65/6 shows that he may have been), for whether or not he believed that the goods were his, he guaranteed, by giving a *mach*, that they were *dilys*, immune from any claim. The *mach* thus guarantees the recipient against loss through third-party claims, but he cannot guarantee that the original transaction shall go through and he is thus, to that extent, an *oferfach* 'useless surety' (65/5).

arwystyl. Originally a gage, *gwystyl*, given instead of *(ar)* something else, perhaps the original debt, but guaranteeing its eventual payment. From this starting-point, the word acquired the more general meaning 'substitute'.

65/4. This rule suggests that the legal worth, *gwerth kyfreyth*, must be at least as much, but very possibly more, than the current market value. This is important for the dating of the sections in the lawbooks detailing legal values: since the Welsh used English coinage and their economy was closely linked with that of England, they are likely to have experienced the inflation of that coinage during the twelfth and thirteenth centuries. The main values are the same in all or almost all texts and correspond to English market values of *circa* 1200. This gives a *terminus ante quem* for those sections in their present form, and suggest that they may have been revised in the late twelfth century. Their unanimity still remains, however, remarkable and unexplained: it appears to presuppose some collective action effective throughout both Gwynedd and Deheubarth.

65/7-8. A text similar to Ior's tractate on suretyship, but varying from it in important respects, is contained in Peniarth MS 35 (G) and will be referred to as the G text. This text, Ior and Col disclose three different stages of legal opinion on the contractual capacity of women (see above pp. 22-27, for Robin Stacey's important observations on this issue, to which what follows is complementary):

(1) In the G text a woman can neither be, nor give, a surety. The latter is the more important disability since it entails incapacity to make a normal contract (*briduw* and *amod* might still, however, be available: cf. 65/11, 68/10).

(2) In Ior a woman may still not be a surety, but she can give a surety. Ior's way of expressing this rule strongly suggests, however, that it is a recent development. Indeed, the rule given in 65/7 probably belonged originally to the earlier stage represented by the G text. The main argument for this conclusion stems from the syntax of the sentence *nyt mach mach gwreyc*, and in particular the phrase *mach gwreyc*. The constructions attested in Ior expressing the relationships of *mach* to some person are as follows:

(a) *mach y gan X* = a surety given by X (the debtor): 58/6 etc.

(b) *mach y X* (*y* = Mod. Welsh *i* 'to') = surety received by and thus belonging to X (the creditor): 63/1, 65/2;

(c) *mach tros X* = surety on behalf of X (the debtor): 66/6;

(d) *y mach* (Mod. Welsh *ei fach* 'his surety') = his (the creditor's) surety: 67/2.

Similarly, the creditor is said to receive (*cymryd*) a surety given by (*rhoi*) the debtor. The surety is thus thought to have come from the debtor, by whom he was initially appointed, but to belong to the creditor, who should also have appointed him. So far, then, one would expect *mach gwreyc* to mean 'the surety belonging to a woman (as creditor)'; but the context shows that this is impossible, for the argument in Ior presupposes that it might mean either 'a woman as surety' or 'a surety given by a woman'.

The examples in Cyfn confirm the conclusions already arrived at, but they also add something more:

(a) *mach dyn* = someone's (the creditor's) surety: Cyfn 20, 36;

(b) *y vach* = his (the creditor's) surety: 4;

(c) *gwadu/diwad mach* = the debtor's denial of the surety: 1; cf. Ior 61/2;

(d) *gwadu/diwad mechniaeth* = the surety's denial of his suretyship: 2, cf. *gwadu hyt nat mach*, Ior 61/2;

(e) *nyt mechni eu mechni* = their (the purported sureties') suretyship is no suretyship: 26.

From this last example one may conclude that, had Cyfn wanted to restate the general proposition, *y rei hynny nyt mechni eu mechni onyt gan ganhat eu arglwydi*, as one about women in particular (who are included in the list), it would have said *nyt mechni mechni gwreic* and not *nyt mach mach gwreic*.

For Gwynedd, a similar conclusion may be drawn from a comparison with a statement of the same issue found in *Llyfr y Damweiniau* (AL IV.iv.4: MSS *EGKU*):

> *Rey a dyweyt nat mach mach gwreyc: nyny a dywedun bot yn uach y mach a rodo gwreyc ceny aller mach o wreyc.*
> Some say that a woman's surety is no surety: we say that the surety a woman gives is a surety, although it is not possible to have a woman as surety.

Here the proposition *nyt mach mach gwreyc* is not reinterpreted, but rejected in favour of the statement *bot yn uach y mach a rodo gwreyc*, 'that the surety a woman gives is a surety.' There is no pretence that the two mean the same thing. Moreover we now have another way in which one could say that a woman could not act as surety: *nyt mach mach o wreyc*. We may conclude, therefore, that Ior has taken an old rule forbidding women from giving sureties and has reinterpreted it as if it expressed current law. The author of Ior was a creative lawyer, but a bad historian.

(3) Col 113 has a revised version of Ior:

> *Tredet ev, nyt mach o wureyc ony byt argluydes, a ny dely gureyc bot yn vach, ac ny dyly guraget guadu mach na reyth wyr arney hytheu y wadu mach; ac urth na uarn keureyth y gureyc uot yn uach a cheny allo gureyc bot en euach, hy a dyly rody mach.*
> The third is, a woman does not act as surety unless she is a lady, and a woman is not entitled to be a surety, and women are not entitled to deny a surety nor should she have a group of men as compurgators against her to deny [her as] a surety; and since the law does not judge that a woman is a surety, and although a woman cannot be a surety, she is entitled to give a surety.

Col is repetitious and keeps the implausible reasoning of Ior (for the probable original function of the argument see above, pp. 25-26). The clause *ony byt argluydes* derives from the Latin lawbooks (e.g. Lat E 15), and ultimately from the Irish *Collectio Canonum Hibernensis* (see the note to Col 113, and also above pp. 21-22). There is now, therefore, a limited recognition of the right of women to act as, and to give, a surety.

65/9. This argument is syllogistic and perhaps smacks a little of the revived logic of the twelfth century. It is, however, obscure because of linking propositions taken for granted. In full it would go as follows:

(1) major premiss: *pwybynnac a allo anylyssv da e kyvreyth a dyweyt bot en kyvreyth ydav y dylyssv;*
    minor premiss: *gwreyc a eyll anylyssv da;*
    conclusion: [*e mae en kyvreyth y wreyc dylyssv da*];

(2) major: [*e mae en reyt mach ar dylysrwyd y kan pop vn a vynno dylyssv da*];

minor: [*e mae en kyvreyth y wreyc dylyssv da*];

conclusion: *e kyvreyth a dyweyt bot en reyt mach ar dylysrwyd y kenthy.*

§66

This section of the tractate continues to be a collection of miscellanea — on the gage, on who can or cannot give or act as a surety, tidying up a minor difficulty caused when the *oet* coincides with one of the three greatest feasts of the liturgical calendar, a brief note on minor exchanges which do not require a surety and finally a pleasant piece on a meeting between a surety and a debtor on a bridge formed by a single log.

66/1-5. The main point of this paragraph is to draw a distinction between the surety and the lord, on the one hand, and the owner of goods involved in a contract, on the other. Though they are in the same boat in that, for all three, a gage is forfeit on the appointed day, the *oet* (66/1-3), nonetheless they are different in that neither surety nor lord are required to give a further surety, apart from themselves, to guarantee that ownership of the gage cannot be claimed by a third party. The surety *ex hypothesi* has the required legal status, and the principle is firmly stated that the lord is an unappointed surety for all 'acknowledged goods'. Quite what this last phrase means is not clear. It should not mean that the ownership of the goods is undisputed, for as soon as the ownership of the gage was disputed the lord's guarantee would then cease. The argument might, however, be in two stages: (1) the lord acts as surety for all goods whose ownership is not in dispute (not specially the gage, but goods exchanged by contract); (2) the lord therefore has the privileges attached to the office of surety, including that of giving a gage without needing to give sureties for its immunity from claim. In practice, of course, it might be out of the question for a subject to challenge the ownership of a gage given by his lord, since it is quite likely that Ior is here thinking of the *arglwydd* as a territorial ruler rather than as a *seigneur* (contrast BA 24 where the lord of a client is an unappointed surety).

66/6-7. The first sentence suggests that suretyship was not confined to those who already enjoyed some authority over the contracting party. The list in 66/7 is a version of one which, in several Welsh lawbooks but not apparently in Ior, stems ultimately from the Irish *Collectio Canonum Hibernensis*: see Mrs Stacey's discussion, above pp. 21-22. The reasoning in 66/7 may, as Mrs Stacey also shows (above, pp. 23-25), be profitably compared with that in 65/8: this sentence demonstrates that the argument in 65/8 originally justified the position taken by the G text, not the position taken by Ior. When compared with similar lists in other texts it is clear that a woman had earlier appeared among the categories disguised under the phrase 'and every person who cannot, without the permission of another, come to serve at law,' although the latter is already in the G text.

66/13. The inclusion of *aryant* 'money' in this list is odd in view of 65/1.

§67

The *oet wrth porth* 'fixed period of delay to seek aid' is a standard element in the procedure of cases concerning land in the law of Gwynedd (Ior 72/7-11, 81/10, AL VII.i.3-4, 9; cf. DwCol 483). The standard *porth* 'aid' consisted of the *cyngaws* and the *canllaw*; while the division between their responsibilities is not clear, they both pleaded on behalf of their client for DwCol 483 shows that their client might choose which plea he preferred, his own, that of the *cyngaws* or that of the *canllaw*. The rule that there can be no delay to seek such aid is consistent with the relative simplicity of the law of suretyship when compared with land-law.

67/2-3. Recourse to law is an option for either side which the other party must not refuse. On the other hand, it is worth noting that, when the debtor refuses to go to law, it is not any agent of the court who takes action, but the surety. In the last resort, enforcement of the debt remains the responsibility of a privately appointed enforcing agent. The explanation in 67/2 is important evidence for the close identification of the surety with the binding force of the contract (cf. the Irish *naidm*, literally 'binding').

67/4. This must be a candidate for the prize for the most involved sentence ever produced by a medieval lawyer. For an explanation, see Col, note on 123-25, where it is pointed out (1) that this issue does not belong to the law of suretyship at all; (2) that the point of the decision may turn upon the order of events in a case concerning land, for the giving of a surety that one will abide by law should come long after the request for a delay for seeking aid. A premature demand for such a surety may thus be treated by the judge as turning the case into one concerning suretyship where there is no delay for seeking aid. What still remains obscure, however, is why the further inference is made that, because there is no delay in a case concerning suretyship, therefore there is no right to a surety that one will abide by law. It is clear, however, that the law's verdict has little to do with the arguments of the parties.

§68

For a detailed discussion see Mr Huw Pryce's chapter, above, pp. 47-71. I shall confine myself to textual issues.

68/1. The form *bridui* in *A* (also in 68/7) is early, before metathesis had converted *dwy* (OW *duiu*) into *dyw*, *duw* (except in names of rivers and in some derivatives or compounds such as *meudwy* 'hermit').

68/8. The error in *AEC* is important evidence for the α group MSS.

§69

In his important essay, 'Celtic Suretyship: fossilized Indo-European Survival?', Professor Binchy argues (as a footnote to his case) that the Welsh *amodwr* corresponds to the Irish *naidm/mac*, and that the Welsh *mach*, although his name is cognate with Irish *mac* 'enforcing surety', is only a paying surety like the Irish *ráth*. This is to attach too much weight to the evidence of the southern lawbooks, where the *mach* is indeed a paying surety, as against that of the lawbooks from Gwynedd. Even Col, the latest of the northern versions of 'Hywel's Book', maintains unwaveringly the view of the *mach* as an enforcing surety. While the equation proposed by Professor Binchy between *amod* and Irish *imtha* in *ben imtha* 'woman of contract' (gen. sg. from **imb(o)tha* to *im-both, im-buith*) is convincing, it does not follow that the *amodwr*, as he is described in the lawbooks, is a more archaic type of surety than the *mach*. In this section the *amodwr* appears to preserve two features of the Irish *naidm*: first, he is a privileged witness to the contract (69/2), and, secondly, he has a role in the ceremony by which the contract is made in that the parties "put it into the hands of the *amodwyr* that they should maintain the contract..." (69/1; cf. 69/7 where a contract that is made by one party putting his hand in that of the other is not an *amod*). This is not born out by 68/8 which does not mention the *amod* at all, but the phrasing is certainly reminiscent of *Berrad Airechta* (*Gaib it láim*, 'Take into your hand', 50b and c). The parallel is hardly a strong argument, however, for the *mach* also has these two features, and the law concerning the *mach* appears to have acted as a model for the other types of surety (cf. 69/3). In fact the most important things about the *amod* are (1) that the enforcing function is discharged by the lord (69/2), not by the *amod*-men; and (2) that the office is not heritable (unless the heir agrees to take it over). Both these points distinguish the *amod*-man from the *mach*, and on both the *mach* is the one which corresponds to the Irish *naidm* or *mac*. It is unfortunately very difficult to suggest what form the *amod* might have taken at an earlier period. It is even possible that the *amod*-man was simply a form of *mach* transformed by the appearance of a greater role for the ruler in the enforcement of contracts. If this were so, *amod* would originally have been a general word for a contract, as indeed it remained in many contexts, and such an *amod* would be enforced by the *mach*.

69/1. This is an obscure sentence: it is likely that the first occurrence of *amvotwr* means 'party to an *amod*' while the second means '*amod*-man', namely the special sort of surety who guaranteed an *amod*. The first lot of *amvotwyr* make the *amvot*, whereas the second guarantee it.

amvot is a reformation of *amot* (Mod. W. *amod*), preserving its original form as a compound of *bod* 'to be', *am − + bod*. The literal meaning is, therefore, 'being around'. It may originally have referred to the guarantee provided by the surety and then have come to refer to the contract itself because of the close identity between the enforcing surety and the contract.

69/3. The syntax is unclear and appears to have been so for the scribes, who tried different ways to improve it. It seems likely that the original stood as in C since that provides a reasonable basis from which the different readings might have arisen. The use of *ehwn* (i.e. *ehun*) without a preceding possessive or infixed pronoun is rare: the meaning appears to be adverbial, 'alone', and to have developed from the starting-point, *un* 'one', independently of the much commoner reflexive use (cf. D. Simon Evans, *A Grammar of Middle Welsh*, §98, p. 90).

69/7. In this sentence and in 69/9 *amvot* appears to have the general meaning contract.

69/8. The witnesses, *tystyon*, are to be distinguished from the *amod*-men in one vital respect: they take no part in the ceremonial binding of the contract by the taking of hands.

69/12. This is a maxim which occurs in several texts including Cyfn 62; cf. Col 140n. and Glanvill's remark, "quippe generaliter enim verum est quod conventio legem vincit" (*Tractatus de Legibus et Consuetudinibus Regni Angliae qui Glanvilla vocatur*, ed. G. D. H. Hall, 129).

§70

The *gorfodog* is a different kind of surety from all those who have already been discussed: he does not guarantee the payment of contractual debt but the lawful conduct of the person whom he takes upon his *gorfodogaeth*. The closest Irish parallel is the *aitire chána*, a surety who guarantees compliance with the rules of a *cáin*, a law promulgated by a king or an assembly consisting of both laymen and ecclesiastics. There may be a time-limit on the responsibilities of the *gorfodog* just as there was for at least some *aitires* (70/4; cf. BA, 65e).

70/1. The *gorfodog*'s responsibilities appear to be retrospective: this caused difficulty to *A* and *E*.

70/2. Cf. BA, 74-75 on the *ráth*-surety. There is no corresponding provision for sureties to enforce the indemnifying of the *aitire*.

iv THE 'CYFNERTH' TEXT
EDITED AND TRANSLATED BY MORFYDD E. OWEN

Dafydd Jenkins has been occupied of recent years with producing what he sometimes refers to as a 'full orchestral score' of the Cyfnerth texts using the contents of all the known manuscripts. Of all the families of Welsh legal texts, that of the Book of Cyfnerth has the most fluid history revealed in the variety of content as well as in the variety of readings found within the tractates dealing with individual legal topics. The textual history of the Tractate on Suretyship conforms with this generally fluid pattern.

The seven manuscripts associated with the Cyfnerth text are listed below. The sigla used are those of Aneurin Owen's *Ancient Laws and Institutes of Wales* (AL), with the exception of *Mk* which takes its name from the Meyrick family of Plas Bodorgan in Anglesey who have owned the manuscript for centuries. Reference is also made to the sigla of William Wotton's *Leges Wallicae* (LW) and to those used in the compilation, known as the *Deddgrawn* or *Corpus Hoelianum*, made by the antiquary William Maurice in the seventeenth century and preserved in N.L.W. Wynnstay MSS 37 and 38.

U: N.L.W. Peniarth 37, the *Morg* of William Maurice's *Deddfgrawn* is a small paged manuscript attributed by Gwenogvryn Evans (RWML i.371) to the late thirteenth century but probably deriving from the fourteenth. It is in the same hand as Ior manuscript *G* and was used by Aneurin Owen as the basis for his Gwentian Code. This is the only one of the Cyfnerth manuscripts which does not contain the Surety Tractate.

V: B. L. Harleian 4353 is a manuscript of the same date. It is in the same hand as the Book of Taliesin (N.L.W. Peniarth 2) as is *W* (see above p. 000). It is the H.3 of LW. The Surety Tractate which is on ff. 35r-37r was printed at WML 85-9.

Mk: A manuscript kept at Plas Bodorgan in Anglesey which is the property of Sir George Meyrick. It was the *M* of LW. This manuscript has been dated to the early fourteenth century by Daniel Huws and its script is closely related to that of *V* and *W*. The Surety Tractate is found on pp. 73-78.

W: B.L. Cotton Cleopatra A. xiv (see above p. 132). The Surety Tractate is found on ff. 74v-78r and sections of it were printed at WML 295-98.

X: B.L. Cotton Cleopatra B v. The Cott 5 of LW is a larger paged more ornately decorated manuscript than the former and is in a loose

Gothic hand. It was dated by Gwenogvryn Evans to circa 1350 (RWML ii. 954). The Surety Tractate is on ff. 215v-316v.

Y: N.L.W. 20143A, though classified as a Cyfnerth manuscript, follows the Blegywryd texts with regard to the Law of Suretyship.

Z: N.L.W. Peniarth 259B. This manuscript known as Ponf in William Maurice's *Deddfgrawn* (see above) is a paper manuscript of the mid-sixteenth century, but probably imitates in its layout and in the forms of its letters an earlier archetype. The Surety Tractate is found on ff. 27r-28r.

In editing the Surety Tractate from Cyfnerth, I have followed the method used by Dafydd Jenkins in WLW. The text printed here is that recorded in *W*. This is the fullest version of the Surety Tractate found in the Cyfnerth manuscripts and includes much material from the Ior tradition (see above p. 33). The text has been divided into numbered sentences. The *W* tractate consists of sentences 1-63. Following the tractate and numbered in sequence, 64-97 are passages concerning suretyship placed elsewhere in *W*, together with passages not found in *W* taken from *U*, *V*, *Mk*, *X* and *Z*.

V, *Mk*, *X*, and *Z* all contain forms of the Surety Tractate which show differences of order and of readings from the version found in *W*. *U* contains only sentences 79 and 80 of our text. The versions of the Tractate found in *V* and *Mk* are closely related; *X* and *Z*'s texts are much shorter and some of the clauses are more compressed.

The main difference between *W* and *Mk/V* lies in the absence of the long section of Cynghawsedd, *W* 37-48 which corresponds to Ior §69. *X* and *Z* have none of the material found in *W* 26-63 and sentences 1-9 of *W*, i.e. the sections concerned with denying a surety, denying suretyship and taking distraint are found in a mixed order at the end of the tractate in those manuscripts. If the texts found in *X* and *Z* represent an early Cyfnerth version of the Surety Tractate, the order followed is different from that found in *V*, *Mk*, and *W*. *X* and *Z* begin with the sections concerning the payment schedule which derive ultimately from an Irish canon (see above p. 29).

Using the numeration followed in the text printed below, the contents of the texts of the Surety Tractate in *V*, *Mk*, *X*, and *Z* can be tabulated in the sequence in which they occur (see Table 2). The asterisks signify that the corresponding sentence occurs in the manuscript though not in the same sequence.

TABLE 2: *The Contents of V, Mk, X and Z*

V	Mk	X	Z
1	1	★	★
2	2	★	
3	3		
4	4	★	★
5	|	★	★
6	6		★
7	7	★	
8	8	★	
82	|		
83	|		
9	9	★	
★	10	10	10
★	11	11	11
★	12	12	12
10	16	★	★
13	13	13	13
14	14	14	14
15	15	15	|
16	16	16	16
10	★	★	★
11	★	★	★
12	★	★	★
16	★	★	★
17	17	17	17
18	18	18	18
21	21	★	★
22	22	★	★
20	20	★	★
★	★	19	19
★	★	20	20
★	★	21	21
★	★	22	22
			79
|	|	|	80
19	19	★	★
23	23	23	23
24	24	24	24
25	25	25	25

TABLE 2: *The Contents of V, Mk, X and Z*

V	Mk	X	Z
26	26	26	26
36	36		
27	27		
29	29		
28	28		
30	30		
|	|		
73	73		
48	48		
49	49		
50	50		
51	51		
84	84		
60	60		
61	61		
62	62		
63	63		
★	★	4	4
★	★	5	|
★	★	7	
★	★	8	
★	★	9	
★	★	1	1
★	★	2	|
★	★		5
★	★		6

The Tractate

Cyfn 1-9

[*W*74v4]

¹Y neb a diwatto mach, rodet 16 seith nyn nessaf y werth; petwar o parth y tat a deu o parth y uam ac ynteu e hunan seithuet. ²Y neb a diwatto mechniaeth, rodet 16 seith nyn yn y kyffelyb vod. ³Ac ony byd y genedyl yn vn wlat ac ef, rodet y 16 e hunan uch pen seith alla6r kyssegyr yn vn cantref ac ef, canys uelly y diwedir bri Duw.

⁴O teir ford yd ymdiueicha mach: vn ohonu o talu o'r talawdyr drostaw; yr eil y6 o rodi oet o'r ha616r y'r tala6dyr yn a6sen y uach; trydyd y6 o d6yn gauel o'r ha616r ar y talat6dyr heb ganhat y uach ac yna, talet tri buhyn cam16r6 y'r brenhin.

⁵Oet mach y ymgoffau ae mach ae nat mach tri dieu. ⁶Yspeit mach y paratoi tal gysseuin, os ef e hunan a'e tal, tri dieu.

⁷O teir ford y differir mach [75r] a chynogyn; o glybot corn y brenhin yn mynet yn lluyd; ac eil y6 o ha6l ledrat; trydyd y6 o ha6l treis, kanys aghen yn aghen y6 pop vn o'r holyon hyn.

⁸Mach a dyly d6yn gauel gyt a'r ha616r hyt yn niogel a godef arna6 y gouit a del; ac ony wna y velly, talet e hunan. ⁹Dyn a dyly kymryt mach ar pop da onyt da a rotho y argl6yd ida6.

¹ diwatto] watto *MkV*
rodet] roddet X rroded Z
16] y 16 *Mk*
seith nyn nessaf] ar y seithuet or dynyon nessaf *MkV*; seithnyn nessa Z
² y neb] enep X
diwatto] a watto *MkV*
mechniaeth] y vechniaeth X
16 seith nyn] y 16 ar y seithuet *MkV*; seithnyn nessaf y gwerth X
³ canys] kanys *MkV*
diwedir] gwedir *MkV*
⁴ o teir ford yd ymdiueicha mach] Tri lle yd ymdiueichya mach gan gyfureith *XZ*
vn ohonu] *MkV omits*; Vn ohonunt X; un onaddunt Z
o talu] Z *omits* o
⁵ y ymgoffau] y 6ybot V; i wybot Z
oet mach y ymgoffau] oed kyfureith yssyd y mach y emgoffa6 X
⁶ tri dieu] na6 nieu *MkV*; dwy wythnos Z
⁷ ac eil y6 o ha6l ledrat; trydyd y6 o ha6l treis] ac o ha6l treis ac o ha6l ledrat *MkVX*
⁸ gouit] gofut V
gauel... ... ... del] gafuael ... y gyt ar kynogyn a godef y gofuud a del arna6 X
ony wna velly] ony wna hynny V

[1] Whoever may deny a surety, let him give the oath of seven men nearest to his wergeld, four from the father's side and two from the mother's side and he himself as seventh. [2] Whoever may deny suretyship, let him give the oath of seven men in like manner. [3] And if the kin be not in the same *gwlad* as he, let him give his own oath above seven consecrated altars in the same *cantref* as himself, since thus is *bri Duw* denied.

[4] It is in three ways that a surety is released: one of them is by the debtor paying on his behalf, the second is by the claimant giving an appointed time to the debtor in the absence of the surety; the third is by the claimant distraining the debtor without his surety's permission, and then let him pay the three kine of *camlwrw* to the king.

[5] Three days is the set time for a surety to recall whether he be a surety or not. [6] Three days is the period for a surety to prepare the first payment, if he himself pays it.

[7] In three ways are surety and debtor protected: by hearing the horn of the king going on a hosting: second, is by a claim concerning theft; third, is by a claim concerning violence; for each of these claims is an urgency in an urgency.

[8] A surety should take distraint together with the claimant into a safe place and suffer whatever trouble may come; and unless he do thus, let him pay himself. [9] A man should accept surety for all goods, save the goods which the lord may give him.

Cyfn 10-18

[10]Y neb a uo mach dros dyn, onys tal y tala6dyr yn oet dyd, oet pymthec niwarna6t a geiff y mach yna, os ar da marwa6l y byd mach. [11]Ac onys tal y tala6dyr yna, oet deg niwarna6t ar hugeint a geiff y mach. [12]Ac ony thal y tala6dyr yna, oet deg niwarna6t a deugeint a geiff y mach yna. [13]Os ar da bywa6l y byd mach ac na thalho y tala6dyr yn oet dyd, oet pymthec niwarna6t a geiff y mach yna. [14]Ac ony thal y tala6dyr yna, oet deg niwarna6t a geiff y mach yna. [15]Ac ony thal y tala6dyr yna, oet pym niwarna6t a geiff yna y mach. [16][75v] Ac ony thal y tala6dyr yna, talet y mach e hunan. [17]A phan gyuarffo y mach a'r tala6dyr, yspeilet ef oc a uo ymdana6 o dillat eithyr y pilyn nessaf ida6. [18]A gunaet uelly uyth yny gaffo tal o g6byl y ganta6.

[10] Y neb] Pwybynac a vo Z
[11] Ac onys tal... ... ...mach] ac ony thal yna oed a geiff y mach yna dec diwyrnawt ar hugeint X; onis tal . . . oed hyd ymhen y permthec niwyrod or hugeint a gaif y mach Z; MkV add yna
[12] Ac onys tal...deugeint] ac onys tal y talawdr yna oed a geiff y mach dec diwarna6d a deugeint X
[13] ac na thalho... ... ...yna] onys tal y talawdyr yn oed y dyd. oed a geiff y mach yna pymthec diwarnawt X; na chao y talawdr talu yn oed y dydd oed xv niwyrnawd a gaif y mach yna Z;
[14] ony thal...mach yna[Ac odyna dec diwarnawt X
[15] oet pym...yna y mach] Ac odyna pymb diwarnawt X
[16] talet y mach e hunan] Ac odyna taled y mach X; yna taled i hunan Z; V add a llyna oeteu mach am da bywa6l
[17] oc a vo] or a vo Z
pilyn] pilin MkVZ
[18] A gunaet uelly...ganta6] ac uelly g6naet byth hyt pan gaffo c6byl tal y ganta6 MkV; ac uelly gwnaed hyd pan gaffo gwbyl X; a gwnaed velly yn wasdad yn i gaffo dal i dda i ganthaw Z

Cyfn 19-20

[19]O'r byd mar6 y tala6dyr ac na chaffo talu y da yn y gymun 6rth neb, dyget y mach y uechniaeth dros y mar6 a thalet y teir ach nessaf ida6, a'r mach bieu kymell kystal ac ar y tala6dyr bei byw; [20]a chyt dycco mach y uechniaeth dros lud argl6yd, ny chyll na dir6y na chaml6r6. [21]O'r byd mar6 mach dyn kyn talu o'r tala6dyr drosta6 y uechniaeth, doet yr ha6l6r ar y seithuet o'r dynyon nessaf y werth uch pen [bed]* y uach a thyget y uot yn uach o'r caffant y bed. [22]Ac ony chaffant y bed, tygent uch yr alla6r gyssegyr y uot yn uach, ac yuelly y keiff y da.

[10] Whoever may be surety for another, unless the debtor pay on the set day, then the surety shall have a set time of fifteen days, if he be surety for dead stock. [11] And if the debtor does not pay it then, the surety shall have a set time of thirty days. [12] And if the debtor does not pay then, the surety has a set time of fifty days. [13] If he be surety on live stock and the debtor does not pay on the set day, the surety shall then have a set time of fifteen days. [14] And if the debtor does not pay then, the surety shall then have a set time of ten days. [15] And if the debtor does not pay then, the surety shall have a set time of five days. [16] And if the debtor does not pay then, let the surety himself pay. [17] And when the surety meets the debtor, let him (the surety) take from him (the debtor) whatever clothes he (the debtor) has about him save the garment next to him. [18] And let him (the surety) do thus until he has received complete payment from him (the debtor).

[19] If the debtor dies and can not in his bequest deliver the goods to someone, let the surety perform his suretyship on behalf of the dead and let the three collateral branches nearest to him pay; and the surety has a right to compel the suretyship just as much as if it were on the debtor were he alive, [20] And though the surety performs his suretyship in the face of the lord's opposition, he forfeits neither a *dirwy* fine nor a *camlwrw* fine. [21] If someone's surety dies before the debtor discharges his suretyship on his behalf, let the claimant come with the six men nearest to his wergeld, to

[19] tala6dyr] kynocnyn Z
ac na chaffo talu y da yn y gymun 6rth neb] ac na chaffo kymynnu y da 6rth neb *MkVX*;
ac na chaffo dalu i gymvn wrth neb i dda *Z*
dros y mar6] *Z adds* hwnnw
nesaf ida6] *Z adds* y da; *X omits everything after* ida6
kymell] y gymhell *MkV*
[20] a chyt] kyt *MkV*
dros lud arglwyd…na chamlwrw] dros 16 arglwyd ny thal na dirwy na chamlwry *X*
[21] ha6l6r] kynogyn *X*; kynocnyn *Z*
ar y seithuet o'r dynyon] ar y seithued *X*
nessaf y werth] nessaf idaw *MkV*; nessa iddaw *Z*; * *not in MS*
thyget] thyngent *V*; thynged *Z*; *X omits*
[22] ony chaffant] *Z adds* wyntau
tygent] tyngent *VZ*; tynghed *X*
y uot yn uach] *MkV add* ac na diwyg6yt drosta6 y vechniaeth tra uu vy6 ac uelly[y keiff y da

Cyfn 23-30

[23] Y neb a adefho dylyu da ida6, talet yn diohir, pan ouynher, eithyr yn y
teir g6yl arbenhic, y Nadolyc a'r Pasc a'r Sul[76r]guyn: nyt amgen o Nos
Nadolyc guedy gosper hyt Duw Kalan guedy efferen; o nos Sadwrn Pasc
guedy dat6yrein hyt Duw Pasc Bychan guedy efferen; o nos Sadwrn Sulguyn
guedy gosper hyt duw Sul y Trinda6t guedy efferen. [24] Kanys ny dyly neb
gouyn y gilyd yn y diewed hyny.
[25] Ny dyly neb kymryt mab yn uach heb ganhyat y tat tra dylyo uot drosta6;
na manach na bra6t heb ganhyat eu habat; nac alldut canyt geir y eir ar
Gymro; na gureic onyt ar yr hyn y medho y hargl6ydiaeth arna6.[3]
[26] Y rei hynny nyt mechniaeth eu mechni onyt gan ganhyat eu hargl6ydi.
[27] Ny dyly neb kymryt mach kynnogyn, kanys deu ardel6 ynt ac na dyly
neb namyn dewis y ardel6. [28] Os mechni a dewis, nyt oes gynnogyn. [29] Os
kynnogyn a dewis, nyt oes uach. [30] Ac 6rth hynny, ny eill neb seuyll yn uach
ac yn gynnogyn.

[23] talet] taler *Mk; MkVX omit* pan ouynher *X omits everything after* eithyr yn y teir g6yl
arbenhic
[24] Kanys ny dyly] kany dyly *Mk V*; *ZX omit* kanys
[25] heb ganhyat] heb ganhat *MkV*; *MkV omit* y hargl6ydiaeth] *MkVZ add* nac yscolheic yscol
heb ganhat y athro
heb ganhyat . . . arna6] heb ganyad y tad tra uo adan y wialen, nac yscolheic heb ganhyad
y athro, na manach heb ganyad y abad, na chaeth heb ganyat y arglwyd, na gwreic heb ganyad
y gwr *X*
[26] nyt mechniaeth eu mechni] nyt mechni eu mechni *MkV*; nyd mach eu machniaeth *X*; a
rrai hyn nid machniaeth *Z*.
[27] namyn] onyt *MkV*
[28] mechni] mach *MkV*

the surety' grave and let him (the claimant) swear that he is a surety if they find the grave. [22] And if they cannot find the grave, let them swear above the consecrated altar that he is surety and thus he (the claimant) will have the goods.

[23] Whoever admits that goods are due from him, let him pay without delay when it be asked, save on the three special feasts, Christmas, Easter and Whitsun: namely from Christmas Eve after vespers until New Year's day after mass; from the night of Easter Saturday after the resurrection until Little Easter day (Low Sunday) after mass; from the night of Whit Saturday after vespers until Trinity Sunday after mass. [24] For no one should make a demand of another during those days.

[25] No one should accept a son as surety without his father's permission as long as he (the father) is obliged to be responsible for him; nor a monk or brother without their abbot's permission; nor an *alltud*, for his word has no validity against that of a Welshman; nor a woman, save for that over which she has dominion. [26] The surety of such persons is no surety save with their lords' permission.

[27] No one should accept a surety-debtor because they are two *arddelw* and no one should do other than choose his *arddelw*. [28] If he choose suretyship there is no debtor. [29] If he choose (to be) a debtor, there is no surety. [30] And for that reason, no one can act as (both) surety and debtor.

Cyfn 31-35

³¹O'r kymer dyn mach ar da a chyn dyuot oet y da, [76v] dehol y tala6dyr
ae o alanas ae o ledrat ae o aghyfreith arall a mynu o'r ha6l6r y da y gan
y uach, sef a wyl kyfreith yna, rannu y collet yn deu hanher yrydunt: nyt
amgen talu o'r mach hanher y da y'r ha(6)l6r*. ³²Kanys aghyfreith y6 talu
o'r mach g6byl ac ynteu yn wiryon; ac nat tegach colli o'r ha6l6r o g6byl
a chredu* ohona6 ynteu y uach. ³³A llyna y trydyd lle y ran kyfreith. ³⁴Ac
o'r da y tala6dyr y'r wlat dracheuyn, 6ynteu a dylyant kymhell y da h6nn6
arna6 ef; a hanher a dyly y mach. ³⁵A llyna yr *vn* lle y byd kymhell6r y
mach ar da ida6 e hun.

³¹ *MS hal6r.
³² MS *a cholli chredu.
³⁵ *punctum delens beneath* vn *in* MS.

Cyfn 36-47

³⁶O'r byd mar6 mach dyn kyn talu y uechniaeth ac ada6 mab ohona6*,
y mab h6nn6 a dyly seuyll yn lle y tat yn y uechni.

³⁷O deruyd y dyn rodi da y arall a mach arna6 a phan delher y ouyn, diwat
o'r tala6dyr a ch6yna6 o'r ha6l6r 6rth yr argl6yd, ia6n y6 d6yn y d6y pleit
y gyt a'r mach [77r] a gouyn udunt ae mach h6n ae nat mach. ³⁸'Mach',
heb yr ha6l6r 'Na uach', heb y tala6dyr. ³⁹Yna, y mae ia6n gouyn y'r mach,
'A 6yt uach ti?' ⁴⁰'Mach' heb ynteu. 'Nac 6yt uach' heb y tala6dyr 'y
genhyf i ar dim'. ⁴¹Heb y mach 'Yr gyfreith y dyly6yf i. Mi a'e
canhebrygaf'. ⁴²'Ac val y mae ia6n y minheu, mi a'e diwadaf', heb y
tala6dyr. ⁴³Yna, y mae ia6n barnu reith, canyt oes eithyr vn taua6t y mach
yn gyrru vn taua6t y tala6dyr y wadu. ⁴⁴Kymryt o'r bra6d6r y creir yn y
la6 a dywedut 6rth y tala6dyr, 'Na6d Duw ragot a na6d dy argl6yd na th6g
anudon'. ⁴⁵Os t6g, tyget y Du6 yn y blaen, ac y'r creir nat mach y ganta6
ef nac ar a dyweit nac ar dim. ⁴⁶Ony 6rtht6g y mach arna6 tra uo yn rodi
y eneu y'r creir, talet y mach y dylyet can adeu6ys y uot yn uach a bit ryd
y tala6dyr*. ⁴⁷Os g6rtht6g a wna y mach, dyget y tala6dyr y reith, nyt
amgen, y 16 ar y seithuet.

³⁶˙ MS ohonona6
MkV omit kyn talu y uechniaeth
⁴⁶ MS bit ryd ynteu y tala6dyr

³¹ If a man take a surety on goods and before the set time for rendering the goods comes, the debtor be banished either for *galanas* or theft or any other unlawful deed and the claimant claims his goods from his surety; this is the view that the law then takes, that the loss be divided in two halves between them; namely, that the surety pays half the goods to the claimant. ³² For it is unlawful that the surety pays all and he himself innocent; nor is it fairer that the claimant should lose all when he had trusted his surety. ³³ And that is one of the three places where the law divides. ³⁴ And if the debtor returns to the *gwlad*, they should enforce (payment of) those goods on him; and the surety has a right to half. ³⁵ And that is the (one) place where the surety is the enforcer of goods for himself.

³⁶ If a man's surety dies before discharging his suretyship and he leaves a son, that son should act instead of the father in his suretyship.

³⁷ If it happens that a man gives goods to another with a surety for them and when someone comes to ask for them, the debtor denies and the claimant complains to the lord, it is right to bring together the two parties with the surety, and ask them whether this man is a surety or not. ³⁸ 'Surety' says the claimant; 'Not a surety' says the debtor. ³⁹ Then it is right to ask the surety 'Are you a surety?'. ⁴⁰ 'Surety' he says. 'You are not a surety' says the debtor, 'for me for anything'. ⁴¹ The surety says 'I am entitled to law. I shall act according to it'. ⁴² 'And as it is right for me, I shall deny it', says the debtor. ⁴³ Then it is right to decree a *rhaith*, since there is nothing save the mach's single tongue compelling the debtor's single tongue to deny it. ⁴⁴ The judge takes the relic in his hand and says to the debtor 'God's protection (being) before you and the protection of your lord, do not swear perjury'. ⁴⁵ If he swears, let him swear first to God and to the relic that he is not a surety for him neither on what he says nor on anything. ⁴⁶ Unless the surety counter-swear against him while he is putting his lips to the relic, let the surety pay the debt, since he has admitted that he is a surety and let the debtor be free. ⁴⁷ If the surety counter-swears, let the debtor bring forward his *rhaith*: namely his oath as one of seven.

Cyfn 48-51

[48] O'r canhata [77v] y tala6dyr y'r mach rodi g6ystyl punt yn lle keinha6c
a chyn dyuot oet y g6ystyl y golli, kyfreith a dyweit na dyly y tala6dyr
tracheuyn namyn dimei, kanys hynny y6 trayan keinha6c* kyfreith; kanys
e hunan a lygr6ys y breint y 6ystyl. [49] O'r dyry mach* peth ma6r y g6ystyl
peth bychan, kyfreith y6 y'r ha6l6r y gymryt; a chyt coller kyn yr oet, ny
diwygir namyn y trayan drachefyn y'r mach. [50] Y mach hagen a di6c yn
g6byl, kanys aghyfreitha6l y duc. [51] O'r dyry dyn kywerthyd punt y g6ystyl
ar geinha6c a'e dyg6yda6, ny 6rthtelir ida6 tra'e geuyn dim.

[48] MS trayan di keinha6c
tala6dyr (2)] kynnogyn (2) *MkV*
rodi g6ystyl punt yn lle keinha6c] kywerthyd punt yg g6ystyl keinha6c *MkV*
a chyn dyuot oet] *MkV omit* dyuot
[49] MS mach *written above* dyn
kyfreith y6] *MkV omits*
y ha6l6r y gymryt] yr ha6l6r a dyly y gymryt *V*
ny diwygir...y'r mach] nys di6c yr ha6l6r yr mach traegefyn namyn y trayan *VMk*
[50] Yn g6byl] o g6byl *V*
kanys aghyfreitha6l y duc] kanys yn aghyfreitha6l y duc *MkV*; *Mk adds* ef
[51] O'r...dim] Or dyry kynnogyn kywerthyd punt yg g6ystyl keinha6c ae dygwydaw ny
diwygir ida6 dim *VMk*

Cyfn 52-63

[52] P6ybynhac a wnel amot kyfreitha6l, doent y gyt y wneuthur. [53] O'r
guna dyn amot ac na mynho y gad6, argl6yd bieu y gymhell. [54] O'r guna
dyn amot ac arall yn gyrru arna6, kyfreith a dyweit na da6 namyn y l6 e
hunan y diwat, ony [78r] byd g6rtht6g arna6. [55] Os g6rtht6g a uyd, galwet
ynteu am vra6t. [56] Sef a uernir ida6, y l6 ar y seithuet yn vn funut ac y diwat
mach ac am oet y reith ac am pop peth. [57] O'r guna dyn amot a'e gilyd heb
amotwyr, os guadu a uyn, ny da6 eithyr* y l6 e hunan y diwat ony cheif
tyston ar y welet. [58] O'r edeu dyn da y arall yg g6yd tyston a mynu eilweith
y wadu, kyfreith a ddyweit na eill y wadu, onyt y tyston a palla y'r llall.
[59] Os edeu ynteu heb neb yn y lle, guadet e hunan, os myn, ar y l6. [60] Ny
dyly neb guneuthur amot dros y llall heb y ganhyat, kany phara amot
namyn yn oes y neb a'e gunel, na that ar tor y mab na mab ar tor y tat,
heb y ganhyat. [61] Kyt gunelher amot yn erbyn kyfreith, dir y6 y gad6.
[62] Amot a tyr ar dedyf. [63] Trech amot no g6ir.

[57] MS eithyr eithyr
[60] ar tor y mab na mab ar tor y tat] dros y vab na mab dros y tat *MkV*

[48] If the debtor allows the surety to give a gage of a pound instead of a penny and before the set time for the gage lapses it is lost, the law says that the debtor has no right to anything save a halfpenny; for that is the third of a legal penny, for he himself has debased the status of his gage. [49] If a man gives a big object as a gage for a small object, the law is that the claimant take it, and though it be lost before the set time, nothing is restored save the third returned to the surety. [50] The surety nevertheless makes complete restoration, since he took it illegally. [51] If a man gives the equivalent of a pound as a gage for a penny and it is forfeit, no repayment is made to him.

[52] Whoever make a lawful *amod*, let them come together to make it. [53] If a man makes a *amod* and he does not wish to keep it, the lord has a right to enforce it. [53] If a man makes an *amod* and another make a claim against him, the law says that nothing save his own oath can come to deny it, unless there be counter-swearing against him. [55] If there be counter-swearing, let him call for a judgment. [56] This is what shall be adjudged to him, his oath as one of seven on the same manner as one denies surety with regard to both the appointed time of the *rhaith* and everything else. [57] If a man make an *amod* with another without *amod*-men, if he wishes to deny, nothing save his own oath can come to deny it unless he (the creditor) finds witnesses who have seen it. [58] If a man promises goods to another in the presence of witnesses and he is determined to deny it subsequently, the law say that he cannot deny it, unless the witnesses fail the other. [59] If he promises with no one present, let him deny it himself, if he wishes, on his oath. [60] No one should make an *amod* for another without his permission, for an *amod* does not last save in the life time of the man who makes it, neither a father for a son nor a son for a father without his permission. [61] Though an *amod* be made against the law, it must be kept. [62] An *amod* cuts through the law. [63] An *amod* is stronger than the law.

Additional material placed elsewhere in W

[W87v10 = X183r6]

[64] Pop g6ystyl a dyg6yd ympen y na6uet dyd eithyr y rei hyn: arueu egl6yssic, ny dylyir eu g6ystla6 a chyt g6ystler ny dyg6ydant; c6lltyr a challa6r a b6ell gynnut ny dyg6ydant uyth kyt g6ystler. [65] Oet vn dyd a *bl6y(dy)n yssyd y eur a llurugeu a llestri goreureit pan 6ystler. [66] Kyfreith benfic y6 y dyuot mal y rother. [67] Y neb a rotho benffic a dyly kymryt tyston rac mynet yn y erbyn. [68] O'r eir en y erbyn a gordiwes o'r perchenna6c arna6, talet yn deudyblic. [69] Y neb (a) adawho da y arall ac os diwat pan delher y ouyn, kyfreith anudon a uyd arna6 ef (os) yn gyhoeda6c y t6g, nyt amgen, tri buhyn caml6r6 y'r brenhin. [70] A chymeret ynteu y penyt am yr anudon; a'r llall o'r byd tyston ganta6, y da a geiff.

[65] MS blwyn
[69] a *and* os *added*

[W93v5]

[71] O'r byd mar6 mach dyn ac adaw mab ohona6, y mab a dyly sefyll yn lle y tat yn y uechni. [72] O'r dyg6yd mechni ar uab dros y tat a goruot y diwat, y gyfreith a dyweit na watta neb o genedyl y uam gyt ac ef amyn kenedyl y tat a chenedyl mam y tat. [73] Argl6yd a uyd mach ar pop da adef.

[71] corresponds to 36; 73 occurs at V36v15 and Mk75.6 within the main body of the Surety Tractate.
[73] pop da adef] pop da adefedic diuach MkV

[W93r10 = X217r16-20]

[74] Oet arwassaf o wlat arall neu am d6uyr ma6r neu am lan6, pythe6nos ac nyt mwy. [75] Oet arwassaf yn vn gymh6t neu yn vn cantref tri dieu. [76] Os yn argl6ydiaeth arall yn agos na6 nieu ac ny dodir teruyn ar du6 Sul nac ar du6 Llun.

[W102v15 = V45v22]

[77] Tri da dilys diuach yssyd: da a rotho y brenin y 6r ac a del ida6 ynteu gan gyfreith; a da a gaffo gureic gan y g6r yn y h6ynebwerth, pan gytyo y g6r a gureic arall; a da a dycker yn ryuel deu argl6yd.

[W104v9]

[78] Tri lle yg kyfreith Hywel y mae pra6f: un ohonu, gureic bieu proui treis ar 6r; eil y6 kynogyn bieu proui uch pen bed y mach y uot yn uach ac na diwyg6yt drosta6 y uechniaeth tra uu uy6; trydyd y6 proui bugeilgi.

[64] Every gage lapses at the end of the ninth day save these: equipment belonging to a church should not be used as gages and though it be used it does not lapse; a coulter and a cauldron and an axe for cutting firewood never lapse though they may be gages. [65] A set time of a year and a day is allowed for gold and mail-coats and gilded vessels when they are gages. [66] The law of borrowing is to return the object as it was given. [67] Whoever shall lend should take witnesses, lest there be opposition. [68] If there be opposition and the owner prevail against him, let him (the borrower) make a twofold payment. [69] Whoever may promise goods to another and if he deny it when he (the borrower) come to ask for it, the law of perjury is to be applied to him if he swear publicly, namely, a three kine *camlwrw* to the king. [70] And let him do penance for the perjury; and the other, if he has witnesses, shall have the goods.

[71] If a man's surety dies and leaves a son, the son should stand instead of his father in his suretyship. [72] If suretyship falls on a son for his father and he is forced to deny it, the law says that none of his mother's kin deny it with him but his father's kin and his father's mother's kin. [73] The lord shall be surety for all acknowledged goods.

[74] The set time for an *arwaesaf* froom another *gwlad* or from the other side of a large (expanse of) water or a tidal water, a fortnight or more. [75] The set time for an *arwaesaf* in the same *cwmwd* or *cantref*, three days. [76] If he be in another lordship nearby, nine days, and no limit is fixed for Sunday or Monday.

[77] There are three kinds of goods which are undisputed without surety: the goods which the king may give his man and which come to him by right of law; and the goods which a wife may have from her husband as insult-payment when her husband has intercourse with another woman; and the goods which may be taken in a war between two lords.

[78] Three instances in Cyfraith Hywel where there is proof: one of them, a wife has the right to prove rape against a man; the second is that a debtor has the right to prove above the grave of a surety that he is a surety and that his suretyship was not discharged while he lived; the third is the proving of a shepherd dog.

Additional material from other manuscripts.,

U

[*U*56.3-9 = *Z*27v6]

[79] Gwerth goruoda6c un vreint a'r neb yd aeth drosta6 ac yuelly am dyn a 6ystler dros arall. [80] Oet goruoda6c y geissa6 y oruodogaeth un dyd a b16ydyn.

V

[*V*38r10 = *Mk*98.9]

[81] Y neb a uo goruoda6c dros arall ony eill y d6yn 6rth gyfreith, dyg6ydet* y goruoda6c yg kyfreith y neb yd aeth ef drosta6. [80] Oet goruoda6c y geissa6 y oruodogaeth vn dyd a b16ydyn.

[81] ˙   MS drost

[*V*35vl]

[82] Mach a adefho peth o'e vechniaeth ac a watto peth arall, g6adet ar y 16 e hunan, os myn.
[83] Tri mach hagen yssyd ac ny cheiff vn ohonunt dwyn y vechniaeth ar y 16 e hunan kyt g6atto ran ac adef ran arall o'e vechni: nyt amgen, dyn a el yn vach y g6yd llys a mach diebredic a mach talu. Beth bynhac a tygho y kyntaf, y llys a dyly tygu ygyt ac ef neu yn y erbyn; y deu ereill beth bynhac a tygho ar y seithuet o'e gyfnesseiueit y t6g; kanys tala6dyr uyd pop vn ohonunt.

[*V*37r6-8 = *Mk*77.14-16]

[84] Po(b)* dadyl yn y hamot. Nyt amot heb amot6yr. Vn diwat yw amot a mechniaeth.

Mk

[*Mk* 99.10]

[85] Unwerth uyd y neb a 6ystler a'r neb y rother yg g6ystyl drosta6.

[*Mk* 119.7]

[86] Teir mefyl6ryaeth mach: g6adu y vechniaeth ac ef yn vach; ac adef y vechniaeth ac na allo y chymhell, a chameturyt y vechniaeth pan dotter arna6.

[*Mk* 24.20]

[87] O tri mod y kedernheir g6ys: o tyston, neu o vechiaeth, neu o auael.

[84] ˙ MS Po.

[79] The value of a *gorfodog* is of the same status as the one for whom he stands, and so it is for a man who is given as hostage for another. [80] The set time for a *gorfodog* to seek his *gorfodogaeth*: a year and a day.

[81] Whoever shall be a *gorfodog* for another, if he is unable to bring him to law, let the *gorfodog* be liable in law for the one on whose behalf he stood. [80] The set time for a *gorfodog* to seek his *gorfodogaeth*: a year and a day.

[82] A surety who may admit part of his suretyship and deny another part, let him deny it on his own oath, if he will.

[83] There are three sureties however, not one of whom can support his suretyship with his own oath, although he deny part and admit part of his suretyship: namely, a person who becomes a surety in the presence of a court and an inefficient surety and a paying surety. Whatever the first shall swear, the court should swear with him or against him; the other two, however, swear with six of their nearest relatives; since each of them is a debtor.

[84] Every (legal) case according to its *amod*. There is no *amod* without *amod*-men. Denials for an *amod* and for suretyship are the same.

[85] The value of a person who may be given as hostage is the same as that of a person, for whom he is given as hostage.

[86] The three shames of a surety: denial of his suretyship and he being a surety; and acknowledging his suretyship but being unable to enforce it, and falsely asserting (the amount) of his suretyship when it be placed on him.

[87] In three ways is a summons confirmed: by witnesses or by suretyship or by distraint.

[88] Teir ouerwys a ellir eu g6adu kyn tyston: g6ys dan tyston ny wneir onyt pan ofynner tir o ach ac etryt. [89] Ac o gofyn[25]nir tir yn amgen no hynny neu peth arall, o g6edir vn wys a'e thygu, tr6y vechniaeth y kymellir yr amdiffynn6r y atteb. [90] Lle y pallo mechniaeth vn weith neu y tremycker y g6ys teir g6eith, yno y dylyir kymryt gauael, ac os am tir y byd y dadyl, y tir a euelir. [91] Pallu mechniaeth y6 na rother mach pan dylyher, neu y rodi a'e tremygu. [92] Tremyc g6ys neu vechniaeth y6 na del y dyn a wyssyer yn gyfreitha6l y le enwedic y atteb y dyd y galwer, neu dyuot ac nat atteppo. [93] Tri dyn ny dylyr eu g6yssya6: tyst a g6arant a g6eithreda6l kyss6yn neu gyfadef, eu mechnia6 a dylyir.

[94] Tri ry6 wadu yssyd: vn y6 g6adu yr holl ouyn a datter ar dyn a hynny a reith ossodedic heb y lleihau na'e hachwanegu; eil y6 adef peth o dadyl drycweithret a g6adu y g6eithret, a h6nn6 a wedy gan achwenegu reith ossodedic, megys y mae yg colofneu kyfreith am gelein, lle y tygei deg wyr a deu vgeint gan wadu llofruthyaeth a'e haffeitheu, yno y t6g cant neu deucant neu trychant gan adef affeith a g6adu llofrudyaeth; trydyd y6 g6adu ran [26] ac adef ran arall o dadyl heb weithret yndi, ac yna gan leihau reith ossodedic y g6edir megys y my6n mechni, lle y tygei y mach ar y seithuet gan wadu y vechniaeth oll; yno y t6g ehunan gan wadu ran ac adef ran arall o'r vechni.

X

[X218v14]

[95] Teir gauael nyd atuerir: un onadunt dros ledrat, a mach a galanas.

Z

[Z65r25]

[96] Paham y dywedir oed dridiav a ddyly mach i ymgofav? Llyma paham: oed dridiav a ddyly ef i wybod ai mach ai nid mach; ac yn yr oed hwnw y dyly wadv neu vadde. Gwedi addeffo i vod yn vach ac edryd i vachnieth, yna y dyly ef oed naw niav; oed dridiav y sydd i'r neb a amhevo edrych mach i geisiaw kreiriav i greiriaw y mach.

[Z68rll]

[97] A oes raith i wadv mach? Nac oes raith i wadv nad mach y sydd, gwedi addefer i vod ef yn vach, nid oes raith i wad[v].*

[96] MS edryd
[97] MS wad

[88] Three futile summons can be denied before witnesses: a summons with witnesses can only be made when land is sought by kin and descent. [89] And if land be [25] sought in some way other than that, or any other thing, if one summons be denied and it be sworn to by oath, it is by suretyship that the defendant be compelled to answer.

[90] Where suretyship fails once or the summons be scorned three times, then distraint should be taken, and if the dispute be about land (it is the land that) is to be seized. [91] Failure of suretyship is that a surety is not given when it should be, or that it be given and scorned. [92] Scorning a summons or suretyship is that the man who may be summoned legally may not come to an appointed place to answer on the day that he be called, or that he come and does not answer.

[93] Three men who should not be summoned; a witness and a warrantor and an alleged or admitted confederate; sureties should be required of them.

[94] There are three kinds of denial: one is to deny all the claim which may be put on a man and that with a *rhaith* of a fixed number no more and no less; second is to admit part in a case of misdeed and to deny the deed and that is denied by adding a fixed *rhaith* as in the columns of law regarding a corpse, where fifty men swore denying homicide and its accessories, there a hundred or two hundred or three hundred swear admitting an accessory but denying homicide; the third is to admit a part and deny another part of the case without a deed in it, and then decreasing the fixed *rhaith* one denies as in suretyship, where the surety swore as one of seven denying all his suretyship, there he swears himself, denying part and admitting another part of the suretyship.

[95] Three distraints which are not restored: one of them for theft, and surety and *galanas*.

[96] Why is it said that a surety should have a set time of three days to recall? This is why: he should have three days to know whether he is a surety or not and within that time he should deny or acknowledge. After he acknowledge that he is a surety and declares his suretyship, then he has a right to a set time of nine days. The set time for anyone, who may doubt the declaration of the surety, to seek relics on which the surety may swear, is three days.

[97] Is there a *rhaith* to deny surety? There is no *rhaith* to deny that there is no surety, after it be conceded that he is a surety, there is no *rhaith* to deny it.

[1] The Introduction to the text is in parts a piece of deliberate plagiarism, echoing Dafydd Jenkins' own Introduction to the Cyfnerth text printed at WLW 132-35. I am grateful to T. M. Charles-Edwards who checked my translation and read the Introduction and to Eurys Rolant who checked my transcript with the manuscripts and made valuable suggestions regarding the translation of some words.

[2] 10-18: these sentences concerning the payment schedule, deriving ultimately from an Irish canon mark the beginning of the Surety Tractate as it is preserved in X and Z.

[3] 25: the list of X includes interesting variants and does not correspond with that of any of the other Cyfnerth manuscripts. It includes the caeth (slave) and the gwraig (wife) mentioned is one who cannot operate without her husbands permission (na gwreic heb ganyad y gwr). This latter reference may concur with the idea that lies behind Ior 66/7 which specifies amongst the list of legal incompetents, 'each person who cannot serve the law without the permission of another' (p(h)ob den ny allo hep kanhyat arall guassanaethu keureyth).

[4] 37-63 derive from the tradition of the Book of Iorwerth (see above p.000). 37-47 contain a compressed version of Ior 62/7-11 and 52-63, a compressed version of Ior 69/1-12.

[5] 79-81: four of the manuscripts, U, Mk, V and Z have two clauses dealing with the gorfodog surety which occur, as in Ior, outside the main Surety Tractate (see Ior 70/1 and above p.196).

[6] 86-92: these triads from Mk correspond to triads in Bleg. 86 = Bleg 40.29-41; 87-94 = Bleg 125.4-126.4.

[7] 95-7: this section of question and answer texts is reminiscent of the style of the Schools, see T. M. Charles-Edwards and F. Kelly, Bechbretha (Dublin, 1983) 25; 20 (1980) Studia Hibernica 141-62. The style is usually found in later Welsh law manuscripts.

V. LATIN REDACTION E
EDITED AND TRANSLATED BY HELEN DAVIES
Merton College MS 323, f. 17r, l.6.

[LTWL 458.17] [1]Debitor principalis debitum non inficiatus absque contradictione soluet. [2]At si dies solutioni prefixus nondum adfuerit, dies expectandus* est.

[3]Qui autem ante diem debitum per accionem petierit, tantum temporis post diem insolutus remanebit.

DE FIDEIUSSIONIBUS

[4]Adstante die solutionis, fideiussor habebit diem ad petendum principalem debitorem. [5]Fideiussor, postquam mortuus fuerit *kynnogyn*, id est, debitor, nihil habens in mundo, reddat dimidium; similiter pro *kynnogyn* qui deserit patriam.

[6]Tres manus oportet convenire ad faciendum* fideiussorem: videlicet dantis, fideiussoris et accipientis. [7]Qui inconsulta dominicali potentia pro debito *gauel*, id est, districtionem acceperit, dato debito priuabitur, et tres vaccas domino reddet. [8]Debitoris districtio non capitur nisi fideiussor tradiderit. [9]Fideiussor, licet soluendo existat pro debitore, minime tamen soluet antequam debitor deficiat. [10]Debitor vero non deficiet dum iuri paruerit. [11]De iure quidem, licet nihil nisi tria indumenta habuerit, duo soluet et tercium sibi retinebit, et sic semper quolibet anno donec totum soluat. [LTWL 459.12] [12]Fideiussor negans fideiussionem cum septem manibus proximorum negabit, vel ipse solus in septem altaribus consecratis et septies super eodem [f. 17v] altari. [13]Si vero partem negat et partem confitetur, solus semel negabit. [14] Et nota quod non debet admitti ad iuramentum qui non est dignus ad proferendum testimonium. [15]Non debet fideiussor dari qui extraneus est, quia verbum eius est nihil super Cambrum, vel fortior seipso, vel mancipium nisi cum licentia domini, vel monachus* nisi consentiente abbate, nec scholaris nisi consentiente magistro neque femina nisi fuerit domina principalis absque licentia mariti, nec filius donec ad etatem legitimam** veniat sine consensu patris. [16]Quamvis fideiussor in fideiussione sua habeat *ystum*, id est, euasionem, non debet contra eum *gwrthtung*, id est, 'αντωμοσία* sed fidei ipsius est credendum.

[17]*[18]Si quis nomine emptionis rem aliquam ab aliquo acceperit, et post qui accepit ab hac vita exiens res suas amicis reliquerit, cum ipse pro se de pretio rei assumpte reddendo fideiussor extiterat, ab amicis prefatis, licet factum ignorantibus et ob hoc diffidentibus, de rebus mortui pretium rei sue

LATIN REDACTION E

[1] The principal debtor who does not deny his debt shall pay without objection. [2] But if the day fixed for payment has not yet come, that day should be awaited. [3] Whoever seeks by suit a debt due to him before the appointed day shall remain unpaid for that length of time after the day.

OF SURETIES

[4] When the day of payment arrives, the surety shall have a day to seek the principal debtor. [5] When the *kynnogyn*, that is, the debtor, has died with no worldly goods, let the surety pay half, as also for the *kynnogyn* who has left the country.

[6] Three hands must come together to make a surety: namely those of the giver, the surety and the recipient. [7] Whoever should take *gauel*, that is, distraint, for a debt, without the lord's authority, shall be deprived of the debt given, and shall pay three cows to the lord. [8] The distraint of the debtor is not taken unless the surety hands it over. [9] Although the surety is there to pay on behalf of the debtor, he shall not do so at all before the debtor defaults, [10] but the debtor shall not default while he obeys the law. [11] For, by law, if he should have nothing except three garments, he shall pay two and keep the third for himself, and similarly each year for ever until he pays the whole debt. [12] The surety who denies his suretyship shall do so with the oaths of seven of his kindred, or alone on seven consecrated altars and seven times on the same altar. [13] If he denies part of the debt and admits the other part, he alone shall deny it once. [14] And note that one who is not worthy to give evidence should not be admitted to take an oath. [15] A surety should not be given who is a foreigner, since his word is as nothing concerning a Welshman; or someone more powerful than himself; or a slave without his master's permission; or a monk without his abbot's permission; or a scholar without his master's agreement; or a woman, unless she be a chief lady, without her husband's permission; or a youth, until he reaches the legal age, without his father's agreement. [16] Whatever *ystum*, that is, excuse, the surety should have in his suretyship, there should be no *gwrthtwng*, that is, (counter-oath) against him, but his word should be believed.

[17]*[18] If someone received something from another as a purchase, and then the receiver died leaving his estate to friends, having stood surety for himself

venditor consequatur. [19]Iurabit tamen prius cum sex viris probatis de proximis suis super sepulcrum debitoris, si possit inveniri — sin autem non possit, super altare consecratum — quod illi rem vendiderit, et quod ipse pro se fideiussor principalis fuerit, et quod ante* mortem nihil de debito solverit. [20]Tribus modis fit liber fideiussor de debito confesso: primo concesserit si creditor debitori alium diem solutionis ultra primum sine eius licentia; secundo si redditur debitum creditori pro eo; tertio si *adauel*, id est, districtio, capitur pro debito sine deliberatione fideiussoris. [21]Si fideiussor fateatur se esse in commercio*, super illum primo venit iuramentum ut fateatur super quod fit [f. 18r] fideiussor. [22]Si totum negat quod non sit fideiussor, super *kynnogyn*, id est, debitorem, primo venit iuramentum. [23]Et si fideiussor contra iuret, *kynnogyn*, id est, debitor, denegat illum cum septem hominibus. [24]Si* manu, id est, fide, confirmatur commercium**, redditur, si negatur, non. [25]*Negatio autum fideiussionis quae dicitur *bri Duw*, id est, Deo teste**, fit cum septem hominibus.

[26]Similiter est fideiussoris negatio, si contra iuretur. [27]Et si non, non debet nisi iuramentum ipsius solius super quod ponatur fideiussor. [28]Nullum commercium* est sine fideiussione vel fide. [LTWL 460] [29]Tribus modis differtur fideiussor et *kynnogyn*, id est, debitor, videlicet, audito cornu regis euntis ad prelium vel exercitum, et *hawl trais*, id est, accio rapinae, et *hawl lledrat*, id est, accio latrocinii. [30]Fideiussor debet *adauael*, id est, districtionem, ducere cum *kynnogyn*, id est, debitore usque ad tutum, et primam verberationem si necesse sit accipere, et litigium omnem sustinere. [31]Si sic non fecerit, reddat ille solus. [32]*[33]Spacium fideiussoris ut sciat an est fideiussor vel non: tres dies.

[34]Quicunque sit *goruodauc*, id est*, fideiussor vel manucaptor in causa capitali, non deliberabitur a suo vadimonio usque ad annum et unum diem. [35]A die solutionis prefixo, nisi ea die principalis debitor debitum creditori soluerit, fideiussori iure duodecim conceduntur dies ad soluendum; deinde viginti; ad ultimam triginta. [36]Postea sine ulla dilatione temporis et contradictione soluet. [37]Alii dicunt quod si super re viua fidem debeat, primo habebit novem dies ad soluendum; deinde quinque. [38]Si vero super re mortua, triginta dies habebit; et postea soluat. [39]In tribus non debet accipi fideiussor: scilicet quando* promittitur aliquid alicui a rege; et quando accipit sacerdos testamentum vel testimonium ab infirmo; et [f. 18v] medicus mercedem ab egro**. [40]In omnibus aliis debet accipi fides vel fideiussor. [41]*[42]Qui debitor est, et non negat, iure debet reddere cui debet sine aliqua temporis delatione cum creditori placuerit, nisi dies solucionis fuit prefixus, vel fideiussor fuerit. [43]Quicumque calumpniatur propter aliquam calumpniam et propter hoc dimittat vel deserat patriam antequam fideiussorem vel fidem de illa calumpnia dari faciat, dominus eius pro ipso

concerning the payment of the price of the article, let the vendor seek the price of the article from the dead man's estate from the friends aforesaid, though it was done without their knowledge and therefore without their oath. [19] He shall swear first with six good men of his kindred on the debtor's grave, if it can be found — if not, on a consecrated altar — that he sold the article to the dead man and that the latter was principal surety for himself and paid none of the debt before his death.

[20] The surety may be freed from an acknowledged debt in three ways: first, if the creditor gave the debtor another date for payment beyond the first without his permission; secondly, if the debt is paid to the creditor on his behalf; thirdly, if *adauel*, that is, distraint, be taken for the debt without consultation with the surety. [21] If the surety acknowledges that he is involved in the bargain, he is to be the first to swear an oath, [namely] that he acknowledges [the debt] for which he is surety. [22] If he wholly denies that he is surety, an oath is first taken by the *kynnogyn*, that is, the debtor. [23] If the surety swears to the contrary, the *kynnogyn*, that is, the debtor, denies him with seven men. [24] If the bargain is confirmed by hand, that is, by oath, it (the debt) is paid; if it is denied, it is not. [25] Let denial of the suretyship called *Bri Duw*, that is, God being witness, be done with seven men.

[26] The denial of the surety is done in the same way if a counter-oath be sworn. [27] And if it is not, there is required only his oath alone as to [the debt] for which he is appointed surety. [28] There is no bargain without suretyship or oath. [29] There are three ways in which the surety and the *kynnogyn*, that is, the debtor, are delayed, namely by hearing the king's horn as he goes to battle or to his army; by *hawl trais*, that is, an action alleging violence; and *hawl lledrat*, that is, an action of theft. [30] The surety should take the *adauael*, that is, the distraint, with the *kynnogyn*, that is, the debtor, to safety, bear the first blow, if necessary, and withstand all dispute. [31] If he does not do this, let him alone pay. [32] * [33] The time allowed a surety to decide whether or not he is a surety is three days.

[34] The *goruodauc*, that is, surety or bail in a capital case, shall not be freed from his gage for a year and a day.

[35] If the principal debtor does not pay the creditor his debt on the day fixed for payment, twelve days are allowed by law to the surety to pay, then twenty, and finally thirty. [36] Then he shall pay with no further delay or objection. [37] Others say that if he stands surety for a live thing, he shall first have nine days to pay, then five. [38] If he stands surety for an inanimate object, he shall have thirty days; then let him pay. [39] Upon three occasions should a surety not be taken: namely when a promise is made by the king, when a priest takes the will or testimony of a sick man, and when a doctor takes a fee from a patient. [40] In all other cases an oath or a surety should be

respondere debet, et si necesse* fuerit reddere vel suum homagium iuramento negare, quia pro ipsa calumpnia ipsum secum non tenuit. ⁴⁴Si fideiussor reddit pro *kynnogyn*, id est, debitore, qui dimisit patriam, cum ille redierit, ipse sibi ius ab eo exquiret. ⁴⁵Et hic est solus locus ubi fideiussor ius suum potest cogere. [*LTWL* 461] ⁴⁶Quilibet *kynnogyn*, id est, debitor*, debet liberare fideiussorem per unum modum e tribus: aut reddendo pro ipso, aut pignus deliberando, aut ipsam** fideiussionem negando.

⁴⁷A vigilia *Nodolic*, id est, Natalis Domini, post vesperas, usque *Calan*, id est, diem Circumcisionis, post missam, et a vigilia Paschae usque ad primam Dominicam sequentem, post missam, et a die *Sulgwyn*, id est, Pentecostes, ad Dominicam usque Sanctae Trinitatis, post missam, nemo debet de sua fideiussione respondere, licet sit dies determinatus ad reddendum. ⁴⁸Si quis fideiussor ante terminum sue fideiussionis aut lepram aut aliquem cultum divinum accepit, nihilominus fideiussionem qua se obligauit exequi debet. ⁴⁹Fideiussio vel promissio vel forefactum* ebrii vel aliud quodcumque dixerit, nihil valebit, nec tenetur pro eis respondere. ⁵⁰Si fideiussor inter *haulvr*, id est, creditorem, et *kynnogyn*, id est, debitor, fuit et uterque non negat, sed [f. 19r] *kynnogyn*, id est, debitor, dicit super minus debitum, *haulvr*, id est, creditor, vero super maius, sed fideiussor dicit se fideiussorem** esse super maiorem quantitatem quam uterque dicit, reddat *kynnogyn*, id est, debitor, tantum quantum dixerit, et residuum fideiussor de rebus propriis persoluat. ⁵¹Si fideiussorem se aliquis inter duos fateatur, et unus ipsorum dicat eum esse fideiussorem super minus, alter super maius, et fideiussor ignorare se firmat super quantum est, illud *ymrysson*, id est, controversum, quod est inter eos dividatur in duas partes et dimidia pars cum re petita *haulvr*, id est, creditori, reddatur.

² *expetandus.
⁶ *faciendam.
¹⁵ *est *deleted*.
**legittimam.
¹⁶ *αὐλωμοσία
¹⁷ *omitted.
¹⁹ *autem.
²¹ *comertio.
²⁴ *sum.
**comercium.
²⁵ *fideiussionis *deleted*.
**testae.
²⁸ *comercium.
³² *omitted.
³⁴ *id est *omitted*.

³⁹ *scilicet quando *omitted*.
**ergo.
⁴¹ *omitted.
⁴³ *neccesse.
⁴⁶ *debitore.
**ipsum.
⁴⁹ *foreisfactum.
⁵⁰ *debitor.
**de fideiussionem.

taken. [41]*[42]The debtor who does not deny his debt should by law pay his creditor without any delay when it pleases the creditor, unless a day was fixed for payment, or there was a surety. [43]If a man was accused and on account of this leaves or abandons the country before he causes a surety or an oath to be given concerning the accusation, his lord should answer for him, and pay if necessary, or deny his homage on oath, since he did not detain the man with him with regard to the accusation. [44]If the surety pays for the *kynnogyn*, that is, the debtor, who left the country, when the latter returns, the surety shall require of him [what is his] right. [45]This is the only occasion upon which the surety can enforce his own rights. [46]The *kynnogyn*, that is, the debtor, should free the surety in one of three ways: by paying on his behalf, or by giving a gage or by denying the suretyship itself.

[47]From the eve of *Nodolic*, that is the day of the birth of Christ, after vespers, to *Calan*, that is, the day of the Circumcision, after mass, and from the vigil of Easter to the first Sunday following, after mass, and from the day of *Sulgwyn*, that is, Pentecost, to Holy Trinity Sunday, after mass, no one should answer for his suretyship, though the day fixed for payment should fall within that time. [48]If a surety should contract leprosy or accept some [position devoted to] divine worship before the end of his suretyship, he should nevertheless perform the suretyship by which he has bound himself. [49]The suretyship, promise or forfeiture of a drunkard, or anything he says, is worthless, and he should not be held to answer for them. [50]If there is a surety between the *haulvr*, that is, the creditor, and the *kynnogyn*, that is, the debtor, and neither denies it, and the *kynnogyn*, that is, the debtor, says that [the surety] is for a lesser debt, and the *haulvr*, that is, the creditor, says [that the surety is] for a greater one, and the surety says that he is surety for a greater debt than either says, let the *kynnogyn*, that is, the debtor, pay as much as he said, and let the surety pay the rest from his own money. [51]If a man acknowledges that he is a surety between two men, and one of them says that he is surety for a lesser sum and the other that his suretyship is for a greater sum, and the surety says that he does not know the amount, let the *ymrysson*, that is, the amount in dispute between them, be divided in two, and let half be paid to the *haulvr*, that is, the creditor, with the rest of the debt.

E II = B III

f. 47r, l. 13

[LTWL 501.14] [1] Si principalis debitor mortuus fuerit, plegius reddet. [2] Si principalis debitor filium habuerit, plegius querat ius suum ab eo si poterit. [3] Si quis negauerit *mach* et *kynnogyn*, id est*, fideiussorem et debitorem, det iuramentum quattuordecim propinquorum suorum ex quibus duae partes erunt ex parte patris, tertia ex parte matris.

[3] *id est *omitted*

[f. 47r, 1. 13]

[1] If the principal debtor is dead, the surety pays. [2] If the principal debtor had a son, let the surety seek his right from him if he can. [3] If anyone denies being *mach* and *kynnogyn*, that is, surety and debtor, let him give the oath of fourteen of his kindred, two thirds from his father's side, and one third from his mother's side.

BERRAD AIRECHTA: AN OLD IRISH TRACT ON SURETYSHIP
TRANSLATED BY ROBIN STACEY

This translation of the principal Irish text on suretyship is based on that of Thurneysen in his fundamental work *Die Bürgschaft im irischen Recht*. The opportunity has been taken, however, to benefit by Thurneysen's own second thoughts and improvements suggested by Bergin, O'Brien and Dr Binchy as well as by the improved text now available in Dr Binchy's *Corpus Iuris Hibernici*, and also to offer, tentatively, some new renderings. The translation does not seek to replace that of Thurneysen: quite apart from its excellence, the appended notes remain invaluable and have in general been followed without any special reference. It is hoped, however, that this version will be useful for those who do not know German. The paragraph numbers are those of Thurneysen and these are followed, in square brackets, by page and line references to CIH. Square brackets are also used to insert words required to fill out the sense of the original, but parentheses are used to insert explanations. Glosses in the MS are enclosed in braces { . . .}.

BERRAD AIRECHTA
'The shaving of the court'[1]

1. [591.9] There are, moreover, transactions within the tribe [which are] entirely immune from claim[2] in Irish law. What is their form?[3] Not difficult. [A transaction] for which neither a *naidm*-surety nor a *ráth*-surety is appropriate to render [the transaction] entirely immune from claim is nevertheless entirely immune from claim, provided that the values of those things which are due [from the other side to each bargain] in respect of them (the contracts) be complete,[4] and provided that they have been given in the presence of witnesses. What are they? The food-rent of a lord, a fief of base-clientship, the [enforcing]-third of a legal agent,[5] alms, offerings, a gift to a poet, the fee for baptism or for reliquaries, lawful gifts to children, chattels [given for future] maintenance, etc.

2. [591.15] The food-rent of a lord, first of all, is entirely immune from claim in Irish law. How is that so? Not difficult. Though stolen food may have been given to a lord in payment of his dues, it is entirely immune from claim for him, and for each person who eats it with him, provided that he does not know that a stolen thing was [given] to him. If he should know it, he is liable to claim. Whatever food [there be] to which the lord is entitled in the tribe is also entirely immune from claim for him, although he may consume it himself at that time, and [also] for each person who eats it with him.

3. [591.20] The price of base clientship is also entirely immune from claim in Irish law, because [the client] does service for it, provided that he (the lord) has been fed from it (the fief) in the presence of 'living candles' (before witnesses). There is also a lord[6] whose fief is forfeit, although he be not fed: a lord who wounds his client. There is also a client whose fief is not immune from claim though he has fed his lord from it twelve times, i.e. a client who wounds his lord.

4. [591.23] The [enforcing]-third of a legal agent, that is also entirely immune from claim for the legal agent in Irish law, i.e. a third of anything[7] that he levies for him (a claimant); his legal activity constitutes his side of the transaction.

5. [591.25] Alms are also entirely immune from claim, provided that he to whom they are given be a Catholic.

6. [591.25] An offering, also: that which is given to God and to the church is entirely immune from claim, provided that the life that is lived there be according to God. That which was given is not immune, however, if it be according to the devil or the world that the church lives.

7. [591.27] A gift to a poet is entirely immune from claim, i.e. that which is given in payment for a poem, provided that the poem is in accordance with truth and propriety.

8. [591.30] The fee for a baptism or for communion is entirely immune from claim, i.e. for a priest, provided that he has not given it to his old woman[8] or to a son born to him after he entered the priesthood.

9. [591.31] Lawful gifts to children are also entirely immune from claim in Irish law. A query: how many gifts to children are there in Irish law? Three, i.e. a gift in exchange for maintenance and a gift of (given to stop?) tears and a gift of love. What is it that makes gifts to children immune from claim? Merit, first of all, makes gifts for maintenance immune from claim, for it is perpetually and entirely immune from claim as the native law recites:...[9]

10. [591.35] A yearling calf every year after that until the termination of fosterage, i.e.e until the end of fourteen years.[10] His son is then returned [to the natural father], and, together with the boy, his horse. If it, i.e. his horse, is not returned, it is [treated as] a fief for which he (the foster-father) is liable [to pay renders]. It is for this reason that an 'after-fief' (fosterage-fee) exists.[11]

11. [591.37] There are, moreover, two legal errors in fosterage. It is an error for the natural father if he stretches out his hand to his son (to take him out of fosterage) after putting him into fosterage until fosterage has been completed, unless a legitimate reason drives him to it. If that be the case, if he is being fostered badly, [the contract of fosterage] is annulled. For if he brings him out [of fosterage] without a legitimate reason, he cannot put him into that fosterage again, and he will receive nothing [back] from the fosterage-fee.

12. [592.5] The second error is for the foster-father to return [the child] before the [end of the proper] period if he has received all of the fosterage-fee. He returns him with the full fosterage-fee as it has been given in its entirety, as the native law recites: "Let him return the boy with his goods...with his goods is [the fosterling] adjudged until the end of fosterage.[12] For the payment of a person who is not benefited from it is not swallowed up". The goods of the fosterage-fee [are to be returned?] from the foster-fathers {he sets them out in *Macslechta*}.[13] There are three ways of judging them (children in fosterage): appearance and weight and clothing.

13. [592.10] The earnings of an adze are also entirely immune from claim in Irish law, provided that they be in return for sweat (hard work). Likewise also the earnings of a smith's tongs are entirely immune from claim in Irish law. Likewise also the earnings of the casting of a fishing net.

14. [592.12] That which a pupil gives to his teacher for teaching him is also entirely immune from claim in Irish law, provided that his teaching to him has been without defect.

15. [592.13] And that which has been given to the doctor as a payment for healing is immune from claim.

16. [592.13] That which has been given across a [tribal] boundary in recompense for a violation of a peace treaty is also entirely immune from claim in Irish law, provided that it has gone across the boundary, though it be stolen property that is given in that case, for the offence has been rendered entirely immune. No payment is made provided that the counter-obligations in the peace treaty have been fully and truly performed by the other side.[14]

17. [592.16] Contracts [made in a state of] drunkenness are also immune from claim. Only three of them are immune from claim, i.e. a promise of a fief for base clientship and an agreement for joint-ploughing[15] and all neighbourhood relationships.

18. [592.18] The promise of a fief, in the first place, is lawful though it may have been promised in a state of drunkenness, provided, however, that service be subsequently given — it is thus that it is then lawful.

19. [592.19] And a contract for joint-ploughing is also entirely immune from claim in Irish law though [it has been made] in a state of drunkenness, for it is that [joint-ploughing] which causes that [drunkenness], and fulfilment of the obligations [of the contract] is required of both parties.

20. [592.21] Neighbourhood relationships are also lawful though [they may have been contracted] in a state of drunkenness, for every person is entitled to them from his partner.[16]

21. [592.22] A question: why is it said that "thou shouldst not bind what thou canst not enforce"? Because there are *naidm*-sureties who bind what they cannot enforce, since their *naidm*-suretyships do not encompass the means whereby they may bind, i.e. the son of a living father upon his father, a client upon his lord, a member of a monastic community[17] upon his superior, an exile(?) upon another. For they do not exact payment from them by force, but their obligations stand in their way.[18]

22. [592.26] A question: why is it said that "thou shouldst not buy from, thou shouldst not sell to, a legal incompetent"? That refers to *naidm*-binding on unfree persons, for their superiors annul them (their contracts) so that they are not enforced against them, for instance a *naidm*-binding on a chief wife, on a fool, on an imbecile, on a lunatic, on an exile — for the latter moves his residence[19] if something be enforced against him — on a man cast ashore by the sea. Likewise for every person who cannot be bound; in the face of every *naidm*-binding[20] they possess mouths behind their backs:[21] not only do they not bind anything on anyone, no one binds anything on them,[22] for their contracts are annulled by their superiors.

23. [592.32] There are *naidm*-sureties who fulfil the responsibilities [of their office] though they may not have been appointed as *naidm*-sureties, for instance a *naidm*-surety for the cattle of a woman — certain and uncertain (close and remote) kin enforce it, etc.

24. [592.34] Moreover, one man of a kindred as against another, a father for his son, a teacher for his pupil, an abbot for his *manaig* (monks and monastic tenants), a lord for his client — [namely] every 'head' for his proper 'limbs' — are [unappointed] *naidm*-sureties [provided] they are not impugned on account of him over whom they are entitled to exercise authority.[23] Therefore is it said: "[A claim] is enforced and [a *naidm*-surety] is not appointed."

25. [592.37] There are also hasty *naidm*-sureties, that is, *naidm*-sureties who guarantee exchanges and contracts without annulling [them] before [the two contracting parties] exchange the goods; [the contracts] are then made fast through these *naidm*-sureties and they do not defraud. Therefore is it said: "*naidm*-sureties make fast and they do not defraud."

26. [592.40] There are one-sided *naidm*-sureties, i.e. many kinsman-*naidm*-sureties with the one contracting party and a single *naidm*-surety consisting of one man from the other. It is for this reason that lots are cast between them to find out which of them, according to the ordeal, should enforce [the claim], and it is thus enforced.

27. [593.2] There are other one-sided *naidm*-sureties, namely *naidm*-sureties who are appointed by the one side, and who are not appointed by the other side. They are one-sided *naidm*-sureties: such *naidm*-sureties do not enforce for a *naidm*-surety does not enforce obligations upon a contracting party unless they enforce [them] with him (with his original consent), unless the obligations have been counter-bound, so that it is said: "Appoint *mac*-sureties, do not enforce obligations [and] do not take [the responsibility for the] enforcement [of a claim] on yourself without being able to enforce [it]." [24] It is also to *naidm*-sureties who are appointed and do not enforce that [the sayings] "contracts of a wood", "contracts of drunkenness" apply. [25]

28. [593.8] A question, then: which of the two is the more to be respected, a *naidm*-surety or entitlement? [26] There is a time when entitlement is more to be respected than a *naidm*-surety , another time when the *naidm*-surety is more to be respected, [and] another time when both are to be respected equally.

29. [593.10] Entitlement is more to be respected, first of all, when it is a transaction of "light with darkness," i.e. a transaction between a sensible person and a fool, or between one fool and another. For although the sensible person has defrauded the fool, or the fool [has defrauded] the other, such a case reverts to entitlement, [27] and *naidm*-sureties do not make fast that fraud.

30. [593.13] When, however, it is a transaction between two competent people, a *naidm*-surety is as much to be respected in that case [28] as is entitlement, for then is it [asked]: "How may it be enforced? [29] How may it be violated?"

31. [593.14] When, however, the sensible person knows that he is being defrauded, a *naidm*-surety is more to be respected with regard to that [transaction], for that excludes entitlement. Therefore is it said: "A *mac*-surety {i.e. a *naidm*-surety [30]} pierces {i.e. pierces [31]} entitlement."

32. [593.16] A *naidm*-surety is as much to be respected as is entitlement when the contract proceeds under the supervision of a *naidm*-surety and a judge, for it turns to entitlement then. [32] A *naidm*-surety is stronger, however, when it is under the supervision of a *naidm*-surety and of witnesses that it proceeds.

33. [593.18] There is a situation in which entitlement is more to be respected than is a *naidm*-surety: when injustice {i.e. a fraud} is dissolved to the dishonour of a *naidm*-surety and entitlement is bound without a *naidm*-surety. Therefore is it said: "[A *naidm*-surety] is appointed and [a claim] is not enforced; [a claim] is enforced and [a *naidm*-surety] is not appointed."[33]

34. [593.22] A question: what are the contracts which entitlement makes valid without a *naidm*-surety? They are those that we have mentioned: i.e. a fief for extra services and a payment for poem etc.

35. [393.24] A question: what are those [contracts] which are dissolved to the dishonour of a *naidm*-surety? i.e. a fief for which food-rent is not given and a fosterage-fee for which [the child] has not been fostered.

36. [593.26] A contract [made] with the son of a living father without the participation of his father [is also dissolved to the dishonour of a *naidm*-surety]. But there are three [types of] sons of a living father in Irish law, i.e. a cold son and a hot son and a fostered son. A cold son: that is a son who is in the cold by virtue of having evaded [his responsibilities towards] his father, so that is it forbidden to harbour and to protect him.[34] Therefore it is said: "Any forbidden person is not acceptable." Forbidding entails invalidity; a contract with such a son is then no contract. The second son is the hot son,[35] that is a son who is in a warm relationship of *pietas* with his father, properly subordinated so that he controls neither foot nor hand. His contract, too, is no contract. The fostered son, that is the son emancipated in the tribe, because the father leaves him with whomsoever he chooses, i.e for the sake of [learning] a craft or farming. That son, however, is capable of making contracts, except for contracts which cling to[36] an inheritance, i.e. monastic or base clientship.

37. [593.35] Any contract, then, which is made with people [requiring the] supervision [of a 'head'] in the absence of the person who protects them is no contract even though *naidm*-sureties and *ráth*-sureties may have guaranteed it, for their contracts are annulled by their 'heads' so that they are not enforced against them, for instance a contract with a woman, with a son, with a slave, with an unfree person, with a member of a monastic community, with an exile, with a *fuidir* (type of half-freeman) with a landless person, with a legally irresponsible person, with a senseless person, with a cottager. A contract of (made through) fear and ignorance and compulsion [is no contract]. Whatever contract, then, in which such *naidm*-sureties act, they do not for their part enforce, for as [contracts] are not enforced against them, so they do not enforce [contracts] with anyone.

38. [594.1] There are, moreover, [situations where], within the tribe, wounding a man is immune from claim, as we have said it, i.e. [wounding] a person who seeks to kill you.[37] Distraint which is prosecuted is also immune from claim, if the period of its forfeiture has expired, though its immunity from claim may not have been bound through oral contracts.[38] Every gage that has lapsed[39] is also immune from claim, provided that it has lapsed according to each propriety, according to [proper] time and notice. [Trespassing?] cattle which have been seized are also immune from claim, provided that each propriety has been remembered.

39. [594.5] Though neither a *naidm*-surety nor a *ráth*-surety may hold them fast, entitlement holds them fast, for time and acknowledgement and proper seizure bind [them]. Therefore is it said: "Possession [of the gage or distraint] is obtained by detaining [it]: they are made fast by [the other party] allowing [possession]; they are made immune from claim by [the other party] recognizing [possession]."

40. [594.8] A question, then: what [fee] does each person receive for his guarantee? Not difficult: a sack [of grain] for the testimony {i.e. the word} of a substantial freeman (*bóaire*), a yearling heifer for his witnessing[40] {i.e. for his witness}, a yearling calf for his appointment {i.e. for his *naidm*-suretyship}, a cow for his *aitire*-suretyship, i.e. one third of his honour-price.

41. [594.10] A *naidm*-surety, however, enforces [a claim equal in value to] his full honour-price. In times past,[41] the substantial freeman used to enforce his *naidm*-suretyship [up to a value of] seven *cumals*, but now it is up to five *séts*.

42. [594.13] There is also a *naidm*-surety who undertakes the responsibilities of a *ráth*-surety: i.e. that is a *naidm*-surety who is circumvented [in his attempt to enforce his suretyship]; he enforces his compensation afterwards by distraint.[42] There is an *aitire*-surety who undertakes the responsibilities of a *naidm*-surety: that is an *aitire*-surety who puts his hand on the breast of a debtor [to enforce a claim] together with a *naidm*-surety. He enforces [the claim] before he has paid. In that way he is free from liability. There is also a *naidm*-surety who performs the responsibility of a *ráth*-surety: that is a *naidm*-surety who guarantees base clientship. He is a *ráth*-surety of base clientship after the client defaults until he brings the lord onto the land.[43]

43. [594.18] A question: what are the three responsibilities of a *naidm*-surety? Preserving [in his memory the value of] the thing for which he is appointed *as surety* lest anything be added to it and lest anything be subtracted from it, [giving] his oath without blemish,[44] and enforcing it (the contract) without neglect.

44. [594.21] If, then, a party to a debt {i.e. a contracting party} should abscond so that the *naidm*-surety is not able to enforce [the claim] against him, what compels him to come face to face with the *naidm*-surety? And to whom does it belong to bring pressure on the *naidm* when there is a witness that it is not he who is a debtor. For the *naidm*-surety says to the claimant: "Let me find the debtor with you, awaiting me in the place appointed for payment, without a chariot, without protection, and I will then, with you, enforce [the claim] against him."

45. [594.26] What, then, are the defences [available to] a debtor [which protect him] from a *naidm*-surety, if he seeks protection? There are three things which protect him from a *naidm*-surety in Irish law, i.e. a high noble (*ánsruth*) and a court and an assembly. This is the high-noble who protects him, i.e. a man whose father and grandfather were high-nobles and who is a high-noble himself, for [a high-noble of only] one generation is not a proper high-noble for this purpose. The noble privilege of a king or a bishop or a church or the chief fort of a king or of a master of poets protects him as well.

46. [594.31] And if the protection does not permit a judgement [to be enforced] against him, his calves are nevertheless then enclosed [apart from their mothers] until he comes [to tend] those [calves], [45] so that his verbal contracts can be made fast upon him.

47. [594.33] And if he should have no calves, are the calves of his kindred taken instead? They are not taken, for ordinary oral contracts do not injure the kindred.

48. [594.35] A question: what is done about it if one should not meet him? One goes to the *ráth*-surety or the *aitire*-surety, if they are securing [an obligation], for those are the five things which exist in order to protect against evasion, i.e. a *naidm*-surety and a *ráth*-surety and an *aitire*-surety and celebrating [a religious ceremony] [46] and a gage. One goes then to the *ráth*-surety after evasion by the debtor. [47]

49. [594.38] Why is a contracting-party (*féchem*) so called? Not difficult: because he is entitled to a debt (*fíach*) or a debt is due from him, [48] for each of these is a contracting party.

50. [595.1] A question: which of the two parties first binds [an obligation] on the other? Not difficult: he who is entitled to something.

51. [595.1] A question: how is it (the obligation) fixed upon him? Not difficult:

a. [595.2] "Take on your hand [49] that [this] debt [will be paid] to me by you on [such-and-such] a future day, in this place appointed for payment, unchanged [and] without alteration, with its full lawful worth and its [proper] appearance (?), with it having been tested, [50] and its immunity from claim and freedom from dispute [guaranteed], in my possession or in the possession of the person who 'kindles' my affairs. There is a single gage and a single period of notice by which the obligations of the *ráth*-surety and of the contracting party are terminated.

b. [595.5] "Take into your hand that, should you not come on that day, as a consequence one third of the debt that is here bound 'runs' (becomes an additional debt).[51] [Let] the debt-payment from you or from the *ráth*-surety who is a guarantor on your behalf [be] immune from claim so that it may be, and may have been paid, in the hand of the creditor, who may take it away. Let each penalty be as immune from claim as the principal of its debt. Find a payment which does not diminish the original [debt]. May you acknowledge also [your obligations] with respect to the place appointed for payment and [with respect to] clarification through witnesses. And [let] this debt be paid to me by you, and [let it be] a complete, secure, faultless debt-payment, [made] without [further] preparation, without delay, without defence. [Let it be] the debt of a living man between two living contracting parties, [a debt] that the death of a *ráth*-surety or of a contracting party or of the man who binds [the obligations][52] or of [the man] on whom they are bound does not diminish.[53] [The obligation] passes on to the heirs of each one of them.[54]

c. [595.13] "Take in your hand likewise [that you will fulfil your obligations] without evasion, without defect,[55] without neglect, without removal, without stipulation, without condition, without difficulty, without neglect, except insofar as counter-services [performed] by you may be a substitute.[56]

d. [595.15] "I appoint [*naidm-sureties*]," says the contracting party from whom [the debt] is due."

52. [595.16] A question: wherein consists the proper treatment and the delivery (proper treatment of the delivery?) of the debt-payment between these two contracting parties? Not difficult: if this contracting party, from whom [the debt] is due, should evade the place appointed for the payment of the debt on the day that debts are due from him, and no lawful exemption should protect him, and the contracting party who is entitled to something should come there, the latter declares {i.e. the latter says} before witnesses: "The debt to which I am entitled here today, I demand it, I claim it. Let it be a [valid] debt-payment, provided that it be in my possession [and] that he has paid it in full,[57] and the side of the contract affecting him will be fulfilled by me according to whatever is due. I have appointed *mac*-sureties that I will behave correctly with respect to receiving and removing [the payment] and [with respect to a declaration of] freedom from loss and renunciation [of any further claims on the debtor], provided that the debt has been paid to me." This debt is then subsequently exacted from the *ráth*-surety with its fines.

53. [595.23] If it should be the debtor who comes there with the debt-payment (and the creditor does not appear), he for his part says in the presence of witnesses: ["As for] the debt that is due from me here today, here it is. I appoint *mac*-sureties [to guarantee] the payment and the repayment [of the debt], with its testing (having been checked) and its immunity from claim and its security from dispute, except insofar as delivering and removing [the payment], [declaration of] freedom from loss and renunciation [of any further claim] and service may take its place (i.e. of part of the debt-payment). It becomes for him a debt [payable only] in a year's time unless a legitimate excuse excuses him for his non-appearance.[58]

54. [595.29] If both parties be responsible for the negligence, the year is divided in two between them.

55. [595.30] Are there obligations that the [one] contracting party would not enforce on the other when he strips (exacts the debt from) the *ráth*-surety or when [the *ráth*-surety's] being stripped instead of him (the debtor) is likely? There are certainly. What are they? Not difficult: "Swear to God that it is an extinction[59] [of the obligation] according to each entitlement, that you have exacted [the debt] entirely, according to each propriety, in accordance with the [correct] times and arrangements, and that you have not stripped my *ráth*-surety at the wrong time or [in contempt of] a lawful excuse."

56. [595.34] A question: are there obligations that the contracting party would not seek from the *ráth*-surety when he declares him free from liability? There are, certainly. What are they? "Swear to God that I have paid, and have not rendered [myself] liable. Do not induce a blush {i.e. a blush} unlawfully. [Swear] that I have paid all at the [correct] times and in accordance with the [correct] arrangements."

57. [595.36] A question: what is the formula with respect to the binding that the contracting party makes which makes fast[60] these obligations? "Appoint *mac*-sureties that [this] debt will be in my possession on the appointed day, in this place. [Let there be] a single gage and a single period of notice by which the obligations of the *ráth*-surety and of the contracting party are terminated."[61]

58. [596.3] THE LAW OF WITNESSING: Why is witness (*fíada*) so called? Because he is a lord (*fíada*), for witnessing cannot be done except by a conscientious responsible person, or else [because] witness (*fíado*) is in the presence of two (*fíad a do*), for [the testimony of] a single man is not lawful in witnessing — two or three persons are [required]. Witnessing (*fíadnaise*), then, [is so called because the transaction] is to be bound (*naisi*)[62] in the presence (*fíad*) of someone, for no contract at which there is no witness present to keep [the details of the transaction] in memory is complete.

59. [596.6] As the native law recites: Where is proof found in Irish law? Do heirs have memories without ogam [inscriptions] on stones,[63] without public lot-casting {i.e. lots}, without *mac*-sureties, without *ráth*-sureties? Although they have been proclaimed, how shall contracts of the [deceased] ancestors be enforced?[64] It is witnesses who make fast proof.[65] Every proof that is confirmed through witnesses is good, for it is false when they are lacking. Unfree men, senseless men {i.e. without a head} lordless men {i.e. without a leader} provide {i.e. go to} proof that is supported [by the responsible testimony of others].[66] A living person {i.e. a contracting party} is exonerated through [the testimony of] living people {i.e. witnesses} for each proof which is not recalled in the memories of witnesses is defective. Why is a report that is heard [about an event which occurred] in the absence [of the person bearing witness] a 'dead-opinion'?[67] For everyone's hearing is a whore, so that a report that is heard is invalid, whether the matter concerning which a rumour {i.e. a tale} is heard be true or untrue. Witnessing is not made fast by a kinsman or a woman or a son or a slave or a half-witted person {i.e. [he is intermittently either] a fool or a sensible person} or a person who is too old. For if he is too old, [his] memory does not reach any distance. Female testimony[68] has no claim beyond [that of] secrets[69] {i.e. beyond confidences}, for nothing [valued at] more than a sack is adjudged to [such] an oath.[70] It is not [valid] witness unless it is ascribed to him in whose presence the action be done.

60. [596.19] As the native law recites: Where does anyone testify to, where does anyone adhere to {i.e. what is the place in which anyone holds fast to} something that he does not see and that he does not hear? For every murmur {i.e. every statement} that is not confirmed through witnesses, about which [a statement] may not be made definite and may not be sworn,[71] is dumb, the boast of an unreasoning person[72] {i.e. of an unwise person} [made] because of rashness, an estimation [made] on the basis of opinion. [It is] a grievous ruin for the judge in a case {lit.: its judge} who judges according to oaths [made on the basis] of opinions — that type of oath is a "clarification of deception", [whether offered] by free persons or unfree persons. [When a case] is not prosecuted before the eyes of an old pair [of witnesses] {i.e. old witnessing}, [it is] the ruin of a lawsuit [and] the destruction of a prosecution.

61. [596.25] Where does a nobleman undertake hosting without base clients? Where does one sue for ale without authority [and] without vassalry? Where is a hundred-fold host sought without arms? Where does every poor person desire [to make a] purchase? Where do judges pass judgements without knowledge? Where does an heir enforce contracts without witnesses after a long time {i.e. after a long time}? It is true that he is no witness who does not see nor hear nor appear [to give evidence?] nor swear to it (his evidence?).[73]

62. [596.29] For those are the seven things which overturn every [attempt at] dissolving [a contract]: valid witnessing, immoveable stones, *ráth*-sureties [as a guarantee] of prescriptive right, a godly old writing, a bequest in respect of death. Those who are more numerous [and] more worthy swear to it; but no one is worthy [to be believed] in his own cause, and no judge by whom a pair [of persons who are parties in a case] is protected is worthy, and no witness who does not testify truth against enemies or friends is worthy, and no oath over which there is no supervision is worthy, and no witness who does not testify is worthy.

63. [596.34] Entertainment does not take away debts; each thing that has been given is to be returned; it is 'filled up' if it is lacking.[74] Any person who does not have *naidm*-surety or a *ráth*-surety or witness[es] in every contract to testify to [their] memories [of the details of the contract] is foolish, so that [that to which he is entitled] be not neglected {i.e. so that neglect be not put upon him}. No one exculpates by oath in respect of something that he does not see and that he does not hear when there is no witness to the obligations [of the contract]. It is true that a contract without a *ráth*-surety, without witnesses, without a *naidm*-surety is not fixed. For it is a *naidm*-surety who enforces [a contract], a *ráth*-surety who gives a gage [for payment], a witness who protects debts together with the obligations [of the contract]. For neither a debt nor a contract is made manifest without witnessing, or until each person has fulfilled his obligations[75] that he has acknowledged of his own free will. A 'pierced-*naidm*-surety' is not fixed nor validated by oath for tribes.[76]

64. [597.4] THE LAW OF *AITIRE* SURETYSHIP: why is an *aitire* ('betweenship') so called? Between (*iter*) two, i.e. between breast and cheek,[77] or between two contracting parties.[78] A question: how many *aitire*-sureties are there in Irish law? Not difficult: three. What are they? An *aitire*-surety of oath and an *aitire*-surety of warranty and an *aitire*-surety of binding.[79]

65. [597.6] How are [his responsibilities] fixed upon an [*aitire*]-surety of an oath? Not difficult:

a. [597.6] ''Swear to God that you will fulfill the duties and the practices and the [established] times and the responsibilities of the *aitire*-suretyship into which you enter, as against me and as against this man, that you will not

evade them, that you will fulfill them. [Swear to God that] you will compel
them according to what pertains to proper justice [fulfilling] completely the
responsibilities that each person for whom you act as surety gives [to you],
by enforcing [the claim] and 'milking'[80] {i.e. on his kindred}, by making
payment without neglect, by fulfilling any [responsibility] that 'reaches' you
according to the decision of the judge that we appoint, by supporting {i.e.
by upholding} his decision, whoever may enforce [the claim], whoever may
acknowledge [judgement?], by payment [of the debt thus] 'unyoking' [the
contract].[81]

   b. [597.11] "Swear to God that you will receive any summons by which
you may be summoned in accordance with the [established] times of an *aitire*-
suretyship according to what is appropriate. [Swear to God] that you will
enforce any meeting [and] any arrangement at which your presence shall be
required (?) with your strength and your power.[82]

   c. [597.13] "Swear to God that you will effect your true prompt meetings
without neglect [and] without negligence, except [if you have] a legal
exemption because of your death or your sickness or [your obligation to
perform the duties associated with] an immediate *naidm*-suretyship of tribes,
so that each person may be bound to his responsibilities anew after [the
expiration of] the legal exemption, i.e. [the parties involved] are to come
after [the expiration of] the legal exemption to the place where there is a
summons to meet.

   d. [597.16] "Swear to God that you will undertake the safe-conduct of
a cleric or a layman to the place in which your meeting is announced to you,
and that you will not keep[83] him from the meeting, and that it (the
responsibility of your office?)[84] will not be removed from you unless I
remove it or unless my legal agent, whom I will appoint, should remove it.

   e. [597.18] "Swear to God of heaven that, wherever an obligation may
'reach' your responsibilities until [the end of the established] time period,
you will yourself undertake it with respect to those responsibilities and
arrangements in accordance with the customs of an *aitire*-surety who best
enforces, who best carries out what is just, who does not evade [his
responsibilities and] who best pays.

   f. [597.21] "Swear to God that you will be ready [and] willing [to put]
your foot in a fetter [and] your neck in a chain, [and] to remain in the stocks
or in prison until you are released from it by debt-payments [by the debtor],
or until you can give a gage {i.e. until you can give a gage} for yourself after
the forfeiture [period].

   g. [597.23] "Swear to God [an oath] without deception, without fault,
without force, without concealing anything, [and that it is] a true oath,

without stipulation, without condition, without difficulty, without negligence, without neglect.''

66. [597.25] If the *aitire*-surety then evades [his responsibilities], how are they enforced upon him? There is no [way to enforce them] except by bringing reproach upon his name.

67. [597.26] What is the compensation of the *aitire*-surety? I.e. [the price of] his maintenance and [of] his disturbance and [of] his [missed] work, and the price of the seven *cumals* of a warrior after forfeiture, i.e. the [ransom] price of a captive, for the *aitire*-surety is a captive after falling forfeit, [and the double of?][85] what he has paid, for he pays all to each person against whom he acts as surety, as it is with an *aitire*-surety of a peace treaty, for it is in respect of a peace treaty that there first was an *aitire*-suretyship of an oath.

68. [597.30] What is an *aitire*-surety of warranty? That [type of *aitire*-surety] gurantees fines. . . [86] Because his *cáin* is not obtained,[87] the principal [of the debt] comes to be equivalent to the fines. These are the four difficulties of (associated with) the protection and the stripping of a *ráth*-surety in accordance with the times established by law between two contracting parties in the pleading of a case. . .(omission?) and when a *ráth*-surety is stripped on behalf of the debtor in this manner, the *ráth*-surety turns to [seek] compensation.

69. [597.34] A query: what is the compensation of this *ráth*-surety? There are two [types of] compensation for a *ráth*-surety according to the times established by law. What are they? Compensation for the opening of [his] milking enclosure without stripping him, and compensation for opening [it] after stripping him, that is after a payment by the *ráth*-surety on behalf of the debtor.

70. [597.37] If it happens that the debtor comes at [the time of] the opening of the milking enclosure [but] before the stripping, he himself pays the principal of the debt and its fines before the *ráth*-surety pays on his behalf, and he pays a cow to the *ráth*-surety for his disturbance and for the opening of his milking enclosure. For there are sixteen days during which a *ráth*-surety is 'disturbed':[88] he receives then a sack every day after that for the disturbance — he thus receives a cow. This is the compensation for the opening of a milking enclosure.

71. [598.4] And the compensation for the opening [of the *ráth*-surety's milking enclosure] after stripping — what is that? When a *ráth*-surety has paid on [the debtor's] behalf, so that his milking enclosure has been stripped to his disadvantage, his compensation is his honour-price according to his rank together with cattle by-products and the young [of his cattle] and interest[89] and the principal of the debt.

72. [598.7] Everyone undertakes suretyship, then, [for an amount up to] that which a third of his possessions can support. The one who is capable of [undertaking] *ráth*-suretyship for every [type of] thing is the one who can do it, or [in other words] he who has goods among his possessions equal in value to the amount for which he undertakes *ráth*-suretyship. For there are three excesses of *ráth*-suretyship, i.e. a *ráth*-surety for a rampart, and for an oratory and for a bronze cauldron, because they perform [special] services.

73. [598.11] What is the *ráth*-surety who undertakes the responsibility of a *naidm*-surety? A *ráth*-surety who enforces [a claim] against a debtor together with a *naidm*-surety before he has been stripped. What is the *naidm*-surety who undertakes the responsibility of a *ráth*-surety? A *naidm*-surety of base clientship.

74. [598.12] A question: how are [his responsibilities] fixed upon the *ráth*-surety in accordance with the times established in law? No one is capable of [himself appointing immediately] a *ráth*-surety [to act] on his behalf in the contract. The freedom from loss of the *ráth*-surety is bound first of all, before the binding [of the *ráth*-suretyship] on [the *ráth*-surety] himself; and the contracting party for whom *naidm*-sureties guarantee [the *ráth*-surety's] freedom from loss appoints [*naidm*-sureties to guarantee the *ráth*-surety's compensation], so that he (the creditor) says:

a. [598.16] "Appoint *mac*-sureties [to guarantee] the complete freedom from loss and the full payment of this *ráth*-surety for anything that he who acts as [*ráth*]-surety for you may pay [on your behalf] in virtue of his *ráth*-suretyship. [Guarantee] full payment, entire payment [such as those with which] the gentle, pure *ráth*-sureties of the *Féni* who are best paid are paid, so that you may leave him fully free from loss and perpetually free from loss, without fault, without offence, without [further] payment [by him], without fines, without loss, without the 'rust [of old claims], without *íarsnae*.[90]

b. [598.19] "Appoint *mac*-sureties that you will pay him after[91] he pays [the debt on your behalf], that your heirs [will] pay his heirs, [and] that you will pay him yourself while you live, so that you and your heirs may leave him free from loss with respect to anything that he may have acknowledged on your behalf in [his] *ráth*-suretyship.

c. [598.22] "Appoint *mac*-sureties [to guarantee] that wherever a payment [made] on your behalf is obtained from him because of your evasion [of your contractual obligations] or because of [your] defective payment which is unlawful, you will pay his compensation, even though you may [eventually] have paid [the debt yourself].[92] Your own house is the place appointed for the payment [of his compensation] — immoveable, without alteration so that they (the items paid in compensation) be not of the same type and of the same value [as those paid out by the *ráth*-surety], unless there be an 'extinction' [of your obligations] according to a judgement or a judge, in accordance with a proclamation of every due, and in accordance with the lawful [periods of] waiting.

d. [598.26] "Appoint *mac*-sureties to him thus without stipulation, without condition, without difficulty, without neglect."

75. [598.27] The *naidm*-sureties say to the debtor: "Do you appoint [us to guarantee] the complete payment of the *ráth*-surety who acts as surety on your behalf, so that he may be fully free from loss and perpetually free from loss with respect to anything that he may acknowledge on your behalf in his *ráth*-suretyship, fully free from loss [as are] *ráth*-sureties of the *Féni* who are paid according to whatever is due?"

76. [598.29] The debt or the contract which [the *ráth*-surety] guarantees is fixed on the *ráth*-surety by the contracting party for whom the *ráth*-surety acts:

a. [598.31] "Appoint *mac*-sureties to guarantee your *ráth*-suretyship with respect to this debt or with respect to entitlement or to the validity of the contract. [Guarantee that it will be] a full *ráth*-suretyship, an unimpaired *ráth*-suretyship, a noble *ráth*-suretyship, [and that you will be] a *ráth*-surety of 'rest' (permanent residence), a *ráth*-surety of the place appointed for payment, a "*ráth*-surety of three deeds",[93] a *ráth*-surety of noble honour, a strong *ráth*-surety. [Guarantee that your suretyship will be one that] is fixed on you by oath and not denied by oath; [guarantee] that you [will] also pay the due payment of a good *ráth*-surety,[94] and that you will act according to the truth of justice until [your *ráth*-suretyship] is extinguished for you according to everything that is due.

b. [598.35] "Appoint *mac*-sureties [to guarantee] that you will give a gage and identify [it?],[95] [and] that you will be ready to give a gage and to enforce and to 'milk', [and] to make the payment which you will promise from your own place of residence[96] by an announcement from the green, by demanding [that the debtor pay his debt?], and by waiting in [your] place of residence [to make payment on the debtor's behalf].

c. [598.38] "Appoint *mac*-sureties [to guarantee] that you are the first *ráth*-surety for this debt [and that it is] the first contract in which each person for whom you act as surety [is involved]. [Guarantee that you will be a *ráth*-surety] of 'rest' and of the place appointed for payment, [and that you will not permit] the contracting party against whom you act as surety to go past the hearth of the contracting party on whose behalf you act as surety [in order to levy the claim directly from you?]. And [guarantee] the entire immunity from claim of anything which you may have given as a gage and anything which may have been paid for your *ráth*-suretyship, though they may not have been bound again [by a contract specifically for the purpose], but that it (the immunity) has been guaranteed by your [own] *ráth*-suretyship.

   d. [599.4] "Appoint *mac*-sureties [to guarantee] that, as against the creditor and as against the one entitled [to payment],[97] you are a *ráth*-surety who is capable of [making a declaration of] freedom from loss (that he is free from loss) and a renunciation [of further claims] with respect to the debt or the contract. [Guarantee that you are a *ráth*-surety] as against [the creditor's] heir and his contract and his base clientship and his legacy. [Guarantee that it will be] a good *ráth*-suretyship that is most fully performed, is guaranteed by gage, is paid, [a *ráth*-suretyship that has priority over your contracts and over your heirs, and over each person who takes responsibility for your offence [and] your *ráth*-suretyship, and who receives the property you leave at death. [Guarantee that your *ráth*-suretyship] is not entangled with monastic clientship or base clientship or the status of a cottager or forfeiture, [and] that what is required of a good *ráth*-surety who is best at giving a gage, at paying and at milking will not be neglected.

   e. [599.10] "Appoint *mac*-sureties to him thus that [this suretyship] is [put] upon you without the amount [involved being] too great, without a counter-suit, without a counter-reckoning, without stipulation, without condition, without difficulty, without negligence, without neglect."

77. [599.12] The *naidm*-sureties say to the *ráth*-surety: "Do you appoint us to guarantee your *ráth*-suretyship and the true fulfilment of your *ráth*-suretyship for the contracting party, and that you will be ready [and] prepared to 'milk', to enforce, to give a gage and to make payment, and that, though the debtor may default, you will not default?"

78. [599.15] Though every contract be bound in the same way between contracting parties, through *naidm*-sureties and *ráth*-sureties [and] in the presence of witnesses, [discrepancies in the value of the goods or services exchanged] are 'cut away' or 'filled up' if the goods or services be not complete [in value].[98]

79. [599.16] As the native law recites:

   Defective understanding dissolves confirmations. A [proper] foundation promotes just bindings (*naidms*). *Ráth*-sureties do not give a gage for the hasty disadvantageous contract of a foolish person or the defrauding of a weak person.

Let [excessive] burdens be attended to, let bad contracts be set straight for contracting parties without mutual fraud according to the law of God and man.

80. [599.21]

A *ráth*-surety gives no gage to guarantee injustice;
Fraud with evil intent does not attain immunity from claim;
The oath of a superior dissolves;
Truth is enforced in spite of an exemption;
Nothing that has been bound is extinguished;
It is not an exemption period unless [the penalty] is taken on account of the offence of a sensible person and a fool (?).[99]

81. [599.24] Every nine-fold custom is formed with nine entrails (?): territory, place, person, invalidity, time, godly [writing], oath, binding, preserving [in memory]. Even lordly *ráth*-sureties cannot give a gage for crooked, pierced bindings in Irish law.[100] It is not unjust though the basis of an invalid suit be inpugned. It is a foot against a stone wall if the goods or services exchanged be not complete. Improper goods or services do not entail immunity, and the reward given for a fraud is not immune from claim.

82. [599.28] Thou shouldst not sell what thou dost not buy. Thou shouldst not buy [anything without ensuring its] immunity from claim. Anything unsound[101] is not immune from claim. Nothing is sound without freedom from loss [and] without restitution. Thou shouldst not buy back if thou hast sold, for that which one sells does not belong to one: it belongs to him who buys [it] in accordance with inspections (?) of good judgement. One does not lend what one does not bind.

83. [599.31] As the native law recites: "Thou shouldst not lend if thou dost not bind, for thou shouldst not swear what thou hast not given. One does not judge something over which one has no control. Estimation precedes judgements. He who does not acknowledge tradition[102] is not a supervisor. He who does not supervise an oath is not a guardian of tradition. It is not an oath without lot-casting. It is not lot-casting without persons equal in status.

84. [599.35] "Thou shouldst not be a witness of 'cutting'. Thou shouldst not be a guardian of strife. A single man is no witness, unless he be devout [and] believing. Thou shouldst not be a swearer to something dubious. Thou shouldst not be negligent of binding (*naidm*, so that thou mayest enforce what thou mayest bind. Thou shouldst not be forgetful of the place appointed for payment. Thou shouldst not be violent in a [judicial] assembly, lest thou be a delayer of the court."

¹ The title is almost certainly an old one: Thurneysen pointed out that it is cited in a later part of the same MS, H.3.18, (p. 433a = CIH 973.13-14). Although the cited text does not occur in our tract the use of *dano* 'moreover' at the beginning of the extant material suggests that something is missing. The cited text might therefore have belonged to the missing portion.

² That is, which cannot be reclaimed after the exchange has been completed, either by the giver of the goods or by a third party who claims ownership. A third party might nevertheless have a good claim against the giver, if, for example, the latter had stolen them: cf. Welsh *aruaesaf*, above, pp. 20n.39, 152, Ior 62/3 below p. 338.

³ *Lluid*, apparently the preterite of *téit*, must be an error for *tucht*: see *Bürgschaft*, p. 6, n. 3 to para. 1 and *cia tucht side* in para. 2.

⁴ Keeping *aruilten* rather than emending to *airitin* with Thurneysen (cf. *Bürgschaft*, p. 6, n. 4 to para. 1). The avoidance of the emendation proposed by Thurneysen depends upon the emendation of *rope toga* to *ropet oga*, suggested by Binchy, CIH 591, n. (h). This is supported by comparison with para. 78, *doathbongatar no forlinaiter mani be togha folaith*, which makes much more sense if emended to *doathbongatar no forlinaiter manibet oga folath*, [discrepancies in the value of the goods or services exchanged] are 'cut away' or 'filled up' if the goods or services be not complete [in value]'; and also para. 81: *is cos fo coraith manipetoga folaith* which must be read *is cos fo coraith manipet oga folath*, 'it is a foot against a stone wall if the *folad* (goods or services promised in contract) be not complete': see CIH 599, nn. (n) and (q). Thurneysen, however, reads *toga* in all three cases.

What is meant by this difficult sentence emerges from para. 4 where the activity of the legal agent (*aigne*), in accordance with the job he has undertaken, is his *folad*, namely what he owes as his side of the bargain which he has made with the person who has employed him. The fee he receives is *ruidles*, entirely immune from claim, provided that the *folad* is complete, in other words provided that he has fully discharged his side of the bargain. More generally, if A owes X to B in exchange for B's delivery of Y to A, thén B's title to X is entirely secure (*ruidles*) provided that B has delivered Y *in toto* to A. For the different senses of *folad* see the glossary s.v.

⁵ For Welsh examples of the 'enforcing-third', see Ior 106/14, 108/3, Col 298, WML 139.2-4 and R. R. Davies, 'The Survival of the Bloodfeud in Medieval Wales', (1969) 54 *History* 345-46.

⁶ The MS has *ata ui fl·*; Binchy's emendation, omitting *ui*, has been followed rather than Thurneysen's *Ataat flaithi*.

⁷ Emending *nech* to *neich*.

⁸ *Caillech*: in this instance the word seems to be roughly equivalent to the *focaria* of twelfth-century reformers.

⁹ Thurneysen joins *amail arachan fenechus* to para. 10, but there appears to be an omission: CIH 591, n. (p).

¹⁰ In both *Cáin Iarraith* (CIH 1768.32 = 1341.8; 1769.1-2 = 1341.17ff.) and *Bretha Crólige* (ed. D. A. Binchy, (1934) 12 (1) *Ériu* 8, para. 7) fosterage ends at seventeen, but *Críth Gablach*, lines 30-34, agrees with *Berrad Airechta*.

¹¹ An etymological gloss: the fee paid to the foster-father is the *íar-rath* 'after-fief'. Whether the explanation of the term given here is correct is uncertain.

¹² The portion left untranslated reads *ma fasaith suide no osath*. *No osath* may be an attempt by the scribe to correct his text. One would expect a pres. subj. verb in the protasis of a conditional clause expressing a general legal rule. This argues against emending to *ma fa-saig-side* 'if the latter annoys him'. *Ma fa-sa-side* 'if the latter should annoy him' seems too violent an emendation to be acceptable, but I have nothing better to suggest.

[13] The translation is based on the following emendations: (a) *nech* to *neich*; (b) *nadet tormaighter tii folad* to *nad tormaigther. Tí folad.* The second is quite uncertain.

[14] Reading *ropet oga* instead of *rope toga*: see above n. 4.

[15] Thurneysen translates *comol* as *gemeinsame Trunk*, taking it as *com-ól* 'joint-drinking', but in SEIL 19 he translates the same phrase *comul comair* by 'der Abschluss einer Pfluggemeinschaft', taking *comul* as the verbal noun of *con-lá*. In this text there may well be a play on words as between *comol* 'joint arrangement' and *comól* 'joint drinking'.

[16] This is the end of the first section of the tract; now begins the section on *naidm*-sureties.

[17] *Manach* can mean either 'monk' or 'monastic tenant'.

[18] Thurneysen's insertion of the pronoun *é* after the copula (anticipating the subject of *gaibte*) may be unnecessary: *Grammar*, para. 815.

[19] *Fo-fúataigh* is to be analysed as *fo-uss-di-n-g* (cf. DIL under **fúataing*). Other examples all appear to be transitive. The vb.n *fúatach* occurs in this text in para. 51c. For the absence of the infixed -*n*- see *Grammar*, para. 550.

[20] Emending to *ar cach nadmaim techtait béolu íarna cúl.* Thurneysen translates "Denn alle [diese] naidms haben einen Mund...nach hinten", but this not only seems to presuppose an un-Irish word-order, but construes adjectival *cach* with a plural noun.

[21] The point is that whatever these legal incompetents do or promise can be annulled by their superiors; hence the 'mouths behind their backs'.

[22] Apart from Thurneysen's emendation of *nach ni* to *noch ni*, it is necessary to emend *fair* to *forru.*

[23] Cf. *Díre* Tract, para. 36, ed. and trans. Thurneysen, *Irisches Recht*, p. 34.

[24] Emending *frisroirsetar* to *frisrairsetar* with Thurneysen (3 pl. pass. perf. pres. subj. to *fris-áraig*). Thurneysen also suggests that MS *aururgi* may be 2nd sg. pres. subj. of a weak verb derived from *ar* and *fuirec.*

[25] Those made with exiles or in secret: Thurneysen, 'Nachträge zur Bürgschaft', (1930) 18 ZCP 396.

[26] *Dliged* refers to what a party to a contract is entitled to in virtue of the ordinary principles of fairness as opposed to the terms of the contract. The *naidm*-surety, inasmuch as he is, in Thurneysen's words, "the contract in person", should in general seek to enforce the terms of the contract. In para. 32, therefore, the judge defends the principles of fairness, whereas the *naidm* maintains the claims of the contract. On the other hand, as several archaic maxims in paras. 81-82 show, a surety was not expected to uphold the integrity of the contract whatever the justice of the case, and the *naidm* could thus co-operate with the judge in 32 even though *dliged* prevailed.

[27] *Tossui for*: cf. *Bechbretha*, ed. T. Charles-Edwards and F. Kelly (Dublin, 1983), n. on para. 25.

[28] Emending *comsruithiu* to *comsruith*: *Bürgschaft*, n. 1 on para. 30.

[29] Part of a legal tract preserved elsewhere: CIH 1290.21ff.

[30] An interlinear gloss: see above pp. 16-17.

[31] *Tris-gata* is the earlier form of *tregtaid* 'pierces' which is used to gloss it.

[32] *Tossui fri*: see n. 27 above. From 29-31 the issue turns on the capacity or knowledge of the parties to the contract. From 32-33, however, it turns on who has authority over the contract. Since *naidm*-surety and judge act together in 32, *naidm* and *dliged* are equally to be respected, *comsruith*, even though the dispute over the contract itself is settled in accordance with *dliged.*

[33] The meaning of the second clause in the quotation is not obvious, but it perhaps refers to the contract once it is revised in accordance with *dliged* 'entitlement'. In its new form it is not the contract which the *naidm*-surety bound and whose details he undertook to

remember. It is thus a contract which is enforced, but it is not the contract for which the *naidm* was appointed. The enforcement of the revised contract may be by 'unappointed' *naidm*-sureties (cf. paras. 23-24) or by distraint rather than by the original *naidm*-surety.
[34] *Lepaith* ɔ *a apuith*: see David Greene, 'Miscellanea', (1954) 2 *Celtica*, 337-39.
[35] Emending *de* to *té*: see D. A. Binchy, 'Some Celtic Legal Terms', (1956) 3 *Celtica*, 229, n. 3. The 'hot son' is the one who has discharged his filial duty, *goire*, towards his parents. On the relationship between *goire* and *gor* 'warm' (and Welsh *gwar* in *mab gwar, mab anwar*) see Thurneysen's edition of *Gúbretha Caratniad*, (1925) 15 ZCP 312-13 and n. 2 on p. 312, D. A. Binchy, 'Celtic Legal Terms', pp. 238-31; Warren Cowgill, 'The etymology of Irish *guidid* and the outcome of *gʷʰh* in Celtic', *Lautgeschichte und Etymologie*, ed. Mayhofer, Peters and Pfeiffer (Wiesbaden, 1980), pp. 55-56 and 62-63. For an example of *goire* in action see Adomnán, *Vita S. Columbae*, II. 39.
[36] Thurneysen takes the verb to be *as-léna* 'pollutes, sullies', but this is doubtful: see Binchy, note to para. 5 of *Coibnes Uisci Thairidne*, (1955) 17 *Ériu* 79, who suggests that it may be a strong verb, *as-len*. This might mean something like 'clings to, sticks to'. Base clientship endures until the death of the lord and may thus be inherited by the heirs of the original client.
[37] See Binchy's note (b), CIH 594, which points to the parallel *Críth Gablach*, 144 (= CIH 779.19), showing that *do-saig* must be supplied before *do cenn*.
[38] Cf. Ior 62/9, Col 96 for the immunity of the Welsh gage even though without a *mach*; on the sense of *dithaim* here see Thurneysen's n. 3 to this passage and D. A. Binchy, 'Distraint in Irish Law', (1973) 10 *Celtica*, 47-48.
[39] *Etaim* is certainly the verbal noun of a cpd. of *do-tuit*, 'falls', but its analysis is uncertain. The earlier theory that it belonged to *in-tuit* cannot be reconciled with the evidence that (1) the *e* is short and (2) *t* stands for [t] (see DIL under *etim*); *ess-taim* runs foul of the second of the above objections, while *ess-di-taim*, the analysis proposed in DIL, should have yielded a palatal *t*, which it admittedly often has in non-legal examples, but in the laws the *t* is generally neutral. For the meaning '*gage*' see DIL under *etim* III.
[40] I have followed Thurneysen (n. 1 *ad loc.*) in taking the gloss to be correct.
[41] Emending to *mad in tan sen* following Thurneysen, n. 1 *ad loc.*
[42] Thurneysen's later proposal to interpret *naidm* here as 'surety' in general rather than *naidm*-surety in particular, and, moreover, to be referring to the *aitire*, 'Nachträge', p. 404, seems to be quite impossible in the context. On the senses of *slán* here and elsewhere in this text see the glossary s.v.
[43] Following CIH in extending *b-* as *beir* rather than as *bé* or *bí*. It appears that if a base client defaulted on his renders or services, and his kindred was unwilling or unable to provide substitutes, his lord could then acquire possession of part of his inherited land: cf. CIH 207.3-4; 908.23-25.
[44] Following Binchy's suggested emendation *cen on*: CIH 594, n. (i).
[45] This method was also used against a king who did not have a 'substitute churl': 'A Text on the Forms of Distraint', ed. D. A. Binchy, (1973) 10 *Celtica*, para. 9, p. 80.
[46] On this see Binchy's note on para. 7 of *Coibnes Uisci Thairidne*, (1955) 17 *Ériu*, 81.
[47] Here ends the second part of the tract, on the *naidm*; now begins the discussion of *féchemain* 'contracting parties'.
[48] Following Binchy's suggestion, CIH 594, note (o).
[49] Welsh contracting parties grasped hands to make a contract: Lat E 6, Lat D in LTWL 368.11-23, Bleg 40.6-20.
[50] *Focal* in this context, and also in para. 53, appears to refer to testing for quality as Thurneysen suggests, comparing *Cáin Aicillne*, para. 8 (ed. Thurneysen, (1923) 14 ZCP 374-51 = CIH 481.26-30). In para. 57, however, it means a formula.

⁵¹ This may be the same percentage charged to a defaulting debtor in Welsh law: see p. 20, note 38.

⁵² The creditor.

⁵³ The debtor.

⁵⁴ The existence of an heir allows the transaction to be "between two living claimants".

⁵⁵ *Esngabál*: the examples of *as-ingaib* CIH 427.22 and 23 (= *Fuidir* Tract, para. 5, ed. Thurneysen, *Irisches Recht*, p. 65) show that the original meaning was not just 'exceeds', but either 'exceeds' or 'falls short of'. *Esngabál* might therefore mean either 'excess' or 'defect'. The latter suits the context here.

⁵⁶ On *fo-reith* see P. Mac Cana, 'Varia', (1966) 20 *Ériu*, 217-21.

⁵⁷ Thurneysen translates *dirir* as 'ohne Richterspruch' (*dí-réir*), but I take it as the third sg. pret. of *dí-ren* 'pays as a penalty'.

⁵⁸ The translation of this last sentence is that of D. A. Binchy, 'Varia', 20 *Ériu*, 230.

⁵⁹ Emending, with Thurneysen, note ad loc., as *noebath* to as *ndibath*.

⁶⁰ Emending *dofuiben* to *dofuidben* (*to-dí-men-*): Thurneysen, note ad loc.

⁶¹ Here ends the section on contracting parties; now begins the archaic material entitled *Córus Fíadnaise* by the compiler (who also added the first paragraph with its etymological glosses).

⁶² *Naisi* could either be the verbal of necessity or the passive preterite of *naiscid*; the latter is preferred by Thurneysen in his translation and by Binchy, 'Bergin's Law', (1979/80) 14-15 *Studia Celtica*, 50.

⁶³ Thurneysen's, emendation to *nibat* was challenged by O'Brien, (1932) 11 *Ériu*, 154-55, who read it as *i n-* 'when, since' + *– bat*: Bergin subsequently pointed out that the substantive verb, rather than the copula, was required, and emended it to *i mbiat la comorbu cuimne* 'when heirs have [only] memories', (1938) 12 *Ériu*, 207, n. 1. *In* may also be the interrog. particle which can retain the *n* before *b* (Thurneysen, *Grammar*, para. 463). The translation assumes this last interpretation because of the rhetorical questions which follow.

⁶⁴ Following Bergin, 12 *Ériu*, 207.

⁶⁵ Emending, with Thurneysen, *tuibaithsir* to *tuidbiat fír*.

⁶⁶ *Diairchinn* may mean 'men who are not "heads"' (as opposed to 'members', i.e. dependants) as Thurneysen suggests (though one might rather have expected *dícinn*), or it may be 'men who lack an *airchinn(ech)*' 'leader', i.e. lordless men, as it is translated here.

⁶⁷ Following O'Brien, art. cit., 155.

⁶⁸ Rather than 'white judgement' as Thurneysen later proposed, 'Nachträge', 397.

⁶⁹ MS *u.e.* for *coice* 'secrets': O'Brien, art. cit., 155-56.

⁷⁰ See C. Watkins, 'Preliminaries to a Historical and Comparative Analysis of the Syntax of the Old Irish Verb', (1963) 6 *Celtica*, 33, corrected in his vol. (III/1) of the *Indogermanische Grammatik* (Heidelberg, 1969), 187.

⁷¹ On the emendation of *farnan bechtae nan tochtaeich* to *fornád bechtai na tochtai* see Binchy, 'Indo-European *Qʷe* in Irish', (1960) 5 *Celtica*, 81-82.

⁷² Emending *anfeith* to *anfeich* with Thurneysen, 'Nachträge', 397.

⁷³ See Thurneysen's and Binchy's notes ad loc.

⁷⁴ On the distinction between *fuillem* ('interest', vb.n. to *fo-sli*) and *fuilled* (earlier *fuilned*, 'filling up', vb.n. to *fo-lína*) see Thurneysen's commentary on *Cáin Aicillne*, 14 ZCP xiv 346, 365-66, 377.

⁷⁵ Reading *coropat oga*: see n. 4 above.

⁷⁶ This is the end of *Córus Fíadnaise*; now begins the section on the various *aitires*.

⁷⁷ This is a reference to the Irish custom of sucking a man's breast and catching hold of his cheek to swear friendship with him or to ask quarter from him: M. A. O'Brien, (1939) 3 *Etudes Celtiques*, 372; D. A. Binchy's note, on para. 5 of his ed. of the Saga of Fergus mac

232 LAWYERS AND LAYMEN

Léti, (1952) 16 *Ériu*, 42.

[78] An etymological gloss, but one which seems likely to be correct: see L. Breatnach, 'On Abstract Nouns from Prepositions in Irish', (1983) 15 *Celtica*, 18-19, who gives other examples of the formation, and P. Russell, 36 *Ériu*, 163-68.

[79] I.e. a *naidm* — not discussed any further here, probably because he had been covered in sufficient detail earlier in the tract.

[80] Thurneysen translated this 'milking' as *Einstehen*, 'standing in for', and understood it as referring to the surety's paying the debt on the debtor's behalf. In the main tract on distraint the word means 'surrogate debtor, kinsman debtor' (D. A. Binchy, 'Distraint in Irish Law', (1973) 10 *Celtica*, 33). The primary meaning of the verb *in-omlig* is, however, 'levies, mulcts' and the verbal noun may therefore mean 'levying, mulcting' here. But cf. n. 93 below.

[81] Thurneysen's emendation may be unnecessary (note *ad loc.*); one may read *cía-sía, cia-dama (n)diul co scor* taking *diul* as a prepositionless dative.

[82] The weak verb *fuichid* and its compound *do-fuichi* are otherwise unknown (neither is included in DIL). *Do-fuichi* occurs here and *fuichid* in 65d. Thurneysen suggested that *fuichid* must mean something like 'fernhalten' and so translated *nach fuic[h]fe di dáil* in 65d by 'das du ihn nicht von der Zusammenkunft fernhalten (?) wirst', and indeed 'keep away' must be the meaning in the context. Here, however, *do-fuichi* may mean something like 'involve, detain, require presence at'. The best clue is the parallel between the following phrases, both in 65b:

(1) na(ch) fócre fond[o]t-ocerthar;
(2) nach dál, nach aidbden tonut-fuichfither.

Since (1) means 'any summons by which you shall be summoned', one might translate (2) by 'any meeting, any representation in which you shall be involved.' If *fuichid* construed with *di* means 'keep away from' then *do-fuichi* may mean literally 'keep to', and one may then compare the relationship between *téit* and *do-tét*; hence the translation suggested 'at which your presence shall be required'. On *aidbden* see Thurneysen, 'Nachträge', 379-82, *Críth Gablach*, p. 35, note on l. 412.

[83] See the previous note.

[84] The infixed pronoun -s- is probably fem. sg. referring to *aitire* in the sense of *aitire*-ship.

[85] Following Thurneysen's suggestion on how to fill an apparent omission in the text.

[86] The text is corrupt at this point. Thurneysen believed that there was a large gap after *fo-sisithar side*. If that were so, it would make it difficult to be sure that the *aitire fóisma* was indeed the *ráth* under another name, for in the gap one might have had a new heading with an introductory etymology for *ráth* to correspond to those already given for *féchem, fíadnaise* and *aitire*. On the other hand, *dam in fasach sin* might be the remains of a gloss so that the text would then run: *fo-sisithar side smachta, óre na[d] n-édar a cháin. For-reith colainn smachta,* 'the latter guarantees fines, since he (the debtor) may not be constrained. The principal of the debt comes to be equivalent to the fines.' According to para. 52, if the debtor defaults (and cannot be constrained to pay), the *ráth*-surety must pay not only the original debt but also fines, *smachta*.

[87] If there is a gap in the text at this point (see previous note), the sense of *cáin* must remain uncertain: the translation given is close to that of Thurneysen.

[88] Emending, with Thurneysen, *immen olrath* to *imme-rolóith*.

[89] With *fuillem* 'interest' here perhaps in error for *fuilled* 'filling up': see Thurneysen's note *ad loc.* and note 74 above.

[90] MS *íarsnae*: Thurneysen originally proposed to emend to *íarsmae* 'remnant', but later withdrew this suggestion ('Nachträge', 398), because of another example in LL 147a (= diplomatic ed. l. 18664). Unfortunately that example occurs in a cheville (*iarsna dosceóil*

deit, perhaps 'the end of a sad story for you'), and it may be worth noting that Mac Neill, in his edition of the poem, identified *íarsnae* with *íarsmae*: (1895) (3rd Ser.) 3 *Proc. Roy. Ir. Acad.*, 546-53.

[91] *Ria* is an error for *iar*: Thurneysen, note *ad loc.*

[92] Following Bergin, 'On the Syntax of the Verb', p. 207.

[93] Pledging, enforcing and 'milking' in 76b and pledging, enforcing and paying in 76d. This may suggest that Thurneysen's interpretation of 'milking' is correct (see above, note 80).

[94] Reading *cene* with Thurneysen, note *ad loc.*, but Binchy's alternative suggestion *cech ni* may be right.

[95] A *gell* 'gage' was sometimes retained in the possession of the person who gave it (see *Críth Gablach*, pp. 94-95); one may suppose that if it then became forfeit, it would have to be identified to the creditor, who would subsequently remove it.

[96] Emending *astoichich* to *as do thig* with Thurneysen, note *ad loc* (or *as do thich*, *Grammar*, para. 130).

[97] Emending *frithilgech* to *fri dligthech*: 'Nachträge', 398.

[98] Reading *Mani bet oga*: see note 4 above.

[99] I have followed Thurneysen in putting these paragraphs into verse form.

[100] Following the form of this sentence that occurs later in H.3.18 (CIH 987.39-40; also cited by Thurneysen, 'Nachträge'; 375-76).

[101] MS *fol-*: Thurneysen suggested *follan* because of the structure of the passage: of two head-words in each clause the second is repeated by the first head-word in the next clause; *follan* is the first head-word in the next clause. This has been followed here though Binchy's *folad* is easier to translate ('without [performance of] obligations').

[102] Thurneysen took *senchas* to be a reference to the *Senchas Már*, but the use of *senchae* in the next sentence is against such an identification.

PART II: LAWMAKERS AND THE LAW

LEGISLATORS, LAWYERS AND LAW-BOOKS
ALAN HARDING

THE TRADITION OF LEGISLATION

The political struggles of early modern Europe generated the idea that the only true law was made by the people out of their wisdom and experience, 'like a silk-worm that formeth all her web out of her self': the written laws were not true laws which were made 'by the Edicts of Princes or by Councils of Estates' and 'imposed upon the Subject before any Trial or Probation made, whether the same be fit and agreeable to the nature and disposition' of the people.[1] Translated into the historical judgement that medieval kings were supposed merely to 'find' the law and not make it, this idea has obscured the growth of the profession of law as well as the extent of conscious legislation in the Middle Ages, since (as this paper will argue) the rôles of the lawyer and the legislator developed in tandem.

The historical judgement was wrong because it underestimated not so much royal power and ambition as the strength and maturity of the legislative tradition within which even the most powerful of kings had to work. Legislative tradition, not the customs of the folk, circumscribed the king's law-making. Aquinas, writing *circa* 1270, does admit as legislation the making of custom by repeated acts which show the necessary conjuction of will and reason.[2] But he sees promulgation in writing by the governor of the community as ultimately essential to law, and goes to some lengths to show that even God's law, though existing from eternity, meets this requirement.[3]

The story of the origin of the Welsh law-books in King Hywel's promulgation of laws in an assembly at Whitland in 942 stands beside the introduction to King Alfred's laws, written half a century earlier, as proof of the recognized legislative function of early medieval kings. Alfred prefaces his laws with the dooms handed down by Almighty God to Moses, 'biddings' which we are reminded that Christ said he came not to destroy but to fulfil, and which the evangelists carried throughout Asia Minor in letters from the Church in Jerusalem. A significant twist is given by Alfred to St Matthew's 'do not do to others what you would not have them do to you': he replaces 'for this is all the law and the prophets' by the statement that a man needs no other 'doom-book' than the maxim that he should judge others as fairly as he would be judged. The purpose of legislation is to serve justice and build up the judicial institutions of the kingdom. As peoples throughout the earth received the faith of Christ, synods of bishops and wise men assembled to lay down the compensation-payments for injury, 'and they wrote them in many synod-books, here one doom, there another.' It is at this point that Alfred announces that he has made his own collection of the laws of previous English kings, choosing the ones he liked and rejecting others, by the advice of his councillors. But wise counsel is not the only restraint upon the legislator: Alfred does not presume to set in writing many laws of his own, simply because he is ignorant of what will please those who 'come after us'.[4]

This misgiving of the legislator who is consciously but cautiously providing for the future was echoed by the Papal council at Rheims in 1148. John of Salisbury records it as approving by general consent a whole series of canons — but not one that banned the wearing of multi-coloured cloaks by the clergy, which was resisted by the German delegation on the grounds that it 'would be disliked by both present and future generations'.[5] From the end of the Roman Empire in the West until the revival of Roman jurisprudence about 1100, the legislative tradition was kept alive by the Church and for its benefit, though it was the business of Christian kings like Clovis, Ethelbert of Kent ('the first of the English to be baptized'[6]), Charlemagne and Alfred to promulgate the laws. Gratian's *Decretum* of *circa* 1140 aimed to draw together and harmonize all the *regulae* made for the Church in the course of a thousand years. Yet Gratian is conscious that he is dealing with an even longer tradition of law-making, which indeed spans the entire history of human society and stretches from Moses; through Mercurius Trismegistus, Solon, the Twelve Tables, the named laws of Republican Rome (such as the *Leges Iuliae* of Caesar and Augustus), the writings of the Imperial jurists, and the decrees of the Christian emperors Constantine and Theodosius; down to the councils and synods of the medieval Church. Law-making in this tradition is not for Gratian a random exertion of power: true laws are framed for the common utility of citizens and not for private advantage; accord with nature and with the usages of the country; and are suitable to the place and the time.[7] Gratian has a quite advanced idea of what legislation means: the function of the law-maker is to develop and correct the organic body of law of a particular community.

The other side of this truth is that communities should be consolidated by the positive law-making of their rulers rather than by some mysterious principle of growth within custom. Although the rebirth of Roman jurisprudence was not needed to turn kings into legislators, it did make explicit a distinction between *leges* and *judicia*, between general laws and the court-judgements with which they are lumped in King Alfred's 'dooms'.[8] Gratian's reworking, at the beginning of the *Decretum*, of the definitions of law which he got from Roman jurisprudence by way of Isidore of Seville, shows how much positive law-making had become the jurists' main preoccupation. Law (*ius*) is made up of laws (*leges*), which are written constitutions, and of long-used customs, which can be taken for law when written constitutions are lacking. Constitutions may be customs put into writing, but what is essential to a proper law is a public authority to promulgate it. The written laws of popes and councils are termed canons, and 'constitutions' in normal usage are the edicts of kings and emperors. But according to Gratian, something more even than writing down by order of the authorities is required to make a law in the truest sense, for this is 'a constitution of the whole people', sanctioned by nobles and plebs together.[9]

The understanding of laws as made for the whole community and in some sense by it, which was already clear in Papinian's definition,

> Lex est commune preceptum, virorum Prudentium consultum: delictorum, quae sponte vel ignorantia contrahuntur coercitio: communis reipublicae sponsio,[10]

had grown stronger through the centuries in which very little real law was written down. The early barbarian 'law-codes' were not much more than lists of injuries and tariffs of the compensation to be paid for them, and the Carolingian capitularies comprised series of instructions to royal agents. There was more law in the charters which granted privileges to individuals, but these lent themselves no more than law-codes or capitularies to the systematic presentation of legal norms.[11] Men bound by laws, not a set of abstract norms, stood in the foreground. Rather than edicts from above, laws were men's rights and obligations, including their wergilds and the forms of proof required of them in court, all of which varied according to rank; and the totality of law was consequently the practice of the courts in dealing out rights to individuals, nearer in its procedures to magic than the application of a rational order, and preserved in the heads of anonymous lawmen who transmitted it by word of mouth.[12] Laws at this period took their names more often from the groups of people who used them than from the magistrates who issued them, as in the examples of the Salic Law (the law of the Salian Franks), the *Lex Romana* by which the clergy continued to live amongst the barbarian nations, and the *Lex Walensis* which we first hear of in 1086.[13] When it was brought into England by the Danes about the time of Alfred, the word 'law' was used for this multiplicity of *leges et consuetudines terrarum*, the whole *ius* or *recht* of a community, as well as for the individual doom, *lex* or *Gesetz* made by the community's ruler; and the

English language has conflated the law with laws ever since.[14] As migration
gave way to settlement, the *folcriht* of the community was transmuted into
the *landriht* or *landlaga* of the settled territory (the *Lex terrae* of Magna Carta).
A territory itself, such as the Danelaw, could be defined by the folkright
prevailing in it.[15]

A law which was so much the tradition of a whole people was not to be
altered lightly by either royal *capitula* or fresh customs. When it was found
necessary to make new laws it was done cautiously and by the advice of
councillors and lawmen. Territorial law was shaped by lords and men
together. 'The wise reeve must know the lord's *landriht* as well as the rights
of the people' in terms of agricultural practice.[16] A kingdom's *landriht* was
the sum of the rights and public obligations of landlords towards the king:
fyrd-service, burgh-building and bridge-building, and 'from many estates,
more *landriht*...under the king's ban'.[17] To the people of a subjugated part
of his territory, a king might propose to give a complete set of new laws,
as King Edgar did to the Danes.[18] Yet it seems always to have been accepted
that kings legislated in partnership with the community, and that they had
no power alone to issue orders which should outlast their lifetimes.[19] King
Alfred and King Guthrum made a peace *for geborene ge for ungeborene* but only
along with *ealles Angelcynnes witan* and 'all the people who were in Eastern
England'.[20] The Anglo-Saxon laws alternate the royal first person with the
plural of the king and his wise men.[21] Only with the advice of his witan
does Alfred claim to reject the laws of his predecessors, and he submits for
their approval the collection of dooms which he wishes to remain in force.[22]
Whether the king should be seen as promulgating the laws made by his
witan,[23] or the witan as witnessing the king's laws in the way that they
witnessed his charters,[24] his councillors' participation in law-making was
apparently essential. The wise men were thus political guardians of the law
of the community, and they can be observed urging the enforcement of
dooms made at previous assemblies and the amendment of others.[25]
Including many churchmen, they were principally concerned about the
morality of the secular law and the punishments it prescribed.[26]

LAWMEN, COURTS AND CUSTOM

But the account of the making of the Welsh laws by Hywel Dda shows
another set of guardians of the law, the local communities, and it is amongst
them that lawyers are to be found, to set over against the legislators. The
earliest (late twelfth-century) Latin text of the laws has the king acting with
the consent of his witan (*sapientium*), but also in the presence of six men 'of

authority and science' from each commote (pagus), and it is by counsel of
these men that later redactions make King Hywel approve in part 'the
ancient laws', partly amend them, partly abolish and partly create anew.[27]
The picture is very like that of Alfred's law-making, except for the
representatives of the localities. It has been suggested that the writers of the
earlier versions of the Welsh laws got the idea of this local committee from
the Norman inquisitio as it was used in the compilation of Domesday Book.[28]
But in a collection of Anglo-Saxon laws there is an agreement between the
Welsh people and the English witan about the policing of the southern
borderlands inhabited by the Dunsaete, an agreement assigned by Liebermann
to the tenth century, which ordains that twelve lawmen (lahmen) shall give
the law (riht taecean) to the Welsh and English, 'six Welshman and six
Englishmen'.[29] The story of King Hywel's commote representatives seems
likely to reflect, not the arrival of the Frankish inquisition in Britain at the
Norman Conquest, but the indigenous development of territorial
administration by the Wessex kings in the tenth century and plausibly by
their Welsh contemporaries.[30] A law which should hold, as King Edgar
insisted, 'everywhere within the bounds of our power, amongst Danes,
English and Britons', required diligent ealdormen and reeves to publish the
king's written instructions in their territories.[31] At the same time, a peace
was binding only insofar as it was accepted and sworn to by a particular
community, and laws were received from the king most deferentially when
they gave a peace which was not general but for the five boroughs, or the
shire of Kent, and suited to local ways.[32]

The landlaga which should be luflice leornian amongst the people therefore
varied from place to place with the ways of the people.[33] To judge just
dooms and pronounce folchriht, the reeve needed (according to King Edward
the Elder) a doom-book to tell him, for instance, the compensation laid
down for harbouring outlaws, which was different in the written peace-
agreements (fridgewritu, scripta pacis) of Wessex, East Anglia and
Northumbria.[34] But even more necessary for the dispensation of law which
varied in its details according to rank as well as to location were lawmen in
the local community. The name of the lahmen, six of whom from each side
were to apportion law to the Welsh and English in the region of Dunsaete,
must have been a tenth-century borrowing from the Norsemen, along with
'law' itself; but the institution may very well have been present in the groups
of elders (meliores, seniores) who we know were regulating transactions in
south Wales in the seventh and eighth centuries. According to Domesday
Book, the Sheriff of Herefordshire was attended in the shire court by six or
seven Welsh meliores.[35] The 'Laws of Edward the Confessor', compiled in
reality in the twelfth century, ordered an inquiry 'per lagemannos et per

meliores homines de burgo vel de hundredo vel villa' as to the reputation
of anyone who bought goods without proper witnesses.[36] As a personal
name, 'lawman' occurs in Domesday Book, and it was also held by an
eleventh-century King of Man and by the twelfth-century poet, Layamon,
a native of the Welsh marches and author of the Brut.[37] We hear of an
hereditary 'lagaman civitatis, quod Latine potest dici legislator vel iudex' at
York in 1106; and it seems likely that the twelve judices civitatis recorded by
Domesday at Chester are equivalent to the lagemanni at Lincoln and Stamford
and the aristocratic Cambridge 'doomsmen'.[38]

Mr Richardson and Professor Sayles argued that when royal justices in
eyre began to go out in 1129, these local 'judges' were shown to be little
more than jurors who presented the crimes of the shires and hundreds and
were punished for doing so corruptly and ignorantly.[39] But the Stamford
group could be called 'iudices legum' as late as 1275, and 'lawman' could be
translated legislator as well as iudex.[40] In Scandinavia, the only legislator was
the lawman or law-speaker who pronounced the law in the public courts,
and it would be anachronistic to try to distinguish between law-making and
the declaration of customary law in what he did.[41] Charlemagne called
'legislators' those who gave 'judicial decisions' on points of Roman or
Lombard law.[42] Legislator, legifer and even legisdoctor were all possible
translations of échevin and doomster.[43] The lawmen who apportioned 'the
right' to Welsh and English in Dunsaete-land can be accepted as making the
law just as much as the king and the royal councillors who set them up.
Intriguingly, it is in this very region that Domesday Book makes the earliest
mention of Welsh law and the first statement of its contents; and tells us
that six or seven Welsh meliores attended the English shire court.[44] In the
law of the early medieval kingdoms, the functions of the legislator, the judge
and the juror seem to have merged into each other.

Yet political and social changes were beginning to separate them out, and
to create an entirely new and recognizably modern distinction between
legislators and lawyers. By the time of Domesday Book, the development
of government, both royal and ecclesiastical, which had got under way three
centuries earlier in the Carolingian empire, was pulling apart the political
law-makers and the professional 'finders' and guardians of the law. Neither
the relationship in classical Roman law between the praetor who prescribed
new legal remedies and the judex, chosen by the parties, who applied them
in particular cases,[45] nor that between the Emperor Justinian who willed,
and his quaestor Tribonian who framed, a complete scheme of law,[46]
provided a model for the juxtaposition which now appeared of the ruler who
continually dispensed rights and status to his subjects and the lawyer who
integrated the ruler's statutes into existing law. As the administrative

capacity of the Carolingians expanded, and (a century further on) that of the Wessex dynasty in England, the balance of responsibility for the law, which Charles the Bald still recognised as made 'by the consent of the people and the constitution of the king' working together,[47] began to pass to the king. Carolingian kings issued capitularies for the protection of the Church, the honour of the kingdom 'and the law and justice of the people committed to our charge';[48] capitularies which were to be 'held for law' (pro lege tenere). The notion of law became more complex as the preservation of the native laws of each of their subjects was joined, amongst the concerns of the Frankish kings, by the administration of 'the equity of the law' through the missi to everyone in any part of the kingdom who complained of oppression.[49] The break-up of the Carolingian empire and development of feudal societies in smaller and in the end more tightly governed kingdoms consolidated the notion of law as a man's personal rights against other men, but rights which were dispensed and enforced by a sovereign lord. With the Établissements of St Louis of France and the Statutes of Edward I of England in the thirteenth century, although these were much concerned with the personal rights of lords and men, legislation achieved its full sense of the willing by a sovereign power of abstract norms of behaviour which were to be universally observed.

As 'Royal Majesty' came to be 'adorned with laws' as well as 'furnished with arms',[50] its need of lawmen only increased, because the law which rulers moulded was a law of jurisdiction and procedure. The practices of the courts were the real substance of the custom which was opposed to lex scripta in the twelfth-century renewal of the ancient debate on the sources of law. Roman jurists had accepted that custom was valid law because people consented to it by use and abrogated it by disuse — and they discovered it in the following of precedents in provincial courts.[51] The Welsh laws also placed the rôle of oral custom in litibus: it was impossible for everything to be recorded in writing, yet the law said that a similar judgement was to be given in similar circumstances.[52] On the other hand, Charlemagne had been so determined that 'judges should judge according to written law and not their own discretion', that in 802 he ordered that the texts of the barbarian laws (such as the Lex Salica) be read out in a great assembly and amended in writing.[53] At the end of the same century, King Alfred proclaimed that a man needs no other doom book (liber judicialis) than the maxim that he should judge others as fairly as he would be judged: but went on to promulgate a selection of the dooms of his predecessors, such as those setting the compensation for misdeeds which he found to have been written in synod-books.[54] In Germany, Frederick II's Constitutio Pacis of 1235 ordered judges to decide according to the reasonable customs of their jurisdictions, but that notaries should record all accusations and judgements so that there should be no ambiguity in later cases of the same sort.[55]

In feudal society, rights of jurisdiction became a main sense of 'custom': customary rights to hold, as well as to plead in, certain types of court. The baronage asserted *consuetudines* to have their own courts.[56] The power of landlords was a compound of liberties granted by the king and jurisdictions which were customary to their status in their home districts; of *herschafte, fryheide, recht und gudegewinde* on the one hand, and on the other of the *privilegia und breve* bestowed by rulers.[57] Charters granting 'customs' like sake and soke were a sort of written law;[58] and monastic chronicles also devoted much space to this type of custom, Battle Abbey's recording, for instance, the extensive jurisdiction and forceful processes operated by the Battle court under 'the power and terror of the royal name'.[59] Usually, however, the king had to resort to sworn inquests, as William I did comprehensively in the Domesday survey, to discover the *consuetudo et ius terrae* which was specific to each locality and deposited in the memory of its inhabitants. When the abbot of Battle exercised his authority in a way which should go down in memory as a precedent, he was careful to have the younger as well as the older monks in court. On the basis of such judicial custom, the Angevin kings were to build the Common Law.[60]

But it was the Papacy that first created a centralised and authoritarian idea of custom as the tradition of the Roman church. In the eyes of the Church, a custom without truth was simply ancient error, and the customs of the people (particularly those of the feudal aristocracy) were often bad. Popular usage must yield to the authority and reason of law, as secular constitutions to ecclesiastical ones. Augustine, though, had emphasized the authority of tradition stretching back through the Fathers to the Apostles; and the practice of the whole *Populus Dei* in matters such as the blessing of the font at baptism was held equivalent to law. The universal customs and traditions of the Church were not to be gainsaid: it was under this heading that Gratian quoted the *Institutes* of Justinian to the effect that *diutini mores consensu utentium approbati legem imitantur*. The emphasis was on universal traditions, however, for 'the locality does not commend the custom, but the custom the locality', as Pope Gregory I told Augustine of Canterbury when the latter was perplexed by the strange practices of the English.[61] The exaltation of apostolic tradition assented to by the whole Church was really a justification for papal legislation, which from the Investiture Contest onwards came into conflict with the *ius terrae* of secular kingdoms in a few but crucial respects (chiefly family law and therefore inheritance).[62] The first confrontation between legislation and local custom was not within particular countries but between the universal legislation which was a chief constituent of the *ius novum* of the Church from Gratian's time, and the amalgam of customary procedures, royal edicts and ecclesiastical *ius antiquum* which made up a nation's *lex terrae*.[63]

In dealings with the papacy, kings came to see the advantage of emphasizing the customs of their peoples. Henry II's 'constitutions of Clarendon' purport to be a record of the customs and privileges of the crown or of the realm of England, as acknowledged by the bishops, barons and elders (*antiquiores*) of the realm.[64] By 1200, the fast-developing procedures of English law could be described as *consuetudo regni* or *consuetudo Anglie*.[65] Even the Empire was governed by the 'customs on fiefs generally observed throughout the empire hitherto';[66] and the Emperor was glad to invoke rights based on 'the custom of the most holy Roman empire observed in Germany from time out of mind, which custom obtains the force of law like other ceremonial customs within the empire, which may not be restricted by laws, since they are above the law.'[67]

The essential diversity of custom was to a great extent a myth, bolstering the sense of law as the creation of the people as a whole. In fact, customary procedures such as the methods of settling feuds, the ordeals, and dispute-settlement in the town courts, varied from place to place only in details, not in general form; and in the case of the towns the variations were caused as much by royal privileges as by communal improvisation. The law which kings made in the course of the extension of their power by adapting the existing practices of courts could reasonably be called 'general' as distinct from 'local' custom.[68] The *Très Ancien Coutumier* of Normandy contains the clearly legislative acts of the twelfth-century dukes (also, of course, kings of England), which are indicated by phrases such as *communi consilio et assensu statutum est*. A chronicler records that Henry II decreed for Normandy the 'statute and custom' (*hoc statutum et consuetudinem statuit*), that vassals should not be distrained for the debts of their lords.[69] Philippe de Beaumanoir's *Customs of Beauvaisis* is full of the *établissements* of thirteenth-century French kings.[70] It is tempting to say that if custom was indeed made by repeated acts, it was by the repeated acts of kings.

In the face of this conscious manufacture of national customs, the duty of lawmen became the preservation of a country's legal tradition by integrating into it the new legislation of princes. Whether they were 'law-speakers' who now performed their ancient functions in the service of kings (as in Norway),[71] or clerks valued for their ability to write down collections of laws, the first professional lawyers were jurists (*jurisperiti*)[72] not mere attorneys or pleaders. They were defined by their relationship to the process of law-making, but they were naturally drawn from the ranks of the holders, judges and clerks of the courts, and it was long before they could distinguish

statute-law from the court-judgements with which it was conflated in the
Latin *decreta judiciorum* and Old English 'doom'.[73] In consequence, they
tended to see the law which they guarded as an arrangement of jurisdictions.

LAWYERS AND LAWBOOKS

The evidence of the roles of legislator and lawyer is in the first secular lawbooks of the Middle Ages, of which the leading examples are the
Sachsenspiegel and other 'mirrors' of German law; the provincial *coutumiers*
of France which reached their zenith in Beaumanoir's *Customs of Beauvaisis*;
the *Livre au Roi* and the *Livre de Jean d'Ibelin* in the Kingdom of Jerusalem;
Glanvill and Bracton writing on the laws and customs of England in a
tradition reaching back to the *Leges Henrici Primi*; for Scotland, the book
called *Regiam Maiestatem* and its antecedents; and the books of Welsh law.
These were the private compilations of a new class of professional lawyers
who endeavoured to impose order on whole bodies of law, just as a new sort
of theologian strove in the twelfth century to give logical coherence to the
propositions of the faith. Yet a study of these books as a group suggests that
it was the steady accumulation of king-made laws, stretching well back
before the rebirth of Roman jurisprudence to the Carolingian capitularies,
which provided the stimulus for the work.

In his study of the development of the Saxon law-books, Gerhard
Theuerkauf has argued that the first *Rechtsbüch* anywhere in Europe was the
Lex Saxonum, the early ninth-century compilation in which an anonymous
lawman brought together the ordinances made by Charlemagne for this
newly-conquered territory with Church law and Saxon customary law.[74]
The immediate stimulus may have been Charlemagne's summoning to
Aachen in 802 of an assembly of prelates and lay magnates, along with the
rest of his Christian people and their law-makers (*legislatores*), to inspect the
rule of St Benedict and the laws of the Church and kingdom, and where
necessary amend them in writing.[75] It seems that 'the law of the Saxons'
mentioned in Charlemagne's *Capitulatio de Partibus Saxoniae* of 785 had never
been written down so that it could be systematically amended.[76] The first
law-book of a particular country (as opposed to that of a tribe or nation) was
apparently created in the process of fitting into the traditional Saxon tariff
of compensation for injuries the draconian capitularies by which
Charlemagne had prescribed death or enormous fines for resisting baptism
and a compensation sixteen times the normal for the breach of the king's
peace within Saxony. There is no explicit arrangement of the *Lex Saxonum*'s
sixty-six terse chapters, mostly listing injuries and the compensation for
them in the manner of the barbarian codes, but Theuerkauf shows that

amongst all these *delicta* (themselves separated into secular and ecclesiastical injuries) there are groups of chapters which can be classed as dealing systematically with the law of persons within the family (cc. 40-49), and with the transfer and inheritance of property, including wives (cc. 61-5).[77]

The great Saxon law-book, the *Sachsenspiegel*, compiled by Eike von Repgow in the 1220s, is ten times longer than the *Lex Saxonum* and proclaims the much more ambitious purpose of holding up a mirror to the Saxon people as a woman does to her face.[78] By then, enormous social and political changes had altered the way a country's law might be understood. From the break-up of the Carolingian empire there had emerged a society of lords and men bound together by the tenure of fiefs; but the empire had been revived in 962 by German, indeed Saxon, kings. In the 1150s, by which time the imperial title had passed to the Swabian family of Hohenstaufen, there began an attempt which continued for the rest of the Middle Ages to impose order on the German Reich by means of *Landfrieden*, detailed sets of regulations for the keeping of the peace issued by the emperor for particular regions and defining offences and the responsibilities of the local courts for punishing them. The *Sachsenspiegel* is therefore divided into: *Lehnrecht*, the law of the feudal aristocracy, which comes second although it probably hardened into a set of customary rules at the earlier date; and *Landrecht*, the mixture of local customs and the laws made from above by lay and ecclesiastical rulers which constituted the general law of Saxony. The impulse to the compilation of *Landrecht*, the first and major part of the work, seems to have been once more the need to incorporate into Saxon law the new laws made by kings, and those made by the Church, two legislative traditions which also had to be integrated with each other to produce a true mirror-image of Saxon society. In the prologue, the Christian kings Constantine and Charles are identified as the founders of society in Saxonland, and the *Landfrieden* of more recent kings make up a good deal of the substance of *Landrecht*. Its form is likely to have been much influenced by the arrangement of Bernard of Pavia's collections of papal legislation.[79]

The recognition of the catalytic role of legislation in the making of the Saxon law-books can be extended with profit to their counterparts in England. English law was *landriht* and partly constituted by *fridgewritu* or *scripta pacis*, before the Norman conquest brought *Lehnrecht* to England.[80] But the first great English law-book was that called the *Leges Henrici Primi*, the author of which Maitland acclaimed as 'engaged on an utterly new task, new in England, new in Europe: he was writing a legal text-book, a text-book of law that was neither Roman nor Canon Law'.[81] It may be suggested that the impulse to the making of this compilation of chiefly Anglo-Saxon laws, a good half-century after the Conquest, came from the

need to fit into them one or two recent acts of royal legislation. Calling the
book 'the laws of Henry I' was not just a device to give spurious authority
to a private work. It begins with Henry I's coronation charter, and the
keystone of the discussion of jurisdiction which immediately follows is the
function of the shire-court, restated in Henry I's ordinance of 1108.[82]

The fact that the crucial legislation of Henry II consisted of the provision
of writs to initiate forms of court action should not be allowed to hide the
more important truth that royal law-making, not merely procedural
improvisation, is what *Glanvill* is about.[83] Both Glanvill and Bracton assert
that the laws of England, though unwritten, are true laws — because they
are promulgated by the king with the counsel of his magnates.[84] Bracton's
treatise exploits a quite new mass of material which had not been available
to Glanvill: almost five hundred cases from the plea-rolls of the king's courts
are used in the book. Yet one of the most interesting features of Bracton's
work is the struggle to keep up to date the law which the cases illustrate,
in the face of the continual making of new laws. It has been suggested that
the famous *addiciones* may be citations of old cases removed from the original
text to the margin by revisers who found them obsolete, and then restored
selectively and variously to the body of the text by copyists who took them
for new material. If this was so, legislation must have been the driving-force
which rendered case-law obsolete.[85]

The *Très Ancien Coutumier* of Normandy has been described as really a
'mirror' of ducal legislation: dispositive phrases like *ne quis audeat* and
statutum est stand out from its text. In his *Coutumes*, Beaumanoir cites a
variety of statutes made by Philip Augustus, Louis IX and Philip III, some
of them not otherwise known, which concern everything from the details
of legal procedure to the substantive law of dower.[86]

In Scotland, legal writing began with collections of assizes or legislation
attributed quite arbitrarily to David I (1124-53), William the Lion
(1165-1214) and Alexander II (1214-1249), and borough customals which
borrow largely from the customs of Newcastle-upon-Tyne but include
privileges granted by King William to Perth. The comprehensive Scottish
law-book is *Regiam Maiestatem*, which was officially recognised by
Parliament in 1425 and subsequently as constituting the main source for the
earlier law of Scotland and the basis for its revision. It was probably compiled
during the reconstruction of Scottish law and government after the War of
Independence, and new laws made by King Robert I in 1318 about
procedure in land actions is worked into material from Glanvill in the first
book.[87] RM stands at the end of the line of *Rechtsbücher*, for thereafter the
rising flood of legislation washed away many of the landmarks of the old
jurisprudence. From that time onwards, statute law has been preserved in

the official records of legislatures, and in England at least lawyers confined themselves in the fourteenth century to making their own collections of recent statutes or writing manuals of procedure or pleading. [88] Yet, without the law-books of the twelfth and thirteen centuries, the lines of statutes which have given European nation-states their legal continuity might never have begun. It was the law-books which ensured that the legislation of kings became the accepted way of developing coherent bodies of national law.

Some of the law-book writers compressed the experience of royal legislation into the myth of the constitution of a country's laws by the single act of a great king of the past. The belief in an original unity and design of a nation's laws was perhaps a necessary myth for those who were having to reduce the spate of new legislation to order. But the crediting of King David I with the foundation of Scots law, in the prologue of the *Regiam Maiestatem*, or of King Hywel the Good with the promulgation of the *Lex Walensis*, at the beginning of the Welsh law-books, rested on a true historical sense of the role of kings in the formation of European societies. The pagan attribution to kings of magical influence on the prosperity of their peoples was reinforced by their part in the conversion of western nations to Christianity. David I had not needed to convert the Scots, but he had brought them reformed monasticism and feudal tenure, and he could reasonably be seen as the king above all others who had constituted Scotland a Christian country. The prologues of barbarian laws had much earlier expressed the king's responsibility for the moral as well as the material welfare of his subjects, in terms of the writing-down of a code from which all pagan elements had been purged; and this is how the *Sachsenspiegel* saw Charlemagne's gift of law to the Saxons. [89]

Because consent was an essential part of the legislative tradition, the story of a king's constitution of a nation's laws might turn into the myth of a contract between king and people, founding the nation's political constitution. [90] The thirteenth-century jurists of the Kingdom of Jerusalem asserted the rights of the feudal aristocracy against their Hohenstaufen sovereigns by appealing to written laws (the *Lettres du Sépulchre*) allegedly agreed between Godfrey of Bouillon and the first Crusaders when Jerusalem was taken in 1099 — laws which they had to reconstruct in their law-books, since the 'letters' had vanished in the disaster of Saladin's reconquest in 1187. What Godfrey was believed to have established by his laws was a system of courts, topped by the Haute Cour which in the thirteenth century effectively controlled the succession to the kingdom. [91] All the law-books set out the political constitutions of the kingdoms in which they were written, because they had first to describe the courts where the law was declared, and in the Middle Ages it was through courts, through jurisdiction, that power was exercised. The first common characteristic of the law-books, and the one which explains their making, is the concern to integrate new legislation into existing law. But this second characteristic — a preoccupation with the powers and duties of judges — explains their substance and internal arrangement.

There were two reasons for this concern: first, that early law-making was about the jurisdiction and procedures of courts which already existed; and second, that the authors of the law-books can only have been judges and administrators responsible for the running of those courts. The rights of jurisdiction belonging to feudal lords were chief amongst the *consuetudines* mentioned in charters, which (as customs) did not need to be described.[92] Kings always wanted the practice of the courts written down, however, 'so that judges would judge by written law' and not be swayed in their judgements by the gifts of the rich: this was the reason which Charlemagne gave for having the tribal laws amended in writing in 802.[93] In some Carolingian manuscripts the sections of the laws and capitularies *De judiciis* — concerned with the responsibilities of judges — are marked out. These were clearly of particular interest to their users.[94] But the authors of the law-books would probably not have drawn a firm line between judging and legislating, which were both included, along with law-enforcement, within the notion of jurisdiction.[95] At the end of the ninth century, King Alfred proclaimed, in the preface to his laws which is almost an embryonic law-book, that a man needs no other 'doom-book' or *liber judicialis* than the maxim that he should judge others as he would be judged; but he went on to promulgate a selection of the dooms of his predecessors.[96] The books of Welsh law, purporting to have been drawn up another half-century on by King Hywel the Good, again with the advice of his *Witan*, are perhaps examples of doom-books for the use of judges — and they prescribe 'instant and permanent retirement' for a judge whose dooms are proved false.[97]

The originality which Maitland attributed to the 'Laws of Henry I' seems to consist in the fact that their author went beyond these moral injunctions and attempted, for the first time in medieval Europe, to give a comprehensive account of the various kinds of court in a particular country and the different types of cases heard in them. We do not need the titles under which the chapters of the *Leges* were grouped, probably after the text was written, to tell us that it sets out as a treatise 'on the conduct and definition or description of law-suits' (*De causarum pertractatione et diffinitione vel descriptione*), and therefore on the courts to which the different cases were to be taken. The crucial distinction, established by the king's ordinance on the shire-court, is between 'the general pleas of the county' and the 'demesne pleas of the king'.[98] But all cases, the *Leges Henrici* insist, 'are to be determined by judges with a true understanding of judgement'.[99]

Bracton greatly elaborates on this warning against unwise judges in what has sometimes been seen as a reflection on the standard of his colleagues, though in fact it simply gives colour to the author's expressed purpose of collecting 'the ancient judgements of just men' in order to instruct these 'lesser judges'.[100] From *Glanvill*, the prologue of *Regiam Maiestatem* gets a rather more complacent statement of the impartiality of the judges of 'our just king' — Henry II presumably reincarnated as Robert I. But the reason why *Regiam Maiestatem* sets off on the same course as Glanvill and the *Leges Henrici* is the appropriateness to the Scottish situation of what comes after the exhortation to just judgement: the division of secular causes into those belonging to the king and those belonging to the sheriffs.[101] (English treatises later than *Glanvill* were less relevant because they treated the shire court increasingly as a mere cog in the machinery of Westminster justice, whereas in Scotland the sheriff's court remained a distinct jurisdiction.) 'Glanvill with the writs removed' (a possible description of *Regiam Maiestatem*) is not so far distant from the *Leges Henrici* as the usual accounts of the transformation, indeed invention, of English law in the twelfth century lead us to believe. If one ceases to be blinded by the procedural elaboration of English law and its writ-system, English as well as Scottish law-books can be seen to fit into the long-term development of the European law-book. They are all concerned to set out the various levels and types of jurisdiction, royal and shrieval, ecclesiastical and feudal, within particular countries.

This concern explains their arrangement. *Regiam Maiestatem* follows the form of the *Institutes* only superficially (they both have four books). The titles of its first two books, *In quo agitur de preparatoriis judiciorum* and *In quo agitur de judiciis*, indicate a preoccupation with courts and judging which had already shown itself in the Scottish borough customals and the treatise called the *Liber de Judicibus*.[102] The duties of a judge actually come last in the *Institutes*, at the end of the treatment of actions,[103] whereas the medieval concern with judging as the form of political power, and with courts as the framework of government, brought judging to the forefront of any exposition of a country's laws.

The *Sachsenspiegel* demonstrates most clearly how, by describing jurisdiction, the jurists provided 'mirrors' of their nations. It points beyond law-making and judging and strictly legal material to a third concern of the law-books, which can only be termed constitutional — an intention to set out the basic institutions and relationships of their societies. The scheme of the work which Theuerkauf has managed to tease out shows it dividing in half, in the middle of the third book of the *Landrecht*, up to which point

Eike is presenting the common law of Saxon freemen. The first of the six sections in this first part of the *Sachsenspiegel* describes the judicial responsibilities of the rulers of Church and State, and the obligations of freemen to attend the different types of court, and goes on to list the orders of free society, which Eike makes up to seven, to match the seven ages. The second section begins with the seven degrees of kinship (which Eike insists still determine inheritance in Saxony although the Pope has reduced the prohibition of marriages to within the fourth degree); and goes on to the law of inheritance in general. The third section is on the property aspects of marriage; but the fourth moves back to jurisdiction in some difficult property cases and to the qualifications and duties of judges. The fifth section is concerned with the law of injuries in an agrarian society, beginning with the definition of the jurisdiction of the Bauermeister; and leads naturally into the sixth, on criminal jurisdiction in Saxony under the emperor's *Landfrieden* — again a matter of *judicia*.

His exposition of the common law of Saxony, very much in terms of its courts and levels of jurisdiction, brings Eike in the second half of his work to consider the place of Saxon society within the historical ordering of the world. This second part (of which *Lehnrecht* is just the concluding section) begins with an account of God's creation of man in his own image, the history of the human race, and the translation of empire from Babylon *via* the Persians and Greeks to the Romans; which leads into the famous denunciation of serfdom as unrighteous custom stemming from an act of political violence (the Saxon conquest of the Thuringians). There is further material about how society had achieved its existing constitution, and especially how the relationship between the ecclesiastical and lay jurisdictions had developed. The Emperor Constantine had given Pope Silvester and the Church the power to hold separate courts for spiritual offences, but the secular and spiritual jurisdictions should work in harmony, respecting the boundaries between them. We are then given the historical geography of jurisdiction and power in Saxony, broken down into five royal palaces, seven banner-fiefs, two archbishoprics and fifteen bishoprics. The king is judge of everyone. The princes are summoned before him by writ and seal and punished by fines of a hundred pounds. Beneath the king's court are ranged the courts of the counts-palatine and other officials to whom the king has delegated jurisdiction (each with its appropriate level of fine), and the courts of the landlords.[104]

The *Sachsenspiegel* is an extraordinary work, but it helps us to see that the law-books as a group were always more than handbooks of court procedure. Distinctions of jurisdiction were not just procedural rules. In the Middle Ages, *judicia* in the sense of a presentation of the various jurisdictions in which litigants must seek their rights, took the place of the *Institutes' personae* as the first section of the model law-book. The list of the different sorts of private persons making up society according to Roman jurisprudence, gave way to the marshalling of the king's officials, as in the Welsh laws of court, and then to a display of the jurisdictions and liberties which they exercised.[105] From distinctions of jurisdiction grew substantive distinctions between the rights which could be claimed in them, and thence distinctions of status between litigants as well as between court-holders. It was in this way that *Rechtsbücher* became mirrors of their societies. In its first three chapters, *Regiam Maiestatem* summarized the political constitution of Scotland by dividing jurisdiction into (1) causes belonging to the Crown and in the cognizance of the Justiciar; (2) causes belonging to the sheriffs, bishops, abbots and (lay) barons; and (3) an addition to Glanvill to suit Scottish circumstances, causes belonging to the Church.[106] The *Sachsenspiegel* had given a territorial survey of the palaces, fiefs and dioceses through which Saxon justice was administered; and a century earlier still, the *Leges Henrici* had divided England into the three provinces of the West Saxons, the Mercians and the Danes; two archbishoprics and fifteen bishoprics (oddly enough the same number as Eike gives for Saxony); and thirty-two counties.[107] The law-books were products of the constitutional process by which communal and feudal courts were moulded into the framework of the earliest territorial states, under the pressure of royal legislation. In that process, too, the lawmen grew into a professional class of lawyers who served and guarded national systems of law.

---

[1] Sir John Davies in the preface to his *Irish reports* (London, 1674). After beginning this article, I found that Dafydd Jenkins had been thinking along the same lines as myself, and has the sub-heading 'Lawbooks, lawyers, and Legislators' in his O'Donnell lecture, 'The Medieval Welsh Idea of Law' (1981) 49 TvR. It will be seen, however, that we have different views of the relative importance of *Volksrecht* and royal legislation in the development of medieval law.

[2] Aquinas, *Summa Theologiae*, 1-2, q. 97, a.3.

[3] ST, 1-2, q. 90, a. 4; 91, a. 1.

[4] LTWL 109; Liebermann, i. 42-6.

[5] *The Historia Pontificalis of John of Salisbury*, ed. and trans. Marjorie M. Chibnall (Edinburgh: Nelson's Medieval Texts, 1956), 8.

[6] Liebermann, i. 46-7 (49.9).

[7] Gratian, *Decretum*, (2nd edn. E. Friedberg, Leipzig 1879, repr. Graz 1959) *distinctiones* IV, VII, XV; Gratian found his list of law-makers in Isidore of Seville's *Etymologiae*, (cf. ed. W. M. Lindsay) V.i.; Aquinas discusses the role of legislation at length in his *Commentary on the Nicomachaen Ethics*, lesson XVI; and see ST, 1-2, q. 95, a. 1, ad. 2, where Aquinas emphasises that legislators make general judgements for the future, while judges make particular decisions about present situations.

[8] For Anglo-Saxon dooms or *iudicia* which seem to make substantive law, see Liebermann, i. 42, 46 (Alfred, introduction, 49 and 49.8), 171 (IV Athelstan, 1,2), 320 (II Cnut, 15.2).
[9] Gratian, *Decretum, distinctiones* I-III, especially II, c. 1.
[10] *Digest*, 1.3.1. Cf. a capitulary of Charles the Bald in 864: 'Et quoniam lex consensu populi et constitutione Regis fit, debent Franci jurare...', *Capitularia Regum Francorum*, 2 vols., (MGH Leges Sectio II) vol. 1 (ed. A. Boretius, Hanover 1883, repr. 1984) 313.35.
[11] The law in the charters is explored in E. John, *Land Tenure in Early England* (Leicester, 1960).
[12] On the various senses of *Lex*, see J. F. Niermeyer, *Mediae Latinitatis lexicon minus* (Leiden, 1954-76) and Du Cange, *Glossarium Mediae et Infimae Latinitatis*, s.v. lex. The late Anglo-Saxon 'Rights and Ranks of People' attempts to set down the law or lex of a Thegn, and the *riht* of the Geneat, the Cottar and the Gebur: Liebermann, i. 444-6. See also *Capitularia Regum Francorum* (MGH Leges Sectio II) vol. 2 (ed. A. Boretius & V. Krause, Hanover 1890-97, repr. 1980/84) 653 s.v. *lex*.
[13] LTWL 92-3.
[14] Liebermann, ii. 129-30, 466-71. For the *leges et consuetudines terrarum*, see i. 452(21).
[15] For *folcriht*, see Liebermann, i. 138 (Prol.), 200 (1.1), 452 (20.1,4); for *Landriht*, 444 (1), 453 (1: '...ge hlafordes landriht ge folces gerihtu'), 477 (6: '...ge burhriht ge landriht'); ii. 566; for *landlaga*, ii. 452 (21); for Danelaw, 132 (7.2), 256 (37), 320 (15.2).
[16] Liebermann, i. 453 (1).
[17] Ibid., 444 (1).
[18] Ibid., 212 (12).
[19] Liebermann, ii. 471 (22). In 1139, the abbot of Battle told King Stephen that the king might 'at will change the ancient rights of the country for his own time', but 'that fact should not establish anything for posterity except with the common consent of the barons of the realm': *The Chronicle of Battle Abbey*, edited and translated by Eleanor Searle (Oxford, 1980), 145.
[20] Liebermann, i. 126 (Prol.).
[21] Liebermann, i. 138-41, ii. 469 (15). See i. 88-9, for King Ine's ordering of right harmony (*coniugium*) and right 'kingdooms' for his folk, under the exhortation and teaching of his father and his bishops, and along with all his *ealdermen* and the older wise men (*yldestan witan*) and a great gathering of the servants of God.
[22] Ibid., i. 46-7 (49. 9-10).
[23] Which is how parts of Aethelred's laws present the situation (ibid., 226 (9), 246 (Prol.); cf. ibid., 171, for the *iudicia* which the *sapientes Anglie* were said to have instituted by the counsel of King Aethelstan.
[24] Ibid., 207 (Prol.).
[25] Ibid., 166 (Prol.), 171, 182-3 (12.1), 226.
[26] Ibid., i. 246-7, ii. 468.
[27] LTWL 109. 193.
[28] Ibid., 5-6.
[29] Liebermann, i. 376, iii. 214-19; Wendy Davies, *Wales in the Early Middle Ages* (Leicester, 1982), 204-5.
[30] Davies, *Wales in the Early Middle Ages*, 131-2.
[31] Liebermann, i. 88 (Prol.), 178-9, 210 (2.2), 214 (15.1).
[32] Ibid., 170 (Aethelstan's peace for Kent), 228 (Aethelred's for the five boroughs): cf. 452 (21.1) for laws to be observed in certain places rather than generally.
[33] Ibid., 452 (21).
[34] Ibid., 138 (Prol.), 145 (5.2).

[35] Davies, *Wales in the Early Middle Ages*, 132.

[36] Liebermann, i. 669 (38.2).

[37] Liebermann, ii. 565-6 (6).

[38] Liebermann, ii. 565 (4).

[39] H. G. Richardson and G. O. Sayles, *The Governance of Mediaeval England* (Edinburgh, 1963), 181-2.

[40] *Rotuli Hundredorum* (2 vols., Record Comm., 1812-18), i. 354; Liebermann, ii. 565 (3b, 4); Niermeyer, *Lexicon minus*, sub vv.

[41] B. Rehfeldt, 'Saga und Lagsaga', (1955) 72 ZRG/GA 47, 54-5; K. Haff, 'Der germanische Rechtsprecher als Träger der Kontinuität', (1948) 66 ZRG/GA 364-8.

[42] *Capitularia Regum Francorum*, (n.10, *Supra*) i. 204.

[43] Niermeyer, *Lexicon minus*, s.vv.; cf. *Novum Glossarium Mediae Latinitatis* (Copenhagen) for *legidoctor*.

[44] LTWL 92-3.

[45] See J. P. Dawson, *The Oracles of the Law* (Ann Arbor, 1968), 101 et s.

[46] Justinian emphasizes the need for change in laws, but also the final authority of his own *corpus*: see Tony Honoré, *Tribonian* (London, 1978).

[47] *Capitularia Regum Francorum*, (n.12, supra) ii. 313.35.

[48] Ibid., i. 212.10, ii, 156.15.

[49] Ibid., i. 67.20, 210.35, ii. 69.30, 74.35.

[50] E. H. Kantorowicz, 'Kingship and Scientific Jurisprudence', in *Twelfth-Century Europe and the Foundations of Modern Society*, ed. Marshall Clagett, Gaines Post and Robert Reynolds (Milwaukee and London: University of Wisconsin Press, 1966), 98-9.

[51] Inst. 2.9; Code 8.53.1; Digest 1.3.32-40 (especially 37-8).

[52] LTWL 394.

[53] *Capitularia Regum Francorum*, (n.10, *supra*) i. 105; Rosamond McKitterick, *The Frankish Kingdoms under the Carolingians* (London, 1983), 88-9.

[54] Libermann, i. 44-47 (49.6 et seq).

[55] *Constitutiones et Acta Publica Imperatorum et Regum* (MGH Leges Sectio IV) vol. 2, 1198-1272 (ed. L. Weiland, Hanover 1896 repr 1963), 242.35, 247.20.

[56] J. F. Lemarignier, 'La dislocation du "pagus" et le problème des "consuetudines" ', in *Mélanges Louis Halphen* (Paris, 1951), 401-10; for jurisdictional custom in Germany, see *Constitutiones, 1198-1272*, op. cit. previous note, 212.10, 419.5, 611.10; *Constitutiones, 1345-1348*, (MGH Leges Section IV) vol. 8 (ed. K. Zeumer and R. Salomon 1910-26, repr 1982) 3.15, 332.15.

[57] *Constitutiones 1345-1348* (op. cit. previous note) 3.15, 332.15.

[58] For the grants of 'customs' by the Anglo-Norman kings, see A. Harding, 'Political Liberty in the Middle Ages', (1980)55 *Speculum* 429.

[59] *The Chronicle of Battle Abbey*, op. cit. n.19 supra, 111.

[61] Ibid., 111.

[61] Gratian, *Decretum*, distinctiones VIII (De differentia juris naturalis, constitutionis et consuetudinis), X (Constitutiones seculares ecclesiasticis subsunt), XI (Consuetudo legibus cedit), XII (Contra consuetudines et traditiones universales non est agendum).

[62] See the assertion of Eike von Repgow, echoed by Henry of Bracton and Philippe de Beaumanoir, that the Pope's legislation altering the prohibited degrees could not affect national laws of inheritance: *Sachsenspiegel (Land- und Lehnrecht)*, ed. K. A. Eckhardt (MGH Fontes Iuris Germanici Antiqui, n.s. vol. 1, Hanover, 1933), 22-3 (1.3.3.); K. G. Hugelmann, 'Der Sachsenspiegel und das vierte Lateranensische Konzil', (1924) 44 ZRG/KA 427-87; *Bracton on the Laws and Customs of England*, trans. S. E. Thorne (4 vols. to date,

Cambridge, Mass., 1968-77), ii. 196 (fol. 67b); Philippe de Beaumanoir, *Coutumes de Beauvaisis*, ed A. Salmon (2 vols., Paris, 1899-1900 repr. 1970), i. 192 (406), ii. 195 (1370).

[63] See especially the refusal of the English barons at the Council of Merton in 1236 to change the laws of England to conform with the Canon law which permitted certain bastards to be legitimized by their parents' subsequent marriage: Bracton (op. cit. previous note) iv. 296 (fol. 417).

[64] W. Stubbs, *Select Charters*, 9th edn. revised H. W. C. Davis (Oxford, 1913), 163-4.

[65] R. E. Latham, *Revised Medieval Latin Word-List* (London, 1965), 110.

[66] *Constitutiones, 1345-1348* (op. cit. n.56) vol. 8, 182.5.

[67] *Constitutiones, 1325-1330* (op. cit. n.56) vol. 6.1, ed. J. Schwalm, Hanover, 1914-27, 519.10.

[68] *Constitutiones, 1345-1348* (op. cit. n.56) vol 8, 315.25.

[69] Jean Yver, 'Le "Très Ancien Coutumier" de Normandie, Miroir de la Legislation Ducale?', (1971) 39 TvR 342-3.

[70] Cf. note 86 below.

[71] *Handwörterbuch zur deutschen Rechtsgeschichte,* ed. A. Erler and E. Kaufmann, i. (Berlin, 1971), 1603.

[72] *Constitutiones* 1273-1298 (op. cit. n.56) vol. 3, ed. J. Schwalm, Hanover, 1904-06), 336.30, 337.45, 338.20, 339.15, 340.15.

[73] *decreta judiciorum* is Bede's phrase for the laws made by King Ethelbert of Kent 'after the example of the Romans': *Baedae Opera Historica*, ed. C. Plummer (Oxford, 1896), i. 90; and cf. D. Jenkins, 'The Medieval Welsh Idea of Law', 344; for *doom*, see Liebermann, ii. 54.

[74] G. Theuerkauf, *Lex, Speculum, Compendium Iuris* (Cologne, 1968), part II.

[75] *Capitularia Regum Francorum,* i (op. cit. n.10, *supra*) 105, 111-13; McKitterick, *The Frankish Kingdoms under the Carolingians* (n.53, *supra*) 62-3, 98-9.

[76] *Capitularia Regum Francorum,* i (op. cit. n.10, *supra*) 68-70 (cap. 33).

[77] *Leges Saxonum und Lex Thuringorum* ed. C. von Scwerin (MGH Fontes Iuris Germanici Antiqui in usum Scholarum separatim editi vol. 4, Hanover & Leipzig, 1918) 27-30, 32-3.

[78] *Sachsenspiegel Land-und Lehnrecht* (op. cit. n.62, *supra*) 9; for the discussion of the *Sachsenspiegel*, see Theuerkauf, *Lex, Speculum, Compendium Iuris*, Part III (n.74, *supra*).

[79] On *Landfrieden* see *Handbuch der Quellen und Literatur der neueren europäischen Privatrechtsgeschichte*, I, *Mittelalter*, ed. H. Coing (Munich, 1973), 588 ets., and H. Angermeier, *Königtum und Landfriede im deutschen Spätmittelalter* (Munich, 1966); for Bernard of Pavia, see Theuerkauf, *Lex, Speculum, Compendium Iuris*, part III (2) (n.74, *supra*).

[80] Liebermann, i.140 (1), 144-5 (5.2.), 441 (1), 453 (1), 477 (6), ii. 412-13, 566.

[81] i PM 100-101.

[82] *Leges Henrici Primi*, ed. with trans. and commentary by L. J. Downer (Oxford, 1972), 81 (1), 98-9 (7.1).

[83] *The treatise on the laws and customs of England commonly called Glanvill*, ed. with intro, notes and tr by G. D. G. Hall (London, 1965), xxxiv-xxxv, 28.

[84] *Glanvill*, (op. cit. previous note) 2; *Bracton*, (op. cit. n.62, *supra*) ii. 19.

[85] Thorne's introduction to *Bracton*, (op. cit. n.62, *supra*) iii, especially xxii, xxxi, xxxvi and xliv 342 et s.

[86] Yver, 'Le "Très Ancien Coutumier" de Normandie (op. cit. n.69, *supra*) 342 et s; Beaumanoir, *Coutumes de Beauvaisis*, ed. Salmon (op. cit. n.62, *supra*) i. 39, 40, 90, 103, 116, 212, 367, 485, 498, ii. 104, 256, 371, 379.

[87] P. Stein, 'Roman law in Scotland', *Ius Romanum Medii Aevi*, part V, 13b (Milan, 1968), 6-21.

[88] The collecting of statutes is discussed by H.-Ph. Genet, 'Droit et histoire en Angleterre:

la préhistoire de la 'Révolution historique'', [1980] *Annales de Bretagne et des Pays de l'Ouest*, 87.

89 *Regiam Maiestatem* in *Acts of the Parliaments of Scotland*, ed. T. Thomson and C. Innes, I (1844), 597; LTWL 109, 193 etc.; *Leges Baiwariorum*, ed. E. de Schwind (*MGH* Leges Sectio I, Leges Nationum Germanicarum vol. 5, Hanover, 1926), 202, lines 3-6; *Sachsenspiegel*, ed. Eckhardt (op. cit. n.62 *supra*), 13-14.

90 The kernel of the idea is already present in Ulpian's *Lex Regia*, according to which the people had originally conferred on the prince his authority and power (*Digest* 1.4.1).

91 *Livre de Jean D'Ibelin*, in *Assises de Jérusalem*, ed. Comte Beugnot (2 vols., Recueil des Historiens des Croisades: Paris, 1841-43), i. 21-25; J. Riley-Smith, *The Feudal Nobility and the Kingdom of Jerusalem, 1174-1277* (London, 1973), 121-144.

92 J. F. Lemarignier, 'La dislocation du "pagus", et le problème des "consuetudines" ' ', in *Mélanges Louis Halphen* (Paris, 1951), 401-10.

93 *Capitularia Regum Francorum*, i. (op cit. n.10, *supra*) 105.20.

94 See Rosamond McKitterick, 'Some Carolingian law books and their function', *Authority and Power: Studies on Medieval Law and Government*, [Festschrift for Walter Ullmann] ed. P. Linehan and B. Tierney (Cambridge, 1980), 21, 26.

95 Cf. Brian Tierney, *Religion, law, and the growth of constitutional thought, 1150-1650* (Cambridge, 1982), chapter 3, 'Origins of jurisdiction', especially p.45, where it is claimed that the powers of government were first divided into legislative, judicial and executive by Hervaeus Natalis in the early fourteenth century, in a treatise *De iurisdictione*.

96 Liebermann, i. 44-6 (49.6-9).

97 LTWL 324-5; D. Jenkins, 'The Medieval Welsh Idea of Law', 331-2, 343.

98 *Leges Henrici Primi*, ed. Downer (op cit. n.82 *supra*) 3, 70-73, 81-82, 98, 108 (10.4).

99 Ibid, 80.

100 *Bracton* (op. cit. n.62, *supra*) ii.19.

101 *Acts of the Parliaments of Scotland*, i. 597-8, 627; *Glanvill* (op. cit. n.83, *supra*) 1-4.

102 Stein, 'Roman Law in Scotland' (op. cit. no. 87 *supra*) 13-15.

103 *Institutes*, book IV, tit. xvii: 'De Officio Judicis. Superest, ut de Officio judicis dispiciamus. Et quidem in primis illud observare debet judex, ne aliter judicet, quam Legibus et Constitutionibus, aut moribus proditum est...'

104 Theuerkauf, *Lex, Speculum, Compendium Iuris* (op. cit. n.74, *supra*) 124ff. and 293 ff., divides the first part of the Sachsenspiegel after 1.3.2, 1.19, 1.32, 2.12, and 2.65, and ends it after 3.41; the crucial historical and constitutional section runs from the beginning of the second part to 3.64 (Eckhardt edition, 129-147).

105 Cf. chapters 29 and 30 of the *Leges Henrici* ('Qui debeant esse judices regis' and 'De libertate procerum in placitis comitatus') with the section *De diversis iudicibus* in Latin redaction D of the Welsh laws: *Leges Henrici Primi* op. cit. n.82 *supra*. 130-3; LTWL 349-50).

106 *Acts of the Parliaments of Scotland*, i. 598.

107 *Sachsenspiegel*, ed Eckhardt, 144-5 (3.62); *Leges Henrici Primi* (op cit. n.82 *supra*) 96-9 (chapters 6,7). Cf. the seven *domus episcopales* of Dyfed in the Welsh laws: LTWL 141, 240; T. M. Charles-Edwards, 'The Seven Bishop Houses of Dyfed', (1970) 24 BBCS, 247-62.

THE ADMINISTRATION OF LAW IN MEDIEVAL WALES: THE ROLE OF THE *YNAD CWMWD (JUDEX PATRIE)*

R. R. Davies

Few subjects are so elusive in the study of native society in medieval Wales in the period before the Edwardian Conquest as the administration of law and the dispensation of justice. The native law-texts, *Cyfraith Hywel*, provide us with a corpus of material on substantive law, on the basic legal principles which governed, or should govern, social relations and behaviour. But the Welsh law-texts, in common with most customary law, are very unforthcoming on how the law is to be operated and administered or in what context legal decisions are made and how they are effected.[1] Even where they lay down some clear procedural rules — as they do in disputes relating to suretyship (*mechnïaeth*) and, above all, to land (*tir a daear*) — we have no means of knowing whether or how far these rules were followed in practice. As one historian has remarked recently in a discussion of early medieval law-texts and legislation, 'it may be that our error is to think too much in terms of the practical application of our texts'.[2] Nor can we resolve the issue by appealing to contemporary documentary sources, for as we know only too well there is virtually no contemporary legal record on the operation of native law in Wales before the end of the thirteenth century. Even the fascinating legal memoranda relating to a land dispute in Arwystli in the early thirteenth century, recently discussed and illuminated by Dr David Stephenson, are as anomalous in their form as they are exceptional in their survival. It is not merely that contemporary legal documents do not survive; it is very unlikely that they ever existed, at least in any number. Native Wales, until at least the thirteenth century, was for most secular purposes a largely preliterate society.[3] It resolved its disputes locally; it reached its decisions by reference to oral or visual testimony or by proof; it retained a record of those decisions through the collective memory of society. Preliterate societies are quite as capable as literate societies of formalising the processes by which disputes are resolved and customs observed; but the framework of assumptions and institutions — or, perhaps, 'occasions' would be a more appropriate word — within which law operates in a preliterate society is often very different from that which pertains in a society in which law has become an academic or professional subject, in which legal records impose their own categories, distinctions and assumptions upon the processes of peace-keeping, and in which kings and lords have largely arrogated to themselves a monopoly of enforcing law and imposing justice. Historians are the prisoners of written records; they study the past through the evidence and, what is more, the categories and assumptions of those records. That is why they are ill at ease with preliterate societies, for they smuggle the categories and distinctions of the later world of the written word into their study of such societies. Nowhere more so than in the study of the operation of law in preliterate societies.[4]

How, then, can we try to recapture something of this largely preliterate phase in the history of native law in Wales, a phase which lasted virtually until the loss of political independence in 1282-83? One way of doing so is through the study of the records and institutions of Welsh law which survive from the post-Conquest period, in the hope that we may thereby catch a glimpse of how native law might have operated in pre-Conquest days as well as of the forms in which it survived in the later middle ages. The present article will concentrate on one particular aspect of the operation of native Welsh law, the office of *ynad* (*judex, judicator*) and on the evidence for its survival and role in parts of late medieval Wales; but before attending to this specific task, and indeed in order to place it in a broader context, it is necessary to make certain preliminary general comments about the way in which law was dispensed in pre-Conquest native Wales as seen through the (possibly distorting) mirror of the late medieval evidence.

What is immediately apparent is that law was part of a more general framework of social rules and customs and that, like those rules and customs, much of it operated outside the formal, regular institutions which we so often associate with the enforcement of law in later centuries. It is, indeed, far from clear that regular and organised courts, held under princely or seignorial authority, were common in Wales before the late twelfth or thirteenth centuries. Just as early medieval law was 'undifferentiated, indeterminate and flexible',[5] so was the dispensing of justice itself. Much of it was arbitrative, dispensed as occasion required and at assemblies or gatherings which were, by later standards, informal. It often took the form of agreements upheld by witnesses, of mediation arranged by friends and neighbours, of decisions made by mutually-agreed arbitrators. In the law-texts themselves, agreement between the parties (*o gyfundeb pleidiau*) and by arbitrators (*cymrodeddwyr*) is seen as an alternative to judgement (*barn, judicium*) as ways of terminating disputes.[6] Such 'extra-curial' arbitration remained much more important in dispute-settlement and in the maintenance of social peace in late medieval England than was appreciated until recently;[7] in native Wales it was, and remained, central to the normal processes of law-enforcement. Edward I recognized as much, at least in part, in the Statute

of Wales in 1284 when he conceded that in land disputes 'the truth may be
tried by good and lawful men of the neighbourhood, chosen by consent of
the parties'.[8] This is why so few land disputes survive in the legal records
of late medieval Wales. They were settled extra-curially, by formally
recognized processes and often according to Welsh law and custom. They
were legally terminated, but outside the framework of the officially
recognized courts. It is to such land disputes and settlements that the handful
of legal documents in Welsh for the late medieval period refer — such as
the partitions of land in Abererch and Dinmael,[9] the arbitration
(cyflafareddiad) regarding debt payable in hay at Abergele,[10] or the fascinating
land plea in Caeo (Carms.) in 1540 published and discussed some years ago
by the late Professor T. Jones Pierce.[11] Such extra-curial settlements were
not confined to land pleas. They were also used, contrary to English practice
and royal prohibition, to terminate criminal pleas, as they would be defined
by English law. Thus in 1330 four arbitrators, one of whom was a local
clergyman, drew up an agreement between the parties in a case of assault in
Dyffryn Clwyd and did so apparently according to Welsh law; in
Aberystwyth in 1441 a similar arbitration was imposed to terminate a
particularly vicious feud and the defendants were to clear themselves of the
charge of intentional homicide by massive public purgation, namely the oath
(asach) of two hundred and three hundred men; while in Pwllheli in 1523
a case of homicide was settled by an agreement drawn up by four
arbitrators.[12] Such examples are probably no more than the tip of the
iceberg; the vast majority of such agreements doubtless went unrecorded.
What these arbitrations reveal is a society devising its own local methods for
solving its problems and for defusing issues which might breed friction and
give rise to feud.

Arbitration and curial judgement were not mutually exclusive in early
societies; it is only our later categories which make them so. Likewise which
assemblies and occasions merit the title 'court' in such societies is far from
clear. Law courts only emerge as specialized assemblies when their status and
functions are delimited, their meetings regularized and their proceedings
formalized. Even when that happens — as it may well have done in much
of native Wales in the twelfth and thirteenth centuries — the communal
element in the dispensing of justice and the settling of disputes often
remained pre-eminent. 'Some kind of collective judgement', so it has
recently been asserted, 'was normal' in the dispensing of law in western
Europe prior to the twelfth century.[13] Wales was no exception. In one of
the earliest examples of dispute-procedure (and of old Welsh) which
survives, it is the 'good men' (degion) who seek to 'make peace'; in the
Arwystli dispute in the early thirteenth century, it is to the decison of

judgement-finders (*dadferwyr*), drawn 'from the better men' of the district (*de melioribus viris de Arwistli*), that the issue is referred; and in the law-texts the role of the local leaders of society (*gwyrda, henuriaid y wlad*) and of the judgement of the *patria* (*dedfryd gwlad*) figures prominently. [14] This collective element remained frequently to the fore in late medieval Wales. In the southern Principality and its contiguous lordships (such as Cydweli), it was the 'suitors of the court' who gave judgement. So likewise in north-eastern Powys: it was the suitors of Bromfield and Yale who declared the law on substantive and procedural issues, while in Chirkland it was the duty of free and unfree to act as doomsmen or judgement-finders, *judicatores curie*. [15] This communal element in the declaration of law, in judgement-finding and in the dispensation of justice survived in native Wales because it was woven into the very texture of law and custom and into the mechanisms which native societies had evolved for settling disputes and preserving order. It would only be gradually ousted as the concepts, categories and processes of English law — and that a precociously professional, formal and royally-enforced law — slowly triumphed in Wales, whether by royal statute (as in 1284 and 1536), by the fiat of local governors (such as those who tried to impose alien customs and habits in west and north-east Wales in the thirteenth and fourteenth centuries), or, most important of all, by the slow diffusion of the forms, practices and methods of the common law.

Native law in Wales, both before and after the Edwardian Conquest, was — if the above interpretation is plausible — to a considerable degree arbitrative in its operation, collective in its judgements, and often, by the standards of later justice, informal in its methods. This did not mean, however, that expertise in the law was at a discount. On the contrary, societies which are governed by customary law frequently defer to the wisdom of men who are regarded as having a special knowledge of that law. Collective judgement and legal knowledge are regarded as complementary, not exclusive. The men who were called upon to give judgement in the Arwystli dispute were chosen not only for their social standing but also for their knowledge of the laws; they were truly law-worthy men. [16] In south Wales, likewise, the suitors who gave judgement were clearly expected to know, or to draw upon knowledge of, the law, for their judgements could be challenged by appeal to experts in Welsh law (*dosbarthwyr*); while the arbitrators who settled land pleas called themselves 'judges' (*barnwyr*), were chosen for their knowledge of Welsh law, and supported their judgements by reference to the law texts (*kyfraith yn dywedut*). [17] Judgement was collective, in that it was given by members of the local community; but it was based not on personal whim but on the knowledge, interpretation and application of an acknowledged corpus of legal lore, transmitted either orally or, increasingly from the thirteenth century, in written form.

It is against this background that we should approach the role of the judge in the administration of law in native Wales in medieval times. We are immediately confronted with a problem of terminology which in turn reflects a diversity of practice within Wales. In the vernacular versions of native Welsh law two terms are used to refer to a judge (using that term itself in the loosest of senses): in the texts associated with north Wales the term *ynad* (plural *ynaid*) is the one normally favoured whereas in south Wales the term preferred was *brawdwr* (plural *brawdwyr*). The distinction was more than one of terminology; it reflected contemporary recognition of a diversity of practice in the status and role of the judge in the administration of law in different parts of Wales.

This deversity is explained with admirable succinctness by the native law texts associated with south-west Wales, *Llyfr Blegywryd*. There are, so it proclaims, three different kinds of judges (*brawdwyr*) according to the law of Hywel Dda: (i) the judge of the royal court (*brawdwr llys*) in the courts of Dinefwr and Aberffraw; (ii) the official judge in each commote or cantref (*brawdwr cwmwd neu gantref herwydd swydd*) in Gwynedd and Powys; and (iii) the judge in respect of land tenure (*brawdwr o fraint swydd*) in every commote or cantref, 'namely every owner of land' *(pob perchennog tir)*.[18] Leaving aside the judge of the royal court (whose functions and privileges are described in the tractate on the laws of the court), there is clearly a fundamental cleavage between the second and third categories of judges, between men who are regarded and possibly appointed as official judges in their localities on the one hand, and local landowners required to act as judges in respect of the land they hold on the other. The distinction is, perhaps, rather overdrawn, since the judges in respect of land tenure in south Wales were certainly expected to be conversant with Welsh law and since 'experts in Welsh law' were specifically recruited in south Wales in the later middle ages. Yet it is a basic distinction and one which highlights the major regional differences in the operation of law within native Wales. It was, at heart, a distinction between professional or quasi-professional lawmen and amateur doomsmen. It was recognized as such in the law-texts: the 'professional' judge was to be paid a fee of fourpence for each judgement whereas his amateur colleague went unrewarded; if a 'professional' judge was convicted of a false judgement, he forfeited his office, his privilege (*braint*) as a judge, and the worth of his tongue, whereas the amateur judge paid only the price of his tongue, for his function as judge was an obligation arising from land tenure, not an official post. It is to the role of the 'professional' local judge in north Wales, the *ynad cwmwd* or *judex patrie*, that we must now turn.[19]

The law-texts make it clear that in north Wales such an *ynad* — and it

is as well to retain the native term since the English word 'judge' is heavily
laden with modern, and possibly misleading, connotations — must be taught
by a law-teacher (*athro*), must master the basic elements of Welsh law as
contained in the Proof Book (*Llyfr Prawf*), must be examined and approved
by the *ynad* of the royal court, and would be formally invested with the
status of *ynad* by the lord or king.[20] The *ynad*'s training, examination and
formal acceptance were, therefore, comparable to those of the professional
poet. Like the poet, he had to qualify for membership of a professional order
and to master the lore of that order. How far and for how long this *cursus*
was observed in practice is difficult to gauge; but references to a man from
Cyfeiliog travelling to north Wales 'to learn the laws of Hywel Dda' and
thereafter being called *ynad* or to an *ynad* being appointed 'who knew the
laws and customs and the Welsh language' suggest that some of its features
survived at least until the late thirteenth century.[21] Such an *ynad*, formally
apprenticed and examined, officially sanctioned and thereafter frequently
appointed, or accepted, as *ynad* in a specific commote or cantref would clearly
command a special status in the administration of Welsh law. Yet that status
would appear to have been complementary to, rather than exclusive of, the
arbitrative and collective features of judgement-finding in Welsh law. He
was a jurist whose knowledge and expertise deserved special respect.[22] He
was not the president of the court; rather was he a legal expert who should
know what formal procedures should be followed and who could bring his
knowledge of legal lore and of the law-texts to bear on the issues to hand.
His position approximated to that of an expert arbitrator.[23] It may well be
that he only acted when he was invited to do so: so much is suggested by
the later medieval evidence and by a reference to an *ynad* 'elected jointly
according to the law and custom of Wales'.[24] His judgement could be
challenged by a formal process of appeal if one of the parties believed that
he had given a false judgement (*cam frawd, cam farn*), in that it did not
conform with the law of the written texts. It was the law that was supreme;
the *ynad* was expected to apply it correctly and faithfully.

Professional local *ynaid* were to be found in most parts of Gwynedd, both
Is Conwy and Uwch Conwy, in the days of the native princes. The evidence
is most clear for north-east Wales — notably Tegeingl, Rhuddlan, Rhos and
Dyffryn Clwyd;[25] but an earlier stray reference indicates that the office was
also taken for granted in the furthest western parts of Gwynedd.[26] During
the bitter dispute about Arwystli in the years 1277-82 the Welsh claimed
that 'judges who are called in the common tongue *ynaid* had been presented
before the king so that they could judge about those lands'; while the *Survey
of Denbigh* of 1334 assuredly reflects pre-Conquest circumstances in its
assumption that there will be an *ynad* (*iudex*) in each commote.[27]

Throughout Gwynedd, therefore, we have reason to believe that there were local *ynaid*; elsewhere in native Wales they are notable by their absence. The evidence for Powys is admittedly rather ambiguous. The law-texts claim that local *ynaid* operated there and Llywelyn ap Gruffudd asserted that they certainly existed in the western commotes of Cyfeiliog and Arwystli.[28] On the other hand, one notable witness before the 1281 commission of inquiry into Welsh law claimed that though the title of *ynad* was bestowed on a Cyfeiliog man who had gone to north Wales to learn the law of Hywel Dda, he had not in fact ever adjudicated;[29] while the absence of any references to such professional *ynaid* in the later records of the lordships of Chirkland and Bromfield and Yale strongly suggests that the institution was not known (or had died out) in eastern Powys. As to west and south Wales there can be no doubt; record and law-text evidence concur that local *ynaid* of the professional variety were unknown there.

By the thirteenth century, therefore, such *ynaid* were restricted to the greater principality of Gwynedd and, possibly, to adjacent commotes in western Powys. Many of them probably exercised their functions hereditarily. In this respect they were very similar to two of the other professional learned orders in native Wales — the bards and the physicians. Indeed, there may have been some overlap between them, especially between the bards and the *ynaid*: Dr David Stephenson has suggested that Einion ap Gwalchmai, a member of a family of court poets, was also *ynad* at the court of Llywelyn ab Iorwerth of Gwynedd, while in later fourteenth-century Ceredigion Rhydderch ab Ieuan Llwyd was a discriminating and informed patron of poets as well as an acknowledged expert in Welsh law.[30] In Ireland, likewise, families of hereditary jurists, such as the Mac Egans and Mac Clancys, were common; they were rewarded by leading magnates, such as the Earl of Ormond, for their professional advice on matters relating to Irish law and were appointed 'ordinary judges' in their localities.[31] The 'judges' or 'dempsters' in Scotland, who served as repositories of ancient custom, also often belonged to hereditary families.[32] It was doubtless from similar families of hereditary jurists that many of the *ynaid* of native Wales were drawn.[33] Dafydd Jenkins, in a seminal article, has drawn attention to the legal dynasty centred on Iorwerth ap Madog ap Rhawd and has shown that its ranks included several of the leading jurists whose names are associated with various redactions of the law-texts.[34] Nor were these men merely antiquarian jurists, for the term *ynad* applied to one of them, Madog Goch Ynad, indicates that they may also have held official positions. This was certainly true of another important redactor of the Welsh law-texts, Cynyr ap Cadwgan. Indeed, Cynyr's career and associations take us as close to the heart of native jurisprudence in thirteenth-century Wales as we are likely to get. He was credited with assembling a revised version of *Cyfraith Hywel*; he founded, or continued, a dynasty of jurists, for his text was transmitted to his son and then to his grandsons; he witnessed a deed as abbot of the ancient *clas* church of Llandinam and was chosen as one of the 'wise men' (*sapientes*) of Arwystli to hear a legal case on appeal; and his sons were said to be '*ex officio* judges, that is *ynaid*, in Arwystli'.[35]

How far did the office of local *ynad* survive the trauma of political conquest and the administrative and legal changes which overwhelmed native Welsh society in the thirteenth century? Profound changes in the substance, procedure and administration of law were already afoot in native Wales well before the Edwardian Conquest. The evidence submitted to Edward I's commission of inquiry in 1280-81, however partial it might be, makes that evident enough. Change was indeed inevitable given the far-reaching social and economic transformation that was taking place within Wales and given also the impact of English legal ideas and practices, whether borrowed directly or mediated through the courts and law of the Marcher lordships. In these circumstances the position and importance of the *ynad* would doubtless be modified. But modified, rather than extinguished. What we know of the resilience and adaptability of Welsh law, of the proliferation of revised copies of the native law texts, of the continuing application of Welsh legal concepts and *dicta* in the settlement of disputes, both within and outside the official courts, in certain parts of Wales well into the sixteenth century suggests that men professionally trained in Welsh law still had a rôle to play in dispensing justice in post-Conquest society. This is indeed what we find, notably in the two north-eastern Marcher lordships of Denbigh and Dyffryn Clwyd (both of them formerly part of the greater Gwynedd, transformed into Marcher lordships by Edward I in the wake of his conquest of 1282-83). It is to the evidence of these two lordships on the position of the local *ynad* — normally referred to in the court- and account-rolls as *iudex* or *iudicator Wallicus* — that we now turn.

There was one officially recognized *ynad* in each of these two lordships throughout the fourteenth and fifteenth centuries. The office seems to have been continued without a break from pre-Conquest days, for we are told that Reginald Grey (d. 1308), 'the first after the conquest of Wales', appointed Madoc ap Heilin ap Ithyk (*sic*) to the post in Dyffryn Clwyd.[36] Most of the *ynaid* held their offices for long periods, often for life. This was certainly so in the case of Bleddyn Llwyd, who had been appointed *ynad* of Dyffryn Clwyd before 1322 and died in office in 1349; it was also probably true of Tudur ab Ieuan Goch, *ynad* of Denbigh for more than a generation after 1409. More interesting is it to note that the hereditary tendencies of the office remained strong. Bleddyn Llwyd's sons clearly regarded the office as heritable on their father's death in 1349 and sold it, as a heritable and vendible commodity, to Madog ap Dafydd Goch and his heirs.[37] The lord did not challenge this claim to heritability; instead, he bought out the rights of both parties to the office in order to grant it to his own nominee. As this incident suggests, the office of *ynad*, as so much else pertaining to Welsh law in the later middle ages, had become a source of seignorial exploitation and profiteering. The *ynad* could be amerced for not coming to perform his duties or for not doing so to the lord's advantage;[38] his fees (*gobrau*) and his share in the profits of justice were diverted into the lord's coffers;[39] the post could even be granted, incongruously, to members of English immigrant families such as Henry Salisbury, *iudex inter Wallicos* in Denbigh 1406-08, or Simon Thelwall, *rhaglaw* and *ynad* in the same lordship in the 1470s.[40]

It is from the Dyffryn Clwyd evidence that we can best gather what sort of issues — or rather, more correctly, which pleas originally initiated in the seignorial court — were referred to the judgement of the *ynad* in the late medieval period. They were mainly civil actions, especially cases of surety, debt, unjust detinue, defamation and trespass; but on occasion, serious criminal offences, initiated by appeal — such as rape, wounding and theft — were also referred to his judgement. His judgement was also very often sought on cases relating to the payment of native dues, notably *amobr* (virginity-due), on cases arising out of the Welsh custom of placing a cross on land in dispute to prohibit counter-claims to it pending a settlement,[41] and on the consequences of a defeated litigant entering the Welsh plea that he had no goods and could not therefore be distrained for damages or amercements (*barn y diddim*).[42] The range of issues referred to the *ynad* was, therefore, wide; but they concentrated on personal actions or on issues arising out of the interpretation of Welsh dues and customs.

By the later middle ages in north-east Wales, the *ynad* was a peripheral figure in the formal administration of justice, called in very occasionally to deal with issues raised by the exploitation of Welsh customs or by the survival of Welsh law. He was, as it were, no more than an extra spoke in a wheel of justice which was rapidly becoming English, at least to outward appearances, in its language, pleas and practices. Yet the glimpse that we are allowed of his rôle in these twilight centuries of Welsh law may also help us to understand his status at an earlier period. In the first place, cases were referred to him, sometimes by the lord or his steward, more often at the request of the parties. In other words, he exercised his judgement-giving function by invitation. The parties to a case, individually or jointly, placed themselves 'in his judgement'.[43] In 1359, for example, in an interesting case of defamation — when a local cobbler claimed that he had been slandered by a shrewish woman and that his trade had suffered accordingly — the defendant 'placed herself in the judgement of the *ynad*' whether damages were payable (she had already conceded the substance of the charge).[44] The *ynad* might also be asked to decide on a procedural issue raised in a case, if it referred to Welsh law. In 1331 a defendant answered a charge of unjustly detaining a Welsh history book (how dearly we would like to know what this book was!) first by pleading illness and sending a proxy to excuse him (*excusator*) 'according to Welsh law' and then by claiming that he had not been summoned properly. The *rhaglaw* immediately interjected that he had summoned the defendant 'according to Welsh law and custom'. It was at this stage that the *ynad* adjudged (*adjudicavit*) that the defendant should indeed answer the charge.[45]

Above all the evidence suggests — and the suggestion probably applies to the pre-Conquest as well as to the post-Conquest period — that the main duty of the *ynad* was to determine, in pleas to be heard by Welsh law, what sort of proof was appropriate, which of the parties should proceed to proof — such as the production of witnesses or pledges or compurgation — and then, in the light of the proof, to make his adjudication and impose the appropriate penalty (*camlwrw*) in accordance with Welsh law. He was thereby the interpreter and arbiter of the processes laid down by law. As the law-texts put it, once the parties have agreed to accept the judgement of law, 'the law is to be under the control of the judges'.[46] Thus, in a case of breach of a cross where plaintiff and defendant had sworn and counter-sworn at the behest of the *ynad* (*secundum consideracionem Judicatoris*), the parties were summoned to the parish church 'according to Welsh law', doubtless to make a more solemn and fuller oath in the presence of relics during mass.[47] He could require a defendant in an appeal of theft to swear an oath 'as Welsh law required'; he could examine pledges in a case of debt or the witnesses (*testes*) of a plaintiff in a family dispute about land. He could await while a graduated test of compurgation — with three, then six, and finally twelve compurgators (at which stage the defendant failed) — was applied before he declared his judgement.[48] In these various ways he was ensuring that the rules of Welsh law were being observed and that judgement was given in accordance with those rules. His authority was founded on the written law of the texts,[49] and his adjudication could be formally challenged by reference to that written law.

The *ynad* was, therefore, the servant of a written, customary law; but he was not a blind servant. Questions might be posed and practical issues raised which required a legal ruling. In Bromfield and Yale, Powys, and west Wales, such a ruling would have been given by the doomsmen of the court. But in Dyffryn Clwyd and Denbigh the task might well fall to the *ynad*.

In 1429 in the court of Isaled (Denbigh), Tudur ab Ieuan Goch as *ynad* ruled (*barn*) on the status and responsibilities of the pledges of a person sworn to keep the peace.[50] Similar rulings were given by the *ynad* in Dyffryn Clwyd: pledges who failed to produce the defendant in a plea of *amobr* are to be held responsible for payment of the due; responsibility for the first *amobr* rests on the land of a woman's father not on the person of the woman herself if she were illegitimate.[51] It is in this fashion that Welsh law, at least in part, grew, as professional jurists construed their texts and applied their learning to new problems. That is why the law texts themselves concede that the jurists occasionally differed in their opinions.[52]

The *ynad*, therefore was primarily an officially acknowledged jurist; but he also, and probably increasingly so, exercised his functions within the context of a pattern of seignorial law-enforcement. This was already probably so in pre-Conquest Wales: as an *ynad cwmwd*, he was not only an expert jurist and an arbitrator in local disputes; he was also a princely or seignorial officer, sanctioned to exercise his office by the prince or lord, rewarded with land and a fee and thereby integrated into the structure of princely or seignorial law-enforcement, administration and reward. He used the machinery and penalties of the local courts to ensure that his authority was upheld: parties who failed to appear before him were amerced;[53] defendants could be ordered to be obedient to him and be required to find pledges to be so; the *rhingyll* (or serjeant) could be ordered to summon a defendant at his behest and be held responsible for failing to do so; anyone breaking a cross placed on land or a crop by his order was amerced.[54] He could determine who was responsible for a forest offence or for paying ale-dues by Welsh law;[55] he could join with the deputy-steward in issuing an ordinance on road repair;[56] he could forbid anyone within the lordship from receiving or succouring a defendant who had pleaded that he had no goods on which he could be distrained (*barn y diddim*);[57] he could be called upon to uphold the lord's interest in a case of naifty;[58] and he could issue a decree that only in the presence of a seignorial officer could a tenant place a cross on his land.[59] The professional jurist was increasingly becoming a seignorial servant; the assimilation of functions, we may well believe, had got under way in the days of the native princes.

Yet the *raison* of the *ynad*'s post lay in his knowledge of native Welsh law. Several of the men who bore the title *ynad* in pre-Conquest Wales are known either to have been individually trained in native law or to have belonged to dynasties in which legal lore and expertise was transmitted from one generation to the next. It is likely that such expertise survived the conquest and that several of the *ynaid* who operated in north-east Wales in the later middle ages were either versed in Welsh law themselves or could call on the service of men who were so versed.[60] Knowledge of Welsh law survived in different parts of Wales — such as Cydweli, Carmarthen, Ceredigion, parts of Powys and north Wales, and Marcher lordships such as Clun — throughout the middle ages and into the Tudor period. Some of it was doubtless antiquarian knowledge, fostered by literary patrons; much of it, one suspects, was no more than a general familiarity with some of the basic substantive and procedural concepts of Welsh law, transmitted from one generation to the next and sustained by social conservatism and seignorial self-interest and by the fact that Welsh law was deeply rooted in the fabric of Welsh society and land inheritance. Yet in certain places the knowledge of Welsh law was much more precise and was founded on an acquaintance with the legal texts. Legal *dicta* could be quoted in court; model plaints could be drawn up; and, as the Llwyn Gwyn evidence demonstrates vividly, formal bills, replications and judgements could be composed as late as 1540 showing a close familiarity with the vocabulary, concepts and texts of native law.[61] Such familiarity was likely to be shared by the post-Conquest *ynaid* of north Wales (especially as some of the model pleas in the later Welsh law-texts emanate from Denbigh and Dyffryn Clwyd); but we are rarely allowed a glimpse of it in the cryptic entries in the seignorial court rolls. For the most part the clerk was content simply to note that the *ynad* had given his judgement 'according to Welsh law' — in cases of theft, trespass, the placing of a cross, *amobr*, or, more esoterically, in a dispute about the ownership of a migrant swarm of bees.[62] It is only very rarely that the reticent and formalized court records hint at a more precise knowledge of native law — as in the reference to the nine days allowed to the *ynad*, in accordance with *Cyfraith Hywel,* to give his judgement or in the penalty of one hundred and six cows imposed in a plea of *galanas* in 1398, as stipulated by the Welsh penalty of the augmented hundred (*Cant yr ardyrchafiad*).[63] Such references allow us a fleeting glimpse of a world in which native law was still the subject of study and the professional *ynad* still a useful functionary.

*　　*　　*　　*　　*

The evidence for the study of the *ynad* in post-Conquest Wales is tantalisingly exiguous. Yet disappointing as it is, it is not without interest. It may help us to understand what role the local *ynad* may have played in the dispensation of justice in native Gwynedd. Post-Conquest records are, of course, not necessarily reliable guides to pre-Conquest conditions, especially as such records were compiled according to English formularies and as part of a seignorial system of law-keeping. Yet since the student of

Welsh law must make a virtue of his dire necessity, they are not to be disregarded. They seem to confirm the view that the *ynad* was a jurist, formally trained in Welsh law, applying his expertise to elucidate and confirm the procedures of that law; that he was a professionally-qualified arbitrator, to whose judgement parties deferred and that his role in this respect is to be seen within the broader arbitrative framework of Welsh law-keeping; that his function was in good measure to ensure that the forms of proof and penalties prescribed by Welsh law were observed; and that his territorial position as an *ynad cwmwd* meant that he was increasingly integrated into the pattern of seignorial or princely governance and associated with other officers such as the *rhaglaw, rhingyll, amobrwr* and *coediwr*.

The *ynad* survived the administrative and legal settlement that followed the Edwardian conquest, at least in the lordships of Dyffryn Clwyd and Denbigh. He did so with seignorial consent and to seignorial advantage; but he did so above all because Welsh law remained resilient. Here it is worth emphasizing that our impression of the *ynad's* activity is likely to be very incomplete; it relates only to those occasions where his adjudication impinged upon and was recorded by the seignorial courts. It is more than likely that he was a central figure in much of the extra-curial litigation and settlement which coexisted and overlapped with the formal, curial system of law-keeping; particularly is he likely to have been involved in the settlement of land disputes, in which the concepts of Welsh law are central and which are notable by their absence from the court records. The *ynad* in Denbigh and Dyffryn Clwyd in the fourteenth and fifteenth centuries was part of an alternative, or at least supplementary, source of justice and dispute-settlement within native society.

Yet his days were numbered. He was blatantly exploited by Marcher lords — possibly here, as elsewhere, following precedents set by native princes — for their own financial gain. Nothing illustrates this better than the fact that the formal cases in which he was most frequently called upon to adjudicate were those relating to liability for and collection of *amobr*. The *ynad* and *amobrwr* in north-east Wales, like the *dosbarthwyr* or experts in Welsh law in south-west Wales, were part of the paraphernalia of native custom deliberately exploited for their financial profit rather than generously allowed to survive out of respect of Welsh law and practices. Furthermore, the *ynad* dwelt very much on the periphery of seignorial justice, even in Denbigh and Dyffryn Clwyd. The number of cases referred to his judgement was minute. The vast majority of pleas were terminated either by the acknowledgement or withdrawal of one of the parties, by the judgement of the steward as president of the court or by the verdict of a jury.[64] Native society was adjusting to the forms and practices of English law-keeping, especially in civil and criminal pleas. One case highlights the change. When Tudur ap Dafydd brought a charge of the unjust detinue of one black foal against Robert Pie in 1374, it was the English defendant who asked for the case to be placed in the judgement of the *ynad*. The plaintiff refused: 'He had begun his plea', so he declared, 'according to the custom of the court and the law of England. He therefore requested that they (the parties) should have judgement according to the custom of the court and not according to the judgement of the *ynad* (*secundum judicium Judicatoris*)'.[65] The *ynad* survived for a century or more after this incident; but increasingly his rôle was becoming peripheral and archaic. Eventually it would become redundant.

[1] Dafydd Jenkins, *Cyfraith Hywel* (Llandysul, 1970), 94-96.
[2] Patrick Wormald, '*Lex Scripta* and *Verbum regis*: Legislation and Germanic Kingship from Euric to Cnut', P. H. Sawyer and I. N. Wood (eds.) *Early Medieval Kingship* (Leeds, 1977), 119.
[3] D. Stephenson, *Thirteenth-Century Welsh Law Courts* (Aberystwyth, 1980), 10-14. It was claimed in 1277 that 'pleas of feoffment and pleas of quitclaim are held in Wales without a charter or writing' and later it was asserted that contracts were made there 'sine scripto': J. Conway Davies (ed.), *The Welsh Assize Roll 1277-1284* (Cardiff, 1940), 245; BL Additional Manuscript, 10,013 fol. 7v.
[4] M. T. Clanchy, 'Remembering the past and the good old law', (1970) 55 *History* 165-76; Susan Reynolds, 'Law and Communities in Western Christendom, *c*.900-1140' (1981) 25 *American Journal of Legal History* 205-24.
[5] S. Reynolds, op. cit., 207.
[6] Bleg 124; LTWL, 357.
[7] I. Rowney, 'Arbitration in gentry disputes', (1982) 67 *History*, 367-76; E. Powell, 'Arbitration and the Law in England in the Late Middle Ages', (1983) 33 THRS (5th series) 49-67; M. T. Clanchy, 'Law and Love in the Middle Ages' in J. Bossy (ed.), *Disputes and Settlements: Law and Human Relations in the West* (1983), 47-67.
[8] AL ii 925.
[9] University College of North Wales, Mostyn Collection, 786 (*c*. 1440-50); E. D. Jones, 'Rhannu Tir Rhys ab Elise' (1943-44) 3 NLWJ 23-28.
[10] Melville Richards, 'Darn o Gymraeg Cyfreithiol', (1963-4) 13 NLWJ 203.
[11] T. Jones Pierce, 'The Law of Wales — The Last Phase', [1963] THSC 7-32, repr. in T. Jones Pierce, *Medieval Welsh Society*, ed, J. Beverley Smith (Cardiff, 1972), 369-389. It is clear from the bond of obligation accompanying the pleadings (N.L.W., Edwinsford Collection, 1913) that the dispute and pleadings took place extra-curially.
[12] PRO Court Rolls (S.C.2), 216/10 m. 14 v.; D. Jenkins, 'The Pryse Family of Gogerddan', 1953-4) 8 NLWJ 81-96 at 86-88; R. R. Davies. 'The Survival of the bloodfeud in Medieval Wales', (1969) 54 *History* 338-57, at 355.
[13] S. Reynolds, 'Law and Communities' (above n. 4), 213.
[14] Dafydd Jenkins and Morfydd E. Owen. 'The Welsh Marginalia in the Lichfield Gospels, Part I', (1983)5 CMCS 37-66 at 51; N.L.W. Wynnstay (1945) Montgomeryshire Collection, 29 (alternatively referred to as N.L.W. Wynnstay no. 34); Bleg 70, 106-7. The other Arwystli memorandum (no. 30) uses the word *dedfryd*.
[15] T. Jones Pierce, *Medieval Welsh Society*, 367, 382-83, 389; R. R. Davies, *Lordship and*

Society in the March of Wales, 1282-1400 (Oxford, 1978), 158-59; G. P. Jones (ed), *Extent of Chirkland 1391-93* (Liverpool, 1933), 60.

16 N.L.W. Wynnstay (1945), Mont. Coll., 29 (ad arbitrium bonorum virorum et iura terre illius scientium).

17 T. Jones Pierce, *Medieval Welsh Society*, 388-89; *idem*, [1963] THSC 29 (for the text of the judgement). The two judges were specifically said to be learned in Welsh law: N.L.W. Edwinsford, 1913.

18 Bleg 98-99.

19 Ibid., 99-101. For the term *iudex patrie* see, for example, LTWL 212-13, 457.

20 Col 237-38 and comments in the notes (86-87).

21 'Calendar of Welsh Rolls' in *Calendar of Various Chancery Rolls, 1277-1326* (henceforth *Cal. Welsh Rolls*), 208; J. Conway Davies (ed), *The Welsh Assize Roll 1277-84* (Cardiff, 1940), 247 (iudice electo...qui sit an idem officium deputatus et sciat leges et consuetudines et linguam Wallensicam (? *rectius* Wallensicas)).

22 Cf. the comments of Eoin Mac Neill in CLP 189-90.

23 Cf. the comments of Dafydd Jenkins in 'Kings, Lords and Princes: the Nomenclature of Authority in Thirteenth-Century Wales', (1974-6) 26 BBCS 451-462 at 456.

24 *Welsh Assize Roll 1277-84*, 247 (iudice electo conjuncto secundum legem et consuetudinem Walensicam iudicare). In the Caeo case of 1540 each of the parties chose one of the 'judges' (*barnwyr*); if the two 'judges' failed to agree, one of them could give the judgement, under the peril of the fine in Welsh law for false judgement, but the other reserved the right to reply: N.L.W. Edwinsford, 1913.

25 *Cal. Welsh Rolls*, 196, 199-200. See also the reference to the 'iudex curie secularis' in the cantref of Rhos quoted in D. Stephenson, *Thirteenth Century Welsh Law Courts*, 8.

26 Rec. Caern 252 (1253).

27 C. T. Martin (ed), *Registrum Epistolarum fratris Johannis Peckham* (Rolls Series, 1882-85), II, 440; P. Vinogradoff and F. Morgan (eds.), *Survey of the Honour of Denbigh 1334* (1914), 48, 152, 209, 270, 314.

28 Bleg 99; *Cal. Welsh Rolls*, 195.

29 *Cal. Welsh Rolls*, 208. The argument in *Welsh Assize Roll 1277-1284*, 318 suggests that in eastern Powys judgement by 'fidedigniores patrie' had taken the place of that of the *ynad* (*quasi loco Eygnad*).

30 D. Stephenson, *Thirteenth-Century Welsh Law Courts*, 6: J. B. Smith, 'Einion Offeiriad', (1962-64) 20 BBCS, 339-47; R. A. Griffiths, *The Principality of Wales in the Later Middle Ages, I. South Wales, 1277-1536* (Cardiff, 1972), 117.

31 K. Nicholls, *Gaelic and Gaelicised Ireland in the Middle Ages* (Dublin, 1972), 46-47; G. Mac Niocaill, 'The Contact of Irish and Common Law', (1972) 23 *Northern Ireland Legal Quarterly* 16-23 at 22-23.

32 G. W. S. Barrow, 'The judex' in *The Kingdom of the Scots* (1973), 69-83; *idem, Robert Bruce* (2nd end., Edinburgh, 1976), 6.

33 Cf. *Cal. Welsh rolls*, 208: 'Being asked if he was a judge by hereditary right, as they were usually in North Wales, ...'

34 'Iorwerth ap Madog' (1953-4)8 NLWJ 164-70.

35 AL ii.X; *Cal. Welsh Rolls*, 195; N.L.W. Wynnstay (1945), Mont. Colls., 29-30.

36 S.C. 2/218/4, m. 15 v (1354). All further references to S.C. 2 documents in this paper refer to the Dyffryn Clwyd court rolls at the PRO.

37 S.C. 2/218/1, m. 18 v. (1350); 218/4, m. 14 v., m. 15 v. (1354).

38 I S.C. 2/218/2, m. 18 (1351); PRO, Ministers' Accounts (S.C.6), 1185/10 (Denbigh 1407-9).

[39] S.C. 2/219/7, m. 20 v. m. 25 (1371).

[40] S.C. 6/1185/10; N.L.W. Coed Coch Collection, 796.

[42] For crosses see especially *Ancient Laws*, IX, xvii; IX, xxv; and (for model pleas), XII, xiii-xiv. There is a detailed account of a plea of cross (*dadl kroes am dir a dayar*) in N.L.W. Peniarth Ms. 67, fols. 97-102. The Enlli agreement of 1252 also refers to *dirwy croes*: Rec. Caern. 252.

[49] Cf. AL XI.iii.32: 'ny dyly brawdwr varnu...namyn kyfreith'.

[50] AL IX.xxxix.3; LTWL 409.

[51] S.C. 2/218/2, m. 18 (1351); 221/8, m. 24 (1417).

[52] For example Ior 154/14: 'herwyd rey o'r egneyt'; but in Col 192 this is rendered 'rey o'r llevreu a dyweyt'.

[53] S.C. 2/217/4, m. 13 (1339); 218/4, m. 7 (1354); 218/9, m. 29 v. (1361): 'non venit ad audiendum judicium Judicis Wallici'.

[54] S.C. 2/216/1, m. 18 (1318); 220/10, m. 29 (1398); 216/14, m. 22 (1334).

[55] S.C. 2/219/4, m. 14 (1367, forest offence); 218/7, m. 10 v. m. 18 (1359, Cwrw Gŵyl San Ffraid).

[56] S.C. 2/218/8, m. 26 (1360).

[57] S.C. 2/219/1, m. (1364); 219/7, m. 24 v. (1371).

[58] S.C. 2/222/5, m. 17 (1446: 'et adjudicatus est per Judicatorem Wallicum quod est nativus et filius nativi').

[59] S.C. 2/222/5, m. 26 v. (1449: per judicium Judicatoris adiudicatus est quod proprietarius solus non posset dare defensam domini sine ballivi vel Ringildrium presencia). Cf. AL IX.xvii.1, 'Kanyt groes onyt un a gymerer o law arglud'.

[60] The *ynad* was allowed time to take advice 'with other discreet men': S.C. 2/218/7, m. 15 v. (1359).

[61] Public Record Office Justices Itinerant (J.I. 1), 1156 m. 6 (a plea of wrong judgement at Cydweli, 1510); AL XII; (1963) THSC 26-29.

[62] S.C. 2/216/9, m. 12 v. (1329, theft); 218/7, m. 4 v. (1359, trespass); 216/6, m. 11 v. (1326, cross); 218/7, m. 22 (1359, *amobr*); 219/2, m. 17 (1365, trespass, swarm of bees).

[63] S.C. 2/218/2, m. 19 (1351); R. R. Davies, (1969) 54 *History* 348.

[64] In one case the judgement of the steward is specifically contrasted with that of the *ynad*: S.C. 2/219/8, m. 4 (1372).

[65] S.C. 2/219/9, m. 26.

THE INNS OF COURT AND LEGAL DOCTRINE

J. H. BAKER

'Law schools,' wrote Maitland, 'make tough law.'[1] He was referring immediately to the durability of the Lombardic law of Pavia, but only by way of introduction to his thesis that the inns of court had saved English law in the age of the Renaissance. Of our inns of court he went on to say that it would be 'difficult to conceive any scheme better suited to harden and toughen a traditional body of law than one which, while books were still uncommon, compelled every lawyer to take part in legal education and every distinguished lawyer to read public lectures'.[2] The exact import of Maitland's Rede Lecture has been itself the subject of academic disputations, but the present essay is not concerned with that problem so much as the seemingly incidental proposition or assumption that law schools have something to do with making law — tough or otherwise. Of the many themes floated in the Cambridge Senate-House on 5 June 1901, this one has been undeservedly neglected by almost all commentators except Professor Jenkins.[3] Yet it may well turn out to have been the most important theme of all. Historians of the common law have naturally tended to seek the threads of legal development in the *jurisprudence* of the year books and plea rolls. Dare we consider the possibility that the *doctrine* or learning of the law schools contributed at least as much to the development of the common law?

The inherent likelihood that law schools in some sense make law has obviously occurred to Maitland, and it has been discussed by Professor Jenkins.[4] That law schools influence the way lawyers think may perhaps be taken for granted. Men do not easily shed the habits of mind which result from attending law courses, especially if the courses are as intellectually demanding as we know the inns of court curriculum to have been in the fifteenth and sixteenth centuries. The certainties of taught law are hard to break down. The doubts and uncertainties of the classroom have a more subtle force, because they implant in the mind possibilities for questioning, innovation, sophistication, or evasion, which may bear fruit far in the future. Any law graduate knows as much, or at least comes to know it, as the years pass. But it is another matter to produce convincing evidence to demonstrate that the law of the fifteenth and sixteenth centuries was in some sense 'made' in the inns of court. It is particularly difficult if we make the assumption, as most lawyers do, that the law of England is limited to what the courts say it is. To make that assumption, however, is to beg the question whether the law might not also be what lawyers say or think it is.

The principal evidential obstacle is the convention of legal argument which made it unnecessary to cite doctrinal authorities in court. Although it is possible to marshal occasional instances where readings were cited in court,[5] they are not sufficiently numerous to prove without more evidence that the inns of court had any influence on the legal mind. Whereas continental law reports abound with references to the lectures and opinions of doctors, an English serjeant or judge put cases and referred to 'common learning'[6] without giving chapter and verse. Very often the hypothetical cases put in argument were those which had been discussed before, but it was not necessary to say so: everyone steeped in the common learning knew. And if a proposition or maxim derived from common learning was right, it was not because Fitzwilliam or Constable had said so, but because it was commonly felt to be right: because no one who had taken the course could think the contrary.

FIFTEENTH-CENTURY READINGS AND COMMON LEARNING

The evidence for the influence of the inns of court is not to be found in the year books, at any rate not for the present.[7] There is strong circumstantial evidence in the mere existence of numerous manuscript readings and moots. The inns of court generated a continuous stream of detailed and subtle doctrine for over two centuries, and given the rate at which manuscripts have been lost it is likely that the bulk of written learning was as great as that of the year books. Moreover, the recently discovered notebook of John Port,[8] if it is typical, shows that a late fifteenth-century law student made more notes in the hall of his inn than in Westminster Hall. It may reasonably be presumed that all this writing had some point to it.

Most of the readings and moots in the fifteenth century are taken up with various aspects of property law, and, so far as a modern observer is able to judge, they were fairly conservative. One may scour the pages almost in vain for discussion of such obvious novelties as uses or common recoveries. But in searching for more subtle changes the absence of citations again presents an evidential difficulty. Since the readers did not usually cite cases, and since the earlier readings are often undated, it cannot always be ascertained whether a proposition is based on a reported case or not. Even where a put case can be found both in the readings and in the year books, it is rarely clear whether it began life in academical exercise or forensic argument, and perhaps that distinction would have meant little to a fifteenth-century lawyer anyway. Undoubtedly, much of the lecture-material was paralleled in the year books, and no doubt much was also based on cases in the readers' own experience. The readers' usual technique was to list example upon example in illustration of the subject-matter. The more examples, and the more comprehensive the set of examples, the better. It does not seem to have mattered too much whether they were examples ever likely to be met with in the real world, though of course the law-teacher's most unlikely academic fantasies have a habit of coming true. The prime purpose seems to have been to exercise the mind, in showing how the principles worked in hypothetical situations, rather than to explore new doctrine, criticise old doctrine, or open up loopholes.

It may help to convey a sense of the fifteenth-century lecture course if we look at a particular topic in detail. Let us therefore examine the treatment of the varieties of entail, and of the forms of words used to create them, in the readings on the Statute of Westminster II, c. 1, *De donis conditionalibus*. The earliest readings — undated, but perhaps from the 1420s — adhere closely to the matters dealt with in the statute, and expatiate only on the law relating to frankmarriage and discontinuance.[9] With respect to forms of gift not expressly mentioned in the statute, they are content with a single instance: land may be given to a man and his heirs female.[10] This alone is telling. The possibility of tail female is mentioned by most of the readers thereafter, and by Littleton,[11] and is still found in the current books on real property; and yet it is extremely doubtful whether any such gift was ever made. The only restriction of sex in practice was to male heirs, and tail male was the only variety established by judicial pronouncement.[12] A strong case could have been made against tail female on the grounds that the exclusion of male heirs was against public policy, as then understood,[13] but so far as we know the point was never argued in court. The teacher's love of variety for its own sake seems to have given rise to an axiom which through repetition became unquestionable. That is one way in which law schools make law, though the example is not a very powerful one, since it had no practical repercussions.

Coke tells us that Littleton himself read on *De donis*, and this must have been in the 1440s. Littleton went further than the earliest readers and discussed the need for words of inheritance. A gift to A and the issue of his body, or to A and his seed, passed only a life estate; but a gift to A and the heirs of his flesh passed a fee tail.[14] The last case, at least, came from the year books.[15] An anonymous reading, perhaps contemporary with Littleton's, discussed the same or similar questions (including a gift to a man *et sanguini suo*) and added the cases where a gift in fee simple is cut down to a tail by the *habendum* or by a condition: to A and his heirs for ever *habendum* to him and the heirs of his body, or to A and his heirs for ever but, if A should die without heirs of his body, remainder to B.[16] These cases also occur in the reports.[17] The reader taught further that a gift in tail male excluded males claiming through females. He was doubtless relying on a reported case of 1431,[18] though the point was not decided in that case and the question became confused as a result of a 1450 case reported in Statham.[19] Littleton's *Tenures* stated the law in accordance with the majority in the 1431 case, and in the following century the other case was dismissed as misreported,[20] but the point was inexplicably dropped from the readings. A third reading from the 1440s occurs in a Gray's Inn sequence connected with the name 'Moyne'.[21] The reading on De donis discussed the flesh and blood cases, and the *habendum* case, but introduced some further subtleties: a gift to A and the heirs of the body of his son,[22] or to A and the heirs of the body of his father,[23] or to A and his mother or sister and the heirs of their bodies.[24] These were apparently treated as life estates with contingent remainders to the heirs, although that terminology was not used. The reader also considered the more straightforward contingent remainder: to A for life, remainder to the heir of the body of B. This he concluded was void if B outlived A, but good if B died first. He added, 'but some say, wrongly, that the remainder is void if B is alive at the time of the gift, unless it is granted to him by a specific name'. The validity of such a contingent remainder had been a moot case in Henry VI's time, but the reader's opinion reflected the learning of the year books.[25] Indeed, most of the additional material in this reading seems to be, once again, inspired by reported cases.

Our first surviving named reading on *De donis* is that given by Richard Welby in Gray's Inn at the end of the 1450s.[26] Welby made most of the points in the earlier readings,[27] but departed from them in upholding a gift to a man and his sister and the heirs of their bodies, on the grounds that a marriage with a sister was good until it was defeated. And he added a few more cases, such as a gift to man and a single woman and the heirs of their bodies,[28] which was a good tail if they later married, and a gift to two men and the heirs of their bodies,[29] which was incapable of being a tail. Yet again the cases were from the year books. Welby, however, added some variations which seem to be of his own devising: to a man and his heirs begotten on the heirs of a named woman, to a single woman and her heirs begotten on a named man, to A in tail remainder to B son and heir of C.[30]

In the later readings the examples began to depart more often from the case law. An anonymous reader from later in the century[31] considered a gift to A and his firstborn or to A *et sequelis suis de corpore* (which passed life estates only), or to A and his heir apparent (which passed a fee simple). Robert Constable, reading in Lincoln's Inn in 1489, considered the less realistic cases of gifts to a dean and chapter and the heirs of their bodies,[32] to a master and scholars and the heirs of their bodies and to a mayor and commonalty and the heirs of their bodies.[33] At the last known reading on *De donis*, by Alan Wood in the Middle Temple in 1548,[34] a number of highly academic possibilities were considered, including a gift to A and the Bishop of Westminster and the heirs of their bodies (which passed joint life-estates) or to A and his heirs *habendum* to A and his heirs of his body for his life (which, rather surprisingly, was held to pass the fee simple). Many of Wood's propositions were marked by a subsequent owner of the manuscript 'non est lex'. Here, perhaps, was the beginning of the trend deplored by Coke whereby readers' cases became 'long, obscure and intricate, full of new conceits, liker rather to riddles than lectures', with the result that readings lost their former authority.[35]

It appears from this series of readings, which we have no reason to think untypical, that the exposition of the land law was based chiefly on points which had arisen in actual cases, varying the cases now and then for the sake of comprehensiveness. For this reason, we cannot suppose that much new law was 'made' at such exercises. But developing new law is only one aspect of lawmaking. What the readers did achieve was the arrangement, consolidation and explanation of unwritten principles which are often glimpsed only fleetingly in the year books. They established a tradition as to what was received learning and what was dubious. The year books contain more undetermined arguments than decisions, much that is passed over in silence or abandoned, much of what Plowden termed the 'sudden opinion' voiced *ex tempore*. It must have been far harder to overturn a proposition which had been constantly laid down in the inns of court than a chance remark of a serjeant at the bar. Indeed, Littleton himself offered to 'prove' a proposition in the *Tenures* by saying that he had often heard it in the readings on Westminster II, c. 3.[36] It will be noted that the reference is not to a specific reader, but to a repeated assertion. The readings were not just individual opinions, but the collective and growing wisdom of the profession,[37] the 'common learning' to which we have referred. To be sure, the readers — and their learned audience — were always testing by disputation the borders of that common learning. It was part of their function to keep alive doubts and to raise queries. But the main function by far was to preserve and elaborate the common learning concerning real property. The debates reported in the year books, so often tortuous and obscured by the exigencies of pleading, presupposed a grasp of principles; and it was in the inns, rather than in Westminster Hall, that those principles were expounded and refined as a coherent body of law. It was in that sense more than any other that the law schools made tough law.

THE INNS AND NEW LEARNING, 1450-1550

In a few particular fields we can make a larger claim for the rôle of the inns of court in developing legal doctrine far beyond what may be found in the reports. The clearest example is that provided by the criminal law. Very few criminal cases were decided in Westminster Hall, and, since the cessation of eyres and of circuit reporting in the fourteenth century, only a relatively small number of criminal cases found their way into the fifteenth-century year books. As a result, the antique learning found in Bracton or Britton and in the abridgments under the title *Corone* remained somewhat stagnant: it provided a framework, but later concerns and newly-emerging distinctions were passed by. New questions must have arisen constantly in the country, and at Newgate, and the inns provided the obvious means for airing them. The benchers were mostly justices of the peace themselves, and the students — if present experience is any guide — would have found questions of criminal law more digestible than the finer points of property law. Surviving readings show that the appropriateness of criminal law for the inns of court curriculum was indeed fully appreciated in the fifteenth century. Of course, readers could not lecture on the common law as such, but there were several provisions in the old statutes which provided the pretext for doing so under the guise of statutory interpretation.[38]

So completely was this literature forgotten that until recently it was thought that criminal law had been a neglected science before the publication of textbooks such as Staundford's *Plees del coron* (1557). In fact, those books only mark a transition from aural to visual learning of the criminal law. Readings on the subject were rare after 1550, but they had already served their purpose. The dozens of extant readings on the law of felony, delivered between about 1450 and 1550, show that nearly all the law in the textbooks — and more besides — had been current for the best part of a century. For instance, in lecturing on homicide, the readers had discussed such novel questions as whether it was felony to cause the abortion of a foetus, to frighten someone to death, to refuse to open one's door to a man fleeing from a murderous assault, to make a suit of armour so negligently that its wearer was killed through a defect of design, to hire out a dangerous horse which threw the hirer to his death, to kill from afar with a machine or trained animal; whether the concept of misadventure extended to shooting and other sporting accidents; whether automatism and drunkenness were defences; and many other questions which did not reach the books till much later.[39] Some of the examples were suggested by real but unreported cases.[40] Others were from Bracton, which continued to possess some influence on the criminal law for want of later authority. It was *via* Bracton that an Inner Temple reader of Henry VIII's time commented on a case first debated by

Mela, Proculus and Ulpian in a remote ancient world.[41] Besides real cases and textbook cases, the readers now and then invented a mind-stretching remote contingency — such as that of the blind Italian who prayed benefit of clergy,[42] or the alleged *bigamus* who prayed clergy in an appeal brought by a bishop and his archbishop.[43] Even if some of these cases never occurred in practice, the readers' attempts to analyse and rationalize doctrine must have borne abundant fruit. It is not too great an exaggeration to say that the criminal law of the early Tudor period was reduced to a coherent and sophisticated science, and in that sense made, by the inns of court.

Perhaps no such confident claim can be made for any other branch of the substantive law, though to a lesser degree it may hold true of everything the readers touched. Contract and tort were rarely mentioned in readings, though it seems that current problems could be raised at moots: it was, after all, in Gray's Inn rather than the King's Bench that Sir John Fyneux made his decisive pronouncement that *assumpsit* would lie for nonfeasance.[44] Revenue law, and the associated subjects of uses and wills, came under close scrutiny with the passage of the Tudor legislation aimed at reviving feudalism. Under the Tudors it also became a common practice for serjeants-elect to lecture on Prerogativa Regis,[45] no doubt as a tribute to their royal patron, but perhaps also to prove their fitness for further advancement—though they did not always press the statute as far as some crown lawyers would have done.[46] Readings on uses began at the end of the fifteenth century, and an important contribution was made by Thomas Audley at the Inner Temple in 1526.[47] Audley argued that uses had been invented for fraudulent purposes and had replaced clear law with the passing whims of lord chancellors: a well-timed diatribe which cannot but have furthered his own claim to the great seal six years later, when drastic changes in the law of uses were under active consideration. In this area the inns of court were not introducing new ideas directly, but debating the interpretation of new measures. They sometimes performed this function ahead of the courts—sometimes, perhaps, too far ahead[48]—and it would be surprising if their attempts at explanation had no impact whatever on Westminster Hall. Were it otherwise, it would have been unnecessary for Audley to warn the readers publicly in the Star Chamber, on behalf of Henry VIII, 'truly and justly to interpret and expound his laws and statutes in the readings and moots'.[49] The warning was delivered in 1540, and the government's concern was that loopholes were being found in the Statute of Uses. Within months the crown acted more directly by promoting the Statute of Wills. The evasions had been found in private conference as much as in the lecture rooms, but the incident affords testimony of a different kind of lawmaking by professional opinion: of lawmaking born of exploration, experiment and critical comment.

OPINION IN THE INNS LOSES AUTHORITY, 1550-1642

During the hundred years before the Civil War, many new topics were made the subject of discussion, and a few classic readings — such as those by James Whitelocke on benefices (Middle Temple, 1619) and Robert Callis on sewers (Gray's Inn, 1622)[50] — circulated very widely in manuscript and remained standard works for many years to come. The moots also retained their vitality, not only in sharpening wits but also in transmitting unprinted learning both old and new.

For example, a collection of Jacobean inns of chancery moots in Cambridge University Library (MS. Kk. 6. 42) shows that even at that supposedly elementary level the students were told of earlier inns of court readings,[51] of cases depending in the courts,[52] and of other unpublished authorities of various kinds. At Clifford's Inn in the summer of 1620, Francis Ould — a barrister of only two years' standing in the Inner Temple — raised as one of the many points in his reading:[53]

> Whether issue born after forty-two weeks is a bastard? It seems it is. It was held accordingly in 18 Edw. II,[54] in the Tower rolls, because it was born *post tempus mulieribus constitutum*. In 14 Jac. in the Star Chamber[55] it was held by Lord Chancellor Egerton and Mountague C.J. of the King's Bench that if someone has issue but is castrated or perpetually frigid, the issue is a bastard. Hobart C.J. of the Common Pleas to the contrary, for it is a legal child though not a natural child. See 17 Jac. in Michaelmas term, Andrewe's case in the King's Bench,[56] to the contrary, that it is not a bastard in our case here.

On this point, then, three unpublished authorities had been cited. Perhaps they had in turn been noted by Ould in the King's Bench when the 1619 case was argued. It can hardly be doubted that by attending such exercises a student could still learn a great deal which he could not easily find elsewhere. That, however, is not quite the same as making law.

The exercises continued in full spate until 1642, when they were curtailed.[57] Despite attempts at revival in 1660 they never recovered their former importance. That might seem the most obvious reason for the cessation of the lawmaking rôle of the inns of court. But in truth the exercises could not have been allowed to disappear had not their functional value already been severely diminished. While it is not correct to suppose, as Holdsworth did,[58] that — through the disinclination of both teachers and taught — the exercises steadily declined in quality until they were mere formalities, it is true that their fifteenth-century role in the transmission of 'common erudition' had virtually ceased. The unwillingness of men to read, and the alleged abstruseness of those who did so, may have been factors in bringing about this change; but again they are far more likely to have been symptoms than causes. Three main reasons may be suggested for the changed state of affairs.

First, there was the inherent difficulty in the transmission of common learning arising from the existence of four separate houses. Perhaps in an earlier period there had been cross influences between the inns,[59] while in the inns of chancery the exercises always remained open to all-comers; but by the end of the fifteenth century the learning of each inn of court seems to have been handed on almost entirely within the inn. It was therefore possible for different traditions to arise, as in the apparent divergences between the Inner Temple and Gray's Inn as to whether a lessor could bring an assize against a tenant for years who held over,[60] or, who had the final authority in deciding whether a convict could read as a clerk.[61] Moreover, when tradition depended on word of mouth and unpublished notes, it was not always firm even within the same inn. Sir John Fyneux's famous statement about *assumpsit* in 1499 has seemed to legal historians a landmark in the history of the law of contract. But it had clearly been forgotten in Gray's Inn a mere seventeen years later.[62] Fitzherbert, who published the remark (which he had heard as a student), had the printing press on his side — and the advent of printing may be considered the second factor in the decline of the inns' authority.[63] The printed year books and abridgments reduced the need to learn by ear, and furnished the whole profession with learning which was more truly 'common' than lectures and lecture-notes. In the case of criminal law, we have seen how the availability of printed books simply put an end to readings on that subject. And it was surely the existence of printed books which drove some of the readers to forsake sound common learning and indulge in the flights of fancy for which Coke was to castigate them. But the effect of printing should not be exaggerated.[64] Even in the 1630s and 1640s, perhaps more than half of the available written learning of the common law was not in print, and a good law library still contained as many manuscripts as printed books.

The third and perhaps the chief reason for the decline of the inns as repositories and makers of law was the increasing authority of the judges in that respect. In the fifteenth century the judges had been most unwilling to decide points of law and clarify obscurities in the common learning. As umpires they did not want the rules to be made more complicated — and unresolved doubts had the salutary effect of inducing compromises. Individual judges had great authority, but it was not obviously greater or different in kind from that of serjeants or readers in court, nor was something a judge said in court of greater authority or different in kind from what he said when attending a reading in Gray's Inn. Legal notebooks of the early Tudor period combine both kinds of learning without distinguishing much between them.[65] The law, it seems, was not confined to pronouncements in court, but was what common lawyers in general believed it to be. This ceased to be true in the course of the sixteenth century. It is a fact that as late as 1573 we hear of an inn of court differing from the judges on an important point:

> Wray C. J. said it was clear that if a lease for years is made to two persons to the use of one of them, or to one person to the use of a stranger, this use is not executed by the statute. He said he had heard it to have been the opinion of the Middle Temple that it should be executed; but all the judges of the law in England are of opinion that it is not... [66]

Perhaps Plowden's oracular presence had given the Middle Temple undue confidence in their opinions, though it is not known whether he participated in this pronouncement. However, it must already have been a matter more of wonder than of concern that the benchers of an inn should hold a view differing from that of the courts. It was in any case contrary to the old idea of common learning for one inn to go off at a tangent: had all four inns differed from the courts, the problem would have been more significant. We may doubt also whether the Middle Temple persisted in its heresy once it was judicially denounced. The main point is that by 1573 the judges had the last word. To borrow again the convenient language of French law, *doctrine* had given way to *jurisprudence*. There is reason to think that something similar happened across the channel also, but that is another story.[67] The transition to judicial lawmaking on the continent has sometimes been referred to as 'the Reception (of Roman law)', because the new courts which gave legal reasons for their decisions were composed of doctors learned in Roman law. There had to be a body of learning in existence before the courts could receive and apply it. On the continent it was the body of Roman law, with the doctrinal literature which had grown around it. In England, as Maitland hinted, it was a more homespun product, the law of the inns of court.

---

[1] F. W. Maitland, *English Law and the Renaissance* (1901), 25.
[2] Ibid., 27-28.
[3] There is no mention of the inns of court in Sir Carleton Allen's thoughtful *Law in the Making* (7th edn., 1964), nor is their lawmaking function considered in J. P. Dawson, *Oracles of the Law* (1968). For works more directly concerned with Maitland's lecture, see D. Jenkins, ' "English Law and the Renaissance". Eighty Years On: in defence of Maitland' (1981) 2 *Journal of Legal History* 107.
[4] Op. cit. previous note, at 134-136.
[5] E.g., *Anon.* (1562) Dyer 219, *per* Jeffreys (William Dalison's reading, Gray's Inn, 1550

or before, on 32 Hen. VIII, c. 33); *Case of Mines* (1567) Plowd. 321, *per* Wray (Richard Hesketh's reading, Gray's Inn, temp. Hen. VIII, on the Carta de Foresta); *Sir Jervaise Clifton's Case* (1586) Godb. 93, pl. 103, *per* Coke (Thomas Frowyk's reading, Inner Temple, temp. Hen. VII, on Quo Warranto); *Butler* v. *Baker* (1591) 3 Co. Rep. 34v ('un auter case fuit cite hor dun reading'); *Hulme* v. *Godfrey* (1592) Cambridge Univ. Lib., MS Ii. 5.16, fo. 190, *per* Godfrey (John Denshill's reading, Lincoln's Inn, Lent 1530, on 4 Hen. VII, c. 24); *Anon. (c.* 1602) ibid., MS. Gg. 2. 31, fo. 464, *per* Egerton L.K. (Robert Norwich's reading, Lincoln's Inn, Lent 1521).

[6] See introduction to *The Reports of Sir John Spelman*, II (94 Selden Soc., 1978), at *161.* For earlier references, see Dawson, *Oracles of the Law*, 64 n. 55.

[7] It may be possible to collate passages in reports and readings more effectively when more readings have been edited and indexed. There are a number of explicit references to inn opinion in the Henry VII year books: see E. W. Ives, 89 LQR at p. 82; J. H. Baker, 94 Selden Soc. at *166-167.*

[8] H. E. Huntington library, San Marino, California, MS. HM 46980. The writer is editing the principal contents of this volume for the Selden Society. The bulk of it consists of Inner Temple notes from the 1490s.

[9] An example (from B.L., MS Lansdowne 465) is printed in S. E. Thorne ed., *Readings and Moots at the Inns of Court*, I (71 Selden Soc., 1952), pp. lxix-lxxiv; and another from MS Lansdowne 466), ibid., pp. cxxcii-cxxxiv. Closely similar are Cambridge Univ. Lib., MS Hh. 3.10, ff. 46-47; MS Ee 5. 19, ff. 65-69; Gray's Inn, MS 25, fo. 202; Lincoln's Inn, MS Misc. 486 (11); Bodleian Lib., MS Rawlinson C. 294, ff. 82-90.

[10] Thorne, *Readings and Moots*, at lxix, line 9.

[11] *Tenures*, s. 22. See also YB Mich. 11 Hen. VI, fo. 13, pl. 28, *per* Cottesmore J.

[12] *Helton v. Brampton* (1344) CP 40/340, m. 368; 18 Lib. Ass. 5; YB Mich. 18 Edw. III, fo. 45, pl. 52; YB 18 & 19 Edw. III (RS) 197: A. K. R. Kiralfy, *A Source Book of English Law* (1957) 83 (which shows that no judgment was entered); *Carbonel's Case* (1359) Fitz. Abr., *Taile*, pl. 5. It is possible that settlors may occasionally have limited a remainder in tail female after a gift in tail male, thinking that this would let in the rest of the issue: but this would have been an error, because such a settlement would have excluded males claiming through females and females claiming through males.

[13] See the heads of such an argument in *Sharington v. Strotton* (1565) Plowd. 298, at fo. 305, *per* Plowden (arguing that a gift in tail male was good consideration).

[14] Cited in Co. Litt. 20b.

[15] 37 Lib. Ass. 15: *si heredem de carne habuit.*

[16] Harvard Law School, MS 13, p. 145.

[17] 35 Lib. Ass. 14; YB Hil. 5 Hen. V, fo. 6, pl. 13; Trin. 19 Hen. VI, fo. 74, pl. 2.

[18] *Farington v. Darel*, YB Trin. 9 Hen. VI, fo. 24, pl. 19 (by all except Martin J.); same case, Mich. 11 Hen. VI, fo. 13 pl. 28, *per* Cottesmore J. The record (CP 40/678 m.312) shows that judgment was never entered on the demurrer. For translations of all these texts, see Kiralfy, *Source Book* (op. cit. n.12, *supra*), 100.

[19] Trin. 28 Hen. VI, Stath. Abr., *Devise, pl.* [12], where it is said to have been decided by all the judges in the Exchequer Chamber that in the case of a devise in tail male, the son of a daughter could claim: but otherwise of a gift in tail male. This was copied in Fitz. Abr., *Devise*, pl. 18; but is not in the printed year book.

[20] Littleton, *Tenures*, s. 24; Plowd. at fo. 414v, *per* Dyer C.J.; Co. Litt. 25.

[21] Cambridge Univ. Lib., MS Ii. 5. 43, ff. 165 (beginning), 154. For the date, see Thorne, *Readings and Moots*, at pp. xxxii, lv. Moyne's name appears after c. 25, so the reading on c. 1 was probably by another.

[22] This was a good tail only if the son predeceased A: if the son was still alive at A's death the land reverted to the donor.

[23] This was a good tail only if the father predeceased A. Cf. *Mandeville's Case* (1324-28) Fitz. Abr., *Taile*, pl. 7, 23; Littleton, *Tenures*, s. 30.

[24] This was void, because even by dispensation a man could not marry his mother. As to brother and sister, cf. Mich. 44 Edw. III, Fitz. Abr., *Taile*, pl. 13; Mich. 17 Edw. III, fo. 51, pl. 24 (treated as separate tails); Welby's reading, cited below (held valid, 1450s); 71 Selden Soc. 174 (held valid by Constable, 1489).

[25] YB Trin. 11 Hen. IV, fo. 74, pl. 14; *Farington v. Darel* (1431-32) Trin. 9 Hen. VI, fo. 23, pl. 19; Mich. 11 Hen. VI, fo. 12, pl. 28. The rule was confirmed in Pas. 32 Hen. VI, Stath. Abr., *Doune*, pl. [7]. It was repeated at Constable's reading (1489): 71 Selden Soc. 179. And at Brudenell's (1941): B.L., MS Lansdowne 87, ff. 55, 57v (remainder to right heirs of X).

[26] Cambridge Univ. Lib., MS Hh. 2. 6, ff. 152-156v. For the date, see Thorne, *Readings and Moots*. at pp. xxiii-xxiv, xxxiii.

[27] He confirmed the validity of a gift to A in tail, remainder to the heirs of B in tail, where B died before A; but he did not say whether the remainder would be good if B survived A but died before A's issue were extinct.

[28] Cf. Hil. 11 Edw. III, Fitz. Abr., *Formedon*, pl. 30.

[29] Cf. 8 Lib. Ass. 33.

[30] Each of these was good. In the last example, the words 'son and heir of C' did not effect an inheritance because the person of B was sufficiently defined: in later language, the words operated only as *designatio personae*.

[31] Cambridge Univ. Lib., MS Hh. 3. 14, ff. 16-26.

[32] Cf. Harvard Law School, MS 125, no. 147: Gray's Inn moot, *c*. 1530 (gift to dean and chapter and the heirs of the body of the dean).

[33] 71 Selden Soc. 171-172. He repeated most of the previous learning as well: ibid., pp. 171-180.

[34] Cambridge Univ. Lib., MS Gg. 5. 9, ff. 19-48.

[35] Co. Litt. 280b.

[36] Littleton, *Tenures*, s. 481: 'de prover que le graund assise doit passer pur le demandant en le cas avauntdit, jeo aye oye sovent la lecture de lestatute de Westminster le second, que commence *In casu quo vir...*' Coke commented (Co. Litt. 280b): 'By the authority of Littleton, ancient readings may be cited for proof of the law; but new readings have not that honour, for that they are so obscure and dark'.

[37] For what Professor Thorne has called the 'inherited core' of learning, see his *Readings and Moots*, at lx-lxviii.

[38] For a bibliography of readings on criminal law, *c*. 1450-1550, see 94 Selden Soc. at *347-350*.

[39] Ibid. *304-316*.

[40] E.g., the abortion case: see 94 Selden Soc. at *306*.

[41] Francis Mountford's reading, Brit. Lib., MS Hargrave 87, fo. 177 — from Bracton fo. 136b — from D. 9, 2, 11. See 94 Selden Soc. at *33* n. 11.

[42] Case put at Thomas Kebell's reading, 94 Selden Soc. at p. *330* n. 8. The problem was: (a) he could not perform the reading test, and (b) a modern form of Latin was his mother tongue. The answer seems to have been that he would have to speak good academic Latin to pass.

[43] Another Inner Temple case, perhaps from Richard Littleton's reading (1493): Port's notebook, Huntington Library, MS. HM 46980, fo. 165v. In the case of the archbishop of Canterbury, the answer was that the certifying would have to be done by the prior of

Christchurch as guardian of the spiritualities: ibid.

[44] Fitz. Abr., *Action sur le case*, pl. 45; 94 Selden Soc. *269-270.*

[45] E.g. Thomas Frowyk (Inner Temple, 1495), Robert Constable (Lincoln's Inn, 1495) and John Spelman (Gray's Inn, 1521). See, generally, S. E. Thorne, *Prerogativa Regis* (1949).

[46] Ibid.: 94 Selden Soc. at *194.*

[47] See 94 Selden Soc. *198-199.*

[48] E.g., John Boise's remarks on the Statute of Uses in 1536; 94 Selden Soc. at *202* n. 4.

[49] Register of the Star Chamber, 23 Feb. 1540, as printed in 94 Selden Soc. at 351.

[50] See J. H. Baker, *English Legal Manuscripts*, I (1975), 18, 32.

[51] E.g., fo. 75v (Robert Hitcham, Gray's Inn, 1605); fo. 78 (John Jackson, Inner Temple, 1606); ff. 84, 226v (Edward Bromley, Inner Temple, 1606); fo. 165 (James Dyer, Middle Temple, 1552).

[52] E.g., fo. 162v ('Sir George Sherlys case ore depending in Communi Banco', 1620).

[53] Cambridge Univ. Lib., MS Kk. 6. 42, fo. 185.

[54] Cited as Trin. 18 Edw. I, rot. 13, in Cro. Car. 541; 1 Rolle Abr. 356, line 43. As Trin. 18 Edw. I, rot. 61, in Co. Litt. 123v. As 18 Ric. II in Palm. 10.

[55] *Done and Edgerton v. Hintons and Starkey* (1617) 1 Rolle Abr. 358, line 1. Not printed till 1668.

[56] *Alsop v. Bowtrell* (1619) Cro. Jac. 541; Godb. 281, pl. 40; sub nom. *Alsop v. Stacy*, Palm. 9; concerning Edward Andrews (d. 1610). None of these reports was printed until the 1650s.

[57] Readings ceased until 1660, but moots continued to some extent.

[58] *History of English Law*, VI, 481-486; refuted in W. R. Prest, *The Inns of Court 1590-1640* (1972), 124 et seq.

[59] Professor Thorne detected similarities between the earliest readings from different inns.

[60] 71 Selden Soc. 14: Henry Spelman (Gray's Inn) said he could not, Morgan Kydwelly (Inner Temple) said he could.

[61] 94 Selden Soc. *328.*

[62] Ibid., *272.*

[63] Holdsworth, *History of English Law*, VI, 482-483, considered it the main reason for the disinclination to read and the decay of readings. Cf. Maitland's 'while books were still uncommon', quoted above.

[64] See Prest, *Inns of Court*, at 132-133.

[65] See 94 Selden Soc. *123-124, 171, 172*; to which must now be added Huntington Library, MS HM 46980 (John Port's notebook, which came to light in 1978).

[66] Reports attributed to Richard Harpur, Cambridge Univ. Lib., MS Ll. 3. 8, fo. 186v; Lincoln's Inn, MS Maynard 87, fo. 183 (translated). It is possible that the Middle Temple opinion had been expressed before the judges had considered the question. The point would have been for the Chancery to decide, and that is where Wray C.J. made his remark.

[67] See 'English Law and the Renaissance' (1985) *Cambridge Law Journal* 46.

Y LLYSOEDD, YR AWDURDODAU A'R GYMRAEG:
Y DDEDDF UNO A DEDDF YR IAITH GYMRAEG
Ei Anrhydedd y Barnwr Watkin Powell

Y mae ymron deunaw mlynedd bellach wedi mynd heibio er pan basiwyd Deddf yr Iaith Gymraeg yn 1967. Cafodd fesur o groeso ond cafodd hefyd ei beirniadu am syrthio'n fyr o'r disgwyliadau a godwyd gan brif argymhelliad Pwyllgor Syr David Hughes Parry ar Statws Gyfreithiol yr Iaith Gymraeg a gyhoeddwyd ddwy flynedd ynghynt.[1] Yr argymhelliad oedd y dylai'r Gymraeg fwynhau statws gydradd â'r Saesneg mewn cyfraith a gweinyddiaeth gyhoeddus. Y fformiwla i gyrraedd y nod oedd datganiad statudol y câi unrhyw weithred neu ysgrifen neu unrhyw beth a wneid yn Gymraeg ddilysrwydd cyfartal â phetai wedi ei wneud yn Saesneg.[2]

Y mae'r Ddeddf ei hun yn hynod o fyr. Pum adran yn unig sydd iddi. Y mae cynnwys y rheini ar yr olwg gyntaf yn ddigon diamwys. Ond y mae iddi Raglith neu ragarweiniad. Bu adeg pryd y gwneid defnydd aml o'r arfer hon. Sonia Coke[3] am raglith fel 'allwedd' i wneud statud yn ddealladwy, ond newidiodd y ffasiwn, ac mor bell yn ôl â 1911 sylwodd y Prif Ustus, yr Arglwydd Alverstone, gyda gofid, fod yr arfer wedi peidio â bod:

> I ... regret that the practice of inserting preambles in Acts of Parliament has been discontinued as they were often of great assistance to the Courts in construing the Acts.[4]

Bellach ni cheir Rhaglith fel arfer ond mewn mesurau sydd yn ymwneud â hawliau, dyletswyddau neu gysylltiadau rhyngwladol.

Y mae Deddf yr Iaith Gymraeg felly yn anghyffredin ymhlith deddfau seneddol y ganrif hon. Yr unig gasgliad y gellir dod iddo yn hyn o beth yw i'r Senedd fynd allan o'i ffordd, o fwriad, i atgyfodi hen arfer. O ganlyniad, y mae i eiriad y Rhaglith hon arwyddocâd arbennig.

Y mae'n datgan priodoldeb tri pheth:

> ... it is proper that the Welsh language should be freely used by those who so desire in the hearing of legal proceedings in Wales ..., that further provision should be made for the use of that language, with the like effect as English in the conduct of other official or public business there; and that Wales should be distinguished from England in the interpretation of future Acts of Parliament.

Wedi'r Rhaglith, daw adrannau'r Ddeddf ei hun. O'u talfyrru y mae pum adran y Ddeddf yn darparu'r canlynol:

Y mae'r adran gyntaf yn rhoi hawl i'r partïon, y tystion neu 'unrhyw berson arall sydd yn dymuno gwneud hynny' ddefnyddio'r Gymraeg ar lafar yng ngweithrediadau'r llysoedd yng Nghymru, yn amodol ar roi rhybudd o fwriad i wneud hynny ymlaen llaw ym mhob llys ar wahân i lysoedd yr ynadon: mae'n ofynnol i'r llys wneud y darpariaethau angenrheidiol ar gyfer cyfieithu.

Rhydd yr ail a'r drydedd adran yr hawl i'r Gweinidog priodol, os myn (y gair goddefol *may* a ddefnyddir), awdurdodi cyfieithiad Cymraeg o unrhyw ffurf ar ddogfen neu eiriau a fynnir neu a ganiateir gan y deddfau a ddaw i rym ar ôl Gorffennaf 27, 1967. Nid yw'n ofynnol iddo wneud hynny.

Y mae'r bedwaredd adran yn dileu gofynion y rhan honno o adran 3 yn Neddf Cymru a Berwick 1746 a fynnai fod y term 'Lloegr' yn cynnwys Cymru. Er 1967 rhaid i bob Deddf Gwlad sy'n ymwneud â Chymru gyfeirio'n benodol ati.

Diffiniadau sydd yn y bumed adran.

Er dyfarniad y Prif Farnwr Pollock yn achos *Salkeld v. Johnson* yn 1848[5] ystyrir y Rhaglith yn rhan o'r statud ei hun; ond nid yw hyn yn golygu fod yr hyn a ddatgenir yn y Rhaglith yn creu hawliau na dyletswyddau. Swyddogaeth sylfaenol rhaglith yw esbonio yr hyn a all fod yn amwys yn adrannau'r statud. Os bydd amwysedd, gall y rhaglith gyfyngu neu ehangu ar ystyr geiriau adrannau'r statud er mwyn rhoi grym i amcan a phwrpas y ddeddf.

Er nad oes ar yr wyneb amwysedd yn adrannau Deddf yr Iaith, cyfyd dau gwestiwn pwysig. Y mae a wnelo'r cyntaf â'r hawl i ddefnyddio'r Gymraeg yn y llysoedd. Y mae a wnelo'r llall ag ystyr ac effaith datganiad y Rhaglith am y priodoldeb o ddarparu ymhellach gogyfer â defnyddio'r Gymraeg i'r un perwyl â'r Saesneg wrth i awdurdodau cyhoeddus eraill (hynny yw, awdurdodau heblaw'r llysoedd) weinyddu yng Nghymru.

Ai goddefol yn unig yw'r geiriau yn adran gyntaf y ddeddf: 'In any legal proceedings in Wales... the Welsh language may be spoken by any... person who desires to use it', neu a oes oblygiadau sydd yn gosod ar y llysoedd ddyletswyddau mwy cadarnhaol ac ehangach na darparu cyfieithwyr yn wyneb geiriau datganiadol y Rhaglith '... it is proper that the Welsh language should be *freely* used by those who desire in the hearing of legal proceedings in Wales...'? Hynny yw, a oes i'r gair *freely* arwyddocâd arbennig wrth ddehongli'r Ddeddf?

Yn ail, ai hyd a lled y datganiad yn y Rhaglith am briodoldeb gwneud darpariaeth bellach ar gyfer defnyddio'r Gymraeg mewn busnes swyddogol a chyhoeddus arall yw'r hyn a geir yn ail a thrydedd adran y Ddeddf, sef rhoi disgresiwn i weinidogion y Goron i ddarparu ffurfiau Cymraeg a fersiynau Cymraeg o eiriau a ffurflenni statudol Saesneg sydd yn ofynnol eu defnyddio yn ôl deddf gwlad? Neu a oes iddo oblygiadau cyfreithiol er nad ydyw'n creu hawliau na dyletswyddau? Os felly, a oes iddo werth neu arwyddocâd ymarferol?

Beth bynnag yw'r feirniadaeth ar y Ddeddf hon, y mae iddi arwyddocâd arbennig yn hanes agwedd Senedd Westminster at le'r iaith Gymraeg mewn gweithgareddau a gweithrediadau cyhoeddus yng Nghymru, ac yn sicr, ym mherthynas ymarferol y llysoedd â'r gyfraith a'r iaith. I gymryd un enghraifft yn unig: wedi i'r Ddeddf ddod i rym, prin y byddai'n agored i unrhyw farnwr honni, fel yr honnodd yr Ustus Widgery brin naw mis cyn hynny,[6] nad oedd gan y sawl a ddefnyddiai'r Gymraeg yng Nghymru fwy o hawl i wneud hynny nag a oedd gan Bwyliad i ddefnyddio'r Bwyleg yn yr Old Bailey yn Llundain. Gyda'r Ddeddf, daeth i ben gyfnod yr hirlwm hir yn hanes yr iaith pan alltudiwyd hi o lysoedd ac o fywyd cyhoeddus y wlad yn gyffredinol. Dau brif amcan Deddf yr Iaith Gymraeg 1967 yw symud y llyffetheiriau gormesol ar ddefnyddio'r Gymraeg yn y llysoedd, a rhwyddhau'r ffordd i'w defnyddio yr un mor ddilys â'r Saesneg wrth weinyddu busnes swyddogol a chyhoeddus. Deddf i ddiwygio sefyllfa a ystyrid yn anfoddhaol gan y Senedd ydyw.

Fel yn achos pob deddf sydd yn honni diwygio, y cwestiwn sylfaenol a ofynnir wrth ei dehongli a'i gweithredu yw: beth yw'r camwri neu'r diffygion y mae'r Ddeddf yn anelu at eu cywiro? Y wireb gyfreithiol am y broses hon yw: 'Ex antecedentibus et procedentibus fiat interpretatio', sef o'i throsi: 'Trwy ystyried y datblygiadau a ragflaenodd ddeddf, y mae ei dehongli'. Dim ond wrth ystyried yr hyn a ragflaenodd Ddeddf yr Iaith felly y gellir iawn fesur i ba raddau y chwyldrowyd y sefyllfa ganddi. Rhaid edrych ar y naill law ar gymalau iaith Deddf 27 Harri VIII pennod 26, Deddf Uno 1536 fel y'i gelwir yn gyffredin, a'r modd y'i gweinyddwyd o 1536 hyd at 1942 ac ar Ddeddf Llysoedd Cymru 1942: ar y llaw arall rhaid ystyried achos tra phwysig a benderfynwyd yn Llys Adrannol Etholiadol Mainc y Frenhines ryw bum mlynedd cyn Deddf yr Iaith, sef achos *Evans v. Thomas.*[7]

Y mae o leiaf ddau beth yn gyffredin i'r Ddeddf Uno ac i Ddeddf yr Iaith. Y mae'r naill fel y llall yn ymwneud â statws yr iaith Gymraeg ac â statws Cymru yn ei pherthynas â Lloegr. Y mae i'r ddwy raglith. Bydd y traethawd hwn yn gyfyngedig i'r iaith a'i statws.

Ymysg materion eraill, datganai'r Rhaglith i'r Ddeddf Uno ffaith gwbl gywir am Gymru benbaladr yn y bymthegfed ganrif (ar wahân i dde Sir Benfro, darn bach o dde-orllewin Caerfyrddin a de-orllewin Gŵyr), sef bod yr iaith a ddefnyddid o ddydd i ddydd

Nothing like ne consonaunt to the natural mother tongue used within this Realme,

sef Lloegr. Âi'r Rhaglith yn ei blaen i ddatgan mai bwriad y Ddeddf oedd:

utterly to extirpe alle and singular the sinister customes

a'i gwahaniaethai oddi wrth Loegr.

Dadleuwyd gan rai mai anelu at gyfraith Cymru, Cyfraith Hywel, a wnâi geiriau chwyrn y Ddeddf, yn hytrach nag at yr iaith Gymraeg. Y gwir yw fod y ddwy dan yr ordd; Cyfraith Hywel, a oroesodd dros rannau helaeth o Gymru am dros chwe chanrif ac a ddileïd yn awr, a'r iaith, a fu'n iaith yr holl wlad am yn agos at un ganrif ar ddeg ac a ddiraddid ac a esgymunid o fywyd cyhoeddus y wlad yn awr. [9] Oherwydd, nid gwneud Saesneg yn unig iaith swyddogol y llysoedd a'u cofnodion a wnâi y Ddeddf, ond gwahardd defnyddio'r Gymraeg gan swyddogion y llysoedd wrth gyflawni eu dyletswyddau, a'r gwaharddiad hwn, yn y pen draw, oedd yr ergyd drymaf a mwyaf parhaol ei heffaith. [9]

Penodwyd Ynadon Heddwch am y tro cyntaf yng Nghymru yn 1536. [10] Fel swyddogion llys fe'u gwaherddid rhag defnyddio'r Gymraeg yn yr achosion a ddeuai ger eu bron. A chan fod dyletswyddau ynadon y pryd hwnnw ac, yn wir, tan ddiwedd y bedwaredd ganrif ar bymtheg, y tu allan i'r bwrdeistrefi, yn ymestyn i'r hyn a ystyriwn ni heddiw yn gyfrifoldeb llywodraeth leol, effaith y gwaharddiad oedd alltudio'r Gymrag o fywyd cyhoeddus.

Nid oedd Deddf 1536 yn rhwystro'r sawl na allai siarad Saesneg rhag defnyddio'r Gymraeg yn y llysoedd nac yn eu hymwneud â swyddogion y llys a'r llywodraeth. Byddai hynny yn amhosibl yng Nghymru Oes y Tuduriaid heb amddifadu trwch y boblogaeth i bob diben o'u holl hawliau. Ni rwystrai chwaith y sawl a oedd mewn swydd rhag siarad Cymraeg ar ei aelwyd ac yn ei ymwneud personol ag eraill y tu allan i'r llys. Y mae digon o dystiolaeth o bob rhan o Gymru fod rhai o siryfion ac ynadon y siroedd Cymreig ymhlith noddwyr y beirdd hyd at ganol yr ail ganrif ar bymtheg a hyd yn oed wedi hynny. [11]

Serch hynny, ni adawai'r gyfraith na'i gweinyddwyr le i neb gredu fod y Gymraeg o unrhyw fantais i'r rheini a oedd â'u bryd ar feddu awdurdod, statws a grym economaidd. Âi'r tri pheth law yn llaw, ac ni bu erioed genhedlaeth o Gymry mwy cignoeth awchus am allu, dyrchafiad a chyfoeth na theuluoedd yr uchelwyr yng nghyfnod y Tuduriaid. Fe wyddai'r rhain yn well na neb nad oedd gan y Cymro uniaith Gymraeg gysgod o obaith am ddyrchafiad na safle. Pris dyrchafiad oedd ymwadu â'r iaith Gymraeg mewn bywyd cyhoeddus.

Ymhen amser, ac fe gymerodd bedair canrif i hynny ddigwydd, dysgodd y Cymro uniaith sut i drefnu sefydliad iddo'i hun wedi ei ganoli ar y capel ymneilltuol, lle nad oedd diffyg Saesneg yn rhwystr i ddyrchafiad a rhyw fesur o ddylanwad yn y gymdeithas, yn enwedig dylanwad moesol. Ond o ran y gyfraith a sefydliadau cyhoeddus, parhaodd y rhwystrau ar ffordd y Gymraeg a'r cyfyngiadau ar gyfle'r Cymro uniaith Gymraeg i ddyrchafiad, bron yn ddigyfnewid, hyd at ein dyddiau ni.

Prin y gellir canmol ansawdd y cyfiawnder, os cyfiawnder hefyd, a weinyddid dan y drefn newydd a grewyd gan y 'Deddfau Uno' rhwng 1536 a 1542.

O'r dechrau 'roedd gan y Sesiwn Chwarter awdurdod eang iawn i ddelio â throseddau. Yn ogystal yr oedd gan y llys awdurdod i oruchwylio llywodraeth leol ac i wneud penderfyniadau ynglŷn â materion llywodraeth leol, swyddogaeth y bu crebachu cynyddol arni gyda thwf Byrddau Lleol a dyfodiad y Cynghorau Sir yn 1888[12] a'r Cynghorau Dosbarth yn 1894.[13] Yn y Sesiwn Chwarter, trwy gyfrwng yr iaith newydd, y teyrnasai'r ysweiniaid o Gymry, yn rhinwedd eu swydd fel Ynadon Heddwch. Y mae hanes yr ymgiprys am swyddi rhwng teuluoedd yr uchelwyr a'r twyll a'r dichell a ddefnyddid i sicrhau rheithgorau ufudd ac i osgoi canlyniadau'r ddeddf pe digwyddai i aelod o'r teulu droseddu, wedi ei groniclo'n bur fanwl erbyn hyn.[14] Ond o leiaf, mae'n fwy na thebyg y deallai'r ynadon cynnar hyn ddigon o Gymraeg i wybod beth a ddywedid gan dyst uniaith Gymraeg, pa un bynnag a ddeallai yntau eu Saesneg hwy ai peidio.

Ond yn Llys y Sesiwn Fawr,[15] lle y gwrandewid ar yr achosion yn ymwneud â throseddau mwy difrifol yn ogystal ag achosion sifil y gyfraith gyffredin Seisnig a siawnsri, yr oedd y sefyllfa yn bur wahanol. Yno, bargyfreithwyr o Saeson oedd y barnwyr. Rhannent eu hamser rhwng bargyfreithia yn Llundain ac eistedd fel ustusiaid Uchel Lys yng Nghymru. Cyflawnent yr un gorchwylion yng Nghymru â barnwyr llawn-amser Llysoedd Mainc y Brenin, y Pleon Cyffredin, y Trysorlys a'r Siawnsri yn Llundain.

Bu Llys y Sesiwn Fawr mewn bodolaeth am 288 o flynyddoedd, o 1542 tan 1830. Yn ystod y cyfnod hwn penodwyd cyfanswm o 217 o farnwyr.[16] O'r rhain, dim ond deg ar hugain oedd yn enedigol o Gymru, ac mae'n amheus a allai mwy na deg o'r rheini na deall na siarad Cymraeg. Saeson oedd y gweddill, llawer ohonynt yn feibion i deuluoedd bonedd y Gororau. Y mae'n arwyddocaol i'r Llys fod mewn bodolaeth am dros dri chwarter canrif cyn i unrhyw un a aned yng Nghymru gael ei benodi'n farnwr; John Jeffreys, mab Sieffre ap Huw o Actwn ger Wrecsam (a thaid yr enwog George, y 'dienyddiwr'), oedd hwnnw. Gwnaed ef yn Ail Ustus Cylchdaith

Môn (a gynhwysai Siroedd Môn, Caernarfon a Meirionnydd) yn 1617. Yn yr un flwyddyn, penodwyd Cymro arall yn Ail Ustus Cylchdaith Brycheiniog (a gynhwysai Siroedd Brycheiniog, Maesyfed a Morgannwg), Andrew Powell, mab Siôn ap Dafydd ap Hywel o'r Trostre, Gwent. Mae'n fwy na thebyg yn yr oes honno, y medrai Jeffreys a Powell ryw gymaint o Gymraeg. Y tro cyntaf i Gylchdaith Caer (a gynhwysai Siroedd Dinbych, Fflint a Threfaldwyn ynghyd â Sir Freiniol Caer) gael Cymro'n farnwr oedd 1622 pan benodwyd Marmaduke Lloyd, aelod o deulu Llwydiaid Maesyfelin, Llanbedr Pont Steffan, yn Ail Ustus. Mae'n anodd meddwl na fyddai ef yn gwbl hyddysg yn y Gymraeg. Nid tan 1642, gan mlynedd union wedi sefydlu Llys y Sesiwn Fawr, y gwnaed Cymro yn ustus, Ail Ustus o ran hynny, ar Gylchdaith Caerfyrddin, a gynhwysai dair sir y de-orllewin. David Jenkins, Castell Hensol, yn nyffryn Elái, Morgannwg, oedd hwnnw. Nid oes amheuaeth nad oedd ef yn medru'r Gymraeg.

Ar wahân i'r blynyddoedd rhwng 1617 a 1642, a diwedd y ganrif honno rhwng 1680 a 1695, pan benodwyd nifer o Gymry, prin iawn yw nifer ustusiaid y Sesiwn Fawr a aned yng Nghymru — dim ond wyth — er bod nifer bychan ychwanegol o dras Gymreig.

Nid annhebyg yw patrwm y penodiadau ar y pedair Cylchdaith i swydd weinyddol y Protonotari a Chlerc y Goron: ni chafodd brodor o Gymru swydd Protonotari Cylchdaith Caerfyrddin tan 1783, ddwy ganrif a hanner ar ôl sefydlu'r Sesiwn Fawr. Un o'r enw Henry Mathias, brodor o Hwlffordd, ydoedd hwnnw.

Er mai amrywiol eu doniau oedd barnwyr Llys y Sesiwn Fawr, 'roedd yn eu plith nifer o wŷr disglair neu ddylanwadol, neu a gyfunai'r ddeubeth, a barnu wrth eu dyrchafiad, ymhen blynyddoedd, i'r llysoedd brenhinol yn Llundain neu Ddulyn. Dyrchafwyd tri yn Arglwydd Ganghellor Iwerddon, ac un, George Jeffreys o anhyfryd goffadwriaeth, yn Arglwydd Ganghellor Lloegr. Dewiswyd deg yn Arglwydd-Brif-Ustusiaid Llysoedd Mainc y Brenin neu'r Pleon Gyffredin a chwech yn Brif Farwniaid Llys y Trysorlys, heb sôn am gynifer â phedwar ar bymtheg arall a ddaeth yn Farnwyr Uchel Lys Lloegr.

Ni waeth pa mor dda oedd safon gyffredinol barnwyr Llys y Sesiwn Fawr, yr oedd naw deg pump y cant ohonynt yn gwbl amddifad o wybodaeth o'r Gymraeg. Mewn maes mor bwysig â chyfraith, lle bo penderfyniadau, dyfarniadau a hawliau dynion yn dibynnu ar ddealltwriaeth y barnwr o'r hyn a leferir, yn anad dim arall, y mae'n anodd dirnad sut yn y byd y gallai'r gwŷr hyn, pa mor ddisglair a chytbwys bynnag eu barn ydoedd llawer ohonynt, weinyddu cyfiawnder, nac yn wir ddychmygu eu bod yn addas i weinyddu cyfiawnder, mewn cymdeithas uniaith Gymraeg na ddeallai beth a ddywedid. Yr oedd yno gyfieithu ond prin bod hynny o gyfieithu a gaed yn fedrus, a dweud y lleiaf. Mae'n debyg na ddaeth erioed i feddwl y mwyafrif o farnwyr Llys y Sesiwn Fawr fod y llysoedd a lywyddent yn offerynnau anghyfiawnder. Ond y gwir yw mai system a sylfaenwyd ar orthrwm ac anghyfiawnder oedd y system gyfreithiol a sefydlwyd rhwng 1536 a 1542.

Mewn llythyr a ysgrifennwyd tua phymtheng mlynedd ar hugain wedi sefydlu Llys y Sesiwn Fawr at Syr Francis Walsingham, un o Ysgrifenyddion Gwladol Elisabeth I, gan William Gerard, yntau'n Sais, yn Ail Ustus Cylchdaith Brycheiniog, aelod (ac is-lywydd) o Lys Cyngor Cymru a'r Gororau ac ar fin cael ei ddewis yn Arglwydd Ganghellor Iwerddon, anogir apwyntio barnwr ychwanegol i'r Ustus Fetiplace ar Gylchdaith Caerfyrddin.

> Note that it were verie convenienté that one of the Justices of assizes did understand the Welche tong, for nowe the Justice of Assize must use som interpretor? And therefore many times the Evidence is tolde accordynge to the mind of the interpretor whereby the Evidence is expounded contrarie to that which is said by the Examynate and so the Judge gyveth a wronge charge.[17]

Rhaid bod y llythyr, sydd heb ddyddiad, wedi ei ysgrifennu rywbryd rhwng penodi'r Ustus Fetiplace yn Awst 1574 a Gorffennaf 1577 pan fu farw. Ni dderbyniwyd cyngor yr Ustus Gerard, er mor wybodus a dylanwadol ydoedd, a phan aethpwyd ati i ddewis olynydd i'r Ustus Fetiplace, ar ôl ei farwolaeth yn 1577, un o Swydd Efrog, John Puckering, a ddewiswyd.[18]

Parheid i benodi Saeson uniaith yn farnwyr yng Nghymru am dros dri chwarter canrif ar ôl pasio'r Ddeddf Uno, ac y mae hyn, yn arbennig yn wyneb y math o argymhellion a wnaeth Gerard, yn awgrymu'n gryf mai polisi cwbl fwriadol oedd hwn ar ran y llywodraeth ganol, polisi a'i wreiddiau'n ddwfn yn y Ddeddf Uno ei hun.[19] Cadarnheir hyn gan y gwrthgyferbyniad amlwg rhwng sefyllfa swyddogol anghyflawn yr iaith Saesneg yn Lloegr a'i sefyllfa swyddogol cyflawn a mwy breiniol yn y Gymru uniaith Gymraeg. Tra gorseddid Saesneg fel unig iaith swyddogol ac ystatudol y llysoedd yng Nghymru ac mewn gweinyddiaeth yn gyffredinol, ar lafar ac mewn dogfennau swyddogol, eto, parhâi'r Lladin a'r Ffrangeg Normanaidd yn briod ieithoedd cofnodion y llysoedd yn Lloegr, er i'r Saesneg gael ei dyrchafu'n unig iaith lafar y llysoedd trwy ddeddf gwlad mor bell yn ôl â 1362.[20]

Felly y parhaodd y sefyllfa yn Lloegr am yn agos i ddwy ganrif ymhellach, ar wahân i gyfnod byr adeg Cromwell pan ddisodlwyd Lladin a Ffrangeg ac y gwnaethpwyd Saesneg yn unig iaith swyddogol y llysoedd, ar lafar ac mewn dogfen, trwy ddeddfwriaeth. Pan ddaeth Siarl II yn ôl i'r orsedd, cafwyd gwared â'r ddeddf arbennig hon, fel yn achos llu o ddeddfau eraill y Weriniaeth. Am rai blynyddoedd wedyn bustachai gwŷr y llysoedd i gofnodi gweithrediadau'r llys mewn cymysgedd o Ladin a Ffrangeg pur amheus eu cystrawen a'u sillafu.[21]

Daeth newid yn 1731 gyda Deddf 4 Geo II pennod 26 a wnaeth y Saesneg yn unig iaith y llysoedd ar lafar ac mewn dogfennau. Er mwyn osgoi amryfusedd, deddfwyd yn 1733 (6 Geo II pennod 14) fod Deddf 1731 yn cynnwys llysoedd Cymru hefyd, er mwyn gwarchod pobl Cymru, yn ôl y Ddeddf, rhag anwybodaeth o gynnwys ditiadau, sef cyhuddiadau yn y llysoedd — rheswm pur wag, os nad ffuantus, o gofio fod y mwyafrif o boblogaeth Cymru o hyd yn uniaith Gymraeg. Ni cheir sôn am y Ddeddf Uno yn y naill Ddeddf na'r llall.

Yn 1879 diddymwyd y ddwy Ddeddf uchod, sef deddfau 1731 a 1733, gan Ddeddf Diddymu Deddfau Trefniadaeth Sifil (*Civil Procedure Acts Repeal Act*) sydd, er gwaetha'i theitl, yn ymwneud â phrosesau pob llys.[22] Y mae'n ddiddorol nodi i'r mesur fynd trwy'r Senedd yn ddiwrthwynebiad a heb ddadl yn unol ag arfer y Senedd wrth ddileu deddfau nad ystyrir bod iddynt ddefnydd pellach. Bid a fo am hynny, yr unig fwriad y gellir ei briodoli i'r Senedd oedd dileu'r Saesneg fel iaith swyddogol statudol y llysoedd gan adael mater iaith i ddisgresiwn a chyfleustra'r llys — yng Nghymru fel yn Lloegr.

Yr oedd y sefyllfa a grewyd gan Ddeddf 1879 yn hollol anghyson â chymalau iaith y Ddeddf Uno. Ac eto, parhaodd y Ddeddf Uno yn un o'r deddfau 'byw' yn argraffiad swyddogol y *Statutes at Large*, a gyhoeddwyd gan Owen Ruffhead, 1762-1765 ac yn yr argraffiad a gyhoeddwyd rhwng 1817 a 1828. Nid yw'r llysoedd yn barod, ond o dan amodau eithriadol, i ddyfarnu fod statud ddiweddarach yn diddymu effaith deddf hŷn trwy ymhlygiad. Ond gan fod y Ddeddf Uno yn cyfyngu ar hawliau cyfran o ddeiliaid y Deyrnas a bod Deddf 1879 yn eu rhyddhau o lyffetheiriau, cyfyd y cwestiwn diddorol, ond academig erbyn hyn, sef a ddiddymwyd yr iaith Saesneg fel unig iaith lafar a chofnod y llysoedd yng Nghymru gan Ddeddf 1879? Os cadarnhaol yw'r ateb, prin bod angen Deddf Llysoedd Cymru 1942 a dweud y lleiaf. Ni ddadleuwyd hyn yng nghyfnod Deiseb yr Iaith 1938-1942 a arweiniodd at Ddeddf Llysoedd Cymru 1942, nac ychwaith yn *Evans v. Thomas*.[23] Cymhlethwyd pethau gan Ddeddf Diwygio Cyfraith Statudol (Statute Law Revision Act) 1887 a ddiddymodd 'cymal 20' o'r Ddeddf Uno. Yn ôl y rhifau a roed yn argraffiad Ruffhead o'r *Statutes at Large*, 20 oedd y rhif a roddwyd i gymal yr iaith. Ond nid felly yn argraffiad 1817-28 a ddefnyddiwyd yn Neddf 1879: yn honno, 17 oedd y rhif a roddwyd i'r cymal hwnnw. Awgrymwyd mai trwy amryfusedd a chymysgu rhifau gwahanol argraffiadau Ruffhead o'r *Statutes at Large* y methwyd â dileu cymal iaith y Ddeddf Uno.[24]

Beth bynnag am y posibiliadau diddorol hyn, ni wnaeth y ffaith, i'r Saesneg golli ei statws fel unig iaith statud llysoedd Cymru a Lloegr, unrhyw wahaniaeth i farn yr awdurdodau a'r cyhoedd, o ran hynny, am le'r Gymraeg yn y llysoedd a bywyd cyhoeddus Cymru, ar wahân i ambell lais yn protestio yn yr anialwch.

Anodd darganfod cyfiawnhad cyfreithiol o fath yn y byd dros farn y Twrnai Cyffredinol, Syr Richard Webster, yn 1889 wrth ateb cwestiwn gan Gyngor newydd Sir Feirionnydd, sef a oedd yn briodol iddynt gadw cofnodion y Sir yn Gymraeg?

> [The] claim to keep records of counties and other resolutions and order in the Welsh Language cannot in my judgment be admitted as legal. [25]

A dyna oedd y farn a dderbyniwyd gan fonedd a gwrêng, hyd yn oed gan y Cymry pybyr yr oedd yr iaith Gymraeg yn iaith gyntaf iddynt, nid yn unig yn y llysoedd ac mewn gweithgareddau cyhoeddus ond yn eu hymwneud ag unrhyw fater a allai esgor ar berthynas neu oblygiadau cyfreithiol. Er enghraifft, mor ddiweddar â'r 1950au danfonwyd agenda cyfarfod Ymddiriedolaeth Eglwys Gymraeg yn y Brifddinas at yr ymddiriedolwyr — wedi ei amgau mewn llythyr Cymraeg — ond â'r agenda ei hun yn Saesneg am ei fod, yng ngeiriau Cymraeg y cynullydd, 'yn ymwneud â mater cyfreithiol'. [26]

Nid oes dim sydd yn dangos yn gliriach agwedd drahaus awdurdodau'r llysoedd at y Gymraeg ar y pryd na datganiad o eiddo un o Arglwydd Gangellorion y bedwaredd ganrif ar bymtheg, yr Arglwydd Hatherley. Ateb oedd y datganiad i brotestiadau chwyrn o Gymru yn dilyn apwyntio Sais uniaith, Homersham Cox, yn Farnwr Llys Sirol ar yr hyn a elwid yn Gylchdaith Canolbarth Cymru, yn 1872. Ar y pryd, cynhwysai'r Gylchdaith hon Sir Feirionnydd ynghyd â rhannau o Siroedd Caernarfon, Trefaldwyn a Cheredigion. Rhoddodd yr Arglwydd Hatherley dri rheswm dros beidio ag apwyntio Cymro Cymraeg i'r swydd.

Yn gyntaf:

> In cases Between an Englishman and a Welshman, a judge selected for his Welsh acquirements would be subject to mistrust on the part of an English litigant.

Yn ail, pwysodd ar 'Adran 17' Deddf 27 Hari VIII c. 26 (Adran 20 yn argraffiad Ruffhead o'r *Statutes at Large*) ar y tir fod yr 'adran' yn gwahardd y sawl a ddefnyddiai'r Gymraeg rhag dal swydd yn y llysoedd.

Yn drydydd:

> The existence of two languages has a tendency to separate two peoples who, as fellow citizens, should be as far as possible united. [27]

Ni roddwyd prinder Cymry Cymraeg addas ganddo fel rheswm dros beidio â dewis un a fedrai'r Gymraeg. Ni allai fod wedi rhoi hyn fel rheswm. Y gwir oedd bod o leiaf hanner dwsin o'r rheini yn meddu gwell cymwysterau na Homersham Cox o ran gallu a phrofiad. Ond yr hyn sydd yn fwy trawiadol fyth o ystyried y rheswm cyntaf a roddodd yr Arglwydd Hatherley dros ei ddewis oedd bod buddiannau Sais o ymgyfreithiwr yng Nghymru, yn ei olwg ef, yn cymryd blaenoriaeth dros fuddiannau'r Cymry yn eu gwlad eu hunain, yn enwedig o gofio fod y mwyafrif o'r boblogaeth yn ardal Cylchdaith Canolbarth Cymru ar y pryd yn uniaith Gymraeg. Diddorol, a dweud y lleiaf, yw nodi mai o enau un a oedd yn aelod o lywodraeth Ryddfrydol Gladstone y daeth y datganiad hwn.

Codwyd y mater ar lawr Tŷ'r Cyffredin gan Osborne Morgan, aelod seneddol Dinbych. Ar ei gynnig ef, ar Orffennaf 4, 1872, pasiwyd penderfyniad:

> That in the opinion of this House, it is desirable in the interest of the administration of justice that the Judge of a County Court District in which the Welsh language is generally spoken should, so far as the limits of selection will allow, be able to speak and understand that language.[28]

Yng nghwrs ei araith, cyfeiriodd Osborne Morgan at anallu cyfieithu i sicrhau cyfiawnder i'r sawl a ddefnyddiai'r Gymraeg. Nid annhebyg oedd ei eiriau i eiddo'r Ustus Gerard dair canrif ynghynt. Meddai Morgan:

> It was chiefly through the difficulty of interpreting the evidence of Welsh witnesses that miscarriages of justice arose... a judge or counsel who had to get his evidence through an interpreter was at a very great (disadvantage).

Teg nodi nad yw'r gwelliant pendant a gafwyd yn safon a dull y cyfieithu yn y llysoedd yn ystod y deuddeng mlynedd diwethaf yn newid dim ar yr egwyddor o gyfiawnder sylfaenol y dylai'r sawl sydd yn cynnal achos yn Gymraeg gael barnwr (a rheithgor mewn achos troseddol) sydd yn abl i ddeall yr iaith (neu'r ieithoedd) gwreiddiol. Ni wireddwyd eto yr hyn a fynnai Gerard ac Osborne Morgan.

Os bu peth lliniaru ar y polisi o benodi Saeson uniaith i weinyddu'r gyfraith yng Nghymru yn sgil ymyrraeth Osborne Morgan, gwrthod symud Homersham Cox i gylchdaith arall a wnaeth yr Arglwydd Ganghellor ar waethaf penderfyniad Tŷ'r Cyffredin. Gorfu i Feirionnydd a'r siroedd cyfagos fodloni ar Homersham Cox am ddeuddeng mlynedd ymhellach.

Prif ganlyniad ymgyrch Osborne Morgan oedd penodi Gwilym Williams, Meisgyn, Cymro ac eisteddfodwr brwd, yn Ynad Cyflog Pontypridd a Rhondda yn 1872. Cafodd ei ddyrchafu'n Farnwr Llys Sirol ar Gylchdaith Canolbarth Cymru yn 1884. Cyn pen hir fe'i symudwyd i Gylchdaith

Morgannwg. O leiaf, ni phetrusai ef ddefnyddio'r Gymraeg yn y llysoedd y llywyddai arnynt. Nid heb gyfiawnhad y mae'r gair 'Gwlatgarwr' wedi ei gerfio ar odre cerflun ohono yng ngwisgoedd ei swydd y tu allan i Lysoedd Caerdydd. Eithriad prin oedd ef.

Ond yn y Frawdlys, a ddisodlodd hen Lys y Sesiwn Fawr yn 1830, nid oedd newid yn y drefn. Os rhywbeth, cryfhau Seisnigrwydd y llys a wnaeth y system newydd am mai Saeson uniaith, gydag ambell Gymro uniaith Saesneg, oedd pob un o'r barnwyr a ddeuai yn eu tro ar Gylchdaith Cymru a Chaer o 1830 tan y 1950au. Er bod Cymry, a rhai ohonynt yn Gymry Cymraeg, yn gadeiryddion rhai o lysoedd Sesiwn Chwarter y siroedd, dilynent arfer y Frawdlys, a dim ond pe digwyddai i rywun fel Gwilym Williams eistedd mewn llys sirol y clywid y Gymraeg o fainc y llysoedd hynny.

Un o ganlyniadau uniongyrchol treial y tri chenedlaetholwr ym Mrawdlys Caernarfon yn 1936 oedd tynnu sylw at statws anfoddhaol yr iaith Gymraeg yn y llysoedd. Gwrthododd y barnwr, yr Ustus Lewis, Cymro di-Gymraeg, adael i'r tri diffynnydd hyd yn oed ateb y cyhuddiad yn Gymraeg, ac wrth grynhoi'r achos rhoddodd y barnwr folawd i gyfraith a chyfiawnder Lloegr gan bwysleisio mai eiddo Lloegr oedd y rhagoriaethau.[29] Un o ganlyniadau'r treial hanesyddol hwn oedd cychwyn Mudiad Deiseb yr Iaith yn Eisteddfod Genedlaethol Caerdydd yn 1938. Hawliai'r Ddeiseb statws swyddogol i'r iaith Gymraeg, cydradd â'r Saesneg yn y llysoedd ac yn y cyrff cyhoeddus eraill. Enillodd gefnogaeth sylweddol iawn ond torrwyd ar draws y gwaith o gasglu enwau gan y Rhyfel. Fe'i cyflwynwyd i'r Senedd yn 1941. Ymhen hir a hwyr ac ar ôl cryn wasgu, daeth Mesur Llysoedd Cymru ger bron y Senedd ac fe'i pasiwyd yn Hydref 1942. Cafodd groeso gwenieithus yn y Senedd.[30] Mae'n gwestiwn a haeddai'r clod a dderbyniodd ar y pryd, oherwydd syrthiodd yn fyr iawn o ddisgwyliadau cefnogwyr y Ddeiseb.

Disgrifir y Ddeddf yn ei theitl (ymhlith pethau eraill) fel:

An Act to repeal section seventeen of the Statute 27. Hen Vii c26 (h.y. y Ddeddf Uno), 'to remove doubt as to the right of Welsh speaking persons to testify in the Welsh language in Courts of Justice in Wales, and to enable rules to be made for the administration of oaths and affirmations in that language, and for the provision and employment and payment of interpreters in such courts.

Ni cheir Rhaglith fel yn Neddf yr Iaith 1967 ond y mae'r adran gyntaf yn cynnwys datganiad o fwriad, sef:

Whereas doubt has been entertained whether section seventeen of the Statute 27 Hen VIII C.26 unduly restricts the right of Welsh speaking persons to use the Welsh language in Courts of Justice in Wales, now therefore, the said section is hereby repealed, and it is hereby enacted that the Welsh language may be used in any Court in Wales by any part or witness, who considers that he would otherwise be at any disadvantage by reasons of his natural language of communication being Welsh.

Y mae i'r adran ddwy ran: y rhan gyntaf yn dileu'r rhwystrau a fu ar ffordd defnyddio'r Gymraeg yn y llysoedd, a'r ail ran yn gosod cyfyngiadau newydd ar yr hawl i'w defnyddio.

Yn ôl ail ran yr adran gyntaf, dim ond y parti neu'r tyst, a ystyriai ei fod o dan anfantais oherwydd mai'r Gymraeg oedd ei iaith naturiol, a feddai'r hawl i ddefnyddio'r Gymraeg. Nid oedd yr hawl y proffesai'r adran ei rhoi fawr ehangach na'r hyn y bu'r llysoedd yn ei ganiatáu i'r Cymro uniaith neu'r Cymro prin ei Saesneg o 1536 ymlaen. Yn ail, ni châi na barnwr nac ynad, bargyfreithiwr na thwrnai, yr hawl i ddefnyddio'r Gymraeg am nad oeddynt yn perthyn i gategori 'parti' neu 'dyst'. Yn drydydd, golygai fod y parti neu'r tyst a fynnai ddefnyddio'r Gymraeg yn gorfod datgan yn gyhoeddus ei anallu yn yr iaith Saesneg — yr union anallu a fu'n rhwystr o dan Ddeddf 1536 i unrhyw swydd a dyrchafiad. Prin y gellid fod wedi dyfeisio dull mwy effeithiol o gael Cymro i beidio â defnyddio'r Gymraeg wrth gyflwyno'i achos neu wrth roi tystiolaeth. Yn bedwerydd, cymerai'r adran yn ganiataol mai Saesneg oedd unig iaith swyddogol a rheolaidd llys barn — cyfeiliornad, os oedd grym o gwbl yn y ddadl fod Deddf Diddymu Trefniadaeth Sifil 1879 wedi diddymu Deddf 1733 a wnaeth Saesneg yn unig iaith statudol llysoedd Cymru. Yn bumed, er gwaethaf geiriad y Ddeddf mai'r parti neu'r tyst oedd i farnu a oeddynt o dan anfantais, penderfynodd Llys Adrannol yr Uchel Lys yn achos *Reg v. Ynadon Merthyr Tudful ex parte Jenkins*,[31] ddehongli'r adran mewn modd cyfyng, ar y tir mai mater i'r llys yr ymddangosai parti neu dyst ger ei fron, oedd barnu dilysrwydd hawl diffynnydd neu dyst ei fod o dan anfantais ieithyddol. Yr oedd yn agored i'r Llys, fel y safai'r gyfraith yn union cyn pasio Deddf yr Iaith, ddehongli Deddf 1942 yn y modd hwn, ond dangosodd cyn lleied o werth mewn gwirionedd oedd i'r 'hawl' a roddwyd gan adran gyntaf Deddf 1942. Diddymwyd yr adran gyntaf gan Ddeddf yr Iaith.

Rhoddai'r ail adran yr hawl i gymryd llw neu i wneud datganiad yn Gymraeg yng Nghymru gan y sawl a fynnai, yn unol â ffurf i'w hawdurdodi gan yr Arglwydd Ganghellor. Yr oedd hon yn hawl newydd. Yr oedd y ddarpariaeth ar gyfer awdurdodi ffurfiau'r llw yn Gymraeg yn angenrheidiol gan fod y ffurfiau Saesneg eisoes wedi eu pennu. Deil yr adran hon mewn grym.

Darperir gwasanaeth cyfieithydd ar bwrs y wlad o dan adran 3(1) y Ddeddf, y tâl i'r cyfieithydd i'w benderfynu gan yr Arglwydd Ganghellor gyda chydsyniad y Trysorlys. Deil yr adran hon hefyd mewn grym.

Yn ymarferol, achosodd y gofyn am benodi tâl y cyfieithwyr gan yr
Arglwydd Ganghellor trwy Orchymyn Statudol — proses araf a chymhleth
— beth anghyfiawnder i gyfieithwyr Cymraeg. Y rheswm am hynny oedd fod
graddfa tâl cyfieithwyr ieithoedd eraill yn cael ei phenderfynu gan swyddog
costau'r llys. Yr oedd ac mae ei ddisgresiwn ynglŷn â thâl twrneiod,
bargyfreithwyr, tystion a chyfieithwyr yn bur eang ac yn ddigon hyblyg i
gyfarfod â chwyddiant gyda'r canlyniad fod graddfa tâl cyfieithwyr ieithoedd
tramor, hyd yn ddiweddar, wedi bod yn sylweddol uwch na graddfa'r
Arglwydd Ganghellor. Adran arall sydd yn cyfyngu ar yr hawl i
ddefnyddio'r Gymraeg yw adran 3(2). Y mae o hyd mewn grym. Yn ôl yr
adran hon y mae'n ofynnol cadw cofnodion holl weithgareddau'r llysoedd
yng Nghymru yn Saesneg, a rhaid i'r barnwr neu'r sawl sydd yn llywyddu'r
llys fynnu bod unrhyw beth a ddywedir neu a ysgrifennir yn Gymraeg yn
ystod y gweithgareddau yn cael ei gyfieithu i'r Saesneg, oni bai ei fod o'r
farn nad yw lles y cyhoedd yn galw am gyfieithu.

Gan na roddai'r Ddeddf hawl i'r barnwr, neu'r sawl a lywyddai mewn
achos, ddefnyddio'r Gymraeg ei hun, sicrhawyd awdurdod a safle'r iaith
Saesneg yng ngweithgareddau'r llys. Nid yw'n syndod bod pobl Cymru, y
Cymry Cymraeg a'r Cymry di-Gymraeg, wedi eu cyflyru i gredu nad oedd
i ddogfen a wneid yn Gymraeg, beth bynnag ei natur, rym cyfreithiol.

Dyma'n union y ddadl ar ran diffynnydd, swyddog etholiadol Sir
Gaerfyrddin, yn achos *Evans v. Thomas*.[33] Yr oedd isetholiad yn Ward y
Betws, Rhydaman, ar gyfer y Cyngor Sir. Penderfynodd nifer o etholwyr
enwebu ffermwr lleol, Mr Gwynfor S. Evans, fel ymgeisydd. Cytunodd
yntau. Yn unol â'r Rheolau Etholiadol rhaid oedd cyflwyno'r papurau
enwebu i'r Swyddog Etholiadol erbyn canol dydd ar 21 Mawrth 1961. Yr
oedd yn ofynnol, yn ôl y Rheolau Ffurflenni Etholiadol, ddefnyddio ffurflenni
yn unol â'r Atodlen Gyntaf i'r Rheolau — '*or forms to like effect. . . with such
modifications as the circumstances shall require*'. Yn Saesneg yn unig yr
oedd y ffurflen a luniwyd. Am 11.15 ar fore 21 Mawrth, tri chwarter awr cyn
amser cau rhestr yr ymgeiswyr, cyflwynodd Mr Evans ffurflen enwebu yn
Gymraeg. Yr oedd yn gyfieithiad cyflawn a chywir o'r ffurflen a bennwyd
gan y rheolau. Rhywbryd rhwng 11.15 a 11.25 gwrthododd y Swyddog
Etholiadol ei derbyn ar y tir ei bod yn ddi-rym am nad oedd y papur enwebu
yn y '*prescribed form as laid down by the Statute*' — hynny yw am ei bod yn
Gymraeg. Gan nad oedd ond un ymgeisydd cydnabyddedig ar ôl pan
drawodd y cloc ddeuddeg o'r gloch, cyhoeddwyd i hwnnw gael ei ethol yn
ddiwrthwynebiad.

Yr oedd yn amlwg mai sail dyfarniad y Swyddog Etholiadol oedd na allai
ffurflen Gymraeg fod yn ffurflen '*to like effect. . .* ' â'r fersiwn Saesneg yn yr
Atodlen. Ni allai'r achos yn erbyn dilysrwydd y Gymraeg mewn dogfennau

cyfreithiol fod wedi ymgrisialu'n eglurach.

Gwnaeth y Swyddog Etholiadol un camgymeriad technegol a olygai nad oedd ei weithred yn gwrthod papur enwebu Mr Evans yn gyfreithlon ac y byddai'n rhaid i'r llys etholiadol ddiddymu'r etholiad a gorchymyn etholiad newydd. Ond yr oedd achos y pleintydd, Mr Evans, gymaint â hynny'n fwy atyniadol ac oherwydd hynny yn gryfach na phetai'n seiliedig ar bwynt technegol yn unig, am fod ganddo ddadleuon seiliedig ar haeddiant ac egwyddor. Y diffyg technegol oedd i'r Swyddog Etholiadol ddyfarnu *cyn* canol dydd nad oedd papurau Mr Evans yn ddilys. Yn ôl y Rheolau Etholiadol yr oedd yn rhaid i'r Swyddog Etholiadol aros tan ar ôl yr adeg olaf i gyflwyno enwebiadau, sef canol dydd, cyn penderfynu a oedd y papurau'n ddilys.

Y ddadl o blaid Mr Evans ar dir haeddiant ac egwyddor oedd bod y cyfieithiad Cymraeg yn ddilys fel fersiwn *'to like effect'* â'r un a benodwyd yn yr Atodlen. Dadl y Swyddog Etholiadol oedd bod y fersiwn Cymraeg, am ei fod yn Gymraeg, yn ddi-ddim yn ôl y gyfraith. *'Nullity'* oedd y gair a ddefnyddiwyd i'w ddisgrifio.

Gwrthodwyd dadl y Swyddog Etholiadol yn bendant gan y ddau farnwr a wrandawai ar yr achos, sef yr Ustus Gorman a'r Ustus Winn. Meddai'r Ustus Gorman:

> I do not consider that the law, whether statute law or common law, requires the nomination form to be in the English language. In my view the returning officer was not in law justified in rejecting the nomination form because it was in the Welsh language.[34]

Ehangodd yr Ustus Winn ar hyn i gynnwys dogfennau cyhoeddus yn gyffredinol:

> ... nothing that has been said in argument or brought to the attention of the court requires me to hold that it is a requirement of the English Common Law that all public documents should be couched in English, or that if any other language be used in such a document it becomes a mere nullity...I have... put upon one side [the]... submission that a public document written in Welsh is a nullity.[35]

Er i'r Llys Adrannol ymwrthod â phenderfynu a oedd gan y Gymraeg statws fel iaith swyddogol gydnabyddedig ac er iddo, yn gwbl gywir, wrthod y ddadl bod Deddf Llysoedd Cymru 1942 eisoes wedi rhoi statws felly iddi, yr oedd ei ddyfarniad o'r pwysigrwydd mwyaf. Yn y lle cyntaf, gan na ellid honni mwyach ei bod yn rhaid i ddogfennau cyhoeddus fod yn Saesneg er mwyn bod yn ddilys, y mae dogfen gyhoeddus sydd yn Gymraeg yn gwbl dderbyniol yn gyfreithiol a'r un mor ddilys â phetai yn Saesneg, oddieithr bod y geiriad wedi ei bennu yn Saesneg yn unig gan statud a'i bod yn ofynnol i ddilyn y geiriau penodedig a'r rheini'n unig. Golyga hyn, er enghraifft, y gallai awdurdod lleol gyhoeddi ei ddogfennau swyddogol yn Gymraeg yn unig, pe mynnai, oddieithr y dogfennau y mae'n rhaid eu cyhoeddi yn uniaith Saesneg neu'n ddwyieithog yn ôl gofyn statud arbennig, neu reolau statudol. Yn ail, er mai â dogfen swyddogol yr oedd a wnelai'r dyfarniad, byddai'n anodd, yn wyneb y dyfarniadau yn *Evans v. Thomas*, i unrhyw lys ddyfarnu bod dogfen breifat, megis cytundeb rhwng dau berson, neu siec, yn annilys ac aneffeithiol yn unig am ei bod yn Gymraeg. Yn drydydd, o iawn sylweddoli goblygiadau'r dyfarniad, dyma ddiwedd ar y dybiaeth a goleddwyd yn gyffredinol yng Nghymru, ac a goleddir o hyd gan lawer, ei bod yn angenrheidiol cwblhau unrhyw ddogfen ac iddi sawr swyddogol neu gyfreithiol yn Saesneg.

Cafodd y dyfarniad groeso yng Nghymru.[36]

Yr oedd y dyfarniad hwn, a Deddf Ffurflenni Etholiad Cymraeg Syr Raymond Gower[37] a'i dilynodd, yn ddïau ymysg y ffactorau a arweiniodd Syr Keith Joseph, Gweinidog Materion Cymreig ar y pryd, i sefydlu Pwyllgor o dan gadeiryddiaeth Syr David Hughes Parry i 'egluro statws gyfreithiol yr iaith Gymraeg ac i ystyried pa gyfnewidiadau y dylid eu gwneud yn y gyfraith'. Ffactor arall, a phwysicach ond odid, oedd y berw a ddilynodd ddarlith radio hanesyddol y Dr Saunders Lewis yn Chwefror 1962 ar 'Dynged yr Iaith'.[38] Argymhellion y grŵp seneddol Cymreig yn y diwedd a sicrhaodd ymateb y Gweinidog.

Sefydlwyd y Pwyllgor ar 30 Gorffennaf 1963. Cyflwynodd ei Adroddiad yn Hydref 1965. Pasiwyd Deddf yr Iaith Gymraeg â chefnogaeth yr holl bleidiau gwleidyddol ar 27 Gorffennaf 1967 — bron pedair blynedd yn union wedi sefydlu'r Pwyllgor.

Y pedwar prif argymhelliad oedd:
(1) y dylid diddymu adran 1 Deddf Llysoedd Cymru a gyfyngai'r hawl i ddefnyddio Cymraeg i'r rhai a'u hystyriai eu hunain o dan anfantais am mai Cymraeg oedd eu hiaith naturiol, ac estyn hawl i barti neu dyst ddefnyddio'r Gymraeg yn y llysoedd yn ddilyffethair.[39] Derbyniwyd yr argymhelliad hwn, ac estynnwyd yr hawl i eraill, yn ogystal â phartïon a thystion, gan Ddeddf yr Iaith Gymraeg.
(2) y dylai Deddf yr Iaith gynnwys datganiad statudol i'r perwyl bod unrhyw weithred neu ysgrifen neu unrhyw beth a wneir yn Gymraeg yng Nghymru i gael yr un grym cyfreithiol â phe gwneid hynny yn Saesneg ac i gyhoeddi'r egwyddor bod i'r iaith Gymraeg statws o ddilysrwydd cyfartal â'r Saesneg yng ngweinyddiaeth barn a gwaith gweinyddol yng Nghymru.[40]

Ni dderbyniwyd mo'r argymhellion hyn. Mae'n amheus a oedd angen rhan gyntaf y datganiad a argymhellwyd yn wyneb dyfarniad y llys yn *Evans v. Thomas*.[33] Am ail ran yr argymhelliad, ni wnaed unrhyw ddatganiad yng nghorff y Ddeddf ond cyhoeddwyd, yn y Rhaglith, y priodoldeb o wneud darpariaeth bellach ar gyfer defnyddio'r Gymraeg *'with like effect as English in the conduct of other official or public business',* hynny yw, mewn meysydd ar wahân i faes y gyfraith lle y ceid darpariaeth arbennig. Gwnaed darpariaeth, serch hynny, yn adran 2 yn rhoi hawl i Weinidog y Goron i awdurdodi trosiad Cymraeg o ddogfen neu eiriau i'w defnyddio neu y gellid eu defnyddio i bwrpas swyddogol neu gyhoeddus.

(3) y dylid dileu'r rhan olaf o adran 3(2) o Ddeddf Llysoedd 1942 sy'n gorchymyn barnwr neu gadeirydd llys i gyfieithu unrhyw ran o'r gweithredoedd lle defnyddir y Gymraeg os nad yw ef yn ystyried nad oes angen gwneud hynny er mwyn sicrhau bod cyfiawnder yn cael ei weinyddu'n briodol ac yn gyhoeddus.[41] Ni dderbyniwyd yr argymhelliad hwn ychwaith. (Argymhellodd y Pwyllgor gadw rhan gyntaf adran 3(2) sy'n deddfu mai yn Saesneg yn unig y dylid cadw cofnodion y llys.)[42] Gadawodd Deddf yr Iaith y cyfan o adran 3(2) Deddf y Llysoedd mewn grym.

(4) y dylid cymryd camau gweinyddol gan y llysoedd, y Gwasanaeth Sifil a sefydliadau cyhoeddus i sicrhau bod y sawl a fyn yn gallu defnyddio'r Gymraeg wrth gynnal trafodaethau â'r cyrff hyn.[43] Teg nodi nad argymhellodd Pwyllgor Hughes Parry fod Deddf yr Iaith i gynnwys datganiad o'r hawl sydd gan ddinesydd yng Nghymru i gyfathrebu yn yr iaith Gymraeg fel y mae Deddf Iaith Quebec, er enghraifft, yn rhoi hawl i ddinasyddion y dalaith honno gyfathrebu â chyrff cyhoeddus a chwmnïau yn Ffrangeg.

Prif amcan Deddf yr Iaith oedd symud llyffetheiriau gormesol ar ddefnyddio'r Gymraeg yn y llysoedd. Er i Ddeddf y Llysoedd Cymraeg 1942 broffesu diddymu Adran 17 o Ddeddf 27 Hen 8 C.26 oherwydd bod 'amheuaeth' a oedd y ddeddf honno'n cyfyngu'n ormodol (*'unduly restricts'*) ar hawl y Cymry Cymraeg i ddefnyddio'u hiaith, gosod llyffetheiriau pellach a wnaeth. Y mae ysbryd ac amcan Deddf 1967 yn doriad llwyr oddi wrth y ddwy Ddeddf hyn er bod gofynion Adran 3 o Ddeddf 1942 o hyd mewn grym. Arwyddocâd y Rhaglith yw'r pwyslais a roddir ynddi fod yr iaith Gymraeg i'w defnyddio'n rhwydd ac yn rhydd ('freely') yng Nghymru gan y sawl a fynno, boed farnwr, ynad, bargyfreithiwr, twrnai, parti neu dyst. Os oes amwysedd yn y Ddeddf ei hun neu wrth ei gweinyddu, yn wyneb geiriad cwbl bendant y Rhaglith, dyletswydd y llys ym mhob achos yw rhwyddhau'r ffordd i'r sawl sydd am ddefnyddio'r Gymraeg a dehongli'r Ddeddf mewn modd a fydd yn sicrhau'r hawl i'w defnyddio'n rhydd. Y mae'n amlwg bod ymhlygiadau gweinyddol sylweddol yn deillio o hyn os yw amcanion y Ddeddf i'w gwireddu.

Nid yw'r Ddeddf yn datgan bod gweithred neu ddogfen neu unrhyw beth a wneir yn Gymraeg i fod â'r un dilysrwydd â phetai wedi ei wneud yn

Saesneg ond prin bod angen hynny yn wyneb y dyfarniad yn *Evans v. Thomas*. Yr unig ddarpariaeth benodol angenrheidiol oedd sicrhau bod dogfennau a ffurfiau a orchmynnwyd neu a awdurdodwyd i'w defnyddio gan offeryn statudol yn Saesneg yn cael eu cyfieithu i'r Gymraeg. Ni wnaed hyn yn orfodol ar unrhyw un o weinidogion y Goron a hynny'n ddiau am fod cynifer o ddogfennau ar gael fel y byddai ei wneud yn orfodol yn gosod straen annerbyniol ar adrannau'r llywodraeth. Y mae'r Rhaglith, serch hynny, yn cymeradwyo'r priodoldeb o wneud darpariaethau pellach i ddefnyddio'r Gymraeg â'r un effaith â'r Saesneg wrth weinyddu busnes swyddogol a chyhoeddus yng Nghymru ac y mae hyn yn awgrymu fod y disgresiwn a roddir i'r Gweinidogion yn un y dylid ei ddefnyddio o blaid, yn hytrach nag yn erbyn, awdurdodi fersiynau Cymraeg o ddogfennau swyddogol.

Cyfyd cwestiwn pellach, sef, a ydyw'r rhan honno o'r Rhaglith sydd yn cymeradwyo'r priodoldeb o ddefnyddio'r Gymraeg gyda'r un effaith â'r Saesneg wrth weinyddu busnes swyddogol a chyhoeddus arall (hynny yw, busnes swyddogol a chyhoeddus ar wahân i weinyddu'r gyfraith) yn *anogaeth* i gyrff eraill, megis awdurdodau lleol a byrddau cyhoeddus, i dderbyn yr un patrwm? Y mae'n anodd dod o hyd i unrhyw reswm pam na ddylid eu hystyried felly, am mai'r awdurdodau lleol presennol, y Cynghorau Sir a'r Cynghorau Dosbarth, a etifeddodd awdurdod yr ynadon a'r Llysoedd Sesiwn Chwarter dros lywodraeth leol. Am fod y gwaharddiad ar ddefnyddio'r Gymraeg a geir yng nghymalau Deddf 1536 yn cynnwys gorchwylion llywodraeth leol yr ynadon, gellir yn deg honni bod y datganiad yn y Rhaglith i Ddeddf 1967 yn ddigon eang i gynnwys busnes swyddogol a chyhoeddus yr awdurdodau lleol. Ni fyddai'n synhwyrol gwahaniaethu rhwng awdurdodau lleol a chyrff cyhoeddus yn gyffredinol. Ond wedi dweud hynny, rhaid pwysleisio nad yw'r Ddeddf yn gosod dyletswydd ar unrhyw awdurdod lleol na chyhoeddus i roi dilysrwydd cyfartal i'r iaith Gymraeg ac felly ni ellir eu gorfodi trwy rym cyfraith. Ar y llaw arall, y mae'n agored i unrhyw awdurdod ddefnyddio'r Gymraeg, neu'r Saesneg, neu'r ddwy iaith, yn sgil dyfarniad y llys yn *Evans v. Thomas* ac ni ellir eu galw i gyfrif na gosod na rhwystr na llyffethair gyfreithiol nac ariannol ar eu ffordd, os defnyddiant y Gymraeg. Golyga hefyd na all unrhyw awdurdod wrthod cydnabod dilysrwydd gohebiaeth Gymraeg oddi wrth drethdalwr neu gwsmer yn unig am mai yn Gymraeg y bu'r ohebiaeth.

Siomedig, a dweud y lleiaf, oedd ymateb llawer o'r llysoedd a'r awdurdodau i'r Ddeddf newydd. Dim ond ar ôl ymgyrchoedd hir a chostus, heb sôn am hunanaberth unigolion a grwpiau, y mabwysiadwyd polisïau a dderbynnir bellach fel rhai cwbl resymol. Er enghraifft, bu ymgyrchu caled dros gael gwysion yn Gymraeg: ond nid cyn i'r Arglwydd Hailsham,[44] yr

Arglwydd Ganghellor, wneud datganiad ym Mangor yn 1972, y dechreuwyd rhoi hysbysrwydd ar wysion Saesneg a ddanfonid allan gan lysoedd ynadon yng Nghymru, y gellid cael fersiwn Cymraeg pe gofynnid am un, a hynny bum mlynedd ar ôl i Ddeddf yr Iaith ddod i rym. Yn y cyfamser, wedi i geisiadau rhesymol fethu, mabwysiadodd nifer luosog o bobl (gan gynnwys personau yr oedd parch arbennig i'w barn) bolisi o dorcyfraith er mwyn gwyntyllu'r sefyllfa'n gyhoeddus, sefyllfa na fyddai'n bodoli petai'r llysoedd wedi ymateb yn fwy pendant ac ynghynt i ofynion Deddf yr Iaith.

Yn ystod y pum mlynedd cyntaf wedi pasio'r Ddeddf, parhâi rhai ynadon i gredu, er mawr syndod, nad oedd dim wedi newid ac nad priodol oedd defnyddio'r Gymraeg yn y llysoedd. Y mae'n anodd esbonio hyn oni bai iddynt gael eu camarwain gan eu clercod, a hynny o anwybodaeth neu o ystyfnigrwydd, neu oherwydd i'r ynadon ddewis anwybyddu'r cyngor a gaent. Y dull mwyaf cyffredin oedd i fainc, yr oedd ei haelodau a'u clerc yn gwbl hyddysg yn y Gymraeg, wrthod y gwahoddiad a ddeuai o du'r diffynyddion iddynt ddefnyddio'r Gymraeg wrth weinyddu a llywyddu'r llys. Mewn un achos o'r fath yn haf 1971, y rheswm a roddodd yr ynadon dros wrthod defnyddio'r Gymraeg oedd mai Saesneg oedd iaith swyddogol y llys.

Ar y llaw arall, yr oedd llysoedd yn siroedd Gwynedd, Ceredigion, Caerfyrddin, ac yng Nghaerdydd, lle'r oedd yr ynadon yn ddigon parod i gynnal achos yn gyfan gwbl yn Gymraeg. Trefnai'r clerc alw ynadon a chlerc llys rhugl eu Cymraeg, pryd bynnag y credai fod diffynnydd yn bwriadu defnyddio'r Gymraeg, neu pan gâi rybudd i'r perwyl hwnnw.

Am y llysoedd uwch, ni chymerwyd unrhyw gam arbennig gan Adran yr Arglwydd Ganghellor rhwng 1967 a diwedd 1971 i gyfarfod â'r sefyllfa newydd a grewyd gan Ddeddf yr Iaith yn y Frawdlys, yr hen 'Assis'. O ganlyniad, pan ddaeth nifer o achosion ger bron y llys yn codi o weithgareddau Cymdeithas yr Iaith yn 1969-71, yr oedd y llysoedd hynny bron yn gyfan gwbl ddibaratoad. Yr oedd hyd yn oed hynny a fu o wasanaeth cyfieithu yn y 1940au a'r 1950au cynnar bron wedi llwyr ddiflannu.

Cafwyd datganiad clir a thrylwyr o hawliau gwahanol bersonau i ddefnyddio'r Gymraeg yn y llysoedd yn achos y *Frenhines v. Francis ac eraill* ym mrawdlys Abertawe ym mis Mai 1971 gan yr Ustus Mars-Jones,[45] barnwr a oedd i chwarae rhan allweddol yn hybu defnyddio'r Gymraeg yn y llysoedd yn fuan wedyn.

Ym mis Tachwedd 1971, am y waith gyntaf erioed, dewisodd cwnsler diffynnydd ddefnyddio'r Gymraeg yn unig wrth gyflwyno achos ei gleient. Achos y *Frenhines v. Bowyer* oedd hwnnw. Gwrandawyd arno gan yr Ustus

Talbot a rheithgor yn Yr Wyddgrug. Defnyddiwyd y Gymraeg wrth holi a chroesholi tystion ac wrth annerch y barnwr a'r rheithgor, a chyfieithwyd y cyfan i'r Saesneg gan mai di-Gymraeg oedd y barnwr ac o leiaf naw o'r rheithwyr. Defnyddiwyd dull cyfieithu brawddeg ar y tro, dull a oedd yn bell o fod yn foddhaol.

Yr oedd y sefyllfa yn rhai o Lysoedd Sesiwn Chwarter Cymru ryw gymaint yn well. Yr oedd gan Sesiynau Chwarter Caernarfon, Ceredigion, Meirionnydd a Môn eu cyfieithwyr swyddogol. Amaturiaid oedd pob un o'r rhain a'u safon yn amrywio o'r ardderchog i'r gwael. Mor gynnar â 1958 gwrandawodd Syr David Hughes Parry ar achos apêl at Sesiwn Chwarter Sir Gaernarfon yn erbyn dyfarniad llys ynadon, yn gyfan gwbl yn Gymraeg, ac fe'i gwnaeth yn gwbl eglur ei fod bob amser yn croesawu defnyddio'r Gymraeg yn y llys pan lywyddai ef. Yn sicr, rhwng 1967 a 1971 gwrandawyd ar nifer o achosion apêl yn Gymraeg yn Sesiynau Chwarter Ceredigion a Meirionnydd ac yn yr olaf, ar brydiau, yn Gymraeg y cynhaliwyd holl fusnes gweinyddol yr ynadon. Hyd y gwyddys, yn Llanbedr Pont Steffan yn 1970 y cynhaliwyd am y tro cyntaf, dreial ar dditiad yn gyfan gwbl yn Gymraeg, ond nid treial ger bron rheithgor ydoedd gan i'r diffynnydd bledio'n euog. Ar wahân i'r hyn a ddigwyddai yn y gorllewin a'r gogledd, prin bod dim newid yn safle'r iaith yn Sesiynau Chwarter y siroedd eraill.

Wedi sefydlu Llys y Goron yn Ionawr 1972 a diddymu'r Frawdlys a Llysoedd y Sesiwn Chwarter, aethpwyd ati yn ddiymdroi i sicrhau bod y llysoedd yn abl i gyfarfod â gofynion Deddf yr Iaith. Yr oedd tair problem fawr. Yn y lle cyntaf, gan nad oedd darpariaeth ar gyfer sicrhau rheithgor a ddeallai'r Gymraeg a'i bod yn annhebygol y byddai pob tyst yn gallu siarad Cymraeg ychwaith, yr oedd yn rhaid wrth wasanaeth cyfieithu y gallai barnwr, rheithiwr, bargyfreithiwr, twrnai a pharti ddibynnu arno. Yn ail, yr oedd angen geirfa dechnegol ar gyfer cynnal achosion yn y Gymraeg. Yn drydydd, yr oedd yn rhaid sicrhau fod digon o farnwyr ac o fargyfreithwyr yn hyddysg yn y math o eirfa y disgwylid iddynt ei defnyddio mewn llys barn.

Yr oedd Cylchdaith Cymru a Chaer yn ffodus i gael yr Ustus Mars-Jones yn ogystal â Sais â chydymdeimlad â'r Gymraeg, sef yr Ustus Talbot yn Farnwyr Llywyddol. Neb llai na Mr Dafydd Jones Williams, a fu'n aelod o Bwyllgor Hughes Parry, oedd Gweinyddwr y Gylchdaith.

Dair wythnos wedi sefydlu Llys y Goron gofynnwyd i un o'r Barnwyr Cylchdaith newydd fynd yn gyfrifol am sefydlu gwasanaeth cyfieithu i'r llysoedd. Nid oedd offer ar gael, nid oedd yr un llys wedi ei addasu ar gyfer system cyfieithu cyfredol, nid oedd cnewyllyn o gyfieithwyr, ac ar ben y cyfan gwnaethpwyd datganiad gan nifer o bersonau a fyddai, o ran cymwysterau, yn gwbl addas i fod yn gyfieithwyr, na fynnent ran yn y cynllun newydd. Ystyrient y byddai cyfieithu yn rhwystr rhag datblygu llysoedd cwbl Gymraeg. Gwrthwynebent hefyd unrhyw amod wrth eu penodi y gwasanaethent ym mhob math o achos. Y gwir amdani, wrth gwrs, ydoedd nad oedd gan y llysoedd ddewis yn wyneb gofynion Adran 3 o Ddeddf Llysoedd Cymry 1942, a oedd yn gofyn am gyfieithu popeth o'r Gymraeg i'r Saesneg.

Penderfynwyd o'r dechrau mai llyffethair ar ddefnyddio'r Gymraeg fyddai cyfieithu fesul brawddeg. Nid oedd dim amdani felly ond system o gyfieithu cyfredol. Golygai hynny sicrhau safon uchel iawn ar ran y cyfieithwyr. Golygai hefyd fod dyletswydd ddeublyg ar farnwr i sicrhau na fyddai cyflymdra hawl ac ateb ac araith yn drech na dawn y cyfieithwyr, ac na fyddai camgyfieithu — tasg anodd a dweud y lleiaf gyda thîm o gyfieithwyr dibrofiad, ond tasg gwbl angenrheidiol.

Sicrhawyd ugain o gyfieithwyr addas ar ôl cwrs carlam yng Ngholeg y Brifysgol, Aberystwyth, yn cynnwys elfennau cyfraith drosedd a threfniadaeth y llysoedd trosedd ynghyd â thechneg ac ymarferion cyfieithu. Dilynwyd hyn gan nifer o gyrsiau byrion rhwng Mai a Rhagfyr 1972. Parheir i gynnal cyrsiau cyffelyb. Gwahoddwyd bargyfreithwyr i fynychu rhai o'r crysiau hyn er mwyn magu ffydd y naill garfan yn y llall a rhoi cyfle iddynt ymarfer eu doniau yn Gymraeg. Cynhaliwyd y treial cyntaf yn Gymraeg ar dditiad ger bron barnwr a rheithgor ym mis Mawrth 1973, ac am y tro cyntaf erioed crynhowyd yr achos i'r rheithgor yn gyfan gwbl yn Gymraeg. Yn Llys 5 yn Llysoedd y Goron, Caerdydd y digwyddodd hynny. Defnyddiwyd offer cyfieithu cyfredol am y tro cyntaf. Darparwyd offer parhaol ar gyfer Llys Caerdydd ym mis Tachwedd 1974 — darpariaeth unigryw yn hanes llysoedd gwledydd Prydain; ac am gyfnod, Caerdydd oedd yr unig ddinas rhwng Brwsel a Quebec yn meddu ar lys wedi ei addasu at glywed achosion dwyieithog. Dyma'r cyntaf o bedwar llys a addaswyd ar gyfer cyfieithu cyfredol yng Nghymru.

Yr ail anhawster i'w oresgyn oedd geirfa'r llys. Er mai geirfa gyffredin bob dydd yw geirfa llys barn am dros naw deg y cant o'r amser (ffaith a anghofir yn aml), y mae gan y llysoedd eirfa arbennig ar gyfer trafod rhai syniadau ac egwyddorion cyfreithiol. Yr oedd Llys y Goron yn hynod o ffodus i Mr Robyn Lewis gyhoeddi ei lyfr rhagorol, *Termau Cyfraith*, yn 1972. Yn 1974, cyhoeddwyd llyfryn o eiddo awdur yr ysgrif hon o dan y teitl, *Ymadroddion Llys Barn*. Cafwyd cyflenwad o ddyfarniadau a chrynhoadau gan farnwyr yr Uchel Lys mewn achosion clasurol oddi wrth Gofrestrydd y Llys Apêl. Cyfieithwyd y rhain i'r Gymraeg a'u dosbarthu ymhlith barnwyr, cofiaduron a chyfieithwyr, a'u defnyddio mewn cyrsiau hyfforddi.

Y drydedd broblem oedd rhoi hyder i farnwyr Cymraeg eu hiaith i
ddefnyddio'r Gymraeg wrth eu gwaith gan gofio fod pob un ohonynt trwy
gydol eu gyrfa, o ddyddiau cynnar eu prentisiaeth, trwy flynyddoedd
ymarfer eu crefft fel bargyfreithwyr ac yn ystod eu tymor fel barnwyr, yn
arfer Saesneg yn unig, neu bron yn unig. Dieithr oedd ymadroddion y
gyfraith iddynt yn Gymraeg. Goresgynnwyd y broblem hon trwy gynnal
cyrsiau-wythnos ar ddechrau Ionawr 1974 a Ionawr 1975 yng Ngholeg
Harlech. Llywydd ac arweinydd y cyrsiau oedd yr Ustus Mars-Jones. Ymhlith
y pethau mwyaf diddorol a ddarganfuwyd yn ystod y cyrsiau hyn oedd mor
hawdd oedd troi at y Gymraeg yn gwbl naturiol a chartrefol ar ôl ychydig
o amser yn unig a chyfoethoced oedd y Gymraeg fel iaith llys a chyfraith.
Erbyn hyn y mae rhyw un ar bymtheg o farnwyr, o wahanol raddau, yn abl
i lywyddu gweithrediadau'r llys yn y Gymraeg, un barnwr Uchel Lys, pum
barnwr Cylchdaith a rhyw ddeg o Gofiaduron a Chofiaduron Cynorthwyol
(y ddau ddosbarth olaf yn farnwyr rhan amser).

Cynhaliwyd cyrsiau pellach i fargyfreithwyr a thwrneiod yng
Nghaernarfon a'r Wyddgrug a daeth rhai o aelodau'r Heddlu, sydd yn arfer
ag erlyn yn llysoedd yr ynadon, i'r cwrs a gynhaliwyd yn Yr Wyddgrug.

Sylweddolwyd yn fuan fod angen cyrsiau hyfforddi trwy gyfrwng y
Gymraeg ar ynadon, gan mai yn llysoedd yr ynadon y mae pob achos
troseddol yn cychwyn ar ei daith a'r ynadon sydd yn delio'n derfynol â naw
deg saith y cant o'r holl achosion troseddol a ddaw ger bron y llysoedd.
Gofynnwyd i'r barnwr â gofal am gyfieithu i fod yn gyfrifol am hybu'r
cyrsiau Cymraeg i ynadon. Yn ystod yr un mlynedd ar ddeg ddiwethaf
cynhaliwyd cyrsiau bob blwyddyn yn Siroedd Gwynedd, Clwyd, a Dyfed,
a bu cwrs preswyl i ynadon y de-ddwyrain yn y Dyffryn ger Caerdydd. At
ei gilydd derbyniodd rhwng 600 a 700 o ynadon hyfforddiant rywbryd yn
ystod eu gyrfa i wneud eu gwaith trwy gyfrwng y Gymraeg. O'r 550 o
ynadon Cymraeg eu hiaith sydd yn gwasanaethu yng Nghymru ar hyn o
bryd, amcangyfrifir fod o leiaf ddwy ran o dair ohonynt wedi bod ar un neu
fwy o'r cyrsiau hyn.

Rhoddwyd cryn hwb i'r datblygiadau hyn gan weithred yr Arglwydd
Ganghellor, yr Arglwydd Hailsham, yn gofyn i'r Arglwydd Ustus Edmund-
Davies yn Hydref 1972 wneud astudiaeth bersonol o ddulliau gweithredu'r
Ddeddf, ac ym mis Mawrth 1973 cwblhawyd y gwaith hwnnw a
chyflwynwyd Adroddiad i'r Arglwydd Ganghellor.

Cyhoeddwyd crynodeb o argymhellion yr Arglwydd Ustus Edmund-
Davies.[46] Fel y gellid disgwyl, yr oedd ei adroddiad yn un pwysig a
dylanwadol.

Cytunai fod angen pwysleisio posibilrwydd yn hytrach nag anawsterau
cael treialon cwbl Gymraeg. Credai fod hyn yn bosibl heb gyfieithu yn

Llysoedd yr Ynadon. Dylid annog erlynwyr ar ran yr Heddlu i gyflwyno'u hachos yn Gymraeg pe dymunai'r cyhuddedig hynny. Ar y llaw arall, nid ystyriai ei bod yn gyfreithiol dderbyniol, oherwydd pwysigrwydd egwyddor dewis-ar-antur, nac yn ymarferol, i sicrhau rheithgorau a oedd yn deall y Gymraeg trwy eu holi am eu cymwysterau ieithyddol, ond dylid sicrhau system gyfieithu cyfredol gan gyfieithwyr o safon uchel, a dylid eu hyfforddi. Mewn achosion sifil, lle defnyddid y Gymraeg, dylid bod yn hyblyg wrth benderfynu ai Cymraeg ynteu Saesneg fyddai prif iaith yr achos. Yr oedd angen hyfforddi barnwyr a chofiaduron i ddefnyddio'r Gymraeg wrth lywyddu mewn llys barn.

Yr oedd rhai o argymhellion yr Arglwydd Ustus Edmund-Davies eisoes yn cael eu gweithredu, megis llysoedd ynadon cwbl Gymraeg, a sefydlu panel o gyfieithwyr a'u hyfforddi. Pwysigrwydd yr argymhellion oedd bod un o farnwyr pennaf a mwyaf galluog y cyfnod y tu cefn iddynt. Yr oedd yr anogaeth i'r Heddlu erlyn yn Gymraeg, pe dymunai'r cyhuddedig hynny, yn un hynod o bwysig o ystyried na ellid gwireddu un o brif ofynion Deddf yr Iaith, sef bod y sawl a ddeuai i ymgyfreitha yn y llysoedd yn *rhydd* i ddefnyddio'r Gymraeg heb greu awyrgylch bendant ffafriol iddi: yn hynny o beth yr oedd (ac y mae) gan yr Heddlu ran allweddol i'w chwarae.

Ym Mehefin 1973 cyhoeddodd yr Arglwydd Ganghellor ei ymateb i argymhellion yr Arglwydd Ustus Edmund-Davies.[46] Derbyniai fod treialon cwbl Gymraeg yn yr ardaloedd Cymraeg eu hiaith yn dderbyniol. Derbyniodd y dylid ehangu'r cyfleusterau i gynnal achosion yn Gymraeg yn Llys y Goron. I gadw'r egwyddor o ddilysrwydd cyfartal rhwng y ddwy iaith ac egwyddor sydd yr un mor bwysig, sef dewis rheithwyr ar antur, cyhoeddodd ei fod yn bwriadu trefnu gosod cyfarpar cyfieithu cyfredol mewn nifer o ganolfannau Llys y Goron. Galwodd yr arbrawf yn un 'diddorol'.

Ni soniodd yr Arglwydd Ganghellor am argymhellion yr Arglwydd Ustus Edmund-Davies ynglŷn â'r awdurdodau erlyn, a hynny yn ddiau am nad oeddynt yn dod o dan ei awdurdod uniongyrchol ef. Ni soniodd chwaith am argymhellion yr Arglwydd Ustus ynglŷn â threfniadaeth ar gyfer defnyddio'r Gymraeg yn y llysoedd sifil.

Yr oedd datganiad o'r fath o'r pwysigrwydd mwyaf, hyd yn oed os na wnâi fwy na mynegi agwedd swyddogol gweinidogion Elisabeth yr Ail, agwedd mor wahanol o'i chymharu ag agwedd swyddogol gweinidogion Elisabeth y Gyntaf bedair canrif yn flaenorol — y ddwy agwedd yn adlewyrchu dwy ddeddf yn ymwneud â'r iaith yn y llysoedd a bywyd cyhoeddus. Diddorol nodi mai yn 1978 y derbyniwyd am y tro cyntaf gais am ysgariad yn yr iaith Gymraeg fel dogfen gwbl ddilys ac effeithiol. Yn 1982 cyhoeddodd yr Arglwydd Ganghellor y gellid cael ffurflenni cwbl Gymraeg mewn unrhyw achos yn y Llys Sirol.

Er i Lys y Goron Caerdydd gael cyfarpar cyfieithu cyfredol parhaol ym mis Tachwedd 1974 (yr oedd cyfarpar dros dro yno er mis Mawrth 1973), araf fu'r cynnydd. Cymerodd bedair blynedd ar ôl datganiad yr Arglwydd Hailsham i offer cyfieithu cyfredol gael ei osod yn Llys y Goron yn Yr Wyddgrug — ym Mehefin 1977. Fe'i defnyddiwyd am y tro cyntaf yn Hydref y flwyddyn honno. Caerfyrddin oedd y nesaf. Cwblhawyd gosod yr offer yn y llys ym Mehefin 1978 ac fe'i defnyddiwyd am y waith gyntaf ym mis Tachwedd 1978. Ni roddwyd offer cyfieithu cyfredol yn Llys Caernarfon tan Chwefror 1980, er mai yno yr oedd yr angen a'r galw mwyaf. Gwaith ailadeiladu'r llys oedd yn gyfrifol am yr oedi. Fe'i defnyddiwyd am y waith gyntaf yno yng Ngorffennaf 1981.

Fel yr oedd y gyfraith pan ofynnwyd i'r Arglwydd Ustus Edmund-Davies wneud adroddiad, a phan gyflwynodd ei adroddiad, nid oedd modd derbyniol i holi rheithwyr yng Nghymru am gymwysterau ieithyddol.

Bu newid sylweddol yn y sefyllfa wedi hynny. Ar 1 Mawrth 1973, daeth Adran 25(4) o Ddeddf Cyfiawnder Troseddol 1972 i rym. Derbyniodd y Ddeddf honno gydsyniad y Frenhines ar 26 Hydref 1972. Ffrwyth Adroddiad Pwyllgor Adrannol ar Wasanaeth Rheithwyr o dan gadeiryddiaeth yr Arglwydd Morris o Borth-y-Gest oedd y Ddeddf honno. Un o'r materion o dan sylw oedd anallu rhai rheithwyr i ddeall Saesneg. Wedi astudio dull rhai o wladwriaethau'r Unol Daleithiau o ddelio â'r broblem honno, cymeradwyodd y Pwyllgor na ddylai neb na allai ddeall, darllen, ysgrifennu a siarad Saesneg gael ei alw i fod yn rheithiwr. Yr egwyddor sylfaenol oedd y dylai rheithiwr ddeall yr hyn a ddywedid yn y llys.

Y mae geiriad Adran 25(4) o Ddedd Cyfiawnder Troseddol 1972 (yn awr, Adran 10 Deddf Rheithwyr 1974) yn arwyddocaol:

> Where it appears to the appropriate officer in the case of a person attending in pursuance of a summons for jury service, that on account of. . . insufficient understanding of English there is doubt as to his capacity to act effectively as a juror, the person may be brought before the judge who shall determine whether or not he should act as a juror and, if not, shall discharge the summons: and for this purpose ''the judge'' means any judge of High Court or any Circuit Judge or Recorder.

Y mae rhyw atsain yng ngeiriad yr Adran o eiriau'r Ustus Gerard wrth ysgrifennu at Walsingham bedair canrif ynghynt, sef y dylai rheithiwr ddeall yr hyn a ddywedir yn yr iaith wreiddiol (os yn bosibl) ac nid 'accordyng to the mynde of the interpretor'.[18]

Yr oedd felly gynsail ar ôl 1 Mawrth 1973, o fewn i'r gyfraith statud, dros gynnal ymchwiliad i ddarfanfod a fedrai rheithiwr ddeall iaith treial. Anodd

gweld sut na ellir addasu geiriau'r ddeddf at gymhwyster ieithyddol
rheithwyr pan elwir arnynt i wrando ar achos y mae'n debygol y defnyddir
yr iaith Gymraeg yn helaeth ynddo. Y mae rhesymau cadarn bellach dros
newid y ddeddf nid yn unig am mai ailorau yw cyfieithiad ar ei berffeithiaf,
ond am fod gorfod bodloni ar gyfieithu ynddo'i hun yn llyffethair ac yn
milwrio yn erbyn pwrpas y ddeddf. Os pwrpas y ddeddf yw sicrhau rhyddid
i ddefnyddio'r Gymraeg ac i *ddileu* drwg effeithiau cymalau iaith y Ddeddf
Uno, y mae achos cryf iawn dros ddiwygio Deddf Rheithwyr 1974, a'i
haddasu i sicrhau gwybodaeth o'r Gymraeg pan fo treial yn cael ei gynnal
yn llwyr neu yn rhannol trwy gyfrwng y Gymraeg.

Ni olygai hyn roi pen ar gyfieithu cywir am ddau reswm: y cyntaf yw
anghenion y Llys Apêl pe bai apêl o Lys y Goron; yr ail yw darparu ar gyfer
aelodau'r cyhoedd nad ydynt yn deall Cymraeg.

Y mae, serch hynny, sawl ffactor arall sydd o hyd yn milwrio yn erbyn
yr hawl a rydd y Ddeddf i ddefnyddio'r Gymraeg yn rhydd. Un o
argymhellion Adroddiad Hughes Parry oedd y dylid sichrau staff weinyddol
hyddysg yn y Gymraeg ar raddfa ddigon eang i alluogi unrhyw un a âi i
swyddfeydd y llys (neu gorff cyhoeddus arall o ran hynny) i gyfathrebu'n
rhydd ac yn rhwydd yn Gymraeg. I'r perwyl hwn, awgrymodd yr
Adroddiad y priodoldeb o ystwythder yn y trefniadau i symud staff o'r
Gwasanaeth Sifil i Wasanaeth yr Awdurdodau Lleol a Chyhoeddus ac i'r
gwrthwyneb.

Ni wnaethpwyd hynny. Yn Llys y Goron a'r Llysoedd Sirol yn arbennig,
ar ôl y penodiadau cyntaf, cadwyd yn glòs at fframwaith dyrchafiad y
Gwasanaeth Sifil gyda'r canlyniad fod prif glercod sawl Llys Sirol yn y
Gymru Gymraeg yn uniaith Saesneg, ac nad oes digon o swyddogion o'r
radd briodol sydd yn abl i weithredu fel clercod yn Llys y Goron — yn
enwedig yn Llysoedd Gogledd Cymru, lle mae'r galw mwyaf am Gymraeg.
Er i Adran yr Arglwydd Ganghellor fynegi parodrwydd i ryddhau'r sawl
sydd am dderbyn hyfforddiant mewn cyrsiau Wlpan a phreswyl a drefnir gan
Brifysgol Cymru, ychydig iawn, ysywaeth, a fanteisiodd ar y cyfle. Y clercod
hyn yw'r swyddogion llys cyntaf gan amlaf y cyferfydd aelodau'r cyhoedd
â hwy wrth fynychu llys barn, ac yng ngofal y swyddogion hyn y mae
rhannau ffurfiol pob treial. Os nad yw clercod llys yn abl a pharod i
ddefnyddio'r Gymraeg yn rhydd ac yn rhwydd, teg yw gofyn sut y gellir
creu awyrgylch sydd yn ffafriol i'r Gymraeg, ac yn bwysicach, sut y gellir
cyfleu i reithwyr, tystion a diffynyddion fod y rhod wedi troi a bod i'r
Gymraeg yr un urddas â'r Saesneg?

Yn ail, y mae tuedd gref yn llysoedd yr ynadon, hyd yn oed yn yr
ardaloedd Cymreiciaf, i weithredu ffurf ar yr hen bolisi o ddefnyddio'r
Gymraeg yn ddigon parod, ond dim ond pan fo angen—egwyddor

'angenrheidrwydd' — egwyddor a wrthodwyd gan Bwyllgor Hughes Parry — sydd yn milwrio yn erbyn yr hawl i ddefnyddio'r Gymraeg yn rhydd gan y neb a fynno hynny. Pan fo gwŷs yn Saesneg a'r cyhuddedig yn gorfod gofyn am fersiwn Cymraeg, nid rhyfedd mai prin yw'r sawl sydd yn gofyn amdani. Yn amlach na pheidio, hyd yn oed yn yr ardaloedd Cymraeg, Saesneg yw'r iaith a glywir o enau'r clerc, Saesneg a glywir o enau'r erlynydd, ac yn rhy aml, Saesneg yw'r iaith gyntaf a glywir o enau cadeirydd y fainc. Ceisiwyd gan lysoedd y Gymru Gymraeg ddanfon allan wysion Cymraeg ar gyfer rhai eisteddiadau, gyda nodyn yn Saesneg yn hysbysu'r diffynnydd o'i hawl i gael copi Saesneg o'r wŷs; a gwysion Saesneg ar gyfer eisteddiadau eraill gyda nodyn cyfatebol yn Gymraeg; yr amcan oedd i'r *holl* weithrediadau fod yn Gymraeg ar ddyddiau ateb i'r wŷs Gymraeg, gyda Saesneg yn cael ei defnyddio pe dymunai'r cyhuddedig, ac yn Saesneg ar ddyddiau ateb y wŷs Saesneg a'r Gymraeg yn cael ei defnyddio pe dymunid. Cafwyd arbrofion mewn dau lys, Pwllheli ac Aberystwyth, ond ysywaeth, terfynwyd yr arbrawf, ac aethpwyd yn ôl at ddefnyddio'r Gymraeg yn ôl yr angen.

Anodd hefyd ddeall amharodrwydd cyffredinol yr Heddlu, fel awdurdod cyhoeddus, i erlyn trwy gyfrwng y Gymraeg, ac i roi tystiolaeth yn Gymraeg. Yng nghwrs achos, neu wrth roi hanes blaenorol y cyhuddedig wedi iddo gael ei ddedfrydu a hynny hyd yn oed mewn achosion lle bo'r diffynnydd yn dewis cyflwyno'i achos yn Gymraeg, eithriad prin, hyd yn oed heddiw, yw i swyddog heddlu gymaint â chymryd y llw yn Gymraeg. Y mae'r un sylwadau, ysywaeth, yn wir am y Gwasanaeth Profiannaeth.

Ymddengys fod y math hwn o ymddygiad yn tueddu'n gryf i barhau'r anghyfiawnder y bwriadodd Deddf yr Iaith ei ddileu, oherwydd yn ymhlyg yn yr agwedd hon y mae'r hen syniad a feithrinwyd ar hyd y canrifoedd, sef mai Saesneg yw iaith 'yr awdurdodau', mai iaith i'w defnyddio gan y sawl sydd yn brin ei Saesneg yw'r Gymraeg, ac mai pobl eithriadol, ac 'eithafol' yw'r rheini.

Ar adeg ysgrifennu'r geiriau hyn, y mae Mesur Sefydlu Gwasanaeth Erlyn Annibynnol i Loegr a Chymru o dan Reolaeth y Cyfarwyddwr Erlyniadau Cyhoeddus yn cael ei ystyried gan y Senedd. Y mae'n gwbl angenrheidiol, os yw Deddf yr Iaith i'w gweithredu'n gyfiawn ac effeithiol, fod y gwasanaeth newydd yng Nghymru yn cael ei weinyddu o fewn i fframwaith Cymreig, yn hytrach nag mewn cydgysylltiad â rhannau o Loegr, a bod cyflenwad digonol o gyfreithwyr, ym mhob rhan o Gymru, sydd yn barod ac yn abl i gyflwyno achosion yn Gymraeg yn cael eu cyflogi gan y gwasanaeth. Oni sicrheir cyflenwad digonol o dwrneiod a bargyfreithwyr hyddysg yn y Gymraeg ac unioni'r diffyg amlwg yn hyn o beth, sy'n bodoli ar hyn o bryd bron iawn trwy Gymru gyfan, yn enwedig yng Ngwynedd a Chlwyd, o bobman, anodd, hyd at amhosibl, fydd cynnal llysoedd yn Gymraeg. Anos fyth fydd creu'r awyrgylch ffafriol i'r Gymraeg yn y llysoedd sydd mor hanfodol i effeithiolrwydd Deddf yr Iaith Gymraeg.

Mewn astudiaeth bwysig a diddorol a wnaed gan aelodau o Adran y Gyfraith, Coleg y Brifysgol, Aberystwyth, a gyhoeddwyd dan y teitl, *The Welsh Language in the Courts*, sylwodd yr awduron na fu fawr o gynnydd yn y defnydd a wneir o'r Gymraeg yn y llysoedd yn sgil Deddf 1967.[47] Nid yw hyn yn syndod yn y byd. Ymhlith y rhesymau a roddant am hynny, rhestrir 'confensiynau cymdeithasol, personol, a chyhoeddus'.[48] Diau bod cysgod yr hen lyffetheiriau o hyd ar y llysoedd ac ar y sawl sydd, o ddewis neu o orfod, yn cymryd rhan yn eu gweithgareddau.[49]

Y mae'n amlwg nad digon ynddo'i hun yw cyhoeddi mewn deddf gwlad hawl y sawl a fynno ddefnyddio'r Gymraeg i'w defnyddio.

Y gwir plaen yw na wireddir yr hawl a roddir gan y Ddeddf i 'barti neu dyst neu unrhyw berson arall i ddefnyddio'r Gymraeg yn y llys' oni fyddo parodrwydd ar ran yr holl lysoedd a'u staff hyd at y swyddog distatlaf, ac ar ran yr awdurdodau cyhoeddus sydd yn defnyddio'r llys, megis yr heddlu a'r swyddogion profiannaeth, i ddangos yn gwbl glir, ar bob adeg, eu bod yn barod ac yn abl i ddefnyddio'r Gymraeg, ac i roi'r un urdas iddi ag a roddant i'r Saesneg. Ac i sicrhau hyn y mae angen polisi cadarn a threfnu gofalus. Oni wneir hyn, llythyren farw fydd Deddf yr Iaith, ei haddewid heb ei anrhydeddu a'i phwrpas wedi ei drechu gan yr union sefydliadau sydd â'r ddyletswydd o gynnal y gyfraith.

Y mae'n hanfodol ymhlyg felly yn Neddf yr Iaith fod dyletswydd ar yr awdurdodau cyhoeddus sydd yn ymwneud â gweinyddu'r llysoedd ac yn ymddangos ynddynt i hyrwyddo defnyddio'r Gymraeg nid yn unig pan fyddo arwyddion yn y dogfennau a'r datganiadau (gan gynnwys cyfweliadau) y defnyddir yr iaith Gymraeg mewn treial ond hefyd yn gyffredinol wrth weinyddu. Mater i'r awdurdodau yw penderfynu sut i fynd ati, ond ni ddylai fod anhawster os defnyddir synnwyr cyffredin ac ewyllys da. Y mae'r Ddeddf ei hun yn ei hanfod ac yn ei geiriad yn aml yn galw am yr ewyllys da hwnnw. Teg ychwanegu bod Gweinyddwr Cylchdaith Cymru a Chaer a'u prif swyddogion, o gychwyn system newydd Llys y Goron, yn gwbl deyrngar i Ddeddf yr Iaith a'i hamcanion a'i hoblygiadau.

Mater i'r sawl sydd yn llywodraethu mewn llys barn yw sicrhau bod yr awdurdodau cyhoeddus perthnasol yn gweithredu'n deg ac yn unol â'r gyfraith wrth gynnal gweithrediadau yn y llysoedd ym mater yr iaith fel ym mhob mater arall.

Y mae, serch hynny, un gwendid cynhenid yn y Ddeddf os ei hamcan yw gorseddu'r Gymraeg mewn bywyd cyhoeddus. Er bod y Rhaglith yn cymeradwyo priodoldeb defnyddio'r Gymraeg gyda'r un effaith â'r Saesneg wrth weinyddu busnes swyddogol a chyhoeddus arall yng Nghymru a bod achos *Evans v. Thomas* yn sail dros ddatgan yn gyffredinol fod gweithred a wneir yn Gymraeg, i gael yr un effaith â phetai wedi ei gwneud yn Saesneg, nid yw'r Ddeddf ei hun yn rhoi hawl i ddinesydd fynnu bod awdurdodau cyhoeddus yn cyfathrebu ag ef yn Gymraeg. Y mae absenoldeb hawl o'r fath yn gwanhau ffydd y cyhoedd yn effeithiolrwydd y Gymraeg fel iaith busnes cyhoeddus ac yn rhwystro amcan a phwrpas y Ddeddf. Y mae dygn angen rhoi'r hawliau hyn ar seiliau cadarn trwy ddatganiad statudol. Y mae'n ganlyniad rhesymegol i Ddeddf yr Iaith. Ond uwchlaw popeth, y mae'n fater o gyfiawnder.

[Yr ydwyf yn ddiolchgar i Mr Tegwyn Jones, o staff Geiriadur Prifysgol Cymru, am ei gymorth wrth olygu'r bennod hon. (Gol.)]

---

[1] *Statws Cyfreithiol yr Iaith Gymraeg* (Gwasg Ei Mawrhydi, Cmnd 2785, 1965).

[2] Co. Litt. 79a.

[3] Co. Litt. 93a.

[4] *L.C.C. v. Bermondsey Bioscope Co.* [1911] 1 KB 445, 451.

[5] (1848) 2 Exch 256, 283.

[6] *Reg. v. Merthyr Tydfil Justices, ex parte Jenkins* [1967] 1 All ER 636. Rhoddwyd y dyfarniad ar 9 Tachwedd 1966.

[7] [1962] 2 QB 350.

[8] Yr unig eithriad i'r polisi o wahardd defnyddio'r Gymraeg mewn gweithgareddau cyhoeddus oedd yng ngwasanaethau'r Eglwys — eithriad pwysig a brofodd yn dyngedfennol i barhad yr iaith (statud 5 Eliz. 1 c. 28). Erbyn hyn (1563) wrth gwrs, yr oedd Thomas Cromwell, pensaer deddfwriaeth y Deddfau Uno, wedi hen fynd i'w aped.

[9] Statud 27 Hen. VIII c. 26, 'Adran 20' yn ôl argraffiad Ruffhead o'r *Statutes at Large*.

[10] Statud 27 Hen VIII c. 5.

[11] G. J. Williams, *Traddodiad Llenyddol Morgannwg* (Caerdydd, 1948), Pennod 3. Ymysg y teuluoedd y mae'n eu henwi, ceir enwau Stradlingiaid Sain Dunwyd, Mawnseliaid Margam, Basetiaid Bewpyr, teulu'r Fan ger Caerffili a Morganiaid Tredegyr; nifer ohonynt wedi magu ynadon. *J. Gwynfor Jones*, 'The Welsh Poets and their Patrons', (1978/9) 9 *Cylchgrawn Hanes Cymru* 245-77, enwir, ymhlith eraill, deuluoedd Gwydir a Chlenennau; J. Gwynfor Jones, 'Governance, Order and Stability in Caernarfonshire *1540-1640*', (1983) 44 *Trafodion Cymdeithas Hanes Sir Gaernarfon* 7-52. Yn yr unfed ganrif ar bymtheg am y tro cyntaf, daeth yr arfer o sarhau'r iaith Gymraeg yn gyhoeddus a'i hanwesu'n breifat i'r amlwg trwy Gymru gyfan — deuoliaeth ryfedd a barhaodd mewn llawn bri hyd at y 1970au ac nad yw eto wedi ei chladdu.

[12] Deddf Llywodraeth Leol 1888, 51/2 Vic. c. 41.

[13] Deddf Llywodraeth Leol 1894, 56/7 Vic. c. 73.

[14] Gweler:
Penry Williams, 'The Political and Administrative History of Glamorgan 1536-1642'. *Glamorgan County History*, (Caerdydd, 1974), Cyfrol IV, Pennod 3; Gareth E. Jones, *The Gentry and the Elizabethan State*, 1541-1689 (Abertawe, 1977). Disgrifia G. J. Williams uchelwyr Morgannwg yn y cyfnod hwn fel 'gwŷr garw, afreolus . . . yn caru ymgyntach a chyfreithio', disgrifiad byr ond cywir o'r dosbarth llywodraethol a gododd yn sgil deddfwriaeth Harri'r VIII, gw. G. J. Williams, op. cit. 76.

[15] 34-5 Hen. VIII c. 26.

[16] W. R. Williams: *The Welsh Judges* (Aberhonddu, 1899), 19. Ceir cyfoeth o wybodaeth am Lys y Sesiwn Fawr yn y llyfr hwn. Yn ychwanegol at y rhestr fanwl o holl farnwr y Llys a'i brif swyddogion o 1542 tan 1830, ceir braslun o dras a gyrfa'r barnwyr. O lyfr W. R. Williams y daw'r wybodaeth am Lys y Sesiwn Fawr yn yr ysgrif hon.

[17] Dyfynir cynnwys y llythyr yn Williams: *The Welsh Judges, 16; Calendar of State Papers Domestic,* 514.

[18] Op. cit. n.16, 163.

[19] Nid oedd diffyg yn y cyflenwad o Gymry (llawer yn sicr yn Gymry Cymraeg) â chymwysterau cwbl addas i'w hapwyntio i Lys y Sesiwn Fawr fel y dengys y nifer a ddyrchafwyd i fainc y barnwyr yn y gwahanol lysoedd brenhinol yn Llundain o ddyddiau Harri VIII hyd at ddiwedd y ddeunawfed ganrif. D. Seaborne Davies: *Welsh Makers of English Law.* Darlith Radio Flynyddol BBC Cymru (Caerdydd, 1967).

[20] 36 Edw. III c. 15. Y mae'r rhesymau a roddwyd yn Rhaglith y Ddeddf hon dros droi i'r Saesneg yn Lloegr yn 1362 yn ddiddorol o gofio amharodrwydd y Senedd, o'r unfed ganrif ar bymtheg hyd at yr ugeinfed, i gymhwyso'r un egwyddorion at y Gymraeg yn enwedig mewn perthynas â'r Gymru Gymraeg. '*Because. . . the Laws be pleaded showed and judged in the French tongue which is much unknown in the. . . Realm so that people which do implead or be impleaded in the King's Court and in the Courts of other have no knowledge nor understanding of that which is said for them or against them by the Sergeants and other pleaders and that reasonably the said laws and customs the rather shall be perceived and known and better understood in the tongue used in this Realm and by so much every man of the Realm may better govern himself without offending the law and the better keep save and defend his heritage and possessions and in divers regions and countries. . . good governance and full rights done to every person because that their laws and customs be learned and used in the tongue of their coutry, the King, desiring the good governance and tranquility of his People and to put out and eschew the harm and mischief which do or may happen in this behalf by the occasion aforesaid hath ordained that all Pleas which shall be pleaded in any Courts whatsoever before any of his justices whatsoever within the Realm shall be pleaded, shewed, defended, answered, debated and judged in the English tongue and that they be entered and inrolled in Latin.*' Nid dyma'r egwyddor a weithredwyd yn achos y Cymry uniaith Gymraeg yn 1536 nac yn y canrifoedd a'i dilynodd. Yr wyf yn ddyledus i'r Dr Clive Knowles, Coleg y Brifysgol, Caerdydd, am dynnu fy sylw at y Ddeddf hon.

[21] Ceir enghreifftiau lu o hyn yn yr adroddiadau o achosion y cyfnod yn arbennig yn adroddiadau Thomas Siderfin, 82 English Reports. Gweler, er enghraifft, yr adroddiad am achos un o'r enw *Fitzgerald* (1662), 'Fuit dit per Twisden Justices que si J.S. soit in execution & hebeas (sic) corpus ad testificandum est direct al gaoler lou J.S. est in custody a porter luy que est son prison.'

[22] Deddf Diddymu Deddfau Trefniadaeth Sifil 1879, 42 & 43 Vict c. 59.

[23] [1962] 2 QB 350.

[24] *Statws Cyfreithiol yr Iaith Gymraeg* (n.1), 41.

[25] Llythyr oddi wrth Syr Richard Webster, y Twrnai Cyffredinol, yn ateb tri chwestiwn a ofynnwyd iddo mewn llythyr oddi wrth Samuel Pope (yr unig aelod o gyngor Sir Feirionnydd na fedrai'r Gymraeg). Nid oes sôn am yr ohebiaeth yng nghofnodion swyddogol Sir Feirionnydd ond y mae hanes yr ohebiaeth yn llawn yn *Baner ac Amserau Cymru,* 6 Mawrth 1889. Rwy'n ddyledus i Mr Meurig Parry o Archifdy Meirion am yr wybodaeth hon.

[26] Daeth hyn i'm sylw trwy fy nhad, un o ymddiriedolwyr Eglwys y Tabernacl, Caerdydd. Dylanwadodd y digwyddiad yn drwn arnaf wrth baratoi'r ddadl dros y Pleintydd yn achos *Evans v. Thomas.* Ni welwn sut, yn ôl cyfraith gwlad, y gellid credu bod cofnod gweithrediadau ymddiriedolwyr capel Cymraeg ei iaith yn llai dilys ac effeithiol yn Gymraeg

nag yn Saesneg. Ni welwn chwaith sut y gellid dadlau bod rhin arbennig yn yr iaith Saesneg cyn y gallai dogfen ysgrifenedig greu perthynas gyfreithiol a gydnabyddid gan y llysoedd fel un ddilys. O hyn y tarddodd y ddadl bwysicaf a roddwyd ger bron y Llys yn *Evans v. Thomas*, sef bod i ffurflen enwebu'r Pleintydd, Mr Evans, yr un dilysrwydd â ffurflen Saesneg gan ei bod 'to like effect'.

[27] 'House of Commons Official report: Parliamentary Debates (*Hansard*)' (Tŷ'r Cyffredin), Trydedd Gyfres, Cyfrol 209 (1872), colofn 1654. Cymharer datganiadau'r Arglwydd Hatherley, yr Arglwydd Ganghellor ar y pryd, y cyfeirir atynt gan Osborne Morgan yn ei araith, a datganiadau tra gwahanol ei olynydd, Arglwydd Hailsham o St Marylebone, yn Nhŷ'r Arglwyddi gan mlynedd yn ddiweddarach, (*Hansard* (Tŷ'r Arglwyddi) Pumed Gyfres, Cyfrol 343 (1973), colofnau 532-9).

[28] *Ibid.*

[29] Dafydd Jenkins: *Tân yn Llŷn* (Aberystwyth, 1937), 142.

[30] *Hansard* (Tŷ'r Cyffredin) Pumed Gyfres, Cyfrol 383 (1942), col. 1667 et seq. Gweler yn arbennig areithiau Lewis Jones, James Griffiths a Robert Richards.

[31] [1967] 1 All ER 636.

[32] Deddf Llysoedd Cymru 1942 (c.40) Adran 3 (1) a Rheolau Llysoedd Cymru (Llwon a Chyfreithwyr) a wnaethpwyd o dan Ddeddf 1942.

[33] [1962] 2 QB 350.

[34] Ibid. §366.

[35] Ibid. §370.

[36] Ni ddenodd yr achos y tyrfaoedd. Deg o bersonau yn unig oedd yn bresennol yn Llys 6 yn y Llysoedd Barn Brenhinol yn Llundain pan wrandawyd ar yr achos, naw ohonynt yn swyddogion llys neu'n fargyfreithwyr. Aelod o'r cyhoedd, Y Parchedig J.M. Jones, Llanbedrog wedyn, oedd y degfed, a'r unig aelod o'r cyhoedd.

[37] Deddf Etholiadau (Ffurflenni Cymraeg) 1964 c. 31.

[38] Saunders Lewis: *Tynged yr Iaith*, Darlith Radio Flynyddol BBC Cymru (Caerdydd, 1962).

[39] Statws Cyfreithiol yr Iaith Gymraeg §§165, 174, 203.

[40] Ibid. §172.

[41] Ibid. §176.

[42] Ibid. §§176 a 208.

[43] Ibid. §233.

[44] Gweler cyfeiriad at y datganiad hwn yn *Hansard* (Tŷ'r Arglwyddi) Pumed Gyfres, Cyfrol 343 (1973), colofn 532.

[45] Trawsysgrif o ddyfarniad yr Ustus Mars-Jones (heb ei chyhoeddi).

[46] *Hansard* (Tŷ'r Arglwyddi), Pumed Gyfres, Cyfrol 343 (1973), colofnau 532-539.

[47] J.A. Andrews ac L.G. Henshaw, *The Welsh Language in The Courts* (Aberystwyth, 1984), 56. Y llyfryn hwn yw'r unig fan lle y ceir Deddfau 1942 a 1967 yn eu crynswth ac yn dilyn ei gilydd mewn ffurf hylaw.

[48] Op. cit. 92.

[49] Er enghraifft, mewn mater mor syml â chymryd y llw yn Gymraeg y mae'n syndod mor amharod yw'r rheithwyr yn yr ardaloedd Cymraeg, y mae'r Gymraeg yn amlwg yn iaith gyntaf naturiol iddynt, i gymryd y llw yn yr iaith honno hyd yn oed pan fyddo'r barnwr (neu'r cadeirydd) yn rhoi blaenoriaeth i'r Gymraeg yn y rhannau ffurfiol o weithrediadau'r llys, megis cyhoeddi, agor a chau'r llys a'i ohirio neu wrth ddatgan hawl rheithwyr i gymryd y llw yn Gymraeg neu Saesneg yn ôl eu dewis.

AN ENGLISH TRAGEDY: THE ACADEMIC LAWYER AS JURIST

Ian Fletcher

I. Introductory

Once upon a time, it seemed to be the most natural and easy of things for the Emperor Justinian to exhort his youthful subjects to undertake the study of law as a fitting preparation for the future role in government and administration for which they (a small proportion of them, at any rate) were destined.[1] In the centuries which have succeeded the 'Age of Justinian', and in regions far beyond the borders even of his audacious ambitions, the academic study of law has indeed become a well established means of intellectual preparation for the accomplishment of great and diverse ends, both in individual and in communal terms. The *cachet* thus long enjoyed by the university law degree in continental Europe and, in more recent times, even further afield including the Americas, renders all the more curious the contrasting position occupied by academic legal studies in England and Wales until well into the present century, and indeed still to be remarked upon to this very day. In celebrating the personal and intellectual achievement of the *honoratus* of the present volume, whose career has so felicitously straddled both practical affairs and academic studies and teaching of the utmost distinction, it is perhaps not inappropriate to reflect on the historic — and still perceptible — want of recognition of the proper role and place of academic law, and of academic lawyers, in our national life. It will be suggested that, while the former neglect of juristic pursuits may have achieved at least one commendable objective, namely that of enabling the Common Law to resist the onset of an incipient civilian reception and thereby to retain its individuality and distinctiveness, the subsequent continuation of this essentially philistine piece of perversity in English tradition is to be deplored for a number of reasons, and above all for the damage perpetually being done to the development, practice and administration of our law in the present day.

If historic factors may be justly blamed for the disadvantaged situation of English academic lawyers up until very recently, the continuation of this unsatisfactory state of affairs, even in a somewhat attenuated form, is a malady for which the academics themselves must assume their proportionate share of the blame. The centuries-long failure of English academics to interest themselves in the study of their native system of law has effectively deprived us of a properly-rooted juristic tradition in this country. It should perhaps be made clear at this point that by 'jurist' we are here to understand a particular type of academic lawyer, namely one whose scholarly investigations, writings and other activities are so conducted as to enable him to make an active contribution to the development of the law itself, whether in relation to its substantive content or in its procedural and administrative aspects. The jurist is therefore a maker of the law, and not merely one who, as teacher endowed with no matter what degree of erudition, merely imparts an understanding of the present or past state of the law to future generations of teachers or practitioners. The dearth of such a tradition in England is perhaps best appreciated in contrast with the very different state of affairs which has long been a prevailing feature of much of continental Europe.

II. THE JURISTIC TRADITION IN EUROPE

In the beginning there were no universities. But there were jurists. The role which the Roman *jurisprudentes* created for themselves during the formative phase of Roman private law effectively ensured that, through all the changing circumstances experienced during the evolution of the civilian legal tradition within Europe, a thriving juristic tradition would simultaneously command recognition — indeed acclaim — as an integral component in the structure and fabric of legal administration. The style and character of the legal education and training which were first received, and subsequently imparted, by a Julian, an Ulpian or a Papinian, proved historically decisive in ensuring that the developed Roman law was properly endowed with the quintessential characteristics of consistency and fidelity to principle, combined with a capacity for responding to changed, or changing, social conditions, which are indispensable to any system of justice which is to be worthy of the name. The development of the techniques whereby this delicate task could be accomplished in a continuous and consistent manner, the imparting of those techniques to further generations of jurists, and the preservation in written form of the wisdom derived from careful observation of the dynamic interaction between principle and theory on the one hand, and living practice on the other, were complementary aspects of an integral and unique process. Fortuitously, the constitutional and political circumstances of the Roman Principate proved to be conducive to the flourishing, in the realm of private law at least, of a liberal tradition of open and public juristic activity, whose antecedents may nevertheless be traced far back into the Republican period when legal wisdom was an arcane privilege enjoyed by the members of the College of Pontiffs. However, despite the superficial appearance of independence of spirit and position enjoyed by the classical jurists, we may discern the efforts of successive emperors to manipulate the careers and influence of certain of these supposedly autonomous individuals, through various forms of imperial patronage and endorsement, ranging from the initial strategem whereby the so-called *ius respondendi ex auctoritate principis* was selectively conferred upon a favoured few, to the subsequent practice of directly harnessing their talents in the service of emperor and state by appointment to the *consilium principis* and to specific, governmental positions. [2]

Although from the third century AD onwards the increasingly authoritarian and bureaucratic form of imperial government proved no longer conducive to the active continuation, or revival, of juristic activities, the preserved fruits of the classical jurists' work were destined to endure and, thanks to the timely labour of Tribonian and his fellow commissioners, undergo preservation in a form capable of serving the needs of subsequent ages and societies within and beyond post-Roman Europe. What is to be remarked upon is the way in which, during the successive phases of the European revival of legal activities leading to the eventual reception of Roman law across much of Europe, and subsequently thereafter, the role of the jurist once again assumed a pre-eminence which transcended any purely academic context in which legal learning might happen to be centred, and recaptured that influence upon the living practice and administration of the law which had been such a remarkable feature of the Roman classical period. This appears to have been true even of the early representatives of the Glossatorial school in their activities during the late eleventh century, but increasingly so of their successors from the early twelfth century onwards: not only were Irnerius and the Four Doctors (Martinus Gosia, Bulgarus, Jacobus and Hugo de Porta Ravennate) personally involved as counsellors and advisors to heads of state, including the Holy Roman Emperor, of their time, but also their classrooms were populated by a cosmopolitan body of students attracted in their thousands from all over Europe and consisting of men primarily destined not for the Bench or Bar, but rather to occupy positions as administrators and legal advisors in Church and State affairs. The modern juristic tradition thus came to be founded in medieval Tuscany by men whose approach to their vocation seems to have been almost consciously moulded upon the examples of their distinguished classical Roman forebears, whose preserved writings also furnished the basic source for their own creative work as well as endowing it with an awesome mystique and authority.

The dominating influence which came to be exercised by the most accomplished and illustrious of the Glossators and commentators, in their respective generations, has been memorably captured for posterity in the form of rhyming epigrams of contemporary origin, which duly proclaim the near-monopoly of all wisdom enjoyed first by Azo (*Chi non ha Azo non vada a Palazzo*) and later by Bartolus (*Nemo jurista nisi sit Bartolista*). Moreover, the singular recognition accorded in 1250 to the *Glossa Ordinaria* of Accursius through its codification as law was likewise commemorated in words which, by declaring that only those parts of the *Corpus Iuris* upon which a gloss had been written would be accepted as worthy law,[3] indicate that Bolognese jurists by that time enjoyed an authority which was *sui generis*, rather than merely being dependent upon the acknowledged status of the *Corpus Iuris* of Justinian, upon which their writings and annotations were based.[4]

The cumulative prestige and authority earned by the Glossators and Commentators by the end of the medieval period duly ensured a perpetual place for a juristic tradition in continental Europe. This tradition, while itself responsible in large part for the progressive reception of Roman law, also served to consolidate the fruits of that reception, and in due course enabled the law to progress along lines of divergence away from the common source, thus establishing distinct and vital national systems of law. It can once again be stressed that social and political circumstances proved highly favourable to the gaining of this ascendancy by members of the revived juristic tradition: they found themselves to be in possession of a scarce and much-needed commodity, namely, a knowledge and understanding of the corpus of transmitted knowledge concerning the principles and techniques for regulating human affairs in accordance with a commonly accepted system of values productive of a sense of justice and order. The jurists' success in establishing themselves as the very arbiters of rectitude and good judgment was greatly facilitated, as Dawson among others has ably demonstrated,[5] by the fact that continental judges, unlike their English counterparts, enjoyed no customary immunity from action or indictment for alleged misconduct in performing their judicial functions but were indeed frequently subjected to a positive form of systematic scrutiny at the hands of their successors in office. These practices, developed in Italy from the thirteenth century onwards and directly inspired by the example of the Roman Law action arising quasi-delictually against a judge '*qui litem suam fecit*', effectively brought about two essential developments. First, they gave rise to a tendency on the part of judges regularly to solicit the opinions of the learned university doctors regarding the appropriate terms of the judgments they were called upon to give. Secondly, this very practice, which initially furnished the judge with a form of 'insurance' against his later undergoing condemnation for '*imperitia*' or '*imprudentia*', effectively established a sense of relativity of status and authority as between *judex* and *sapiens*, with the former quite demonstrably subordinate to the latter. Thus, there became established the ingrained attitudes, and habits of thought and behaviour, which to this day remain characteristic of continental jurisprudence, namely the sense of comparative unimportance attending the judicial personality and the individual judicial decision, to be contrasted with the general recognition of the vital role played by the jurists in maintaining and developing the totality of the law in a consistent and intellectually satisfying manner. The acceptance of juristic doctrine as a formal source of law, and the concomitant practice of freely receiving the citation in court of the works of authors both living and dead to whom the status of 'authority' has been conceded, are but two of the most notable discrepancies between the continental and the English legal traditions.

It must be observed, especially in view of what will shortly be said below, that although the foregoing developments were originally associated with the movement for the revival and reception of Roman civil law, the juristic techniques and practices established out of the work of the schools of Glossators and Commentators were in some regions of Europe appropriated and applied to alternative legal traditions, with historically important consequences. Thus, from the sixteenth century onwards there emerged in the northerly part of France (the *pays de droit coutumier*) a parallel juristic tradition to that of the romanists belonging to the *pays de droit écrit*. In the *pays de droit coutumier*, where the Germanic customary laws had been rendered into written form in fulfilment of the *ordonnance* of Charles VII promulgated midway through the fifteenth century, there existed in consequence the source-material upon which to found a rival, national school of juristic studies based upon the customary laws. It is greatly to the credit of such men as Dumoulin, Loisel, D'Argentré and Coquille that from the sixteenth century onwards such a dual-track development took place. By this means not only was the inexorable progress of Roman law in France checked to a large degree, and the perpetuation of a rich and characteristic vein of French law secured, but also a significant demonstration was given to the adacemic world of the possibilities for serious and valuable juristic studies to be undertaken in relation to an indigenous legal tradition whose origins were not to be found in centuries-old documents and treatises, but whose roots were scarcely less ancient, while being frequently more in harmony with popular feelings and instinct.

Similar movements to secure the preservation, and even the revitalisation, of a native legal tradition occurred, albeit with far less conspicuous success, in Germany and in northern Italy. In neither case, it is true, did the achievements of the non-civilians match those of their French counterparts, who effectively brought about the curious paradox that the French *Code*

Civil of 1804 was destined to embody far more elements traceable to Germanic customary laws than were to be found in the German *BGB* of 1900. Nevertheless, the point can be made that both in Italy, the cradle of the rebirth of Roman law, and in Germany, the country in which the reception of Roman law ultimately enjoyed its most spectacular successes, dedicated academic traditions for the study, respectively, of the Lombardic laws and of Germanic customary laws survived until the eighteenth and nineteenth centuries. Thus, it was by no means inevitable that in a jurisdiction such as England, where there is evidence for university legal studies since at least the middle of the twelfth century, the serious and systematic study of English law, as opposed to Roman and Canon law, as an established part of the university curriculum should to all intents have been postponed until late in the nineteenth century. Yet such was to be the case.

III. THE NON-EMERGENCE OF A JURISTIC TRADITION IN ENGLAND

Much has been written concerning the identifiable reasons for the ultimate non-reception of Roman law in England, and it is invariably agreed that key factors among the developments occuring in the crucial period between the reigns of Henry II and Edward I were the successive achievements of the monarchy, first in establishing a centralised administration of justice, and subsequently in creating what was effectively a *cordon sanitaire* around the nascent common law system. Of these accomplishments the former ensured, among other things, an organised resistance to the type of 'rolling reception' of Roman law which was to occur elswehere, notably in Germany, while the latter had the effect of precluding any form of 'intellectual reception' of Roman law resulting from a formalized interaction between jurists and judiciary in the manner which was described above. By the severing of ties between the academic and the professional centres of legal learning and instruction, and the development at the Inns of Court of a self-contained system within which practitioners and apprentice practitioners of the common law were exclusively concentrated, the destiny of English law was effectively determined. The teaching of Roman law and Canon law in the universities of Oxford and Cambridge continued, but its exponents did not see fit to devote themselves to the scholarly investigation of the law as actually practised within the courts of the country in which they were living. The enduring scandal attaching to the doctors of law at the English universities until the last century is that they displayed a permanent want of intellectual curiosity towards the common law, and thus confined their scholarly pursuits to the two areas mentioned. Within the restricted field of practice available to the denizens of Doctors' Commons, where a specialised monopoly in probate, divorce and admiralty endured until the passing of the Judicature Acts of 1873-75, the English civilians could legitimately claim to be actively engaged in the shaping and development of the law of the land. But across the major part of English law generally, the civilians inside and outide the universities failed to make any significant impact. The common law thus maintained its integrity and survived to attain its maturity as a distinct tradition with unique and important properties which the comparative lawyer of the present age can properly appreciate for their contribution to 'genetic diversity' among the legal systems of the world, out of which fertile and dynamic legal development can take place. But it is the present writer's regretful conclusion that some of the very factors and arrangements which enabled the common law to resist assimilation into the Romanist legal family have, in the long term, brought about a serious impairment of our system's capability to function at the optimum levels of attainment of which it is inherently capable. This, it is submitted, is the price which has been paid historically, and which continues to be paid at the present time, for the failure of the English common law to encourage the growth of a native juristic tradition, coupled with the collateral failure of the English universities to cultivate such a tradition even in the face of judicial and professional antagonism. Thus the 'philistine' propensities of the common law system itself are exemplified by the sustained application of a rule forbidding the citation in court of the writings or opinions of any author until after his death, and then only after the writings of the said author have belatedly and begrudgingly been accorded the status of 'books of authority'. This restrictive rule, though technically to be classified only as a rule of etiquette, was for so long rigidly maintained and applied as to enjoy as much *de facto* force as any formal rule of law, its progressive relaxation having effectively commenced only in the latter half of the twentieth century.[6] This resolute exclusion from English courtrooms of all non-judicial expressions of opinion concerning the law undoubtedly helped to ensure that the common law would not fall prey to the continental practice whereby (partly no doubt arising from the circumstances explained above, but chiefly on account of the eminence and excellence of their scholarly opinons) the writings and pronouncements of jurists came progressively to be acknowledged as formal sources of law, in some instances indeed with binding effect.[7] But the corollary to this state of affairs during the centuries-long development of the common law was that the so-called 'common law' of England became, in the hands of an isolated, enclosed and self-selecting body of practitioners and judges, an arcane, remote and impenetrable science — a conglomeration rather than a system — lacking even the redeeming virtues of intellectual coherence and conceptual consistency. By reason of these two important qualities, the otherwise increasingly abstract and rarified products of continental jurisprudence could at least be partially justified in the face of criticism from lay quarters. It is surely a paradox replete with much irony that the English, who so pride themselves upon their pragmatism and common sense, should in the end have created a system of law whose substantive contents, as well as its procedural functioning, are in their own way frequently as far remote from the comprehension and intuitive acceptance of ordinary persons as is the case elsewhere with the most intricate elaborations of the high art of *Professorenrecht*. The conscious spurning of an intellectual dimension on the part of the common law has not in the end served to render that system either more accessible or more intelligible to the population whose needs it is supposed to serve.

It could indeed be observed that, by means of the policy described above of obstinate self-immunisation from the possible effects of an academic legal education, the English Bar and Judiciary simultaneously ensured that the system of which they remained the perpetual, if self-appointed, custodians would remain practically inaccessible to all save those who had the means, and the cast of mind and character, to submit themselves to the system of training prescribed and administered from within. And while the quality of general education imparted by the Inns of Court during the formative period of their development, and down to Tudor times at least, might well be said to have compared favourably with that to be derived from a period of residence and study at the majority of contemporary universities, even this aspect of the Inns' functioning fell increasingly into desuetude, so that it came to be the case that they provided neither a rigorous intellectual training for the law, nor a suitably-rounded training for life. Severed from the humanities, and from all broadening contact with cosmopolitan society and culture, English professional legal training became increasingly moribund, lacklustre and introverted. Indeed, by the nineteenth and twentieth centuries it had become customary for those whose destiny lay at the Bar — and potentially thereafter on the Bench — to resort to one of the Universities for the purpose of completing their general education. But it is notable that, even until very recent times, such persons would almost without exception have regarded the study of law as the very last thing to which they should dedicate their undergraduate years. Indeed, it might be argued with some validity that, by the period of which we are now speaking, an intensive study of Roman and Canon law offered little that seemed of relevance to the future needs of one destined to practise within a distinctively non-romanist system of law, but it might rather have served to confuse and bemuse him. But more to the point, it must be said, was the complete absence within the university law faculties of any established tradition for the systematic, critical and scholarly study of the common law itself, a state of affairs which effectively persisted until the onset of the first generation of truly authoritative teachers of English law, represented by such figures as Pollock,Maitland, Dicey, Holland and Anson. It may be objected that there were earlier, historically significant innovations in the teaching of English law at our universities, for were not Blackstone's lectures delivered at Oxford from 1753 onwards, was not the Vinerian Chair of English Law created there in 1758, and the Downing Chair at Cambridge founded in 1800, and was not a Chair in English Law held by John Austin at the newly-founded University College London between 1828 and 1832? The answer to all these questions must be in the form of a guarded 'Yes, but...'. Of Blackstone it may be observed that his original aspirations had been directed towards the Chair of Civil Law at Oxford; and that his *Commentaries*, and the lectures out of which his *magnum opus* developed, were inspired by a strong personal reaction towards the totally negative quality of the education for the Bar which he encountered in the Middle Temple between 1743 and 1746; and that the *Commentaries* themselves were destined to prove more directly influential in the United States than in their native England. Of both the Vinerian and the Downing Chairs, it must be remarked that, Blackstone apart, neither Chair succeeded in attracting, among its early incumbents, men of the calibre and dedication necessary for the successful inauguration of an intellectually respectable tradition for the study of English law. Nor can the unhappy and ill-fated experiences of John Austin during his four-year tenure of a Chair of English Law at University College be counted as anything other than a demonstration of the extent of the apathy, if not indeed hostility, encountered by the very notion of an attempt to found an academic profession of law in early nineteenth-century England. Thus it was not until the last quarter of the nineteenth century, with the simultaneous flourishing at Oxford and Cambridge of the generation of *illustres* already referred to (the majority of whom had not themselves, for obvious reasons, read law as undergraduates), that regular and established programmes of instruction in English law properly commenced.[8] The amount of lost ground to be made up was by that time enormous, and there was practically no established foundation upon which to begin building: the report of the Select Committee on Legal Education of 1846 had revealed the abysmal condition in which all legal education, both academic and professional, was then to be found.[9]

Despite the undoubted brilliance and imagination of the first torchbearers of the late renaissance of English legal studies, they were destined to find their efforts opposed and frustrated on almost every conceivable front.

Among the ranks of the Bar and the Bench, the age-old prejudices and conspiracies of interest were encountered whenever any purposeful initiatives in reforming legal education presented themselves. Such, for example, was the case with the abortive proposals for the creation of a 'College of Law' and a 'Legal University' in response to the recommendations of the Report of the Select Committee of 1846, and of the Royal Commission of 1855.[10] These successive projects perished, among other reasons, because they came to be too closely identified with simultaneous movements designed to promote fusion between the barristers' and solicitors' professions, and in this guise they drew upon themselves fire from entrenched positions within the Inns and on the Bench, to the majority of whose members any encroachment upon the professional and institutional *status quo* was completely anathema. Thus it came about that the limited intellectual resources available for the establishment of a proper tradition for the teaching of English law were dissipated between the nascent university law faculties, and the separate and rival institutions developed somewhat belatedly by the two wings of the legal profession as their own responses to the censorious comments directed at their respective programmes of training by the Reports of 1846 and 1855. It had been one of the main exhortations of the Select Committee Report that the universities should be taken into partnership, so to speak, in the provision of a two-stage education in law, with the professional stage only to be provided by a special institution to be run by the professions themselves. Rather than defer to this suggestion, the professions each elected to develop separate institutions and programmes for training their own recruits, taking no account of such facilities for the provision of a general academic training in law as the universities might have been able to offer. The possession of a law degree — or indeed of any degree — thus remained a matter of formal indifference to both branches of this supposedly 'learned' profession until far more recent times, when the obtaining of a university degree of some kind (albeit still not necessarily in law) has become the more usual, but still not the invariable, preliminary to entry into the legal profession.

But if the university law schools continued to encounter, until well after the Second World War, sustained prejudice and hostility from among the entrenched establishment of the professions and the Bench itself, it must have seemed doubly demoralising for the academic laywers to find themselves disparaged and derided from within the universities themselves, by members of other faculties who took exception to what they considerd to be the uduly vocational, non-academic nature of legal studies. Thus, the academic lawyers found their credentials simultaneously rejected by their academic peers, on account of the excessively vocational nature of their activities, and by the legal professions, because of their alleged *lack* of vocational and professional relevance! Small wonder, then, that the character of the typical English academic lawyer frequently appears to be marked by a special type of inferiority complex, mingled with certain elements even of paranoia. From one generation of law teachers to the next, it would seem, these unfortunate mental dispositions have been engendered as a result of the constant need to justify and defend one's rôle and existence within the university structure by deploying a particular set of arguments, while at other times, and by other quite contradictory arguments, striving to maintain one's dignity and self-respect in the face of dismissive or — worse — at times, patronising attitudes displayed by judges and practitioners of high degree and low. What must it have felt like for example, to sit in the audience at the annual meeting of the Society of Public Teachers of Law in 1958 and listen to the distinguished guest speaker — the future Lord Devlin — solemnly declaring that 'The function of the academic lawyer is that of the critic of the finer points of play'?[11] Nor could it be particularly reassuring to read, in a popular textbook supposedly written for law students, that 'it is open to question whether law is a very suitable subject for academic study'.[12] Inevitably, in the face of unsympathetic attitudes and pronouncements from both the quarters to which they would naturally look for recognition and acceptance, academic lawyers as a profession have at times behaved erratically and performed disappointingly. At times, claims concerning the vocational relevance of academic legal courses have been exaggerated in an attempt to win the favourable estimation of the profession. On other occasions academics may, like Peter, have been surprised to hear themselves denying the very foundations of their own discipline and creed in the face of some real or imagined accusation of guilt by association. Thus, sadly, it has come about that despite the proliferation of university law schools in recent times, and despite the commensurate increase in the numbers of those teaching and studying therein, the academic lawyer's crisis of identity has remained unresolved, and he or she frequently exists in a state of doubt (nonetheless real for being too often unacknowledged) as to whether what is being undertaken is merely the provision of a preparatory training for future practitioners or an academic pursuit, valid and complete in itself as an educational experience, from which students will derive much benefit regardless of their ultimate career or vocation, but which is utterly indispensable for anyone actually proposing to make a profession in the law. The latter state of mind, which is perhaps all too readily taken for granted by continental academics, does not yet prevail here. Instead, an uneasy attitude of mistrust, suspicion and at times open hostility characterises many aspects of relationships between academics and practising lawyers. At its most pernicious, this can give rise to confrontations of the most damaging kind, as where a student body, the majority of whom already aspire to a career in the law, discover that their university studies are taking place within a Faculty whose members, either openly or at least privately, profess to despise and disdain the careers into which their pupils are destined to enter. Thus, a mood of cynicism, nihilism and alienation ultimately prevails on both sides of the classroom, with students emerging from their academic experience shorn of their ideals, disillusioned and dispirited. It is small wonder then that, if they are to re-establish some semblance of self-respect and develop faith in the validity of their own chosen career in life, many law graduates quickly develop a defence mechanism in the form of a conscious or subconscious rejection of the 'academic' standpoint itself, and thereby participate in confirming and perpetuating the fundamental antagonism between academic and professional lawyer. During the most recent phase of the evolution of legal education in England, many of these destructive and negative conditions have been, if anything, even more sharply exposed as a result of the false dawn, and the subsequent series of disappointing developments, associated with the publication of the Ormrod Report in 1971.[13]

IV. ORMROD AND AFTER

In December 1967 the then Lord Chancellor, Lord Gardiner, appointed a Committee on Legal Education under the chairmanship of Mr. Justice Ormrod. The Committee's terms of reference were:

(1) To advance legal education in England and Wales by furthering co-operation between the different bodies now actively engaged upon legal education;

(2) To consider and make recommendations upon training for a legal professional qualification in the two branches of the legal profession, with particular reference to:

    (a) The contribution which can be made by the Universities and Colleges of Further Education; and

    (b) The provision of training by The Law Society and The Council of Legal Education, the co-ordination of such training, and of qualifying examinations relating thereto;

(3) To consider and make recommendations upon such other matters relating to legal education as the Lord Chancellor may from time to time refer to it or as the Committee itself, with the approval of the Lord Chancellor, decides to consider.

When in due course that Committee presented its Report in March 1971, [14] its recommendations seemed to hold the promise of a new era for legal education, and for the academic legal profession, and to open the way for a fresh start in the development of relationships between the academics and the practising profession. Prominent among the Report's conclusions — albeit in many ways they amounted to no more than a reaffirmation of the proposals of the Select Committee of 1846 — were the declaration that an integrated and coherent programme of training for the legal profession should be developed through collaboration between those responsible for the academic and the vocational stages respectively, with the former stage to be provided by a university or college. [15] It was further urged that the obtaining of a law degree should become the normal mode of entry into the profession, and that a law degree obtained after at least a three-year full-time course should be recognised *per se* as completing the academic stage, and to that extent as forming part of the qualification to practise, instead of merely furnishing the basis for a selective entitlement to exemption from some of the professional examinations. [16] It was emphasized that all the then existing three- or four-year, full-time degree courses in law offered by universities and colleges in England and Wales 'should forthwith be recognised as completing the academic stage for the purposes of professional qualification', and that the professional bodies should recognise new degree courses to be offered in future 'normally on the same principles, without attempting to specify the contents of the curriculum of such courses as a condition of recognition, subject, however, to the right of the professional bodies, in the last resort and after consultation, to withold or withdraw recognition if the curriculum, either as proposed...or as altered...is manifestly inadequate as a professional qualification'. [17]

It is submitted that the Ormrod principles could, if they had been adopted and implemented by all the relevant parties in a sincere and open spirit, have led to a new and fertile age of educational development from which great benefits could have ensued. At the time of the Report's initial publication it did indeed seem possible to envisage that the university law schools would at long last assume an honoured and established place within the framework of English law and English education generally, and that a genuine juristic tradition could begin to develop therein. It was possible to imagine an exciting diversity of approaches being undertaken at various university centres, each of which would be free to develop an individuality of character and approach to legal studies, reflecting the particular talents and predilections of its incumbent staff. Out of such diversity a healthy, dynamic legal culture could be expected to flourish. But it was not to be.

Before such ambitious dreams could be realised, the Ormrod Report itself had to undergo implementation, a task which it fell to Lord Gardiner's successor as Lord Chancellor, Lord Hailsham, to superintend. Admittedly, the far-reaching reforms called for in the Report affected some of the most powerful and well-entrenched professional interests within the realm of the English establishment, and it could be remarked that all previous attempts to promote such changes by means of legislative measures had been effectively frustrated by forceful opposition deployed both inside and outside Parliament. Rather than undertake a further attempt at promoting reform through Government action Lord Hailsham elected to leave the entire destiny of the Ormrod recommendations to be resolved through the agency of a further standing committee, of uncertain status and authority, which was set up in 1972 under the initial chairmanship of Lord Cross. While it is true that the Ormrod Committee had recommended the setting up of a standing Advisory Committee on Legal Education to act as a link between the universities and colleges and the profession,[18] it is clear from the Report that such a committee was envisaged as having an important role to play within the future structure of legal education in this country, *assuming* that the other Ormrod recommendations underwent implementation more or less as they stood. It was at all times accepted that the functions of the Advisory Committee would be, as its very name suggests, merely of a consultative and advisory nature. In the event, the Advisory Committee as actually established served as the unhappy medium through which, under the pretext of 'carrying out the process recommended by the Ormrod Report', the profession contrived to achieve the very opposite result from that which the Report itself had advocated. For in the early months of its existence (in which the present writer ruefully admits to having participated) the Advisory Committee produced reports in which, despite strenuous protests from most of the academic members of the Committee, the Ormrod principles were effectively stood on their heads. In its first report, the Committee purported to advise the professions as to the acceptability of law degrees as providing the academic stage of training envisaged by Ormrod. Early in the deliberations of the Committee, two diametrically opposite points of view had emerged. The academic representatives broadly sought to affirm the Ormrod principles as they stood, while the representatives of the two branches of the profession proposed that recognition of a law degree for the purpose of admission to the professional stage of training should be conditional upon the inclusion, within the curriculum of subjects studied and passed, of certain, specified subjects. These, as initially enumerated, amounted to five subjects (constitutional law; contract; torts; land law and criminal law), but were lated 'firmed up' to six, with the addition of an explicit requirement that the law of trusts be covered. Unhappily, no way was found of bridging the differences between the two points of view formed by members of the Committee, diverging largely along 'party lines', and hence the First Report simply presented its supposed 'advice' in the form of successive paragraphs in which the two, contradictory points of views were summarised. Thereupon, and somewhat predictably, the professions elected to follow that strain of 'advice' which corresponded to the view already advanced by their own representatives on the Committee. Thus were born the regulations in which the six 'core subjects', as they have become to be known, were elevated to the status of a *sine qua non* for professional recognition of any single-honours law degree.

The First Report of the Advisory Committee therefore produced results which amounted to a total rejection of the Ormrod proposal that existing law degrees should be accepted *per se* as fulfilling the academic stage. Moreover, the prospects of a diversified and individualistic range of approaches to the teaching and study of law in the academic stage were instantly dealt a mortal blow. The constraints imposed upon the curriculum by the need to incorporate the six indispensables have proved too stultifying, and the ensuing years have seen little in the way of genuinely radical innovation in the shaping of the entire curriculum in any given law school. Indeed, there have even been suggestions that some innovatory proposals advanced by individual law schools regarding methods of teaching or assessment of certain courses have encountered considerable resistance from one or other of the professional bodies. Given the existence of the ultimate sanction of withdrawal of recognition of the degree as a whole, coupled with the further sad, if inevitable, fact that no law school would in these times of uncertainty have the audacity to persist with a degree scheme from which professional recognition had been withdrawn, the deleterious effects of conservative constraints applied from outside the academic system are becoming all too aparent.

But worse was to follow, because the Advisory Committee, in its Second Report submitted in November 1973, proceeded to deal with the position of the so-called 'mixed' degree, in which the study of law is combined with some other discipline. Here again, the Advisory Committee perpetrated a travesty of the letter and spirit of Ormrod, by recommending that any mixed degree in which the six designated 'core' subjects had been studied should be *equally* as valid and efficacious as a full, single-honours law degree for the purposes of qualifying for entry into the vocational stage, and should moreover earn exactly the same exemption from professional qualifying examinations as would be accorded to the holders of a law degree proper. It may be remarked, for the record, that the Second Report effectively represented the opinion of a narrow majority of the Committee, and that six of the academic representatives jointly signed an open Note of Dissent to its contents. [20] However, the advice contained in the body of the Second Report was once again instantly and eagerly adopted by the professions as their policy for the future. In retrospect it can be seen that the combined effect of the developments resulting from the first two reports of the Advisory Committee has been to elevate the six 'core' subjects [21] to a level of supreme importance, while simultaneously relegating all other legal subjects, and all other aspects of an intensive academic study of law, to the category of 'optional luxuries'. Certainly there has been an understandable proliferation of mixed degree schemes which are, for the most part, worthwhile and useful in themselves. But in the meantime the 'straight' law degree with its much greater potential for academic adventure in the course of an extensive encounter with legal studies, has remained largely in the doldrums. Both *de iure* and *de facto*, the Ormrod injunction, viz. that law courses should *not* be treated merely as the basis for selective entitlement to exemption from some of the professional examinations, [22] has been completely inverted.

The demoralisation, and sense of personal devaluation, of the would-be academic jurist is as complete now as ever heretofore. With hindsight, one can discern the trusting naïvety with which the academic representatives on the Advisory Committee during those early sessions patiently sought to deploy the traditional techniques of their calling — rational argument and tolerant debate — in the hope of convincing their other colleagues of the intrinsic merits of the law degree, viewed as a total educational experience. Ingenuously, too, the academics persisted in adhering scrupulously to the ethical tenets of free and open discussion of all matters arising in committee, and eschewed such tactics as pre-agreed 'block' voting, or the resort to hectoring or prevarication in order to achieve a particular objective. Finally, despite some hesitations, the academic members of the Advisory Committee, and the professional associations of which they were the representatives, persuaded themselves that no useful or positive purpose would be served by the act of resignation and withdrawal from the further work of the Committee, even in spite of the unsatisfactory way in which it was working in practice, and the quite calamitous results of its early reports. In consequence, it has been possible for both branches of the legal profession to claim, perfectly correctly, that the changes in arrangements regarding legal education which have taken place since 1972, though amounting to a travesty of the Ormrod proposals, have taken place in response to the successive recommendations of the Advisory Committee, upon which academic lawyers served, and continue to serve, as active participants. Thus was the spirit of Ormrod subverted and laid to rest, and with it were interred, perhaps for another century or longer, the prospects for the development of an English juristic tradition.

V. THE FUTURE

The foregoing picture has been necesssarily a pessimistic one: some may argue, excessively so. No doubt also it will be objected that the allegations which have been made are unduly broad and generalised. The writer, however, remains convinced that the history of English legal education down to and including the present time consists of a series of missed opportunities resulting in an intellectual impoverishment both of English law and of the profession which administers it. Above all, it is submitted, the very combination of circumstances and policies which served to facilitate the creation and survival of the common law as an intact and independent system of law, ultimately resulted in the perpetuation of a state of antagonism between academic and practitioner, and have proved largely responsible for the fact that English law lacks a proper and established juristic tradition, in the sense in which that term has been conceived and employed throughout this paper.[23]

What prospects exist for an amelioration of this problem in the reasonably near future? In the face of such besetting and entrenched attitudes of mutual mistrust, and even disapproval, it is difficult to be very sanguine, but at least some seeds of hope exist. In recent years, for one thing, it has become more or less acceptable for the written views of still-living academics to be invoked by counsel in the course of their courtroom argument, and while not in any sense commanding the status of formal legal authority, the writings of some individuals have begun to be regarded as 'authoritative' by reason of their having consistently received some measure of approval from the Bench. One important innovation, also the outcome of the most fruitful Chancellorship of Lord Gardiner, has been the creation of the Law Commission for England and Wales (with its Scottish counterpart), in which a small but effective team, with a changing membership drawn from the ranks of both academic and practising lawyers, is involved in a permanent programme of investigation designed to bring about the reform and improvement of the law.[24] Here, obviously, is one body through which, either as serving members or as participants in the Commission's consultative processes which have become an integral part of its *modus operandi*, academic lawyers can aspire to play a genuine juristic role. It is thus to be hoped that ever-increasing numbers of them will seek to involve themselves in its work in one way or the other.

In the wider context, however, it is believed that the deeply ingrained attitudes (on both sides) which have for so long impeded the formation of a harmonious relationship between academic and practising lawyers can only be dispelled by gradual means, in which each side would need to exhibit a readiness to move towards a better appreciation of the merits of the other's rôle and vocation. Perhaps initiatives could be taken within universities to create opportunities for practitioners, and also for judges, to spend periods of time in residence, engaged both in personal research and in active teaching and academic discussion. For their part, the practitioners might respond by enabling law teachers to enjoy reciprocal opportunities to visit them in their working context, for the purpose of observing and absorbing the realities of legal practice. This, perhaps obvious-seeming, possibility has in fact been rendered more than ever desirable in recent years, since the modified arrangements for completing the professional stage of training have had the incidental effect that far fewer of the entrants to the ranks of university teachers than heretofore have the opportunity to undertake the acquisition of a professional legal qualification in addition to obtaining a further degree in law as a way of preparing themselves to compete for a permanent university post. Another worthwhile innovation would be the development of a system of 'judicial clerkships', whereby younger academics could be seconded as assistants to senior judiciary — of the Court of Appeal and above — rather along the lines of the 'legal secretaryships' currently established at the European Court of Justice. One further possibility, which is already a long-established tradition in other parts of the common law world, as well as in countries belonging to the civilian tradition, would be the appointment of at least one eminent academic lawyer at any one time to serve as a member of our supreme judicial body, the House of Lords. That so common-sense a manner of serving the national interest by thus deploying some of our most distinguished legal intellects has been resisted for so long, is an eloquent testimony to the wasteful consequences of the conditions and events which have formed the main theme of this paper. In a society so traditionally insistent upon the principle of the rule of law, there ought surely to be an honoured and productive place for the thoroughbred jurist — the person whose very *raison d'être* is to acquire through study and reflection a complete understanding of the theoretical and practical aspects of the law, and to place that expertise at the disposal of society so that it may help to develop and enhance the law itself. Despite the numerous setbacks and discouragements, this is still an attainable goal, towards which every academic lawyer, at every level of seniority and eminence, ought to be striving as a matter of course. It may perhaps justifiably be said of former generations of academic lawyers that their talents went unharnessed largely because they themselves neglected to apply them in a manner capable of serving contemporary national interest to good advantage. That failing is now a diminishing one, and it is greatly to be hoped that the correct means will be found in the future to ensure that academic lawyers, and academic legal education, are together enabled to confer upon the nation the full benefits of which they are assuredly capable[25].

[1] Justinian, Institutes, Prooemium (*"cupidae legum iuventuti"*) 21 November, AD 533.

[2] e.g. Salvius Julianus served on the *consilia* of four successive emperors from Hadrian onwards, and held a variety of governmental posts, including the Praetorship, two Consulships, several Provincial Governorships, and the post of Controller of the state and military treasuries; Aemilianus Papinianus, friend and confidant of the Emperor Septimius Severus, occupied the position of Prefect of the Praetorian Guard, the highest office of state next to the Emperor himself. On the *Consilium Principis*, see the book bearing that title by J. A. Crook (Cambridge, 1955).

[3] *Quidquid non agnoscit glossa nec agnoscit curia.*

[4] Vinogradoff aptly described the books comprising the *Corpus Iuris* of Justinian as "sacred books" in the estimation of the mediaeval doctors of the law: *Roman Law in Mediaeval Europe* (Oxford, 1929), 57.

[5] See John P. Dawson, *The Oracles of the Law* (ann Arbor, 1968), esp. at 128-145.

[6] See e.g. *Hopes v. Hopes* [1949] P.227, 238 C.A., *per* Denning L. J. (Citing views of Gower and Goodhart); but see *Wheatley v. Wheatley* [1949] 2 All E.R. 428, 429 C.A., *per* Goddard, L. C. J.

[7] See Dawson, op.cit. *supra* n.5, esp at 138-145 (Italy) and 196-213 (Germany).

[8] The Honour School of Jurisprudence at Oxford was founded in 1872; the Law Tripos at Cambridge was instituted in 1873.

[9] House of Commons, 25 August 1846. An incisive summary of the report's factual discoveries in this matter is to be found in the Report of the Committee on Legal Education (The Ormrod Committee, q.v. *infra*, section IV), March 1971, Cmnd. 4595, at para. 14.

[10] Report of the Royal Commission on the Arrangements in the Inns of Court and Inns of Chancery for promoting the study of Law and Jurisprudence, 1855: *British Parliamentary Papers 1854-5*, Vol. 18.

[11] (1957-8) 4 JSPTL 206, 207.

[12] Radcliffe and Cross, *The English Legal System*, 4th Edn. 1964 (by Sir Geoffrey Cross and G.D.G. Hall), pp.419-420. The passage cited, and the chapter from which it is taken, appeared in the work for the first time in the 4th edition. In the preface to that edition, sole authorship of the new chapter is claimed by the surviving original author of the book, then a puisne Judge. In 1972, as a Lord of Appeal in Ordinary, the same author was destined to become the first chairman of the Advisory Committee on Legal Education (q.v. *infra*, section IV). In the light of subsequent events, the entire section with which the fourth edition of Radcliffe and Cross concludes (section 8 of chapter 23, headed "The legal Profession") is ominously portentous.

[13] Cmnd. 4595, mentioned *supra*, n.9.

[14] Ibid.

[15] Ibid., paras. 85, 98-100.

[16] Ibid., paras. 101-103, 106-111.

[17] Ibid., paras. 108, 185 (Summary of Conclusions and Recommendations, point 10).

[18] Ibid., paras. 107, 116-117.

[19] Advisory Committee on Legal education, First Report 1972, esp. paras. 5-8.

[20] The Note of Dissent was prepared by Mr J. A. Jolowicz, and was jointly signed by five others (including the present writer) from among the eight ''academic'' representatives on the Committee.

[21] These have subsequently undergone a further ''firming up'' with the inclusion of a specific requirement that aspects of Administrative Law must be expressly covered. Rumours persist that further subjects may be added as 'core' subjects by the same, unilateral process.

[22] Loc. cit. *supra*, n.16.

[23] See Section I, *supra*.

[24] Law Commissions Act 1965, s.3(1).

[25] [See also the report to the Social Sciences and Humanities Research Council of Canada by the Consultative Group on Research and Education in Law (Chairman, Harry W. Arthurs), published as *Law and Learning/Le Droit et Le Savoir* (Ottawa, 1983), and reviewed by the author in (1984) 4 *Legal Studies* 349-356 (Ed.)].

GLOSSARY

This glossary, like that in WLW, aims to be useful rather than exhaustive. Terms already explained in the glossary in WLW are not included here.

aitire, pp. 74, 100 etc. The Old Irish term *aitire* was used, like *ráth* and *naidm*, in two senses: (1) in general, for suretyship or a surety; (2) for a particular kind of surety. *Aitire* means literally 'betweenship' and thus characterizes the function of a surety as a go-between, guaranteeing the performance of an obligation by one party to the other. It is more commonly used, however, for the person who has the function, for the surety rather than his suretyship. When *aitire* means a special kind of surety (as opposed to *naidm* and *ráth*), it usually refers to a person who guarantees obligations of political importance. Thus the *aitire* acts as security for a treaty between two tribal kingdoms (*aitire chairdi*) or for the obedience of subjects to the edict of a king or leading churchman or a synod (*aitire chána*). It is possible that he may have guaranteed the settlement of a feud within a kingdom, a function he certainly performed for kingdoms linked by a treaty (*cairde*). The range of matters in which he acted remains, however, uncertain.

The office, unlike that of the *ráth*, was not hereditary. If the obligations guaranteed were not discharged, the *aitire* had to deliver himself into the control of the aggrieved party and remain in detention for a period of days. If the obligation was still undischarged, he could then pay what was due and ransom himself, whereupon he became entitled to heavy compensation from the person or persons for whom he was acting. For further details see CG 74-75, *Bürgschaft*, 61-74.

anudon, 'perjury', p. 56. The term *anudon* means literally 'un-oath', 'evil oath' and embodies an ancient word for 'oath', *ud*, cognate with Old Irish *óeth*, English 'oath'. Elsewhere *ud* has been replaced by *llw*, just as the normal Irish term was *luge*. According to the canon law of the thirteenth century, perjury was primarily a sin and thus came under the jurisdiction of the Church. This claim was not fully accepted in Welsh law where the thirteenth century rule is that a perjurer is liable to pay a fine of three cows or fifteen shillings to the king (*camlwrw*) but is also subject to the jurisdiction of the Church. The Church, therefore had jurisdiction, but not exclusive jurisdiction. The Welsh situation is closely comparable to that found in Cnut's laws (c. 36). Cf. PM ii, 189-90, 541-43.

arwaesaf, Ior 65/3. The simplex *gwaesaf* also occurs in the laws: e.g. Bleg 44.12 and note on p. 186. The Irish cognate *fóessam* 'guarantee' (*fo-sessam* 'standing under') is used in BA 76a, 77. The Welsh terms *gwaesaf* and *arwaesaf* have acquired a more specialized meaning. They refer, it is true, either to the person who guarantees or to the guarantee he provides, but only in the context of a case in which one person claims to be the owner of something in the possession of another. Even if the claim is correct, however, the person in possession may not have committed any wrong, and he may defend himself by claiming that he received the thing in good faith from a third party. If this third party then acknowledges the transaction, the defendant has a guarantor (in English law a warrantor), an *arwaesaf,* and is cleared of any suspicion: see Ior 114/6-115/1. In the southern lawbooks, *gwaesaf* and *arwaesaf* have largely been replaced by *gwarant* (from Anglo-Norman *warrant* or its Latin and English derivatives), though *gwarant* has a wider application: Bleg 44.8-46.3; LTWL 244, 353-54. In 65/3, therefore, the seller (who gave the *mach*) is the *arwaesaf.*

arwystl, 'substitute', Ior 65/3. The original meaning was presumably 'gage (*gwystl*) given instead of (*ar*) something else'. It is used at least once in Medieval Welsh to translate *pignus,* see H. Lewis a P. Diverres, *Delw y Byd* (Caerdydd, 1928), 23. In other words, it was a gage given when the particular thing owed could not be given on the appointed day; it thus bought further time. From this starting-point, the word acquired the general meaning 'substitute', cf. Ior 57/9 where it is used for an animal sent as substitute for an injured animal. The same development is also attested in Breton. In CR the word occurs once only, *me dedisse illam rem proprietatis meae in* **aruuistl** *propter solidos vi.* with the meaning gage cf. L. Fleuriot, *Dictionnaire des gloses en vieux breton,* (Paris, 1964), s.v. *aruuistl.*

bara offeren, 'mass-bread', Ior 60/3 and pp. 53-55. The term referred to bread which was blessed but not consecrated and was distributed at the end of the mass to those of the congregation who had not received communion. See under *eulogia.*

barn, a term used infrequently in the Welsh law texts for an opinion or judgment as in *barn tremyg* or *barn y diddim,* see WLW 191; cf. *brawd.*

barnu, is the verb commonly used in the law texts meaning to judge or administer the law. The medieval Welsh judge often did not decide which party won the case but rather which party had the right to prove his case and how, whether through witnesses or by oath and what kind of witnesses or oath.

bedydd esgob, p. 58, literally, 'the baptism of a bishop', is the term used for confirmation at the hand of a bishop and is one of the seven sacraments traditionally recognised by the Christian church. A Medieval Welsh list, *Seith Rinwedd yr Eglwys* (The Seven Virtues of the Church) which lists the sacraments as: *bedydd, bedydd esgob, kymmyn, penyd, angennu neu olew, urdeu, priodas* (baptism, confirmation, eucharist, penance, extreme unction, [holy] orders and marriage) was published by Sir John Prys in 1546. See R. Geraint Gruffydd, 'Yny Lhyvyr Hwnn: The Earliest Welsh Printed Book', (1969) 23 BBCS 110-11. The Welsh list corresponds to the list in Peter Lombard's Sentences, Bk 4, dist. 1, num. 2.

benedicamus, 'let us give blessing (to God)', Ior 60/3 and pp. 54-55. *Benedicamus* was the initial word of one of the formulae of dismissal used at the end of the mass. It is uncertain when it was used instead of *Ite missa est* (the formula which survived into the post-Tridentine liturgy).

brawd, translated *iudicium* in the Latin texts of the laws, is the usual word for a judgment or legal decision; cf. E. P. Hamp, 'barnu brawd' (1976) 11 *Celtica* 68-76.

brawdwr, p. 262, the normal word for a judge in the South Wales texts means literally the one who issues a *brawd*, judgment or decree. In South Wales, the judging of cases in local courts was not in the hands of professional lawmen as in Gwynedd. Administering the law in the local courts was part of the responsibility of the landowners and thus a less high standard might be expected than that given by a trained *ynad*. Nevertheless the texts emphasize that the responsibilities of the judge who made a wrong judgment was a heavy one, cf. Bleg 17-18. If one of the parties doubted the correctness of judgment, he could challenge the judge to defend it and show the authority of a book for his judgment. Failure of judgment meant that the judge had to pay a fine equal in value to his tongue. A record from Is Cennen shows how a lawman in the fifteenth century paid the fine given in the lawbooks when his judgment failed. Such a wrong judgment also implied loss of office (PRO/Just/1156,6), D. Jenkins and M. E. Owen, (1982) 18 *Carmarthenshire Antiquary* 24, 27, n. 49.

The lawtracts refer to three kinds of *brawdwr*, a *brawdwr llys* or the court judge who was an official of the king's court and who seemed to be the chief judge of the territory, a *brawdwr cwmwd* or *cantref* and a *brawdwr* by right of land Bleg 98.28-99.6.

briduw, 'honour of God' or 'power of God', Ior §68 and pp. 47-71. In early MSS it is often written as two words. It is a special form of suretyship by which 'God is taken [as security] in place of a *mach*' (Ior 68/9). *Briduw* appears to have been an alternative, not a supplement, to ordinary suretyship, *mechnïaeth, mechni.* It thus provided a place in the law for an agreement enforceable without surety. It also had other important features: *briduw* could be given by a woman as well as a man, and even by minors of seven years and over. Until shortly before the date of Ior (early thirteenth century) this was probably the only way in which women in Gwynedd could make contracts. Cf. *godborh.*

cam farn, p. 263, a false opinion or judgement, see *barn.*

cam frawd, p. 263, a false judgement, see *brawd.*

canonwyr, 'canons'. The term is used in the section on *dirwy* (fine) in court and church, *llys a llan,* in Bleg (43.7, 9). If fighting occurs within the precinct of the church, a fine is payable; half goes to the abbot and the other half to the priests and to the *canonwyr.* In place of 'the priests and the canons' WML has *meibon lleyn yr eglwys* (114.3). The term *mab lleyn* derives from the Welsh church before the Norman reforms: it corresponds to Irish *mac legind* 'youth undergoing ecclesiastical education'. In WML it appears to be used of a portioner of a church and is comparable to the similar use of *scolóc* in medieval Scotland and perhaps to the sense of *yscolhaig* in *Manawydan uab Llyr* (PKM 61). An order of canons, clearly separate from that of the monks, came into existence as a result of the reforms of Louis the Pious and Benedict of Aniane at the Aachen synod of 816, but it only penetrated Wales with the Normans: see F. G. Cowley, *The Monastic Order in South Wales* (Cardiff, 1977), 28-37.

cantref, p. 262, literally *can* 'a hundred' *tref* 'holding(s)'. The largest administrative unit in Medieval Wales, it was according to Sir J. E. Lloyd, the successor of the old *tud,* see *History of Wales* i, (London, 1948), 302. The earliest usage is to be found in LL 134; the word has been compared with the English hundred. The term is however unlikely to show a borrowing from the English, since John Bannerman has shown that a cognate term, *cét treb,* was used by the Celtic peoples of Scotland at a very early date. See Bannerman (1968) 8 *Celtica* 97-98.

coediwr, p. 270, woodward.

contract may, for the purposes of Welsh law, be defined as a legally enforceable agreement. In Middle Welsh *amod* is used for contract in general as well as for a special form of contract (D. Jenkins, *Cyfraith Hywel,* 81). The normal way in which contracts were enforced in medieval law was through the surety and thus suretyship was central to the law of contract. It is likely that *amod* derives from a Celtic word for contract since there is evidence for an Irish cognate *imbuith* or *imboth* (Binchy in CLP 115). The normal Irish word *cundrad* comes from **con-dúrad* 'jointly enduring' and may originally have meant the purely 'executory' contract in which neither party performs immediately but promises to do so in the future.

crair, 'relic', see pp. 51-53. In the pre-Christian period it was not uncommon to use some object to act as the focus of the ceremony of oath-taking and thus to enhance the solemnity of the procedure; for example, the Lombards used weapons. With the gradual Christianization of European law and politics in the early middle ages such objects were replaced by relics. It is likely, however, that the word *crair* already meant the object used as the focus of oath-taking before this function came to be discharged by relics since it is derived from *cred,* the base of *credu* 'believe' and comparison with Irish *cretair, cretid* shows that the term goes back to Common Celtic.

cyflafareddiad, p. 260, literally 'a speaking together' is the word for arbitration used in a case regarding a debt payable in hay at Abergele (1943-4) 3 NLWJ 23-28.

cymrodeddwyr, p. 259, is used in Lat D (LTWL 357.34) to gloss *arbitros* 'arbitrators' in the triad which in Bleg begins *Tri therfyn cyfreithiol* (the three legal teminations) Bleg 124.5-8. In the triad the three legal terminations are cited as agreement between parties, termination through arbitrators and termination by judgment. Dafydd Jenkins has shown (1984) 7 CMCS 111, that the medieval Welsh lawyer was as fond as his modern counterpart of avoiding going to judgment. Extra-curial arbitration was common in Wales as in the rest of Europe and continued to be so after the Edwardian Conquest.

cynnogn, 'debtor' as opposed to the *hawlwr* 'claimant' or 'creditor'.

Cynnogn is often replaced by *talawdyr* 'payer' in Cyfn and Bleg. In many contracts (i.e. 'bilateral' contracts) each side would be both *cynnogn* and *hawlwr* since they would have agreed to exchange assets and thus each would have both a right and an obligation as against the other.

dadferwyr, p. 261, judgment-finders drawn 'from the better men' of the district who functioned in cases of dispute settlement in later medieval Wales. GPC quotes an example of the word being used to gloss *arbitros* in NLW Wynnstay Deeds, 34.

dedfryd gwlad, p. 261, literally, the 'verdict of the country or *patria*'. According to Bleg 70.6-16, 107.1-8, *dedfryd gwlad* was the judgment of the elders (*henuriaid*) given after due consideration and compurgation (*racreitha*) and proclaimed by the judges (*brawdwyr*).

dempster, p. 264. The medieval Scottish dempster or *judex* was a survival from Celtic Scotland and may be compared to the Irish *brithem* (*breitheamh*): see G. W. S. Barrow, 'The *judex*', in his *The Kingdom of the Scots* (London, 1973), 69-82.

deorad Dé, 'exile of God', p. 60 n. 93 **Deorad Dé** was an Old Irish term *peregrinus pro amore Dei*, a person who has chosen exile for the love of God. The *deorad Dé* was held to be the special representative of God and was thus expected to enforce contracts for which God had been invoked as guarantee (cf. *briduw*).

dilis, dilisid(us), p. 74, see under *dilys*.

dilys, 'unobjectionable, inactionable'. To be *dilys*, Breton *dilis,* Irish *díles,* is to be immune from legal objection or claim: see *llys* 'objection, bar' in the glossary to WLW. The term then has two principal senses depending on whether the person under consideration is disadvantaged by this state of affairs. If the immunity from legal objection consists in the thing having passed irrevocably out of his possession so that he can bring no action to recover it, it is *dilys* 'forfeit', i.e. inactionable in circumstances when he would have wished to bring an action. This sense is fading in Middle Welsh but is still present in Ior 52/4, Latin A 52/21 (WLW 152, 174). When the person in question is not disadvantaged, it may often be translated 'valid' or, in respect of title, 'secure' and the negative *anilys* is then 'insecure, invalid'. In exchanges by contract the issue arises as to whether the vendor's title is secure, namely whether the thing to be sold is *dilys* to him. Only if that is so, is he entitled to sell it and only then is the surety entitled to guarantee the contract. The reason is that the contract purports to make the thing *dilys* (to *dilysu* the thing) for the buyer, and if it was not *dilys* for the vendor, he and the surety cannot make it *dilys* for the buyer: this is one of the three useless suretyships of Ior 65/3-6.

The Breton *dilis* was the base for one of the terms for a surety found in the Cartulary of Redon, *dilisid(us)*. It is apparently equivalent to *fideiussor* (q.v.). The term *securator* 'one who makes secure' may be another Latin equivalent designed to render the meaning of *dilisidus*. Though the word *dilisidus* lays stress on one of the functions of a surety, there is good reason to suppose that he performed the full range of a surety's functions and that there was thus no difference between him and the *fideiussor*: see pp. 74-75.

dosbarthwyr, p. 261, men learned in native Welsh law whose names appear as consulting specialists in the court rolls for the period after the Norman conquest. One of the most notable *dosbarthwyr* of the fourteenth century was Rhydderch ab Ieuan Llwyd who was called upon as *dosbarthwr* in Carmarthenshire and Cardiganshire between 1380 and 1392 see R. A. Griffiths, *The Principality of Wales in the later Middle Ages* (Cardiff, 1972), 117. In the law texts the verb *dosbarthu* is used for the process of settling/classifying suits in a court. The verb used to correspond to it in the Latin texts is *discernere,* see Bleg 7.25-30, and compare LTWL 325.28-30. *Dosbarthwr* means literally the man who creates the *dosbarth*.

dwfr swyn, 'holy water', presumably originally 'sign water' namely water used to make the sign of the cross etc., pp. 53-55 and Ior 60/3. At the entry of the congregation for solemn mass, they were sprinkled with water which had been blessed (the *Asperges*). What was left was then kept to be distributed to the congregation at the end of mass, together with blessed but unconsecrated bread, *bara offeren* (q.v.). The people could then use the water to sprinkle their homes and livestock. *Dwfr swyn* was thus a quasisacramental bond between church and home.

eulogia, (ἡ εὐλογία), the blessing, that which has been blessed). An early medieval term for the bread in the Gallican liturgy of which part was consecrated at the Eucharist, distributed at the end of Mass to those present; identical with the *pain bénit* distributed after the principal Sunday Mass in some French and Québec churches until the liturgical reforms of the IInd Vatican Council (cf. *pane benedetto, gesegnetes Brot*; and the *antidoron*, 'in place of the Gifts', still so distributed in the Byzantine rite). Originally intended for those who did not communicate, it came to be given to all present,

communicants or not. See e.g. MGH Capit. I, *Capitulare Monasticum, a.*
817, c. 68 (at p. 347): *Ut eulogiae fratribus a presbyteris in refectorio dentur;*
MGH *Leges § Caspitula Episcoporum* (ed. P. Brommer, 1984), 2nd Capitulary
of Bishop Hildegar of Meaux, Province of Sens, a. 868, c. 8 (at p. 199): *Ut
fideles omni die dominico eulogias accipiant* The *capitulum* states that while
Holy Communion is apt for the salvation of the body and soul, nevertheless
laymen are reluctant to communicate daily *propter fragilitatem carnis*; it is
therefore decreed (*decernimus*)

> *ut omni die dominico et precipuis festivitatibus cuncti fideles eulogias accipiant de
> bendicto pane cuius participatione roborati diabolicas sive humanas viriliter possint
> superare insidias,*

'that every Sunday and major festival all the faithful (laity) are to receive
the *eulogiae* of blessed bread, the partaking whereof gives strength to
overcome the snares both of the devil and of our human nature'.

féchem, 'contracting party'. The *féchem* is the person involved in a *fiach,*
debt, either as creditor or as a debtor; see BA, 49. The word is formed from
fiach (earlier *féch*) by means of the agent suffix -*em*. Another term for a party
to a contract, *cobach* (from *com-* + *fiach* 'one who has a joint debt' similarly
lays stress on the bond between the two parties and their common
involvement in the debt.

fiach, see *féchem.*

fiadu, fiadnaise, BA, 58. Old Irish *fiadu* is the witness, *fiadnaise* the
testimony that he gives. In both cases it is solely eye-witness, namely witness
concerning that which is *fiado* 'in his presence': cf. Welsh *gwybyddiad,*
especially the definition given at AL VII.i.14, and Binchy in CLP, 118-19.

fideiussio, (from *fideiubeo* 'become surety') (1) The normal suretyship of
Roman law from 1st cent. BC, i.e. from the start of the classical period of
Roman law, and the sole form under Justinian. The *fideiussor* stood surety
for what the debtor in fact owed, but his obligation was accessory to the
debtor's and came to be limited by a number of restrictions affecting his
liability if called upon to pay. In the classical period the chief of these were
(a) the *lex Cornelia,* by which no-one could stand surety to any other in any
one year for more than 20,000 sesterces, any excess being void (probably
made under Sulla, c. 138-78 BC); (b) *beneficium divisionis,* where one of plural
sureties could obtain from the Praetor a ruling that his liability be *per capita*

proportionate with his fellow-(solvent) sureties, upon proof that the latter were also liable (first granted under Hadrian, AD 117-138, probably by 131 when the Praetor's Edict was standarised); (c) *b. cedendarum actionum,* where a surety assumed liability only after taking an assignment of the creditor's claims against the (solvent) debtor, whom the surety then sued to recover what he had paid the creditor (see e.g. D. (Julian) 46.1.17: Julian lived *c.* AD 100-169). Justinian's reforms affecting *fideiussores,* especially the 4th Novel (AD 535), added the *b. excussionis* or *ordinis* by which sureties could resist the creditor's claim against them if the principal debtor had not been unsuccessfully sued. (The names of these *beneficia* are conventional, not contemporary). See generally Buckland §CLVI (445 et seq.), Kaser, RPR §57 (tr.232 et seq.) and RPr §278 (vol. 2, 457 et seq., cf. §§ 155-6 & 279) for the details and a discussion of earlier forms, e.g. *sponsio,* displaced by *fideiussio.* (2) The Latin term widely adopted in medieval secular and canon law for suretyship, irrespective of whether Roman or customary rules applied, e.g. in Lombardic law (Liutprand cc. 36-40), Frankish law (*Capitula Legis Salica addita* c. 73 §7 in PLS 246, MGH Capit. 2:3, index s.vv. *fideiussio, -or*), Welsh law (LTWL Index IV s.v. surety, e.g. at A 125) and in Canon law (*Liber Extra* 3.22, *de fideiussoribus,* E. Friedberg (ed.) *Corpus Iuris Canonici* vol. 2 Leipzig 1879 col 529-531; and see Bernard of Pavia, *Summa Decretalium* ed. E. A. T. Laspeyres, (Regensburg, 1860; repr. Graz, 1956), 3.28 (pp. 86-8) for the reception of Roman law into Canon law. The term was also used in the middle ages for a variety of rôles: sureties of various kinds (for example the Welsh *mach* and the Irish *ráth*), persons who gave gages and even oath-helpers.

fideiussor, a surety; see *fideiussio.*

fides, (vb. *fido, affido*), *fides facta* (*fidem facere*). *Fides,* faith, has the double sense of having another's trust reposed in one so as to be answerable to him for it, and the promise or profession of that trust. Medieval law, like the laws of antiquity, recognized that mutual faith or trust between persons not otherwise bound by ties of kinship or alliance could be created by the exchange of undertakings (by contract, in effect), whether the parties were equal or stood in the relationship of superior and inferior. For example, faith might be 'pledged' or '(en)gaged', 'made' or 'given' by a convicted or admitted wrongdoer who, or whose kindred, was debtor for the composition to avoid the feud, due to the victim's kin. If time was needed to raise the sum, instead of offering gage and sureties the debtor might make his faith that payment could be forthcoming. In so doing, he pledged his honour; in societies where honour was prized above all, this was no light pledge. The church adapted or paralleled the pledge of honour with the pledge of one's religious faith, again no light undertaking for a believer. Under Christian influence 'faith' embraces the subject-matter of 'right belief', so that faith and belief become interchangable terms (see *cred*, (below)).

fides facta, *gwystl ffydd,* the pledge of faith, can be illustrated from medieval Welsh literature. In *Culhwch ac Olwen* the hero and his companions ask Custennin's wife (sister to Culhwch's mother) to send for Olwen saying:

'Will she come here if she is sent for'?

The woman replies:

'... I will not betray the one who would trust in me (*am crett6y*). But if you give your faith (*o rod6ch cret*) you will do her no harm, I will send for her...' This they granted...

(WM 238 col 475.13). For cred as 'undertaking (*ymrywmiad*) on one's faith' see Col § 426; DwCol § 244, *na kymerer...gedernit*) where AL V.ii. 20 has *na chymerer cret.* Welsh versions of the Book of Common Prayer express the exchange of vows in the marriage service as *yr ydwyf yn rhoddi* (or *y rhoddaf*) *i ti fy nghred* for the English 'I plight thee my troth'. *Troth* is loyalty, good faith: trothplight, *rhoddi cred*, is *fides facta.*

For *fides* in Frankish law, e.g. emphasizing loyalty to the Emperor over other human loyalties, see MGH Capit I, the General or 'Programmatic' capitulary for the *Missi*, a.802, cc. 2-9 at pp. 92-3, tr. Loyn & Percival, *The Reign of Charlemagne* (London, 1975), 74-6, and comment by F. L. Ganshof, *Frankish Institutions under Charlemagne* (Providence, Rhode Island, 1968), 6,7; and see generally Niermeyer, s.v. *Fides* 5,7,8 & 10. For comment on *fides facta* see PM ii. 186-192; J. Goebel, *Felony & Misdemeanour* (New York/Oxford, 1937), esp. 117-122; and Walters, *supra* (101-106) III, *Leistungsbürgen.*

folad, p. 229 n. 13. On this Old Irish term see D. A. Binchy, 'Irish History and Irish Law: II', (1976) 16 *Studia Hibernica*, 26-31. Its meaning underwent a considerable development in the Irish law of contract, which may be set out as follows:

(1) The initial sense is 'wealth' (cf. its Welsh cognate *golud*). A good example is *Cáin Adamnáin*, ed. K. Meyer (Oxford, 1905), para. 42, where, as Plummer noted in his copy, one should read *mad céthin do foluth no dona muccaib no dona conaib. Foluth* is equivalent to *bíastaib*

cenntaib 'tame beasts' in the previous clause, so that one may translate 'if it be a first offence by the cattle (*foluth*) or by the pigs or by the dogs' (cf. S. Welsh *da* 'cattle').

(2) Contracts were most commonly sales of movable wealth, especially cattle. *Folad* thus came to have the sense 'goods' owed in virtue of contract'.

(3) From this it was an easy step to make *folad* stand for services as well as goods owed by contract. *Folad* remained distinct from *fíach* 'debt' in that it referred to what was owed rather than to the debt itself.

(4) Central issues in the Irish law of contract were (a) whether the *folad* of one party matched the *folad* of the other, and (b) whether one or both parties had delivered or performed their *folad* in full. In such contexts *folad* tends to be used from the point of view of an aggrieved party who may be questioning the adequacy of the other party's *folad*. The aggrieved party may, for these purposes, be termed the creditor. If the *folad* is defective, the creditor may be entitled to annul the contract; if it does not match what he has delivered or performed, then again he may have grounds for annulling the contract or having its terms revised. In this context, then *folad* is equivalent to the English legal term 'consideration' and the issue is one of 'defective consideration'.

(5) Sometimes the relationship of the *folad* of one party to a contract to the *folad* of the other is expressed by the pair of terms *folad* and *frithfolad* 'counter-*folad*'. If the *folad* of the one party has been delivered or performed, its *frithfolad* is due.

(6) *Folad* and *frithfolad* may also be used for obligations arising from an offence (from delict as opposed to contract), as in *Cáin Adamnáin*, para. 43, which prohibits the setting off of a compensation due to A for an offence by B against the compensation due to B for an offence by A: "There is to be no *frithfolad* nor balancing of offences in the Law of Adamnán."

gage, see *uuadio,* below and Note on Terminology.

gell, Old Irish for a gage (or pledge), a thing given to guarantee an obligation, as opposed to the *gíall,* 'hostage', i.e. person given to guarantee an obligation. In Welsh a single word, *gwystl* (Old Breton *guistl*), stands for both, but the distinction made by the two Irish forms is old (*gell* < *g^whistlon, gíall* < *g^wheistlos* are distinguished by both ablaut and gender).

gíall, Old Irish for a hostage, see *gell.*

god-borh, Old English term for 'God-surety', p. 60-61. The word is found only in Alfred's laws, c. 33, where a procedure is prescribed which is comparable, but not identical, with that given by some of the Welsh laws for *briduw*.

gwlad, 'country, lordship, *patria*', p. 261. *Gwlad* is generally used for a lordship consisting of one or more cantrefs or commotes, units comparable with the English shire and hundred, or the Frankish *pagus* and *centena*. The Old Irish cognate may be used of the lordship or kingdom (territorial sense), of the lord himself or of the lordship that he wields. A similar flexibility may be attested in Welsh at a very early date by *The Poems of Taliesin* VII. 53, where *gwacsa gwlat da wrth uruwyn* may best be translated 'a good lord is useless compared to Urien'.

gwrthdwng 'counter-swearing', refers to the oath sworn to rebut a previous oath by the other party. In Ior's tractate on suretyship it is only used for the second stage in the hearing of a case, when both sides swear on relics (59/5-7), not for a counter-assertion in the first stage, even for the solemn denial in 58/8 introduced by *dyoer* 'God knows'.

gwyrda, p. 261, literally, the good men, the *gwyrda* can be compared with the *boni viri* mentioned in CR. *boni viri* and *boni homines* are found in many continental systems during the later Middle Ages. In the Welsh law texts, they are the leaders of society who were active members of legal tribunals and seem to have had and advisory role collaborating with the lord in deciding disputes about boundaries etc. See (1948) 7 CMCS 110-11.

gwystl stands for both 'gage' and 'hostage'. See Irish *gell* and *gíall* (q.v.).

gwystl ffydd, p. 47. See under *fides*.

halidom, Old English for 'relic' p. 00. III Aethelred 2,1 (Liebermann, i, 228) shows that a person making an oath on relics would be given the relic to hold in his hand. The hold-oath given in *Swerian,* c. 1 (Liebermann, i, 396) shows the same connection as in Ior 59/3-4 between an appeal to the relic and an appeal to God: "By the Lord, before whom this *haligdom* is *halig* (holy), I will be faithful and true to N."

henuriaid y wlad, p. 261, literally 'the elders of the land' used like '*gwyrda*' q.v. for the leaders of society who participated in law-suits particularly in land suits. cf. Bleg 70.6-16.

iudex A general term for a judge. In Latin texts and documents relating to Welsh law it is used for different kinds of judges—*ynad, brawdwr,* q.v. see R. R. Davies, above, n.18 for the passage at Bleg 98.28-99.11; for Bleg's Latin source see LTWL 349.27-36 (mixed Latin and Welsh) repeated (Latin alone) at 382.26-32, viz. the *iudex curiae regis* and *iudex patriae* who are judges *virtut officiorum,* and another kind of *iudex patriae* who acts as such per *dignitatem terrae.* The two first are comparable with the *ordinarius iudex* of Romano-Canonical law, who if ecclesiastical derives his jurisdiction from the Pope and if secular from the sovereign (cf. Bernard of Pavia, *Summa Decretalium,* 1.21.1, *Ordinarius iudex est qui in ecclesiasticus ab Apostolico, in seclaribus ab Imperatore totalem quandam habet iurisdictionem*). These ordinary judges are contrasted with judges-delegate and with arbitrators, assessors and auditors.

iudicator or **sectator.** Judgment, in the sense of a decision according to law, might be given in Welsh and Marcher law collectively by local men of appropriate status and knowledge of the laws, called in the Latin documents *iudicatores* (or *sectatores,* 'suitors': see R. R. Davies, *Lordship & Society in the March of Wales 1282-1400* (Oxford, 1978), 158-9 esp. his n.47). cf. *dadfrewyr, gwyrda, henuriaid y wlad* and *seniores.*

mach, 'surety'. Derivatives are *mechni, mechnïaeth* 'suretyship'.

machtiern, p. 81 ff., cognate with the Welsh *mechdeyrn,* 'overlord, king' and the Cornish *myghtern* 'king', the word probably derives from '*mach*', 'surety' and '*teyrn*' 'king, lord', L. Fleuriot, 'Un fragment en latin des tres anciennes lois bretonnes-armoricaines du VI siecle', (1971) 78 *Annales de Bretagne* 194-221. *Machtiern* is the term used for the local headman or official in CR. J. G. T. Sheringham 'Les Machtierns' (1981) 58 *Memoires de la Societe d'Histoire et d'Archeologie de Bretagne,* 61-72) considers the *machtiern* as fourth in importance in the hierarchy of public power following the duke, the count and the viscount. Acting as guarantor himself, he could initiate dispute settlement proceedings. Machtiernships were often hereditarily submitted through families whose property interests spanned two or three *plebes.* They were not appointees of the government but their responsibility was to the village community.

mair, p. 80, is cognate with Welsh *maer,* used to gloss *prepositus,* and Cornish *mair,* used to gloss *prepositus* and *gerefa.* The Welsh maer was one of the king's administrative officials, directly accountable to him and responsible for the supervision of his lands and collection of his dues. The

Breton word occurs glossing both *prepositus* and *actores* in Old Breton, see L. Fleuriot, *Dictionnaire des gloses en vieux breton*, (Paris, 1964), 253.

naidm, an Old Irish term for a 'binding-surety' or 'enforcing-surety'. *Naidm* is the verbal noun to *naiscid* 'binds'; in BA it is sometimes used for the binding of a contract upon the parties (*Bürgschaft*, 33-34), but more usually for the 'binding-surety' who binds the contract by taking the hands of both parties (see pp. 217-219). He is thus, in his person, the bond or obligation. If a debtor defaults, it is his job to try to compel him to discharge his obligation. The older term for the binding-surety, preserved notably in the formulae in BA was *mac(c)*, cognate with Welsh and Breton *mach*. In the tractate in Ior the Welsh *mach* preserves much of the character of the Irish *macc* or *naidm*: see above, pp. 19-27.

obses, 'hostage', 'hostage-surity', p. 19, n. 38. *Obses* is glossed by *guistl* in Old Breton. See under *gell*.

patria, p. 261,, used in the Latin texts to translate *cantref* or *gwlad* q.v.

plebes, p. 81, the term used for the village-based units of agrarian society described in CR (cf. Welsh *plwyf*, Breton *plou*).

pledge, See Note on Terminology. The modern English word does duty for *plight* (see above, *fides facta*), cognate with Ger. *Pflicht*, OHG *phliht* 'duty undertaken', but assimilated to 'pledge' as derived through French from *plevium*. The phrase, 'to pledge one's word or honour', shows the assimilation.

pledge of faith, p. 47: see *fides*.

precium, p. 79, used in CR for wergild or life-price.

principal, p. 11, the person whose obligation the surety secures or guarantees.

principes, p. 73, the term used for the successors of the ninth-century Nominoe who ruled Brittany firstly as representative of the Carolingian rulers and latterly more or less independently of them.

rad, 'surety', glosses *stipulationes*, (q.v.) in Old Breton. See under *ráth*.

ráth, Old Irish for 'paying-surety', one who undertakes to discharge the debt if his principal defaults (either by refusing or by being unable to pay). The *ráth* acts if the *naidm* has been unable to compel the debtor to pay. His office, unlike that of the *aitire* but like that of the *naidm,* was hereditary. In function, the *ráth* corresponds quite well to the *mach* of Cyfn and Bleg, but not to that of Ior. On the basis of Jeremiah, 32.11, the Irish canonists introduced the native *ráth* into Irish canon law, and in its Latin form *rata* it was incorporated into the early eighth-century *Collectio Canonum Hibernensis.* That text passed to Brittany where it was glossed. The Breton glossator used a term *rad* to gloss *stipulatio,* (q.v.). This *rad* is probably derived from *rata* in the sense given it in the *Collectio,* for it cannot be cognate with *ráth.* It is thus very doubtful if *rad* was ever a genuine term of Breton law. See Thurneysen, *Bürgschaft,* 35-56, (1930) 18 ZCP 364-75.

rhaglaw, p. 266. The chief resident officer in the commote during the Middle Ages. A civil officer representing the lord and having general authority over the *maer* and the *rhingyll,* the *rhaglaw* supervised the collection of rents, the issuing of summonses and the making of arrests. He assisted in the commote court and enforced its decisions receiving a shilling from every amercement paid. His fees were considerable and included the maintenance of his horse and groom together with a yearly commorth or grant from the community, William Rees, *South Wales and the March, 1284-1415,* (Oxford, 1924), 95-98; R. A. Griffiths, *The Principality of Wales in the Later Middle Ages* (Cardiff, 1972), 59-69.

rhingyll, 'beadle', p. 270. In South Wales, after 1282, the *rhingyll* was essentially the local officer in the commote charged with collecting the *gwestfa,* the money (originally food-rent) paid by freemen to the crown. Other officers were appointed to collect the more important rent of assize. In the north he retained responsibility for a wider range of dues and also for the fees paid by local officials. Some *rhingylls* in the north-east had still wider powers being the chief officers of the commote. See R. A. Griffiths, *The Principality of Wales in the Later Middle Ages* (vol. i, Cardiff, 1972), 60-69: *The Survey of the Honour of Denbigh,* ed. P. Vinogradoff and F. Morgan (London, 1914), lxxxii-lxxxiii.

sapientes, p. 265 the wisemen of Arwystli appointed to hear a legal case on appeal who included Cynyr ap Cadwgan, abbot of Llandinam, redactor of a Welsh law-text and founder of a dynasty of jurists.

scabini, p. 80, were permanent 'judgment-finders' first created by

Charlemagne at the beginning of his reign, and probably initially in Northern Francia, to replace the *rachemburgii* who had discharged the same function but had been chosen in a more *ad hoc* and informal way. The *scabini* acted in the *mallus*, the county court, in a panel of at least seven, and were closely attached to the count who presided over the court, either in person or through his deputy. They were recruited from the *pagenses,* people native to the *pagus* or *pays.* See F. L. Ganshof. *Frankish Institutions under Charlemagne* (Providence, Rhode Island, 1968), 76-81.

securator, one of the terms for a surety in the CR, p. 75. Cf. *dilisidus* under *dilys* above.

seniores, p. 80, local elders who functioned as sureties in some of the transactions recorded in CR.

slán, a very common Old Irish legal term which occurs several times in BA and in slightly different senses. It occurs as an adjective, as a noun standing for a person (when it is masculine) and as a noun standing for a transaction or relationship (when it is neuter). The nouns appear to be substantivisations of the adjective. The fundametal sense of the adjective is 'healthy', from two aspects. On the one hand, it is used simply for a state of health, on the other, for a person having entered into a state of health or, by transference, for a thing having caused someone to enter into a state of health. When it became a legale term *slán* continued to have the same nuances. These can best be explained by a diagram:

		Primary	Secondary
(1) state	(a) persons	healthy	free from liability or loss
	(b) things/ transactions	maintaining health	complete

(2) having entered into state/having caused someone to enter a state		
(a) persons	recovered from sickness	compensated for loss or injury
(b) things/ transactions	restorative of health	made whole/ completed

stipulatio, the principal formal contract of Roman law. In the republican period, the *stipulation* was an oral contract made by the parties making formal promises beginning with the word *spondeo* 'I promise'. Any written document was evidence that the contract had been made, not the means by which it was made. Under the empire, however, the written document, often known as the *cautio,* came to constitute the decisive act. In the early middle ages this later Roman law is reflected in the Germanic laws of southern Europe, notably in those of the Lombard king Liutprand. It is likely, however, that in northern Europe the oral contract recovered its earlier predominance. The term is used in the *Collectio Canonum Hibernensis* apparently for a surety: this can be explained by the influence of the vernacular *naidm* which was used both for the binding of the contract and for the surety who bound it. As used in the *Collectio,* the term was then glossed by Breton *rad* (q.v.).

testis In this book, according to the context, 1. a participant in a legal transaction or in legal proceedings, other than a principal, whose intervention is necessary for validity; a witness to the transaction or proceedings, not to events prior to them; 2. a person who solemnly swears to the credibility of another's word, a compurgator. The modern sense of a witness to facts prior to the proceedings etc. at which the witness is called to give evidence, is rare. The early Latin **ter-stis, *tri-stis* (from *tres,* three) also supports the sense of 'one present as a third party'. Cf. *tyst.*

tir a daear, p. 258, literally 'land and earth' a hendiadys of type commonly found in Medieval Welsh (cf. *llid a bar* 'fury and anger'), *dadlau tir adaear,* cases of 'land and earth', is the phrase commonly used for land-suits.

tyst, 'witness'. The old distinction between *gwybyddiad* 'eye-witness' (see under *fiadu* and Binchy in CLP 118-19) and *tyst,* other forms of witness is not generally preserved in Welsh law. In the most detailed discussion in Ior (paras. 79-81/4) *tyst* appears to be equivalent to *gwybyddiad.* In Lat B 214.38-215.36 (= Lat D 365.30-366.29, Bleg 36.9-37.28) the two appear to be distinct but on what basis it is impossible to say since the text appears to be a fragment and the context is unclear. On the other hand the distinction is clearly stated at AL VII.i.14-17, and it therefore appears to have survived in some legal circles but not in others. The witnesses required for contracts were undoubtedly *gwybyddiaid.*

uuadio, (see Niermeyer s.v. *wadium* for variant spellings): the primary sense is gage (see Note on Terminology). Cf. Gothic *wadi*; arra, earnest-money; OE *wed(d),* gage and Latin *uas, uadis* (hence *uadimonium*), an early kind of surety to guarantee the defendant's appearance in court, i.e. a *Gestellungsbürge.* In medieval texts the prevailing sense is of a security effected symbolically in favour of the creditor by reference to some physical object (perhaps even the body of the gagor or debtor) which was passed to the creditor or some intermediary, pending performance of the obligation, actual process against the gage (animate or not) only taking place in the event of the debtor's default (see Walters, above, 107). See the long entry in Niermeyer, s.vv. *wadium, wadiaria* and the following entries. *Rewadiare* is sometimes used of self-pledge, not, as with *fides facta,* by pledge of honour or faith, but by handing over a gage as a symbolic substitute for self-surrender. *Wadium* is not used, however, for distraint, for which the common term is *namium,* vb. *namiare,* For *vadium* in Welsh law see e.g. LTWL, 508.4-12 (and for *namium* e.g. 458.-8).

venditio, normally 'sale' but in CR also used for the giving of gages (pledges) of land, see p. 77.

ynad, p. 259, 262, see WLW, 220-21; Nesta Lloyd a Morfydd E. Owen, *Drych yr Oesoedd Canol* (Caerdydd, 1986), §§27-29, and *brawdwr* and *iudex* above.

A BIBLIOGRAPHY OF THE WRITINGS OF
DAFYDD JENKINS 1935-1983

Philip Henry Jones

Because of the range and diversity of Dafydd Jenkins's interests this does not claim to be a comprehensive bibliography of his writings. In particular, no attempt has been made to list systematically all his contributions to Welsh newspapers. The attribution of anonymous items has been restricted to those for which the internal evidence for authorship appeared conclusive.

1935

'Traddodiad eglwys Caergaint'. *Y Llenor*, 14 (1935), 140-51.

1936

Joint editor of *Heddiw* from volume 1, no. 1 to volume 4, no. 3 (November, 1938).
'Dyddiadur Cymro'. *Heddiw*, 1 (1936-7), 59-64, 107-9, 133-6, 173-6.
'Heddiw'. *Heddiw*, 1 (1936-7), 7-9.
'"Ond yw hi'n fach ddel?"' *Tir Newydd*, 4 (1936), 8-11. [Short story].
Review of H. I. Bell, *The development of Welsh poetry*. *Heddiw*, 1 (1936-7), 73-5.
Review of T. Gwynn Jones, *Astudiaethau*. *Heddiw*, 1 (1936-7), 76-8.
Review of Gwilym Owen, *Mawr a bach*. *Heddiw*, 1 (1936-7), 32-3.
Review of D. J. Williams, *Storïau'r tir glas* and G. Dyfnallt Owen, *Y machlud a storïau eraill*. *Heddiw*, 1 (1936-7), 200-4.
Review of the 1936 British and Foreign Bible Society edition of the *New Testament* in modern Welsh orthography. *Heddiw*, 1 (1936-7), 160.

1937

'Ar degwch Ceredigion'. *Llawlyfr Cymdeithas Ceredigion Llundain*, 4 (1937-8), 28-32.
'Beth a ddaw o Gymry Llundain?' *London Welsh Annual 1937-1938*, pp. 44-6.
'Cylchgronau'. *Heddiw*, 2 (1937), 39-40.

'Dyddiadur Cymro'. *Heddiw*, 1 (1936-7), 223-7; 2 (1937), 23-6, 62-5.
'Golygyddol'. *Heddiw*, 2 (1937), 161-2. [*In memoriam* Idwal Jones].
'Golygyddol: beth yw rhyfel?' *Heddiw*, 2 (1937), 121-3.
'Golygyddol: dau fyd y Cymro'. *Heddiw* 2 (1937), 81-4.
'Golygyddol: "Democratiaeth"'. *Heddiw*, 2 (1937), 202-4.
'Golygyddol: Democratiaeth eto'. *Heddiw*, 3 (1937-8), 1-4.
[Under pseudonym 'Myrddin Gardi'] 'Nadolig Llawen'. *Heddiw*, 3 (1937-8), 167-74. [Short story].
Tân yn Llŷn: hanes brwydr gorsaf awyr Penyberth... Aberystwyth: Gwasg Aberystwyth, 1937. pp. 196.
'Teivy Dairy'. *Y Llenor*, 16 (1937), 98-106. [Short story].
'Trem ar Gymru'. *Heddiw*, 2 (1937), 163-70. [Review article discussing *The second industrial survey of South Wales* and R. G. Stapledon, *A survey of the agricultural and waste lands of Wales*].
[Under pseudonym 'Myrddin Gardi'] 'Yr ymgyrch lên ar gered yn Sir Gâr'. *Y Ddraig Goch*, Hydref 1937, p. 12.
[Translator] 'A summer day'. In: *Welsh short stories: an anthology*. London: Faber & Faber, 1937, pp. 50-7. [Translation of Kate Roberts, 'Dydd o haf'].
Review of D. Cadwaladr, *Storïau Dilys Cadwaladr. Heddiw,* 1 (1936-7), 242-4.
Review of R. O. Davies, *Elfennau cemeg. Heddiw*, 3 (1937-8), 150-5.
Review of F. Elwyn Jones, *Hitler's drive to the East. Heddiw*, 2 (1937), 33-7.
Review of W. Hughes Jones, *Wales drops the pilots* and J. E. Daniel, *Welsh nationalism: what it stands for. Heddiw*, 3 (1937-8), 38-9.
Review of W. Hughes Jones, *What is happening in Wales?* and Eiluned and Peter Lewis, *The land of Wales. Heddiw*, 2 (1937), 156-60.
Review of E. Matthews, *Y Nadolig cyntaf a storiau eraill o'r Beibl. Heddiw*, 2 (1937), 80.

1938

'Diwyg llyfrau Cymraeg'. *Heddiw*, 3 (1937-8), 329-32 [i.e. 429-32].
[Under pseudonym 'Myrddin Gardi'] 'Eiddo a chyfalaf'. *Y Ddraig Goch*, Mawrth 1938, pp. 8-9.
'Golygyddol: y gyfraith a'r proffwydi'. *Heddiw*, 3 (1937-8), 237-40 [i.e. 337-40].
Monmouthshire: the case for Wales. Caernarfon: Welsh Nationalist Party, 1938. pp. 12.
'Pwmp y pentre'. *Y Ddraig Goch*, Ionawr 1938, p. 11; Chwefror 1938, p. 6; Mawrth 1938, p. 6; Ebrill 1938, p. 6; Mehefin 1938, p. 11; Gorffennaf 1938, p. 11; Medi 1938, p. 6; Tachwedd 1938, p. 11; Rhagfyr 1938, p. 11. [Series of articles on local councils].

Review of J. Bodvan Anwyl, *Geiriadur Saesneg a Chymraeg* (11th edn.) and *Geiriadur Cymraeg a Saesneg* (13th edn.). *Heddiw*, 3 (1937-8), 264-8.
Review of *Efrydiau Athronyddol I. Heddiw*, 4 (1938-9), 35-6.
Review of Daniel Owen, *Y Siswrn. Heddiw*, 3 (1937-8), 268-72 [i.e. 368-72].
Review of *Welsh short stories. Heddiw*, 3 (1937-8), 232-40.

1939

[Under pseudonym 'Myrddin Gardi'] 'Am rai llyfrau'. *Heddiw*, 5 (1939-40), 147-51, 203-9, 366-70.
'Y Ddeiseb hyd yma'. *Heddiw*, 4 (1938-9), 137-40.
[Under pseudonym 'Myrddin Gardi'] 'Dyddiadur Cymro'. *Heddiw*, 5 (1939-40), 308-14.
[Under pseudonym 'Myrddin Gardi'] 'Imperialaeth a heddwch'. *Heddiw*, 5 (1939-40), 69-75.
'Pwmp y pentre'. *Y Ddraig Goch*, Chwefror 1939, p. 11; Ebrill 1939, p. 4. [Conclusion of series of articles on local councils commenced in January 1938].
'The Welsh language petition'. *Welsh Review*, 1 (1939), 152-6.
[Translator] 'The condemned'. *Welsh Review*, 1 (1939), 72-8. [Translation of Kate Roberts, 'Y condemniedig'].
[Translator] 'Samuel Jones's harvest thanksgiving'. *Welsh Review*, 1 (1939), 63-8. [Translation of E. Tegla Davies, 'Samuel Jones yr Hendre yn diolch am ei gynhaeaf'].
Review of W. J. Griffith, *Storïau'r Henllys Fawr* and J. O. Williams, *Tua'r gorllewin ac ysgrifau eraill. Heddiw*, 5 (1939-40), 43-5.

1940

[Under pseudonym 'Myrddin Gardi'] 'Am rai llyfrau'. *Heddiw*, 6 (1940-1), 114-15.
[Under pseudonym 'Myrddin Gardi'] 'Cymru grefyddol'. *Heddiw*, 5 (1939-40), 439-42.
[Under pseudonym 'Myrddin Gardi'] 'Dyfodol Cymru—llythyr agored'. *Heddiw*, 5 (1939-40), 479-83.
[Editor] William Rees 'Gwilym Hiraethog', *Helyntion bywyd hen deiliwr*. Aberystwyth: Y Clwb Llyfrau Cymreig, 1940. pp. lxvi, 201. [Introduction by D. J. traces the early development of the novel in Welsh].
'Y milwyr: Ionor 1940'. *Heddiw*, 5 (1939-40), 465. [An *englyn*].
'Rhy hwyr'. *Cyfansoddiadau a beirniadaethau... Eisteddfod Genedlaethol 1940 (Aberpennar)*, pp. 189-95. [Short story].

[Under pseudonym 'Myrddin Gardi'] 'Statws dominiwn'. *Heddiw*, 5 (1939-40), 408.

[Translator] 'Pwll yr Onnen'. In: *Welsh short stories*. Ed. Gwyn Jones, Harmondsworth: Penguin, 1940, pp. 157-65. [Translation of D. J. Williams, 'Pwll yr Onnen'].

Review of *Efrydiau Athronyddol II. Heddiw*, 5 (1939-40), 463.

1941

[Under pseudonym 'Myrddin Gardi'] 'Am rai llyfrau'. *Heddiw*, 6 (1940-1), 303-6.

[Under pseudonym 'D. Meurig Rhys'] 'Bugeilio... gwenith gwyn'. *Heddiw*, 6 (1940-1), 276-9.

'Deddfgrawn William Maurice'. *National Library of Wales Journal*, 2 (1941-2), 33-6.

'Dyddiadur Cymro'. *Heddiw*, 6 (1940-1), 208-11, 236-9, 254-7.

Economeg heddwch. Pamffledi Heddychwyr Cymru: Cyfres 1, Rhif 4. Dinbych: Gwasg Gee, [1941]. pp. 26.

'Llyfr y proffwyd Eric Gill'. *Heddiw*, 6 (1940-1), 283-6.

'Un o ganolfannau hyfforddi'r Crynwyr'. *Heddiw*, 6 (1940-1), 314-17.

Review of D. Tegfan Davies, *O ganol Sir Gâr. Heddiw*, 6 (1940-1), 180-1.

Review of D. J. Williams, *Storïau'r tir coch. Heddiw*, 6 (1940-1), 334-6.

1942

Review of *Efrydiau Athronyddol IV. Heddiw*, 7 (1941-2), 90.

Review of T. Rowland Hughes (ed.), *Storïau radio. Heddiw*, 7 (1941-2), 89-90.

Review of Stephen J. Williams and J. Enoch Powell, *Cyfreithiau Hywel Dda yn ôl Llyfr Blegywryd. Heddiw*, 7 (1941-2), 120-4.

1943

'Gobaith gwleidyddiaeth'. *Yr Efrydydd*, 8(2) (1942-3), 23-5.

Treth incwm y ffermwr. [Aberystwyth]: Gwasg Aberystwyth, [1943]. pp. 24.

1944

'"Rhaid eich geni drachefn"'. *Yr Efrydydd*, 9(2) (1943-4), 8-16.

Review of J. E. Meredith (ed.), *Credaf. Yr Efrydydd*, 9(1) (Rhifyn y gaeaf) (1943-4), 27-9.

1945

[Translator] 'The court cupboard'. *Wales*, 5(8-9) (1945), 74-81. [Translation of D. J. Williams, 'Y cwpwrdd tridarn'].

[Translator] 'Two storms'. *Welsh Review*, 4 (1945), 94-9. [Translation of Kate Roberts, 'Dwy storm'].

1946

'Y crefftwr'. *Y Fflam*, 1 (1946), 20-3. [Short story].

[Translator] 'A summer day'. In: *A summer day and other stories*. Cardiff: Penmark Press, 1946, pp. 63-9. [Reprints translation first published in 1937].

[Translator] 'Two storms'. In: *A summer day...* pp. 17-26. [Reprints translation first published in 1945].

[Translator] 'The wind'. In: *A summer day...* pp. 27-37. [Translation of Kate Roberts, 'Y gwynt'].

1947

Review of W. Ambrose Bebb, *Calendr coch*. *Y Fflam*, 2 (1947), 61.

Review of T. Rowland Hughes, *Chwalfa*. *Y Fflam*, 2 (1947), 65-6.

1948

'The agriculture of Wales'. *Cymru'r Groes*, 4 (1948-9), 54-8.

'D. J. Williams'. In: *Gwŷr llên: ysgrifau beirniadol ar weithiau deuddeg gŵr llên cyfoes...* Ed. Aneirin Talfan Davies, Llundain: W. Griffiths a'i Frodyr, 1948, pp. 229-40.

Y nofel: datblygiad y nofel Gymraeg ar ôl Daniel Owen. Caerdydd: Llyfrau'r Castell, 1948. pp. 43.

[Under pseudonym 'D. Meurig Rhys'] 'R. T. Jenkins'. In: *Gwŷr llên...* pp. 23-39.

Thomas Johnes o'r Hafod 1748-1816. Caerdydd: Gwasg Prifysgol Cymru, 1948. pp. 84.

1949

'Amddiffyniad i'r cominasiwn'. *Y Llenor*, 28 (1949), 209-16.

1950

[Under pseudonym 'D. Meurig Rhys'] 'Dyddiadur'. *Y Genhinen*, 1
 (1950-1), 47-51, 113-17, 180-4, 250-3. [Last part under title
 'Dyddiadur Eisteddfodwr'].
'Some impressions of Irish co-operation'. *Rural Wales: a yearbook of Welsh
 agricultural co-operation, 1949-50*, pp. 53-7.
'Wales'. *Year book of agricultural co-operation 1950*, pp. 88-94.
Beirniadaeth: Y stori fer. *Cyfansoddiadau a beirniadaethau Eisteddfod
 Genedlaethol Caerffili 1950*, pp. 178-84.

1951

Ar wib yn Nenmarc. Aberystwyth: Y Clwb Llyfrau Cymraeg, 1951. pp. 86.
'Cyfarwyr hanner canrif'. *Lleufer*, 7 (1951), 136-40.
'Llawysgrif goll Llanforda o gyfreithiau Hywel Dda'. *Bulletin of the Board
 of Celtic Studies*, 14 (1950-2), 89-104.
'Trawscoed'. *Llawlyfr Cymdeithas Ceredigion Llundain*, 6 (1950-1), 27-37.
 [Transcript of a talk broadcast in the BBC series 'Gwin newydd'].
'Wales'. *Year book of agricultural co-operation 1951*, pp. 90-6.
Beirniadaeth: Nofel i ieuenctid oddeutu 25,000 o eiriau. *Cyfansoddiadau a
 beirniadaethau Eisteddfod Genedlaethol Llanrwst 1951*, pp. 170-3.

1953

'Iorwerth ap Madog: gŵr cyfraith o'r drydedd ganrif ar ddeg'. *National
 Library of Wales Journal*, 8 (1953-4), 164-70.
'Thomas Johnes, amaethwr'. *Llawlyfr Cymdeithas Ceredigion Llundain*, 9
 (1953-4), 9-15. [Transcript of a talk broadcast 17 May 1951].
Contribution to *Y Bywgraffiadur Cymreig hyd 1940*. 'Johnes, Thomas
 (1748-1816)'.

1954

'Cristnogaeth ddoe a heddiw'. *Llafar*, 4(1) (1954-5), 22-8. [Transcript of a
 talk broadcast 16 September 1953].
'Wales'. *Year book of agricultural co-operation 1954*, pp. 85-8.

1955

'Storïau diweddar D. J. Williams'. *Y Genhinen*, 6 (1955-6), 7-12.
'Wales'. *Year book of agricultural co-operation 1955*, pp. 24-9.

1956

'Wales'. *Year book of agricultural co-operation 1956*, pp. 109-13.

[Translator] 'Two storms'. In: *Welsh short stories*. Ed. Gwyn Jones, London: Oxford University Press, 1956, pp. 243-52. [Reprints translation first published in 1945].

[Translator] 'Pwll-yr-Onnen'. In: *Welsh short stories...* pp. 313-22. [Reprints translation first published in 1940].

Review of Islwyn Ffowc Elis, *Ffenestri tua'r gwyll*. *Lleufer*, 12 (1956), 71-4.

1957

'Agricultural co-operation in Wales 1955-56'. *Year book of agricultural co-operation 1957*, pp. 74-7.

'Kate Roberts, nofelydd'. *Lleufer*, 13 (1957), 83-8.

'Sånga—Säby: the Swedish College of Agricultural Co-operation'. *Rural Wales*, 5 (1957), 68-73.

1958

'Agricultural co-operation in Wales 1956-57'. *Year book of agricultural co-operation 1958*, pp. 115-19.

Law for co-operatives. Oxford: Basil Blackwell, 1958. pp. xvi, 312.

1959

Ar wib yn Sweden. Aberystwyth: Cymdeithas Lyfrau Ceredigion, 1959. pp. 146.

'Crymmych & District Farmers' Association Limited'. In: *Crymmych and District Farmers' Association Limited Jubilee Souvenir 1908-1958*. Haverfordwest: Printed by the Western Telegraph, [1959], pp. 9-33.

'Priod-ddull a throsiad'. *Y Genhinen*, 9 (1958-9), 161-5.

'Woodland co-operatives in Wales'. *Year book of agricultural co-operation 1959*, pp. 89-99.

[Translator] 'The court cupboard'. In: *Welsh short stories*. Ed. G. Ewart Evans, London: Faber & Faber, 1959, pp. 232-41. [Reprints translation first published in 1945].

Review of Dyddgu Owen, *Brain Borromeo* and Bobi Jones, *Nid yw dŵr yn plygu*. *Lleufer*, 15 (1959), 148-51.

1960

'Agricultural co-operation in Wales 1957-1959'. *Year book of agricultural co-operation 1960*, pp. 83-7.

Review of Melville Richards (ed.), *Cyfreithiau Hywel Dda o lawysgrif Coleg Iesu, Rhydychen, LVII. Welsh History Review*, 1 (1960-3), 106.

1961

Ar wib yn Sweden. Aberystwyth: Cymdeithas Lyfrau Ceredigion, 1961. pp. 146. [Reissue in paperback of work first published in 1959].

'Iorwerth ap Madog a Hywel Dda'. *Lleufer*, 17 (1961), 17-33.

Beirniadaeth: Portreadau o chwe chymeriad gwreiddiol o unrhyw ardal. *Cyfansoddiadau a beirniadaethau Eisteddfod Genedlaethol Frenhinol Cymru Dyffryn Maelor 1961*, pp. 107-11.

1962

'Co-operative law in Sweden and the United Kingdom'. *Year book of agricultural co-operation 1962*, pp. 59-70.

Hanes Eifionydd Farmers' Association Limited 1908-1958. S.L.: S.N., 1962. pp. [2], 74.

[With Erik Anners] 'A Swedish borrowing from Welsh medieval law?' *Welsh History Review*, 1 (1960-3), 325-33. [Revised summary of an article by Anners first published as 'Götalagarnas lekarerätt—en Keltisk influens?' *Rättshistoriska Studier*, 2 (1957), 8-25].

[With Alun Thomas] 'Wales: seed growers' co-operation'. *Year book of agricultural co-operation 1962*, pp. 85-92.

1963

'Agricultural co-operation in Wales 1961-62'. *Year book of agricultural co-operation 1963*, pp. 80-90.

'Gwyddoniaeth a llywodraeth'. *Barn*, 7 (1963), 205.

'Legal and comparative aspects of the Welsh laws'. *Welsh History Review*, Special number (1963), pp. 51-9.

Llyfr Colan: y gyfraith Gymreig yn ôl hanner cyntaf llawysgrif Peniarth 30. Bwrdd Gwybodau Celtaidd, Prifysgol Cymru, Cyfres Hanes a Chyfraith, Rhif 19. Caerdydd: Gwasg Prifysgol Cymru, 1963. pp. xliv, 214.

Review of J. Lloyd Jones, *Geirfa barddoniaeth gynnar Gymraeg (rhan 8)*. *Barn*, 14 (1963), 52.

Review of Alun T. Lewis, *Blwyddyn o garchar* and Jane Edwards, *Dechrau gofidiau*. *Barn*, 7 (1963), 212-13.

Review of Undeb yr Annibynwyr Cymraeg, *Llyfr Gwasanaeth*. *Barn*, 14 (1963), 51-2.

Beirniadaeth: Nofel hanes. *Cyfansoddiadau a beirniadaethau Eisteddfod Genedlaethol Llandudno a'r cylch 1963*, pp. 119-20.

1964

Agricultural co-operation in Sweden. Occasional paper no. 23. London: Plunkett Foundation for Co-operative Studies, 1964. pp. [6], 54, [24].

'Comisiwn y Ffiniau a'r Gymraeg'. *Barn*, 15 (1964), 113-14.

Review of R. M. Jones, *Emile Jean-Jacques Rousseau. Detholion*. *Barn*, 18 (1964), 170.

1965

'Y Babell Lên'. *Barn*, 36 (1965), 347.

'Chwe stori o *Ystorïau Heddiw*'. *Barn*, 32 (1965), 236-7. [Discussion of R. G. Berry, 'Wyn, M.A. (Oxon.)'; W. J. Gruffydd, 'Dygwyl y meirw'; T. Gwynn Jones, 'Dau o'r hen do'; W. J. Griffith, 'Eos y Pentan'; J. O. Williams, 'Pnawn Sadwrn'; Amy Thomas 'Henrietta'].

'Cyfrol deyrnged D. J. Williams'. *Taliesin*, 11 (1965), 110-13. [Review article discussing J. Gwyn Griffiths (ed.), *D. J. Williams, Abergwaun*].

'Nofelau'r goler gron'. *Taliesin*, 11 (1965), 98-104. [Review article discussing John Rowlands, *Ienctid yw 'mhechod*, G. Parry, *Plant yr ecsodus* and T. Wilson Evans, *Nos yn yr enaid*].

[With Hywel Moseley] 'Pa alwedigaeth?' *Barn*, 27 (1965), 87; 28 (1965), 116-17.

'Y priod-ddullgwn'. *Barn*, 29 (1965), 140-1.

Review of Elizabeth M. Mrowiec, *Teithio Pŵyl*. *Barn*, 38 (1965), 56.

1966

'Creu gelynion'. *Barn*, 49 (1966), 14.

'Nodiadau cymysg: [1] arianfys; efyddfys; goldfinger; [2] blwyddau'. *Bulletin of the Board of Celtic Studies*, 21 (1964-6), 308-9.

'Rhagor am y cynllun uno'. *Barn*, 45 (1966), 237-8.

Y stori fer Gymraeg. Cyfres pamffledi llenyddol Cyfadran Addysg Aberystwyth, Rhif 2. Llandybïe: Llyfrau'r Dryw, 1966. pp. 20.

1967

'Ateb i John R. Jones, Llangoed'. *Barn*, 53 (1967), 124.
'Bil yr Iaith Gymraeg'. *Barn*, 58 (1967), 262.
'The Black Book of Chirk: a note'. *National Library of Wales Journal*, 15 (1967-8), 104-7.
'"Camsyniadau F. W. Maitland"': y genedl alanas yng nghyfraith Hywel'. *Bulletin of the Board of Celtic Studies*, 22 (1966-8), 228-36.
'Diwygio diwyg llyfrau—tybed?' *Baner ac Amserau Cymru*, 26 Ionawr 1967, p. 7.
'A lawyer looks at Welsh land law'. *Transactions of the Honourable Society of Cymmrodorion*, 1967, pp. 220-48.
'Nodiadau cymysg: [1] distain; [2] nythod: nisi: llamysten; [3]cestyll: castra: lluesteu'. *Bulletin of the Board of Celtic Studies,* 22 (1966-8), 127-9.
'Welsh laws'. *Encyclopaedia Britannica*, 1967 edn.
[With Alwyn Hughes Jones] Beirniadaeth: Traethawd Cymraeg neu Saesneg: Yr awdurdodau lleol a datblygiad economaidd cefn gwlad Cymru. *Cyfansoddiadau a beirniadaethau Eisteddfod Genedlaethol Frenhinol Cymru Y Bala 1967*, pp. 110-13.

1968

'Y nofel'. In: *Gwŷr llên y bedwaredd ganrif ar bymtheg a'u cefndir*. Ed. Dyfnallt Morgan, Llandybïe: Llyfrau'r Dryw, 1968, pp. 245-54. [Transcript of talk broadcast in 1964].
'Yr Ynad Coch'. *Bulletin of the Board of Celtic Studies*, 22 (1966-8), 345-6.

1969

'Cywirdeb'. *Barn*, 77 (1969), 123.
'The essence of the contract'. *Cambridge Law Journal*, 27 (1969), 251-72.
[Translator] 'Mab y Dyn'. *Taliesin*, 18 (1969), 42. [Translation of a work by Harald Kidde].

1970

'Corporate liability in tort and the doctrine of *ultra vires*'. *The Irish Jurist*, NS 5 (1970), 11-29.
'Cyfamodi yng Nghymru'. *Barn*, 90 (1970), 148-9.
Cyfraith Hywel: rhagarweiniad i gyfraith gynhenid Cymru'r oesau canol. Llandysul: Gwasg Gomer, 1970. pp. viii, 131.

'The date of the Act of Union'. *Bulletin of the Board of Celtic Studies*, 23 (1968-70), 345-6.

'The language of the law'. *Cambrian Law Review*, 1 (1970), 22-8.

'Law and government in Wales before the Act of Union'. In: *Welsh studies in public law*. Ed. J. A. Andrews, Cardiff: University of Wales Press, 1970, pp. 7-29.

'R. T. Jenkins: Maitland Cymru'. *Y Traethodydd*, 125 (1970), 98-109.

'Ysgar mewn cyfraith a chrefydd'. *Y Traethodydd*, 125 (1970), 35-47.

Review of T. L. Williams, *Caradoc Evans*. *Barn*, 94 (1970), 276.

1972

'Hugh James a'i gyfnod'. In: *Farmers together: golden jubilee volume of the Welsh Agricultural Organisation Society*. Ed. Elwyn R. Thomas, Aberystwyth: Welsh Agricultural Organisation Society, 1972, pp. 133-52.

Review of *Craies on statute law* (7th edn.) and *Stroud's judicial dictionary of words and phrases* (4th edn.). *Cambrian Law Review*, 3 (1972), 100-3.

1973

[Editor] *Celtic law papers introductory to Welsh medieval law and government: studies presented to the International Commission for the History of Representative and Parliamentary Institutions XLII... Aberystwyth 1971*. Bruxelles: Les editions de la librairie encyclopédique, 1973. pp. viii, 212.

Cyfraith trosedd. Cyhoeddiadau cyfraith Coleg Prifysgol Cymru, Rhif 1. Aberystwyth: Adran y Gyfraith Coleg Prifysgol Cymru, 1973. pp. [2], 15.

'Cymraeg y gyfraith'. *Taliesin*, 26 (1973), 136-42. [Review article discussing R. Lewis, *Termau cyfraith*].

D. J. Williams. Writers of Wales Series. [Cardiff]: University of Wales Press on behalf of the Welsh Arts Council, 1973. pp. [4], 96.

Damweiniau Colan: Llyfr y Damweiniau yn ôl llawysgrif Peniarth 30. Aberystwyth: Cymdeithas Lyfrau Ceredigion, 1973. pp. xviii, 82.

'A family of medieval Welsh lawyers'. In: *Celtic law papers...* pp. 121-33.

'Law and government in Wales before the Act of Union'. In: *Celtic law papers...* pp.23-48. [Reprints paper first published in 1970].

'Nodiadau amrywiol: [1] Gwad cyn dedfryd; [2] Sabrina/Severn/Hafren: s- > h-; [3] cael: fa; [4] llydyn; hych'. *Bulletin of the Board of Celtic Studies*, 25 (1972-4), 112-18.

1974

'G. K. Chesterton'. *Barn*, 142 (1974), 434-5.

1975

[Editor] *Legal history studies 1972: papers presented to the Legal History Conference Aberystwyth, 18-21 July 1972.* Cardiff: University of Wales Press, 1975. pp. viii, 155.

'Skinning the pantomime horse: two early cases on limited liability'. *Cambridge Law Journal*, 34 (1975), 308-21.

Tân yn Llŷn . . . Caerdydd: Plaid Cymru, 1975. pp. 198. [New edn. of work first published in 1937].

1976

Cyfraith Hywel: rhagarweiniad i gyfraith gynhenid Cymru'r oesau canol. Llandysul: Gwasg Gomer, 1976. pp. x, 133. [2nd edn., with corrections and a revised bibliography, of a work first published in 1970].

'Cynghellor and chancellor'. *Bulletin of the Board of Celtic Studies*, 27 (1976-8), 115-18.

'Kings, lords, and princes: the nomenclature of authority in thirteenth-century Wales'. *Bulletin of the Board of Celtic Studies*, 26 (1974-6), 451-62.

1977

'Abaty, albate, albadeth'. *Bulletin of the Board of Celtic Studies*, 27 (1976-8), 216-21.

'Amdiffyn dyneiddiaeth'. *Y Faner*, 12 Awst 1977, pp. 11-12.

'Collfarnu iaith'. *Y Faner*, 4 Tachwedd 1977, pp. 21-2.

Hywel Dda a'r gwŷr cyfraith: darlith agoriadol. Aberystwyth: Adran y Gyfraith Coleg Prifysgol Cymru, 1977. pp. 19.

'The significance of the law of Hywel'. *Transactions of the Honourable Society of Cymmrodorion*, (1977), pp. 54-76.

1978

'Canllath o gopa'r mynydd'. *Y Faner*, 8 Rhagfyr 1978, p. 22.

'O archifau'r Blaid'. *Llais Llyfrau*, Gwanwyn 1978, pp. 25-6.

1979

'At olygydd *Taliesin*'. *Taliesin*, 39 (1979), 91.
'Camliwio enbyd'. *Y Faner*, 11 Mai 1979, p. 5.
'*Heddiw* (1936-1942)'. *Y Faner*, 16 Mawrth 1979, pp. 12-13.
'Sinderela'r Eisteddfod?' *Barn*, 198-9 (1979), 87-8. [Contribution to a discussion concerning the Prose Medal of the National Eisteddfod].
'Y stori fer Gymraeg'. In: *Y stori fer, 'Seren wib llenyddiaeth'*. Ed. John Jenkins, Abertawe: Christopher Davies, 1979, pp. 36-48. [Reprints study first published in 1966].

1980

'Aneirin Talfan Davies 1909-1980', *Y Faner*, Rhifyn yr Eisteddfod 1980, pp. 14-15. [Correction in *Y Faner*, 15 Awst 1980, p. 3].
[Editor and translator] 'The "Cyfnerth" Text'. [Of the tractate on the law of women]. In: *The Welsh law of women...* pp. 132-45.
'Fel y dangosodd y Refferendwm, rhaid i ni fel Cymry...' *Y Traethodydd*, 135 (1980), 19-28. [Contribution to a symposium].
'Property interests in the classical Welsh law of women'. In: *The Welsh law of women...* pp. 68-92.
'Sylwadau ar y *Surexit*'. *Bulletin of the Board of Celtic Studies*, 28 (1978-80), 607-12.
[With Morfydd E. Owen] 'Gwilym Was Da'. *National Library of Wales Journal*, 21 (1979-80), 429-30.
[Joint editor with Morfydd E. Owen] *The Welsh law of women: studies presented to Professor Daniel A. Binchy on his eightieth birthday 3 June 1980*. Cardiff: University of Wales Press, 1980. pp. xiv, 253.

1981

'English law and the Renaissance eighty years on: in defence of Maitland'. *Journal of Legal History*, 2 (1981), 107-42.
'Llawlyfr I ac A'. *Y Traethodydd*, 136 (1981), 204-9.
'The medieval Welsh idea of law'. *Tijdschrift voor Rechtsgeschiedenis*, 49 (1981), 323-48.
'Precedent and the Court of Appeal'. *Legal Studies*, 1 (1981), 340-2.
'Tegla'. *Taliesin*, 42 (1981), 9-24.

1982

Agricultural co-operation in Welsh medieval law. [Sain Ffagan]: Amgueddfa
Werin Cymru, 1982. pp. 18.

'Chwarae teg i'r Ysbryd Glân!' *Y Faner*, 3 Medi 1982, p. 6.

'''Cymraeg Coleg Bangor'''. *Barn*, 229 (1982), pp. 13-14.

'Druan o'r diwydiant cyhoeddi Cymraeg'. *Llais Llyfrau*, Hydref 1982, p. 8.

'Gwenogvryn Evans's ''Facsimile of the Chirk Codex'''. *National Library
of Wales Journal*, 22 (1981-2), 470-4.

'Milltir sgwâr Dinefwr'. *Barn*, 239-40 (1982-3), 409-10.

'Pwy yw Ficer Crist?' *Y Faner*, 23 Gorffennaf 1982, p. 6.

[With Morfydd E. Owen] 'Welsh law in Carmarthenshire'. *Carmarthen
Antiquary*, 18 (1982), 17-27.

1983/4

[With Morfydd E. Owen] 'The Welsh marginalia in the Lichfield Gospels'.
Cambridge Medieval Celtic Studies, 5 (1983), 37-66; 7 (1984), 91-120.

BIBLIOGRAPHICAL ABBREVIATIONS

(Some standard legal abbreviations, e.g. QB for Queen's Bench, are not given.)

Abt	The Laws of Æthelberht in Liebermann, i, 3-8, or in F. L. Attenborough, *The Laws of the Earliest English Kings.* Cambridge, 1922. pp.4-17.
AL	*Ancient Laws and Institutes of Wales.* Ed. A. Owen, London, Record Commission, 1841; published in two forms, a two vol. octavo and a single vol. folio; the pagination is different in the two, and references are therefore best given by book, chapter and paragraph; e.g. AL VII.i.9 = Book VII, chap. i, para. 9. For the first vol. of the octavo and the corresponding part of the folio references are given to the 'codes'; e.g. VC III.ii.2 = Venedotian Code, Book III, chap. ii, para. 2.
AN	Anglo-Norman.
Arch. Camb.	*Archaeologia Cambrensis.*
BA	Berrad Airechta. CIH 591.8-599.38; trans. *Bürgschaft*; see above, 210-227.
BBCS	*Bulletin of the Board of Celtic Studies.*
Beyerle, 'Der Upsprung der Bürgschaft'	F. Beyerle, 'Der Ursprung der Bürgschaft', (1927) 14 ZRG/GA, 567-645.
Binchy	'Celtic Suretyship' D. A. Binchy, 'Celtic Suretyship, a Fossilized Indo-European Institution?', first published in *Indo-European and the Indo-Europeans, Papers Presented at the Third Indo-European Conference at the University of Pennsylvania.* Ed. G. Cardona, H. M. Hoenigswald and A. Senn. Philadelphia, 1970. Pp.355-67. Reprinted in (1972) 7 Irish Jurist (N.S.), 360-72. Page references are given to both in order of publication in the form 360 (365).
Bleg	*Llyfr Blegywryd.* Ed. S. J. Williams and J. E. Powell. 2nd edn., Cardiff, 1961. References are given in the form 60.1 = p. 60, line 1.

Bracton	Bracton, *De Legibus et Consuetudinibus Angliae*. Cited by the foliation of the Vulgate edition of 1569, which is reproduced in all subsequent editions. The standard edition is *On the Laws and Customs of England*. Ed. G. E. Woodbine and trans. S. E. Thorne. Cambridge, Mass., 1968-.
Brunner	H. Brunner, *Deutsche Rechtsgeschichte*. 2nd edn., i, Leipzig, 1906, ii, ed. C. von Schwerin, Munich and Leipzig, 1928.
Buckland	W. W. Buckland, *A Textbook of Roman Law from Augustus to Justinian*. 3rd edn. by P. Stein, Cambridge, 1963.
Bürgschaft	R. Thurneysen, *Die Bürgschaft im irischen Recht. Abhandlungen der Preussischen Akademie der Wissenschaften, Phil- hist. Klasse*, No. 2, 1928.
CG	*Críth Gablach*. Ed. D. A. Binchy, Medieval and Modern Irish Series, Dublin, 1941. References to the text are by line.
CIH	*Corpus Iuris Hibernici*. Ed. D. A. Binchy. 6 vols., Dublin, 1978. References are by page and line.
CLP	*Celtic Law Papers introductory to Welsh Medieval Law and Government*. Ed. D. Jenkins. *Studies presented to the International Commission for the History of Representative and Parliamentary Institutions*, xlix, Brussels, 1973.
CMCS	*Cambridge Medieval Celtic Studies*.
Col	*Llyfr Colan*. Ed. D. Jenkins. Board of Celtic Studies, History and Law Series XIX, Cardiff, 1963. References are to the no. of the sentence.
Conrad	H. Conrad, *Deutsche Rechtsgeschicte: Frühzeit und Mittelalter*. Karlsruhe, 1954.
Councils and Synods	*Councils and Synods with other Documents relating to the English Church*. Vol. i, parts i and ii, A.D. 871-1204. Ed. D. Whitelock, M. Brett and C. N. L. Brooke. Oxford, 1981. Vol. ii, parts i and ii, A.D. 1205-1313. Ed. F. M. Powicke and C. R. Cheney, Oxford, 1964. References are in the form *Councils and Synods*, 1:1, 254 = vol. i, part i, p.254.
Cyfn	*Llyfr Cyfnerth*; see above, 179-180. One version is edited by A. W. Wade-Evans, *Welsh Medieval Law*.

	Oxford, 1909. Another forms the 'Gwentian Code' in AL (G.C.).
Decretum	Decretum Gratiani, in *Corpus Iuris Canonici* vol. 1 Ed. E. Friedberg, Leipzig, 1879.
Digest	*Iustiniani Digesta.* Ed. Theodore Mommsen and P. Krüger, *Corpus Iuris Civilis,* vol. 1, 11th edn. Berlin, 1908 and subsequent editions.
DIL	*Dictionary of the Irish Language* and *'Contributions to a Dictionary of the Irish Language'.* Dublin, 1913-75.
DwCol	*Damweiniau Colan: Llyfr y Damweiniau yn ôl Llawysgrif Peniarth 30.* Ed. D. Jenkins. Aberystwyth, 1973. References are given by the no. of the sentence.
Edictus Rothari	Ed. F. Beyerle, *Leges Langbardorum, 643-866.* Germanenrechte, N. F., Westgermanisches Recht. 2nd edn., Witzenhausen, 1962. Also ed. F. Bluhme, *Leges Langobardorum,* MGH Leges, 1868.
Gilissen	J. Gilissen, 'Esquisse d'une histoire comparée des sûretés personelles: essai de synthèse général', (1974) 28 *Rec. Soc. Jean Bodin,* 5-127.
Glanvill	*Tractatus de Legibus et Consuetudinibus Regni Anglie qui Glanvilla vocatur.* Ed. G. D. G. Hall. London and Edinburgh, 1965.
GMW	*A Grammar of Medieval Welsh,* D. Simon Evans, Dublin 1976.
GMWL	*A Glossary of Medieval Welsh Law,* T. Lewis, Manchester 1913.
GPC	*Geiriadur Prifysgol Cymru.* Cardiff, 1950-.
Grammar	R. Thurneysen, *A Grammar of Old Irish.* Trans. by D. A. Binchy and O. J. Bergin, Dublin, 1946.
H&S	A. W. Haddon & W. Stubbs, *Council & Eccles. Documents relating to Great Britain & Ireland (after Spelman & Wilkins),* 3 vols. Oxford 1869-78.
Holmes	O. W. Holmes. *The Common Law.* Boston, 1881, and numerous subsequent printings.
Hübner	R. Hübner, *A History of German Private Law.* Trans. F. S. Philbrick. The Continental Legal History Series, 4. Boston, 1918.
Ior	*Llyfr Iorwerth.* Ed. A. Rh. Wiliam. Board of Celtic Studies, History and Law Series, xxix, Cardiff, 1960.

	References are given in the form 66/3 = para. 66, third sentence.
Ir. Recht	R. Thurneysen, *Irisches Recht. Abhandlungen der Preussischen Akademie der Wissenschaften*, Phil.-hist. Klasse, No. 2, Berlin, 1931.
Kaser, RPR	M. Kaser, *Roman Private Law*. 2nd English edn., trans. of 6th German edn. R. Dannenbring. Durban, 1968.
Kaser, RPr	M. Kaser, *Das römische Privatrecht. Handbuch der Altertumswissenschaft*, X.3.3.1-2. 2 vols., Munich, 2nd revised edn, 1971, 1975.
Latham	R. E. Latham, Revised Medieval Latin Word-list from British & Irish Sources. British Academy/Oxford, 1965 (or later edn.).
LHEB	K. Jackson, *Language and History in Early Britain*. Edinburgh, 1953.
LHP	*Leges Henrici Primi*. Ed. L. J. Downer. Oxford, 1972.
LL. Lang.	Leges Langobardorum. For editions see above under *Edictus Rothari*.
LQR	*Law Quarterly Review*.
LTWL	The Latin Texts of the Welsh Laws. Ed. H. D. Emanuel. Board of Celtic Studies, History and Law Series, xxii, Cardiff, 1967.
Lat A, B, C, D, E	Latin Recensions A, B, C, D, E in LTWL.
Lex Ribuaria	*Lex Ribvaria*. Ed. F. Beyerle and R. Buchner. MGH Leges, I.III.II.
Liebermann	*Die Gesetze der Angelsachsen*. Ed. F. Liebermann. 3 vols., Halle, 1903-1916.
Mansi	*Sacrorum Conciliorum nova et amplissima collectio*. J. D. Mansi et al., 1759-., repr. Leipzig & Paris, 1901-25 in 57 vols.
MGH Capit.	*Monumenta Germaniae Historica, Capitularia Regum Francorum*. Vol. i, ed. A. Boretius, 1883; vol. ii, ed. A. Boretius and A. Krause, 1897.
MGH Const.	*Monumental Germaniae Historica, Constitutiones et Acta Imperatorum et Regum*, 11 vols. to date, a.911-1356 Hannover, 1893-1984.
MGH Leges	*Monumenta Germaniae Historica, Leges in Quarto*.
Migne, PL	*Patrologiae cursus completus, series Latina*, J.-P. Migne, Paris 1841-64, 222 vols.

Niermeyer	J. F. Niermeyer, *Mediae Latinitatis Lexicon Minus*. Leiden, 1954-76.
NLWJ	*National Library of Wales Journal (Cylchgrawn Llyfrgell Genedlaethol Cymru)*.
PKM	*Pedeir Keinc y Mabinogi*. Ed. Ifor Williams. Cardiff, 1930.
PLS	*Pactus Legis Salicae*. Ed. K. A. Eckhardt, MGH Leges, I.IV.I., Hannover, 1962.
PM	F. Pollock and F. W. Maitland, *A History of English Law*. 2 vols., Cambridge, 1895.
PRIA	*Proceedings of the Royal Irish Academy*.
Plucknett	T. F. T. Plucknett, *A Concise History of the Common Law*. 5th edn., London, 1956.
Planitz/Eckhardt	H. Planitz and K. A. Eckhardt, *Deutsche Rechtsgeschichte*. 2nd edn., Graz, 1961.
Rec. Caern	*Registrum vulgariter nuncupatum 'The Record of Caernarvon' e codice MS. Harleiano 696 descriptum*, ed. Sir Henry Ellis, Record Commission, London 1898.
Rec. Soc. Jean Bodin	*Recueils de la Société Jean Bodin pour l'histoire des institutions*.
RIDA	*Revue internationale des droits de l'antiquité*.
RM	*The Text of the Mabinogion...from the Red Book of Hergest*. Ed. J. Rhŷs and J. Gwenogoryn Evans, Oxford, 1887.
SC	*Studia Celtica*.
SEIL	R. Thurneysen et al., *Studies in Early Irish Law*. Dublin, 1936.
SS	Publications of the Selden Society.
THSC	*Soc. Transactions of the Honourable Society of Cymmrodorion*.
TRHS	*Transactions of the Royal Historical Society*.
TvR	*Tijdschrift voor Rechtsgeschiedenis/Revue de l'histoire de droit/Legal History Review*.
VC	Venedotian Code (in AL).
VSB	*Vitae Sanctorum Britanniae et Genealogiae*. Ed. A. W. Wade-Evans, Board of Celtic Studies History and Law Series IX, Cardiff, 1944.
WHR	*Welsh History Review*.

WLW	*The Welsh Law of Women: Studies presented to Professor Daniel A. Binchy on his Eightieth Birthday.* Ed. D. Jenkins and M. E. Owen. Cardiff, 1980.
WM	*The White Book Mabinogion.* Ed. J. Gwenogvryn Evans. Pwllheli, 1907.
WML	*Welsh Medieval Law.* Ed. A. W. Wade-Evans, Oxford, 1909.
WTL	T. P. Ellis, *Welsh Tribal Law & Custom in the Middle Ages.* 2 vols., Oxford 1926.
ZCP	*Zeitschrift für celtische Philologie.*
ZRG/GA	*Zeitschrift der Savigny-Stiftung für Rechtsgeschichte, Germanistische Abteilung.*
ZRG/KA	*ZRG Kanonistische Abteilung.*
ZRG/RA	*ZRG Romanistische Abteilung.*
de Zulueta, *Gaius*	*The Institute of Gaius.* Ed. F. de Zulueta. 2 vols., Oxford, 1946, 1953.

INDEX TO PASSAGES
OF WELSH LAW CITED

This list omits the references to Ior 58/1-71/1 found in the commentary on those passages, pp.164-78; it also omits the references to the contents of the suretyship tractate printed in Table 1 pp.44-46. References to words are to the articles in the Glossary under the respective keywords.

AL (*Ancient Laws and Institutes of Wales*, 1841)
vol.i

G.C. II.vi.18:	50 & n.24
G.C. II.xxxvii.1:	65 n.39

vol.ii

IV.iv.4:	25 n.62, 174
IV.vi.4:	38 n.10
V.ii.20:	115 n.111, *fides facta*
V.ii.63:	41 n.80
V.ii.66:	41 n.80
V.ii.68:	41 n.80
V.ii.96:	70 n.96
VI.i.40:	68 n.75
VI.i.65:	41 n.80
VII.i.3-4:	176
VII.i.9:	165, 176
VII.i.13-19:	165
VII.i.14:	*fiadu, fiadnaise*
VII.i.14-17:	*tyst*
VII.i.21-22:	165
VII.i.43:	37 n.5
VIII.i.1-11:	31 n.99
VIII.i.7:	63 n.17
VIII.i.8:	31 & n.100
VIII.iii.6:	41 n.80
VIII.v.2:	37 n.5
VIII.x.6:	39 n.38
VIII.xi.29:	41 n.29
VIII.xi.29:	41 n.80
IX.vi.4:	55 & n.64
IX.xvii:	273 n.59
IX.xxxix.3:	267 n.50
X.v.9:	41 n.80

X.vii.27:	37 & n.118
X.vii.39:	27 & nn.59, 73
X.vii.40-43	19 & n.30(1)
X.vii.44:	41 n.92
XI.ii.1-2:	65 n.32
XI.iii.32:	267 & n.49
XI.v.43:	63 n.17
XII:	269 n.61
XII.xiii-xiv:	273
XIV.i.10:	63 n.17
XIV.iii.12, 24:	63 n.17
XIV.xiii.4:	62
XIV.xxi.16:	63 n.17
XIV.xxii.2:	67 n.74
XIV.xxii.1,2,4:	63 n.17
XIV.xxii.10:	38 n.10
XIV.xxv.4:	41 n.80
XIV.xxxvi.4:	63 n.17
XIV.xl.31:	63 n.17
XIV.xli.12:	41
p.925:	271 n.8

Bleg/Blegywryd (S.J. Williams and J.E. Powell, *Cyfreithiau Hywel Dda yn ôl Llyfr Blegywryd*, 1942/61)

7.25-30:	*dosbarthwyr*
17.2-7:	65 n.38
17-18:	*brawdwr*
37.17-25:	56 & n.71
38.18-20:	19 & n.33
40.2:	20 & n.35
40.6-22:	16 & n.9, 19 & n.30
40.6-20:	230
40.14-22:	64 n.26
40.29-41:	200 n.6

41.1-3:	20 n.40
41.1-4:	20 n.36
41.4-8:	29 & n.83, 36 & n.114
41.7-8:	29 n.87, 37 n.7
41.9-15:	63 n.14
41.14-15:	67 n.93
41.16-25:	31 & n.97, 36 & n.115
41.16-25:	36 n.115
42.1-7:	38
42.7-12:	29 & n.87
42.16-12:	21 & n.46
43.7,9:	canonwyr
44.8-46.3:	arwaesaf
44.12:	arwaesaf
50.16-22:	66 n.24
63.15-22:	64 n.24
63.18:	64 n.28
70:	271 n.14
70.6-16:	dedfryd gwlad, henuriaid
71.1-3	53 n.51
98.28-99.11:	iudex
106-107:	271 n.14
107.1-8:	dedfryd gwlad
111.5-11:	111 n.29
124:	259 & n.6
124.5-8:	cymrodeddwyr
125.4:	115 n.111
125.4-126.4:	200 n.6
126.5-13:	41 n.80

Col (D. Jenkins, *Llyfr Colan*, 1963): references unless otherwise noted are to the numbered sentences of the texts.

52:	40 n.65
78-79:	18 & n.31
81n.:	167
p.86:	124 & n.11
pp.87-8:	124 & n.12
88:	19 & n.33
92:	20 & n.40, 39 & n.38
92-99:	20 & n.36
93:	19 & n.34
93n.:	170
96:	230 n.38
98:	38 n.24
101:	20 & n.38, 43 n.115
107:	29 & n.87

111-113:	172
113:	25 & n.64
116:	21 & n.46, 22 & n.51
126-131:	65 n.33
128:	53 & nn.53, 57
129:	67 n.72
130:	68 n.75
131:	58 & n.73, 68 n.77
192:	273 n.52
355:	65 n.37
367:	65 n.38
426:	64 n.24
455:	53 & n.51
496:	65 n.37
502:	115 n.111
529:	56 n.71

Cyfn/Cyfnerth (the parts of the Cyfnerth text published here except where noted: for other 'Cyfnerth' material, see WML and AL:G.C.)

Cyfnerth 73/24a = WLW 138:	26 & n.66
1-3:	53 n. 54
2:	42 n.104
3:	70 n.96
4:	20 & n.35, 116, n.119, 164
6:	30 & n.93, 115 n.118
8:	20 & nn.36, 40, 27 & n.76, 35 & n.110, 42 & n.104, 116 n.119, 168
11:	19 & n.31
10-16:	167
10-18:	29 & n.89
17-18:	29 & n.90, 37 n.7, 41 n.81
19:	29 & n.87, 42 & n.104
20:	173
21-22:	35 & n.107
25-26:	21 & nn.44, 46
27-30:	33 & n.103
31:	42 & n.104
31-35:	33 & n.103
36:	33 & n.103, 173
37-47:	33 & n.103
48:	33 & n.103

49, 50:	33 & n.103
51:	33 & n.103
62:	178
73:	33 & n.103
74-76:	33 & n.103
82:	19 & n.33
82:	67 n.73
83:	41 n.80

DwCol (D. Jenkins, *Damweiniau Colan*, 1973); references are to numbered sentences.

128:	67 n.69
131-33:	52 & n.40
244:	115 n.111
371:	68 n.79
390, 397:	19 & n.33
402:	41 & n.80
462-65:	172
462-68:	16 & n.9, 19 & n.30
472:	65 n.32
483:	176

Ior/Iorwerth (A.R. Wiliam, *Llyfr Iorwerth*, 1960, and the text here printed)

45/8:	68 n.79
46/9, 10:	25 n.66
47/1:	64 n.24
47/4:	167
52/4:	34
55/2:	25 & n.65
56/5:	19 & n.33
57/3:	78 & n.17
57/9:	*arwystl*
58-60:	23 & n.56, 42 n.104, 51
58-9:	33 & n.103
58-70:	65 n.34
58/7:	56 & n.72
58/8:	19 & n.31
58/8:	*gwrthdwng*
59/1:	37 n.5
59/1-2:	19 n.31
59/3:	52 & n.39
59/3-4:	*halidom*

59/5:	27 & n.72, 39 n.102
59/5-7:	*gwrthdwng*
60/2:	53 & n.54
60/3:	54
60/3:	*bara offeren, benedicamus, dwfr swyn*
60/4:	56 & n.69
60/-6:	27 & n.72
60/6:	32 & n.102
61/1-4:	51
61/2-4:	42 n.104
61/5:	57 & n.73
62:	107
62/1:	32 & n.101, 111 n.29
62/1-4:	20 & n.36, 32 & n.101
62/2:	39 nn.38, 39
62/3:	20 & n.40, 39 n.39, 107
62/3-4:	27 & nn.73, 76, 35 & n.110, 42 n.104
62/5-6:	20 n.34
62/7:	33 & n.103, 39 n.38, 200
62/8:	33 & n.103
62/9:	230
62/10-11:	27 & n.73
62/12:	32 & n.101, 38 n.24, 41 n.95
62/12-13:	113 n.68
63/1:	19 & n.32
63/2:	33 & n.103, 43 n.115
63/3:	41 n.95
63/10:	68 n.80
64/1-3:	27 & n.78
64/1-4:	33 n.103
64/5:	16 & n.8, 33 n.103, 42 n.107
64/6-7:	38 n.23
64/8-10:	57 & n.78
64/8, 11:	33 & 103
64/10:	29 & 87
64/13:	33 & n.103
65/3:	78 & n.17, *arwaesaf*
65/3-6:	75 & n.9
65/11:	53 & n.56
65/7-10:	24 & n.60
65/7-11:	22 & n.54
66/7:	21 & nn.44, 46, 22 & n.55, 26 & n.67
67/2:	19 & n.32

67/4:	105
68:	65 & n.33, *briduw*
68/1:	51, 57
68/1-6:	51
68/2-3:	51
68/5:	53 & n.57
68/6:	56 & n.69, 57
68/7:	67 n.74
68/7-10:	51
68/8:	16 & n.9, 19 & n.30, 57
68/9:	61 & n.101, 68 & n.79, *briduw*
68/10:	58
69:	51
69/1-12:	200 n.4
70:	51
70/1:	31 & n.98, 200 n.5
70/2, 3:	105
72/7-11:	176
77/36:	115 n.111
77/37:	115 n.111
77/37:	111 n.29
79-81/4:	*tyst*
80/4-8:	165
81/10:	176
81/13:	62 & n.107
83/10:	65 n.32
87/5-6	62 & n.107
97/6:	68 n.83
106/9:	65 n.41
111/17-20:	167
113/3:	166
114/6-115/1:	*arwaesaf*
115:	58 & n.80
117/4:	64 n.24
154/14:	273 n.52

IOR (G)

Peniarth 35, f.23r   24 & nn.58-9

Latin texts (H.D. Emanuel, *Latin texts of the Welsh Laws*, 1967 and the texts here printed); references are to the pages and lines of Emanuel's edition. These have been equated with Mrs Robnin Stacey's numbering of the sentences in the surety tractates (see pp.15-46 *passim*, especially pp.43, 44-46)

Lat A

109:	257 n.89
123.23-26:	64 n.24
124.18	19 & n.33

Lat A 5
= 125.4-6:	29 & n.90, 37 n.7

Lat A 3-5
= 125.2-6:	29 & n.83, 36 & n.114, 41 n.83

Lat A 6
= 125.6-7:	29 & n.86, 36 & n.114

Lat A 7
= 125.8-11:	21 & n.46, 29 & n.86

Lat A 8
= 125.12-14:	29 & n.86

Lat A 8-9
= 125.12-15:	29 & n.89

Lat A 10-11
= 125.16-18:	20 & nn.36, 27 & n.76, 40, 35 & n.110

Lat A 13-14
= 125.19-27:	31 n.97, 36 n.115
125.23-26:	67 n.73
125.33-36:	48 & n.15
125.34-35:	53 & n.55

Lat A 21-23:   29 & nn.86.87
131.19-21:	53 & n.51
132.11-12:	56 & n.71
141:	257 & n.107
143.37-41:	64 n.24

Lat A 52/49-51
= WLW 156:	26 n.66

Lat A 52/21
= WLW 152:	*dilys*

Lat B
212.1-5:	64 n.24
212-213:	272 n.19
215.38-215.36:	*tyst*
216.8:	19 & n.33

Lat B I/1
= 216.20-21:	29 & n.86

Lat B I/4
= 216.25-26:	29 & n.86

Lat B I/6
= 216.29-30:	36 & n.114

Lat B I/10-12
= 216.36-38:	29 & nn.83, 90 36 & n.114

Lat B I/12
=   216.17-38:   37 & n.7
Lat B I/15
=   217.6-10:   21 & n.46, 29 & n.86
217.1-4:   67 n.73
217.2-3:   63 n.16
Lat B I/16-17
=   217.9-17:   31 & n.97, 36 &
n.115

Lat B II/1
=   217.31-32:   20 & n.35
217.33-218.4:   50 & n.21
217.36-37:   53 & n.55
217.37:   64 n.26
217.37-38:   51
218.5-7:   64 n.28
218.12-14:   20 & n.36, 27 & n.76
Lat B II/13-14
=   218.12-14:   20 & n.40, 27 & n.76,
35 & n.110

Lat B II/15
=   218.15:   30 & n.94
226.33-36:   53 & n.51
235.33-36:   65 n.37
240:   257 n.107
244:   238 & n.4
Lat B III/1-2
=250.23-25:   35 & n.113
253-54:   36
254.1-3:   56 n.71
Lat B IV/1-2
=   254.6-8:   29 n.87
Lat B V/1-3
=   254.28-38:   35 n.113
Lat B VII/1-4
=   256.26-31   29 n.89, 35 n.113
Lat D
288.18:   53 n.51
324-5:   250 & n.97
325.28-30:   dosbarthwyr
343.14-18:   64 n.24
349.27-36:   iudex
349-50:   257 n.105
352.28-30:   dosbarthwyr
357:   259 n.6
357.34:   cymrodeddwyr
365.30-366.29:   tyst
366.21-26:   56 & n.71
357.4-5:   19 & n.33

Lat D 1
=   367.38-39:   29 & n.86
Lat D 6
=   368.7-9:   20 & n.35
Lat D 8-13
=   368.11-23:   16 & n.9, 19 & n.30
368.11-23:   228 n.49
368.17-23:   64 n.26
Lat D 14
=   368.25-27:   30 & n.94
Lat D 18
=   368.32-33:   20 & n.40
Lat D 18-19
=   368.32-34:   20 & n.36
Lat D 19
=   368.33-34:   36 & n.114
Lat D 20-22
=   368.34-38:   29 & n.83, 36 & n.114
Lat D 22
=   368.37-38:   29 & n.90, 37 n.7
369.1-2:   53 & n.55
369.1-5:   63 nn.13, 14
369.3-4:   67 n.73
Lat D 26-27
=   369.6-14:   36 & n.115
Lat D 30-31
=   369.19-24:   38 n.8
Lat D 32-33
=   369.24-29:   29 & n.87
Lat D 35
=   369.32-36:   29 & n.86
Lat D 35-36
=   369.32-37:   21 & n.46
378.10-14:   64 n.24
382.26-32:   iudex
383.12-18:   53 n.51
385.35-41:   63 n.13
388.29-33:   166
Lat E
409:   271 & n.50
452.9-13:   64 n.24
457:   272 n.19
458.3:   19 & n.33
Lat E I/1
=   458.17-18:   29 & n.86
Lat E I/8
=   458.29-30:   36 & n.114
Lat E I/9
=   458.31-33:   167

Lat E I/9-11
 = 458.31-35:   29 & n.83, 36 &
                   n.114
Lat E I/11
 = 458.33-35:   29 & n.90, 37 n.7
459 n.1:   63 n.16
459.1-2:   63 n.16
Lat E I/15
 = 459.6-9:   21 & n.46, 29 n.86,
                   174
Lat E I/18-19
 = 459.15-23:   31 & n.97, 36 &
                   n.115
Lat E I/20
 = 459.24-25:   39 n.35
459.26-35:   50 & n.21
Lat E I/30-31
 = 460.3-5:   20 & nn.36,40, 27 &
                   n.76, 35 & n.110, 168
Lat E I/32
 = 460.6:   30 & n.94
Lat E I/35
 = 460.11-13:   29 n.86
Lat E I/35-38
 = 460.11-17:   29 n.89, 35 n.113, 167
Lat E I/41
 = 460.22-24:   35 n.113
Lat E I/42-43
 = 460.25-32:   35 n.113

Lat E I/45
 = 460.34-5:   172
Lat E I/50
 = 461.12-17:   41 n.80
473.21-5:   64 n.24
Lat E II/1-2
 = 501-14-16:   29 & n.87
504-11-13:   26 & n.69
504.14-15:   26 & n.69
508.4-12:   uuadio
508.12-13:   39, n.38

WML (A.W. Wade-Evans, *Welsh Medieval
Law*, 1909): references are to the page and
line, see also Cyfn/Cyfnerth.
47.23-48:   66 n.51
52.11-13:   166
85.4-11:   48 & n.9
85.12-17:   164
97.9:   52 & n.50
108.20-109.5:   67 n.69
114.3:   canonwyr
119.8-120.6:   56 & n.71
129.17-22:   65 n.38
330   171

GENERAL INDEX

A

Aachen, 802, assembly of, 246
Abbey Dore, MS of, 122
Aberconwy, 130
Abererch, partition of land in, 260
Abergele, arbitration concerning debt at, 260
Aberystwyth, arbitration of feud at, 260
academic lawyers, 324-32
  low esteem for in England, 324-26
  roles of in subversion of proposals of Ormrod Committee, 331-32
Accursius, 319
Act of Union, 289-94, 298, 302-303
  and *Cyfraith Hywel*, 290
  forbids use of Welsh by court officials, 290
  inconsistency with Civil Procedure Acts Repeal Act, 294
addicti, 103
administration of justice, centralised by Henry II and Edward I, 321
Advisory Committee on Legal Education, 329
  First Report of, 330
  Second Report of, 330-31
Aeschylus, *Agamemnon* of, 102
aitire 74, 100, 103
aitire chána, 178
Alexander II, king of Scotland, 248
Alfred, king of Wessex, 243
  introduction to his laws, 237-38
  laws of, 239
    c. 33, 60-61
  preface to laws of, 250
  treaty with Guthrum, 240
Allen, Thomas, 136
Alverstone, Lord, 387
amobr, cases of, 269
amobrwr, 270
amod, 169
  enforced by lord, 177

amodwr, 176-77
  as kind of surety, 177
  as party to *amod*, 177
  office not heritable, 177
amvot, as reformation of *amod* (q.v.), 177
Angevin kings, 244
Anglo-Saxon laws, 84-85
Anson, 324
anudon, 56, 166
  Church's jurisdiction over, 56
anudon (perjury), 51
Aphrodite, 96
Aquinas, 237
arbitration, 259-61
archaic society, meaning of, 92
Ares, 96
arglwyddes (see *domina*)
Armagh, Book of, 4
aruuistl, used for gage of land, 75, 78
Arwystli, 260
  dispute concerning (1277-82), 263
  land dispute in, 258
  land-suit in, 261
  local *ynaid* operate in, 264
sapientes of, 265
arwystyl, 172
asperges, 54
assumpsit lies for nonfeasance, 280
Athens, 102
auctor, 84
Audley, Thomas, 280
Augan, 81, 82
augmented hundred (*Cant yr arddyrchafiad*), 269
Augustine of Canterbury, 244
Augustine of Hippo, 244
Augustus, 238
Austin, John, 324
authorities, doctrinal, convention that it is unnecessary to cite them in court, 275

Azo, 319

B

bail, 94

Bains, 75, 77, 81, 82, 83

bara offeren, 53-55

barbarian law-codes, 239

bards, 264

barn y diddim, 266, 268

barnwyr, 261

Bartolus, 319

Basingwerk, Abbey of, 128

Battle Abbey, 244

Batz, 82

Be wifmannes beweddunge, 94

Beaumanoir, Philippe de, 245-46, 248

Beauvaisis, see customs of Beauvaisis bell
   of saint, as relic on which oaths were
   sworn, 53

ben imtha, 177

Benedicamus Domino, 54-55

Bernard of Pavia, 247

Bernold of Constance, 54

Berrad Airechta, not concerned with debtor's
   denial of surety, 169

Bidiau, 126, 128

Binchy, D.A., 3, 47, 60, 74, 92, 100, 104,
   169, 176-77

Blackstone, Sir William, 324

Bleddyn ap Llwyd, *ynad* of Dyffryn Clwyd,
   265

Blegywryd, Book of, 17-18
   on three kinds of judges in Wales, 262

blood-feud, 97

Book of Taliesin (Peniarth MS 2), 133

borh, 10

Bracton, 246, 248, 251, 279

Brain, 77, 83

brawd, 167

brawdwr, term preferred in South Wales, 262

brawdwr cwmwd neu gantref herwydd swydd,
   262

brawdwr llys, 262

brawdwr o fraint swydd, 262

Breton surety
   also found in more Frankish areas, 84
   distinguished from ordinary witnesses, 84
   enforcing surety's role in dispute settle-

      ment, 80
   functions of, 75-78, 84
   his witness has special status, 78
   not distinctively Breton, 84-86
   payments to, 84
   police function of, 80
   secures ownership, 77-79
   social and economic status of, 81-83

Breton suretyship
   absence of state interest in, 87
   not distinctively Celtic, 86

briduw
   denial of in Ior and Col imitates denial of
      mach 51, 56
   enforcement by Church and king, 57
   etymology of, 47
   function of, 61-62
   not derived from canon law, 49
   origin of term, 60

Brittany, 3-4

Britton, 279

Bromfield and Yale, 261, 267
   professional *ynaid* absent from, 264

Broughton, Richard, 127

Brut y Brenhinedd, MSS of, 121

Bulgarus, 318

Byzantine Italy, 84

C

cadernid, 105-106

cadernid, 115, n. 111

Caeo, land-plea in, 260

Callis, Robert, reading on sewers, 281

Cambridge, University of, Downing Chair
   of English Law at, 324

Cambridge University Library MS Kk. 6.,
   42, 281

camlwrw, 267

canllaw, 6, 176

canon law, 8

Canon law, at universities of Oxford and
   Cambridge, 321

canon law, perjury an offence against, 166

canon lawyers, 9

Capitula presbyteris data (Hincmar of Reims,
   852), 54

capitularies, 242

Capitulatio de Partibus Saxoniae, 246

Carentoir, 75-79, 82-83

Carmarthen, survival of Welsh law in, 269
Carolingian capitularies, 239
Carolingian empire, 242
  break-up of, 243, 247
central courts of English crown, 8
Ceredigion, survival of Welsh law in, 269
Charlemagne, 78, 238, 242, 243, 246-47, 250
Charles II, 293
Charles the Bald, 77, 243
Charles VII, king of France, 320
Charles-Edwards, T.M., 17, 24
charters, as a form of written law, 244
Chirkland, 261
  professional ynaid absent from, 264
Church
  claim to jurisdiction over perjury, 56
  growth in jurisdiction of, 62
Church of Wales Trust, 295
churchyard (see mynwent)
civil law, 8
civil lawyers, 9
Civil Procedure Acts Repeal Act, 294
civilian legal tradition, 317-21
Clayton, Thomas, 136
Clerk of the Crown, appointments to office of, 292
Clifford's Inn, 281
Clovis, 238
Clun, lordship of, survival of Welsh law in, 269
Code Civil of 1804, Germanic elements in, 320-21
Code (Justinian), 84
coediwr, 270
Coibnes Uisci Thairidne, 60
Coke, Sir Edward, 276, 278, 287
Coleg Harlech, 307
Collectio Canonum Hibernensis, 29-30, 34, 85, 174-75
  influence of on Book of Cyfnerth and Latin lawbooks, 21-22
Commentators, 319-20
commercium, 50
Common Law, 244
  intellectual deficiencies of, 322-24
  resists civilian reception, 316
'common learning', 275, 278
compurgation, 165-68

disadvantageous to be driven to, 165
  for briduw, 53
compurgators, 165-67
consent, as part of legislative tradition, 249
Constable, 275
Constable, Richard, 277
Constantine, 238, 247, 252
Constitutio Pacis of Frederick II, 243
Constitutions of Clarendon, 245
consuetudines, 244
consuetudo et ius terrae in Domesday Book, 244
contract
  form of, 11-12
  rarely mentioned in readings, 280
contracting-party, death or exile of, 171
Coquille, 320
correctus, 128
Cotton Caligula A. iii, 119-32
  influence of early insular gospel books on, 123
  influence of Latin codices on, 125
  place of origin, 125, 127-30
  Test Book in, 121, 124-25
Cotton Cleopatra A. xiv, 132-35
Cotton MS Titus D ix, 137
Council of Wales and the Marches, 293
courts, 1
  regular courts possibly rare in Wales before twelfth century, 259
coutumiers, 246
Cox, Homersham, 295-96
crair, meaning of in laws, 53
criminal law, made coherent by inns of court, 280
Cromwell, Oliver, 293
Cross, Lord, standing committee under the chairmanship of, 329
cross, placing of, 269
Crown Courts, 305
Culhwch ac Olwen, 50
custom
  as law of Empire, 245
  as opposed to lex scripta in the twelfth century, 243
  as rights of jurisdiction in feudal society, 244, 250
  as the tradition of the Roman church, 244
  English law c. 1200 as, 245

in Welsh law, 243
local variations only in detail, 245
made by repeated acts of kings, 245
Customs of Beauvaisis, 245-46, 248
Cwmhir, 135
Cydweli, 261
survival of Welsh law in, 269
Cyfeiliog, 263
local *ynaid* operate in, 264
Cyfnerth, Book of, 3, 17-18, 179
briduw in section's influence on Latin D,
48
influence of Ior on MSS of, 117
MSS of, 179
version found in MS *U* (Peniarth MS 37),
17
cyfraith anudon, 56
Cyfraith Hywel, 15
Latin redactions of, 20
learnt in North Wales, 263
prologues to, 240-41, 249
Cyfraith Hywel as doom-books for use of
judges, 250
Cyfreithiau Gwlad, intended to be in one
quire in *C*, 121
cyngaws, 6, 176
cynghawsedd, 16, 18
cynghawsedd (pleading), 5-6, 164-68
Cynyr ap Cadwgan, 264-65

D
dadferwyr, 261
Dafydd ap Llywelyn (prince of North
Wales 1240-46), relic of, 52
damweiniau, 16, 18
Damweiniau, Book of, 25
Danelaw, 240
D'Argentré, 320
David I, king of Scotland, 248-49
Davies, Gwilym Prys, 47
Dawson, J.P., 319
De donis, readings on, 276-78
de Zulueta, F., 103
debt
disagreement on amount of, 167
inheritance of by son or kinsman, 29
legal meaning of, 92-93
payment-schedule after initial default,
29-30

debt-bondage, 102-103
dedfryd gwlad, 261
Dee, John, 135-36
children of, 136
Delphic oracle, 102
Demodocus, 96
dempster (doomster), 242
Denbigh, 130, 267-70
lordship of, 265
model pleas from, 269
Denholm-Young, N. 133
denial of surety, 164
deorad Dé, 60
Devlin, Lord, 326
Dicey, A.V., 324
Die Bürgschaft im irischen Recht (Thurneysen),
3
Digest (Justinian), 84
dilis, 75
dilisidus, 74-75
dilmaine, 172
dilse, 172
dilys, 172
Dinefwr, 52
Dinmael, partition of land in, 260
discontinuance, 276
dishonour, sanction behind suretyship, 103
distraint, 105
distraint by surety, 20
Doctors' Commons, 322
doctrine, given way to *jurisprudence* before
1573, 283
dogn-fanag, 166
Domesday Book, 241, 242, 244
domina (*arglwyddes*) as giver of surety, 22, 25
doom-book, 237
doom-book (*liber-judicialis*), 243, 250
doomsmen, 1, 261, 267
amateur, 262
at Cambridge, 242
doomster, see dempster, doomsmen and
lawman
dosbarthwr, 270
dosbarthwyr, 261
dower, 94
Dumoulin, 320
Dunsaete agreement, 241
duty, contrasted with liability, 94-101
dwfr swyn, 53-55

Dyffryn Clwyd, 263, 266-270
 case in settled by arbitration, 260
 lordship of, 265
 model pleas from, 269

E
échevin, see *scabinus*
Edgar, king of England, 240, 241
Edmund-Davies, Lord Justice, 307-308
Edward ap Rhys, 130
Edward ap Rhys ap Dafydd of Eglwyseg, 129
Edward ap Roger Eytton, 129
Edward I, king of England, 259
Edward I
 statute of Merchants, 61
 statutes of, 243
Edward the Confessor, laws ascribed to, 241
Edward the Elder, 241
Edwardian conquest, 265
Edwards, Robart, 127, 129-30
Edwards, Robert of Stansty, 130
Edwards, Sir Goronwy, 17
Egerton, Lord Chancellor, 281
Einion ap Gwalchmai, as *ynad*, 264
elders (*meliores, seniores*), 82, 241
Ellis, T.P., 53, 55
Emanuel, H.D., 136
emperor, Holy Roman, 318
enforcing surety, 11, 104
 as privileged witness, 19
 as stakeholder, 107
 evolution into paying surety, 107
 role in securing Breton gages of land, 79
 takes debtor's gage, 169-70
enforcing surety (see also *mach* and *naidm*)
England, 85
 as including Wales by Wales and Berwick Act (1746), 288
English
 not sole language of law in England before 1731, 293-94
 sole official language of courts in Wales, 293
English law
 as *consuetudo*, 245
 as limited to what the courts say it is, 275

 as what common lawyers in general believed it to be, 283
 impoverished by antagonism between academic and practitioner, 332
 in Wales, 261
 lack of juristic tradition injurious to legal development, 316
 lacks a proper juristic tradition, 332
 writ system of, 251
Etablissements of Louis IX, 243
Ethelbert, king of Kent, 238
eucharist, rarity with which laity communicated, 54
eulogia, 53
European Court of Justice, 333
Evans, Gwynfor S., 299-300
Evans, J. Gwenogvryn, 119
Evans v. Thomas, 289, 299, 301, 303, 313
Excerpta de Libris Romanorum et Francorum, 85
excommunication, 57
eye-witnesses, see *gwybyddiaid*
Eyton, Roger, 130
Eytton, Roger, 127, 129-30

F
festuca, 107
fideiussio, 107
fideiussor, 74-75, 84
fides, 50
 Church claims jurisdiction over transactions guaranteed by, 51
fides facta, 101
Finley, M.I., 102
First Crusade, 249
Fitzherbert, 282
Fitzwilliam, 275
folcriht, 240
Forderung, 95
Fougeray, 82
Four Doctors, 318
Francia, 85
Frankish Gaul, 53
Frankish law, 101
frankmarriage, 276
Frankpledge, 104
Franks, fluctuating control of eastern Brittany, 73
Frederick II, Hohenstaufen, 243

friðgewritu (*scripta pacis*), 241, 247
Fyneux, Sir John, 280, 282
Fyrnwy, 130

G
gage, 105, 175
  associated with enforcing surety, 107
  associated with paying surety, 107
  characteristic of *ráth* not *naidm*, 170
  debtor's taken by *mach*, 41-42, n. 95
  function, 2-3
  meaning of, 10-11
  symbolic, 107
  taken by surety, 32
  value of, 20, 171
gage of land, 77-79
Gaius, *Institutes*, 103
galanas, 17-18
  plea of (1398), 269
Gallican liturgy, 54
Gardiner, Lord Chancellor, 327, 329, 332
Geisel, 111, n. 29
Geisel, 95, 96
Gerald of Wales, 52-53
Gerard, William, 293, 296, 309
Germanic customary laws, study of in Germany, 321
Gestellung, 96
Gestellungsbürgschaft, 96, 104
gíall, 99-100
Gierke, O., 4, 95, 99
Gilissen, J., analysis of forms of suretyship, 108-109
Gladstone, liberal goverment of, 296
Glamorgan circuit, 296-97
Glanvill, 178, 246, 248, 251, 253
Glossa Ordinaria, 319
Glossators, 318-19, 320
godborh, 60-61
Godfrey of Bouillon, 249
'good men' (*degion*), 260
gorfodog, 105
  pecuniary liability of, 31
gorfogog, 178
Gorman, Mr. Justice, 300
Gospel book, as relic on which oaths were sworn, 53
Gower, Sir Raymond, 301

Grafio, 101
Gratian, 244-45
Gratian, *Decretum*, 126, 128, 238, 239
Gray's Inn, 277, 280, 282
Great Session, court of, 291-93
  careers of Judges of, 292
  judges' knowledge of Welsh, 291-93
Gregory I, 244
Gruffud Hiraethog, 127, 129-30
Gryffyth, Jasper, 130
Guer, 82
Guérande, 75, 82, 83
Gutyn Owain, 128
gwahardd, 57
Gwawl, 105
gwir Duw, 70, n. 99
gwlad, may be equivalent to *cantref*, 48
gwybyddiaid, advantage of being entitled to produce, 165-66
Gwynedd, 6-7
  Is Conwy, 263
  Uwch Conwy, 263
gwyrda, 261

H
Haeldetuuid, Abbot, 77
Hafter, 95
Haftung, 4, 94-101, 104
Hailsham, Lord Chancellor, 303-304, 307, 329
haildom, 53
hand-plighting, 19-57
Harleian MS 4353, 133
Hatherley, Lord Chancellor, 295-96
Haycock, Marged, 133
Henry I, king of England
  1108 ordinance of, 248
  coronation charter of, 248
Henry II, king of England, 245, 251
Henry VIII, 280
henuriaid y wlad, 261
Hephaestus, 96, 106
Herakles, debt-bondage of, 102
Herefordshire, sherrif of, 241
Hincmar of Reims, 54
Hobart, C.J., 281
Hohenstaufen family, 247
Hohenstaufen kings of Jerusalem, 249
Holdsworth, Sir William, 281

Holland, 324
Holland, Hugh, 127
honour ('face'), 100
honour of surety as creditor's security, 104
hostage, 94, 99
hostage-surety, 96, 105
hostageship, political, 103
Hughes Parry, Sir David, 305
  commission under the chairmanship of,
    287, 301
Hugo de Porta Ravennate, 318
Huws, D. 117, 138
Hywel, law of (see *Cyfraith Hywel*)
Hywel Dda, 136, 237, 240-41, 249, 250

I
imboth (imbuith), 177
influencing surety, 104
inn of court, opinion differing from that
  of judges, 283
Inner Temple, 279, 280, 281, 282
inns of court, 274-83, 321
  decline of intellectual quality of, 323
  lack of communication between, 282
inquisitio, 241
Institutes of Justinian, 244
insular gospel books, influence on C, 123
Iorwerth, Book of, 3, 4, 17-18
  archaism of, 21
  cynghawsedd in, 32
  damweiniau in, 32
  influence on MSS of Cyfn and Latin texts,
    117
  tractate on land-suits, 165-66, 167
  tractate on suretyship, 19
  tractate on women, 37
  use of early material in suretyship trac-
    tate, 31-34
Iorwerth, Book of (see also Test Book)
Iorwerth ap Madog, 125
Iorwerth ap Madog ap Rhawd, 264
Ireland, hereditary jurists in, 264
Irish law, 16
Irnerius, 318
Isaled, commote court of, 268
Isidore of Seville, 239
Ite missa est, 54
iudex, Roman, 242

iudex Wallicus, 265
iudicati, 103
iudicator Wallicus, 265
ius antiquum of Church, 245
ius novum of Church, 245
ius respondendi ex auctoritate principis, 318
ius terrae, 244

J
Jacobus, 318
James, Richard, 136
Jeffreys, George, 291
Jeffreys, John, 291
Jenkins, D., 121, 125, 179, 264, 274
Jenkins, David (Hensol), 292
Jerusalem, kingdom of, 246, 249
John, abbot of Valle Crucis, 129
John ap Rhys, of Rhisgog, 129
John ap Rhys (John Price), 129
John of Salisbury, 238
Jones, John (John Jones, Gellilyfdy), 127
Jones Pierce, T., 17-18
Jones-Williams, D.W., 305
Joseph, Sir Keith, 301
judex patrie, see *ynad cwmwd*
judge
  as arbitrator, 1-2
  control of court proceedings, 165
  in land-suits, 6
  misleading term applied to Welsh *ynad*,
    262-63
judgement-finders, see *dadferwyr*
judges
  continental
    lack immunity from action, 319
    seek advice from jurists, 319
  increasing authority of, 282
  Welsh-speaking not familiar with legal
    Welsh, 307
judicatores curiae, 261
Judicature Acts of 1873-75, 322
judicial clerkship, 333
Julian, 317
Julius Caesar, 238
Jungmann, J.A., 54
jurist
  antedates universities, 317
  definition of, 317

role revives with revival of Roman law,
    318
Roman, 317-18
    appointed to *consilium principis*, 318
    manipulated by emperors, 318
juristic doctrine, accepted as formal source of
    law in civilian tradition, 320
juristic tradition, extends from *pays de droit
    écrit* to *pays de droit coutumier*, 320
jurists
    Bolognese, 319
    Roman, 238, 243
justices in eyre, 242
Justinian, 242, 316

L
land-suits, 6, 258
Landfrieden, 247, 252
landgage (see gage of land)
landlaga, 240, 241
Landrecht, 247
landriht, 240, 247
Langford, Richard, 127
Langon, 77, 83
Lateran, Fourth Council of, 54, 58
Latin lawbooks, as evidence of interchange of
    texts between North and South Wales,
    117
Latin Redaction B
    briduw material related to Ior and Col, 49
    on *briduw*, 49-51
Latin Redaction E, 26
    concordance with other lawbooks, 44-46
law
    academic study of
        lack of prestige in England and Wales,
            316-17
        prestige in Europe and America, 316-21
    ambiguity of word, 239-40
    as a man's personal rights against others,
        243
    as consisting of rights and obligations, 239
    as made for and by the community, 239
    as promulgated by public authority, 239
    composed of written *leges* and also
        customs, 239

of *regnum*, 244-45
sacral element in, 7
secularization in 12th and 13th centuries,
    62
students of in administrative careers,
    318-19
thought to be 'found' not made, 237
written, argued not to be true law, 237
Law Commission for England and Wales,
    332
law schools
    English, lack of innovation in, 330
    in universities, 325-32
law-speaker in Scandinavia, 242, 245
law-teacher (*athro*), 263
lawbook, 2, 8
lawbooks, 246-53
    concerned to integrate new legislation into
        old law, 246-50
    concerned with judges, 250-51
    constitutional concerns of, 251-53
    Welsh, 17
lawman
    as personal name, 242
    at York in 1106, 242
    translated both *legislator* and *iudex*, 242
lawmen
    at Lincoln and Stamford, 242
    judices civitatis at Chester, 242
lawmen (*lahmen*), 241
laws, foundation myth of, 249
'Laws of Edward the Confessor', 241
Laws of Women, Welsh lawbooks' tractate
    on, 25
lawyers, professional lawyers, 1-2
Layamon, 242
lecture (see reading)
legal argument, mode of, 174-75
legal education, 7, 9
    English, six 'core subjects' in, 329-31
    oral character of, 8
legal incompetents, 21-27
    in Latin texts, 36
    women as, 21-27
legal profession, 1
legal secretaryships at European Court of
    Justice, 333
legal values, 172-73
Leges Henrici Primi, 246, 247, 250, 253

Leges Iuliae, 238
legislation
    of Tudors reviving feudalism, 280
    papal, 244-45
legislator, function of merged with those of judge and juror, 242
Lehnrecht, 247
Leistung, 95
Leistungsbürge, Leistungsbürgschaft, 95-96, 104-106
Lettres du Sepulchre, 249
Lewis, Mr. Justice, 297
Lewis, Saunders, 301
Lewis, Timothy, 47, 137
Lex Poetilia, 103
Lex Romana, 239
Lex Salica, 243
Lex Saxonum, 8, 246
lex scripta, 61
lex terrae, 240, 245
Lex Walensis, 239, 249
liability, contrasted with duty, 94-101
Liber de Judicibus, 251
Liber Probationis, see Test Book
Liebermann, F., 241
Lincoln's Inn, 277
Littleton, 276-78
Livre au Roi, 246
Livre de Jean d'Ibelin, 246
Llandaff, Book of, 43, n. 117
Llandinam, *clas* church of, 265
Llanfor, 128
Llanstephan MS 1, 128, 130
Lloyd, John, of Blaen-y-ddol, 130
Lloyd, Marmaduke, 292
Llwyn Gwyn, 269
Llyfr Colan, 5, 20
    section on *briduw*, 51-58
Llyfr Cynghawsedd, see Pleading, Book of
Llyfr Cynog, 24
Llyfr Prawf, see Test Book
Llyfr y Damweiniau, 174
    on relics, 52
llyfr y Ty Gwyn, 128
Llywelyn ab Iorwerth, 264
Llywelyn ap Gruffud, 52, 61, 264
Llywelyn ap Iorwerth, 61
Loisel, 320
Lombard Italy, 85

Lombardic laws, study of in Italy, 321
lord, as unappointed surety, 175
Louis IX, king of France, 243
    statutes made by, 248
Lusanger, 76

M
Mabinogi
    First Branch of, 105-106
    Third Branch of, 60
Mac Clancy family, 264
Mac Egan family, 264
macc, 16
macc (see *naidm*)
mach, 16, 18-21, 107
    as enforcing surety, 20-21, 105, 168
    as paying surety, 105, 106
    as privileged witness, 19-20
    distrains debtor, 169
    evolution into a paying surety, 28-31
    giving of gage by reminiscent of Irish *ráth*, 170
    guarantees title, 172
    in Ior corresponds to Irish *naidm*, 170
    later financially liable, 27
    not liable for principal's debt, 27
    relation to *amodwr*, 176-77
    takes debtor's gage, 169-70
    whether woman entitled to give, 173-74
    woman not entitled to act as 173-74
mach addefedig, 168
mach cynnogn, dvandva compound, 171
machtiern, 73-74, 82
    origin of term, 82
Madog ap Dafydd Goch, 266
Madoc ap Heilin ap Ithyk, 265
Madog Goch Ynad, 264
mair, 81
Maitland, F.W., 1, 101, 247, 250, 274, 283, 324
Man, King of, 242
manus, 97
manuscripts, sigla of, 137
Marcher lordships, as mediators of English legal ideas and practices, 265
Mars-Jones, Mr Justice, 304-305, 307
Martinus Gosia, 318
mass-bread (see *bara offeren*)

Mathias, Henry, 292
Maurice, William, 179
Mela, 280
Mercurius Trismegistus, 238
Merioneth, County Council of, 295
Merton College, Oxford, MS 323, 117-18, 135-36
Middle Temple, 278, 283
  negative quality of education at, 324
Molac, 75, 82
Montgomery, Treaty of, 61
moot, 2
moots, 275, 280
  retain vitality 1550-1642, 281
Morgan, Osborne, 296
morning-gift, 94
Morris, Lord, of Borth-y-Gest, 309
Morus ap Hywel ap Tudur, 129
Mostyn MSS, 117, 133
Mountague, C.J., 281
Mudiad Deiseb yr Iaith, 297
munt, 97
mynwent as place for court proceedings, 52

N
naidm, 16, 18-21, 35, 74, 99-101, 169, 176-77
  as E-S, 20
  not liable for principal's debt, 27
  as privileged witness, 19-20
Nau Kynywedi Teithiauc, 37
Naw affeith galanas, 124
nawdd, 166
negyddiaeth, should be in presence of mach, 171
negyf, 167-68
nestigan, 97
Newcastle-upon-Tyne, customs of, 248
Newgate, 279
nexus, 103
Nominoe, 77, 79
Norway, 245

O
oath
  on relics, 51-53
  on seven altars, 48
  religious quality of, 5
oath on relics, 165, 167-68
oath (see also promissory oath)
oath-helpers, 5
obligatio, 103
obligation
  involuntary, 2-3
  voluntary, 2
Odyssey, 96
oed wrth borth, 176
oral tradition, 7
ordeal, 5
Ormond, Earl of, 264
Ormrod, Mr Justice, committee under the chairmanship of, terms of reference of, 327
Ormrod Report, 327-32
  professional opposition to, 329-30
  recommendations in, 328
  value of, 328
Ould, Francis, 281
outlawry, 97
Owain Glyndwr, 130
Owen, Aneurin, 17, 119
Oxford, University of, Vinerian Chair of English Law at, 324
Oxyrhynchus, bond of suretyship from, 106-107

P
Pactus Legis Salicae, 101
papacy, 4, 62, 244-45
Papinian, 317
  definition of law, 239
paterfamilias, 97
Pavia, Lombardic law of, 274
paying surety, 11, 106-108
  absent from Ior, 30-32, 41, n.95
  evolution of, 28
  in Cyfn, 30
  in Ior MSS F and G, 31
  in Latin texts, 36
Peckham, Archbishop, 62
Peillac, 81, 82
Peniarth MS, 128, 130; 134, 129
Peniarth MS 27ii, 128
Peniarth MS 2, 133
Peniarth MS 34 (F), 124

Peniarth MS 35, 173
  'G text' in, 175
Peniarth MS 35, (G), 24
Peniarth MS 44, 44, 130
Peniarth MS 6iv, 133
Pennant, Thomas (Abbot of Basinwerk), 128
penny
  clipped according to Welsh law 39, n. 38
  legal according to Welsh law, 39, n. 38
Peredur, 50
periglor
  connected with sacrament of pennance, 69, n. 85
  going 'under the hand of', 57-58
  meaning of term, 58
  origin of term, 68-69, n. 84
perjury (see *anudon*)
personal security, 94, 96, 98-99
Perth, privileges granted to, 248
Pfand, 95, 97
Philip Augustus, statutes made by, 248
Philip III, king of France, statutes made by, 248
physicians, 264
pignorantiae, 75
pignoratio, 75
pignus, 75
Pipriac, 80
plea-rolls, 274
Pleading, Book of (Llyfr Cynghawsedd), 165
plebs, Breton, 73-74, 75, 81-82
pledge of faith, 65, n. 30
pledge of faith (*gwystl ffydd*), 47
pledge of land (see gage of land)
plegius, 10
Plowden, 278, 283
Plucknett, T.F., 107
Pollock, Chief Baron, 288
Pollock, F., 324
Pontypridd, 296
pope, 166
  on prohibition of marriages, 252
Port, John, note-book of, 275
porth, as consisting of *cyngaws* and *canllaw*, 176
Poseidon, 96, 106
Powell, Andrew, 292
Powys, 6-7, 261, 264, 267
  survival of Welsh law in parts of, 269

praetor, 242
preamble, as part of statute, 288
Prerogativa Regis, lectures on, 280
Price, see John ap Rhys
principal, meaning of, 11
principalis debitor, 22, 29
principes, Breton, 73
printing, advent of as undermining authority of inns of court, 282
Proculus, 280
professional lawyers, 245
  Welsh lawyers as new class of, 246
promissory oath, 64-65, n. 30
proof, sacral modes of, 4
Proof Book, see Test Book
Prosecution Service, Bill for establishing independent, 311
Protonotary, appointments to office of, 292
Puckering, John, 293
Pwllheli, case of homicide at settled by arbitrators, 260
Pwyll, 105-106

Q
Quarter Sessions, courts of, 291

R
rachinburgi, 101
ráth, 19, 29, 74, 100-101, 106-107, 169, 178
reader (in inns of court), 276
readers, authority in court, 282
readers (at inns of court), cannot lecture on common law as such, 279
reading (lecture), 8
readings, 275
readings (at inns of court)
  lose authority 1550-1642, 281-83
  on law of felony, 279
real security, 94, 96, 98-99
rearing-fee, 94
Reception of Roman law, 283
Redon
  cartulary of, 4, 72
  monastery of, 72, 80
    foundation, 72
    monks and abbot of, 79

Regiam Maiestatem, 246, 248-49, 251, 253
Reginald Grey (ob. 1308), 265
relics, 5
  kinds used by Welsh, Irish and Scots, 53
  oath on, 165
  oaths on, 51-53
Renac, 77, 80, 82, 83
Repgow, Eike von, 247, 252-53
reprisal-taking surety, 104
rhaglaw, 270
Rheims, 1148 Council of, 238
Rhiannon, 105-106
rhingyll (serjeant), 268, 270
Rhondda, 296
Rhos, 263
Rhuddlan, 263
Rhydaman, 299
Rhydderch ab Ieuan Llwyd, 264
Rhys ap Gruffudd (the Lord Rhys), 52
Ríagail Phátraic, 58
Richardson, H., 242
Robert I, king of Scotland, 248, 251
Robert Pie, 271
Roman jurisprudence, revival of, 238-39
Roman law, 60, 317-21
  absence of reception of in England, 321
  at universities of Oxford and Cambridge, 321
  Reception of, 283
  reception of, 319
  twelfth-century revival of, 22
Rome
  College of Pontiffs, 317
  Principate, 317
  Republican period of, 317
Royal Commission on Inns of Court and Inns of Chancery (1855), 325
Ruffhead, Owen, 294-95
Ruffiac, 77-78, 82-83
Ruthin, 130

S
Sachsenspiegel, 8, 246-47, 249, 251-53
St Asaph, bishop and chapter of, 52
St Benedict, 246
sake and soke, 244

Saladin, 249
Salic Law, 239
Salisbury, Henry, *iudex inter Wallicos*, 266
sapientes, 7
Sayles, G.O., 242
scabinus, 81, 242
Schuld, 4, 94-101, 104
Schuldner, 96
Scotland, legal writing in, 248-49
Scottish borough customals, 251
scripta pacis, 241
securator, 75
security, meaning of, 93
Selbstverknechtung, 96
Select Committee on Legal Education (1846), 324-25, 328
self-surety, 94
self-suretyship, 96
Senchas Már, 8
senior, 81, 82
serfdom as unrighteous custom, 252
serjeant, 275
serjeants, 8
  authority in court, 282
Sieffre ap Huw, 291
Silvester, pope, 252
Sixt, 82
Society of Public Teachers of Law, 326
Solon, 238
Solo, laws on debt-bondage, 102-103
Stacey, R.C., 168, 173, 175
Star Chamber, 280
Statham, 277
Statute of Uses, 280
Statute of Wales (1284), land disputes in, 259-60
statutes, principles to be followed in interpreting, 289
Staundford, *Plees del coron* (1557), 279
Stephenson, D., 258, 264
stipulatio, 84, 85
Strata Florida, 135
Strata Marcella, 128
  charters of, 122
suitors, 1
supervising surety, 104
sureties, plurality of, 167
surety
  as authoritative witness, 12

definition of, 92
denies suretyship, 167
enforcing-surety, 4
for appearance in court (see also
  Gestellungsburge), 104-105
for performance, 104, 106-108
paying surety, 27-32
persons incompetent in law to act as (see
  legal incompetents)
surety (see also Breton surety)
suretyship, 258
  essential to society, 2
  forms of, 108-109
  Irish, 99-101
  Latin texts on, 36
  meaning of, 10
Survey of Denbigh (1334), assumes that there
  will be one *iudex* to each commote, 263
synod-book, 238, 243

T
Talbot, Mr Justice, 304-305
Tate, Francis, 127
Tegeingl, 263
teithi, 27, 109
terra pignorantiae, 75
Test Book, 123-25, 138
  comprising quires 6-8 in *C*, 121
  preface to, 124
Test Book (*Llyfr Prawf*), 263
The Welsh Language in the Courts, 312
Thelwall, Simon, rhaglaw and *ynad*, 266
Theodosian Code, 85
Theodosius I, 238
Theuerkauf, G., 246, 251
Thomas ap Ieuan ap Deicws, 129
Thurneysen, R., 3, 74
toredula, 128
tort, rarely mentioned in readings, 280
tractates in Welsh law, 17-18
treaties, securing of, 61-62
Très Ancien Coutumier, 245, 248
triads
  buckle suretyships, 172
  useless suretyships, 172
  ways to free a surety, 164
Tribonian, 242, 318
Tudur ab Ieuan Goch, 268

ynad of Denbigh, 265
Tudur ap Dafydd, 271
Twelve Tables, 238

U
Ulpian, 280, 317
universities, English, lack of study of
  Common law at, 321-24
University College, London, Chair of
  English Law at, 324
uses, readings on, 280
uuadiatio, 75
uuadio, 75

V
Valle Crucis, 128-30
venditio, sometimes used for gaging land,
  78
Visigothic Spain, 85

W
Wales
  Edwardian conquest of, 258
  post-conquest, 7
  West, 267
Walsingham, Sir Francis, 293
Watson, A., 135
Webster, Sir Richard, 295
wed, 10
Welby, Richards, 277
Welsh Courts Act (1942), 289, 297-98, 300,
  302
  limited nature of rights conferred by, 298
Welsh language, 7
  continuous interpretation from or to, 306
  legal status of, 287-313
  use in chapel, 291
Welsh Language Act (1967), 287-89, 301,
  302
  implications of preamble to, 288-89
  preamble to, 287-89
  slow implementation of, 304-12
Welsh law
  after the Edwardian conquest
    arbitrative in operation, 261
    collective in its judgements, 261

informal in its methods, 261
survival after Edwardian conquest, 265
Welsh lawbooks
  as private compilations, 246
  classified as northern or southern, 117
  compared with customary law, 258
  unforthcoming on administration of law,
    258
Welsh laws of court, 253
Welsh lawyers, as new class, 246
Welsh territorial ruler (*brenin* or *arglwydd*), 6
Wessex, kings of, 241, 243
Westminster Hall, 275, 278
Whitelocke, James, reading on benefices,
  281
Whitland, 135
Widgery, Mr Justice, 289
William, A.R., 58, 117, 137
  edition of Iorwerth, Book of, 123-25
William I, king of England, 244
William the Lion, king of Scotland, 248
Williams, Gwilym (Meisgyn), 296-97
Winn, Mr Justice, 300
witan (wise men, *sapientes*), role in law-
  making, 240
witnesses, 5
woman
  as giver of surety, 21-27
  as surety, 21-27
  married, 24
women
  as compurgators, 25-26
  not entitled to act as sureties, 173-74
  only royal women involved in land-grants,
    43, n. 117
  whether entitled to make a contract,
    173-74

Wood, Alan, 278
Wotton, *Leges Wallicae*, 179
Wray, C.J., 283
Wynnstay MSS 37 and 38, 179

Y
year-books, 274-75
  jurisprudence of, 274
ynad, 6-7
  as expert arbitrator, 263
  as seignorial servant, 268, 270
  fees of, 266
  heritable and vendible office, 266
  judgement of can be challenged, 263
  main duty to determine which proof was
    appropriate, 267
  office became source of seignorial exploit-
    ation, 266
  peripheral figure in later middle ages,
    266-67, 271
  role modified after Edwardian conquest,
    265
  terms preferred in North Wales, 262
ynad cwmwd (*judex patrie*), 262-71
ynaid
  comparable to bards and physicians, 264
  hereditary, 264

Z
Zahlbürge (*Zahlungsbürge*) (see also surety
  and paying surety), 28, 96
Zeus, 96

TABLE OF CASES*

Evans v. Thomas [1962] 2 QB 350 .... 289, 294, 301, 314 n.26

Hopes v. Hopes [1949] P 277 334

LCC v. Bermondsey Bioscope Co. [1911] 1 KB 445 313

R. v. Bowyer (1971; unreported) 304

R. v. Francis & others (1971; unreported) 304

R. v. Merthyr Justices, ex parte Jenkins [1967] 1 All ER 636 298

Salkeld v. Johnson (1848) 2 Exch 256 288

Wheatley v. Wheatley [1948] 2 All ER 428 334

*For the cases from the Year Books, Abridgments and early Reports, including anonymous cases and those from the Abridgments cited not by name but by subject-matter, and which are referred to in Dr J.H. Baker's paper, see his notes at pp. 283-6.